FORD AEROSTAR

MID-SIZE VANS 1986-1988

SHOP MANUAL

By
KALTON C. LAHUE

ALAN AHLSTRAND
Editor

CLYMER PUBLICATIONS

World's largest publisher of books
devoted exclusively to automobiles and motorcycles

A division of INTERTEC PUBLISHING CORPORATION
P.O. Box 12901, Overland Park, Kansas 66212

FIRST EDITION
First Printing February, 1989

Printed in U.S.A.

ISBN: 0-89287-458-9

COVER: Photographed by Mark Clifford.

Chapter One
General Information 1

Chapter Two
Troubleshooting 2

Chapter Three
Lubrication, Maintenance and Tune-up 3

Chapter Four
4-cylinder OHC Engine 4

Chapter Five
V6 Engines 5

Chapter Six
Fuel, Exhaust and Emission Control Systems 6

Chapter Seven
Cooling, Heating and Air Conditioning Systems 7

Chapter Eight
Electrical System 8

Chapter Nine
Clutch and Transmission 9

Chapter Ten
Front Suspension, Wheel Bearings and Steering 10

Chapter Eleven
Rear Suspension, Differential and Drive Shaft 11

Chapter Twelve
Brakes 12

Index 13

CONTENTS

QUICK REFERENCE DATA IX

CHAPTER ONE
GENERAL INFORMATION 1

Manual organization
Service hints
Safety first
Expendable supplies
Shop tools
Emergency tool kit
Troubleshooting and tune-up equipment

CHAPTER TWO
TROUBLESHOOTING 9

Starting system
Charging system
Ignition system
Engine performance
Engine oil pressure light
Fuel system (carburetted)
Fuel system (fuel injected)
Fuel pump test (mechanical and electric)
Emission control systems
Engine noises
Electrical accessories
Cooling system
Clutch
Manual transmission/transaxle
Automatic transmission
Brakes
Steering and suspension
Tire wear analysis
Wheel balancing

CHAPTER THREE
LUBRICATION, MAINTENANCE AND TUNE-UP 33

Hoisting, jacking and lift points
Towing
Weekly checks
Owner safety checks
Scheduled maintenance
Non-scheduled maintenance
Engine tune-up
Ignition service
Fuel system adjustments

CHAPTER FOUR
4-CYLINDER OHC ENGINE 61

Engine identification
Engine service
Engine removal/installation
Disassembly checklists
Valve cover
Upper and lower intake manifold
Exhaust manifold
Camshaft belt outer cover
Camshaft belt
Sprockets and engine front seals
Auxiliary shaft
Oil pan
Oil pump
Cylinder head
Camshaft
Valves and valves seats
Piston/connecting rod assembly
Rear main oil seal
Crankshaft
Flywheel or drive plate
Pilot bearing
Cylinder block
Core plug replacement

CHAPTER FIVE

V6 ENGINES 98

Engine identification
Engine service
2.8L V6 engine removal/installation
3.0L V6 engine removal/installation
Disassembly checklists
Rocker arm covers removal/installation (3.0L V6)
Intake and exhaust manifolds (3.0L engine)
Manifold inspection
Rocker arm assemblies (2.8L)
Rocker arm assemblies (3.0L)
Crankshaft pulley and damper
Front cover and timing gears (2.8L V6)
Timing cover, seal, sprockets and timing chain (3.0L V6)
Camshaft
Oil pan
Oil pump
Cylinder head
Valves and valve seats
Piston/connecting rod assembly
Rear main oil seal replacement
Crankshaft
Flywheel or drive plate
Pilot bearing
Cylinder block
Core plug replacement

CHAPTER SIX

FUEL, EXHAUST AND EMISSION CONTROL SYSTEMS 152

Air cleaner system
Fuel quality
Carburetor
Quick-disconnect fittings
Multi-point fuel injection (2.3L EFI)
Multi-point fuel injection (3.0L EFI)
Fuel pump
Fuel tank and lines
Exhaust system
Emission control systems

CHAPTER SEVEN

COOLING, HEATING AND AIR CONDITIONING SYSTEMS 183

Cooling system
Cooling system checks
Cooling system leakage test
Coolant level check
Cooling system flushing
Thermostat
Radiator
Cooling fan
Water pump
Drive belts
Heater system
Air conditioning
Refrigerant
Routine maintenance

CHAPTER EIGHT

ELECTRICAL SYSTEM 215

Battery
IAR charging system
Starter
TFI-IV ignition system
Lighting system
Ignition switch
Headlight switch
Wiper/washer switch
Coolant temperature switch
Oil pressure switch/sending unit
Instruments
Horn
Windshield wipers and washers
Electrical circuit protection
Turn signals
Hazard flasher

CHAPTER NINE
CLUTCH AND TRANSMISSION 253

Clutch
Clutch hydraulic system (1986-1987)
Clutch hydraulic system (1988-on)
Manual transmission
Automatic transmission

CHAPTER TEN
FRONT SUSPENSION, WHEEL BEARINGS AND STEERING 276

Front suspension
Wheel alignment
Wheel bearings
Steering system
Steering wheel and column

CHAPTER ELEVEN
REAR SUSPENSION, DIFFERENTIAL AND DRIVE SHAFT 299

Rear suspension
Drive shaft
Rear axle and axle shafts
Ford integral axle
Dana model 30 axle
Differential

CHAPTER TWELVE
BRAKES 317

Front disc brakes
Rear drum brakes
Brake adjustment
Master cylinder
Brake bleeding
Power brake vacuum booster
Combination valve
Dual brake warning lamp system
Stoplight switch
Parking brake
Brake pedal
Brake hoses and tubing

INDEX 343

QUICK REFERENCE DATA

MAINTENANCE SCHEDULE

Every 7,500 miles (12 months)	• Engine oil change* • Chassis/suspension lubrication* • Check manual transmission • Check exhaust system • Check brake system • Check power steering system • Check automatic transmission shift cable
First 7,500 miles, then every 15,000 miles	• Check and rotate tires • Change engine oil filter*
First 7,500 miles, then every 30,000 miles	• Change manual transmission fluid • Check 2.8L V6 engine valve clearance
Annually	• Check cooling system operation • Check coolant condition and protection
Every 2 years	• Drain, flush and refill cooling system • Replace cooling system hoses
Every 30,000 miles	• Replace spark plugs* • Check spark plug and ignition coil wires • Replace air cleaner filter • Clean, repack and adjust wheel bearings* • Clean choke linkage (2.8L V6) • Inspect fuel tank, cap and lines (EEC system) • Check brake and clutch master cylinder reservoir fluid level • Check brake system operation • Check exhaust system • Lubricate suspension ball-joints • Check suspension bushing, arm and spring condition • Lubricate throttle ball stud
Every 60,000 miles	• Replace PCV valve • Replace spark plug wires • Check Thermactor system hoses • Replace EGR valve • Replace EGR vacuum solenoid filter • Replace HEGO sensor**
Every 100,000 miles	• Change automatic transmission fluid and strainer*

* SEVERE SERVICE OPERATION: If the vehicle is operated under any of the following conditions, change engine oil @ 3,000 miles or 3 month intervals and oil filter @ alternate oil changes. Repack wheel bearings every 15,000 miles.

Change rear axle lubricant every 15,000 miles. Change PCV valve every 15,000 miles. Clean and regap spark plugs every 6,000 miles. Lubricate chassis and suspension every 6,000 miles. Change automatic transmission fluid and filter every 30,000 miles.

a. Extended idle or low-speed operation (short trips, stop-and-go driving).
b. Trailer towing.
c. Operation @ temperatures below 10° F for 60 days or more with most trips under 10 miles.
d. Very dusty or muddy conditions.

** If equipped with an emissions maintenance warning lamp, replace @ specified interval or whenever the warning lamp lights, whichever comes first.

APPROXIMATE REFILL CAPACITIES

	qt.	pt.
Engine crankcase		
I4		
With filter	5.0	
Without filter	4.0	
2.8L V6		
With filter	5.0	
Without filter	4.0	
3.0L V6		
With filter	4.5	
Without filter	3.5	
Automatic transmission**		
After rebuild		19.0
After fluid change		10.0
Manual transmission		5.9
Differential		
Ford		3.5
Dana		2.5
Cooling system		
I4		
Manual transmission	6.8	
Automatic transmission	7.6	
2.8L V6	8.0	
3.0L V6	11.8	

RECOMMENDED LUBRICANTS

Crankcase	API Service SF oil
Engine coolant	Ford cooling system fluid or equivalent meeting Ford spec. ESE-M97B44-A
Brake and clutch master cylinder	Ford Heavy Duty or other DOT 3 or DOT 4 fluid
Power steering pump	Motorcraft Type F automatic transmission fluid
Manual transmission	Standard transmission lubricant part No. D8DZ-19C547-A or equivalent
Rear axle	
Ford	Ford hypoid gear lubricant part No. EOAZ-19580-A or equivalent
Dana	Ford hypoid gear lubricant part No. C6AZ-19580-A or equivalent
Automatic transmission	
1986-1987	DEXRON II automatic transmission fluid
1988	MERCON automatic transmission fluid
Parking brake cable	Ford speedometer cable lubricant part No. D2AZ-19581-A or equivalent
Disc brake caliper rails	Ford disc brake caliper slide grease part No. D7AZ-19590-A or equivalent

(continued)

RECOMMENDED LUBRICANTS (continued)

Throttle control kickdown and ball stud	Ford multipurpose lubricant part No. C1AZ-19590-B or equivalent
Manual steering gear housing	Ford steering gear grease part No. C3AZ-19578-A or equivalent
Hinges, latches and seat tracks	Ford polyethylene grease part No. D7AZ-19584-A or equivalent
Lock cylinders	Ford lock lubricant part No. D8AZ-19587-A
Suspension ball-joints	Ford multipurpose lubricant part No. C1AZ-19590-A or equivalent

INTRODUCTION

This detailed, comprehensive manual covers the 1986-1988 Ford Aerostar rear wheel drive van. The expert text gives complete information on maintenance, repair and overhaul. Step-by-step instructions and hundreds of illustrations guide you through jobs ranging from simple maintenance to complete overhaul.

This manual can be used by anyone from a first-time do-it-yourselfer to a professional mechanic. Easy to read type, detailed drawings and clear photographs give you all the information you need to do the work right and guide you through every step. The book includes all you need to know to keep your Aerostar running right.

Where repairs are practical for the owner/mechanic, complete procedures are given. Equally important, difficult jobs are pointed out. Such operations are usually more economically performed by a dealer or independent garage.

Where special tools are required or recommended, the tool numbers are provided. These tools can often be rented from rental dealers, but they can also be purchased from Owatonna Tools, Inc., Attn: Ford Order Desk, Owatonna, Minnesota 55060.

A shop manual is a reference. You want to be able to find information fast. As in all Clymer books, this one is designed with such use in mind. All chapters are thumb tabbed. Important items are indexed at the rear of the book. All the most frequently used specifications and capacities are summarized on the *Quick Reference Data* pages at the front of the book.

Keep this shop manual handy in your tool box and use it often. It can save you hundreds of dollars in maintenance and repair bills and keep your vehicle reliable and performing well.

CHAPTER ONE

GENERAL INFORMATION

The troubleshooting, tune-up, maintenance, and step-by-step repair procedures in this book are written for the owner and home mechanic. The text is accompanied by useful photos and diagrams to make the job as clear and correct as possible.

Troubleshooting, tune-up, maintenance, and repair are not difficult if you know what tools and equipment to use and what to do. Anyone not afraid to get their hands dirty, of average intelligence, and with some mechanical ability can perform most of the procedures in this book.

In some cases, a repair job may require tools or skills not reasonably expected of the home mechanic. These procedures are noted in each chapter and it is recommended that you take the job to your dealer, a competent mechanic, or machine shop.

MANUAL ORGANIZATION

This chapter provides general information and safety and service hints. Also included are lists of recommended shop and emergency tools as well as a brief description of troubleshooting and tune-up equipment.

Chapter Two provides methods and suggestions for quick and accurate diagnosis and repair of problems. Troubleshooting procedures discuss typical symptoms and logical methods to pinpoint the trouble.

Chapter Three explains all periodic lubrication and routine maintenance necessary to keep your vehicle running well. Chapter Three also includes recommended tune-up procedures, eliminating the need to constantly consult chapters on the various subassemblies.

Subsequent chapters cover specific systems such as the engine, transmission, and electrical systems. Each of these chapters provides disassembly, repair, and assembly procedures in a simple step-by-step format. If a repair requires special skills or tools, or is otherwise impractical for the home mechanic, it is so indicated. In these cases it is usually faster and less expensive to have the repairs made by a dealer or competent repair shop. Necessary specifications concerning a particular system are included at the end of the appropriate chapter.

When special tools are required to perform a procedure included in this manual, the tool is illustrated either in actual use or alone. It may be possible to rent or borrow these tools. The inventive mechanic may also be able to find a suitable substitute in his tool box, or to fabricate one.

The terms NOTE, CAUTION, and WARNING have specific meanings in this manual. A NOTE provides additional or explanatory information. A CAUTION is used to emphasize areas where equipment damage could result if proper precautions are not taken. A WARNING is used to stress those areas where personal injury or death could result from negligence, in addition to possible mechanical damage.

SERVICE HINTS

Observing the following practices will save time, effort, and frustration, as well as prevent possible injury.

Throughout this manual keep in mind two conventions. "Front" refers to the front of the vehicle. The front of any component, such as the transmission, is that end which faces toward the front of the vehicle. The "left" and "right" sides of the vehicle refer to the orientation of a person sitting in the vehicle facing forward. For example, the steering wheel is on the left side. These rules are simple, but even experienced mechanics occasionally become disoriented.

Most of the service procedures covered are straightforward and can be performed by anyone reasonably handy with tools. It is suggested, however, that you consider your own capabilities carefully before attempting any operation involving major disassembly of the engine.

Some operations, for example, require the use of a press. It would be wiser to have these performed by a shop equipped for such work, rather than to try to do the job yourself with makeshift equipment. Other procedures require precision measurements. Unless you have the skills and equipment required, it would be better to have a qualified repair shop make the measurements for you.

Repairs go much faster and easier if the parts that will be worked on are clean before you begin. There are special cleaners for washing the engine and related parts. Brush or spray on the cleaning solution, let it stand, then rinse it away with a garden hose. Clean all oily or greasy parts with cleaning solvent as you remove them.

WARNING

Never use gasoline as a cleaning agent. It presents an extreme fire hazard. Be sure to work in a well-ventilated area when using cleaning solvent. Keep a fire extinguisher, rated for gasoline fires, handy in any case.

Much of the labor charge for repairs made by dealers is for the removal and disassembly of other parts to reach the defective unit. It is frequently possible to perform the preliminary operations yourself and then take the defective unit in to the dealer for repair, at considerable savings.

Once you have decided to tackle the job yourself, make sure you locate the appropriate section in this manual, and read it entirely. Study the illustrations and text until you have a good idea of what is involved in completing the job satisfactorily. If special tools are required, make arrangements to get them before you start. Also, purchase any known defective parts prior to starting on the procedure. It is frustrating and time-consuming to get partially into a job and then be unable to complete it.

Simple wiring checks can be easily made at home, but knowledge of electronics is almost a necessity for performing tests with complicated electronic testing gear.

During disassembly of parts keep a few general cautions in mind. Force is rarely needed to get things apart. If parts are a tight fit, like a bearing in a case, there is usually a tool designed to separate them. Never use a screwdriver to pry apart parts with machined surfaces such as cylinder head and valve cover. You will mar the surfaces and end up with leaks.

Make diagrams wherever similar-appearing parts are found. You may think you can remember where everything came from — but mistakes are costly. There is also the possibility you may get sidetracked and not return to work for days or even weeks — in which interval, carefully laid out parts may have become disturbed.

Tag all similar internal parts for location, and mark all mating parts for position. Record number and thickness of any shims as they are removed. Small parts such as bolts can be identified by placing them in plastic sandwich bags that are sealed and labeled with masking tape.

Wiring should be tagged with masking tape and marked as each wire is removed. Again, do not rely on memory alone.

When working under the vehicle, do not trust a hydraulic or mechanical jack to hold the vehicle up by itself. Always use jackstands. See **Figure 1**.

Disconnect battery ground cable before working near electrical connections and before disconnecting wires. Never run the engine with the battery disconnected; the alternator could be seriously damaged.

Protect finished surfaces from physical damage or corrosion. Keep gasoline and brake fluid off painted surfaces.

Frozen or very tight bolts and screws can often be loosened by soaking with penetrating oil like Liquid Wrench or WD-40, then sharply striking the bolt head a few times with a hammer and punch (or screwdriver for screws). Avoid heat unless absolutely necessary, since it may melt, warp, or remove the temper from many parts.

Avoid flames or sparks when working near a charging battery or flammable liquids, such as brake fluid or gasoline.

No parts, except those assembled with a press fit, require unusual force during assembly. If a part is hard to remove or install, find out why before proceeding.

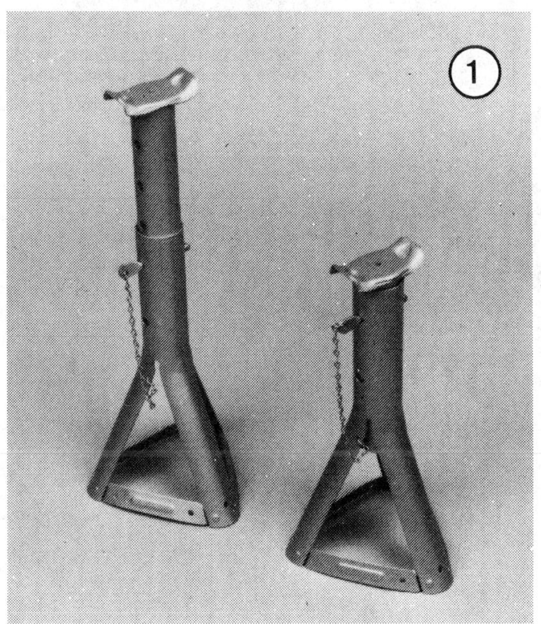

Cover all openings after removing parts to keep dirt, small tools, etc., from falling in.

When assembling two parts, start all fasteners, then tighten evenly.

The clutch plate, wiring connections, brake shoes, drums, pads, and discs should be kept clean and free of grease and oil.

When assembling parts, be sure all shims and washers are replaced exactly as they came out.

Whenever a rotating part butts against a stationary part, look for a shim or washer. Use new gaskets if there is any doubt about the condition of old ones. Generally, you should apply gasket cement to one mating surface only, so the parts may be easily disassembled in the future. A thin coat of oil on gaskets helps them seal effectively.

Heavy grease can be used to hold small parts in place if they tend to fall out during assembly. However, keep grease and oil away from electrical, clutch, and brake components.

High spots may be sanded off a piston with sandpaper, but emery cloth and oil do a much more professional job.

Carburetors are best cleaned by disassembling them and soaking the parts in a commercial carburetor cleaner. Never soak gaskets and rubber parts in these cleaners. Never use wire to clean out jets and air passages; they are easily damaged. Use compressed air to blow out the carburetor, but only if the float has been removed first.

Take your time and do the job right. Do not forget that a newly rebuilt engine must be broken in the same as a new one. Refer to your owner's manual for the proper break-in procedures.

SAFETY FIRST

Professional mechanics can work for years and never sustain a serious injury. If you observe a few rules of common sense and safety, you can enjoy many safe hours servicing your vehicle. You could hurt yourself or damage the vehicle if you ignore these rules.

1. Never use gasoline as a cleaning solvent.

2. Never smoke or use a torch in the vicinity of flammable liquids such as cleaning solvent in open containers.

3. Never smoke or use a torch in an area where batteries are being charged. Highly explosive hydrogen gas is formed during the charging process.

4. Use the proper sized wrenches to avoid damage to nuts and injury to yourself.

5. When loosening a tight or stuck nut, be guided by what would happen if the wrench should slip. Protect yourself accordingly.

6. Keep your work area clean and uncluttered.

7. Wear safety goggles during all operations involving drilling, grinding, or use of a cold chisel.

8. Never use worn tools.

9. Keep a fire extinguisher handy and be sure it is rated for gasoline (Class B) and electrical (Class C) fires.

EXPENDABLE SUPPLIES

Certain expendable supplies are necessary. These include grease, oil, gasket cement, wiping rags, cleaning solvent, and distilled water. Also, special locking compounds, silicone lubricants, and engine cleaners may be useful. Cleaning solvent is available at most service stations and distilled water for the battery is available at most supermarkets.

SHOP TOOLS

For proper servicing, you will need an assortment of ordinary hand tools (**Figure 2**).

As a minimum, these include:

a. Combination wrenches
b. Sockets
c. Plastic mallet
d. Small hammer
e. Snap ring pliers
f. Gas pliers
g. Phillips screwdrivers
h. Slot (common) screwdrivers
i. Feeler gauges
j. Spark plug gauge
k. Spark plug wrench

Special tools necessary are shown in the chapters covering the particular repair in which they are used.

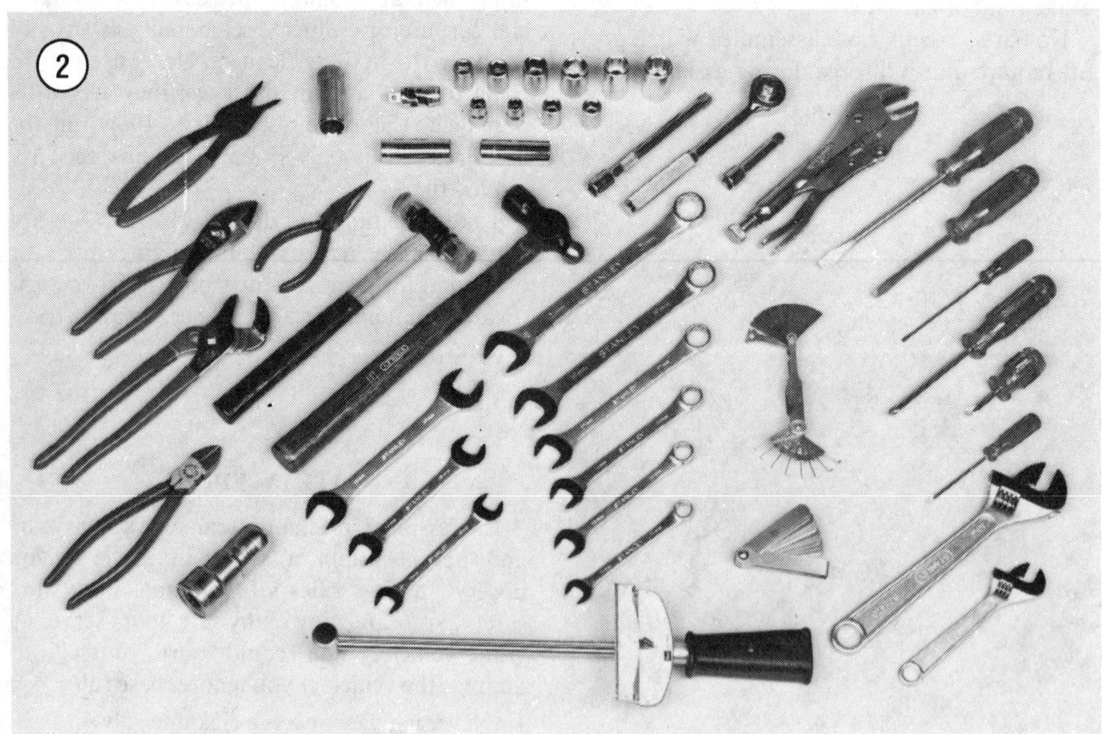

Engine tune-up and troubleshooting procedures require other special tools and equipment. These are described in detail in the following sections.

EMERGENCY TOOL KIT

A small emergency tool kit kept in the trunk is handy for road emergencies which otherwise could leave you stranded. The tools listed below and shown in **Figure 3** will let you handle most roadside repairs.

a. Combination wrenches
b. Crescent (adjustable) wrench
c. Screwdrivers — common and Phillips
d. Pliers — conventional (gas) and needle nose
e. Vise Grips
f. Hammer — plastic and metal
g. Small container of waterless hand cleaner
h. Rags for clean up
i. Silver waterproof sealing tape (duct tape)
j. Flashlight
k. Emergency road flares — at least four
l. Spare drive belts (water pump, alternator, etc.)

TROUBLESHOOTING AND TUNE-UP EQUIPMENT

Voltmeter, Ohmmeter, and Ammeter

For testing the ignition or electrical system, a good voltmeter is required. For automotive use, an instrument covering 0-20 volts is satisfac-

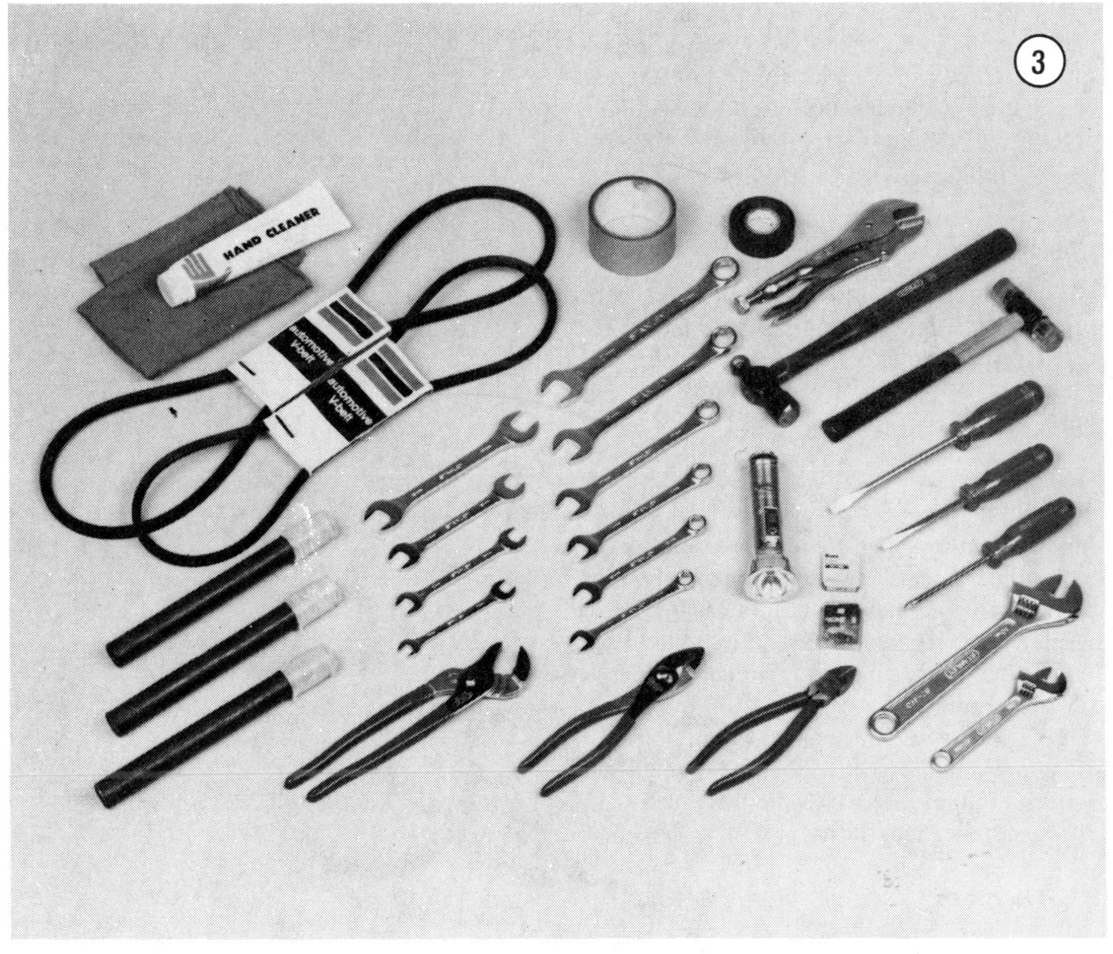

tory. One which also has a 0-2 volt scale is necessary for testing relays, points, or individual contacts where voltage drops are much smaller. Accuracy should be ± ½ volt.

An ohmmeter measures electrical resistance. This instrument is useful for checking continuity (open and short circuits), and testing fuses and lights.

The ammeter measures electrical current. Ammeters for automotive use should cover 0-50 amperes and 0-250 amperes. These are useful for checking battery charging and starting current.

Several inexpensive VOM's (volt-ohm-milliammeter) combine all three instruments into one which fits easily in any tool box. See **Figure 4**. However, the ammeter ranges are usually too small for automotive work.

Hydrometer

The hydrometer gives a useful indication of battery condition and charge by measuring the specific gravity of the electrolyte in each cell. See **Figure 5**. Complete details on use and interpretation of readings are provided in the electrical chapter.

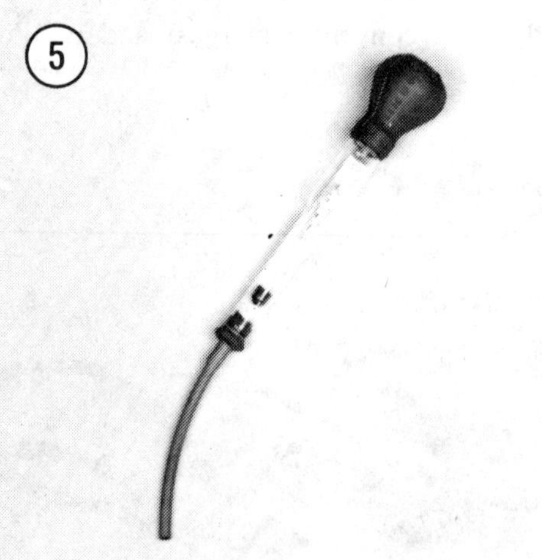

Compression Tester

The compression tester measures the compression pressure built up in each cylinder. The results, when properly interpreted, can indicate general cylinder and valve condition. See **Figure 6**.

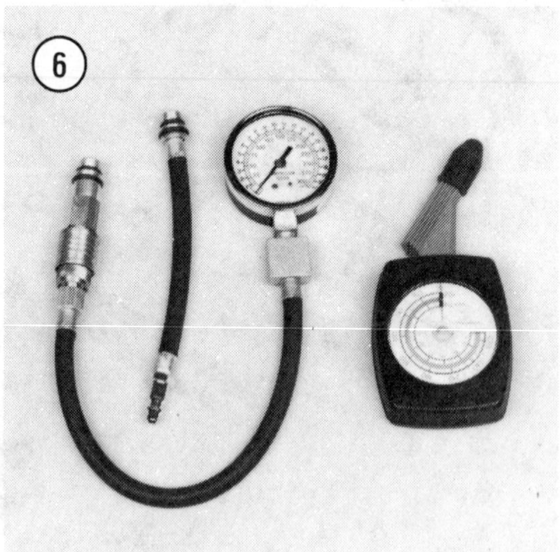

Vacuum Gauge

The vacuum gauge **(Figure 7)** is one of the easiest instruments to use, but one of the most difficult for the inexperienced mechanic to interpret. The results, when interpreted with other findings, can provide valuable clues to possible trouble.

To use the vacuum gauge, connect it to a vacuum hose that goes to the intake manifold. Attach it either directly to the hose or to a T-fitting installed into the hose.

NOTE: *Subtract one inch from the reading for every 1,000 ft. elevation.*

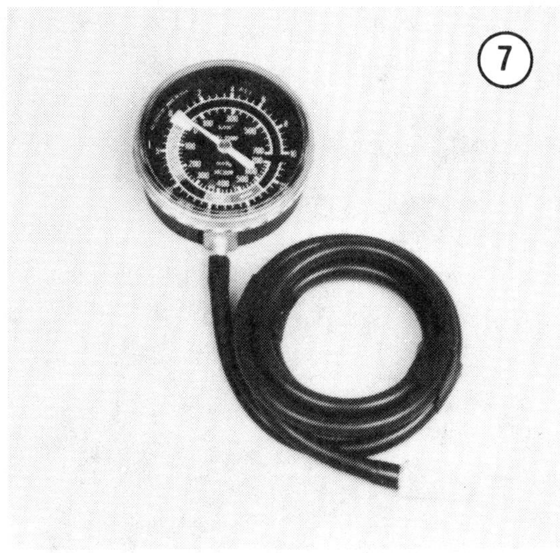
7

Fuel Pressure Gauge

This instrument is invaluable for evaluating fuel pump performance. Fuel system troubleshooting procedures in this manual use a fuel pressure gauge. Usually a vacuum gauge and fuel pressure gauge are combined.

Dwell Meter (Contact Breaker Point Ignition Only)

A dwell meter measures the distance in degrees of cam rotation that the breaker points remain closed while the engine is running. Since this angle is determined by breaker point gap, dwell angle is an accurate indication of breaker point gap.

Many tachometers intended for tuning and testing incorporate a dwell meter as well. See **Figure 8**. Follow the manufacturer's instructions to measure dwell.

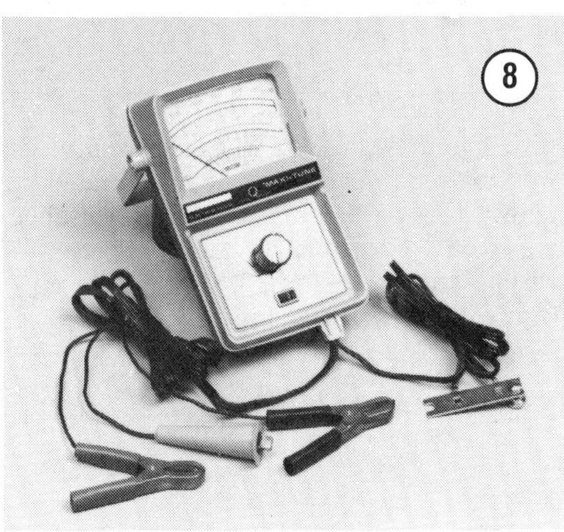
8

Tachometer

A tachometer is necessary for tuning. See **Figure 8**. Ignition timing and carburetor adjustments must be performed at the specified idle speed. The best instrument for this purpose is one with a low range of 0-1,000 or 0-2,000 rpm for setting idle, and a high range of 0-4,000 or more for setting ignition timing at 3,000 rpm. Extended range (0-6,000 or 0-8,000 rpm) instruments lack accuracy at lower speeds. The instrument should be capable of detecting changes of 25 rpm on the low range.

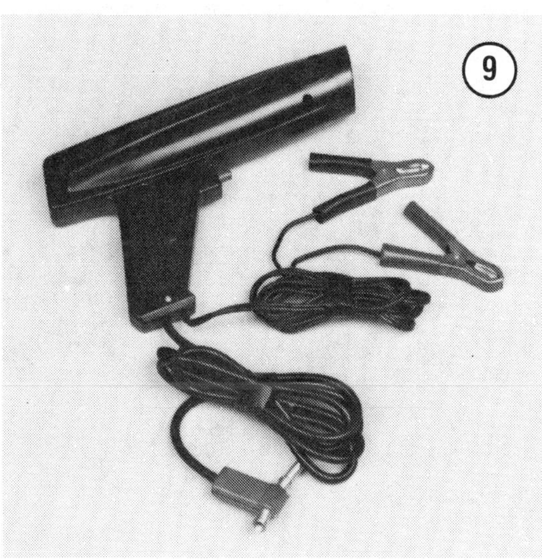
9

Strobe Timing Light

This instrument is necessary for tuning, as it permits very accurate ignition timing. The light flashes at precisely the same instant that No. 1 cylinder fires, at which time the timing marks on the engine should align. Refer to Chapter Three for exact location of the timing marks for your engine.

Suitable lights range from inexpensive neon bulb types ($2-3) to powerful xenon strobe lights ($20-40). See **Figure 9**. Neon timing lights are difficult to see and must be used in dimly lit areas. Xenon strobe timing lights can be used outside in bright sunlight. Both types work on this vehicle; use according to the manufacturer's instructions.

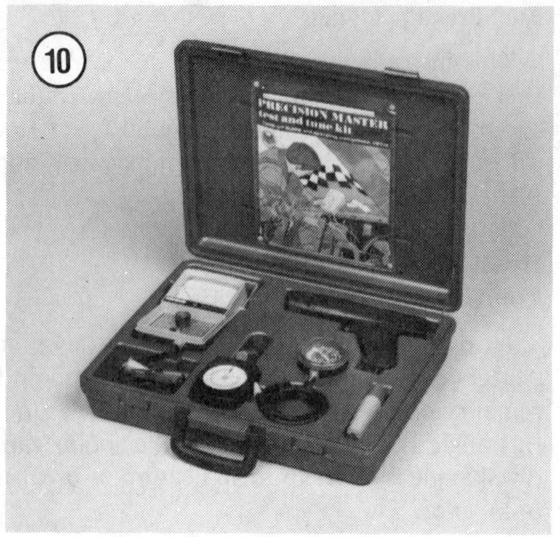

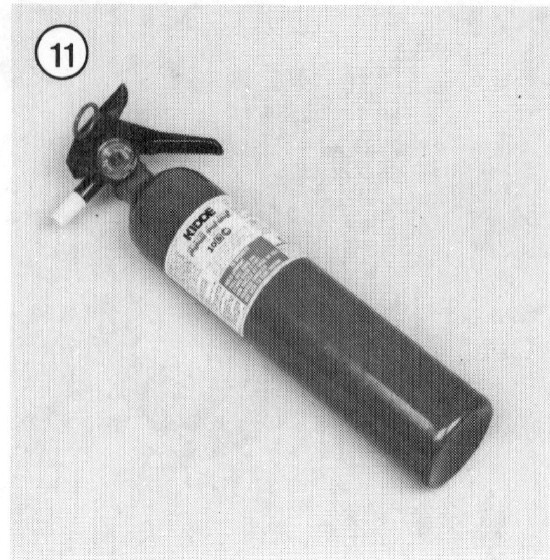

Tune-up Kits

Many manufacturer's offer kits that combine several useful instruments. Some come in a convenient carry case and are usally less expensive than purchasing one instrument at a time. **Figure 10** shows one of the kits that is available. The prices vary with the number of instruments included in the kit.

Fire Extinguisher

A fire extinguisher is a necessity when working on a vehicle. It should be rated for both *Class B* (flammable liquids—gasoline, oil, paint, etc.) and *Class C* (electrical—wiring, etc.) type fires. It should always be kept within reach. See **Figure 11**.

CHAPTER TWO

TROUBLESHOOTING

Troubleshooting can be a relatively simple matter if it is done logically. The first step in any troubleshooting procedure must be defining the symptoms as closely as possible. Subsequent steps involve testing and analyzing areas which could cause the symptoms. A haphazard approach may eventually find the trouble, but in terms of wasted time and unnecessary parts replacement, it can be very costly.

The troubleshooting procedures in this chapter analyze typical symptoms and show logical methods of isolation. These are not the only methods. There may be several approaches to a problem, but all methods must have one thing in common — a logical, systematic approach.

STARTING SYSTEM

The starting system consists of the starter motor and the starter solenoid. The ignition key controls the starter solenoid, which mechanically engages the starter with the engine flywheel, and supplies electrical current to turn the starter motor.

Starting system troubles are relatively easy to find. In most cases, the trouble is a loose or dirty electrical connection. **Figures 1 and 2** provide routines for finding the trouble.

CHARGING SYSTEM

The charging system consists of the alternator (or generator on older vehicles), voltage regulator, and battery. A drive belt driven by the engine crankshaft turns the alternator which produces electrical energy to charge the battery. As engine speed varies, the voltage from the alternator varies. A voltage regulator controls the charging current to the battery and maintains the voltage to the vehicle's electrical system at safe levels. A warning light or gauge on the instrument panel signals the driver when charging is not taking place. Refer to **Figure 3** for a typical charging system.

Complete troubleshooting of the charging system requires test equipment and skills which the average home mechanic does not possess. However, there are a few tests which can be done to pinpoint most troubles.

Charging system trouble may stem from a defective alternator (or generator), voltage regulator, battery, or drive belt. It may also be caused by something as simple as incorrect drive belt tension. The following are symptoms of typical problems you may encounter.

1. ***Battery dies frequently, even though the warning lamp indicates no discharge*** — This can be caused by a drive belt that is slightly too

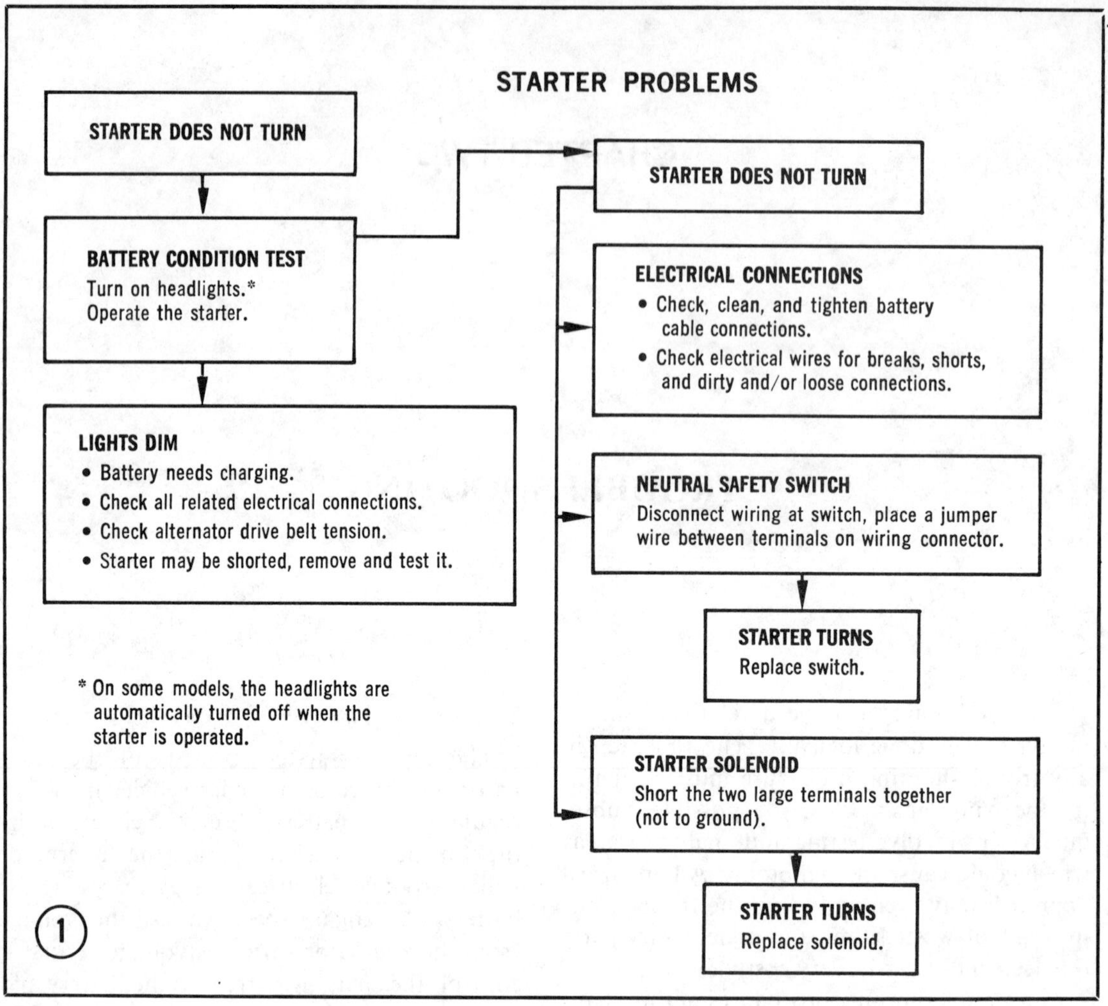

STARTER PROBLEMS
STARTER DOES NOT TURN
BATTERY CONDITION TEST
Turn on headlights.*
Operate the starter.
LIGHTS DIM
• Battery needs charging.
• Check all related electrical connections.
• Check alternator drive belt tension.
• Starter may be shorted, remove and test it.
* On some models, the headlights are automatically turned off when the starter is operated.
STARTER DOES NOT TURN
ELECTRICAL CONNECTIONS
• Check, clean, and tighten battery cable connections.
• Check electrical wires for breaks, shorts, and dirty and/or loose connections.
NEUTRAL SAFETY SWITCH
Disconnect wiring at switch, place a jumper wire between terminals on wiring connector.
STARTER TURNS
Replace switch.
STARTER SOLENOID
Short the two large terminals together (not to ground).
STARTER TURNS
Replace solenoid.
1

STARTER PROBLEMS
STARTER TURNS
DOES NOT ENGAGE WITH ENGINE
Check pinion or solenoid shifting fork and teeth on flywheel gear.
ENGAGES WITH ENGINE — WILL NOT RELEASE
Check for sticking solenoid or jammed pinion onto flywheel.
LOUD GRINDING NOISE
Check flywheel to pinion alignment. The overrunning clutch may be broken.
Remove the starter and examine the gear teeth; replace if necessary.
2

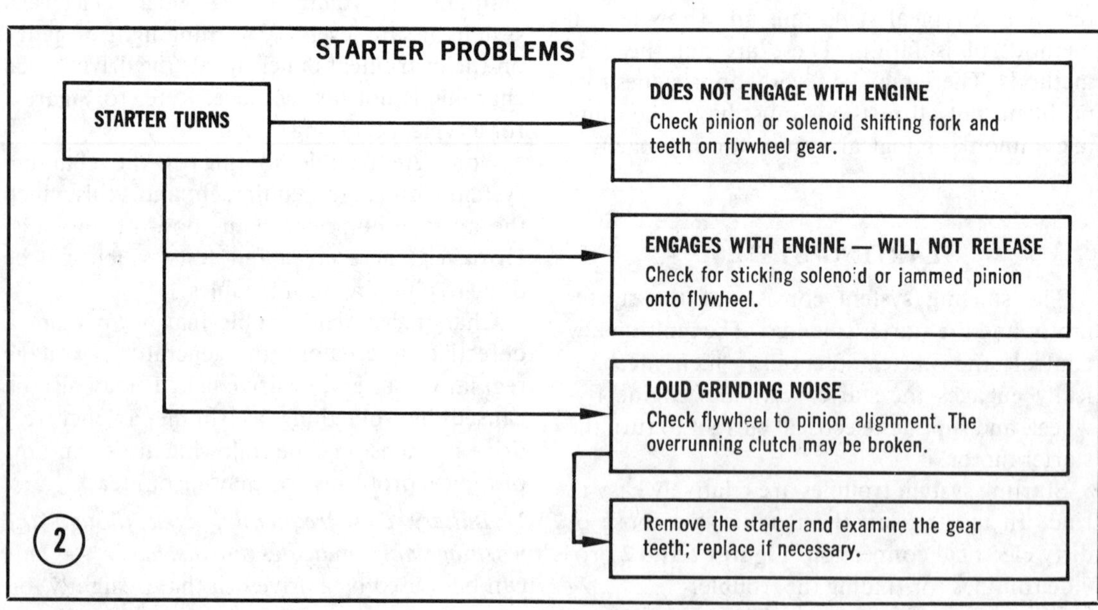

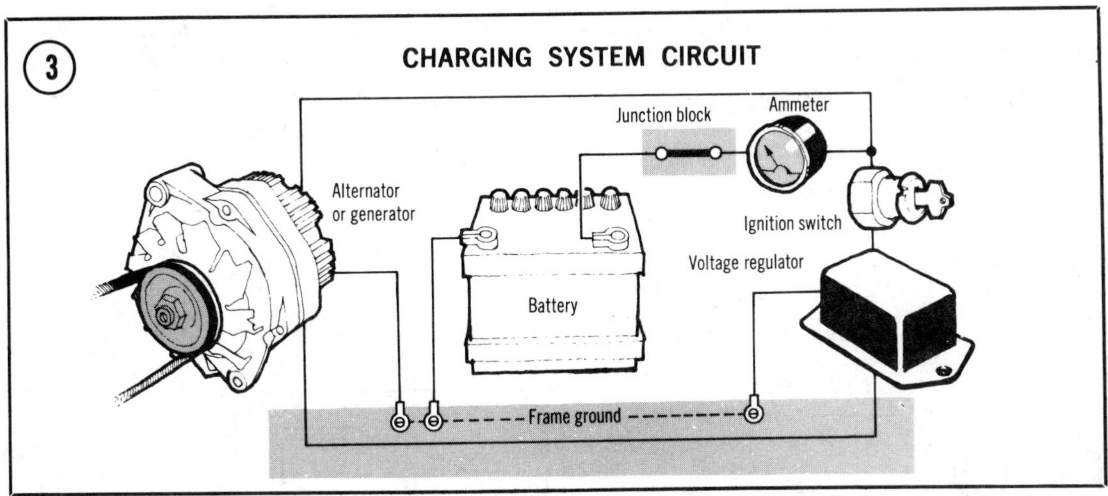

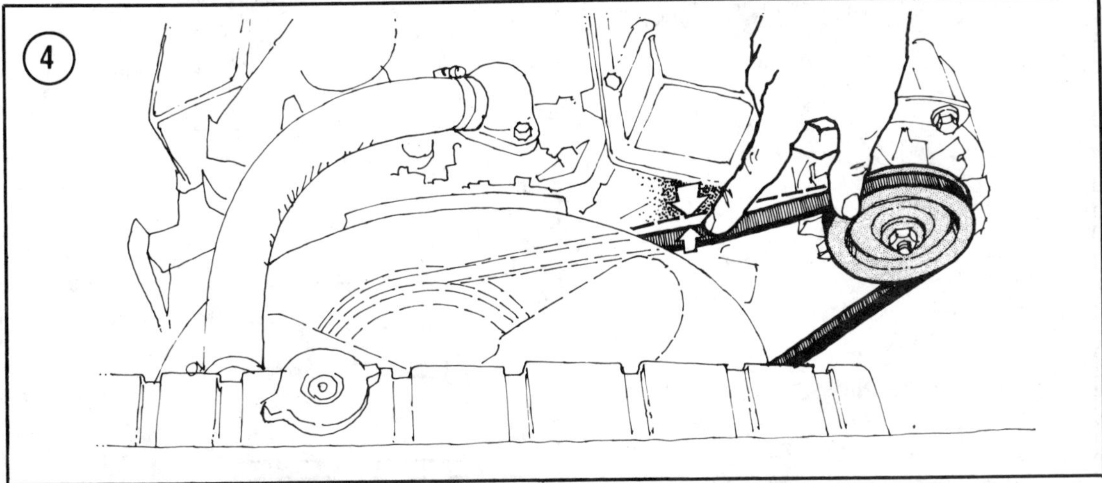

loose. Grasp the alternator (or generator) pulley and try to turn it. If the pulley can be turned without moving the belt, the drive belt is too loose. As a rule, keep the belt tight enough that it can be deflected about ½ in. under moderate thumb pressure between the pulleys (**Figure 4**). The battery may also be at fault; test the battery condition.

2. ***Charging system warning lamp does not come on when ignition switch is turned on*** — This may indicate a defective ignition switch, battery, voltage regulator, or lamp. First try to start the vehicle. If it doesn't start, check the ignition switch and battery. If the car starts, remove the warning lamp; test it for continuity with an ohmmeter or substitute a new lamp. If the lamp is good, locate the voltage regulator and make sure it is properly grounded (try tightening the mounting screws). Also the alternator (or generator) brushes may not be making contact. Test the alternator (or generator) and voltage regulator.

3. ***Alternator (or generator) warning lamp comes on and stays on*** — This usually indicates that no charging is taking place. First check drive belt tension (**Figure 4**). Then check battery condition, and check all wiring connections in the charging system. If this does not locate the trouble, check the alternator (or generator) and voltage regulator.

4. ***Charging system warning lamp flashes on and off intermittently*** — This usually indicates the charging system is working intermittently.

Check the drive belt tension (**Figure 4**), and check all electrical connections in the charging system. Check the alternator (or generator). *On generators only*, check the condition of the commutator.

5. ***Battery requires frequent additions of water, or lamps require frequent replacement*** — The alternator (or generator) is probably overcharging the battery. The voltage regulator is probably at fault.

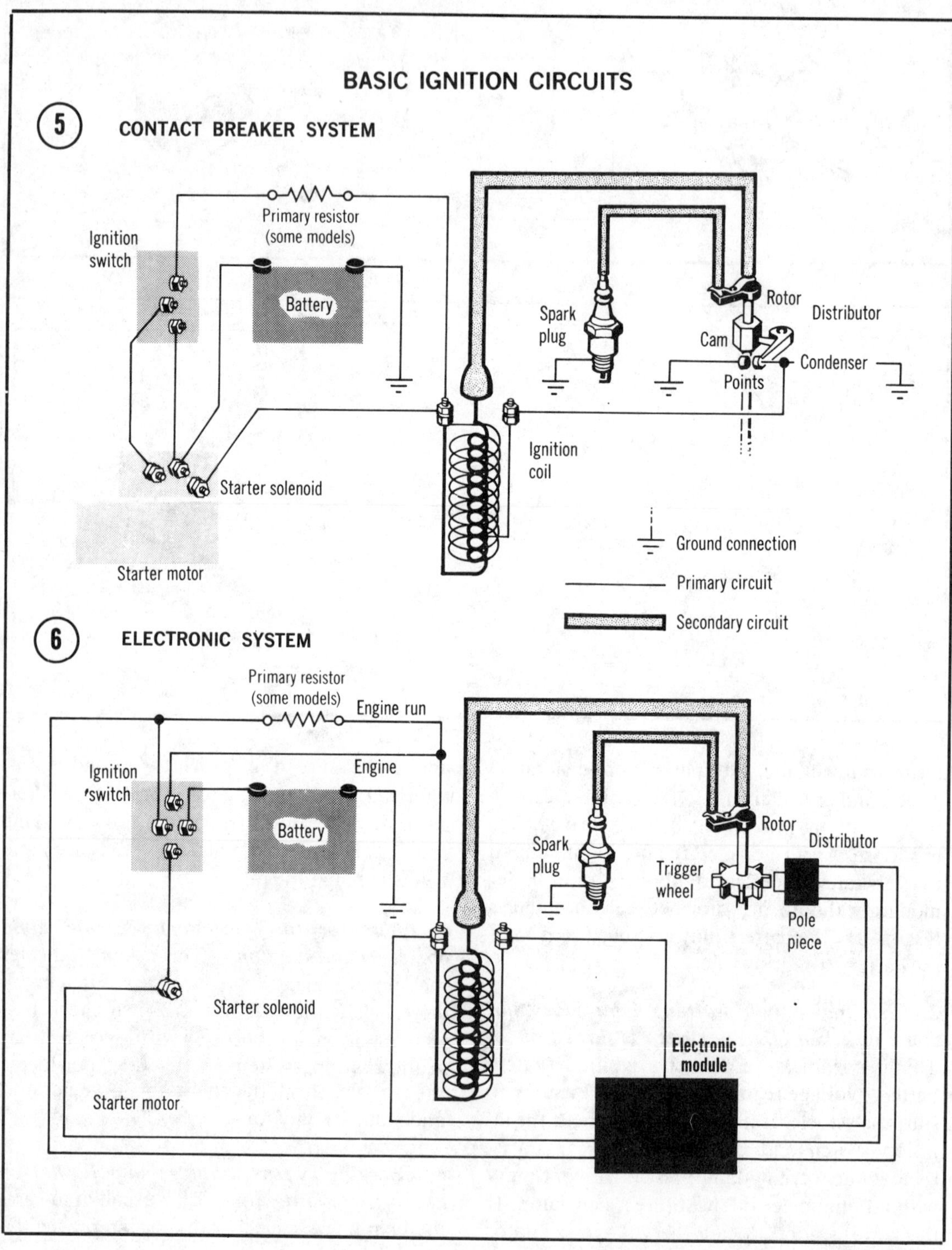

6. ***Excessive noise from the alternator (or generator)*** — Check for loose mounting brackets and bolts. The problem may also be worn bearings or the need of lubrication in some cases. If an alternator whines, a shorted diode may be indicated.

IGNITION SYSTEM

The ignition system may be either a conventional contact breaker type or an electronic ignition. See electrical chapter to determine which type you have. **Figures 5 and 6** show simplified diagrams of each type.

Most problems involving failure to start, poor performance, or rough running stem from trouble in the ignition system, particularly in contact breaker systems. Many novice troubleshooters get into trouble when they assume that these symptoms point to the fuel system instead of the ignition system.

Ignition system troubles may be roughly divided between those affecting only one cylinder and those affecting all cylinders. If the trouble affects only one cylinder, it can only be in the spark plug, spark plug wire, or portion of the distributor associated with that cylinder. If the trouble affects all cylinders (weak spark or no spark), then the trouble is in the ignition coil, rotor, distributor, or associated wiring.

The troubleshooting procedures outlined in **Figure 7** (breaker point ignition) or **Figure 8**

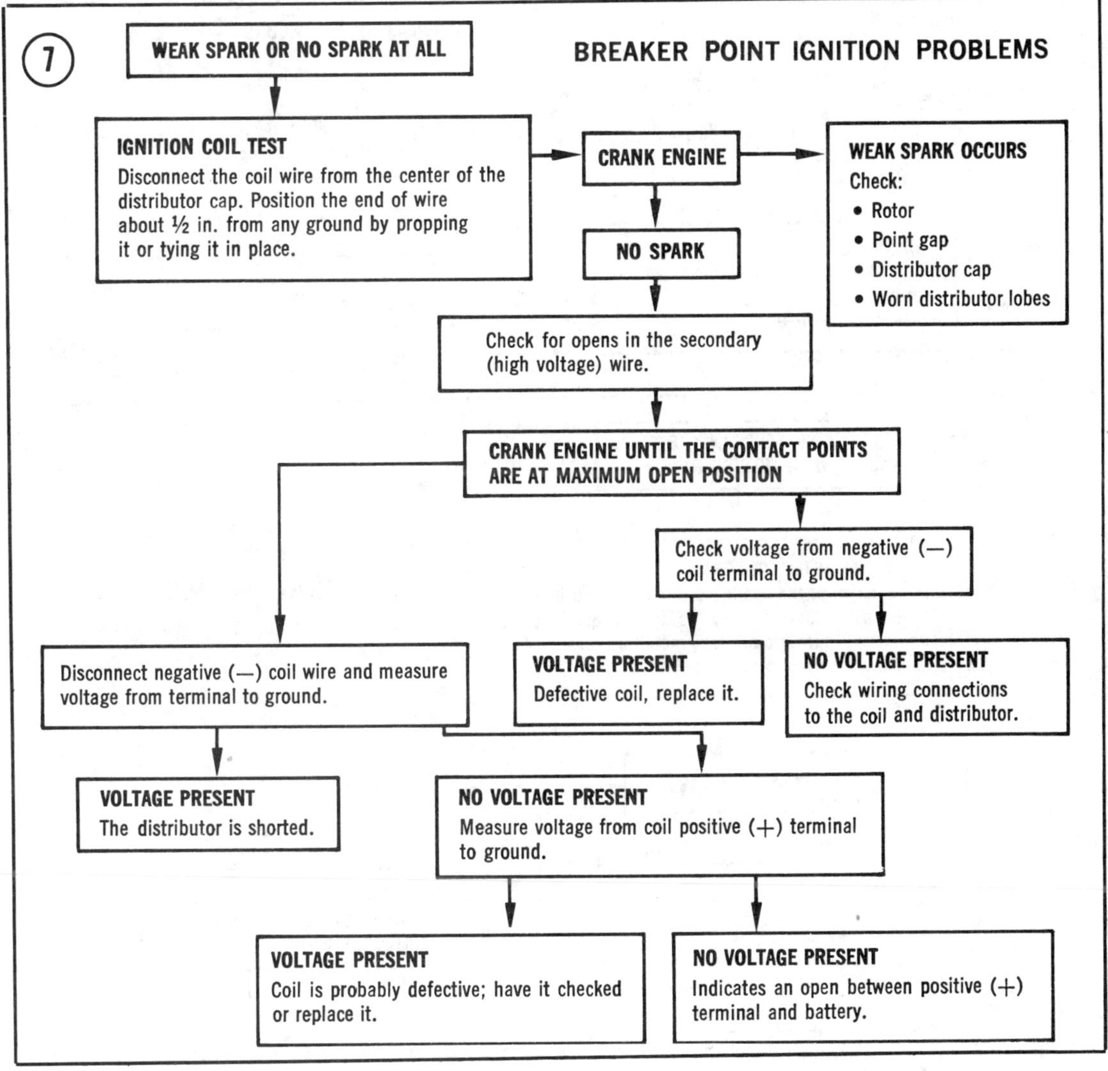

(electronic ignition) will help you isolate ignition problems fast. Of course, they assume that the battery is in good enough condition to crank the engine over at its normal rate.

ENGINE PERFORMANCE

A number of factors can make the engine difficult or impossible to start, or cause rough running, poor performance and so on. The majority of novice troubleshooters immediately suspect the carburetor or fuel injection system. In the majority of cases, though, the trouble exists in the ignition system.

The troubleshooting procedures outlined in **Figures 9 through 14** will help you solve the majority of engine starting troubles in a systematic manner.

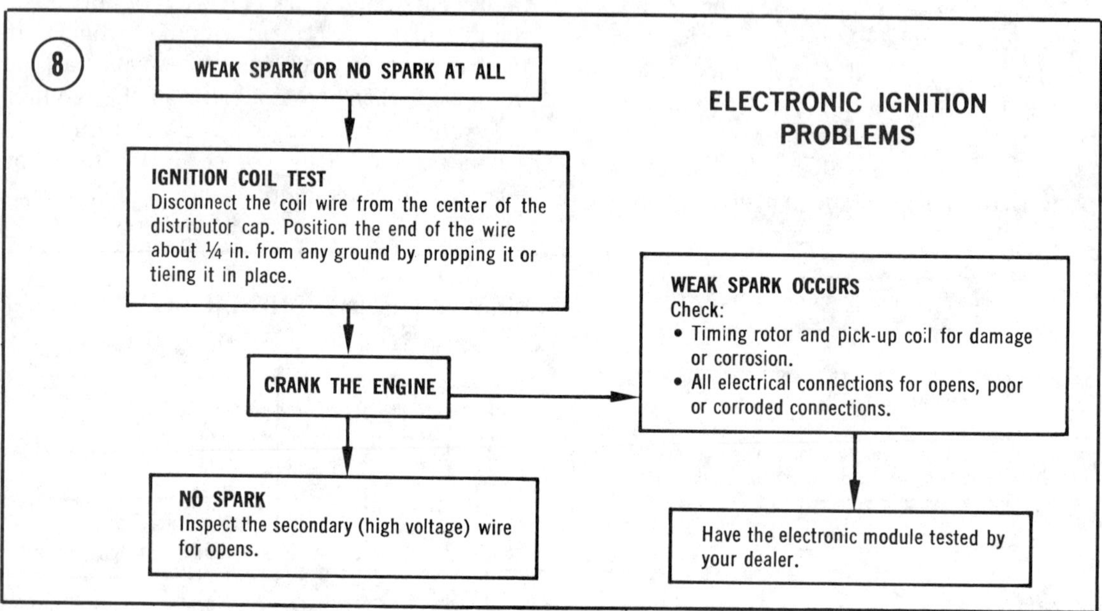

8
WEAK SPARK OR NO SPARK AT ALL
ELECTRONIC IGNITION PROBLEMS
IGNITION COIL TEST
Disconnect the coil wire from the center of the distributor cap. Position the end of the wire about ¼ in. from any ground by propping it or tieing it in place.
CRANK THE ENGINE
WEAK SPARK OCCURS
Check:
• Timing rotor and pick-up coil for damage or corrosion.
• All electrical connections for opens, poor or corroded connections.
NO SPARK
Inspect the secondary (high voltage) wire for opens.
Have the electronic module tested by your dealer.

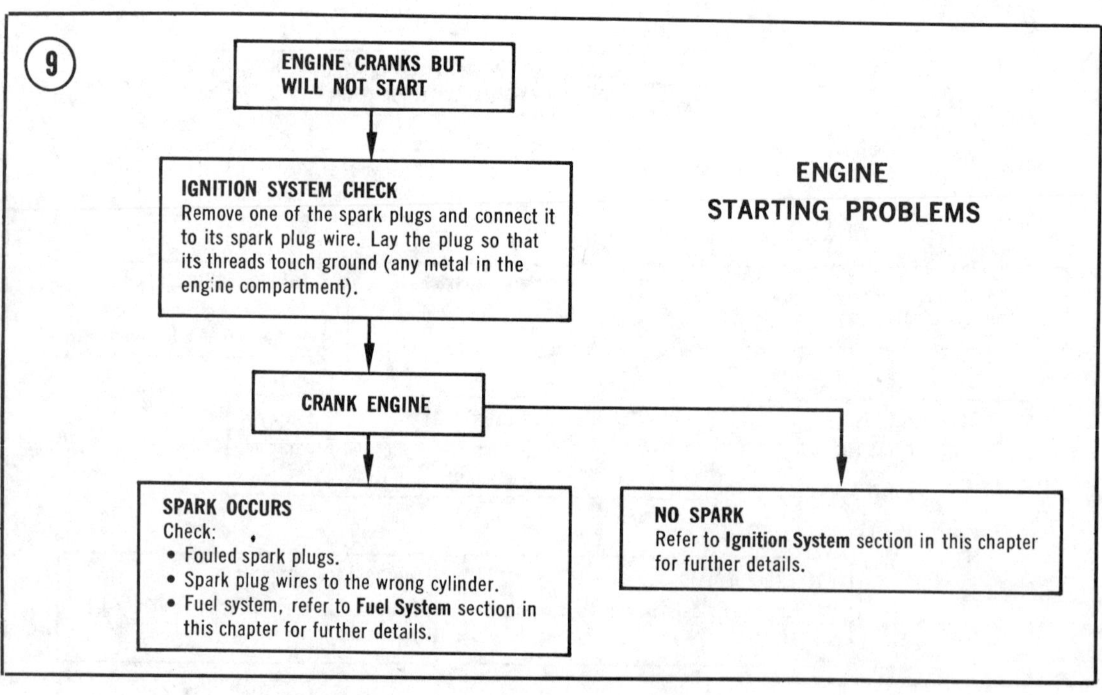

9
ENGINE CRANKS BUT WILL NOT START
ENGINE STARTING PROBLEMS
IGNITION SYSTEM CHECK
Remove one of the spark plugs and connect it to its spark plug wire. Lay the plug so that its threads touch ground (any metal in the engine compartment).
CRANK ENGINE
SPARK OCCURS
Check:
• Fouled spark plugs.
• Spark plug wires to the wrong cylinder.
• Fuel system, refer to Fuel System section in this chapter for further details.
NO SPARK
Refer to Ignition System section in this chapter for further details.

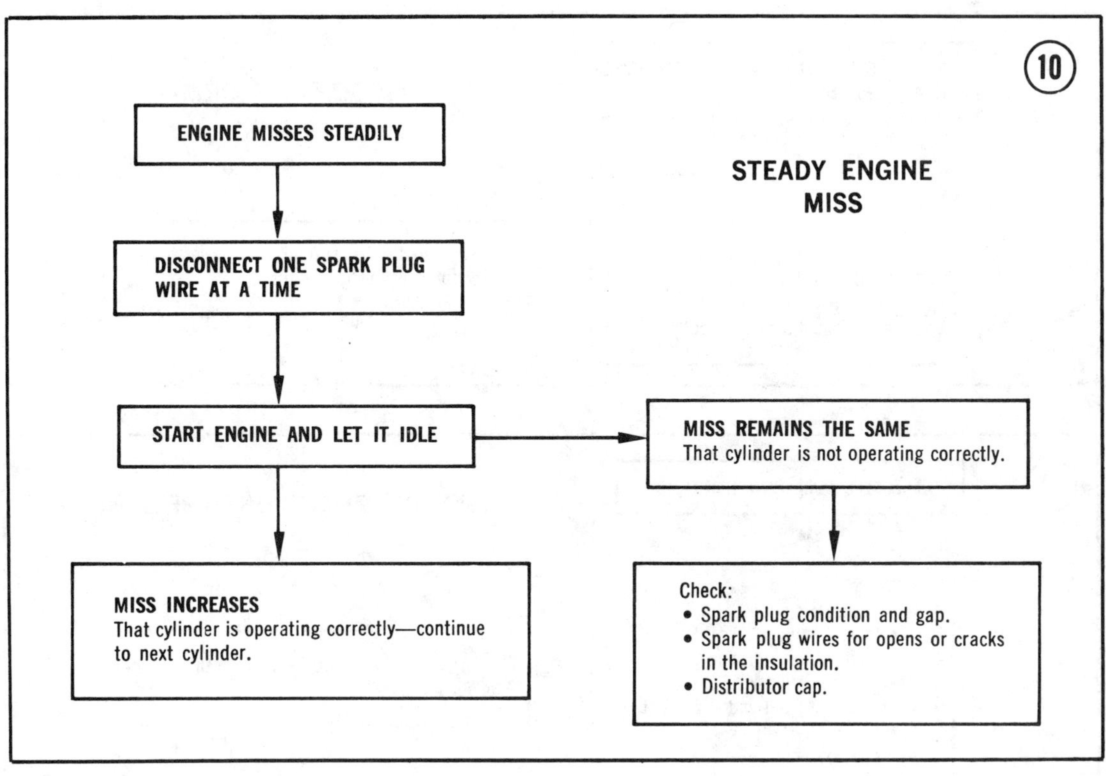
10
STEADY ENGINE MISS
ENGINE MISSES STEADILY
DISCONNECT ONE SPARK PLUG WIRE AT A TIME
START ENGINE AND LET IT IDLE
MISS REMAINS THE SAME
That cylinder is not operating correctly.
MISS INCREASES
That cylinder is operating correctly—continue to next cylinder.
Check:
• Spark plug condition and gap.
• Spark plug wires for opens or cracks in the insulation.
• Distributor cap.

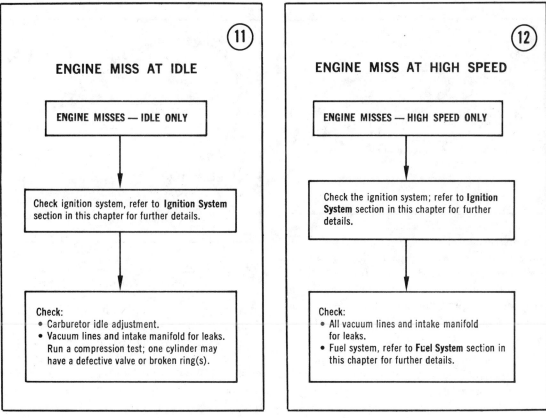

(11)

ENGINE MISS AT IDLE

ENGINE MISSES — IDLE ONLY

↓

Check ignition system, refer to **Ignition System** section in this chapter for further details.

↓

Check:

- Carburetor idle adjustment.
- Vacuum lines and intake manifold for leaks. Run a compression test; one cylinder may have a defective valve or broken ring(s).

(12)

ENGINE MISS AT HIGH SPEED

ENGINE MISSES — HIGH SPEED ONLY

↓

Check the ignition system; refer to **Ignition System** section in this chapter for further details.

↓

Check:

- All vacuum lines and intake manifold for leaks.
- Fuel system, refer to **Fuel System** section in this chapter for further details.

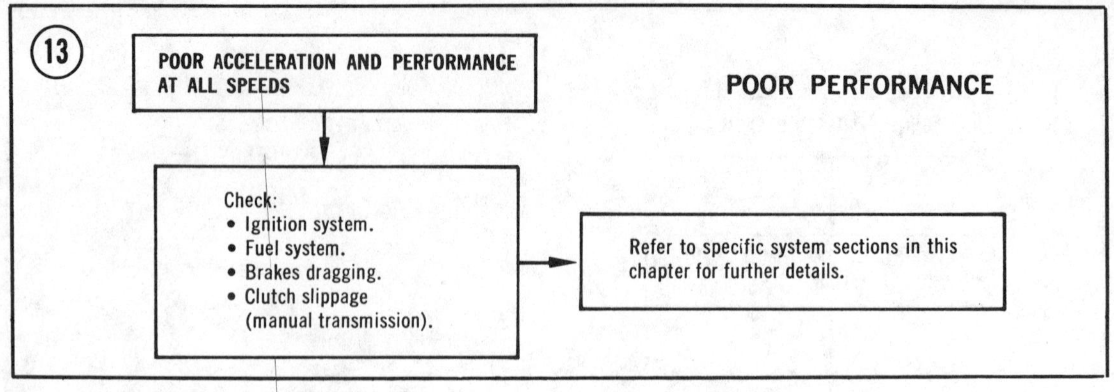

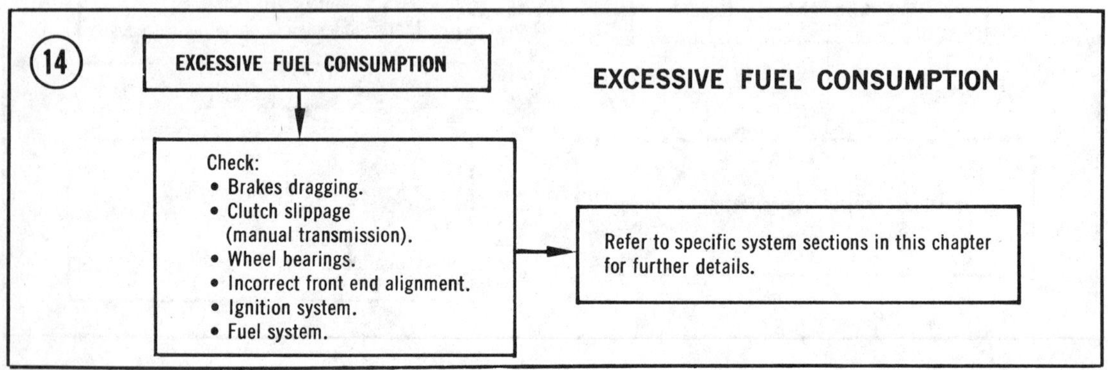

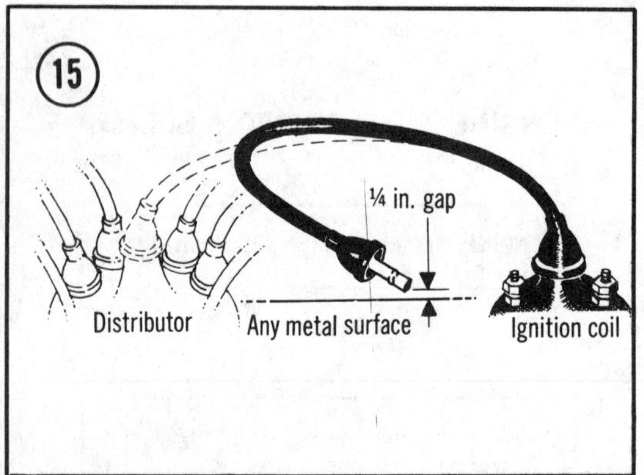

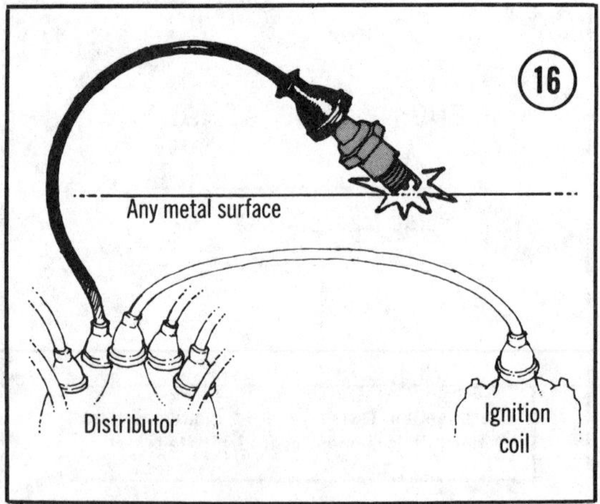

Some tests of the ignition system require running the engine with a spark plug or ignition coil wire disconnected. The safest way to do this is to disconnect the wire with the engine stopped, then prop the end of the wire next to a metal surface as shown in **Figures 15 and 16**.

WARNING

Never disconnect a spark plug or ignition coil wire while the engine is running. The high voltage in an ignition system, particularly the newer high-energy electronic ignition systems could cause serious injury or even death.

Spark plug condition is an important indication of engine performance. Spark plugs in a properly operating engine will have slightly pitted electrodes, and a light tan insulator tip. **Figure 17** shows a normal plug, and a number of others which indicate trouble in their respective cylinders.

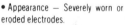

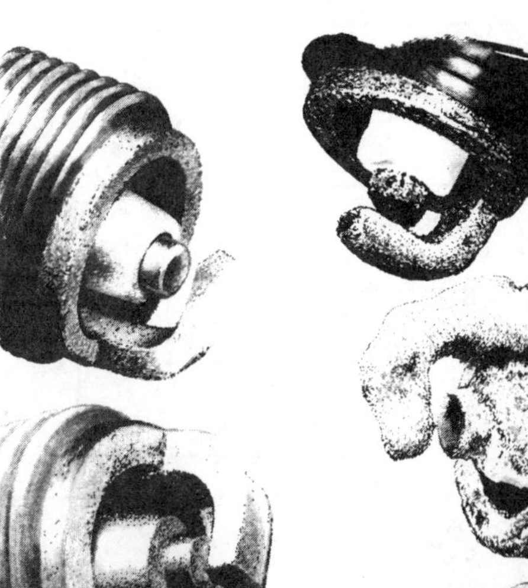

• Appearance—Firing tip has deposits of light gray to light tan.
• Can be cleaned, regapped and reused.

• Appearance—Glazed yellow deposits with a slight brownish tint on the insulator tip and ground electrode.
• Replace with new plugs.

• Appearance — Brown colored hardened ash deposits on the insulator tip and ground electrode.
• Caused by—Fuel and/or oil additives.
• Replace with new plugs.

• Appearance—Dull, dry black with fluffy carbon deposits on the insulator tip, electrode and exposed shell.
• Caused by—Fuel/air mixture too rich, plug heat range too cold, weak ignition system, dirty air cleaner, faulty automatic choke or excessive idling.
• Can be cleaned, regapped and reused.

• Appearance — Severely worn or eroded electrodes.
• Caused by—Normal wear or unusual oil and/or fuel additives.
• Replace with new plugs.

• Appearance—Wet black deposits on insulator and exposed shell.
• Caused by—Excessive oil entering the combustion chamber through worn rings, pistons, valve guides or bearings.
• Replace with new plugs (use a hotter plug if engine is not repaired).

• Appearance — Melted ground electrode.
• Caused by—Overadvanced ignition timing, inoperative ignition advance mechanism, too low of a fuel octane rating, lean fuel/air mixture or carbon deposits in combustion chamber.

• Appearance — Yellow insulator deposits (may sometimes be dark gray, black or tan in color) on the insulator tip.
• Caused by—Highly leaded gasoline.
• Replace with new plugs.

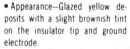

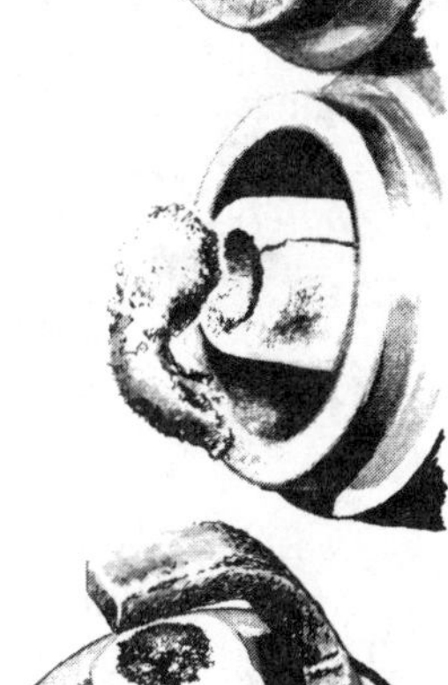

• Appearance—Melted center electrode.
• Caused by—Abnormal combustion due to overadvanced ignition timing or incorrect advance, too low of a fuel octane rating, lean fuel/air mixture, or carbon deposits in combustion chamber.
• Correct engine problem and replace with new plugs.

• Appearance—Yellow glazed deposits indicating melted lead deposits due to hard acceleration.
• Caused by—Highly leaded gasoline.
• Replace with new plugs.

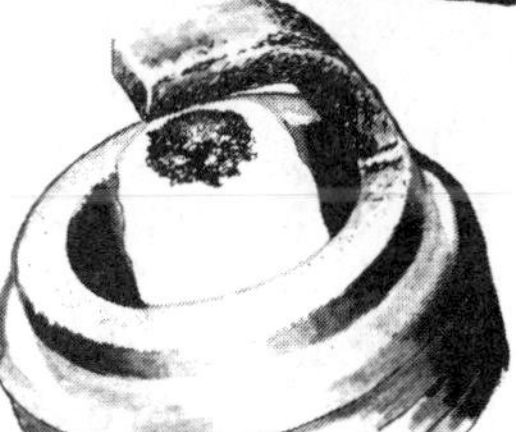

• Appearance—Melted center electrode and white blistered insulator tip.
• Caused by—Incorrect plug heat range selection.
• Replace with new plugs.

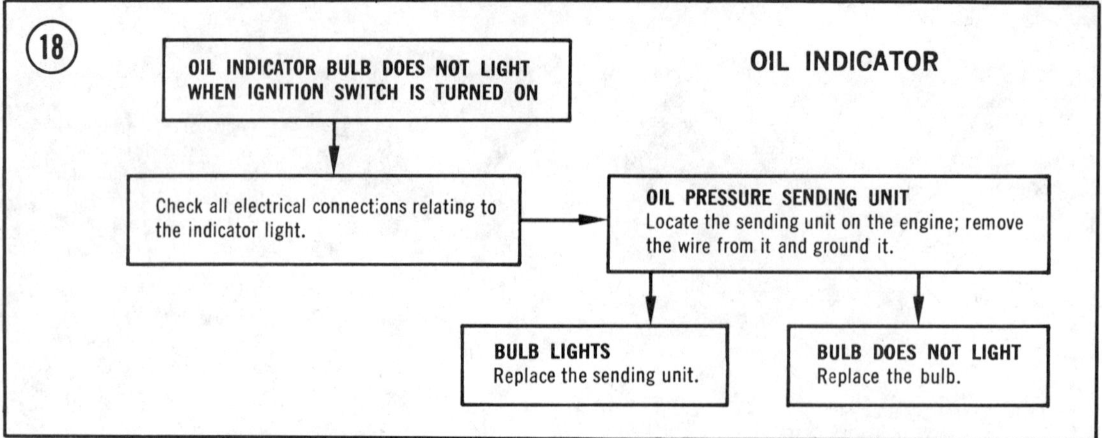

ENGINE OIL PRESSURE LIGHT

Proper oil pressure to the engine is vital. If oil pressure is insufficient, the engine can destroy itself in a comparatively short time.

The oil pressure warning circuit monitors oil pressure constantly. If pressure drops below a predetermined level, the light comes on.

Obviously, it is vital for the warning circuit to be working to signal low oil pressure. Each time you turn on the ignition, but before you start the car, the warning light should come on. If it doesn't, there is trouble in the warning circuit, not the oil pressure system. See **Figure 18** to troubleshoot the warning circuit.

Once the engine is running, the warning light should stay off. If the warning light comes on or acts erratically while the engine is running there is trouble with the engine oil pressure system. *Stop the engine immediately*. Refer to **Figure 19** for possible causes of the problem.

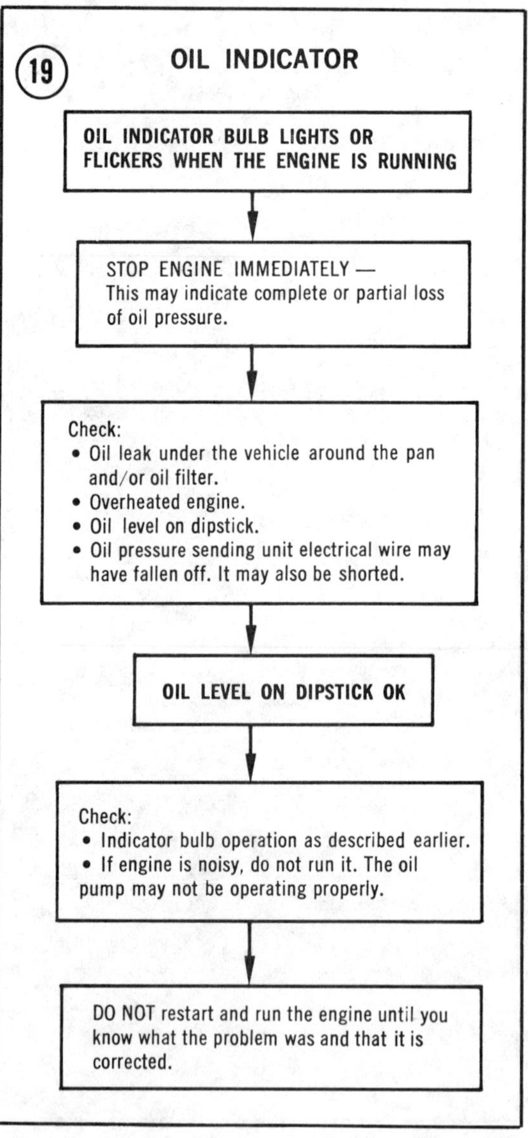

FUEL SYSTEM (CARBURETTED)

Fuel system problems must be isolated to the fuel pump (mechanical or electric), fuel lines, fuel filter, or carburetor. These procedures assume the ignition system is working properly and is correctly adjusted.

1. ***Engine will not start*** — First make sure that fuel is being delivered to the carburetor. Remove the air cleaner, look into the carburetor throat, and operate the accelerator

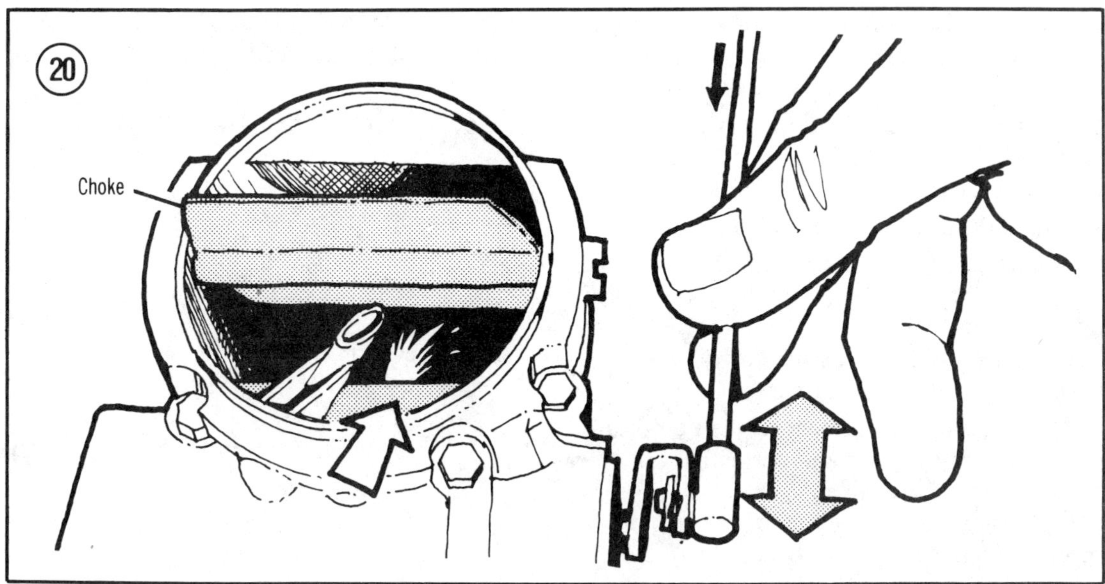

linkage several times. There should be a stream of fuel from the accelerator pump discharge tube each time the accelerator linkage is depressed (**Figure 20**). If not, check fuel pump delivery (described later), float valve, and float adjustment. If the engine will not start, check the automatic choke parts for sticking or damage. If necessary, rebuild or replace the carburetor.

2. ***Engine runs at fast idle*** — Check the choke setting. Check the idle speed, idle mixture, and decel valve (if equipped) adjustment.

3. ***Rough idle or engine miss with frequent stalling*** — Check idle mixture and idle speed adjustments.

4. ***Engine "diesels" (continues to run) when ignition is switched off*** — Check idle mixture (probably too rich), ignition timing, and idle speed (probably too fast). Check the throttle solenoid (if equipped) for proper operation. Check for overheated engine.

5. ***Stumbling when accelerating from idle*** — Check the idle speed and mixture adjustments. Check the accelerator pump.

6. ***Engine misses at high speed or lacks power*** — This indicates possible fuel starvation. Check fuel pump pressure and capacity as described in this chapter. Check float needle valves. Check for a clogged fuel filter or air cleaner.

7. ***Black exhaust smoke*** — This indicates a badly overrich mixture. Check idle mixture and idle speed adjustment. Check choke setting. Check for excessive fuel pump pressure, leaky floats, or worn needle valves.

8. ***Excessive fuel consumption*** — Check for overrich mixture. Make sure choke mechanism works properly. Check idle mixture and idle speed. Check for excessive fuel pump pressure, leaky floats, or worn float needle valves.

FUEL SYSTEM (FUEL INJECTED)

Troubleshooting a fuel injection system requires more thought, experience, and know-how than any other part of the vehicle. A logical approach and proper test equipment are essential in order to successfully find and fix these troubles.

It is best to leave fuel injection troubles to your dealer. In order to isolate a problem to the injection system make sure that the fuel pump is operating properly. Check its performance as described later in this section. Also make sure that fuel filter and air cleaner are not clogged.

FUEL PUMP TEST (MECHANICAL AND ELECTRIC)

1. Disconnect the fuel inlet line where it enters the carburetor or fuel injection system.

2. Fit a rubber hose over the fuel line so fuel can be directed into a graduated container with about one quart capacity. See **Figure 21**.

3. To avoid accidental starting of the engine, disconnect the secondary coil wire from the coil or disconnect and insulate the coil primary wire.

4. Crank the engine for about 30 seconds.

5. If the fuel pump supplies the specified amount (refer to the fuel chapter later in this book), the trouble may be in the carburetor or fuel injection system. The fuel injection system should be tested by your dealer.

6. If there is no fuel present or the pump cannot supply the specified amount, either the fuel pump is defective or there is an obstruction in the fuel line. Replace the fuel pump and/or inspect the fuel lines for air leaks or obstructions.

7. Also pressure test the fuel pump by installing a T-fitting in the fuel line between the fuel pump and the carburetor. Connect a fuel pressure gauge to the fitting with a short tube (**Figure 22**).

8. Reconnect the coil wire, start the engine, and record the pressure. Refer to the fuel chapter later in this book for the correct pressure. If the pressure varies from that specified, the pump should be replaced.

9. Stop the engine. The pressure should drop off very slowly. If it drops off rapidly, the outlet valve in the pump is leaking and the pump should be replaced.

EMISSION CONTROL SYSTEMS

Major emission control systems used on nearly all U.S. models include the following:

a. Positive crankcase ventilation (PCV)
b. Thermostatic air cleaner
c. Air injection reaction (AIR)
d. Fuel evaporation control
e. Exhaust gas recirculation (EGR)

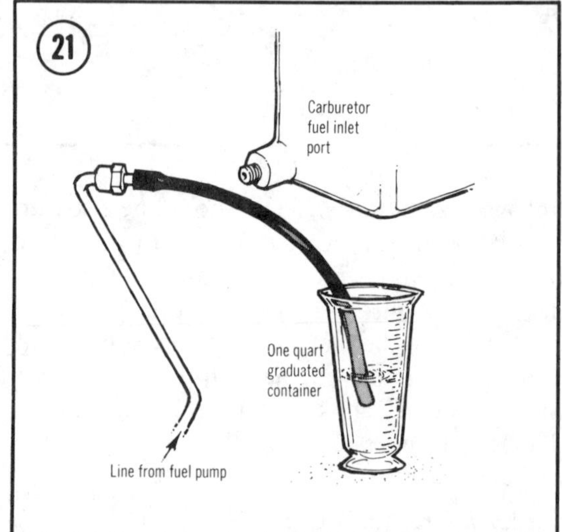

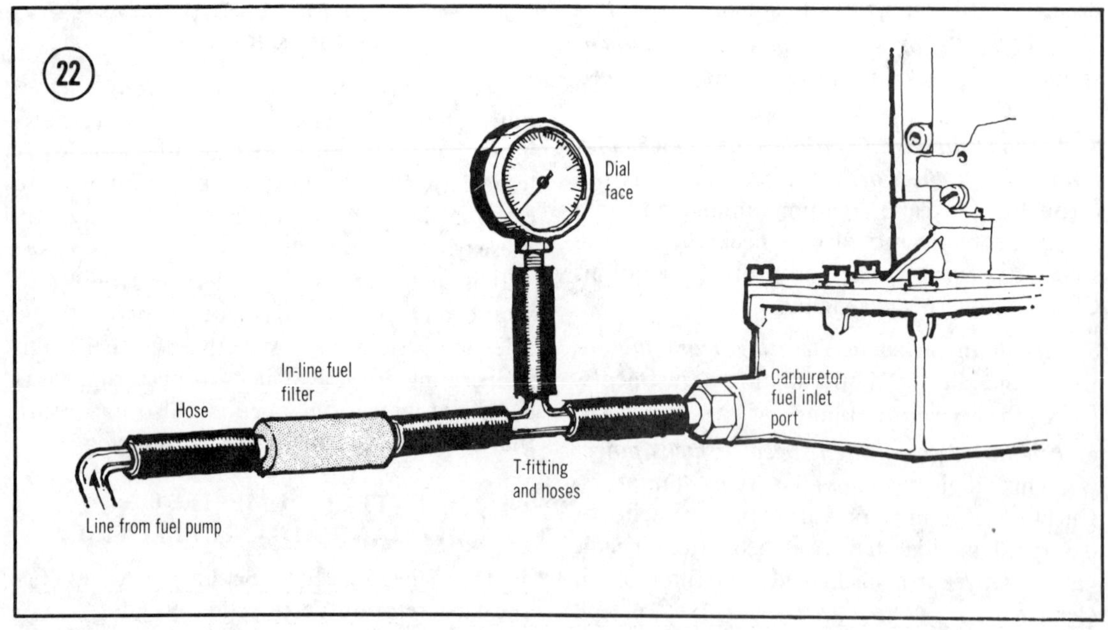

Emission control systems vary considerably from model to model. Individual models contain variations of the four systems described here. In addition, they may include other special systems. Use the index to find specific emission control components in other chapters.

Many of the systems and components are factory set and sealed. Without special expensive test equipment, it is impossible to adjust the systems to meet state and federal requirements.

Troubleshooting can also be difficult without special equipment. The procedures described below will help you find emission control parts which have failed, but repairs may have to be entrusted to a dealer or other properly equipped repair shop.

With the proper equipment, you can test the carbon monoxide and hydrocarbon levels. **Figure 23** provides some sources of trouble if the readings are not correct.

Positive Crankcase Ventilation

Fresh air drawn from the air cleaner housing scavenges emissions (e.g., piston blow-by) from the crankcase, then the intake manifold vacuum draws emissions into the intake manifold. They can then be reburned in the normal combustion process. **Figure 24** shows a typical system. **Figure 25** provides a testing procedure.

Thermostatic Air Cleaner

The thermostatically controlled air cleaner maintains incoming air to the engine at a predetermined level, usually about 100°F or higher. It mixes cold air with heated air from the exhaust manifold region. The air cleaner in-

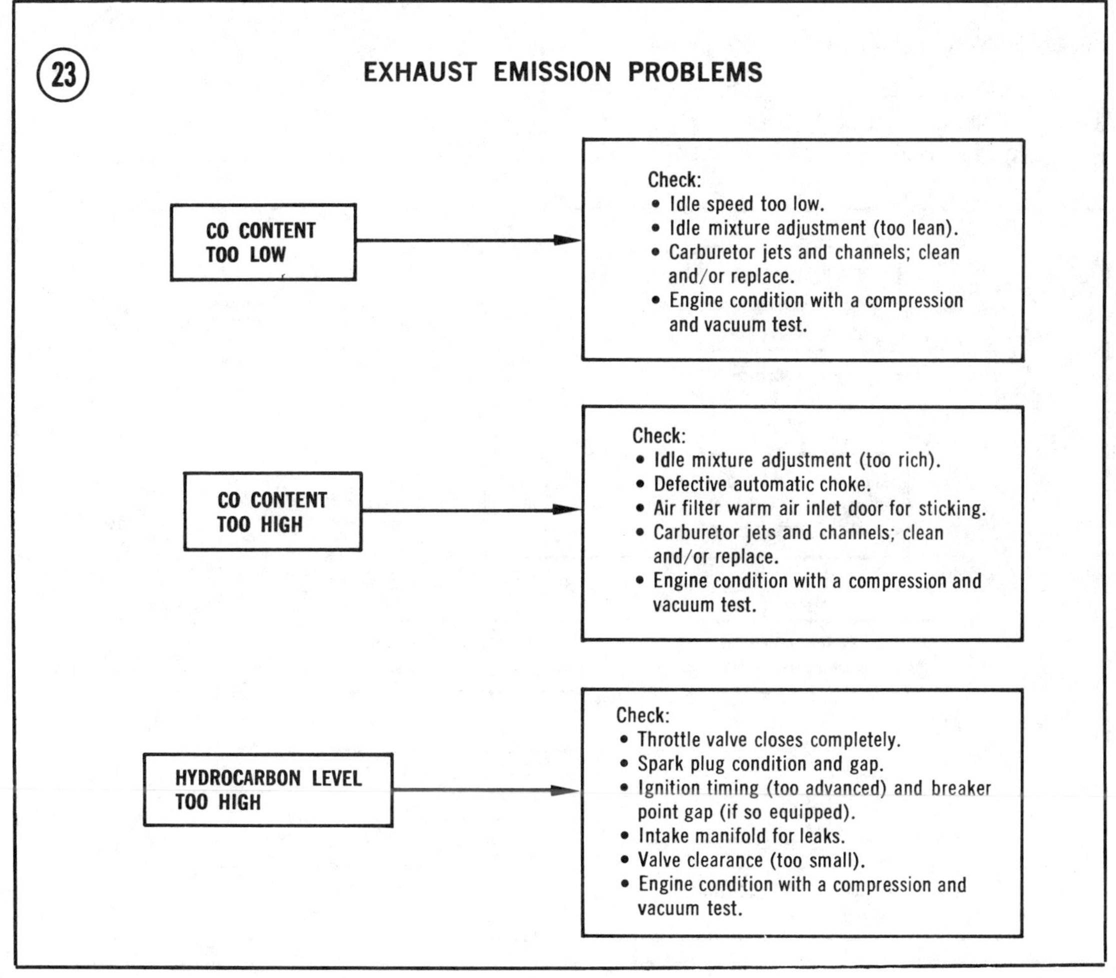
23
EXHAUST EMISSION PROBLEMS
CO CONTENT TOO LOW
Check:
• Idle speed too low.
• Idle mixture adjustment (too lean).
• Carburetor jets and channels; clean and/or replace.
• Engine condition with a compression and vacuum test.
CO CONTENT TOO HIGH
Check:
• Idle mixture adjustment (too rich).
• Defective automatic choke.
• Air filter warm air inlet door for sticking.
• Carburetor jets and channels; clean and/or replace.
• Engine condition with a compression and vacuum test.
HYDROCARBON LEVEL TOO HIGH
Check:
• Throttle valve closes completely.
• Spark plug condition and gap.
• Ignition timing (too advanced) and breaker point gap (if so equipped).
• Intake manifold for leaks.
• Valve clearance (too small).
• Engine condition with a compression and vacuum test.

cludes a temperature sensor, vacuum motor, and a hinged door. See **Figure 26**.

The system is comparatively easy to test. See **Figure 27** for the procedure.

Air Injection Reaction System

The air injection reaction system reduces air pollution by oxidizing hydrocarbons and carbon monoxide as they leave the combustion chamber. See **Figure 28**.

The air injection pump, driven by the engine, compresses filtered air and injects it at the exhaust port of each cylinder. The fresh air mixes with the unburned gases in the exhaust and promotes further burning. A check valve prevents exhaust gases from entering and damaging the air pump if the pump becomes inoperative, e.g., from a fan belt failure.

Figure 29 explains the testing procedure for this system.

Fuel Evaporation Control

Fuel vapor from the fuel tank passes through the liquid/vapor separator to the carbon canister. See **Figure 30**. The carbon absorbs and

24

Air
Filtered air
PCV valve
Carburetor
Fuel-air mixture
Piston
Blow-by gases
Filtered air
Crankcase oil

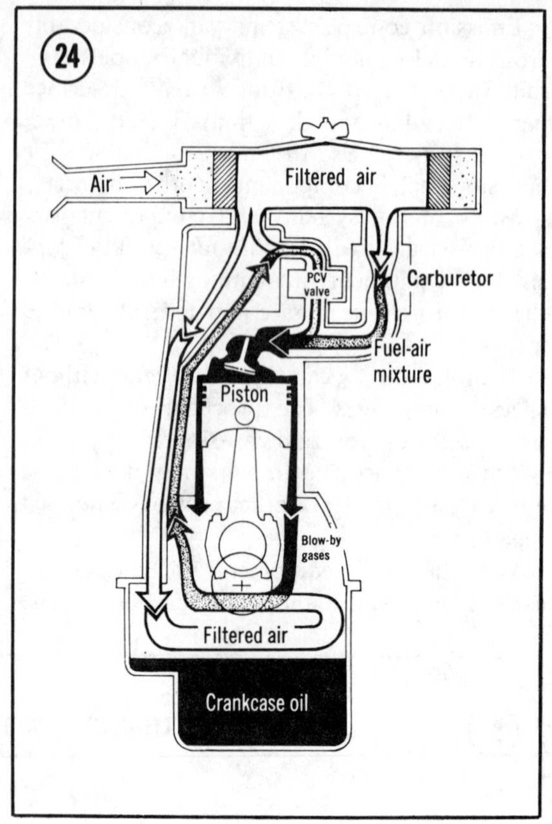

25

PCV VALVE TEST
START ENGINE
Let it idle, remove oil fill cap and place a piece of paper over the opening. The paper should be sucked onto the opening by vacuum.
VACUUM PRESENT
Valve is operating correctly.
NO VACUUM PRESENT
Valve is stuck closed.
Remove PCV valve and shake it, it should rattle.
VALVE RATTLES
Check hose from valve for obstructions. Clean out or replace it.
VALVE DOES NOT RATTLE
Take it apart and clean or replace it.

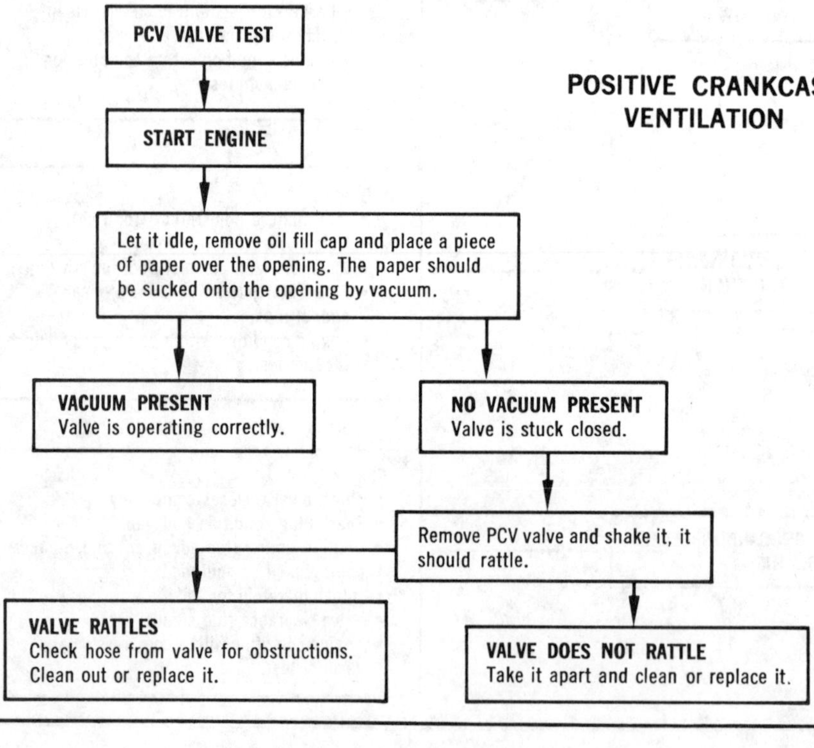

POSITIVE CRANKCASE VENTILATION

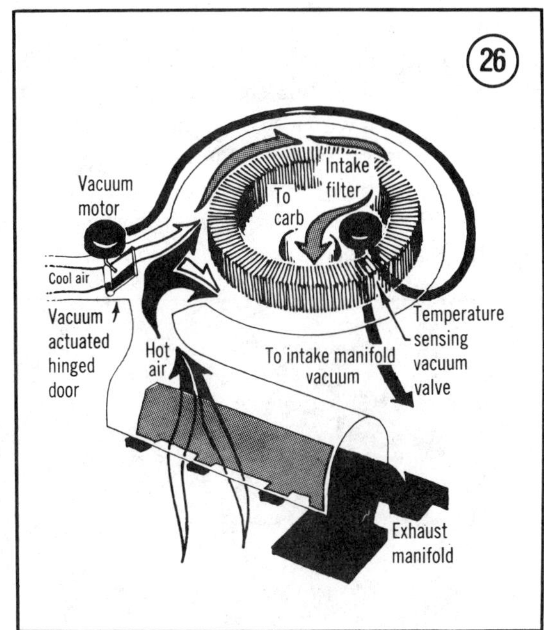
26
Vacuum motor
Intake filter
To carb
Cool air
Vacuum actuated hinged door
Hot air
To intake manifold vacuum
Temperature sensing vacuum valve
Exhaust manifold

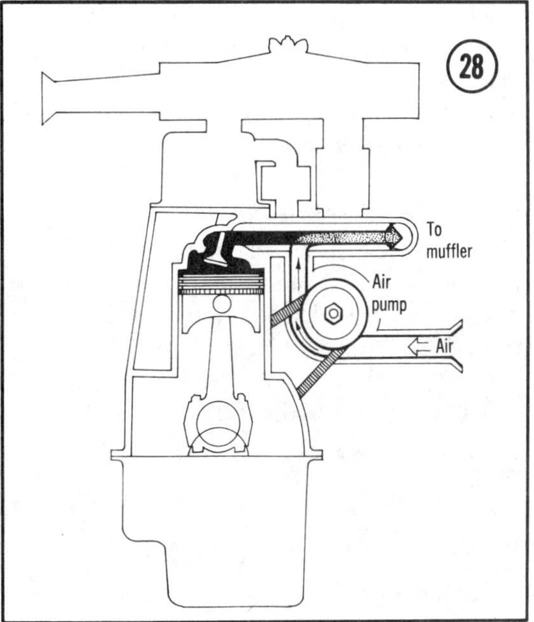
28
To muffler
Air pump
Air

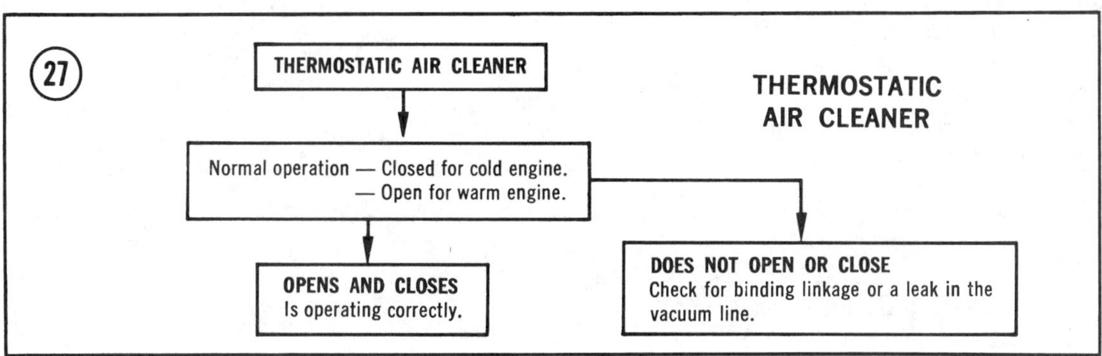
27
THERMOSTATIC AIR CLEANER
Normal operation — Closed for cold engine.
— Open for warm engine.
OPENS AND CLOSES
Is operating correctly.
DOES NOT OPEN OR CLOSE
Check for binding linkage or a leak in the vacuum line.

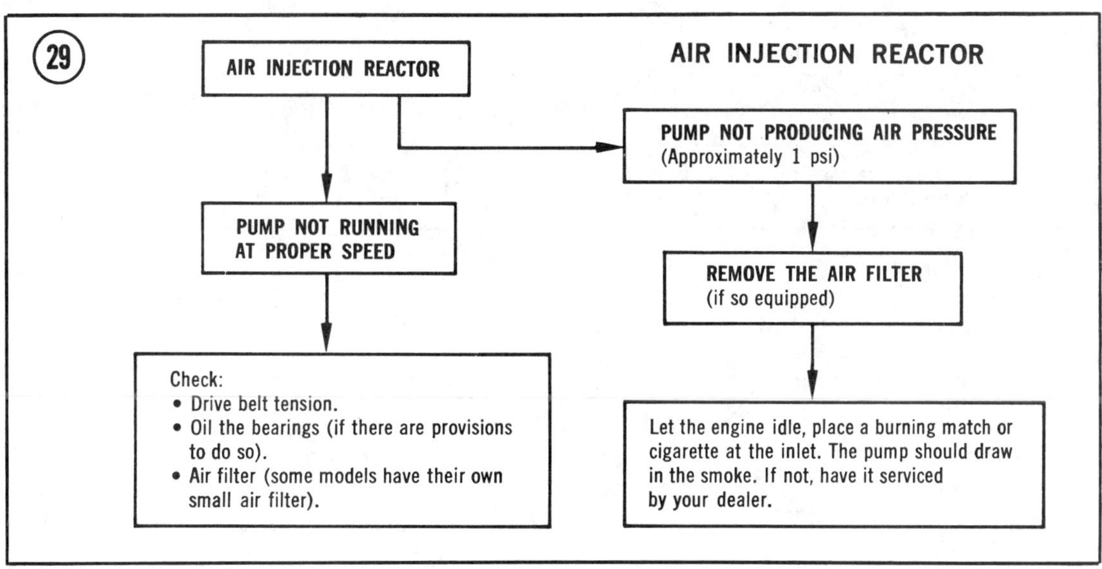
29
AIR INJECTION REACTOR
PUMP NOT PRODUCING AIR PRESSURE
(Approximately 1 psi)
REMOVE THE AIR FILTER
(if so equipped)
Let the engine idle, place a burning match or cigarette at the inlet. The pump should draw in the smoke. If not, have it serviced by your dealer.
PUMP NOT RUNNING AT PROPER SPEED
Check:
• Drive belt tension.
• Oil the bearings (if there are provisions to do so).
• Air filter (some models have their own small air filter).

THERMOSTATIC AIR CLEANER

AIR INJECTION REACTOR

stores the vapor when the engine is stopped. When the engine runs, manifold vacuum draws the vapor from the canister. Instead of being released into the atmosphere, the fuel vapor takes part in the normal combustion process.

Exhaust Gas Recirculation

The exhaust gas recirculation (EGR) system is used to reduce the emission of nitrogen oxides (NOx). Relatively inert exhaust gases are introduced into the combustion process to slightly reduce peak temperatures. This reduction in temperature reduces the formation of NOx.

Figure 31 provides a simple test of this system.

ENGINE NOISES

Often the first evidence of an internal engine trouble is a strange noise. That knocking, clicking, or tapping which you never heard before may be warning you of impending trouble.

While engine noises can indicate problems, they are sometimes difficult to interpret correctly; inexperienced mechanics can be seriously misled by them.

Professional mechanics often use a special stethoscope which looks similar to a doctor's stethoscope for isolating engine noises. You can do nearly as well with a "sounding stick" which can be an ordinary piece of doweling or a section of small hose. By placing one end in contact with the area to which you want to listen and the other end near your ear, you can hear

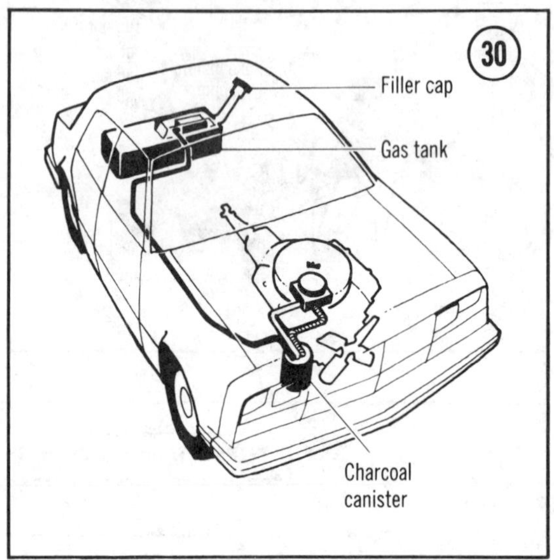
30
Filler cap
Gas tank
Charcoal canister

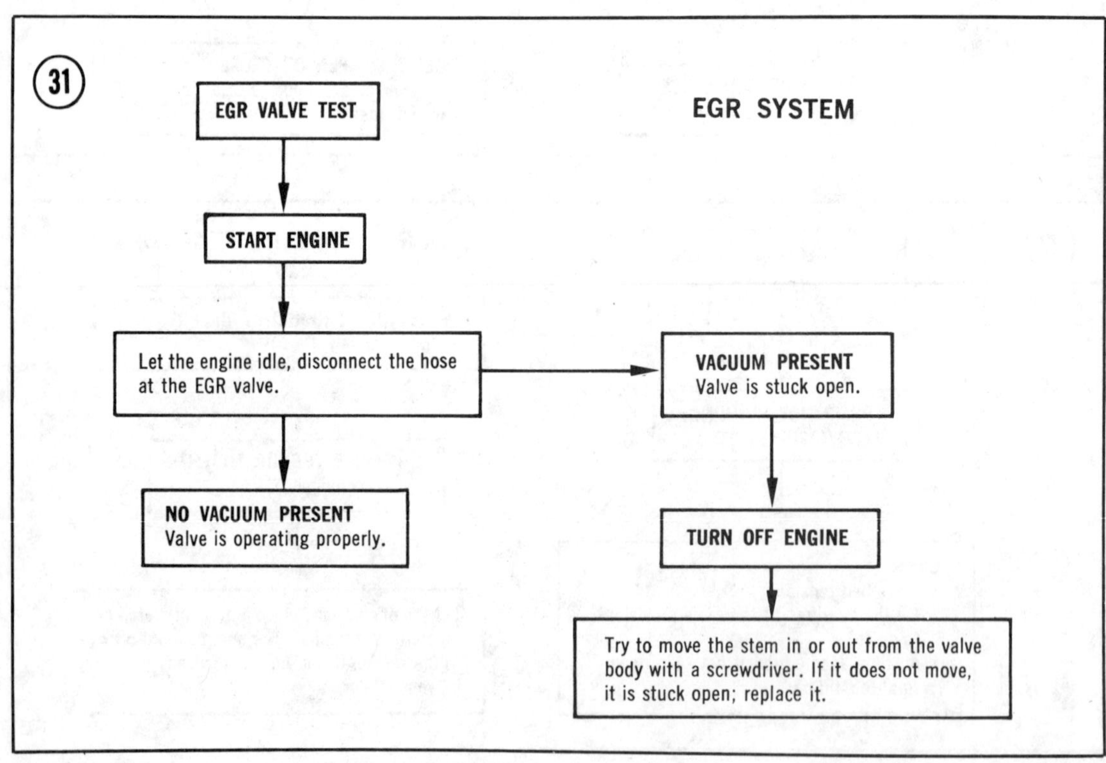
31
EGR VALVE TEST
EGR SYSTEM
START ENGINE
Let the engine idle, disconnect the hose at the EGR valve.
VACUUM PRESENT
Valve is stuck open.
NO VACUUM PRESENT
Valve is operating properly.
TURN OFF ENGINE
Try to move the stem in or out from the valve body with a screwdriver. If it does not move, it is stuck open; replace it.

sounds emanating from that area. The first time you do this, you may be horrified at the strange noises coming from even a normal engine. If you can, have an experienced friend or mechanic help you sort the noises out.

Clicking or Tapping Noises

Clicking or tapping noises usually come from the valve train, and indicate excessive valve clearance.

If your vehicle has adjustable valves, the procedure for adjusting the valve clearance is explained in Chapter Three. If your vehicle has hydraulic lifters, the clearance may not be adjustable. The noise may be coming from a collapsed lifter. These may be cleaned or replaced as described in the engine chapter.

A sticking valve may also sound like a valve with excessive clearance. In addition, excessive wear in valve train components can cause similar engine noises.

Knocking Noises

A heavy, dull knocking is usually caused by a worn main bearing. The noise is loudest when the engine is working hard, i.e., accelerating hard at low speed. You may be able to isolate the trouble to a single bearing by disconnecting the spark plugs one at a time. When you reach the spark plug nearest the bearing, the knock will be reduced or disappear.

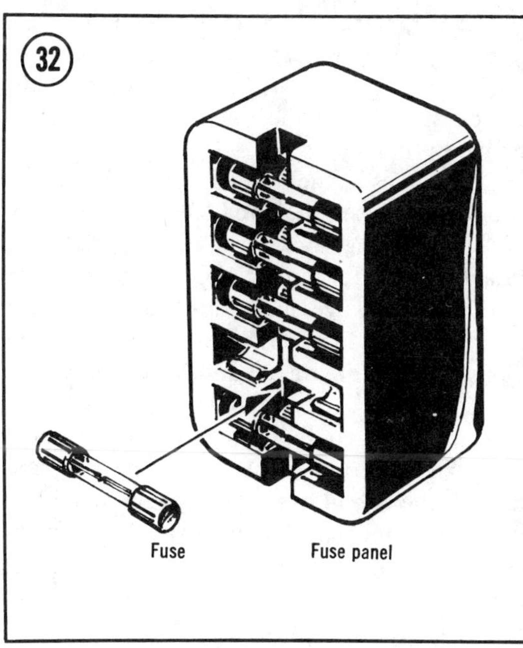

Worn connecting rod bearings may also produce a knock, but the sound is usually more "metallic." As with a main bearing, the noise is worse when accelerating. It may even increase further just as you go from accelerating to coasting. Disconnecting spark plugs will help isolate this knock as well.

A double knock or clicking usually indicates a worn piston pin. Disconnecting spark plugs will isolate this to a particular piston, however, the noise will *increase* when you reach the affected piston.

A loose flywheel and excessive crankshaft end play also produce knocking noises. While similar to main bearing noises, these are usually intermittent, not constant, and they do not change when spark plugs are disconnected.

Some mechanics confuse piston pin noise with piston slap. The double knock will distinguish the piston pin noise. Piston slap is identified by the fact that it is always louder when the engine is cold.

ELECTRICAL ACCESSORIES

Lights and Switches (Interior and Exterior)

1. ***Bulb does not light*** — Remove the bulb and check for a broken element. Also check the inside of the socket; make sure the contacts are clean and free of corrosion. If the bulb and socket are OK, check to see if a fuse has blown or a circuit breaker has tripped. The fuse panel **(Figure 32)** is usually located under the instrument panel. Replace the blown fuse or reset the circuit breaker. If the fuse blows or the breaker trips again, there is a short in that circuit. Check that circuit all the way to the battery. Look for worn wire insulation or burned wires.

If all the above are all right, check the switch controlling the bulb for continuity with an ohmmeter at the switch terminals. Check the switch contact terminals for loose or dirty electrical connections.

2. ***Headlights work but will not switch from either high or low beam*** — Check the beam selector switch for continuity with an ohmmeter

at the switch terminals. Check the switch contact terminals for loose or dirty electrical connections.

3. ***Brake light switch inoperative*** — On mechanically operated switches, usually mounted near the brake pedal arm, adjust the switch to achieve correct mechanical operation. Check the switch for continuity with an ohmmeter at the switch terminals. Check the switch contact terminals for loose or dirty electrical connections.

4. ***Back-up lights do not operate*** — Check light bulb as described earlier. Locate the switch, normally located near the shift lever. Adjust switch to achieve correct mechanical operation. Check the switch for continuity with an ohmmeter at the switch terminals. Bypass the switch with a jumper wire; if the lights work, replace the switch.

Directional Signals

1. ***Directional signals do not operate*** — If the indicator light on the instrument panel burns steadily instead of flashing, this usually indicates that one of the exterior lights is burned out. Check all lamps that normally flash. If all are all right, the flasher unit may be defective. Replace it with a good one.

2. ***Directional signal indicator light on instrument panel does not light up*** — Check the light bulbs as described earlier. Check all electrical connections and check the flasher unit.

3. ***Directional signals will not self-cancel*** — Check the self-cancelling mechanism located inside the steering column.

4. ***Directional signals flash slowly*** — Check the condition of the battery and the alternator (or generator) drive belt tension (**Figure 4**). Check the flasher unit and all related electrical connections.

Windshield Wipers

1. ***Wipers do not operate*** — Check for a blown fuse or circuit breaker that has tripped; replace or reset. Check all related terminals for loose or dirty electrical connections. Check continuity of the control switch with an ohmmeter at the switch terminals. Check the linkage and arms for loose, broken, or binding parts. Straighten out or replace where necessary.

2. ***Wiper motor hums but will not operate*** — The motor may be shorted out internally; check and/or replace the motor. Also check for broken or binding linkage and arms.

3. ***Wiper arms will not return to the stowed position when turned off*** — The motor has a special internal switch for this purpose. Have it inspected by your dealer. Do not attempt this yourself.

Interior Heater

1. ***Heater fan does not operate*** — Check for a blown fuse or circuit breaker that has tripped. Check the switch for continuity with an ohmmeter at the switch terminals. Check the switch contact terminals for loose or dirty electrical connections.

2. ***Heat output is insufficient*** — Check the heater hose/engine coolant control valve usually located in the engine compartment; make sure it is in the open position. Ensure that the heater door(s) and cable(s) are operating correctly and are in the open position. Inspect the heat ducts; make sure that they are not crimped or blocked.

COOLING SYSTEM

The temperature gauge or warning light usually signals cooling system troubles before there is any damage. As long as you stop the vehicle at the first indication of trouble, serious damage is unlikely.

In most cases, the trouble will be obvious as soon as you open the hood. If there is coolant or steam leaking, look for a defective radiator, radiator hose, or heater hose. If there is no evidence of leakage, make sure that the fan belt is in good condition. If the trouble is not obvious, refer to **Figures 33 and 34** to help isolate the trouble.

Automotive cooling systems operate under pressure to permit higher operating temperatures without boil-over. The system should be checked periodically to make sure it can withstand normal pressure. **Figure 35** shows the equipment which nearly any service station has for testing the system pressure.

33

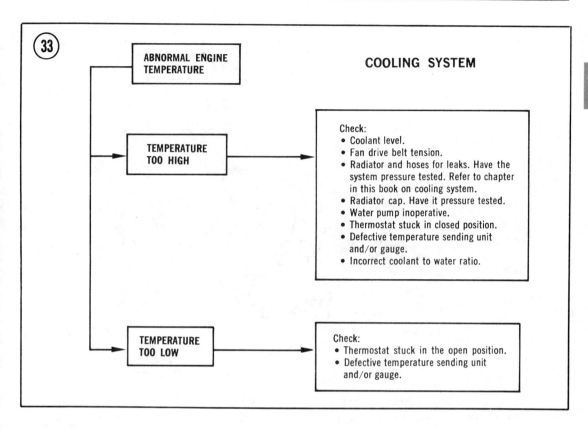

ABNORMAL ENGINE TEMPERATURE

COOLING SYSTEM

TEMPERATURE TOO HIGH

Check:
- Coolant level.
- Fan drive belt tension.
- Radiator and hoses for leaks. Have the system pressure tested. Refer to chapter in this book on cooling system.
- Radiator cap. Have it pressure tested.
- Water pump inoperative.
- Thermostat stuck in closed position.
- Defective temperature sending unit and/or gauge.
- Incorrect coolant to water ratio.

TEMPERATURE TOO LOW

Check:
- Thermostat stuck in the open position.
- Defective temperature sending unit and/or gauge.

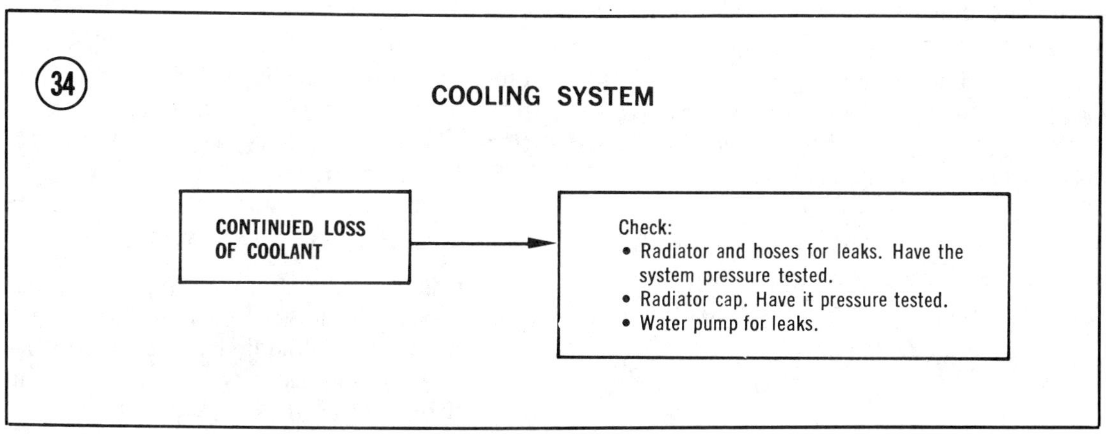

CLUTCH

All clutch troubles except adjustments require transmission removal to identify and cure the problem.

1. ***Slippage*** — This is most noticeable when accelerating in a high gear at relatively low speed. To check slippage, park the vehicle on a level surface with the handbrake set. Shift to 2nd gear and release the clutch as if driving off. If the clutch is good, the engine will slow and stall. If the clutch slips, continued engine speed will give it away.

Slippage results from insufficient clutch pedal free play, oil or grease on the clutch disc, worn pressure plate, or weak springs.

2. ***Drag or failure to release*** — This trouble usually causes difficult shifting and gear clash, especially when downshifting. The cause may be excessive clutch pedal free play, warped or bent pressure plate or clutch disc, broken or

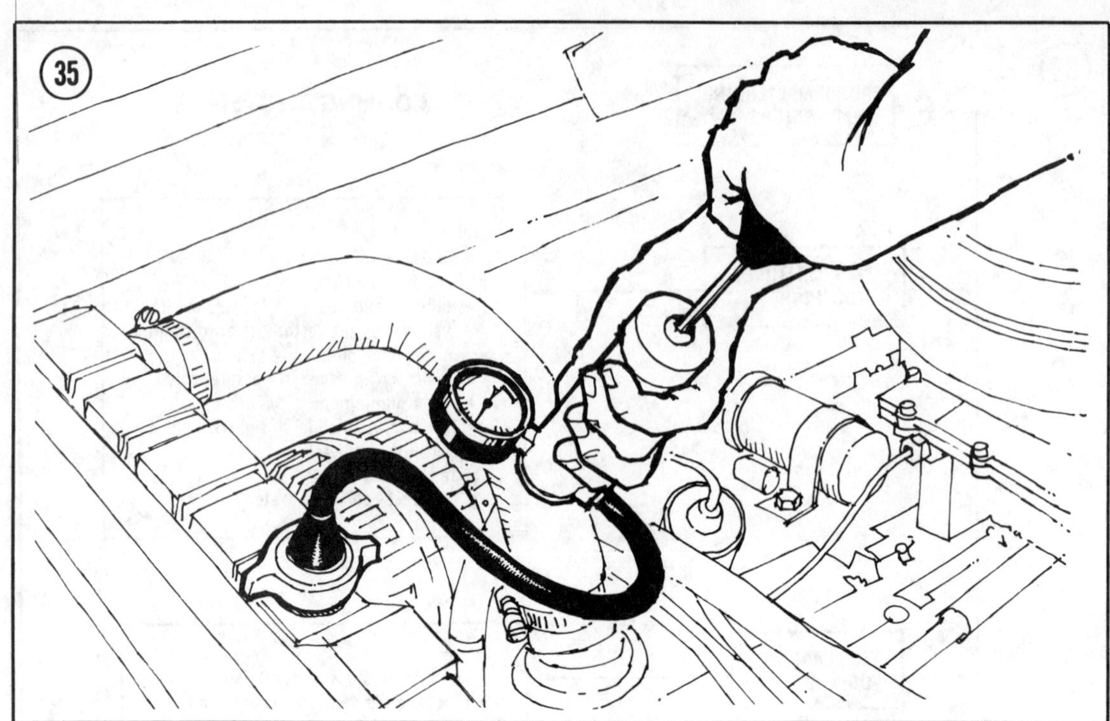
35

loose linings, or lack of lubrication in pilot bearing. Also check condition of transmission main shaft splines.

3. *Chatter or grabbing* — A number of things can cause this trouble. Check tightness of engine mounts and engine-to-transmission mounting bolts. Check for worn or misaligned pressure plate and misaligned release plate.

4. *Other noises* — Noise usually indicates a dry or defective release or pilot bearing. Check the bearings and replace if necessary. Also check all parts for misalignment and uneven wear.

MANUAL TRANSMISSION/TRANSAXLE

Transmission and transaxle troubles are evident when one or more of the following symptoms appear:

a. Difficulty changing gears
b. Gears clash when downshifting
c. Slipping out of gear
d. Excessive noise in NEUTRAL
e. Excessive noise in gear
f. Oil leaks

Transmission and transaxle repairs are not recommended unless the many special tools required are available.

Transmission and transaxle troubles are sometimes difficult to distinguish from clutch troubles. Eliminate the clutch as a source of trouble before installing a new or rebuilt transmission or transaxle.

AUTOMATIC TRANSMISSION

Most automatic transmission repairs require considerable specialized knowledge and tools. It is impractical for the home mechanic to invest in the tools, since they cost more than a properly rebuilt transmission.

Check fluid level and condition frequently to help prevent future problems. If the fluid is orange or black in color or smells like varnish, it is an indication of some type of damage or failure within the transmission. Have the transmission serviced by your dealer or competent automatic transmission service facility.

BRAKES

Good brakes are vital to the safe operation of the vehicle. Performing the maintenance speci-

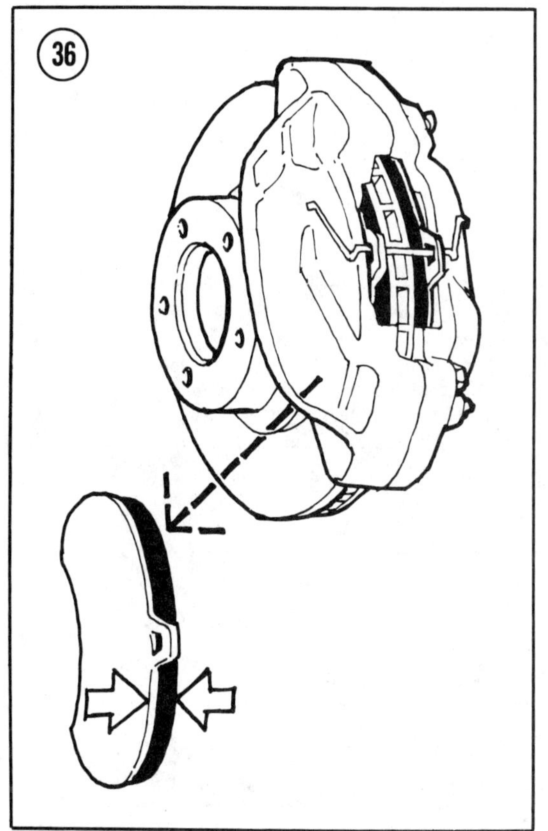

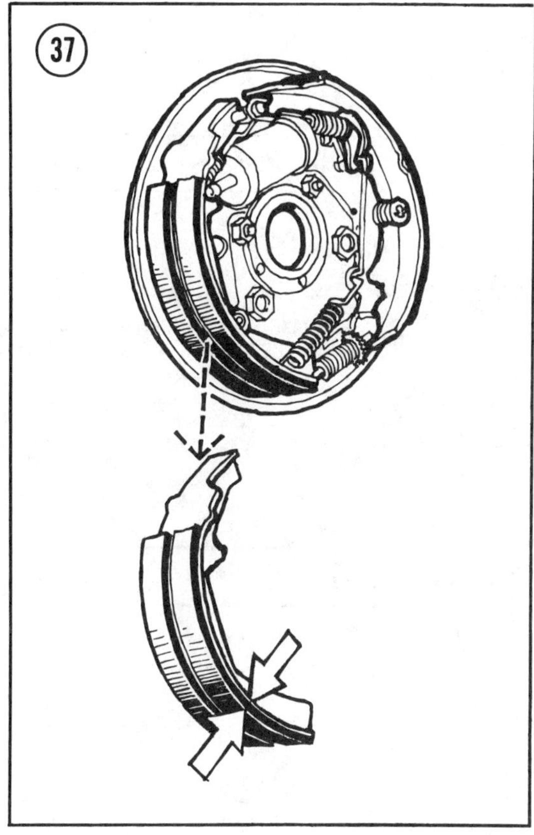

fied in Chapter Three will minimize problems with the brakes. Most importantly, check and maintain the level of fluid in the master cylinder, and check the thickness of the linings on the disc brake pads (**Figure 36**) or drum brake shoes (**Figure 37**).

If trouble develops, **Figures 38 through 40** will help you locate the problem. Refer to the brake chapter for actual repair procedures.

STEERING AND SUSPENSION

Trouble in the suspension or steering is evident when the following occur:

a. Steering is hard
b. Car pulls to one side
c. Car wanders or front wheels wobble
d. Steering has excessive play
e. Tire wear is abnormal

Unusual steering, pulling, or wandering is usually caused by bent or otherwise misaligned suspension parts. This is difficult to check without proper alignment equipment. Refer to the suspension chapter in this book for repairs that you can perform and those that must be left to a dealer or suspension specialist.

If your trouble seems to be excessive play, check wheel bearing adjustment first. This is the most frequent cause. Then check ball-joints (refer to Suspension chapter). Finally, check tie rod end ball-joints by shaking each tie rod. Also check steering gear, or rack-and-pinion assembly to see that it is securely bolted down.

TIRE WEAR ANALYSIS

Abnormal tire wear should be analyzed to determine its causes. The most common causes are the following:

a. Incorrect tire pressure
b. Improper driving
c. Overloading
d. Bad road surfaces
e. Incorrect wheel alignment

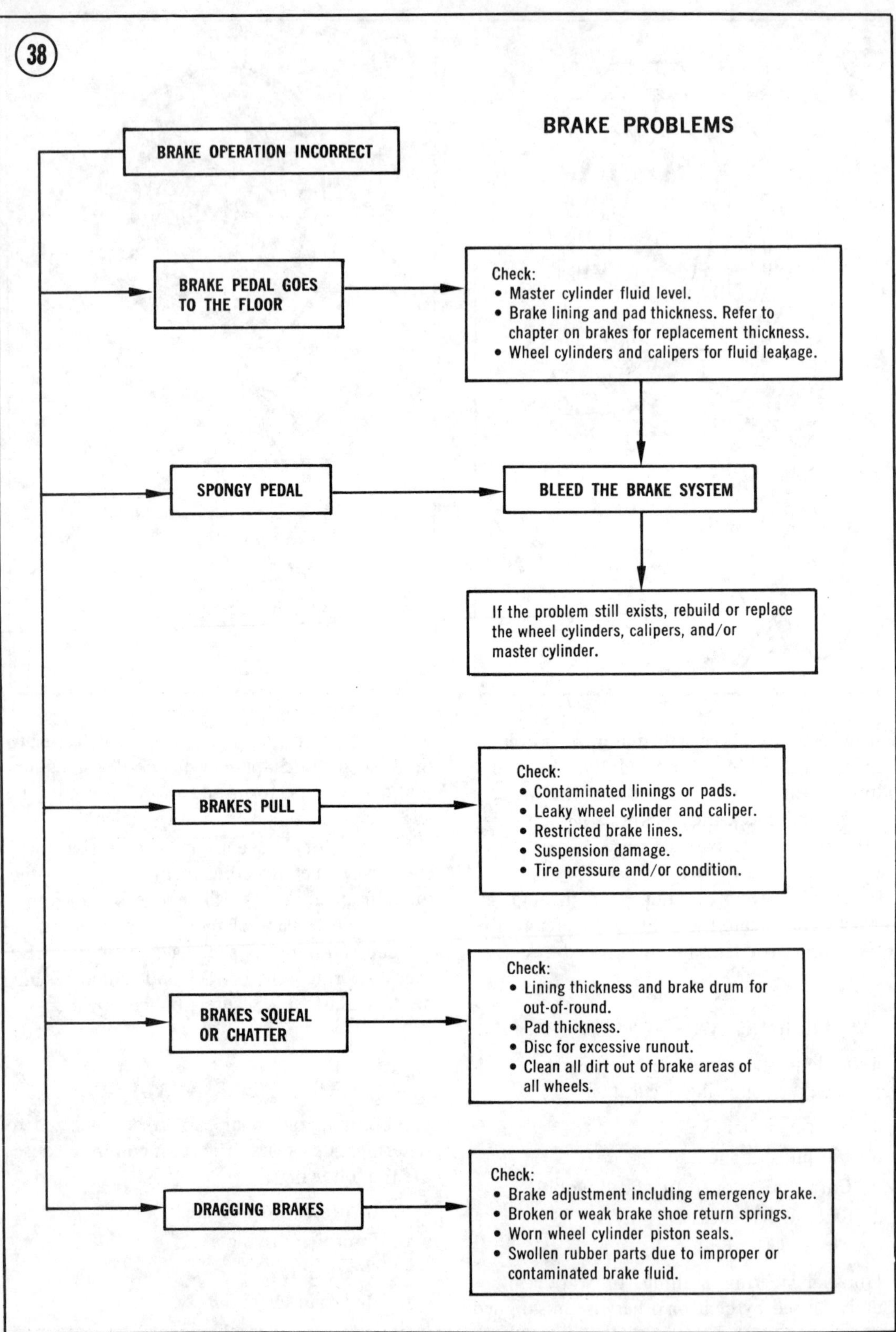
38
BRAKE PROBLEMS
BRAKE OPERATION INCORRECT
BRAKE PEDAL GOES TO THE FLOOR
Check:
• Master cylinder fluid level.
• Brake lining and pad thickness. Refer to chapter on brakes for replacement thickness.
• Wheel cylinders and calipers for fluid leakage.
SPONGY PEDAL
BLEED THE BRAKE SYSTEM
If the problem still exists, rebuild or replace the wheel cylinders, calipers, and/or master cylinder.
BRAKES PULL
Check:
• Contaminated linings or pads.
• Leaky wheel cylinder and caliper.
• Restricted brake lines.
• Suspension damage.
• Tire pressure and/or condition.
BRAKES SQUEAL OR CHATTER
Check:
• Lining thickness and brake drum for out-of-round.
• Pad thickness.
• Disc for excessive runout.
• Clean all dirt out of brake areas of all wheels.
DRAGGING BRAKES
Check:
• Brake adjustment including emergency brake.
• Broken or weak brake shoe return springs.
• Worn wheel cylinder piston seals.
• Swollen rubber parts due to improper or contaminated brake fluid.

39

BRAKE PROBLEMS

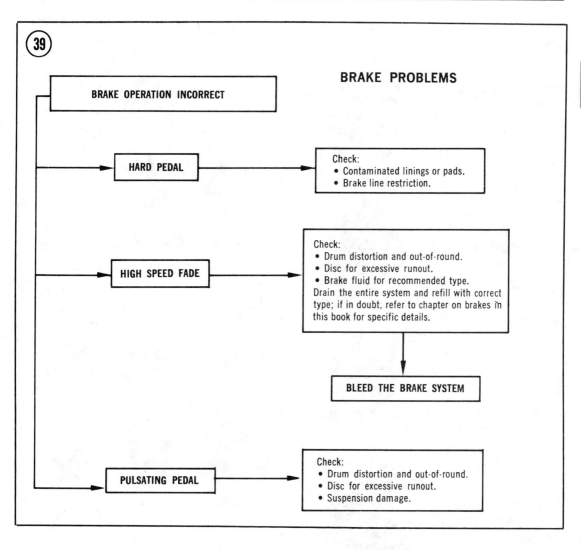

BRAKE OPERATION INCORRECT

HARD PEDAL → Check:
- Contaminated linings or pads.
- Brake line restriction.

HIGH SPEED FADE → Check:
- Drum distortion and out-of-round.
- Disc for excessive runout.
- Brake fluid for recommended type.

Drain the entire system and refill with correct type; if in doubt, refer to chapter on brakes in this book for specific details.

→ BLEED THE BRAKE SYSTEM

PULSATING PEDAL → Check:
- Drum distortion and out-of-round.
- Disc for excessive runout.
- Suspension damage.

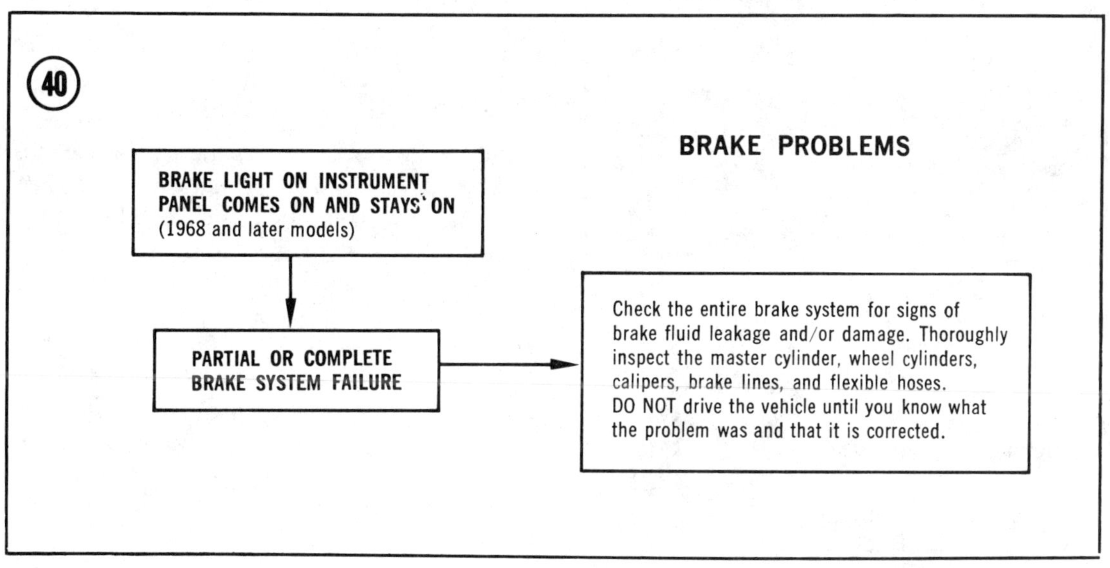

40
BRAKE PROBLEMS
BRAKE LIGHT ON INSTRUMENT PANEL COMES ON AND STAYS ON (1968 and later models)
PARTIAL OR COMPLETE BRAKE SYSTEM FAILURE
Check the entire brake system for signs of brake fluid leakage and/or damage. Thoroughly inspect the master cylinder, wheel cylinders, calipers, brake lines, and flexible hoses.
DO NOT drive the vehicle until you know what the problem was and that it is corrected.

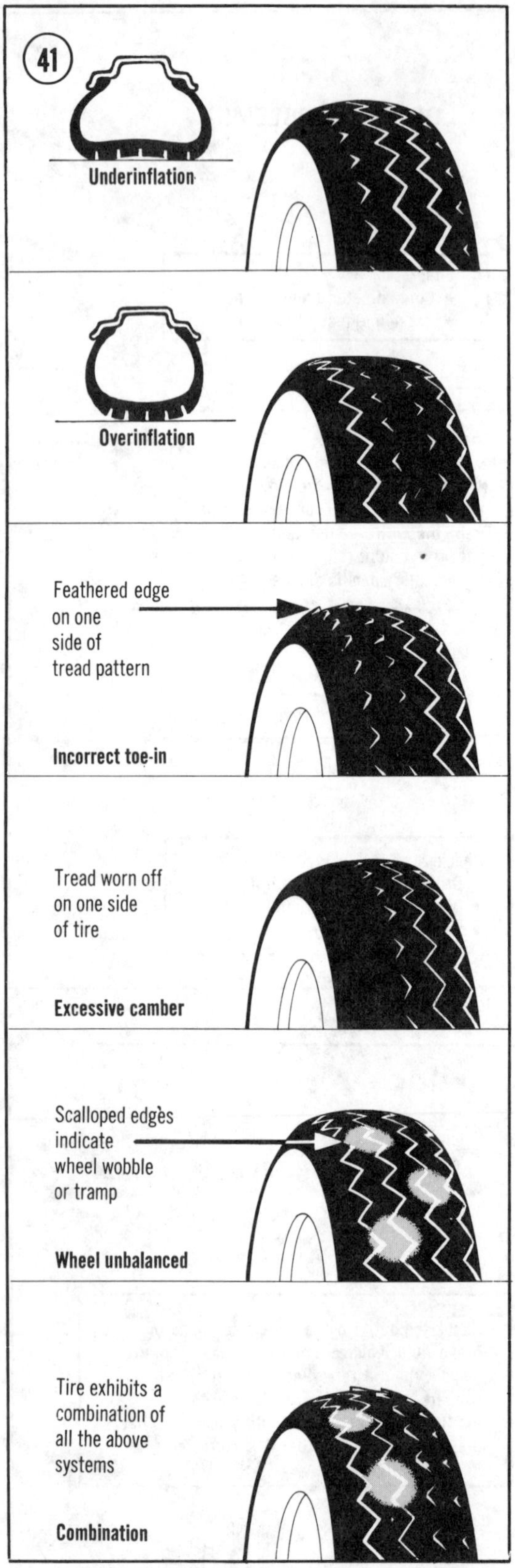

41

Underinflation

Overinflation

Feathered edge on one side of tread pattern

Incorrect toe-in

Tread worn off on one side of tire

Excessive camber

Scalloped edges indicate wheel wobble or tramp

Wheel unbalanced

Tire exhibits a combination of all the above systems

Combination

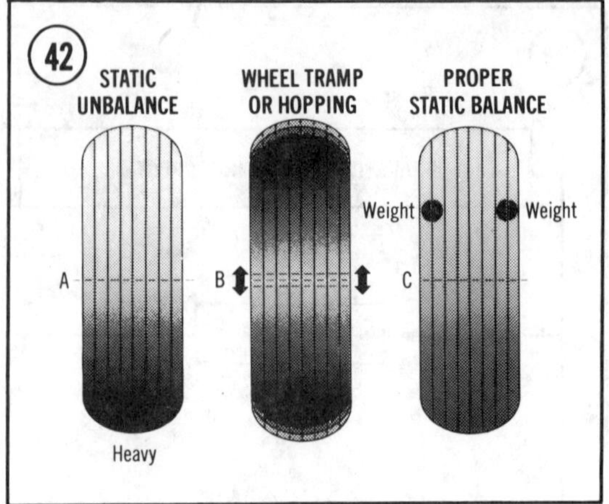

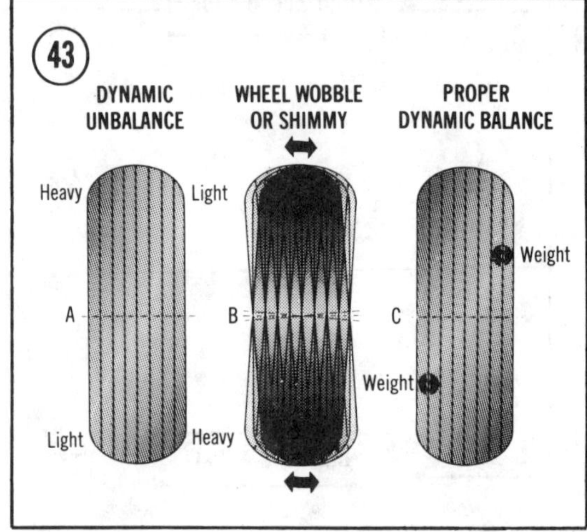

Figure 41 identifies wear patterns and indicates the most probable causes.

WHEEL BALANCING

All four wheels and tires must be in balance along two axes. To be in static balance **(Figure 42)**, weight must be evenly distributed around the axis of rotation. (A) shows a statically unbalanced wheel; (B) shows the result — wheel tramp or hopping; (C) shows proper static balance.

To be in dynamic balance **(Figure 43)**, the centerline of the weight must coincide with the centerline of the wheel. (A) shows a dynamically unbalanced wheel; (B) shows the result — wheel wobble or shimmy; (C) shows proper dynamic balance.

CHAPTER THREE

3

LUBRICATION, MAINTENANCE AND TUNE-UP

This chapter deals with the normal maintenance required to keep your Aerostar running properly. **Table 1** gives the maintenance intervals for vehicles given normal use. Some procedures are done at fuel stops; others are done at specified mileage or time intervals.

Vehicles driven under severe conditions require more frequent maintenance. This is specified in **Table 1**. Such conditions include:

a. Frequent short trips.
b. Stop-and-go driving.
c. Extremely cold weather.
d. Trailer towing.
e. Dust.

Some maintenance procedures are included under *Tune-up* in this chapter and detailed instructions will be found there. Other steps are described in the following chapters. Chapter references are included with these steps.

Tables 1-5 are at the end of the chapter.

HOISTING, JACKING AND LIFT POINTS

Special precautions should be taken when raising the vehicle with a jack or a hoist and when positioning jackstands. Incorrect jack or jackstand placement can cause suspension or drive train damage. The service jack provided with the vehicle is intended only for emergency use in changing a flat tire.

Refer to the Owner's Manual when using this jack. Do not use it to lift the vehicle up while performing other services.

When lifting one wheel of the vehicle, as when changing a tire, dismantling a hub or removing a brake drum, make sure the vehicle is resting as level as possible and firmly block the wheels at the opposite end of the vehicle. Set the parking brake and place the transmission in PARK (automatic transmission) or REVERSE (manual transmission). Position the jack carefully to provide maximum contact at the points shown in **Figure 1** or **Figure 2**. The jack should be as close as possible to the wheel being raised and positioned exactly vertical.

Raise the jack until it just begins to support the axle. Loosen all wheel lug nuts about 1/4-1/2 turn. Continue to raise the jack slowly until the wheel just clears the ground and will rotate freely. Unscrew the lug nuts and remove the wheel. When reinstalling the wheel, tighten the lug nuts securely, lower the vehicle to the ground and remove the jack, then tighten all of the lug nuts to specifications.

A floor jack or other type of hydraulic jack is recommended to raise the front or rear of the vehicle as required for service. Always place jackstands at the appropriate points to hold the vehicle stable. Relying upon a single jack to hold the vehicle without the use of jackstands can lead to serious physical injury.

The front of the vehicle can be safely lifted with a hydraulic jack placed under the center of the front crossmember. Make sure the jack does not lift against or contact any sheet metal, suspension or steering components or the bottom of the radiator. Check to see that it does not touch electrical leads, hydraulic lines or oil/fuel lines.

The rear of the vehicle can be safely lifted by placing the hydraulic jack under the center of the rear axle housing. After the vehicle has been lifted with the jack, support it on jackstands located under the frame rails or the rear axle. Do *not* run the engine when the rear wheels are jacked up if the vehicle is equipped with a limited-slip differential.

WARNING
Never work beneath the vehicle when it is supported only by a jack.

When raising the vehicle on a service station hoist, position the front hoist arms or lifting pads to provide maximum contact at the points shown in **Figure 1** (single-post hoist) or **Figure 2**

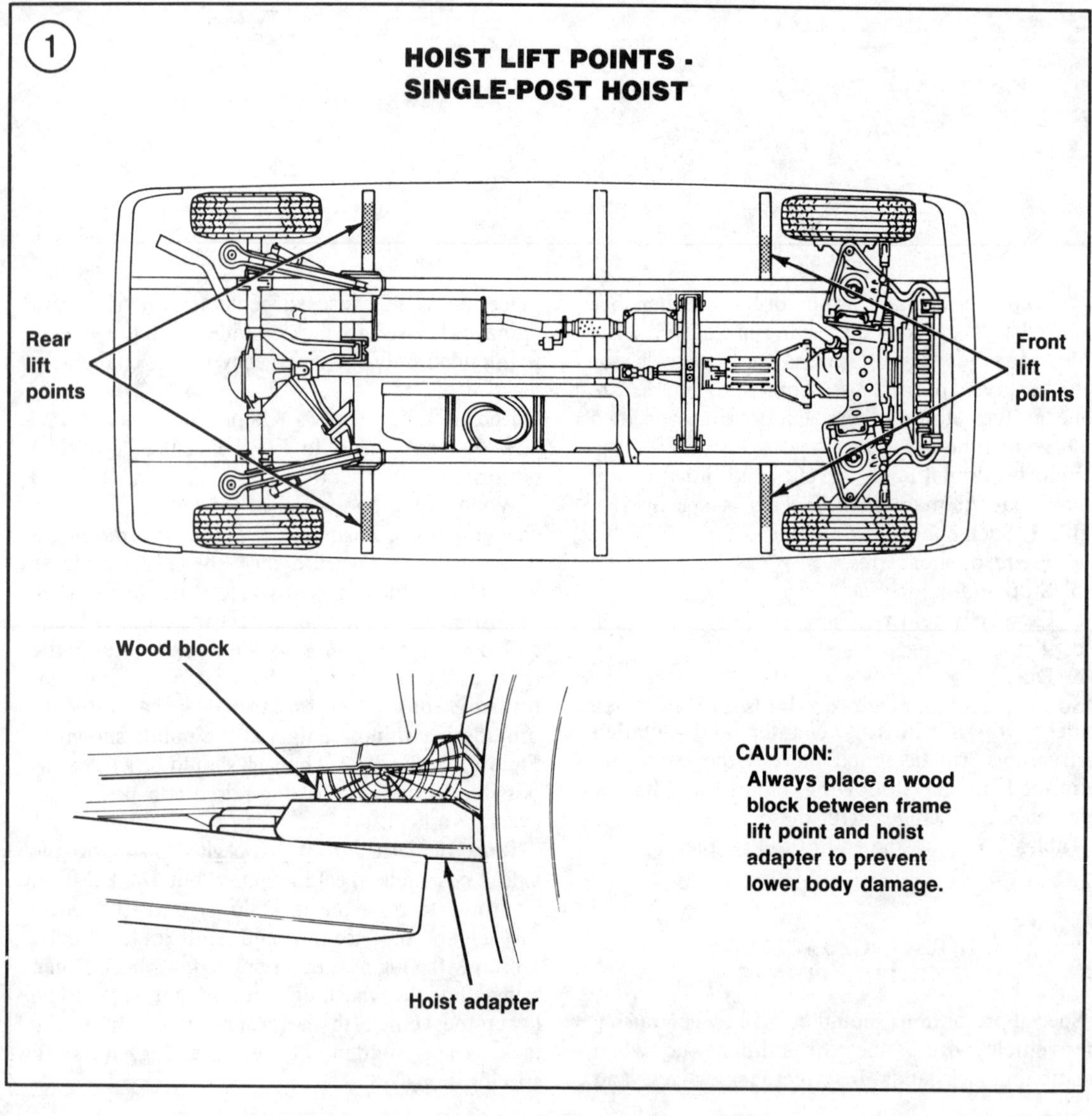

(twin-post hoist), making sure they do not touch the steering linkage.

WARNING
On vehicles equipped with an under-chassis mounted spare tire, remove the tire, wheel or tire carrier before raising the vehicle to a high-lift position. This will avoid any sudden weight release from the chassis that might affect vehicle positioning on the hoist.

TOWING

CAUTION
Tow a vehicle only as described in this chapter and with a minimal load. Improper towing techniques can result in serious transmission damage.

As a general rule, the vehicles covered in this manual should be towed with their rear wheels off the ground. If the rear wheels cannot be raised, either disconnect the drive shaft or tow the vehicle with the aid of a dolly.

If the vehicle is towed with its front wheels on the ground, clamp the steering wheel in a straight-ahead position with a wheel clamping device designed for towing. Do *not* rely upon the steering column lock.

If the vehicle is towed with the front wheels off the ground, do not exceed speeds of 35 mph or distances of 50 miles unless the rear drive shaft is disconnected. Vehicles towed with the rear wheels off the ground should not exceed speeds of 35 mph (rough pavement) or 50 mph (smooth pavement).

WEEKLY CHECKS

Many of the following services were once routinely performed by service station attendants during a fuel stop. With the advent of the self-service station and the extra cost for "full service," you may want to perform the checks yourself. Although simple to perform, they are important, as such checks give an indication of the need for other maintenance. Typical engine compartment component location is provided in **Figure 3** (I4), **Figure 4** (2.8L V6) or **Figure 5** (3.0L V6).

Engine Oil Level

Engine oil should be checked before the vehicle is started each day. At this time, all the oil is in the crankcase and the dipstick will give a true reading. If you find it necessary to check the oil after the

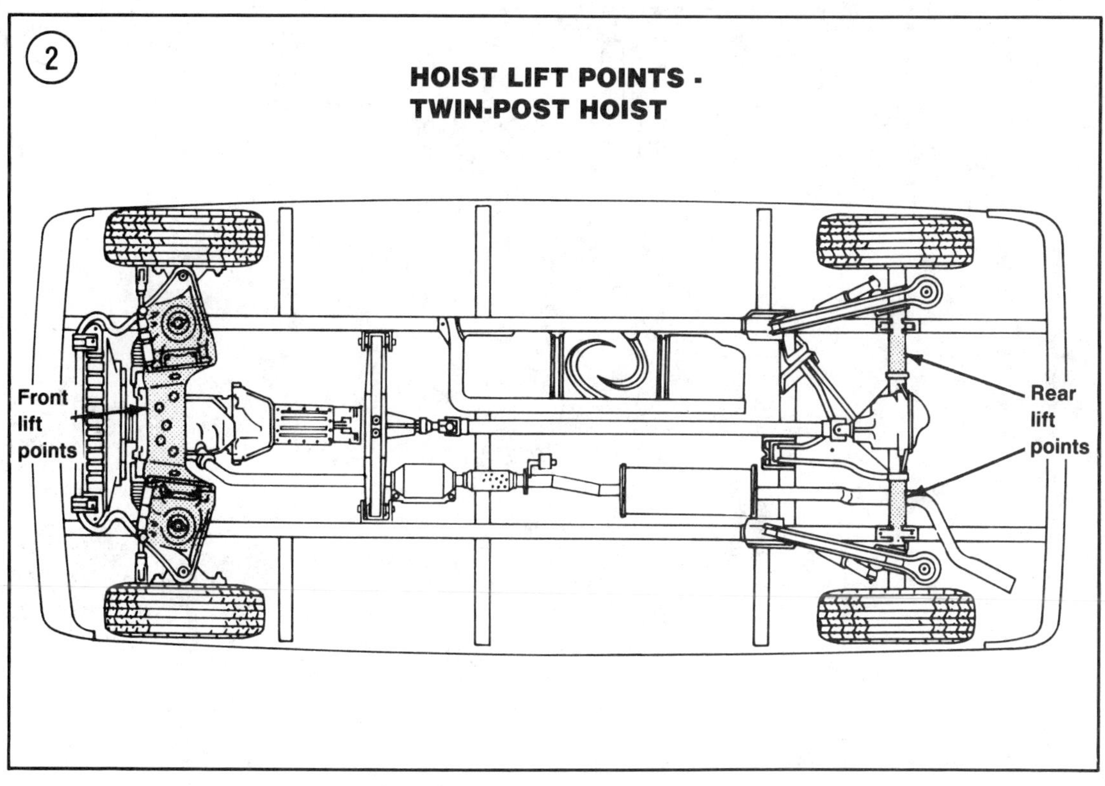

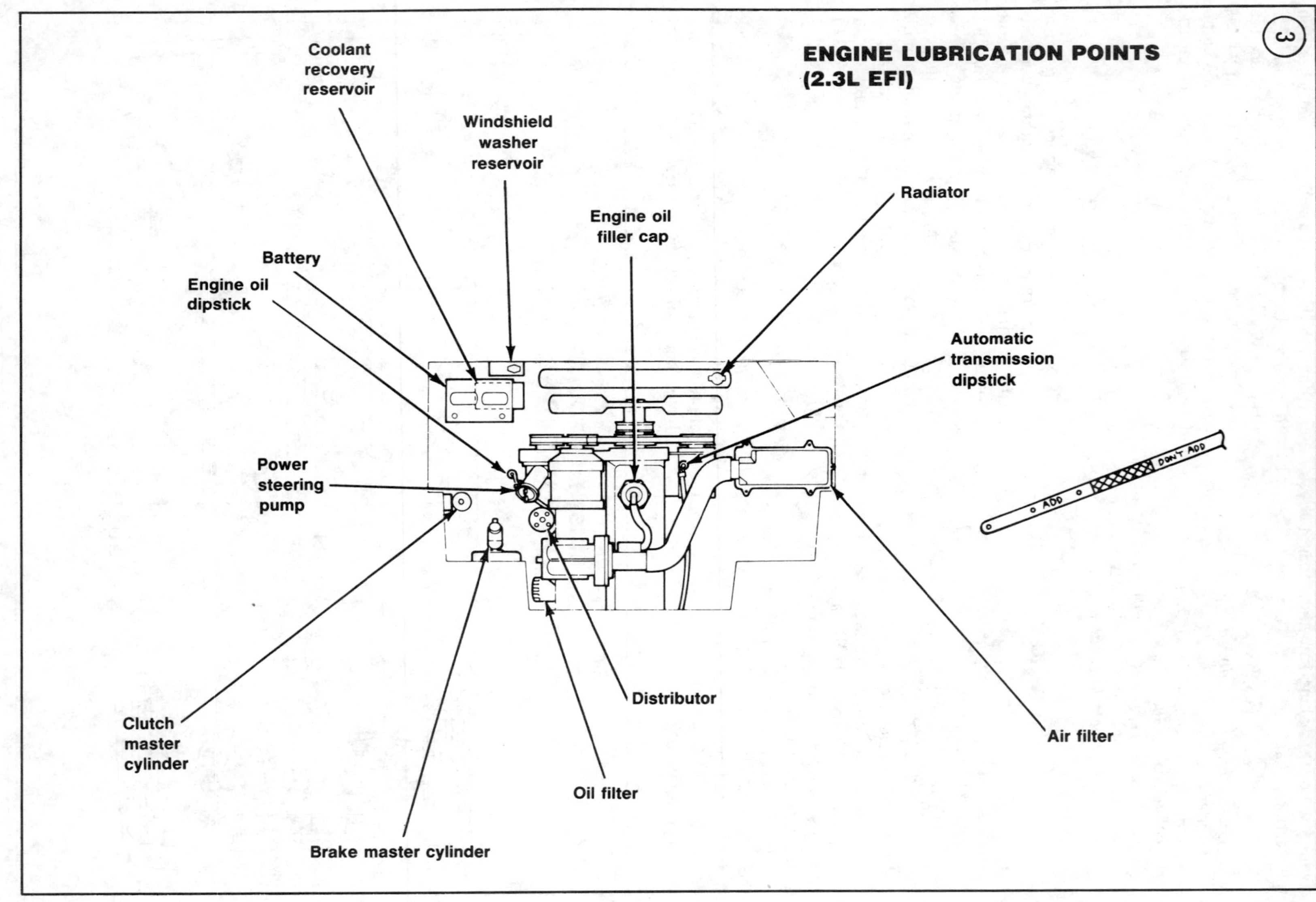

ENGINE LUBRICATION POINTS (2.3L EFI)

ENGINE LUBRICATION POINTS (2.8L V6)

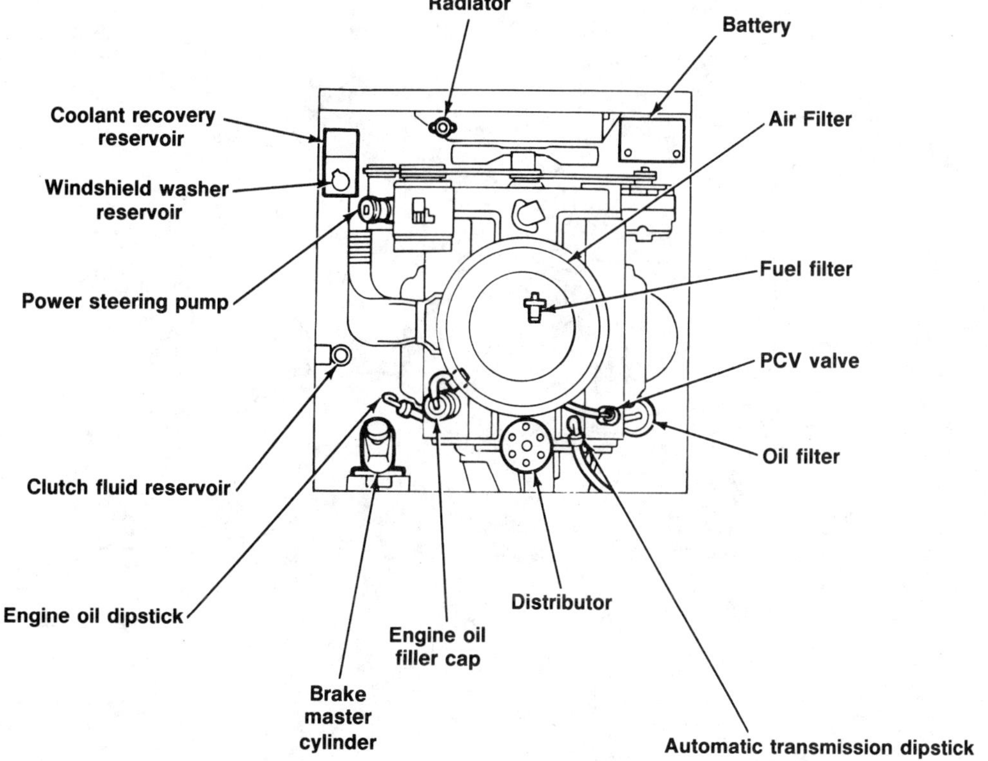

3

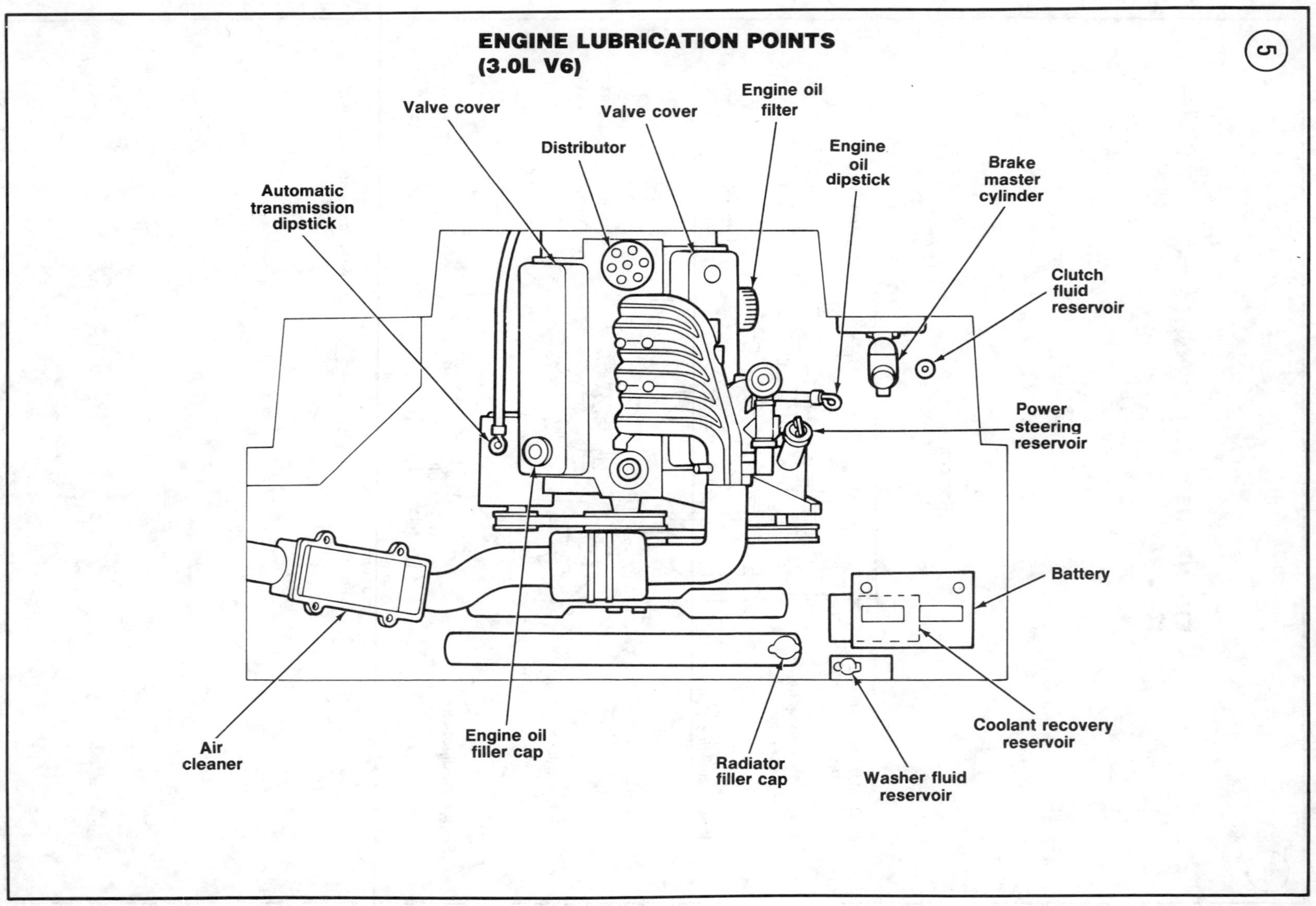

ENGINE LUBRICATION POINTS (3.0L V6)

engine has been started, let the vehicle sit for an hour to allow oil in the upper part of the engine to drain back into the crankcase.

With the engine cold and off, pull out the engine oil dipstick. See **Figure 6** (typical). Wipe the dipstick with a clean rag or paper towel and reinsert it in the dipstick tube. Be sure to push the dipstick all the way down. Pull the dipstick out again and check the oil level on the end of the dipstick. A small circle on the dipstick (**Figure 7**) indicates the *maximum* oil fill limit. Any oil level between the circle and the upper SAFE limit should be considered acceptable. If the oil level is above the circle, drain the oil until the level is at or slightly below the circle. Reinsert the dipstick and push it all the way into the dipstick tube.

Top up to the SAFE or crosshatched mark on the dipstick, if necessary. See **Figure 7**. Use *only* an SF grade oil. See **Table 2** for proper oil viscosity. Add oil through the valve cover opening (I4) or oil fill tube (V6). See **Figure 8** (I4) or **Figure 9** (V6).

Coolant Level and Condition

WARNING
Do not remove the radiator cap when the engine is warm or hot, especially if an air conditioner has been in use. You may be seriously scalded or burned.

Check coolant level by removing the radiator cap. The translucent recovery tank is located under the battery tray and access to it is blocked in most models. With the engine cold, the coolant level should be at the base of the radiator filler neck (**Figure 10**). Top up as needed with a 50/50 mixture

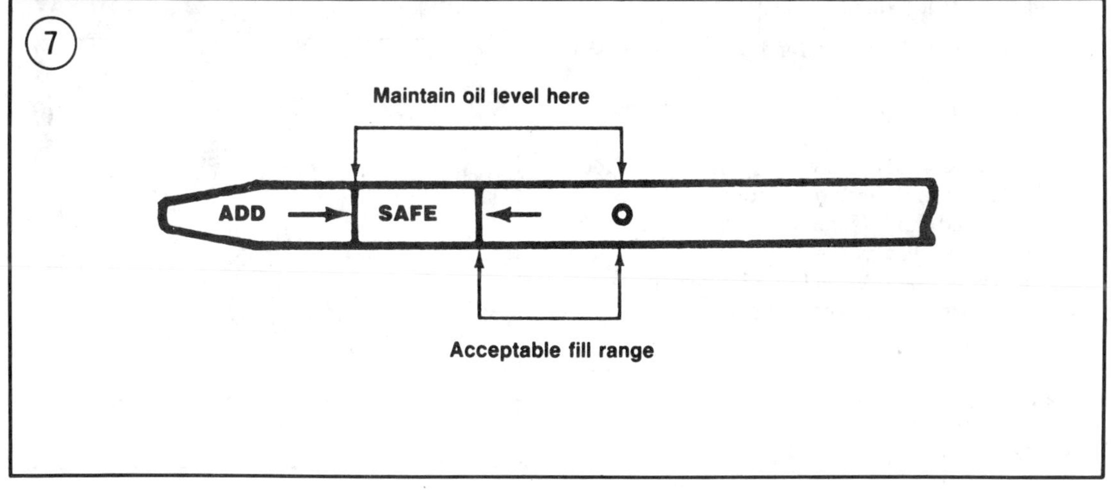

3

of ethylene glycol antifreeze and water, adding it to the radiator.

WARNING
The radiator cap should not be removed when the engine is warm or hot. If this is unavoidable, cover the cap with a thick rag or wear heavy leather gloves. Turn the cap slowly counterclockwise against the first stop (about 1/4 turn). Let all pressure (hot coolant and steam) escape. Then depress the cap and turn counterclockwise to remove. If the cap is removed too soon, scalding coolant may escape and cause a serious burn.

Check the condition of the coolant. If it is dirty or rusty, drain the radiator and flush the cooling system, then refill it with fresh coolant as described in Chapter Seven.

Battery Electrolyte Level

Unsealed batteries have individual cell vent caps or 2 bars with vented plugs, each of which fits across 3 cells. To check electrolyte level with this type of battery, remove the vent caps or vent bars and observe the liquid level. With unsealed black batteries, it should be even with the bottom of the split vent wells. See **Figure 11**. On unsealed translucent batteries, it should be between the marks on the battery case (**Figure 12**).

If the level is low, add distilled water until the level contacts the bottom of the vent well. Do not overfill, as this will result in loss of electrolyte and shorten battery life. Carefully wipe any spilled water from the battery top before reinstalling the vent caps or bars.

Periodic electrolyte level checks are not required for sealed maintenance-free batteries.

Windshield Wipers and Washer

Check the wiper blades for breaks or cracks in the rubber. Blade replacement intervals will vary with age, the weather, amount of use and the degree of chemical reaction from road salt or tar.

Operate the windshield washer and wiper blades. At the same time, check the amount and direction of the sprayed fluid. If the blades do not clean the windshield satisfactorily, wash the windshield and the blades with a mild undiluted detergent. Rinse with water while rubbing with a clean cloth or paper towels.

If the wiper pattern is uneven and streaks over clean glass, replace the blades.

Check fluid level in the windshield washer reservoir. See **Figure 13** (typical). Fill the reservoir with a mixture of water and windshield washer solvent or equivalent (a mixture of ammonia or vinegar and water works equally well). The reservoir should be kept full, except during winter months when filling it only 3/4 full will allow for expansion if the fluid freezes. Never use radiator antifreeze in the windshield washer reservoir, as it can damage painted surfaces.

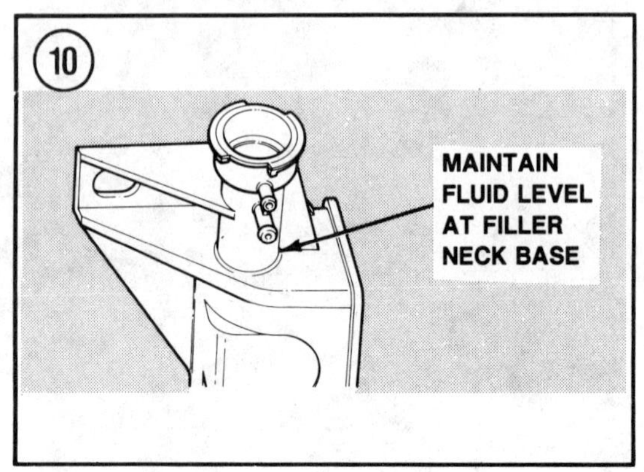

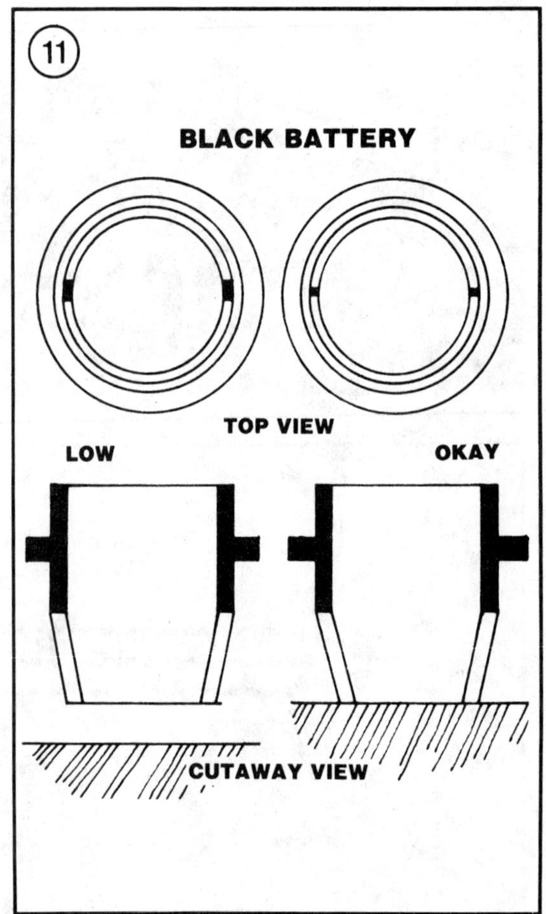

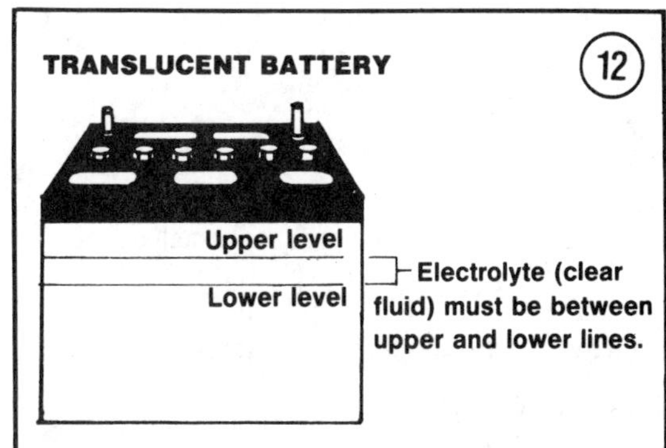

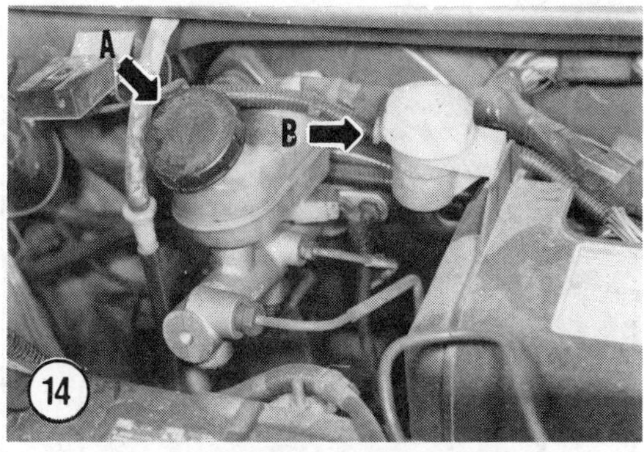

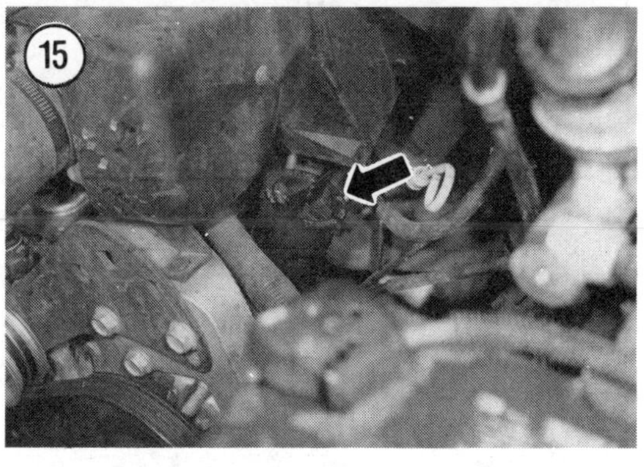

Brake Fluid Level

Clean the master cylinder reservoir and cap (A, **Figure 14**) to remove any possible contamination that might get into the fluid when the cap and diaphragm assembly is removed. Check the fluid level through the translucent reservoir. If the level is not above the embossed line on the reservoir, top up with a brake fluid marked DOT 3 and reinstall the cap and diaphragm assembly.

WARNING

Do not use fluid from a previously opened container that is only part full. Brake fluid absorbs moisture and moisture in the brake lines can reduce braking efficiency.

Hydraulic Clutch Fluid Level

Check the fluid level in the clutch master cylinder reservoir located near the master cylinder (B, **Figure 14**). The fluid level can be seen inside the translucent reservoir and should be above the embossed line on the side of the reservoir. If not, top up with DOT 3 brake fluid.

Power Steering Fluid Level

Check fluid level in the power steering pump reservoir, if so equipped. See **Figure 15** (typical). With the engine at normal operating temperature (upper radiator hose hot), turn the steering wheel lock-to-lock several times, then shut the engine off. Remove the pump reservoir cap with dipstick, wipe clean and reinsert. The fluid level should be between the HOT and COLD marks on the dipstick. Top up if necessary with Motorcraft Type F automatic transmission fluid. Reinstall the dipstick.

OWNER SAFETY CHECKS

The following simple checks should be performed on a daily basis during normal operation of the vehicle. Some are driveway checks. The others can be performed while driving. If any result in unsatisfactory operation, see your dealer to have the condition corrected.

Steering Column Lock

The ignition key should turn to LOCK position only when the transmission selector is in PARK (automatic transmission) or REVERSE (manual transmission).

Parking Brake and Transmission PARK Mechanism

Check holding ability by setting the parking brake with the vehicle on a fairly steep hill. Check the automatic transmission PARK mechanism by placing the transmission selector in PARK and releasing all brakes.

WARNING

You should not expect the PARK mechanism to hold the vehicle by itself even on a level surface. ***Always*** *set the parking brake* ***after*** *placing the transmission selector in PARK. When parking on an incline, you should also turn the wheels to the curb before shutting off the engine.*

Transmission Shift Indicator

Make sure the automatic transmission shift indicator accurately indicates the gear position selected.

Neutral Safety or Clutch Interlock Switch

The starter should operate only in PARK or NEUTRAL positions (automatic transmission) or in NEUTRAL with the clutch fully depressed (manual transmission).

Steering

With the vehicle on level ground, and with the front wheels lined up straight ahead, grasp the steering wheel and turn it from right to left to check for rotational free play. The free play should not exceed about one inch (**Figure 16**) and the steering should not make harsh sounds when turning or parking. Try to move the steering wheel in and out to check for axial play. If any play is felt, check the tightness of the steering wheel center nut.

Attempt to move the steering wheel from side to side without turning it. Movement is an indication of loose steering column mounting bolts or worn column bushings. Check and tighten the mounting bolts if necessary, and if the movement is still present, take the vehicle to a dealer or front end specialist for corrective service.

Wheel Alignment and Balance

Wheel alignment and balance should be checked periodically by a dealer or an alignment specialist. Visually check the tires for abnormal wear. If the vehicle pulls either to the right or left on a straight, level road, an alignment problem is indicated. Excessive vibration of the steering wheel or front of the vehicle while driving at normal highway speeds usually indicates the need for wheel balancing.

Brakes

Observe brake warning light during braking action. Also check for changes in braking action, such as pulling to one side, unusual sounds or increased brake pedal travel. If the brake pedal feels spongy, there is probably air in the hydraulic system. Bleed the brakes (Chapter Twelve).

Exhaust System

Be alert to any smell of fumes in the vehicle or to any change in the sound of the exhaust system that might indicate leakage.

Defroster

Turn on the heater, then move the control to defrost (DEF) and check the amount of air directed to the windshield.

Rear View Mirror and Sun Visors

Make sure that the friction mounts are adjusted so that mirrors and visors stay in selected positions.

Horn

Check the horn to make sure that it works properly.

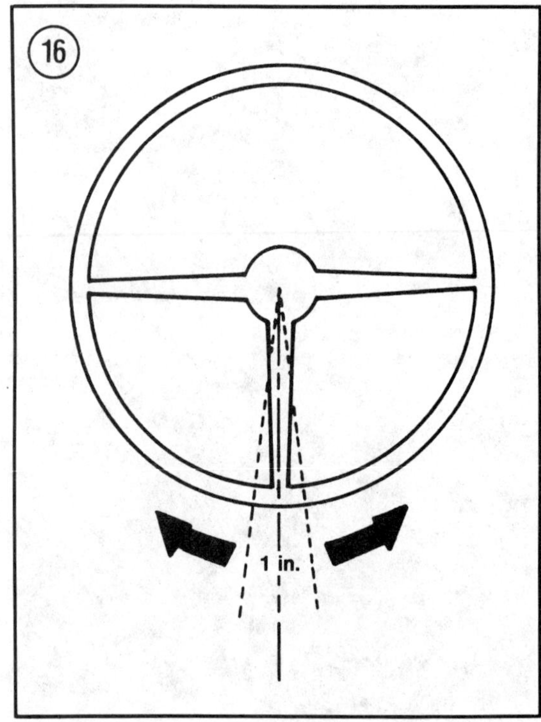

Lap and Shoulder Belts

Check all components for proper operation. Make sure that the anchor bolts are tight. Check the belts for fraying.

Head Restraints

If the seats are equipped with head restraints, check to see that they will adjust up and down properly and that no components are missing, loose or damaged.

Lights and Buzzers

Verify that all interior lights and buzzers are working. These include the seat belt reminder light and buzzer, ignition key buzzer, interior lights, instrument panel illumination and warning lights.

Check all exterior lights for proper operation. These include the headlights, license plate lights, side marker lights, parking lights, turn or directional signals, backup lights and hazard warning lights.

Glass

Check for any condition that could obscure vision or be a safety hazard. Correct as required.

Door Latches

Verify positive closing, latching and locking action.

Fluid Leaks

Check under the vehicle after it has been parked for awhile for evidence of fuel, coolant or oil leaks. Water dripping from the air conditioner drain tube after use is normal. Immediately determine and correct the cause of any leaking gasoline fumes or liquids to avoid possible fire or explosion.

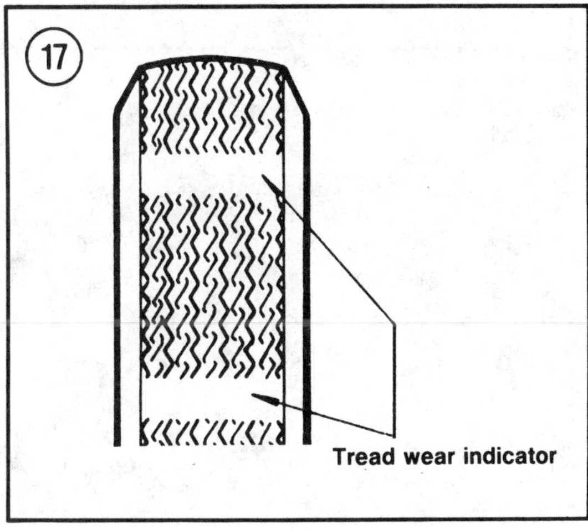

Tires and Wheels

Inspect the tire tread and sidewall condition. Original equipment and many replacement tires have tread wear indicators molded into the bottom of the tread grooves. Tread wear indicators will become visible as shown in **Figure 17** when tread depth becomes approximately 1/16 in. Tires should be replaced at this point. Wear patterns are a good indicator of chassis and suspension alignment. If detected early, alignment problems can be corrected before the tires have worn severely.

CAUTION

For satisfactory operation, all 4 wheels must be equipped with the same size tires, of equal circumference and identical or near identical tread pattern. In addition, bias ply and radial tires should not be mixed; mixing will result in severe and even hazardous handling problems. Damage to the drive train components may also result.

Look for nails, cuts, excessive wear or other damage. Remove all stones or other objects wedged in the tread. Pay particular attention to signs of severe rock damage. This is usually found in the form of fractures and cuts in the tread and sidewalls. This type of damage presents an extreme driving hazard when the vehicle is operated at highway speeds. A damaged tire should be replaced as soon as possible.

WARNING

Do not repair a radial tire by installing a tube. Radial tires have cooling ridges cast inside the casing. Use of a tube prevents this cooling effect from taking place. Since air in the tires expands when heated, use of a tube in a radial tire will cause excessive pressure to develop and can result in a dangerous blowout at high speed.

Check the tire valves for air leaks; replace any leaking valve as soon as possible. Replace any missing valve caps. Check the tire pressure when the tires are cold in the morning or after the vehicle has been parked for at least 3 hours after being driven less than one mile. When the tires heat up from driving, the air inside them expands and gives false high-pressure readings.

NOTE

If tire pressure must be checked when the tires are warm, it will be about 3 psi higher following a low-speed drive and about 7 psi higher following a high-speed drive.

Use a reliable pressure gauge and adjust air pressure to agree with that specified for the tires. Pressure specifications for tires furnished with the vehicle are found on the tire placard attached to the rear edge of the driver's door lock pillar. Maintain the compact spare tire, if so equipped, at 60 psi.

NOTE
Because of the variety of tire types and makes used on the vehicles covered in this manual, it is impractical to print all possible tire pressure ranges. When buying tires other than original equipment sizes, check with the tire dealer for recommended pressures. In all cases, never exceed the maximum pressure embossed on the side of the tire.

SCHEDULED MAINTENANCE

Various services are required at the intervals stated to assure that the emission control systems are maintained at the levels required by law. The maintenance services and intervals provided in **Table 1** are a compilation and simplification of the manufacturer's schedule designed to offer maximum protection. If you follow this table, your vehicle will receive periodic maintenance that will meet all of the manufacturer's requirements.

Engine Oil and Filter

For average use, the engine oil and filter should be changed at the intervals stated in **Table 1** at the end of this chapter. If driving is primarily short distances and in stop-and-go traffic, change the oil and filter twice as often as for average use. If the vehicle is only driven a few hundred miles each month, change the oil and filter every 6-8 weeks. If the vehicle is driven for long periods in extremely cold weather (when the temperature is frequently below 10° F), change the oil and filter twice as often as for average use.

CAUTION
Non-detergent, low-quality oil should never be used. The use of oil additives is unnecessary and not recommended.

Engine oil should be selected to meet the demands of the temperatures and driving conditions anticipated. Refer to **Table 2** to select a viscosity that is appropriate for the temperatures you expect to encounter during the next maintenance interval. Ford recommends the use of a high quality motor oil with an API classification of SF for all gasoline engines, regardless of the model year or previous oil recommendations. The rating and viscosity range are plainly marked on top of the can (**Figure 18**) or on the label of the plastic bottle.

To drain the oil and change the filter, you will need:

a. Drain pan (6 quarts or more capacity).
b. Oil can spout or can opener and funnel.
c. Filter wrench.
d. Sufficient oil (see **Table 3**).
e. Adjustable wrench.
f. New oil filter.
g. Paper towels or shop cloths.

There are several ways to discard the old oil safely. The easiest way is to pour it from the drain pan into a gallon bleach or milk container. The oil can then be taken to a service station for dumping or, where permitted, thrown in your household trash. Oil disposal kits are available from auto parts stores. These contain a substance similar to sawdust which absorbs the oil for clean and easy disposal. After pouring the oil into the box, it can

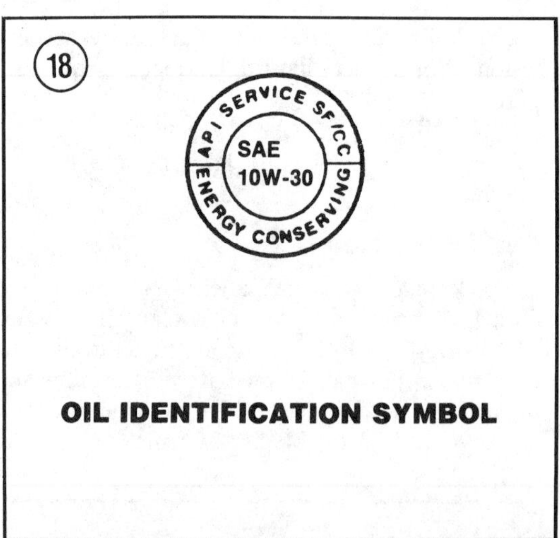

OIL IDENTIFICATION SYMBOL

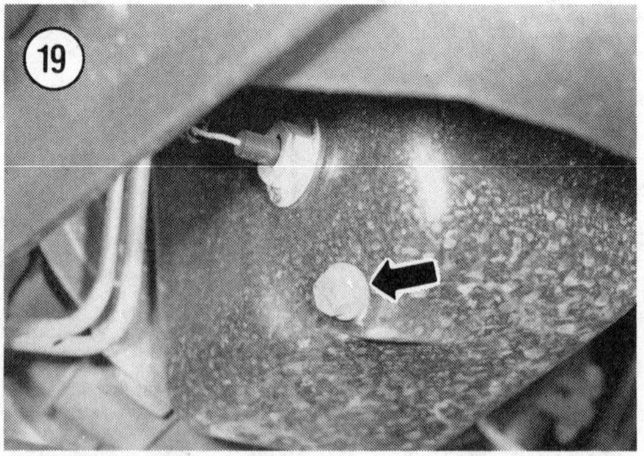

be disposed of in compliance with state and local regulations.

NOTE

Some service stations accept oil for recycling. Check local regulations before disposing of oil in trash. Never let oil drain on the ground.

The drain pan can be cleaned with solvent or paint thinner, if available. If not, hot water and dishwashing liquid will work satisfactorily.

1. With the vehicle on a level surface, warm the engine to operating temperature, then shut it off.
2. Set the parking brake and block the rear wheels so the vehicle will not roll in either direction.
3. Place a suitable container under the oil pan to serve as a drain pan.
4. Remove the oil filler cap on the valve cover (I4) or oil fill tube (V6) to promote faster draining. See **Figure 8** (I4) or **Figure 9** (V6).
5. Remove the dipstick (**Figure 6**) and wipe it clean with a cloth or paper towel.
6. Remove the drain plug with a suitable wrench or socket. See **Figure 19** (typical).
7. Clean the drain plug and check its gasket. Replace the gasket if damaged.

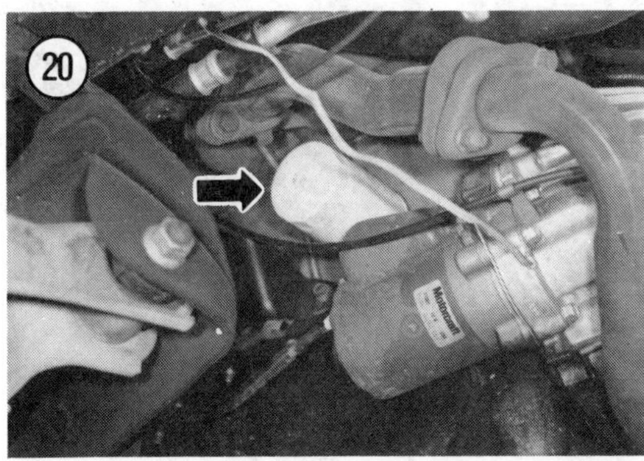

8. Allow the oil to drain completely (10-15 minutes), then reinstall the drain plug and gasket.
9. Relocate the drain pan beneath the oil filter. **Figure 20** shows the V6 filter; the 4-cylinder location is similar.
10. Unscrew the filter counterclockwise. Use a filter wrench if the filter is too tight or too hot to remove by hand. Remove and discard the filter.
11. Wipe the engine mounting pad clean with a lint-free cloth or paper towel.
12. Coat the neoprene gasket on the new filter with a thin film of clean engine oil. Screw the filter in place *by hand* until it contacts the mounting pad surface. Tighten 3/4 turn further *by hand.* Do not overtighten, as this can cause an oil leak.
13. Fill the crankcase with oil through the filler cap or tube hole. Wipe up any spills on the valve cover or oil fill tube with a clean cloth or paper towel and reinstall the filler cap.
14. Reinstall the dipstick. Wait a few seconds, then withdraw the dipstick. The oil level on the dipstick should be very close to the correct mark if the proper quantity of oil was used in Step 13.
15. Start the engine. The engine warning or oil pressure light will stay on for several seconds. Allow the engine to idle for several minutes.

CAUTION

Do not operate the engine at more than idle speed until the oil has had a chance to circulate through the engine or damage may result.

16. Check the area under and around the drain plug and filter for leaks while the engine is idling. Shut the engine off.

Air Cleaner Filter

A disposable paper element filter is used. Service to a paper element filter consists of replacement only. Elements should not be cleaned with an air hose, tapped, washed or oiled. Air cleaner filters should be replaced at specified intervals.

Fuel injected engine

Loosen the air cleaner cover screws enough to allow the cover to be lifted up (**Figure 21**). Remove the filter element from the air cleaner housing and wipe the inside of the housing with a damp rag to remove any dust, dirt or debris. Install a new filter element and reinstall the cover, tightening the screws securely. Check the air cleaner hoses and ducts when servicing the filter. Replace any hose or duct that is damaged.

Carburetted engine

Unscrew the wing nut and remove the air cleaner cover. Lift out the old filter and wipe the inside of the air cleaner housing with a damp paper towel to remove dust, dirt and debris. Install a new filter and reinstall the cover, tightening the wing nut snugly. Check the air cleaner hoses and ducts when servicing the filter. Replace any hose or duct that is damaged. Check to make sure the air control valve in the air cleaner snorkel operates freely. Locate and correct any cause of valve binding or sticking.

Chassis/Suspension Lubrication

Inspect and lubricate the following components. If the vehicle is driven under severe service conditions as described in **Table 1**, perform this service every 3,000 miles or 3 months.

a. Upper control arm ball-joints (**Figure 22**).
b. Lower control arm ball-joints (**Figure 23**).
c. Automatic transmission linkage (**Figure 24**).
d. Parking brake cable.
e. Throttle linkage.

During winter weather, keep the vehicle in a heated garage for at least 30 minutes prior to lubrication so the joints will accept the lubricant.

Wipe around the grease fittings with a clean rag to remove any accumulated road dirt (**Figure 22** and **Figure 23**). On some vehicles, plugs may be installed instead of grease fittings. To lubricate such components, it is necessary to remove the plug and temporarily install a suitable grease or "zerk" fitting. When lubrication has been completed, remove the fitting and reinstall the plug.

CAUTION
Do not overfill until lubricant escapes from boot. This will destroy the weathertight seal.

Any lubricants used should be applied sparingly and the excess wiped away to prevent it from attracting dirt which will also accelerate wear and contribute to difficult operation.

Positive Crankcase Ventilation (PCV) System

The PCV system should be checked for proper operation at the interval stated in **Table 1**. More frequent checks and/or replacement should be made if the vehicle is operated under severe service conditions.

PCV Valve Replacement

The vehicles covered in this manual use PCV valves with different flow rates calibrated to the engine and model year. A new PCV valve should be of the same design and bear the same part number as the one being replaced.

4-cylinder engine

1. Locate the PCV valve in the vent hose between the upper and lower intake manifolds. It should be close to the distributor.
2. Disconnect one hose from the PCV valve with a rotating and pulling motion.
3. Remove the PCV valve from the other hose with a rotating and pulling motion.

NOTE
Do not attempt to clean and reuse a plugged PCV valve.

4. Install the new valve in one hose with a downward rotating motion.
5. Install the other hose over the exposed end of the PCV valve with a downward rotating motion.

V6 engine

1. Disconnect the hose from the PCV valve. See **Figure 25** (typical).
2. Remove the PCV valve from the valve cover grommet with an upward rotating motion. Discard the valve.

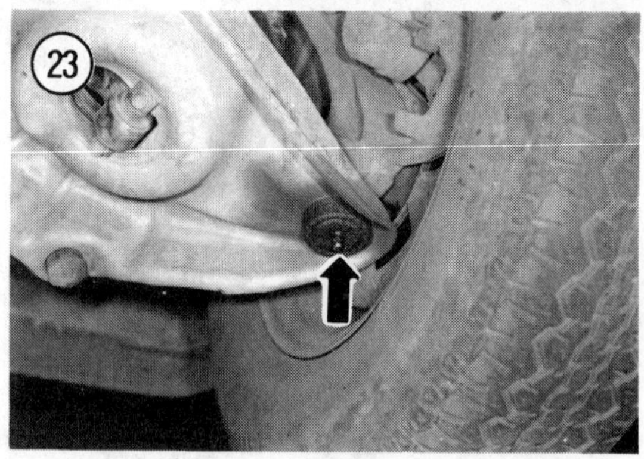

NOTE
Do not attempt to clean and reuse a plugged PCV valve.

3. Check the condition of the valve cover grommet and replace as required.
4. Install the new valve in the valve cover grommet with a downward rotating motion.

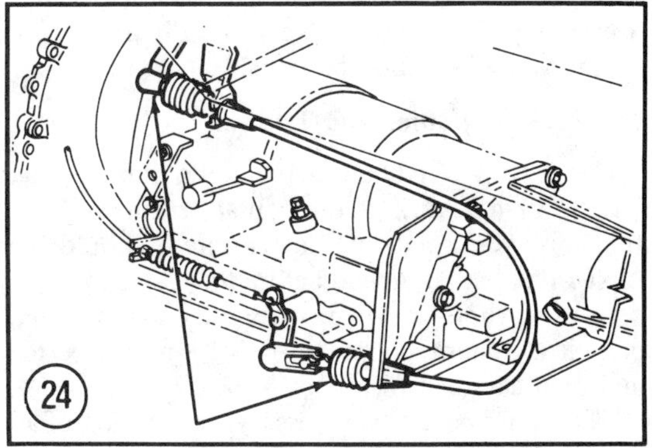

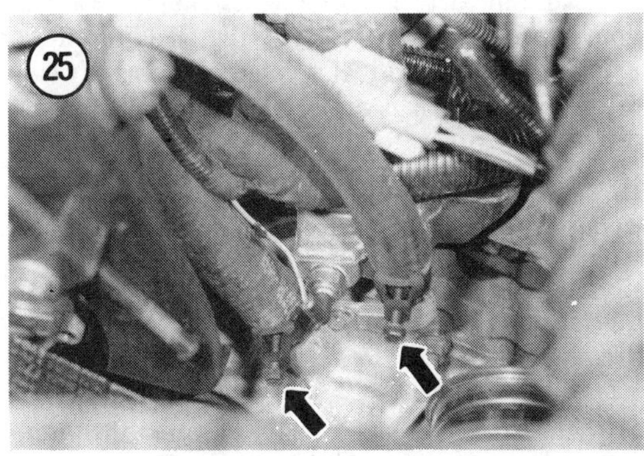

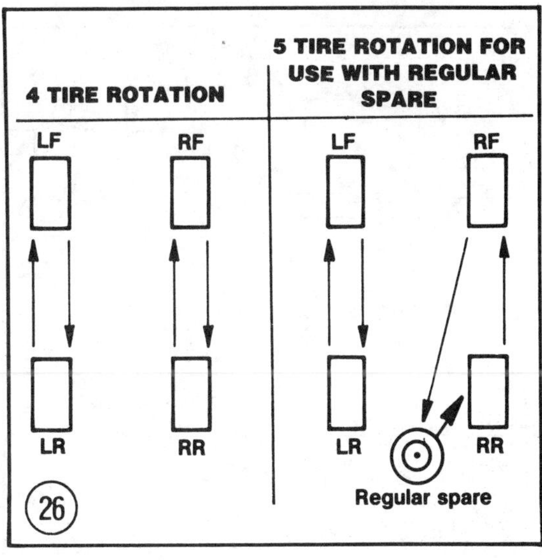

5. Position the valve with the vacuum nipple facing the PCV hose. Reconnect the hose to the valve.

Brake System

Check the brake master cylinder fluid level as described in this chapter.

Inspect all brake lines, hoses and fittings for abrasion, kinks, leakage and other damage; replace as necessary. Any line that is less than perfect should be replaced immediately.

Check all connections to make sure they are tight and look for any signs of leakage which might indicate a cracked or otherwise unserviceable connection. As with lines and hoses, any connections that are less than perfect should be replaced.

Always bleed the brakes after opening a system connection. See Chapter Twelve.

Check all brake shoe linings (disc and drum) for signs of brake fluid, oil or grease contamination on the friction material. If any contamination is present, the linings must be replaced regardless of how much material remains.

Measure the linings to determine their serviceability. If any brake shoe lining (disc or drum) has worn down to within 1/16 in. of a rivet head or the backing plate on bonded shoes, replace the linings on both wheels.

Cooling System

WARNING
Personal injury is possible. Perform cooling system service when the engine is cold.

Clean exterior of radiator and air conditioning condenser with compressed air and inspect radiator and heater hoses at least once a year for cracks, checks, swelling or other signs of deterioration. Make sure that all hoses are correctly routed and installed and that all clamps are tight. See **Figure 26** (typical). Replace hoses at every coolant change.

Remove the radiator cap and check the condition of the coolant. If it is dirty or rusty, the system should be drained, flushed and refilled with fresh coolant regardless of the mileage. Replace the coolant every 24 months or 30,000 miles. See Chapter Seven.

Choke Linkage

Check for damaged or missing parts. Work the choke lever back and forth to check for interference or binding. Spray the choke mechanism and housing with Ford automatic choke cleaner part No. D8AZ-19A501-A or equivalent while moving the choke lever, fast idle lever and fast idle cam. Blow linkage dry with compressed air and repeat the cleaning procedure until all dirt buildup has been removed.

Exhaust System

Check the entire exhaust system from exhaust manifold to tailpipe. Look for broken, damaged, missing, corroded or misaligned components, open seams, holes, loose connections or any other defect that could allow exhaust gases to enter the passenger compartment.

Inspect the catalytic converter heat shields (if so equipped) for looseness or damage. Tighten or replace as required. Remove any debris that may have lodged or accumulated in or around the shields. Make sure there is adequate clearance between the exhaust system components and nearby body areas.

Whenever the muffler requires replacement, replace the exhaust pipe and resonator to the rear of the muffler (if so equipped) to maintain exhaust system integrity.

Front Wheel Bearings

Clean, repack and adjust bearings. See Chapter Ten.

NON-SCHEDULED MAINTENANCE

Some tasks formerly included in factory maintenance schedules are now considered as non-scheduled maintenance on the vehicles covered in this manual. Ford Motor Co. continues to recommend they be performed, but on an "as required" or "periodic" basis.

Fuel Tank, Cap and Lines

Inspect the fuel tank, cap and lines for leaks or damage. Remove the fuel cap and check the gasket for an even filler neck imprint.

Body Care and Lubrication

All hood and door hinges, latches, locks and seat tracks should be lubricated periodically to ensure smooth operation and reduce wear. Recommended lubricants are given in **Table 4**.

1. Clean latch and hinge area of accumulated dirt or contamination.
2. Apply the specified lubricant sparingly, operating the mechanism several times to aid penetration.
3. Wipe off any excess lubricant with a clean, dry cloth to prevent it from attracting dirt and from soiling clothes, carpeting or upholstery.

Tire Rotation

Inspect the tires for cracks, bumps, bulges or other defects. Look for signs of excessive wear. Rotate radial tires at the first 7,000 miles, then every 15,000 miles thereafter. Rotate bias-belted tires every 6,000 miles. Refer to **Figure 26** for recommended rotation patterns.

Drive Belt Condition and Tension

Check the V-ribbed drive belts for fraying, glazing or cracking of the contact surfaces. Belts that are damaged or deteriorated should be replaced (Chapter Seven) before they fail and cause serious problems from engine overheating, electrical system failure or reduction of steering and/or brake control.

Check and adjust (if necessary) the tension of all drive belts (Chapter Seven). A belt that is too loose will cause the driven components to operate at less than required efficiency. A belt that is adjusted too tightly will wear rapidly and place unnecessary side loads on the bearings of driven components, which can cause premature wear or failure of the components.

Fluid Leak Check

Inspect the underbody of the vehicle for signs of fluid leakage. Clean and correct as necessary.

Power Steering

Check the power steering fluid level in the pump reservoir as described in this chapter.

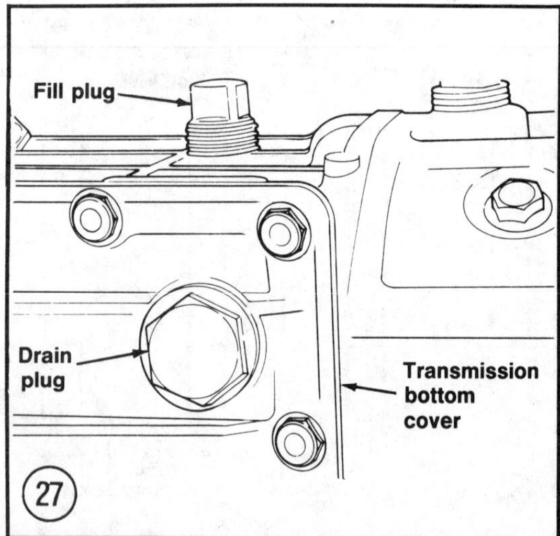

Check all power steering hoses and lines for proper connections, leaks or deterioration. If abrasion or excessive wear is evident, locate and correct the cause immediately.

Manual Transmission and Rear Axle Lubricant Level

Check the manual transmission fluid level whenever leakage or contamination is present. Loosen the fill plug (**Figure 27**) slowly. If fluid starts to seep out from around the plug threads, the fluid level is satisfactory. Tighten the plug to 18-29 ft.-lb. (25-39 N•m).

If the fluid does not seep out from around the plug threads when the fill plug is loosened, remove the plug and fill with the recommended lubricant (**Table 4**) until the fluid runs out of the fill hole. Install the fill plug and tighten to specifications above.

To change the manual transmission fluid, place a suitable container under the drain plug (**Figure 27**). Remove the plug and let the lubricant drain, then reinstall the plug and tighten to 29-43 ft.-lb. (40-58 N•m). Remove the fill plug and fill the transmission with the recommended lubricant. See **Table 4**. Install and tighten the fill plug as described above.

Automatic Transmission Service

Automatic transmission fluid will deliver 100,000 miles of service at normal operating temperature (approximately 175° F) before oxidation occurs. When a transmission operates at above normal temperature, the service life of its fluid is cut in half with each 20° F increase in temperature. See **Table 5**.

If fluid operating temperature is allowed to reach 500° F, the metals inside the transmission will start to warp rapidly. For this reason, rocking a vehicle out of snow, mud or sand by rapidly shifting from FORWARD to REVERSE and back should be avoided if at all possible. If attempted, do not rock the vehicle for more than 1-2 minutes.

Fluid color and smell are no longer valid indicators of fluid condition. DEXRON II turns dark early in its service life and will emit a burned smell after only a few hundred miles of use.

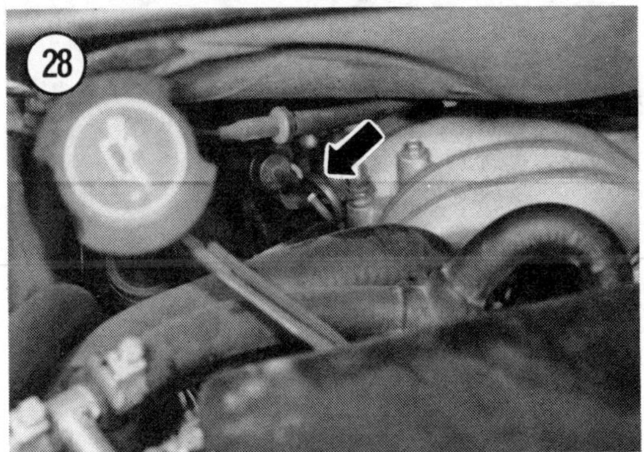

Level Check

1. Check the fluid level with the transmission at operating temperature, engine running and the vehicle parked on level ground with the parking brake set and the transmission selector in PARK.
2. Clean all dirt from the transmission dipstick cap. See **Figure 28** (typical). Pull the dipstick from the tube, wipe with a clean, lint-free cloth and reinsert until the cap seats fully. Wait a few seconds, then remove the dipstick a second time and note the reading. It should be between the 2 embossed squares or arrows on the dipstick.
3. If the fluid level is low, add sufficient automatic transmission fluid of the recommended type (**Table 4**) to bring it to the proper level on the dipstick. Reinsert the dipstick and make sure it is fully seated in the tube.

CAUTION
Do not overfill the transmission. Too much fluid can cause damage to the transmission.

Fluid Change

Under normal circumstances, automatic transmission fluid is changed at 100,000 mile intervals. If the vehicle has been subjected to constant severe service such as those stated in **Table 1**, drain and refill the fluid at 15,000 mile intervals.

1. Drive the vehicle several miles to bring the lubricant to normal operating temperature.
2. Set the parking brake and block the drive wheels.
3. Raise the front of the vehicle with a jack and place it on jackstands.
4. Place a drain pan underneath the transmission.
5. Loosen all pan attaching bolts a few turns with a 13 mm socket. Tap one corner of the pan with a rubber hammer to break it loose and let the fluid drain.
6. When the fluid has drained to the level of the pan flange, remove the pan bolts at the rear of the

pan (**Figure 29**). This will let the pan drop at the rear and drain slowly.

7. When all fluid has drained, remove the 18 pan bolts. Remove the pan (**Figure 30**) and let the filter screen drain.

8. Remove any gasket or sealant residue from the pan and transmission case mating flanges.

9. Discard the gasket and clean the pan thoroughly with solvent and lint-free cloths or paper towels.

10. Remove the 10 mm filter screen attaching bolt. Remove the filter screen from the transmission valve body (**Figure 31**).

11. Install a new filter screen and tighten the bolt snugly.

12. Install the pan on the transmission with a new gasket and tighten the attaching bolts to 8-10 ft.-lb. (11-14 N•m) in a crisscross pattern.

13. Insert a clean funnel containing a fine-mesh filter in the filler tube and pour approximately 4 quarts of fresh automatic transmission fluid into the transmission. See **Table 4** for recommended type.

14. Start the engine and let it idle for 2 minutes with the gear selector in PARK. Increase the engine speed to approximately 1,200 rpm and let it run until it reaches normal operating temperature.

15. Depress and hold the foot brake. Slowly move the selector lever through each gear range, pausing long enough for the transmission to engage. Return to the PARK position.

16. Remove the dipstick and wipe it with a clean, lint-free cloth. Reinsert the dipstick in the filler tube until it seats completely.

CAUTION

Do not overfill the transmission. Too much fluid is harmful. If the fluid level is above the specified mark on the dipstick with the fluid at normal operating temperature, drain enough fluid to correct the level.

17. Remove the dipstick and check the fluid level. Add sufficient fluid as required to bring the fluid to the appropriate level on the dipstick.

18. Once the fluid level is correct, check for and correct any leaks at the filler tube connection and around the edge of the oil pan.

19. Road test the vehicle to make sure the transmission operates properly. After driving the vehicle approximately 100 miles, recheck the fluid level and correct, if necessary.

Fuel Filter

Carburetted engines use a carburetor fuel inlet filter screen (**Figure 32**). No maintenance is

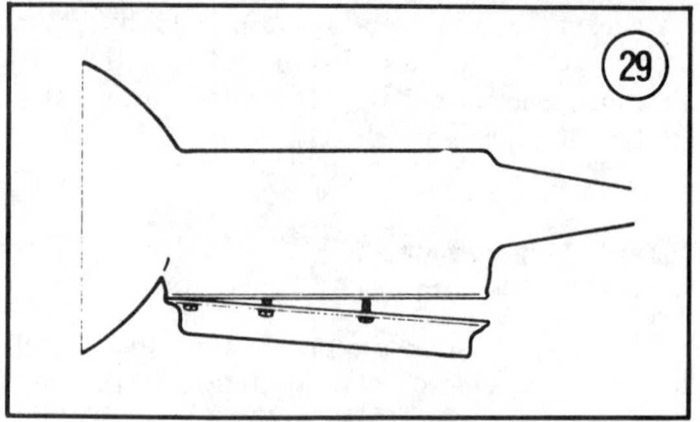
29

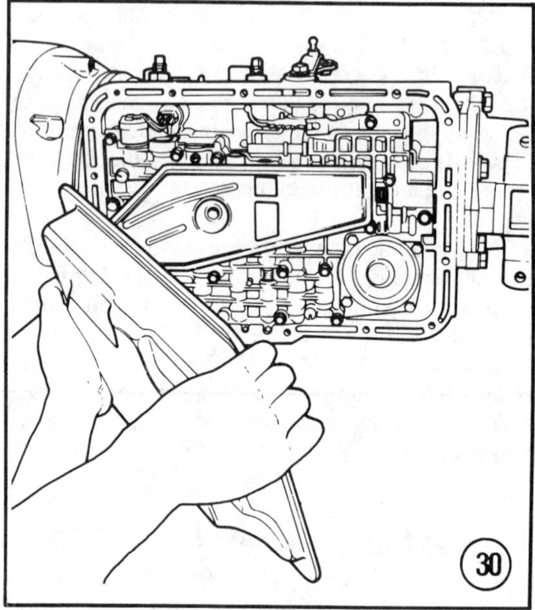
30

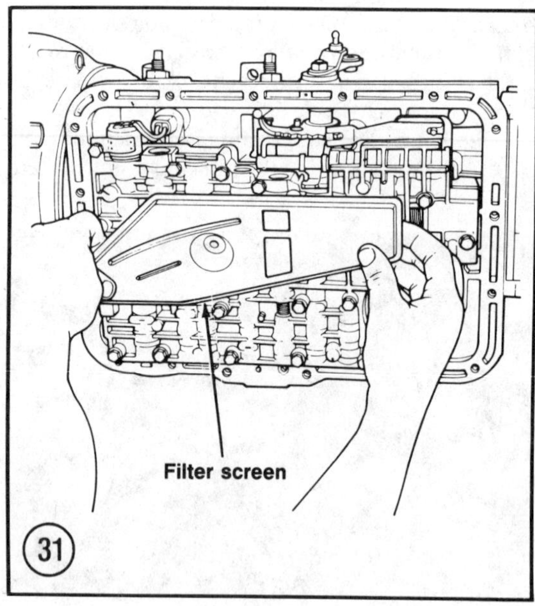

31

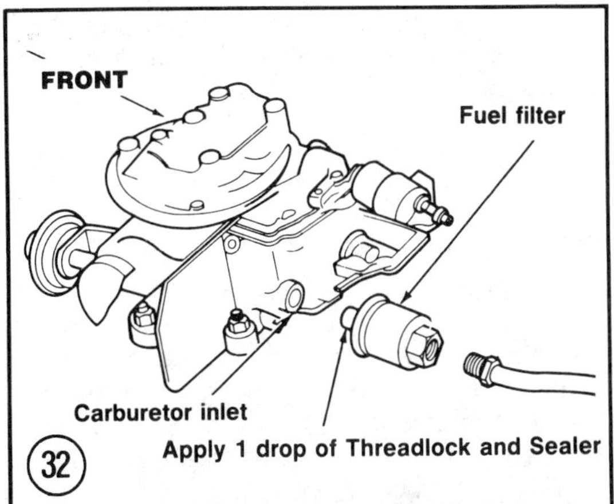

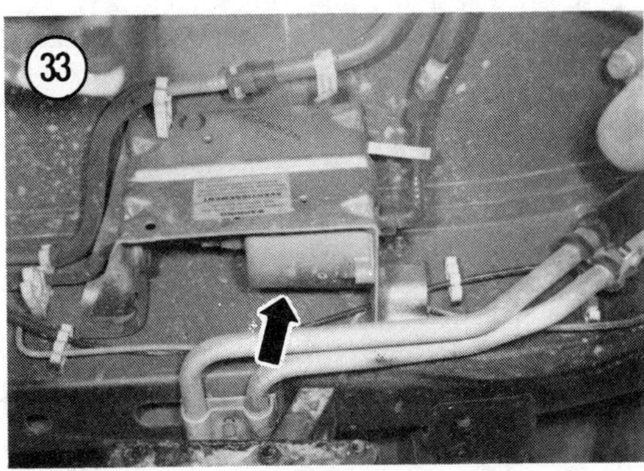

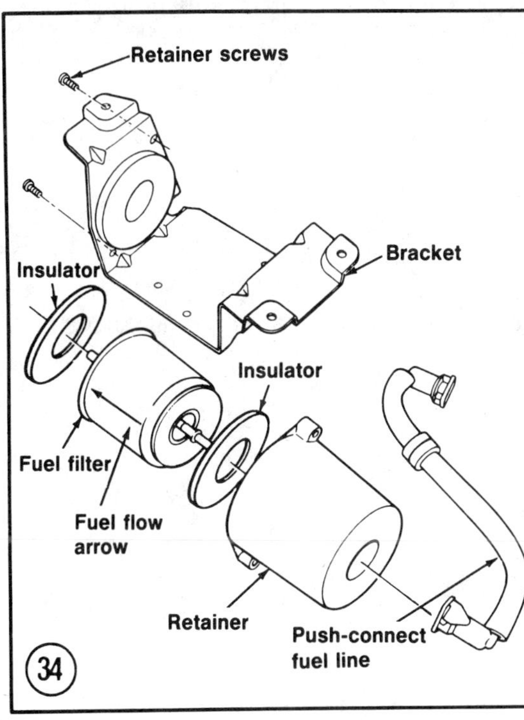

specified other than to replace the filter if it becomes restricted.

All fuel injected engines use an in-line filter assembly, bracket-mounted under the passenger side of the vehicle (**Figure 33**). If the injection system uses an external fuel pump, the pump is mounted on the outside of the protective bracket. Ford states that the filter should last for the life of the vehicle under normal driving conditions.

All vehicles are equipped with an in-tank filter screen assembly attached to the fuel pump or sending unit. See Chapter Six. Fuel injectors use a non-serviceable filter screen. If the injector screen becomes plugged, the entire injector must be replaced.

3

Carburetor fuel inlet filter screen replacement

Refer to **Figure 32** for this procedure.

1. Remove the engine cover panel in the passenger compartment.
2. Remove the air cleaner assembly. See Chapter Six.
3. Hold the filter assembly with an 11/16-in. wrench and loosen the fuel line nut with a 5/8-in. wrench. Disconnect and cap the fuel line to prevent leakage.
4. Remove the filter from the carburetor with the 11/16-in. wrench.
5. Apply a single drop of Threadlock and Sealer (part No. EOAZ-19554-A), Loctite Hydraulic Sealant No. 69 or equivalent on the external threads of the new filter.
6. Thread the new filter into the carburetor inlet by hand, then tighten to 6.5-8.0 ft.-lb. (9-11 N•m).
7. Lubricate the fuel line nut and flare with clean engine oil, then fit the line into the filter opening and hand-start the nut.
8. Hold the filter with an 11/16-in. wrench and tighten the fuel line nut with the 5/8-in. wrench. Tighten the fuel line nut to 15-18 ft.-lb. (20-24 N•m).
9. Start the engine and check for leaks. Reinstall the air cleaner assembly (Chapter Six).

Fuel injected engine in-line filter replacement

Refer to **Figure 34** for this procedure.

1. Relieve system pressure as described in Chapter Six.
2. Set the parking brake. Place the transmission in 1st gear (manual) or PARK (automatic). Raise the vehicle with a jack and place it on jackstands.
3. Disconnect the fuel line push-connect fittings at each end of the filter. See Chapter Six.

4. Unbolt and remove the filter assembly and retainer from its mounting bracket.
5. Remove the rubber insulator ring from the filter and discard it.
6. Remove the filter from the retainer and discard it.
7. Install a new filter in the retainer with its flow arrow pointing away from the retainer.
8. Install a new rubber insulator ring.
9. Position the filter assembly on the mounting bracket and tighten the bolts to 51-60 in.-lb. (5.8-6.8 N•m).
10. Install the fuel line push-connect fittings to the filter ends. Use new retainer clips in each fitting. See Chapter Six.
11. Start the engine and check for leaks. Correct as required.
12. Remove the jackstands and lower the vehicle to the ground.

ENGINE TUNE-UP

A tune-up consists of a series of inspections, adjustments and parts replacements to compensate for normal wear and deterioration of engine components. Regular tune-ups are important for proper emission control and fuel economy. Emission control systems, improved electrical systems and other advances make these engines especially sensitive to improperly operating or incorrectly adjusted parts.

Since proper engine operation depends upon a number of interrelated system functions, a tune-up consisting of only one or two corrections will seldom give lasting results. For improved power, performance and operating economy, a thorough and systematic procedure of analysis and correction is necessary.

Vehicle Emission Control Information (VECI) Decal

Federal government regulations require that a VECI decal be located on the valve cover or elsewhere in the engine compartment. This decal contains the required tune-up specifications and procedures necessary to keep the engine emissions within specified levels for the make, model and model year vehicle. Since running changes which affect emission control are instituted at the factory, these specifications and procedures may vary considerably during a model year. For this reason, it is important that you consult the VECI decal for your vehicle to obtain the proper specifications and procedures. If either varies from the information provided in this manual, *always* follow the decal instructions, as they represent the most current information available concerning your vehicle.

To prevent loss of this information in the event of decal damage or a collision involving damage to the front end of the vehicle, it is a good idea to copy the specifications on a 3x5 in. file card and keep it in the glove compartment.

NOTE
Ford Motor Co. does not provide general tune-up specifications. You must refer to the VECI decal for this information.

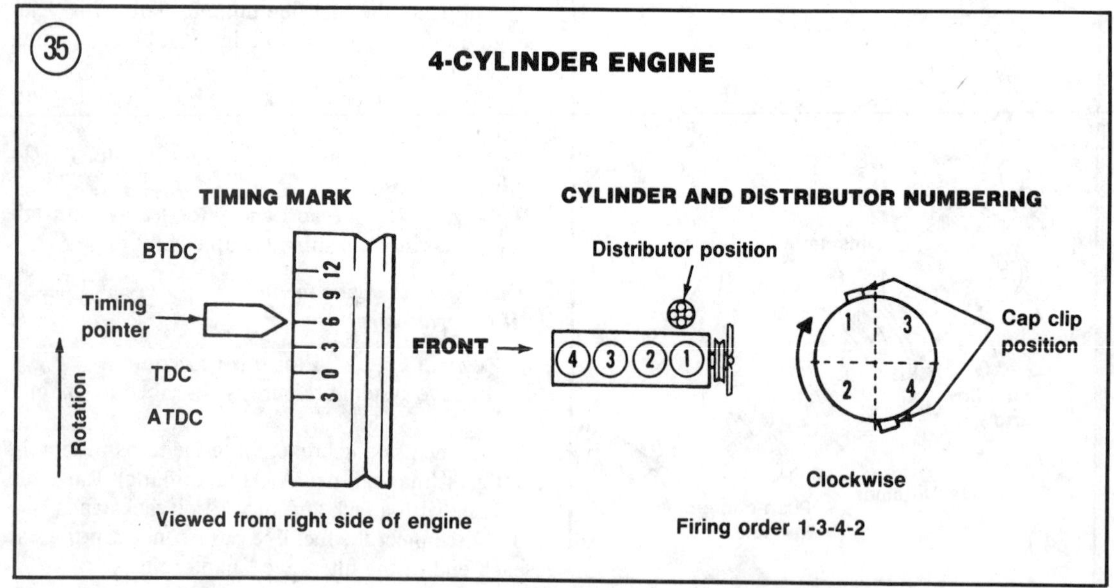

Tune-Up Sequence

Because different systems in an engine interact, the tune-up should be carried out in the following order.

a. Valve adjustment (2.8L V6 only).
b. Engine compression check.
c. Ignition system inspection and adjustment.
d. Fuel system inspection and carburetor adjustment.

Firing Order

The cylinder firing order for 4-cylinder engines is 1-3-4-2 (**Figure 35**). On the V6, it is 1-4-2-5-3-6 (**Figure 36**).

Valve Adjustment (2.8L V6)

See Chapter Five.

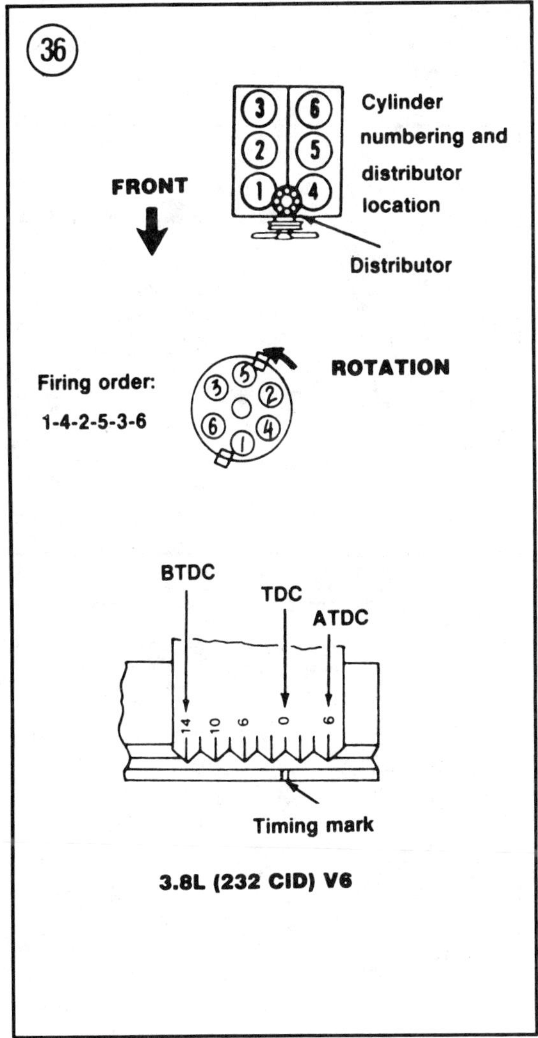

Compression Test

An engine with low or uneven compression cannot be properly tuned. Whenever the spark plugs are removed from the engine, it is a good idea to run a compression test. A compression test measures the compression pressure built up in each cylinder. Its results can be used to assess general cylinder and valve condition. In addition, it can warn of developing problems inside the engine.

1. Warm the engine to normal operating temperature (upper radiator hose hot). Shut the engine off. Make sure the choke and throttle valves are wide open on carburetted models.
2. Remove all spark plugs as described in this chapter.
3. Connect a remote start switch to the starter solenoid according to manufacturer's instructions. Leave the ignition key in the OFF position.
4. Connect a compression tester to the No. 1 cylinder according to manufacturer's instructions.

NOTE
*The No. 1 cylinder is the front cylinder on the I4 engine and the front cylinder on the right (passenger side) bank on the V6. See **Figure 35** or **Figure 36**.*

5. Crank the engine at least 5 turns with the remote start switch or until there is no further increase in compression shown on the tester gauge.
6. Remove the compression tester and record the reading. Relieve the tester pressure valve.
7. Test the remaining cylinders in the same manner.

When interpreting the results, actual readings are not as important as the differences in readings. The lowest must be within 75 percent of the highest. A greater difference indicates worn or broken rings, leaking or sticking valves or a combination of these problems.

If the compression test indicates a problem (excessive variation in readings), isolate the cause with a wet compression test. This is done in the same way as the dry compression test, except that about 1 teaspoon of oil is poured down the spark plug hole before performing Steps 5-7. If the wet compression readings are much greater than the dry compression readings, the trouble is probably due to worn or broken rings. If there is little difference between the wet and dry readings, the problem is probably due to leaky or sticking valves. If 2 adjacent cylinders read low in both tests, the head gasket may be leaking.

Spark Plug Replacement

Spark plugs should be replaced at intervals specified in **Table 1**. Spark plug replacement is not an easy task on any of the Aerostar engines. The vehicle must be raised to a satisfactory working level and the wheel/tire assemblies removed to provide access through the wheel wells. Even then, it is very much a remove-and-replace-by-feel procedure, as much of the time you will not be able to see what you are doing. You should plan on allowing plenty of time to complete spark plug replacement and work slowly and carefully. You will be working by touch in an area with limited access and a loss of patience can result in bruised knuckles and scraped fingers. You also will need a variety of different length socket wrench extensions.

CAUTION
Whenever the spark plugs are removed, dirt from around them can fall into the spark plug holes. This can cause expensive engine damage.

1. Blow out any foreign matter from around the spark plugs with compressed air. Use a compressor if you have one. Cans of compressed inert gas are available from photo stores.
2. Disconnect the spark plug wires by twisting the wire boot back and forth on the plug insulator while pulling upward (**Figure 37**). Pulling on the wire instead of the boot may cause internal damage to the wire. Wire removal with spark plug terminal pliers (**Figure 37**) is recommended where there is enough clearance for their use.
3. Remove the plugs with a 13/16 in. spark plug socket. Keep the plugs in order so you know which cylinder each one came from.
4. Examine each spark plug. Compare its condition with the illustrations in Chapter Two. Spark plug condition indicates engine condition and can warn of developing trouble.
5. Discard the plugs. Although they could be cleaned, regapped and reused if in good condition, they seldom last very long. New plugs are inexpensive and far more reliable.
6. Remove the plugs from the box. Tapered plugs do not use gaskets. Some plug brands may have small end pieces that must be screwed on before the plugs can be used.
7. Determine the correct gap setting from the VECI decal. Use a spark plug gapping tool to check the gap. See **Figure 38** for one common type. Insert the appropriate size wire gauge between the electrodes. If the gap is correct, there will be a slight drag as the wire is pulled through. If there is no drag or if the wire will not pull through, bend the side electrode with the gapping tool (**Figure 39**) to change the gap and then remeasure with the wire gauge.

CAUTION
Never try to close the electrode gap by tapping the spark plug on a solid surface. This can damage the plug internally. Always use a spark plug tool to open and close the gap.

8. Check spark plug hole threads and clean with an appropriate size spark plug chaser if necessary before installing plugs. This will remove any corrosion, carbon build-up or minor flaws from the threads. Coat the chaser with grease to catch chips or foreign matter. Use care to avoid cross-threading.
9. Apply a thin film of engine oil or anti-seize compound to the spark plug threads and screw each plug in by hand until it seats. Very little effort is required. If force is necessary, the plug is cross-threaded. Unscrew it and try again.

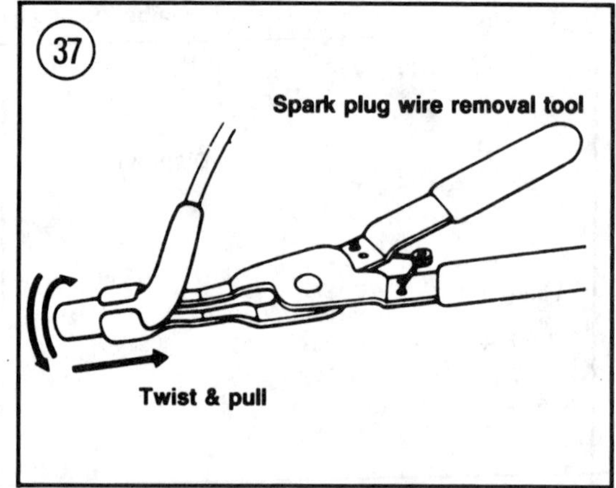

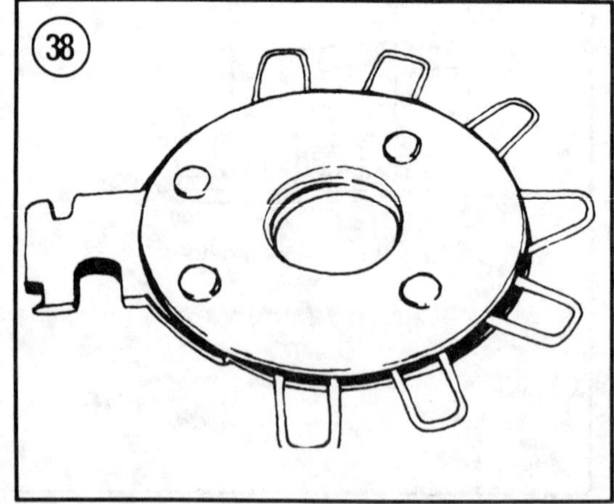

NOTE
On V6 engine installations, access to all cylinder spark plug wells is limited. To install such plugs more easily, slip a 10 in. length of fuel line hose over the end of the plug. This will serve as a flexible handle and allow you to screw the plugs in easily and quickly.

10. Tighten each spark plug by hand until it makes contact, then tighten an additional 1/4-3/8 turn. If you have a torque wrench, tighten to 7-15 ft.-lb. (10-20 N•m). Do not overtighten the plugs, as excessive torque may change the gap setting.
11. Inspect the spark plug wires before installing them to their correct cylinder locations. If the insulation is oil soaked, brittle, torn or otherwise damaged, replace the wire(s).

IGNITION SERVICE

Distributor Cap, Wires and Rotor

The distributor cap, wires and rotor should be inspected every 30,000 miles or whenever the spark plugs are replaced.

1. Loosen the 2 distributor cap latch screws. Lift the cap straight up and off to prevent rotor blade damage.
2. Check the carbon button and electrodes inside the distributor cap for dirt, corrosion or arcing. Check the cap for cracks. Replace the cap and rotor as a set, if necessary.

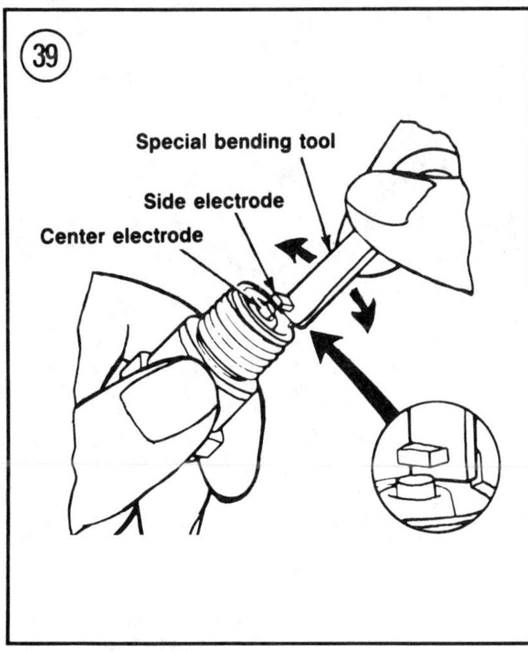

3. Replace the wires if the insulation is melted, brittle or cracked.

NOTE
The silicone compound normally applied to the rotor blade on 1986 models may be thrown from the rotor to the distributor cap terminals by centrifugal force. While such deposits of silicone compound may look like a contaminant, they are normal and result in no performance loss. Do not replace this cap or rotor because of this condition.

4. Loosen the 2 rotor screws on 1986 models. Lift the rotor straight up and off the distributor shaft.
5. Wipe the rotor with a clean, damp cloth. Check for burns, arcing, cracks or other defects. Replace the cap and rotor as a set, if necessary.
6. Reinstall the rotor on the distributor shaft. On 1986 models, tighten the attaching screws and coat the rotor blade with a 1/32-in. application of Ford Silicone Dielectric Compound (part No. D7AZ-19A331-A) or equivalent.
7. Reinstall the distributor cap. Tighten the 2 cap screws securely.

Ignition Timing

Ignition timing on all engines is controlled by the EEC-IV microprocessor. There is no need to adjust timing unless the distributor has been removed from the engine for service (Chapter Eight).

Use the following procedure to set base timing *only* when the distributor has been removed from the engine and is being reinstalled.

1. Set the parking brake and place the transmission in PARK (automatic) or NEUTRAL (manual). Make sure the air conditioning and heater are off.
2. Check the VECI decal to determine the timing specifications, if this information is not already known.
3. Connect an inductive (clamp-on) timing light and tachometer to the engine according to the manufacturer's instructions. Refer to **Figure 35** or **Figure 36** as required for the location of the No. 1 plug wire (its location also is molded on the distributor cap).
4. Disconnect the single wire connector near the distributor. Refer to the VECI decal in the engine compartment and disconnect any other leads specified.
5. Clean the timing marks with a stiff brush. See **Figure 35** (I4) or **Figure 36** (V6) for typical timing marks.

6. Mark the timing mark and pointer with white paint or chalk for better visibility. The paint makes the marks easier to see under the timing light.

WARNING
Keep your hands and hair clear of all drive belts and pulleys. Although they seem to be standing still, they are actually spinning at more than 10 times per second and can cause serious injury.

7. Start the engine and let it warm to normal operating temperature (upper radiator hose hot). Check the curb idle speed and compare to specifications on the VECI decal in the engine compartment. Also note any changes in procedure that differ from the steps given here. If there are differences, follow the VECI decal. If idle speed is incorrect, take the vehicle to a dealer (idle speed is computer-controlled).

8. Aim the timing light at the timing marks. They will appear to stand still or waver slightly under the light. If the timing marks are aligned, the timing is satisfactory.

9. If the timing is incorrect, loosen the distributor hold-down clamp bolt enough to rotate the distributor body. The use of a distributor wrench is recommended.

WARNING
Never touch the distributor's thick wires when the engine is running. This can cause a painful shock, even if the insulation is in perfect condition.

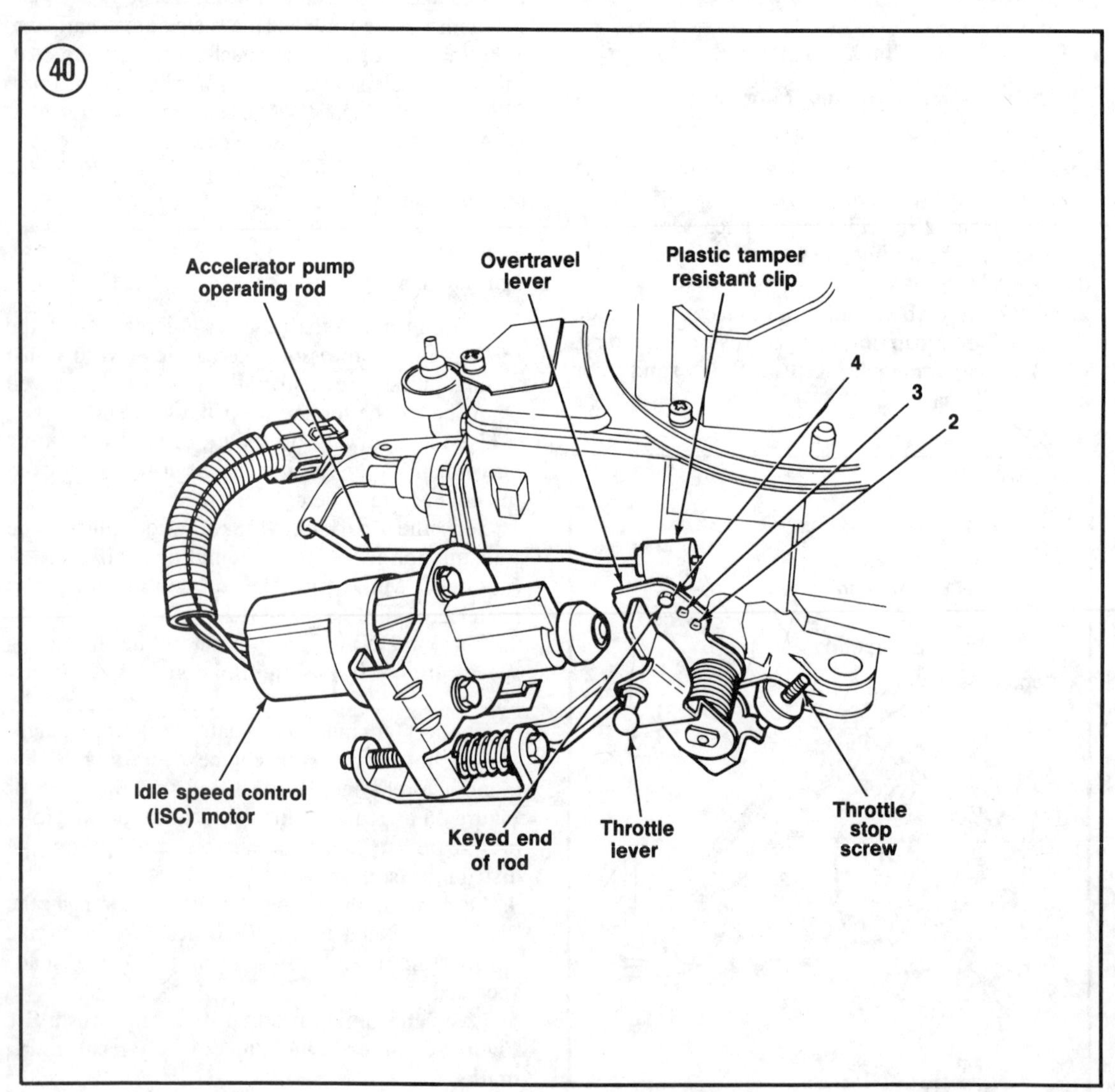

10. Grasp the distributor cap and rotate the body clockwise or counterclockwise as required to align the timing marks. When the marks are properly aligned, tighten the hold-down clamp bolt snugly without disturbing the distributor position and recheck the timing.
11. Disconnect and remove the test equipment. Reconnect the single wire connector. Perform any other steps specified on the VECI decal.

FUEL SYSTEM ADJUSTMENTS

Idle Speed

No attempt should be made to adjust the curb idle or fast idle speed settings on the 1986 carburetted V6 engine. An ISC motor (**Figure 40**) controls idle speed. The EEC-IV microprocessor controls engine rpm precisely, eliminating the need for idle and fast idle speed adjustments. Fuel injected engines require no idle speed adjustment. A throttle air bypass valve mounted on the throttle body or air cleaner housing maintains the correct idle speed according to signals from the EEC-IV microprocessor.

Attempting to adjust idle speed on either the carburetted or fuel injected engine will only make matters worse, since it will affect the input signals received by the EEC-IV microprocessor, which will then send incorrect output signals. If idle speed seems to require adjustment, see your Ford dealer.

Idle Mixture

The idle mixture screw is located under a plug seal on all carburetors in accordance with Federal regulations governing unauthorized adjustment. The carburetors are flow-tested and pre-set at the factory. Idle mixture on fuel injected engines is controlled by the EEC-IV microprocessor. If the idle mixture seems to require adjustment for any reason, see your Ford dealer.

Tables are on the following pages.

Table 1 MAINTENANCE SCHEDULE

Every 7,500 miles	• Engine oil change*(12 months) • Chassis/suspension lubrication* • Check manual transmission • Check exhaust system • Check brake system • Check power steering system • Check automatic transmission shift cable
First 7,500 miles, then every 15,000 miles	• Check and rotate tires • Change engine oil filter*
First 7,500 miles, then every 30,000 miles	• Change manual transmission fluid • Check 2.8L V6 engine valve clearance
Annually	• Check cooling system operation • Check coolant condition and protection
Every 2 years	• Drain, flush and refill cooling system • Replace cooling system hoses
Every 30,000 miles	• Replace spark plugs* • Check spark plug and ignition coil wires • Replace air cleaner filter • Clean, repack and adjust wheel bearings* • Clean choke linkage (2.8L V6) • Inspect fuel tank, cap and lines (EEC system) • Check brake and clutch master cylinder reservoir fluid level • Check brake system operation • Check exhaust system • Lubricate suspension ball-joints • Check suspension bushing, arm and spring condition • Lubricate throttle ball stud
Every 60,000 miles	• Replace PCV valve • Replace spark plug wires • Check Thermactor system hoses • Replace EGR valve • Replace EGR vacuum solenoid filter • Replace HEGO sensor**
Every 100,000 miles	• Change automatic transmission fluid and strainer*

* SEVERE SERVICE OPERATION: If the vehicle is operated under any of the following conditions, change engine oil @ 3,000 miles or 3 month intervals and oil filter @ alternate oil changes. Repack wheel bearings every 15,000 miles.Change rear axle lubricant every 15,000 miles. Change PCV valve every 15,000 miles. Clean and regap spark plugs every 6,000 miles. Lubricate chassis and suspension every 6,000 miles. Change automatic transmission fluid and filter every 30,000 miles.

a. Extended idle or low-speed operation (short trips, stop-and-go driving).
b. Trailer towing.
c. Operation @ temperatures below 10° F for 60 days or more with most trips under 10 miles.
d. Very dusty or muddy conditions.

** If equipped with an emissions maintenance warning lamp, replace @ specified interval or whenever the warning lamp lights, whichever comes first.

Table 2 ENGINE OIL VISCOSITY

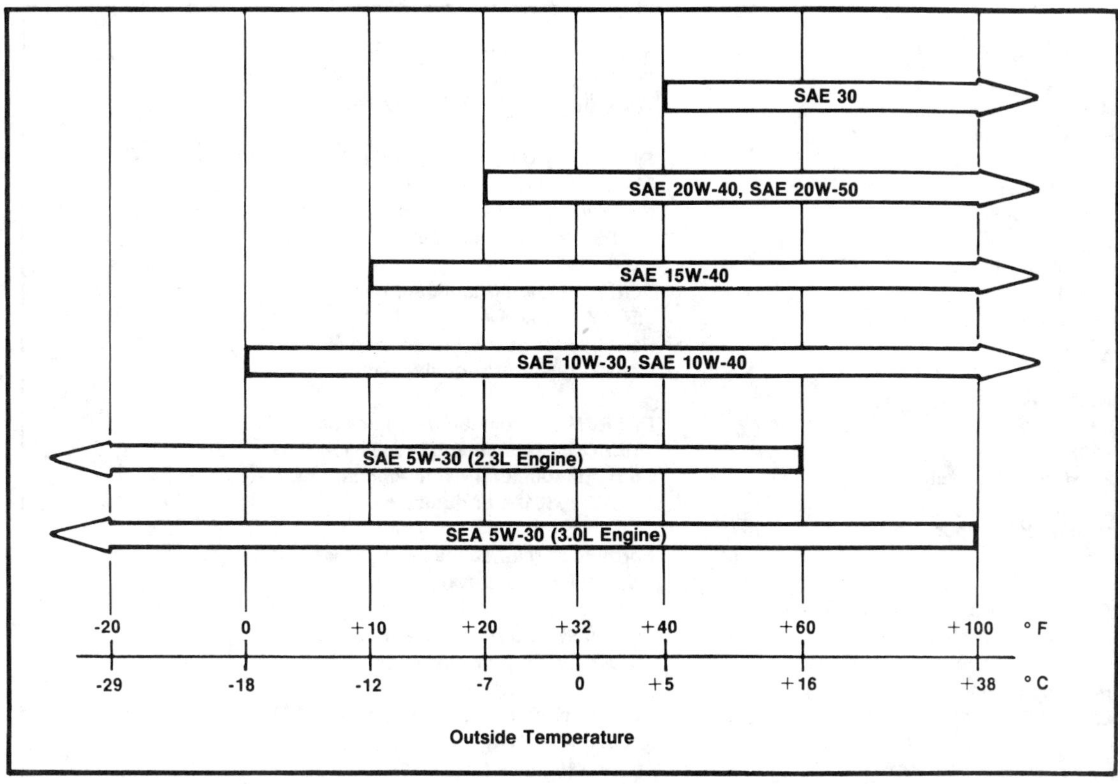

Table 3 APPROXIMATE REFILL CAPACITIES

	qt.	pt.
Engine crankcase		
I4		
With filter	5.0	
Without filter	4.0	
2.8L V6		
With filter	5.0	
Without filter	4.0	
3.0L V6		
With filter	4.5	
Without filter	3.5	
Automatic transmission		
After rebuild		19.0
After fluid change		10.0
Manual transmission		5.9
Differential		
Ford		3.5
Dana		2.5
Cooling system		
I4		
Manual transmission	6.8	
Automatic transmission	7.6	
2.8L V6	8.0	
3.0L V6	11.8	3-4

Table 4 RECOMMENDED LUBRICANTS

Crankcase	API Service SF oil
Engine coolant	Ford cooling system fluid or equivalent meeting Ford spec. ESE-M97B44-A
Brake and clutch master cylinder	Ford Heavy Duty or other DOT 3 or DOT 4 fluid
Power steering pump	Motorcraft Type F automatic transmission fluid
Manual transmission	Standard transmission lubricant part No. D8DZ-19C547-A or equivalent
Rear axle	
Ford	Ford hypoid gear lubricant part No. EOAZ-19580-A or equivalent
Dana	Ford hypoid gear lubricant part No. C6AZ-19580-A or equivalent
Automatic transmission	
1986-1987	DEXRON II automatic transmission fluid
1988	MERCON automatic transmission fluid
Parking brake cable	Ford speedometer cable lubricant part No. D2AZ-19581-A or equivalent
Disc brake caliper rails	Ford disc brake caliper slide grease part No. D7AZ-19590-A or equivalent
Throttle control kickdown and ball stud	Ford multipurpose lubricant part No. C1AZ-19590-B or equivalent
Manual steering gear housing	Ford steering gear grease part No. C3AZ-19578-A or equivalent
Power steering system	Motorcraft Type F automatic transmission fluid
Hinges, latches and seat tracks	Ford polyethylene grease part No. D7AZ-19584-A or equivalent
Lock cylinders	Ford lock lubricant part No. D8AZ-19587-A
Suspension ball-joints	Ford multipurpose lubricant part No. C1AZ-19590-A or equivalent

Table 5 AUTOMATIC TRANSMISSION FLUID OXIDATION

Temperature (degrees F)	Life expectancy (in miles)
175	100,000
195	50,000
212	25,000
235	12,000
255	6,250
275	3,000
295	1,500
315	750
335	325
355	160
375	80
390	40
415	Less than 30 minutes

CHAPTER FOUR

4-CYLINDER OHC ENGINE

The base engine in 1986 and 1987 models is a 2.3L (140 cid) fuel injected 4-cylinder OHC engine. The engine uses a lightweight cast iron cylinder block. The crankshaft is supported by 5 main bearings. The No. 3 bearing provides the crankshaft thrust surfaces.

The camshaft is supported by 4 bearings. It operates the valves through pivot-type rocker arms with hydraulic valve lash adjusters at the fulcrum point of the rocker arm. The camshaft is driven from the crankshaft by a cogged belt which also operates an auxiliary shaft. The auxiliary shaft drives the oil pump and distributor. Tension is maintained on the camshaft drive belt by a locked idler pulley riding on the outside of the belt. The water pump, alternator and cooling fan are driven from the crankshaft by conventional V-belts.

Specifications (**Table 1**) and tightening torques (**Table 2**) are at the end of the chapter.

ENGINE IDENTIFICATION

An engine identification label is attached to the front of the timing belt cover (**Figure 1**). The data on the label identifies each engine. The change level and engine code number tell which parts are unique to particular engines. This data should be used when ordering replacement parts to assure that the correct parts are furnished.

The engine code is the 8th digit/letter of the vehicle identification number (VIN). The engine code for 2.3L Aerostar engines is A. The VIN is the official identification for title and vehicle registration. The VIN is stamped on a metal vehicle identification plate attached to the top left of the instrument panel (**Figure 2**).

ENGINE SERVICE

Access to the 2.3L Aerostar engine is very limited. The engine fills the engine compartment and reaching many components such as the PCV valve is difficult at best without removing the engine from the vehicle. **Figure 3** shows the location of numerous components on the 1986 and 1987 engines that you will not be able to visually see with the hood open. The small engine

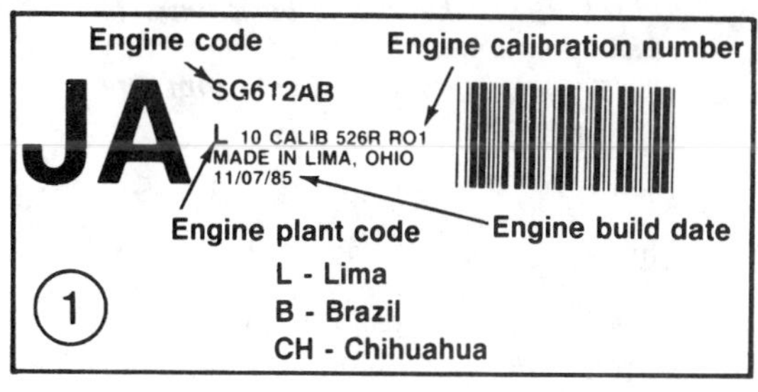

compartment panel underneath the instrument panel in the passenger compartment does not provide as much access as the traditional engine cover found in full-size vans.

The engine is removed and installed from the bottom of the vehicle and requires removal of the suspension. While many of the tasks detailed in this chapter can be performed with the engine in the vehicle, progress will be slow and require the use of an extensive selection of metric tools, including a variety of long and short socket extensions.

Before attempting any procedure, you should study the engine compartment and this chapter, then make a determination whether engine removal will make the task easier and faster. In most cases, the choice will depend upon your skill level as an owner/mechanic. Whatever the choice, expect that many service procedures will require more time than you first think, and be prepared to work slowly and patiently. You even may find it more convenient to perform some of the steps from underneath the engine, even though the procedure does not specify raising the engine.

ENGINE REMOVAL/INSTALLATION

WARNING

The engine is heavy, awkward to handle and has sharp edges. It may shift or drop suddenly during removal. To prevent serious injury, always observe the following precautions.

1. Never place any part of your body where a moving or falling engine may trap, cut or crush you.

2. If you must push the engine during removal, use a board or similar tool to keep your hands out of danger.

3. Be sure the hoist is designed to lift engines and has enough load capacity for your engine.

4. Be sure the hoist is securely attached to safe lifting points on the engine.

5. The engine should not be difficult to lift with a proper hoist. If it is, stop lifting, lower the engine back onto its mounts and make sure the engine has been completely separated from the vehicle.

WARNING

Before opening any fuel system connection on a fuel injected engine, relieve system pressure as described in Chapter Six.

1. Raise and support the hood.
2. Disconnect the negative battery cable.
3. Drain the cooling system. See Chapter Seven.
4. Disconnect the air cleaner outlet tube at the air intake throttle body.
5. Unclamp and disconnect the upper and lower radiator hoses at the radiator. Unclamp and disconnect the heater hoses at the water pump and thermostat housing (**Figure 4**).

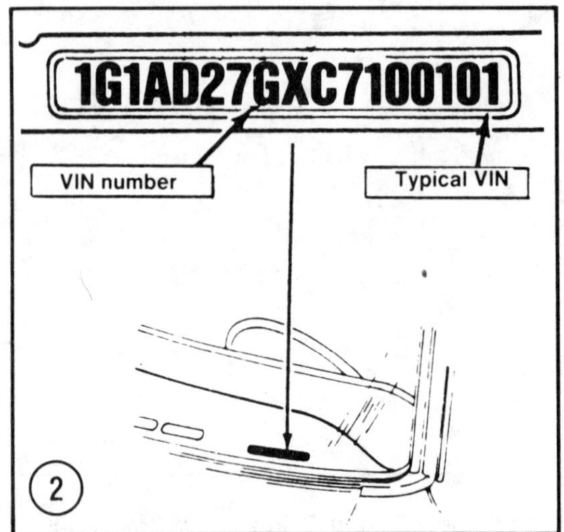

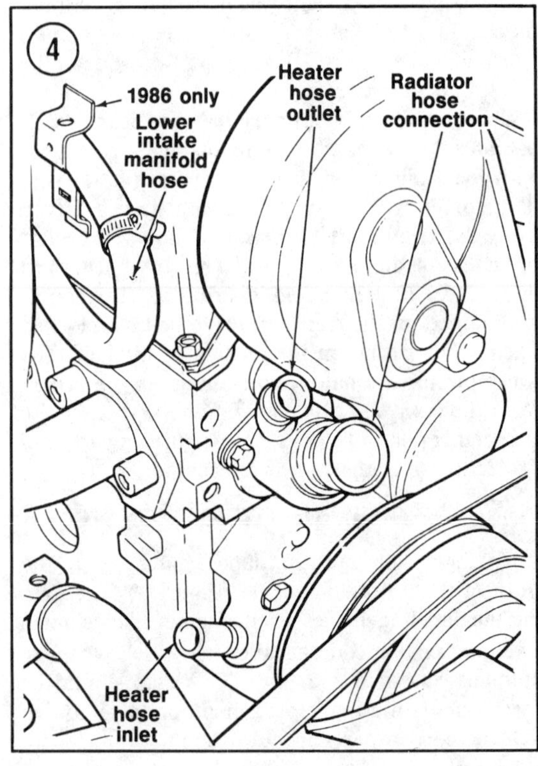

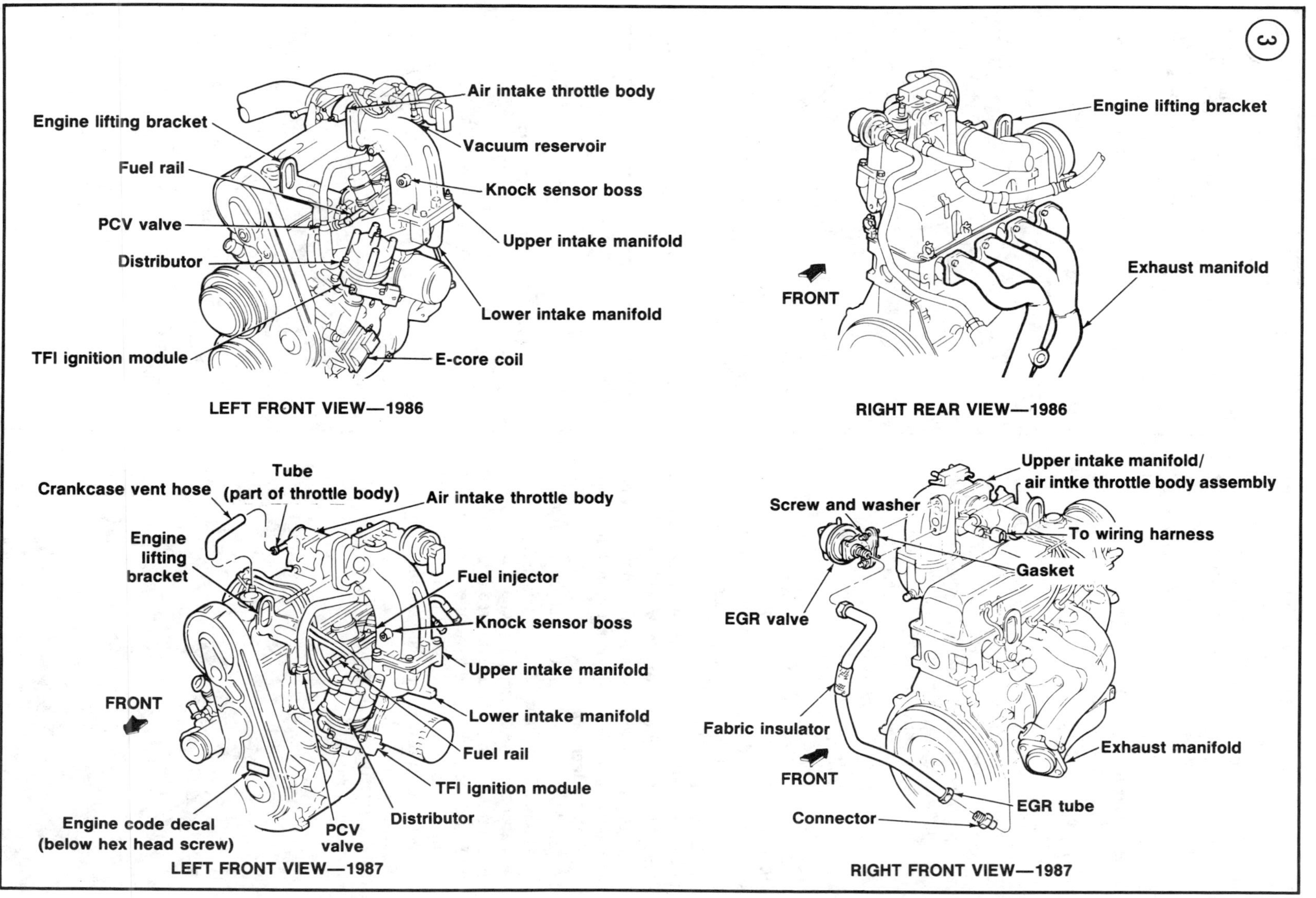
3
Engine lifting bracket
Fuel rail
PCV valve
Distributor
TFI ignition module
Air intake throttle body
Vacuum reservoir
Knock sensor boss
Upper intake manifold
Lower intake manifold
E-core coil
LEFT FRONT VIEW—1986
Engine lifting bracket
FRONT
Exhaust manifold
RIGHT REAR VIEW—1986
Tube
Crankcase vent hose
(part of throttle body)
Air intake throttle body
Engine
lifting
bracket
Fuel injector
Knock sensor boss
Upper intake manifold
FRONT
Lower intake manifold
Fuel rail
TFI ignition module
Engine code decal
(below hex head screw)
PCV
valve
Distributor
LEFT FRONT VIEW—1987
Upper intake manifold/
air intke throttle body assembly
Screw and washer
To wiring harness
Gasket
EGR valve
Fabric insulator
Exhaust manifold
FRONT
EGR tube
Connector
RIGHT FRONT VIEW—1987

6. 1986—Disconnect the lower intake manifold hose at the heater hose tee fitting.
7. Unbolt and remove the fan shroud.
8. Unplug the 2 electrical connectors at the alternator (**Figure 5**).
9. Remove the shield over the throttle linkage. Disconnect the throttle cable (and speed control cable, if so equipped) at the air intake throttle body (**Figure 6**). Unbolt the cables from the bracket and place them out of the way.

WARNING
The air conditioning system contains pressurized refrigerant which can cause frostbite if it touches skin and blindness if it touches the eyes. If discharged near an open flame, the refrigerant forms poisonous gas. Never disconnect air conditioning system lines unless the system has been discharged and evacuated by a professional.

10. If equipped with air conditioning, have the system discharged, then disconnect the suction and discharge hoses at the compressor. Unplug the clutch switch. See **Figure 7**.
11. Reach under the left front of the engine and unplug the ignition coil connectors (**Figure 8**).
12. Reach under the lower intake manifold and carefully unplug the TFI-IV ignition module at the distributor (**Figure 8**).
13. Unplug the knock sensor electrical connector. See **Figure 3** and **Figure 8**.
14. Label and disconnect all vacuum lines at the upper intake manifold vacuum tree (**Figure 9**).
15. Reach behind the rear of the upper intake manifold and unplug the EGR valve electrical connector, then disconnect the vacuum line at the valve. See **Figure 10**.
16. Remove the small engine cover panel inside the passenger compartment.

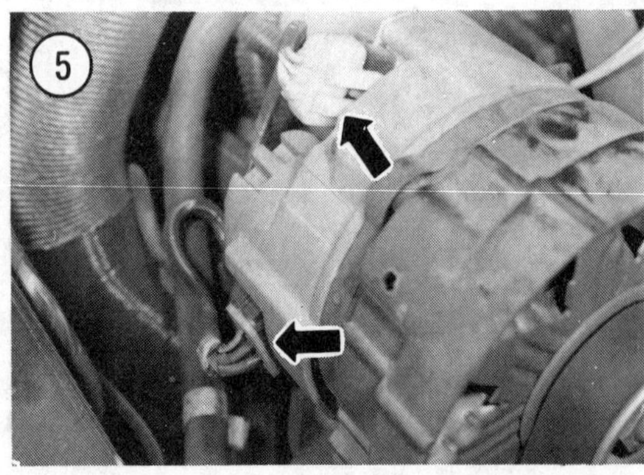

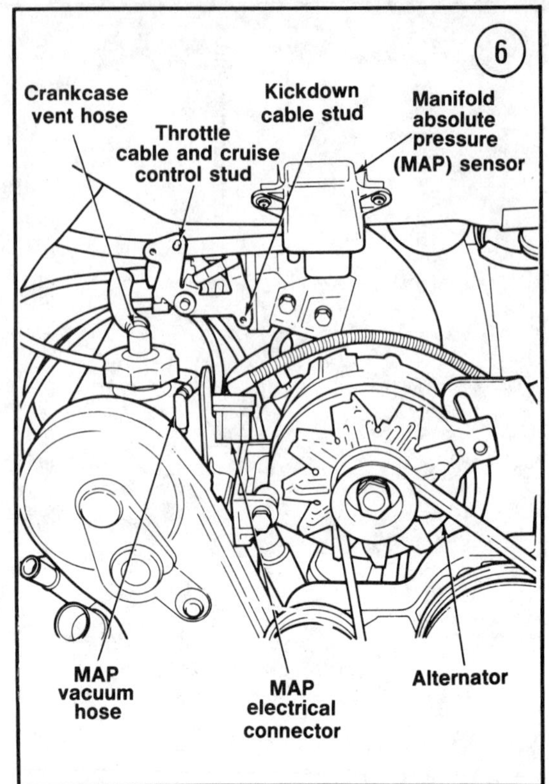

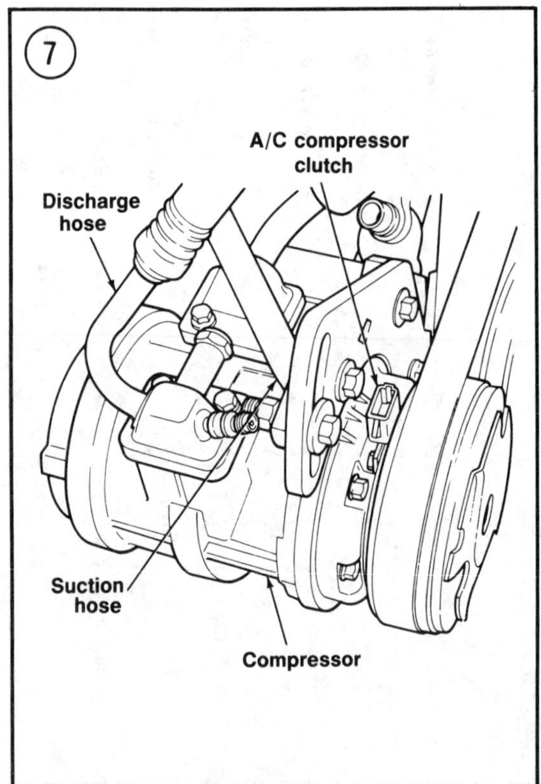

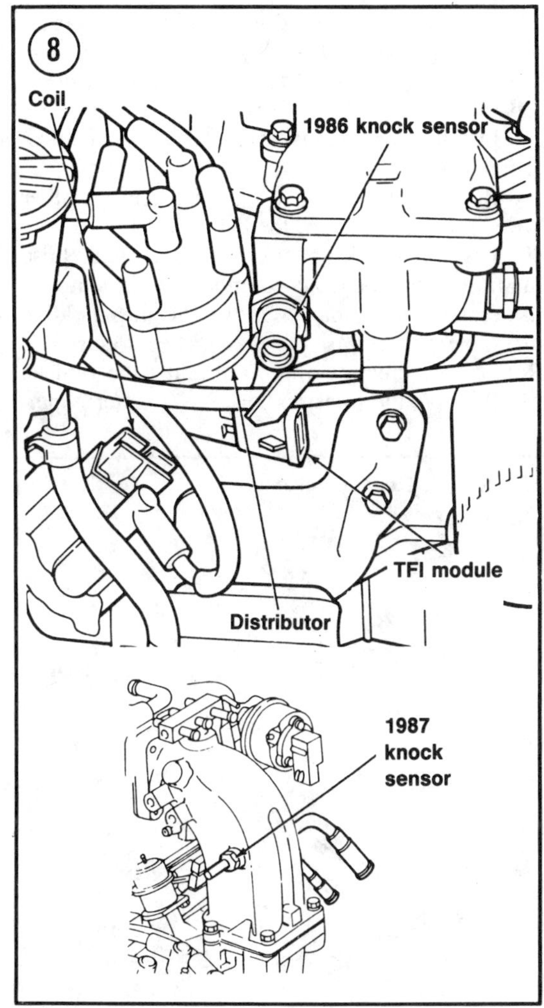

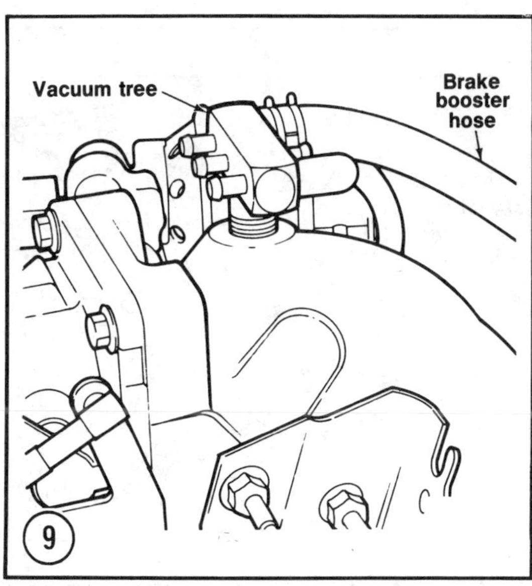

17. Refer to **Figure 11** and unplug or disconnect the following:
   a. Throttle position sensor.
   b. Oil pressure sender electrical elbow.
   c. Fuel injection wiring harness connector.
   d. Air charge temperature sensor.
   e. Coolant temperature sensor.
18. Disconnect the fuel return and supply lines (**Figure 11**). See Chapter Six. Plug or cap the lines to prevent leakage.
19. Remove the nut on the lower part of the engine lifting eye and disconnect the ground strap.
20. Manual transmission—Remove the shift lever. See Chapter Nine.
21. Securely block the rear wheels so the vehicle will not roll in either direction.
22. Loosen the front wheel lug nuts, then raise the front of the vehicle with a jack and place it on jackstands.
23. Remove the wheel/tire assemblies.
24. Automatic transmission—Disconnect the oil cooler lines at the radiator. If equipped with quick-disconnect fittings, see Chapter Six.
25. Power steering—Unplug the pressure switch connector at the steering gear.
26. Unbolt and disconnect the intermediate steering column shaft from the steering gear. See **Figure 12**.
27. Remove the starter motor. See Chapter Eight.
28. Manual transmission—Disconnect the slave cylinder hydraulic line. See Chapter Nine.

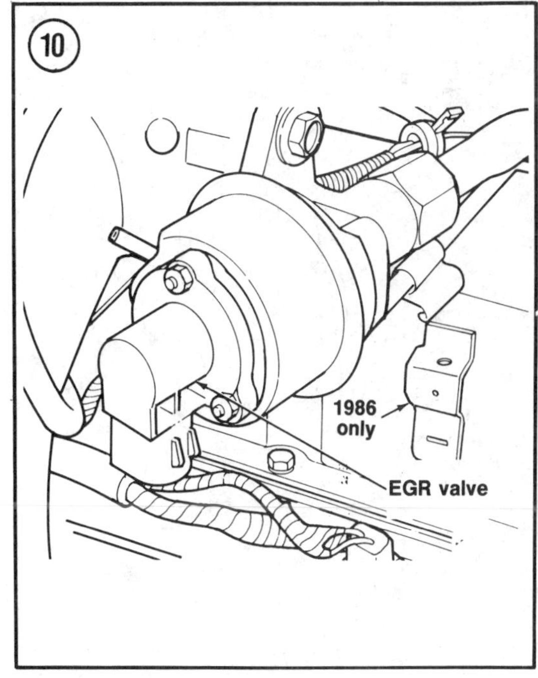

29. Unplug the exhaust gas oxygen sensor connector. See **Figure 13**.
30. Disconnect the catalytic converter at the exhaust manifold. Remove the exhaust pipe and catalytic converter. See Chapter Six.
31. Disconnect all electrical connectors at the transmission. See Chapter Nine.
32. Automatic transmission—Disconnect the selector and kickdown cables at the transmission. See Chapter Nine.
33. Remove the drive shaft. See Chapter Eleven.
34. Disconnect the stabilizer bar at the lower control arm. See Chapter Ten.
35. Disconnect the front brake lines at the frame brackets.
36. Place a jack under the lower control arm and raise the jack enough to apply tension to the control arm.
37. Remove the bolt and nut holding the spindle to the upper control arm ball-joint (**Figure 14**). Lower the jack until the spindle and ball-joint separate.
38. Install safety chains around the lower control arm and spring seat.
39. Repeat Steps 35-37 to disconnect the other lower control arm from the ball-joint.
40. Position a jack under the transmission. Raise the transmission enough to unbolt the insulator at the crossmember, then remove the nuts holding the crossmember to the frame. See **Figure 15**. Remove the crossmember from under the vehicle.
41. Remove the transmission. See Chapter Nine.

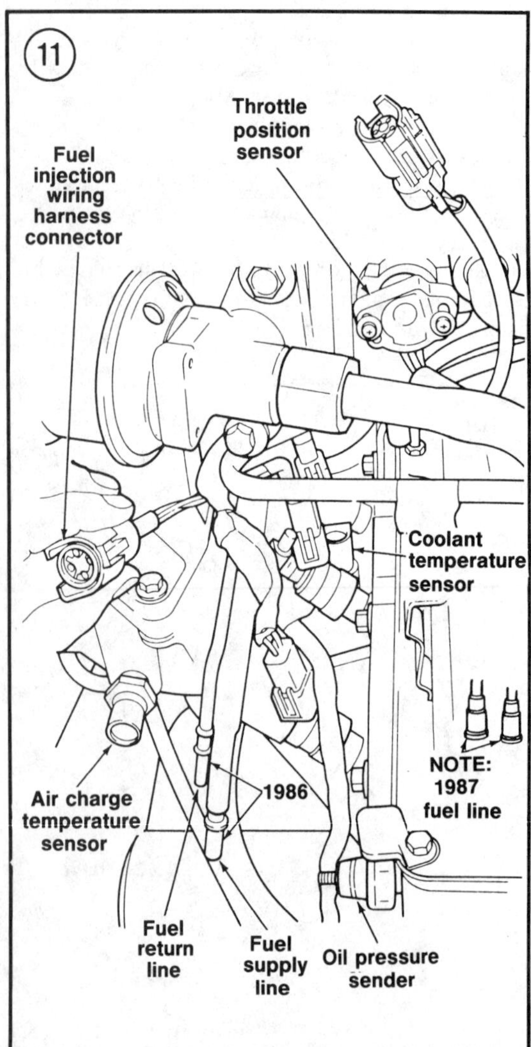

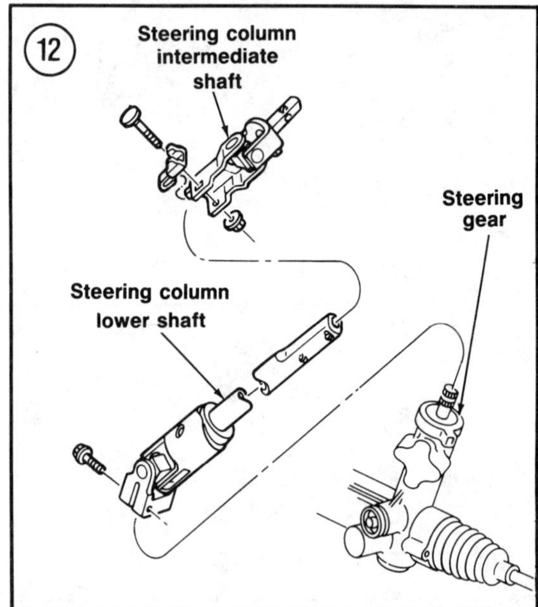

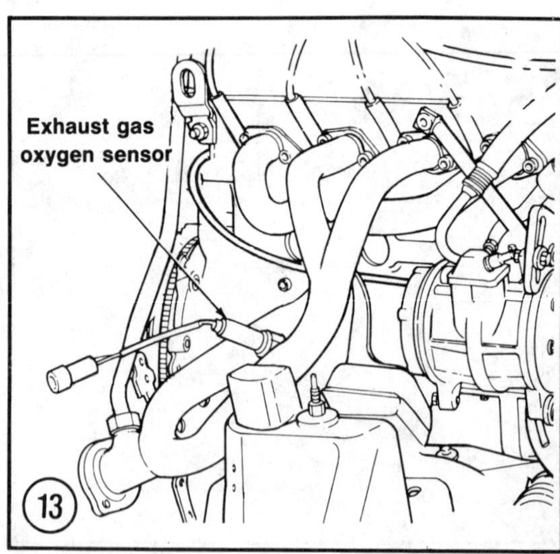

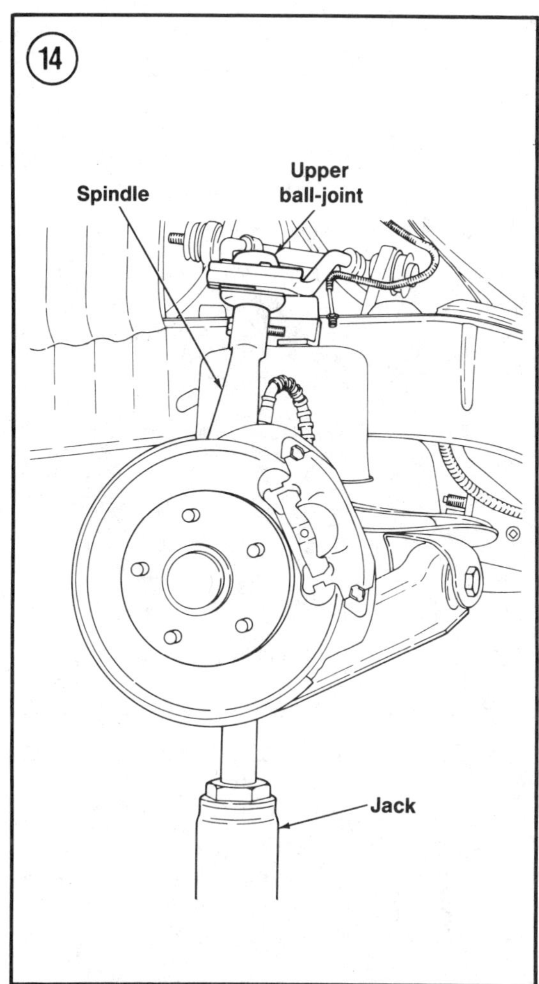

42. Position a suitable support table under the engine and crossmember assembly. Ford recommends the use of Rotunda table part No. 109-0002.

43. Slowly lower the vehicle until the crossmember rests on the support table. Position suitable wooden blocks under the front crossmember and rear of the engine block to keep the assembly level, then install safety chains around the table and crossmember.

44. Remove the fasteners holding the engine and crossmember assembly to the frame on each side of the vehicle. See **Figure 16**.

NOTE

At this point, there should be no hoses, wires or linkages connecting the engine to the body. Recheck to be sure nothing will hamper engine removal and that all accessories, hoses, tubes and wires are positioned out of the way.

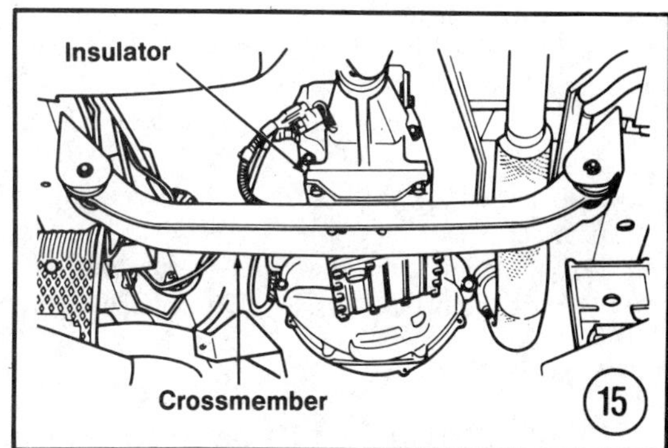

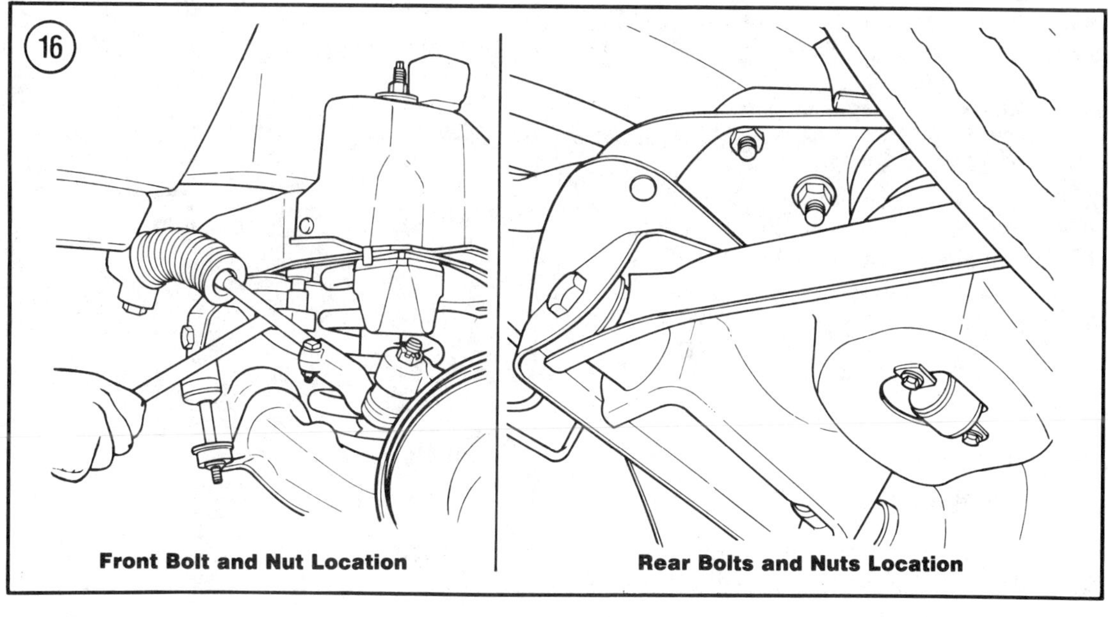

Front Bolt and Nut Location | **Rear Bolts and Nuts Location**

45. Slowly raise the vehicle until it clears the engine and crossmember assembly on the support table **(Figure 17)**. Roll the support table with the engine and crossmember assembly out from underneath the vehicle.
46. Attach an engine hoist chain or sling to the engine lifting bracket eyes.
47. Power steering—Disconnect the hydraulic fluid hoses at the power steering pump. Plug the lines and cap the fittings to prevent leakage.
48. Apply tension to the hoist chain or sling, then remove the nuts holding the engine to the crossmember assembly. Lift the engine up and off the crossmember assembly **(Figure 18)**.
49. Once the engine is clear of the crossmember assembly, lower it to a suitable support or engine stand. Fasten the engine in the support or engine stand, then disconnect the hoist and lifting chain or sling. Inspect the rubber motor mounts and insulators for wear or damage. If these conditions exist, replace the mounts or insulators before reinstalling the engine.
50. Engine installation is the reverse of removal, plus the following:
   a. Tighten all fasteners to specifications **(Table 1)**.
   b. Fill the engine with an oil recommended in Chapter Three.
   c. Fill the cooling system. See Chapter Seven.
   d. Adjust the drive belts. See Chapter Seven.

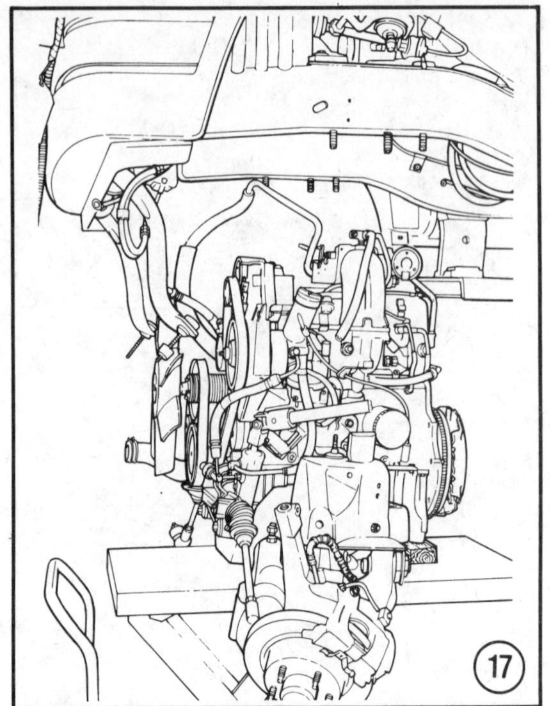

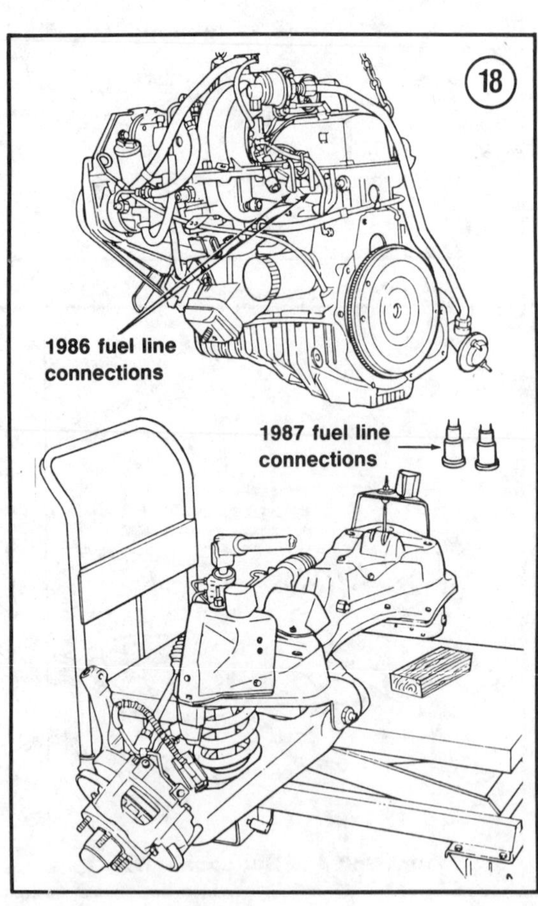

DISASSEMBLY CHECKLISTS

To use the checklists, remove and inspect each part in the order mentioned. To reassemble, go through the checklists backwards, installing the parts in order. Each major part is covered in its own section in this chapter, unless otherwise noted.

Decarbonizing or Valve Service

1. Remove the valve cover.
2. Remove the intake and exhaust manifolds.
3. Remove the rocker arms.
4. Remove the cylinder head.
5. Have valves removed and inspected. Have valve guides and seats inspected, repairing or replacing as required.
6. Assemble by reversing Steps 1-4.

Valve and Ring Service

1. Perform Steps 1-5 of *Decarbonizing or Valve Service.*
2. Remove the oil pan and oil pump.
3. Remove the pistons with connecting rods.

4. Remove the piston rings. It is not necessary to separate the pistons from the connecting rods unless a piston, connecting rod or piston pin needs repair or replacement.
5. Assemble by reversing Steps 1-4.

General Overhaul

1. Remove the engine. Remove the clutch (Chapter Nine) from manual transmission vehicles.
2. Remove the flywheel (manual) or drive plate (automatic).
3. Remove the mount brackets and oil pressure sending unit from the engine.
4. If available, mount the engine on an engine stand. These can be rented from equipment rental dealers. The stand is not absolutely necessary, but it will make the job much easier.
5. Remove the following accessories or components from the engine, if present:
   a. Alternator and mounting bracket.
   b. Power steering pump and mounting bracket.
   c. Spark plug wires and distributor cap.
   d. Fuel lines.
   e. Oil filter.
6. Check the engine for signs of coolant or oil leaks.
7. Clean the outside of the engine.
8. Remove the distributor. See Chapter Eight.
9. Remove all hoses and tubes connected to the engine. **Figure 19** shows the PCV system.
10. Remove the intake and exhaust manifolds.
11. Remove the thermostat housing and water pump. See Chapter Seven.
12. Remove the valve cover and rocker arms.
13. Remove the crankshaft pulley and timing belt outer cover.
14. Remove the cylinder head.
15. Remove the camshaft sprocket and camshaft.
16. Remove the auxiliary shaft.
17. Remove the oil pan and oil pump.
18. Remove the pistons and connecting rods.
19. Remove the crankshaft and main bearings.
20. Inspect the cylinder block.
21. Assemble by reversing Steps 1-19.

VALVE COVER

Removal/Installation

Valve cover design differs slightly between 1986 and 1987 models. Refer to **Figure 20** for this procedure.

1. Unclamp the air cleaner tube at the air intake throttle body.

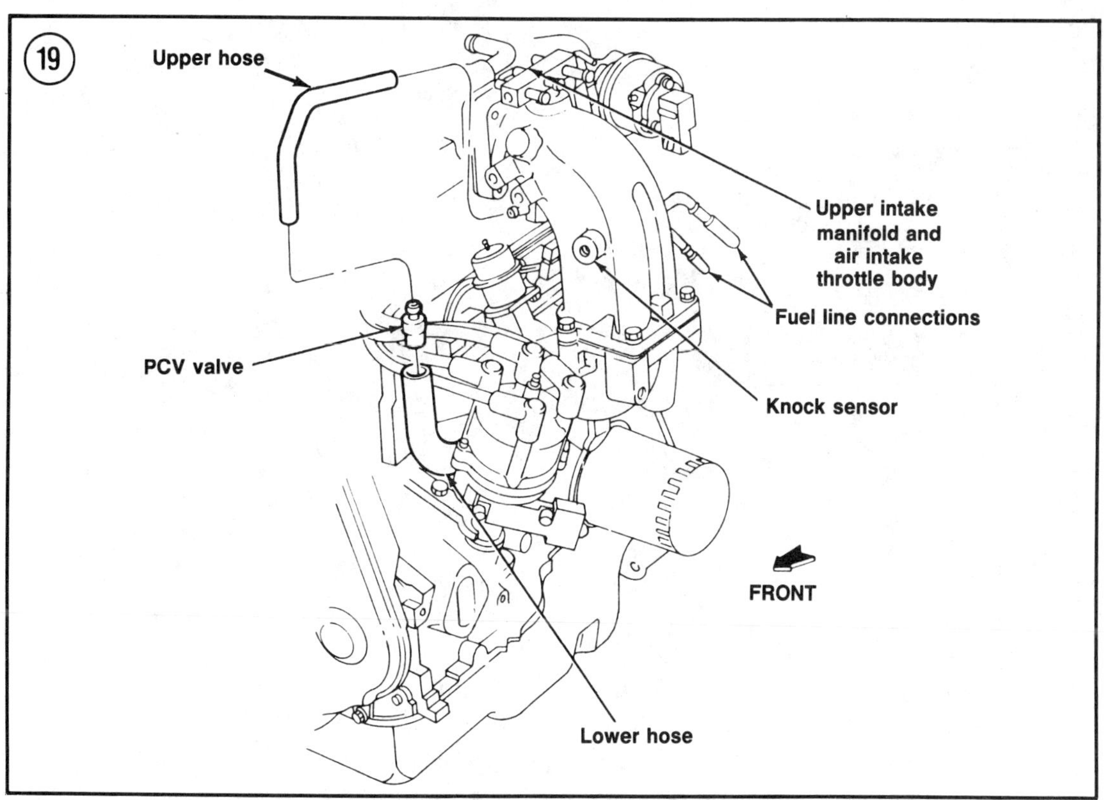

2. Remove the shield over the throttle linkage. Disconnect the throttle cable (and speed control cable, if so equipped) at the air intake throttle body (**Figure 6**). Unbolt the cables from the bracket and place them out of the way.
3. Unplug all electrical connectors and vacuum lines attached to the air intake throttle body. Unbolt and remove the throttle body from the upper intake manifold.
4. Disconnect the spark plug wires at the spark plugs and remove the wire loom from the valve cover. Place the wire loom and wires out of the way.
5. 1986—Remove the screw holding the heater hoses to the valve cover.
6. Remove the valve cover attaching bolts and studs.

NOTE

If the cover refuses to come free in Step 7, bump the end with a rubber mallet. If this does not break the gasket seal, carefully pry the cover loose with a screwdriver. Use caution to prevent distorting the cover sealing flange.

7. Remove the valve cover and gasket. Discard the gasket.
8. Clean all gasket residue from the valve cover and cylinder head mating surfaces.
9. Installation is the reverse of removal. Use a new gasket and coat it on the valve cover side with an oil-resistant sealer such as Ford Gasket and Seal Adhesive (part No. D7AZ-19B508-A). Coat cylinder head mating surfaces with the same material. Let adhesive dry and install gasket in valve cover with locating tabs properly positioned in cover slots. Fit valve cover over guide pins (if used) and hand-start all fasteners. Tighten fasteners to specifications (**Table 2**). Run the engine at fast idle and check for oil leaks.

Removal/Installation

1. Remove the upper intake manifold with air intake throttle body as described in this chapter.
2. Rotate the camshaft by hand until the low side of the camshaft lobe contacts the rocker arm being removed.

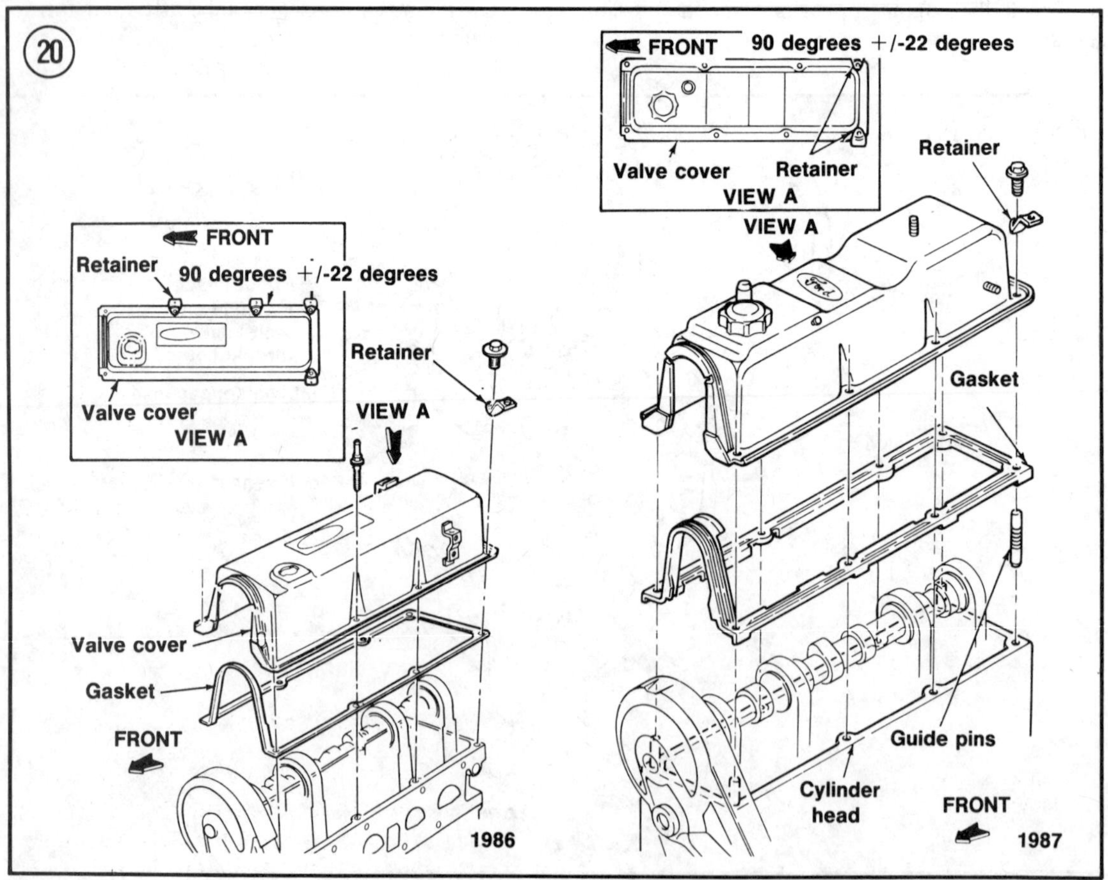

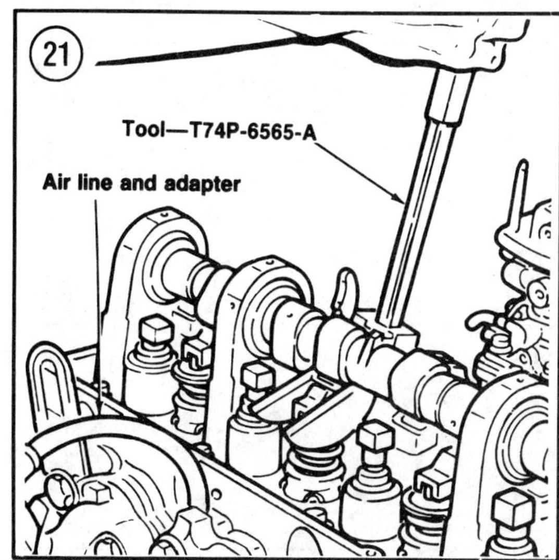

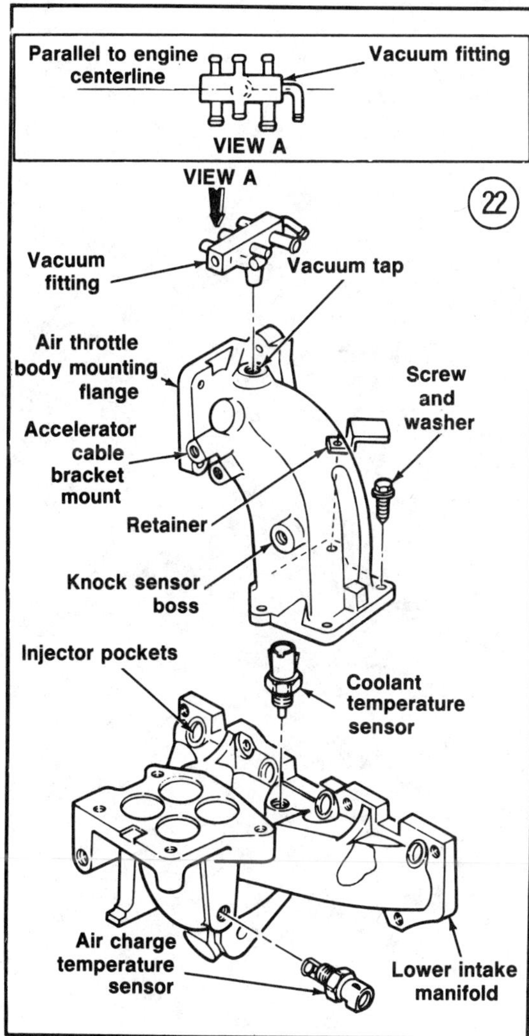

3. Using Ford tool part No. T74P-6565-A, collapse the valve spring and slide the cam follower over the lash adjuster and out of the head. See **Figure 21**. If necessary, lift the lash adjuster out of the head.
4. Repeat Step 2 and Step 3 for each rocker arm to be removed.
5. Installation is the reverse of removal. Each valve spring must be collapsed and released after the camshaft follower is reinstalled before rotating the camshaft to another position.

UPPER AND LOWER INTAKE MANIFOLD

The intake manifold consists of 2 components: the upper intake manifold with air intake throttle body and the lower intake manifold with fuel charging assembly. The 2 components can be removed separately or as a unit. See **Figure 22**.

Removal/Installation

See *Multi-Point Fuel Injection (2.3L EFI), Fuel Charging Assembly Removal/ Installation,* Chapter Six.

EXHAUST MANIFOLD

A header-style exhaust manifold is used on both 1986 and 1987 models.

Removal/Installation

Refer to **Figure 23** for this procedure.
1. Remove the EGR line at the exhaust manifold, then loosen the EGR tube.
2. 1986—Remove the screw holding the heater hoses to the valve cover.
3. Unbolt the inlet pipe from the exhaust manifold.
4. Remove the 8 manifold attaching capscrews. Remove the exhaust manifold from the cylinder head. Remove and discard the gasket.
5. Installation is the reverse of removal. Use a new gasket and tighten all fasteners to specifications (**Table 2**) working from the center to the outside in both directions.

MANIFOLD INSPECTION

Intake and Exhaust Manifolds

1. Check the intake and exhaust manifolds for cracks or distortion. Replace as necessary.
2. Check the sealing surfaces for nicks or burrs. Small burrs may be removed with an oilstone.
3. Place a straightedge across the manifold sealing surfaces and measure any gap between the

straightedge and sealing surface with a flat feeler gauge. Measure from end to end and diagonally. If the sealing surface is not flat within 0.006 in. (0.15 mm) per foot of manifold length, replace the manifold.

CAMSHAFT BELT OUTER COVER

Removal/Installation

Refer to **Figure 24** for this procedure.

1. Disconnect the negative battery cable.
2. Drain the cooling system, then disconnect the upper radiator hose at the radiator. Remove the fan blade and water pump pulley. See Chapter Seven.
3. Loosen the alternator pivot and adjusting bolts. Move the alternator to one side and remove the drive belt.
4. If equipped with power steering, loosen the power steering pump and mounting bracket and move the pump to one side out of the way without disconnecting any hydraulic lines.
5. Remove the camshaft belt outer cover bolts. Remove the outer cover.
6. Installation is the reverse of removal. Tighten the cover bolts to specifications (**Table 2**). Refill the cooling system and adjust the drive belt (Chapter Seven).

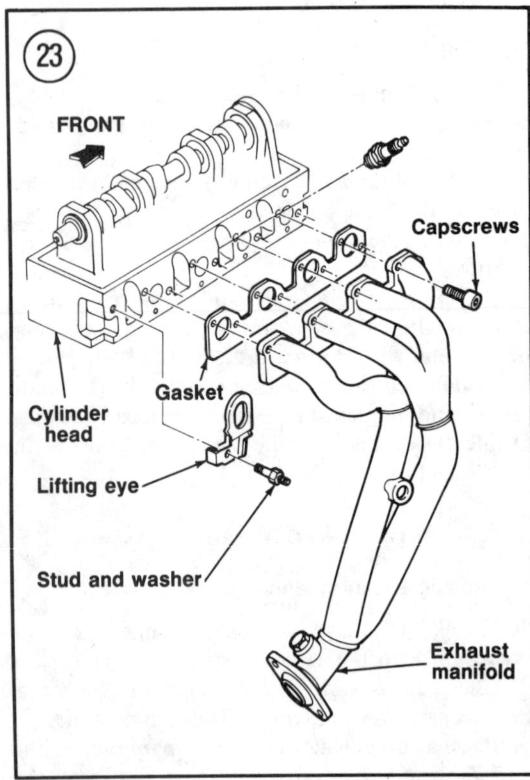

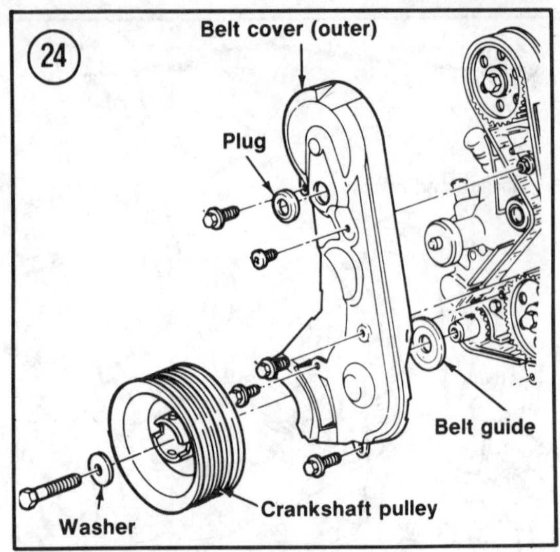

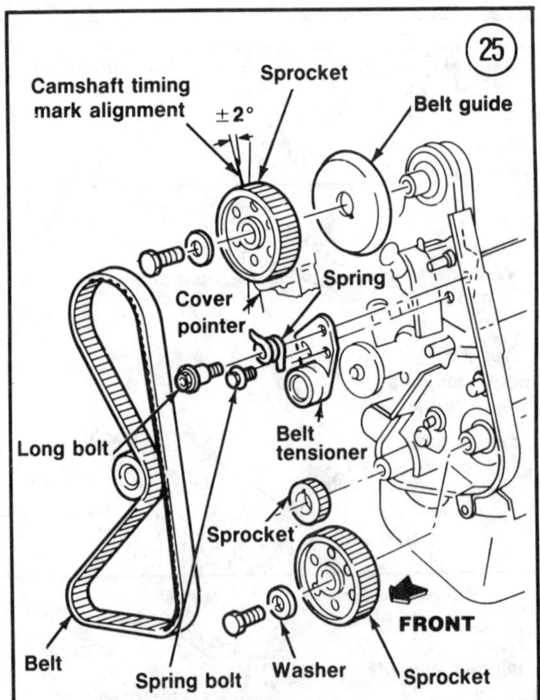

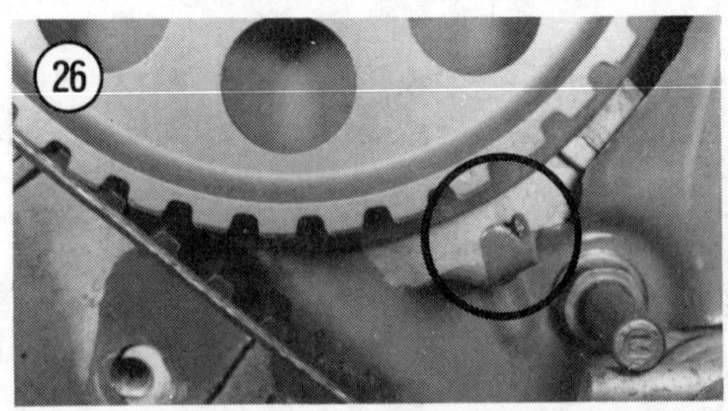

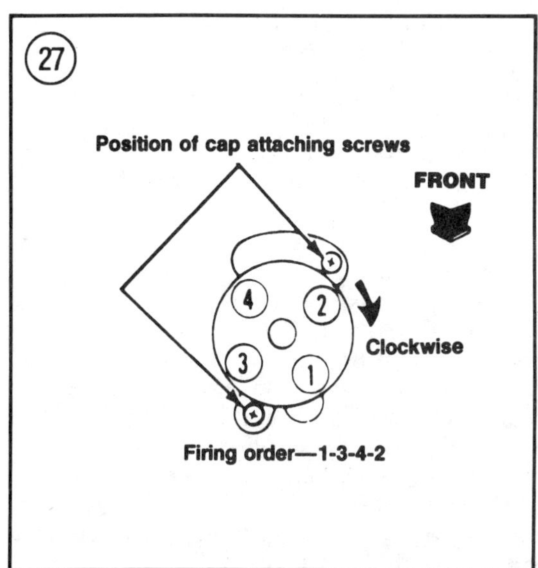

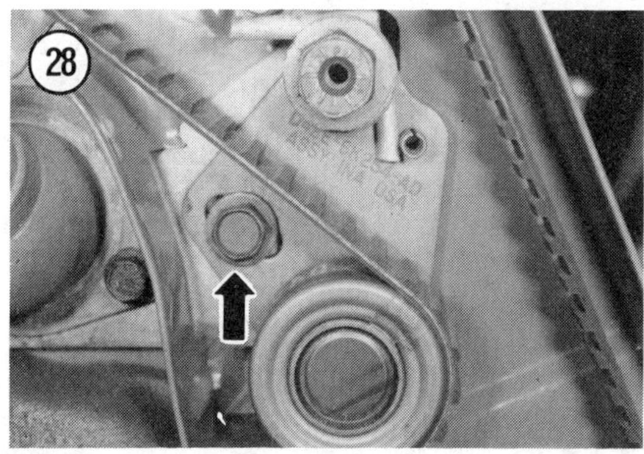

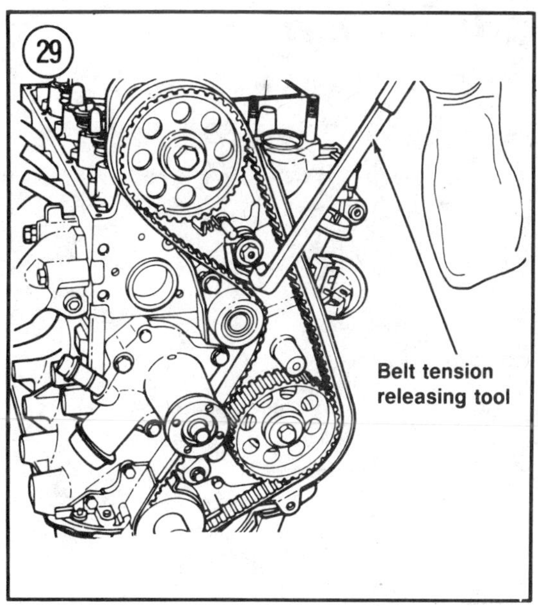

CAMSHAFT BELT

Removal/Installation

Refer to **Figure 25** for this procedure.

1. Remove the camshaft belt outer cover as described in this chapter.
2. Draw an arrow on the camshaft belt with chalk to indicate normal direction of rotation (clockwise as seen from the front). If the belt is to be reused, it must be reinstalled to move in the same direction.

CAUTION
Rotate the engine only in its normal direction (clockwise as seen from the front of the vehicle). Rotating the engine backward may cause the camshaft belt to slip on the sprockets, changing the valve timing.

3. Place a wrench on the crankshaft pulley bolt and rotate the engine in a clockwise position until the No. 1 piston is at top dead center on the compression stroke. When the crankshaft is positioned correctly, the 0° (TDC) mark on the vibration damper will align with the timing pointer on the front of the engine and the camshaft timing mark will align with the camshaft sprocket timing mark (**Figure 26**). Remove the distributor cap and make sure the rotor is pointing to the No. 1 terminal in the cap (**Figure 27**).
4. Loosen the camshaft belt tensioner adjustment bolt (**Figure 28**) and install tensioner releasing tool part No. T74P-6254-A on the tension spring roll pin (**Figure 29**). Use the tool to release the belt tension as far as possible, then tighten the adjustment bolt to hold the tensioner in its fully released position.
5. Remove the crankshaft pulley attaching bolt, the crankshaft pulley and vibration damper and the camshaft timing belt guide.
6. Remove and check the camshaft belt for wear, missing teeth or other damage. Replace the belt if any of these conditions are found.

CAUTION
Do not bend or twist the belt. Do not use sharp instruments to pry it off. Handle the belt with clean hands and keep grease and oil from touching it as they will cause the belt to deteriorate, resulting in a premature failure. Do not rotate any of the belt sprockets while the belt is removed, as that would change engine timing.

4

7. Make sure the timing marks on the camshaft sprocket and timing pointer are properly aligned and that the distributor rotor points toward the No. 1 terminal in the distributor cap. See **Figure 27** and **Figure 30**.
8. Install the camshaft belt around the 3 drive sprockets and camshaft belt tensioner as shown in **Figure 25**. Align the belt properly on the sprockets.
9. Loosen the belt tensioner adjusting bolt and let the tensioner move against the belt.

CAUTION
The spark plugs must be removed in Step 10 prior to rotating the engine or the camshaft belt may jump the sprocketed teeth during engine rotation.

10. Remove the spark plugs. Rotate the crankshaft clockwise (as seen from the front) 2 complete revolutions to remove any slack from the camshaft belt.
11. Tighten the tensioner adjusting and pivot bolts to specifications (**Table 2**).
12. Recheck alignment of timing marks as described in Step 7.
13. Install the camshaft belt guide, crankshaft pulley and damper and the crankshaft pulley bolt. Tighten the pulley bolt to specifications (**Table 2**).
14. Install the camshaft belt outer cover as described in this chapter.

SPROCKETS AND ENGINE FRONT SEALS

This section contains replacement procedures for:

a. The camshaft drive sprocket.
b. The auxiliary shaft drive sprocket.
c. The crankshaft sprocket.
d. The camshaft seal, auxiliary shaft seal and camshaft belt cover seal.

A multi-purpose puller (Ford part No. T74P-6256-A) is required to remove and install the camshaft or auxiliary sprockets. Ford tool part No. T74P-6306-A is required to remove and install the crankshaft drive sprocket. A seal remover (part No. T74P-6700-B) is required to remove each of the 3 seals. Seal installer part No. T74P-6150-A is used to install each of the seals.

1. Remove the camshaft belt cover and camshaft belt as described in this chapter.
2. If the camshaft, auxiliary shaft or crankshaft drive sprockets are to be removed, refer to the tool list above and use the proper tool. **Figure 31** shows removal of the camshaft sprocket. The same tool and method are used to remove the auxiliary shaft sprocket. **Figure 32** shows removal of the crankshaft sprocket.
3. Installation of the sprocket is the reverse of removal. The threaded insert in the sprocket puller

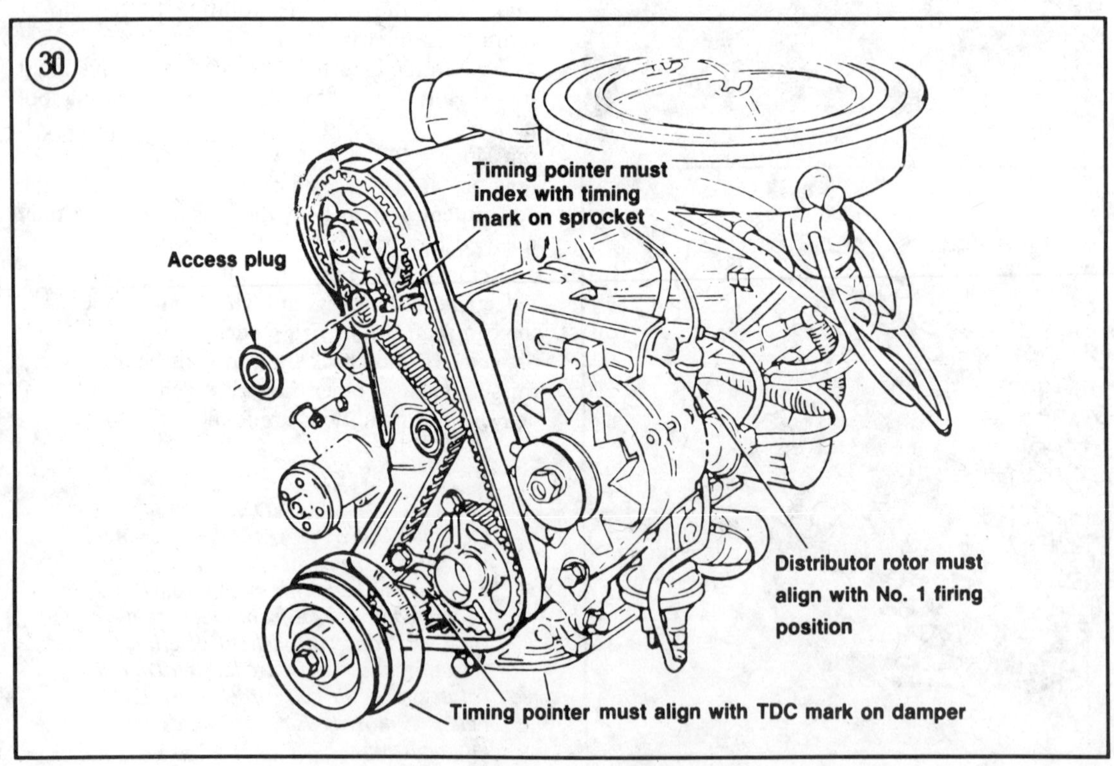
30
Timing pointer must index with timing mark on sprocket
Access plug
Distributor rotor must align with No. 1 firing position
Timing pointer must align with TDC mark on damper

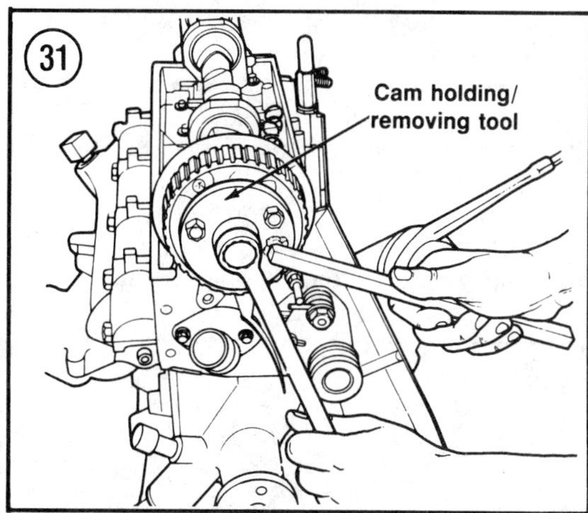

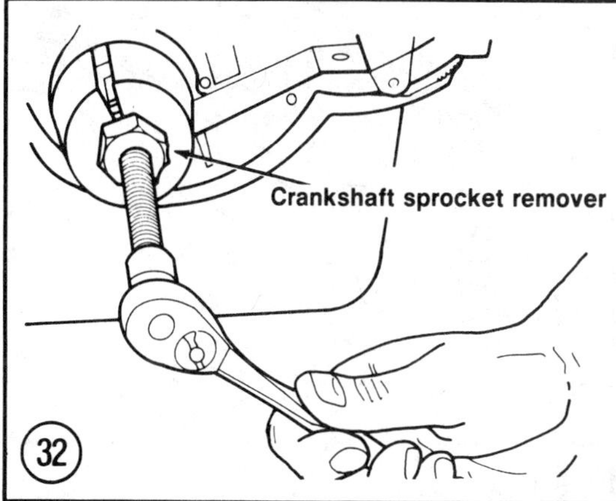

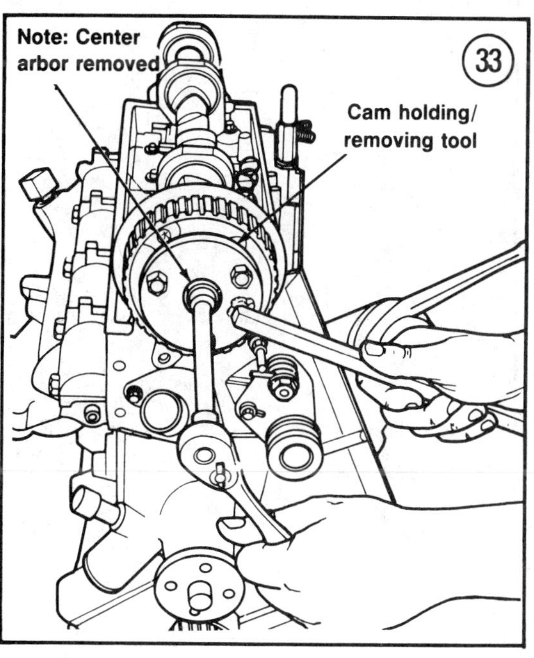

must be removed during camshaft or auxiliary shaft sprocket installation (**Figure 33**) so the center attaching bolt can be installed and tightened. Torque values are provided in **Table 2**. No special tool is necessary to install the crankshaft sprocket.

CAUTION
Always use a new camshaft sprocket bolt or wrap the old bolt threads with Teflon tape. If Teflon tape is not available, coat the bolt threads with Teflon paste.

4. To replace the camshaft seal or auxiliary shaft seal, use the proper seal removal tool. **Figure 34** shows the camshaft seal being removed; auxiliary shaft seal removal is similar. When removing the camshaft seal, make sure the jaws of the tool grip the thin edges of the seal very tightly before operating the jaw-screw part of the tool.
5. To replace the camshaft belt cover seal, install the proper seal removal tool (described in the list above) as shown in **Figure 35**, then remove the old seal. Use tool part No. T74P-6150-A to install the new seal as shown in **Figure 36**.

AUXILIARY SHAFT

Removal/Installation

Refer to **Figure 37** for this procedure.

1. Remove the camshaft belt outer cover, camshaft belt and auxiliary shaft sprocket as described in this chapter.

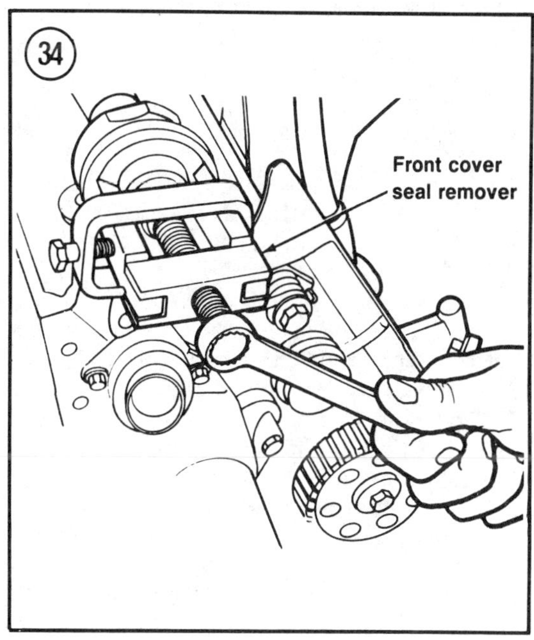

NOTE
Front cover removal is not absolutely necessary. If the cover is not removed, trim the portion of the cover gasket which fits under the auxiliary shaft cover. Use this as a template to cut a matching portion from a new gasket and position it under the auxiliary cover when it is reinstalled.

2. Remove the cylinder front cover.
3. Remove the distributor (Chapter Eight).
4. Remove the auxiliary cover from the block.
5. Remove the 2 screws holding the auxiliary shaft retaining plate to the engine block. Remove the retaining plate.
6. Carefully withdraw the auxiliary shaft from the engine block, making sure that the distributor drive gear does not touch the auxiliary shaft bearing surfaces.
7. Check the auxiliary shaft bearings for wear or damage. If any bearing is visibly worn or defective, remove all with an internal puller (part No. T58L-101-A) and a slide hammer.

NOTE
If the engine is out of the vehicle and you do not have the necessary tools for bearing replacement, take the engine block to a dealer or competent machine shop.

8. Installation is the reverse of removal. If the auxiliary shaft bearings were removed, use a hollow drift of suitable size or tool part No. T57T-7003-A to install the new bearings. Tighten all fasteners to specifications (**Table 2**).

CAUTION
Make sure the oil holes in the auxiliary shaft bearing align with those in the engine block during installation.

OIL PAN

Removal

1. Open and support the hood.
2. Remove the bolt holding the crankcase dipstick bracket. Remove the dipstick and dipstick tube.
3. Remove the engine mount nuts.
4. Automatic transmission—Disconnect the oil cooler lines at the radiator. Cap the lines and fittings to prevent leakage.
5. Unbolt and remove the fan shroud.
6. Automatic transmission:
   a. Remove radiator retaining bolts.
   b. Pull radiator upward and wire in place to the hood.
7. Securely block both rear wheels so the vehicle will not roll in either direction.
8. Raise the front of the vehicle with a jack and place it on jackstands.
9. Drain the crankcase and remove the oil filter. See Chapter Three.
10. Remove the starter motor. See Chapter Eight.
11. Disconnect the exhaust manifold from the inlet pipe bracket at the Thermactor check valve.

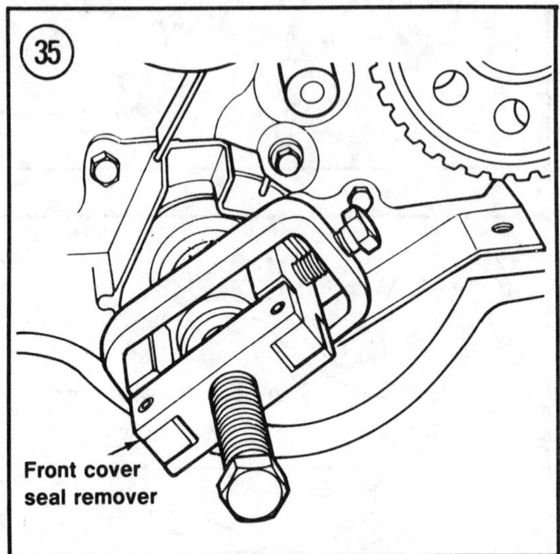

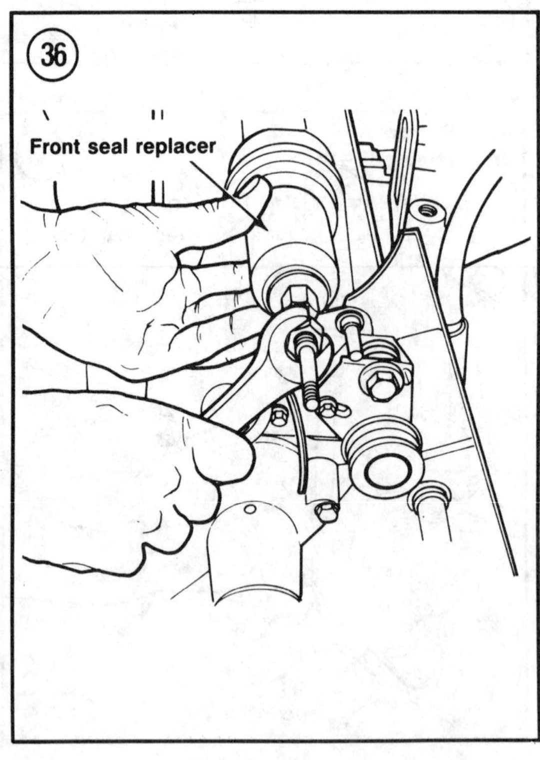

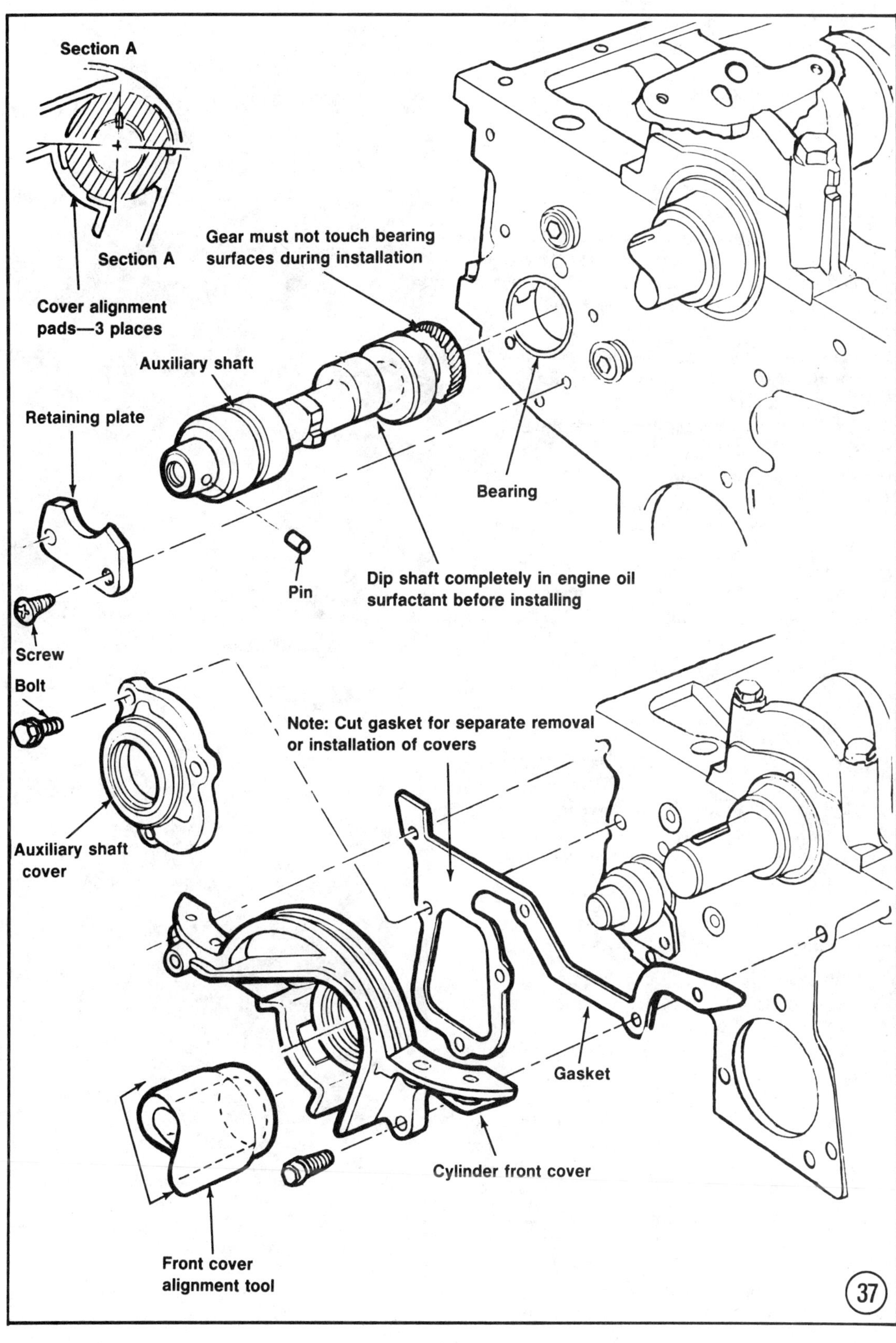
Section A
Section A
Gear must not touch bearing surfaces during installation
Cover alignment pads—3 places
Auxiliary shaft
Retaining plate
Bearing
Pin
Dip shaft completely in engine oil surfactant before installing
Screw
Bolt
Note: Cut gasket for separate removal or installation of covers
Auxiliary shaft cover
Gasket
Cylinder front cover
Front cover alignment tool
37

12. Remove the nuts holding the transmission mount to the crossmember. See **Figure 38**.
13. Automatic transmission:
    a. Remove bellcrank from torque converter cover.
    b. Disconnect the oil cooler lines from the engine block retainer.
    c. Remove the front crossmember.
14. Manual transmission—Disconnect the lower end of the RH front shock absorber. See **Figure 39**.
15. Place a hydraulic jack underneath the engine. Raise the engine about 2 1/2 in. and place a suitable wooden block under the engine block, then remove the jack.
16. Automatic transmission—Place a hydraulic jack underneath the transmission. Raise the transmission slightly.
17. Unbolt the oil pan and lower it to the chassis crossmember.
18. Remove the oil pump drive and pickup tube assembly as described in this chapter to provide clearance for oil pan removal. Place the pump assembly in the oil pan.
19. Remove the oil pan. The oil pan should come out toward the front of the vehicle on automatic transmission vehicles and toward the rear on manual transmission models.
20. Remove and discard the oil pan gasket.

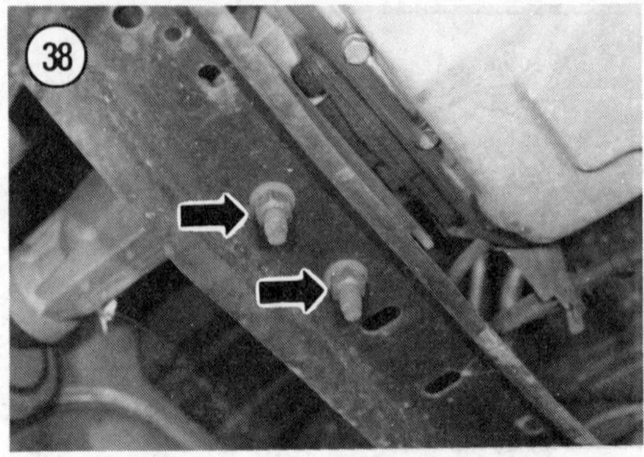

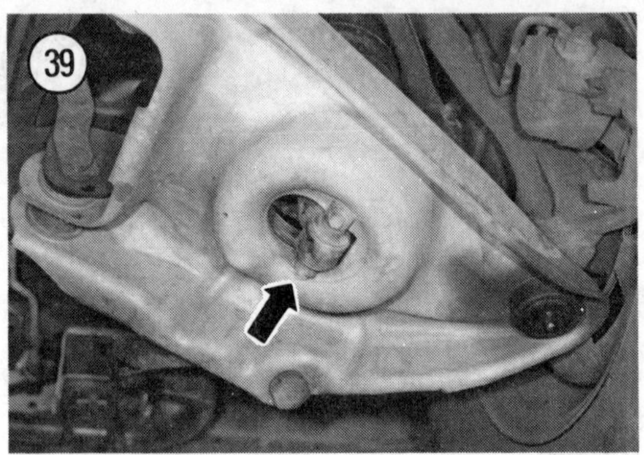

Inspection

1. Remove all gasket or sealant residue from the pan and block sealing flanges.
2. Clean the pan thoroughly in solvent.
3. Check the aluminum oil pan for dents or warped sealing surfaces. Replace the pan as required.

Installation

Refer to **Figure 40** for this procedure.

1. Clean all gasket or sealer residue from the cylinder block, front cover and rear main bearing cap. Be sure to clean the seal groove in the front cover and rear main bearing cap. Be careful not to gouge the sealing surfaces.
2. Run a 1/4 in. bead of Ford RTV sealer part No. D6AZ-19662-A or -B along the seams at the front cover and the rear main bearing cap.
3. Install a new one-piece cork/rubber high-swell gasket in the groove machined in the oil pan flange.
4. Install the oil pan and gasket to the engine block. Tighten the bolts enough to compress the gasket to the point that the 2 oil pan-to-transmission tapped holes align with their

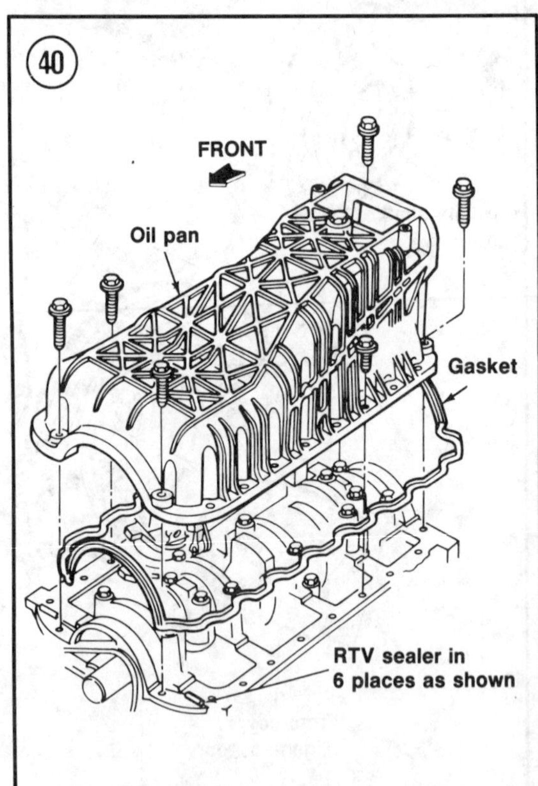

corresponding holes in the gasket, but not tight enough to prevent the pan from moving in relation to the block.

5. Install the 2 oil pan-to-transmission bolts and tighten to 30-39 ft.-lb. (40-54 N•m) to align the oil pan and transmission, then loosen the bolts 1/2 turn.
6. Tighten the oil pan flange bolts to specifications (**Table 2**). Tighten the 2 oil pan-to-transmission bolts to 29-37 ft.-lb. (40-50 N•m).
7. Reverse Steps 1-15 of *Removal.*

OIL PUMP

The oil pump is mounted at the bottom of the engine block inside the oil pan and is serviced as an assembly.

Removal/Installation

Refer to **Figure 41** for this procedure.

1. If the engine is in the vehicle, remove the oil pan as described in this chapter.
2. If the engine is out of the vehicle, remove the oil pan fasteners. Remove the oil pan and discard the gasket.
3. Remove the main bearing cap nut and washer holding the pickup tube bracket.
4. Remove the 2 pump attaching screws and washers. Remove the oil pump and intermediate shaft assembly.

NOTE
Prime the pump by filling it with engine oil and rotating the pump drive shaft to circulate oil throughout the pump before installation.

5. Installation is the reverse of removal. Tighten all fasteners to specifications (**Table 2**).

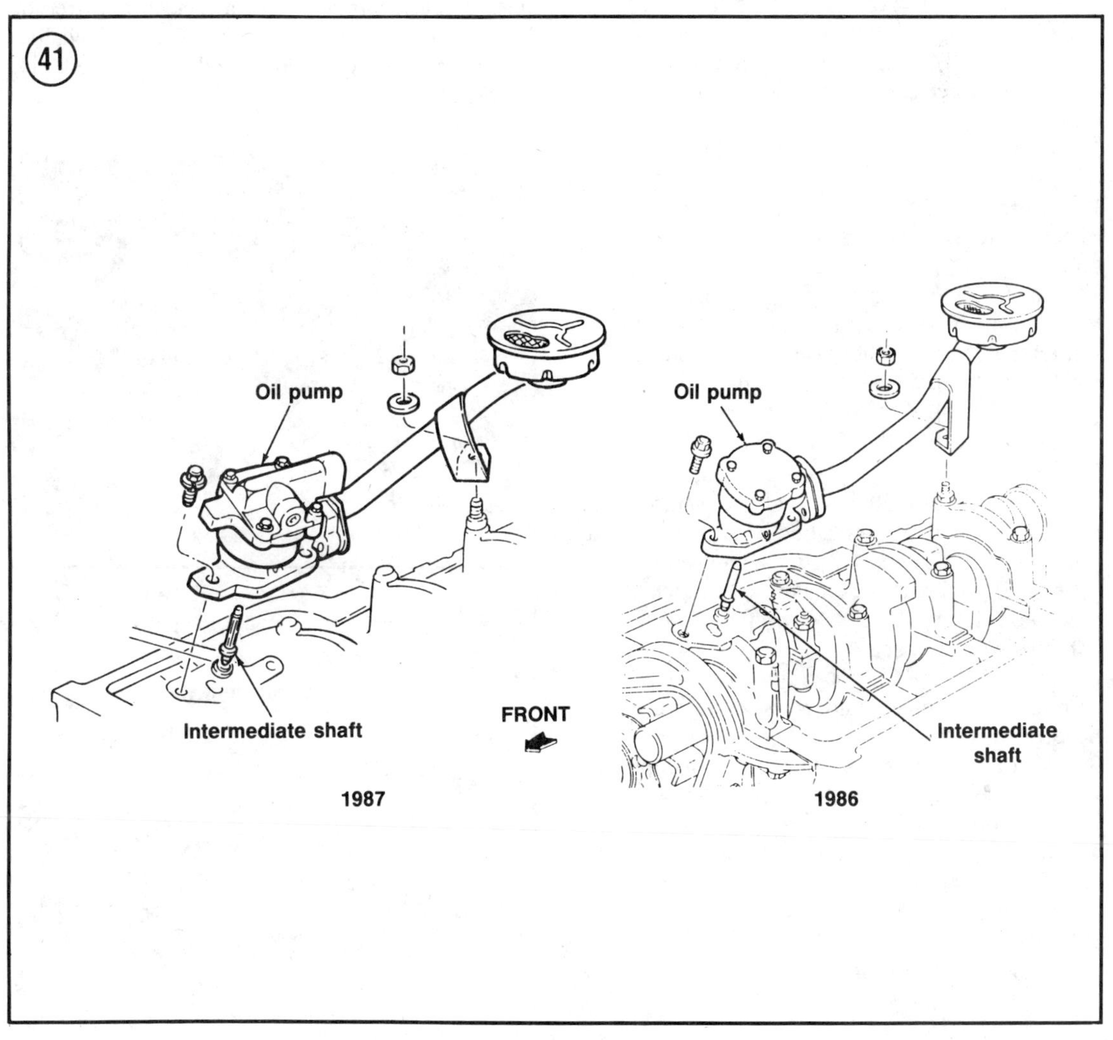

4

CYLINDER HEAD

Removal

1. Disconnect the negative battery cable.
2. Drain the cooling system. See Chapter Seven.
3. Remove the air cleaner resonator assembly (**Figure 42**). See Chapter Six.
4. Disconnect the spark plug wires at the spark plug, then remove the distributor cap and wire assembly. See Chapter Three.
5. Remove the spark plugs. See Chapter Three.
6. Remove the alternator. See Chapter Eight.
7. Remove the upper and lower intake manifolds. See *Multi-Point Fuel Injection (2.3L EFI), Fuel Charging Assembly Removal/ Installation,* Chapter Six.
8. Disconnect the upper radiator hose at each end and remove it from the engine compartment.
9. Remove the exhaust manifold as described in this chapter.
10. Remove the camshaft belt outer cover as described in this chapter.
11. Remove the camshaft belt as described in this chapter. Remove the cam belt idler and idler stop spring.
12. Unplug the oil pressure sending unit electrical connector.
13. Loosen the cylinder head bolts in progressive stages to prevent warping of the head. Remove the bolts.
14. Lift the cylinder head off the block. Place the head on its side on a soft surface to prevent scratching or otherwise damaging the head-to-block surface.
15. Remove and discard the head gasket.

Decarbonizing

1. Without removing the valves, remove all deposits from the combustion chambers, intake ports and exhaust ports. Use a fine wire brush dipped in solvent or make a scraper from hardwood. Be careful not to scratch or gouge the combustion chambers.
2. After all carbon is removed from the combustion chambers and ports, clean the entire head in solvent.
3. Clean away all carbon on the piston tops. Do not remove the carbon ridge at the top of the cylinder bore.
4. Clean the bolt holes. Use a cleaning solvent to remove dirt and grease.

Inspection

1. Check the cylinder head for signs of oil or water leaks before cleaning.
2. Clean the cylinder head thoroughly in solvent. While cleaning, look for cracks or other visible signs of damage. Look for corrosion or foreign material in the oil and water passages.
3. Clean the passages with a stiff spiral brush, then blow them out with compressed air.
4. Check the cylinder head studs for damage and replace if necessary.
5. Check the flatness of the cylinder head-to-block surface with a straightedge and feeler gauge (**Figure 43**). Measure diagonally, as well as end to end. Maximum permissible head warp is 0.003 in. for any 6 in. length of the head surface or 0.006 in. overall. If cylinder head warpage is excessive, have the head milled by a dealer or competent machine shop. If more than 0.010 in. must be removed from the head, replace it.

Installation

1. Be sure the cylinder head, engine block mating surfaces and cylinder bores are clean and free of deposits, sealant or other debris. Check all visible oil passages in the cylinder head and engine block for cleanliness.

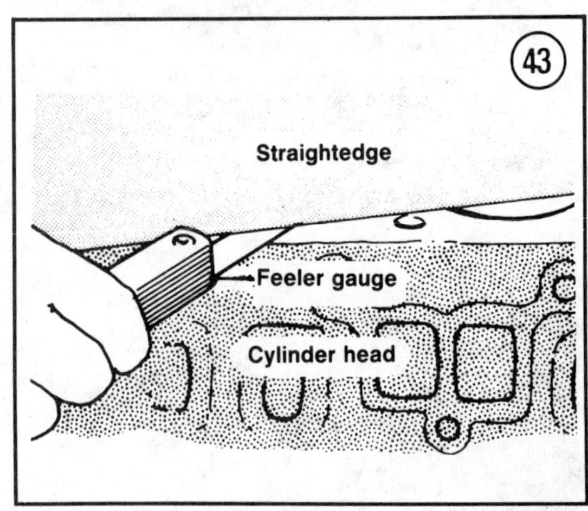

2. Install a new cylinder head gasket on the block mounting dowels.
3. Position the cylinder head on the block and align with the head gasket. If old head bolts are being reinstalled, coat threads with engine oil (new bolts have a preservative coating). Install the head bolts in their mounting holes and insert through the head gasket into the engine block.

NOTE
If the head and gasket are difficult to align, make guide pins by cutting the heads off 2 extra cylinder head bolts. Install the guide pins in diagonally opposite mounting holes in the block. Be sure the guide pins will protrude far enough through the top of the head to permit removal once the head is in place.

4. Remove the guide pins (if used). Tighten the cylinder head bolts in the sequence shown in **Figure 44**. Tighten bolts in 2 stages:
   a. Step 1—50-60 ft.-lb. (68-81 N•m).
   b. Step 2—80-90 ft.-lb. (108-122 N•m).
5. Reverse Steps 1-12 of *Removal* to complete installation.

CAMSHAFT

Removal/Installation

Refer to **Figure 45** for this procedure.
1. Disconnect the negative battery cable.
2. Drain the cooling system. See Chapter Seven.

3. Remove the air cleaner resonator assembly (**Figure 42**). See Chapter Six.
4. Disconnect and remove the upper radiator hose from the engine compartment.
5. Remove the valve cover as described in this chapter.
6. Remove the camshaft belt outer cover as described in this chapter.
7. Remove the camshaft belt as described in this chapter.
8. Remove the hydraulic lash adjusters as described in this chapter.
9. Remove the camshaft sprocket and seal as described in this chapter.
10. Check camshaft end play before removal. Push the camshaft as far as it will go toward the rear of the engine. Install a dial indicator on the front of the cylinder head with its plunger touching the front of the camshaft sprocket. Set the indicator gauge to zero, then pry the camshaft forward as far as possible with a large screwdriver. If the dial gauge reading exceeds specifications (**Table 1**), replace the camshaft retaining (thrust) plate during installation.
11. Remove the retaining (thrust) plate from the rear camshaft support stand of the cylinder head. See View A, **Figure 45**.
12. Securely block both rear wheels so the vehicle will not roll in either direction.
13. Raise the vehicle with a jack and place it on jackstands.
14. Remove the through-bolts from the engine front supports on each side of the vehicle. Remove the lower joint-to-bracket bolts from each support.
15. Place a hydraulic jack under the engine oil pan. Position a block of wood and the jack and raise the engine as far as possible. Insert a suitable block of wood between each engine mount and chassis bracket, then remove the jack.
16. Remove the jackstands and lower the vehicle to the ground.
17. Carefully withdraw the camshaft from the cylinder head support stands (**Figure 45**) with a rotating motion. Do not let the cam lobes touch or nick the support stand bearings.
18. Installation is the reverse of removal. If installing a new camshaft, make sure the threaded plug is installed in the rear of the shaft. If not, transfer the plug from the old camshaft. Coat the lobes with Ford polyethylene grease and the journals with clean engine oil. Carefully install the camshaft with a rotating motion to prevent bearing damage. Tighten the thrust plate to specifications (**Table 2**). Align all timing marks as described for camshaft belt installation.

4

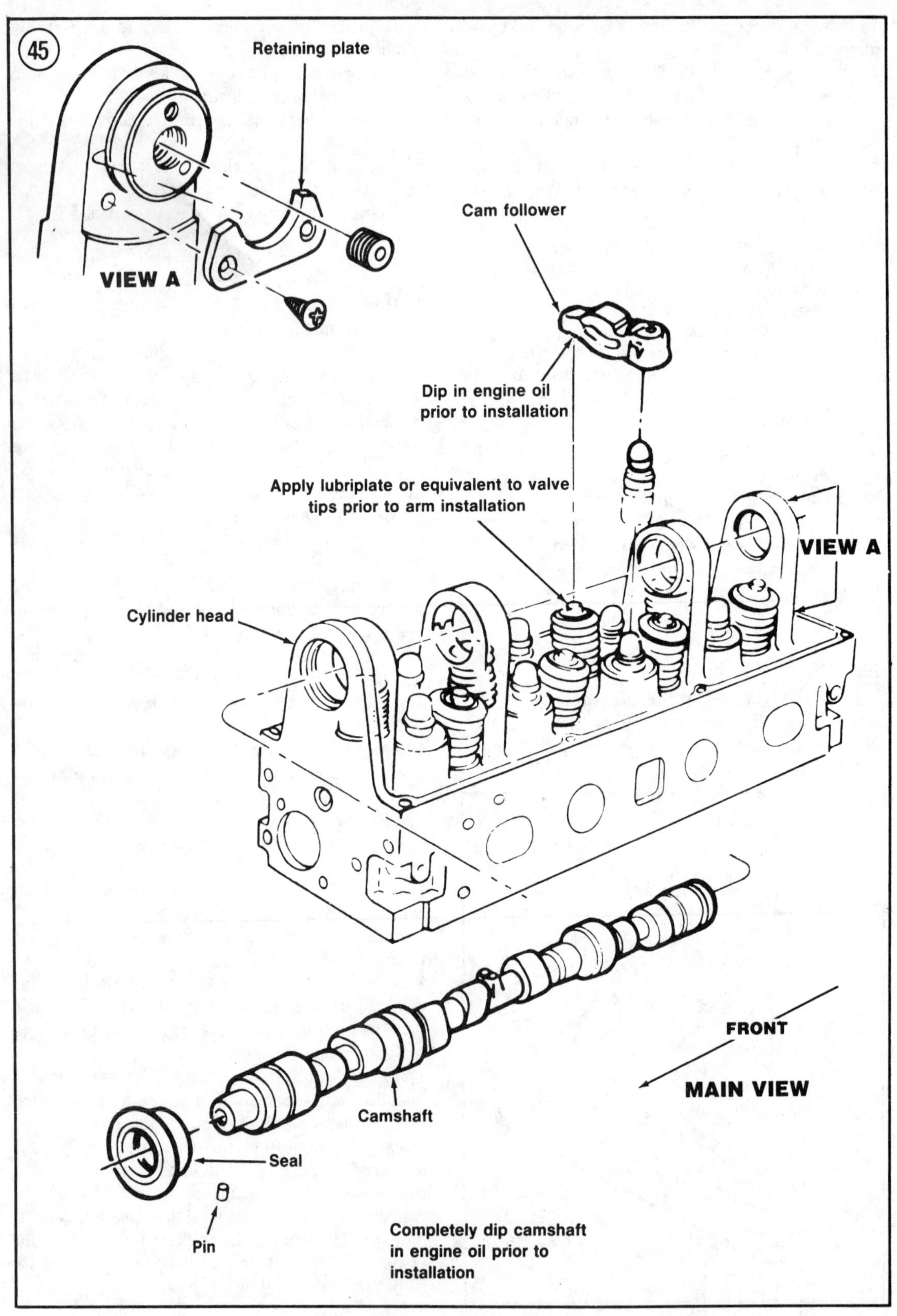
45
Retaining plate
VIEW A
Cam follower
Dip in engine oil
prior to installation
Apply lubriplate or equivalent to valve
tips prior to arm installation
VIEW A
Cylinder head
FRONT
MAIN VIEW
Camshaft
Seal
Pin
Completely dip camshaft
in engine oil prior to
installation

Inspection

1. Check all machined surfaces of the camshaft for nicks or grooves. Minor defects may be removed with a smooth oilstone. Severe damage or wear beyond that specified in **Table 1** requires camshaft replacement.
2. Measure the outer diameter of the camshaft journals with a micrometer (**Figure 46**). Compare this measurement with the specifications in **Table 1**. Replace the camshaft if the journals exceed the wear or out-of-round specification.
3. Check the support stand camshaft bearings. If the bearings are excessively worn, grooved, pitted or scored, have them replaced by a dealer or competent machine shop.

CAUTION
All camshaft bearings should be replaced, even if only one bearing is worn. If not, the camshaft may be out of alignment when reinstalled.

4. Measure the inner diameter of the support stand camshaft bearings. Subtract the measurements obtained in Step 2 to determine the bearing-to-journal clearance. If this clearance exceeds that specified in **Table 1**, either the camshaft bearings, the camshaft or both are worn and must be replaced. Compare both the journal and clearance measurements with specifications to determine which must be replaced.

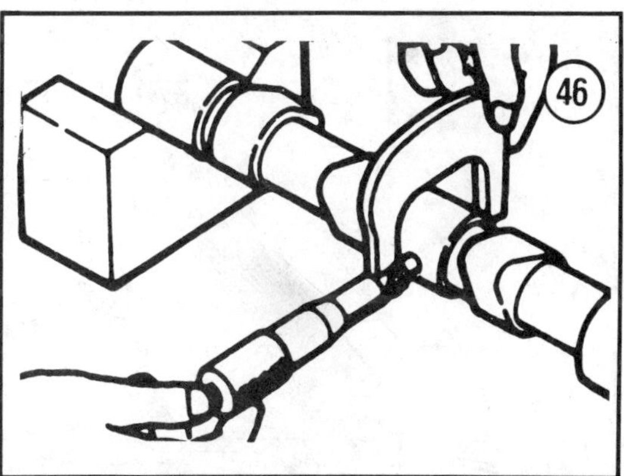

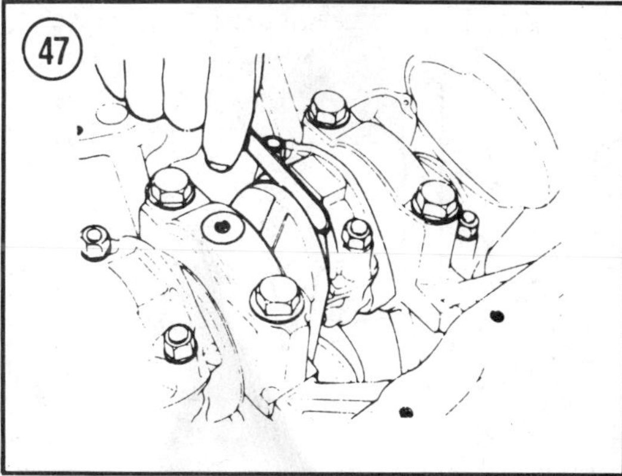

VALVES AND VALVE SEATS

Servicing the valves, guides and valve seats requires special knowledge and expensive machine tools. A general practice among those who do their own service is to remove the cylinder head, perform all disassembly except valve removal and take the head to a dealer or machine shop for inspection and service. Since the cost is low relative to the required effort and equipment, this is usually the best approach, even for experienced mechanics.

PISTON/CONNECTING ROD ASSEMBLY

Piston/Connecting Rod Removal

1. Remove the cylinder head and oil pan as described in this chapter.
2. Rotate the crankshaft until one piston is at bottom dead center. Pack the cylinder bore with clean shop rags. Remove the carbon ridge at the top of the cylinder bores with a ridge reamer. These can be rented for use. Vacuum out the shavings, then remove the shop rags.

WARNING
Make sure manual transmissions are in NEUTRAL before performing the next step. Otherwise, rotating the engine may roll the vehicle forward off the jackstands, causing it to fall on you.

CAUTION
Rotate the engine in its normal direction (clockwise, viewed from the front of the vehicle) during the next step. Otherwise the timing belt may slip on its cogs and change valve timing.

3. Rotate the crankshaft until the connecting rod is centered in the bore. Measure the clearance between the connecting rod and the crankshaft with a flat feeler gauge (**Figure 47**). If the clearance exceeds specifications (**Table 1**), replace the connecting rod during reassembly.
4. Remove the nuts holding the connecting rod cap. Lift off the cap, together with the lower bearing insert.

NOTE
If the connecting rod caps are difficult to remove, tap the studs with a wooden hammer handle.

4

5. Use the wooden hammer handle to push the piston and connecting rod from the bore.

NOTE

*Mark the cylinder number on the top of each piston with quick-drying paint. Check the cylinder numbers or identification marks on the connecting rod and cap. If they are not visible, make your own (**Figure 48**).*

6. Remove the piston rings with a ring remover (**Figure 49**).
7. Repeat Steps 1-6 for all remaining connecting rods.

Piston Pin Removal/Installation

The piston pins are press-fitted to the connecting rods and hand fitted to the pistons. Removal requires the use of a press and support stand. This is a job for a dealer or machine shop equipped to fit the pistons to the pins, ream the pin bushings to the correct diameter and install the pistons and pins on the connecting rods.

Piston Clearance Check

Unless you have precision measuring equipment and know how to use it properly, have this procedure done by a machine shop.

1. Measure the piston diameter with a micrometer (**Figure 50**) at the piston pin centerline height, 90° to the piston pin axis.
2. Measure the cylinder bore diameter with a bore gauge (**Figure 51**). **Figure 52** shows the points of normal cylinder wear. If dimension A exceeds dimension B by more than 0.010 in., the cylinder must be rebored and a new piston/ring assembly installed.

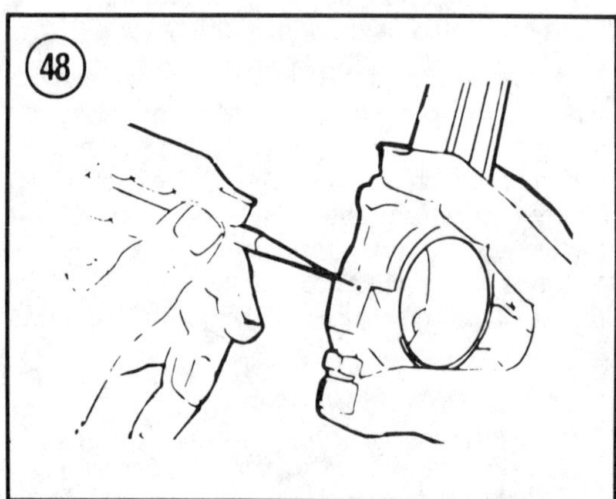

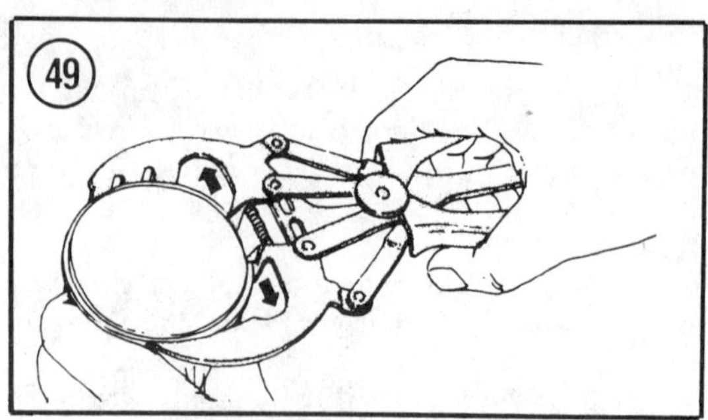

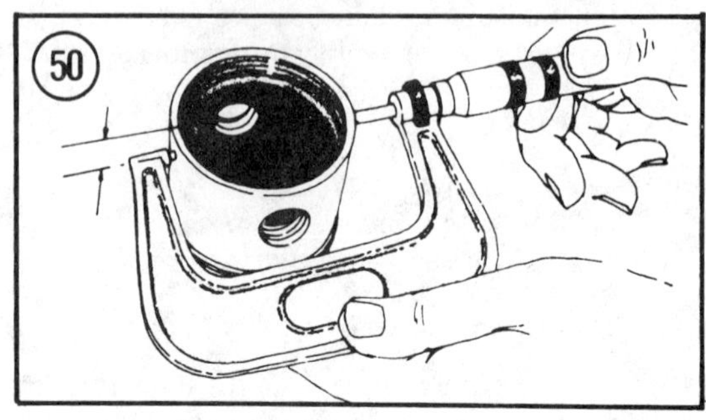

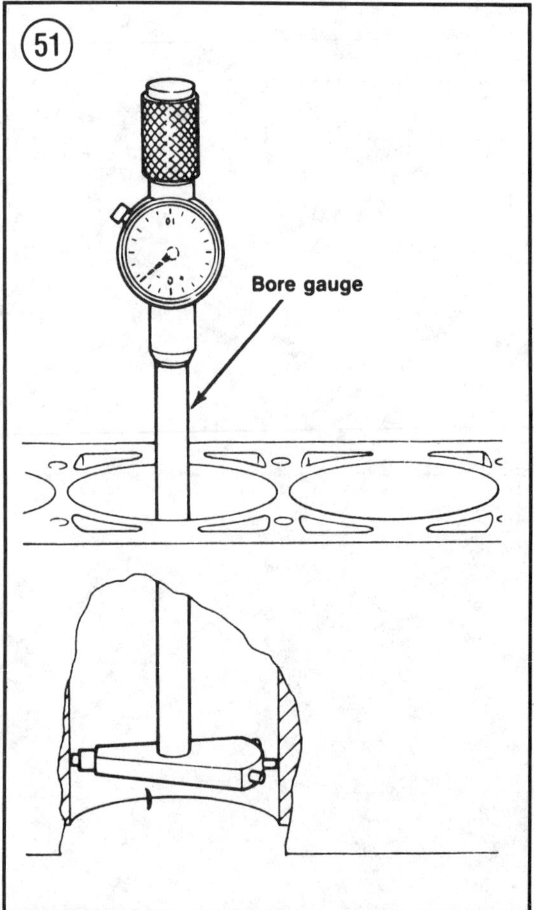

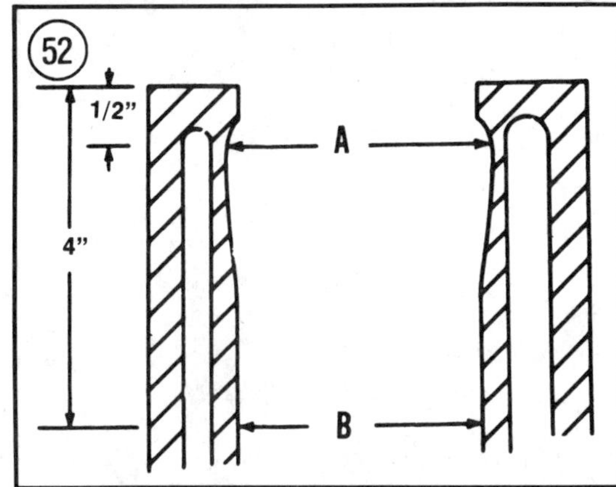

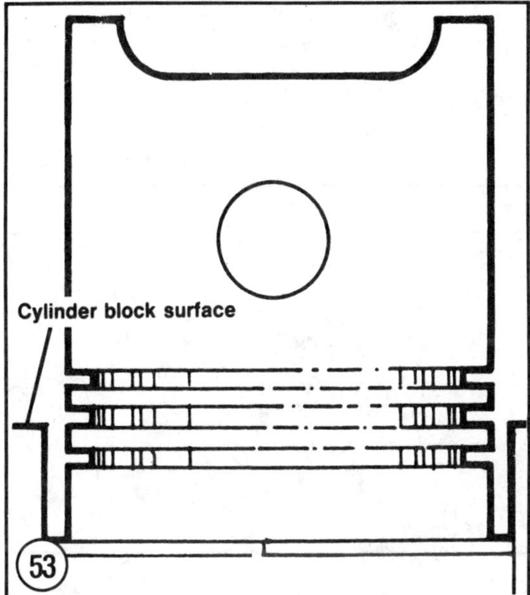

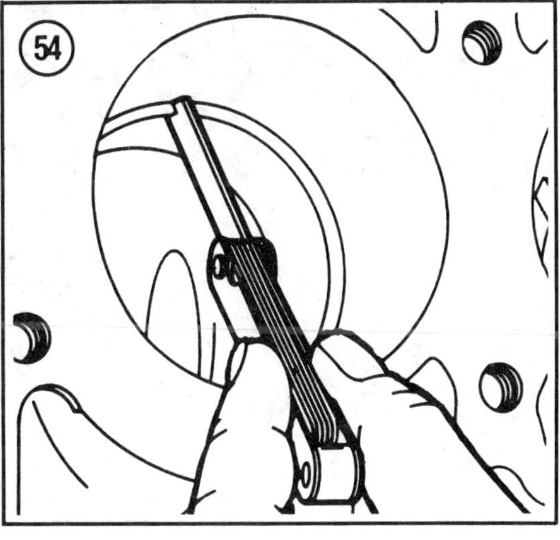

3. Subtract the piston diameter from the largest cylinder bore reading. If it exceeds the specifications in **Table 1**, the cylinder must be rebored and an oversized piston installed.

NOTE
Obtain the new piston and measure it to determine the correct cylinder bore oversize dimension.

Piston Ring Fit/Installation

1. Check the ring gap of each piston ring. To do this, position the ring at the bottom of the ring travel area and square it by tapping gently with an inverted piston. See **Figure 53**.

NOTE
If the cylinders have not been rebored, check the gap at the bottom of the ring travel, where the cylinder is least worn.

2. Measure the ring gap with a feeler gauge as shown in **Figure 54**. Compare with specifications in **Table 1**. If the measurement is not within specifications, the rings must be replaced as a set. Check gap of new rings as well. If the gap is too small, file the ends of the ring to correct it.

3. Check the side clearance of the rings as shown in **Figure 55**. Place the feeler gauge alongside the ring all the way into the groove. The feeler gauge should slide all the way around the piston without

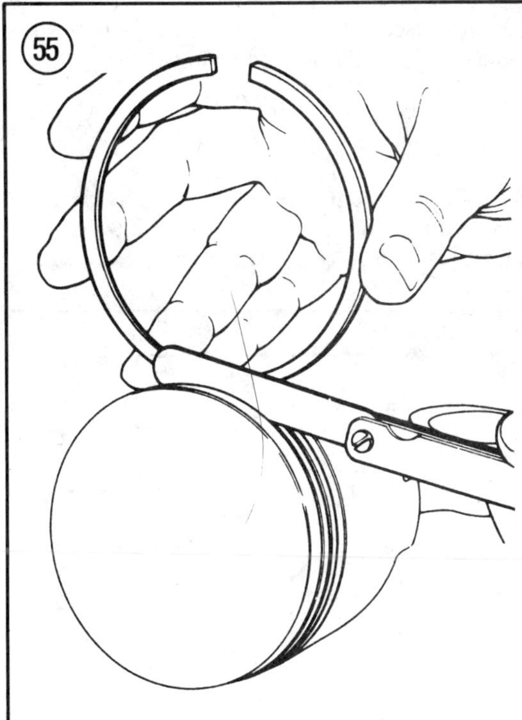

binding. Any wear that occurs will form a step at the inner portion of the ring groove's lower edge. If large steps are discernable (**Figure 56**), replace the piston. Compare the inserted feeler gauge size with the specifications in **Table 1**. If the measurement is not within specifications, either the rings or the ring grooves are worn. Inspect and replace as required.

4. Using a ring expander tool (**Figure 49**), carefully install the oil control ring, then the compression rings. Oil rings consist of 3 segments. The wavy segment goes between the flat segments to act as a spacer. Upper and lower flat segments are interchangeable. The second compression ring is tapered. The top of each compression ring is marked and must face upward.
5. Position the ring gaps as shown in **Figure 57**.

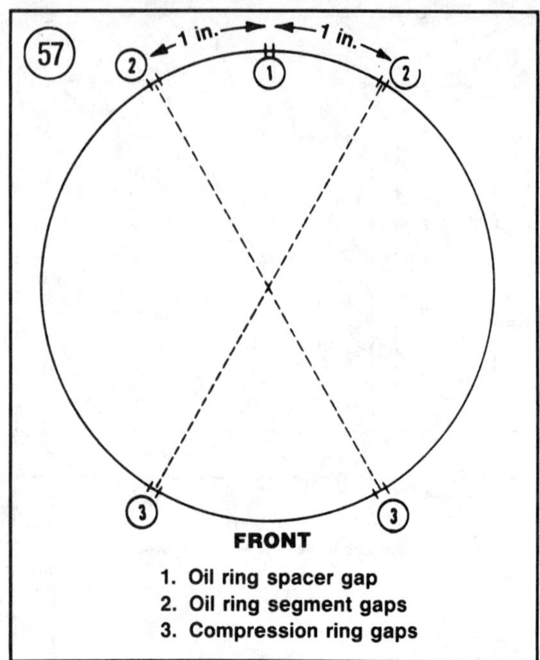

1. Oil ring spacer gap
2. Oil ring segment gaps
3. Compression ring gaps

Connecting Rod Inspection

Have the connecting rods checked for straightness by a dealer or machine shop. When installing new connecting rods, have them checked for misalignment before installing the piston and piston pin. Connecting rods can spring out of alignment during shipping or handling.

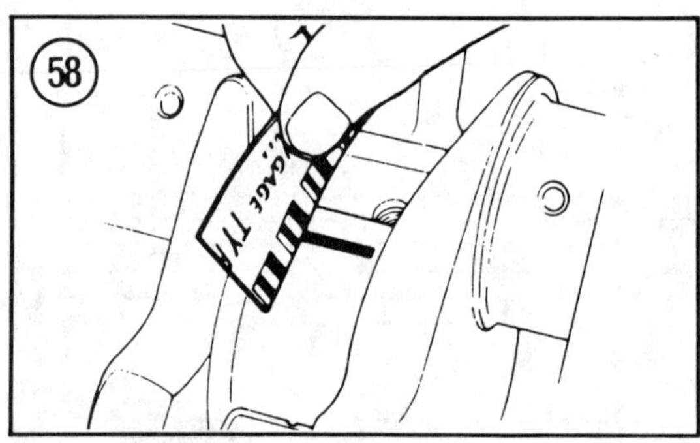

Connecting Rod Bearing Clearance Measurement

1. Place the connecting rods and upper bearing halves on the proper connecting rod journals.
2. Cut a piece of Plastigage the width of the bearing. Place the Plastigage on the journal, then install the lower bearing half end cap.

NOTE
Do not place Plastigage over the journal oil hole.

3. Tighten the connecting rod cap to specifications (**Table 2**). Do not rotate the crankshaft while the Plastigage is in place.

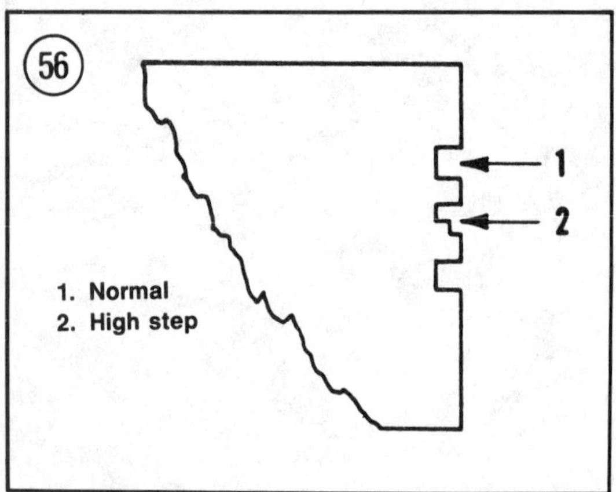

1. Normal
2. High step

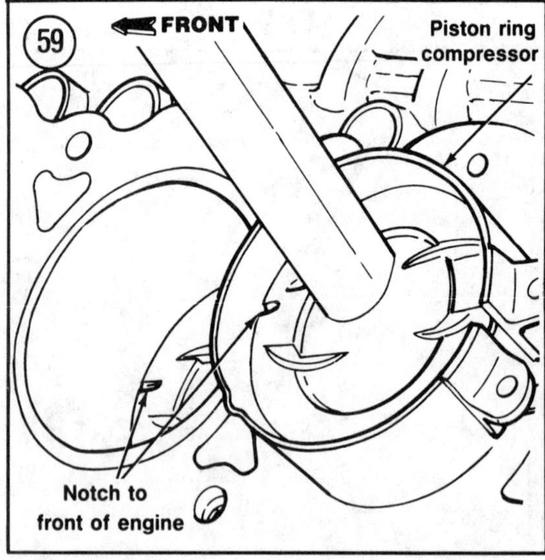

4. Remove the connecting rod caps. Bearing clearance is determined by comparing the width of the flattened Plastigage to the markings on the envelope (**Figure 58**). If the clearance is excessive, the crankshaft must be reground and undersize bearings installed.

Piston/Connecting Rod Installation

1. Make sure the pistons are correctly installed on the connecting rods, if they were separated.
2. Make sure the ring gaps are positioned as shown in **Figure 57**.
3. Slip short pieces of hose over the connecting rod studs to prevent them from nicking the crankshaft. Tape will work if you do not have the right diameter hose, but it is more difficult to remove.
4. Immerse the entire piston in clean engine oil. Coat the cylinder wall with oil.

CAUTION
Use extreme care in Step 5 to prevent the connecting rod from nicking the crankshaft journal.

5. Install the piston/connecting rod assembly in its cylinder with a piston ring compressor. The piston crown notch should face toward the front of the engine. See **Figure 59**. Tap lightly with a wooden hammer handle to insert the piston. Make sure that the piston number painted on top before removal corresponds to the cylinder number, counting from the camshaft belt end of the engine.
6. Clean the connecting rod bearings carefully, including the back sides. Coat the journals and bearings with clean engine oil. Place the bearings in the connecting rod and cap.
7. Turn the crankshaft throw to the bottom of its stroke. Push the piston downward until the connecting rod and bearing fit into place against the crankpin. Remove the protective hose or tape and lightly lubricate the connecting rod bolt threads with SAE 30W engine oil.
8. Install the connecting rod cap. Make sure the rod and cap marks align. Install the cap nuts finger-tight.
9. Repeat Steps 4-8 for each remaining piston/connecting rod assembly.
10. Tighten the cap nuts to specifications (**Table 2**).
11. Check the connecting rod big-end play as described under *Piston/Connecting Rod Removal* in this chapter.

REAR MAIN OIL SEAL

Replacement

Refer to **Figure 60** for this procedure.

1. Remove the engine as described in this chapter.

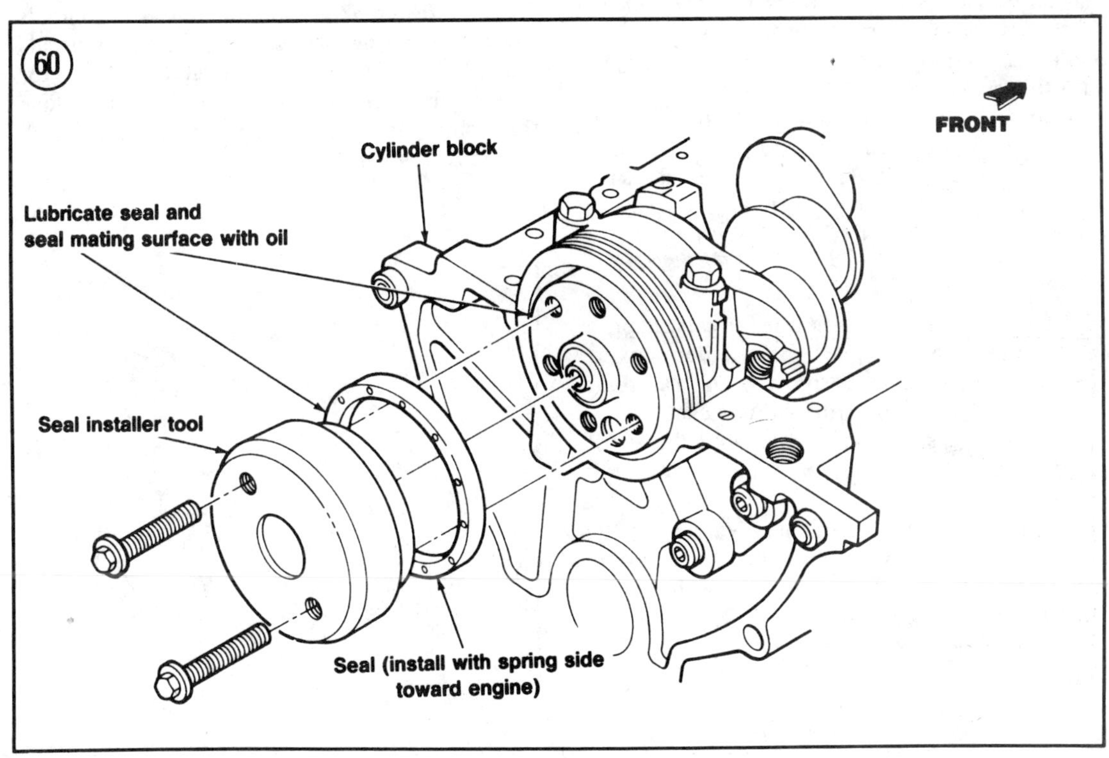

2. Remove the flywheel (manual) or drive plate (automatic) from the rear of the crankshaft as described in this chapter.
3. Install 2 sheet metal screws into the seal. Place small wooden blocks against the cylinder block and pry against the screws with a pair of large screwdrivers to remove the seal. Work slowly and carefully to avoid any possible damage to the crankshaft seal surface.
4. Clean the oil seal recess in the block and main bearing cap.
5. Wipe the seal-to-block surface of the new seal with engine oil. Lubricate the crankshaft and seal contact surfaces with Lubriplate or equivalent.
6. Fit the new seal on installer part No. T82L-6701-A or equivalent. Place tool and seal in position. Alternately tighten the bolts until the seal is seated within 0.005 in. (0.127 mm) of the rear face of the block.
7. Remove the seal installer tool and reinstall the flywheel or drive plate as described in this chapter.

CRANKSHAFT

End Play Measurement

1. Pry the crankshaft to the rear of the engine with a large screwdriver.
2. Install a dial indicator on the engine block so that its contact point rests against the crankshaft flange. Set the indicator dial to zero.
3. Pry the crankshaft to the front of the engine with the screwdriver.
4. Compare the dial indicator reading to specifications (**Table 1**). If the end play is less than specified, check the No. 3 main bearing surfaces for scratches, nicks, burrs or dirt. If end play is excessive, replace the No. 3 main bearing.

Removal

1. Remove the engine as described in this chapter.
2. Remove the camshaft belt outer cover, camshaft belt, crankshaft sprocket and camshaft belt cover oil seal as described in this chapter.
3. Remove the spark plug wires from the spark plugs, then remove the spark plugs from the cylinder head.
4. Remove the flywheel (manual) or drive plate (automatic) from the rear of the crankshaft as described in this chapter, then remove the engine rear cover plate.
5. Remove the oil pan and oil pump as described in this chapter.
6. Rotate the crankshaft to position one connecting rod at the bottom of its stroke.
7. Remove the connecting rod bearing cap and bearing. Move the piston/rod assembly away from the crankshaft.
8. Repeat Step 6 and Step 7 for each piston/rod assembly.
9. Check the caps for identification numbers or marks. If none are visible, clean the caps with a wire brush. If marks still cannot be seen, make your own with quick-drying paint.
10. Unbolt and remove the main bearing caps and bearing inserts.

NOTE
If the caps are difficult to remove, lift the bolts partway out, then pry them from side to side.

11. Carefully lift the crankshaft from the engine block and place it on a clean workbench.
12. Remove the bearing inserts from the block. Place the bearing caps and inserts in order on a clean workbench.

Inspection

1. Clean the crankshaft thoroughly with solvent. Blow out the oil passages with compressed air.

NOTE
If you do not have precision measuring equipment, have a machine shop perform Step 2.

2. Check the crankpins and main bearing journals for wear, scoring or cracks. Check all journals against specifications (**Table 1**) for out-of-roundness and taper. See **Figure 61**. Have the crankshaft reground, if necessary, and install undersize bearings.

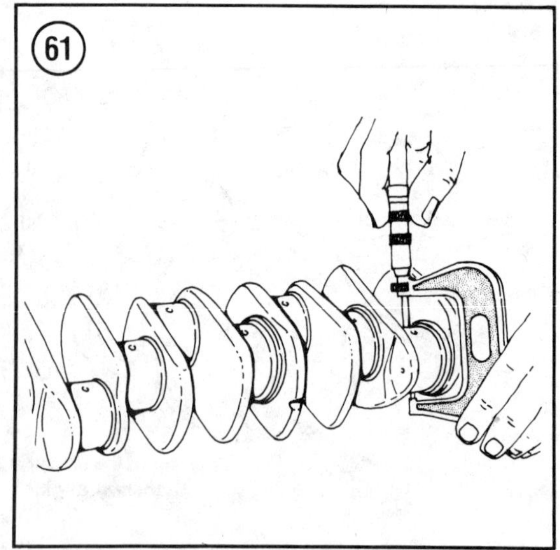

Main Bearing Clearance Measurement

Main bearing clearance is measured with Plastigage in the same manner as the connecting rod bearing clearance described in this chapter. If wear exceeds that specified in **Table 1**, a 0.001 or 0.002 in. undersize bearing may be used on one-half of the journal in combination with the standard bearing on the other half. If undersize bearings are used on more than one journal, the undersize bearing should be installed in the cylinder block, not in the main bearing cap. If this does not produce the correct crankshaft-to-main bearing clearance, the crankshaft should be reground by a dealer or a competent machine shop and undersize main bearings installed.

Installation

1. With the main bearings removed from the bearing caps and cylinder block, clean the main bearing bores in the block, the main bearing caps and main bearing inserts with lacquer thinner to remove all contamination.
2. If the old main bearings are being reinstalled, be sure they are reinstalled in the main bearing caps and cylinder block bores from which they were removed. If new bearings (or undersize bearings) are being installed, be sure they are installed in the proper locations.
3. Make sure the bearing locating tangs are correctly positioned in the cylinder block and bearing cap notches.
4. Coat the main bearing surfaces and the crankshaft journals with a thick coat of clean, heavy engine oil.
5. Carefully place the crankshaft in the main bearings installed in the cylinder block, taking care not to damage the sides of the No. 3 (thrust) bearing.
6. Install all main bearing caps, except the rear cap and the No. 3 cap. Make sure the arrows on the top of the caps face toward the front of the engine.
7. Apply a 1/16 in. diameter bead of silicone rubber sealant to the area of the cylinder block and rear main bearing cap shown in **Figure 62**.

NOTE
Check cap bolts for thread damage before reuse. If damaged, replace the bolts.

8. Lubricate the threads of all cap bolts with SAE 30W engine oil. Install the cap bolts and tighten to specifications (**Table 2**).
9. Install the No. 3 bearing cap and tighten the bolts finger-tight.
10. Use a large screwdriver or pry bar to force the crankshaft as far to the rear of the block as possible

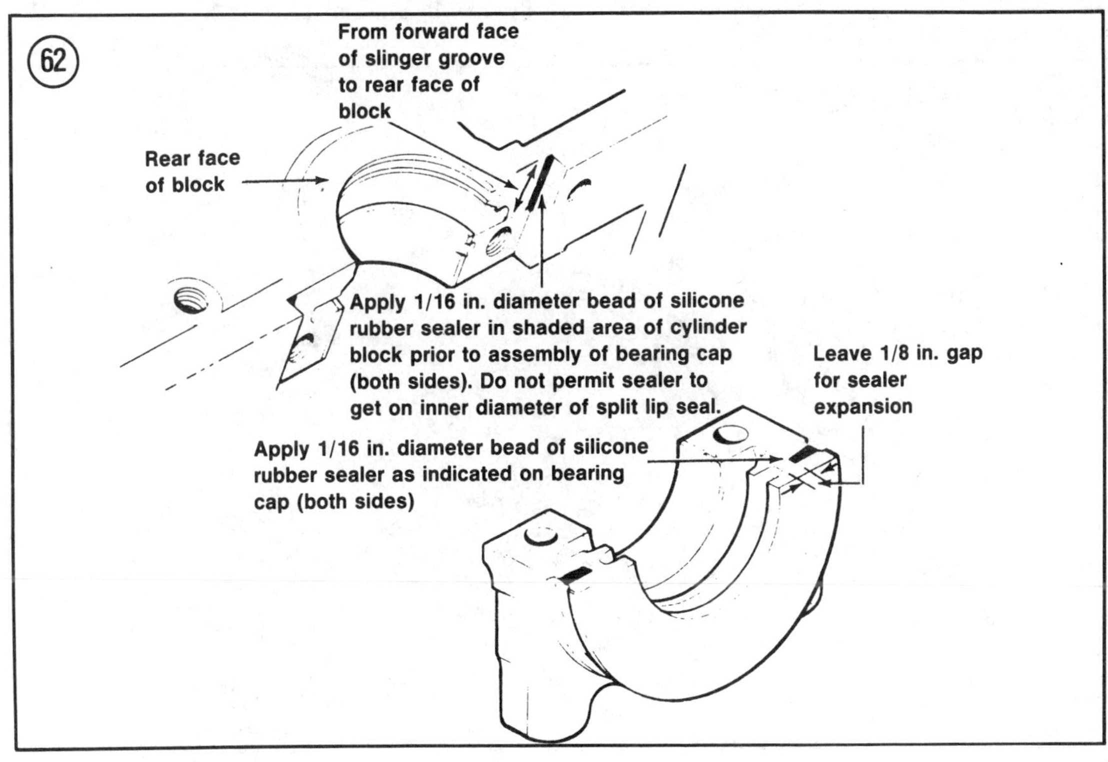
62
From forward face of slinger groove to rear face of block
Rear face of block
Apply 1/16 in. diameter bead of silicone rubber sealer in shaded area of cylinder block prior to assembly of bearing cap (both sides). Do not permit sealer to get on inner diameter of split lip seal.
Leave 1/8 in. gap for sealer expansion
Apply 1/16 in. diameter bead of silicone rubber sealer as indicated on bearing cap (both sides)

and the No. 3 bearing cap as far to the front as possible. This aligns the 2 halves of the thrust bearing. Holding the crankshaft and thrust bearing cap in this position, tighten the cap bolts to specifications (**Table 2**).

11. Rotate the crankshaft during tightening to make sure it turns smoothly without binding at the flywheel rim. If not, remove the bearing caps and crankshaft and check that the bearings are clean and properly installed. Make absolutely certain that bearings are the correct size, especially if the crankshaft has been reground. Never use undersize bearings (except as specified under *Main Bearing Clearance Measurement* in this chapter) if the crankshaft has not been reground.
12. Reinstall the connecting rods and caps on the crankshaft.
13. Reverse Steps 1-5 of the removal procedure to complete installation.

FLYWHEEL OR DRIVE PLATE

Removal/Installation

Refer to **Figure 63** or **Figure 64** for this procedure.

1. Remove the engine as described in this chapter.
2. Remove the clutch on manual transmission vehicles. See Chapter Nine.
3. Remove the 6 bolts holding the flywheel or drive plate to the crankshaft. Remove the flywheel or drive plate.
4. Installation is the reverse of removal. Gradually tighten the flywheel/drive plate bolts to specifications (**Table 2**) in a diagonal pattern. Wipe all oil, grease and other contamination from the flywheel surface before reinstalling the clutch on manual transmission vehicles.

Inspection

1. Visually check the flywheel or drive plate surfaces for cracks, deep scoring, excessive wear, heat discoloration and checking. If the surface is glazed or slightly scratched, have the flywheel/drive plate resurfaced by a machine shop. Replace the flywheel if damage is severe or if more than 0.045 in. (1.143 mm) must be removed to restore the surface.
2. Measure flywheel runout with a dial indicator. Replace or resurface the flywheel if runout exceeds 0.005 in.

NOTE
The ring gear is an integral part of the drive plate on automatic transmission models. If defective, the entire assembly must be replaced.

3. Inspect the flywheel ring gear teeth. If the teeth are chipped, broken or excessively worn, check the starter motor drive teeth for similar wear or damage. Have a new ring gear shrunk onto the flywheel by a machine shop.

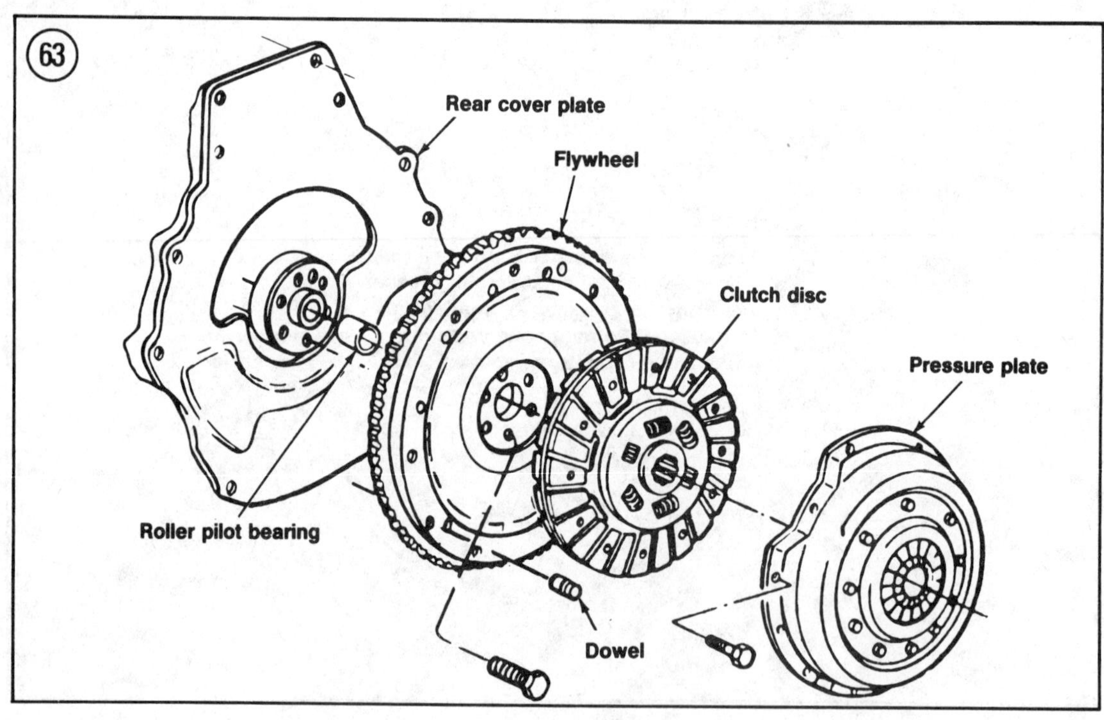

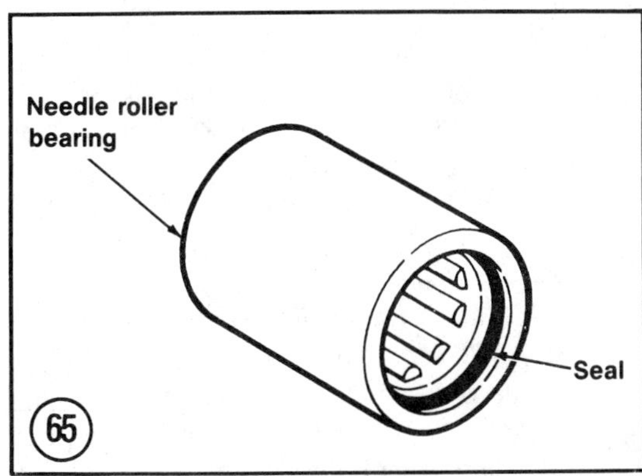

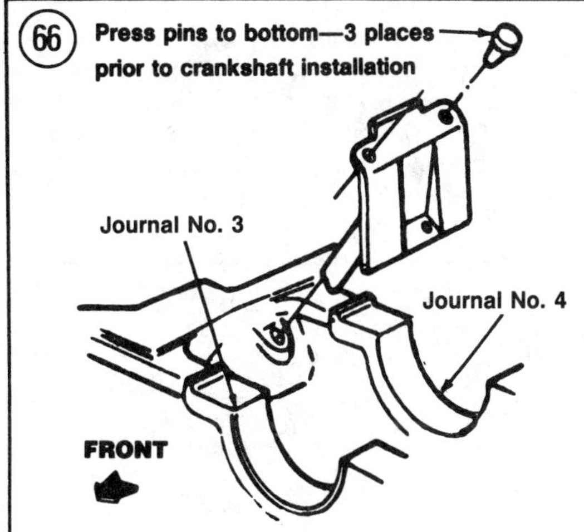

PILOT BEARING

Engines fitted to manual transmissions are equipped with a sealed roller bearing clutch pilot. See **Figure 65**.

1. Remove the clutch and transmission. See Chapter Nine.
2. Remove the bearing with tool part No. T58L-101-A and a slide hammer.
3. Wipe crankshaft pilot bearing bore with a light coat of Ford Multi-purpose Long-life Lubricant (part No. C1AZ-19590-B) or equivalent.
4. Install the new bearing with tool part No. T71P-7137-C.

CYLINDER BLOCK

Cleaning and Inspection

1. Clean the block thoroughly with solvent. Remove any RTV sealant residue from the machined surfaces. Check all core plugs for leaks and replace any that are suspect. See *Core Plug Replacement* in this chapter. Remove any plugs that seal oil passages. Remove the PCV baffle located between the No. 3 and No. 4 crankshaft journals (**Figure 66**), if so equipped. Check oil and coolant passages for sludge, dirt and corrosion while cleaning. If the passages are very dirty, have the block boiled out by a machine shop. Blow out all passages with compressed air. Check the threads in the head bolt holes to be sure they are clean. If dirty, use a tap to true up the threads and remove any deposits.

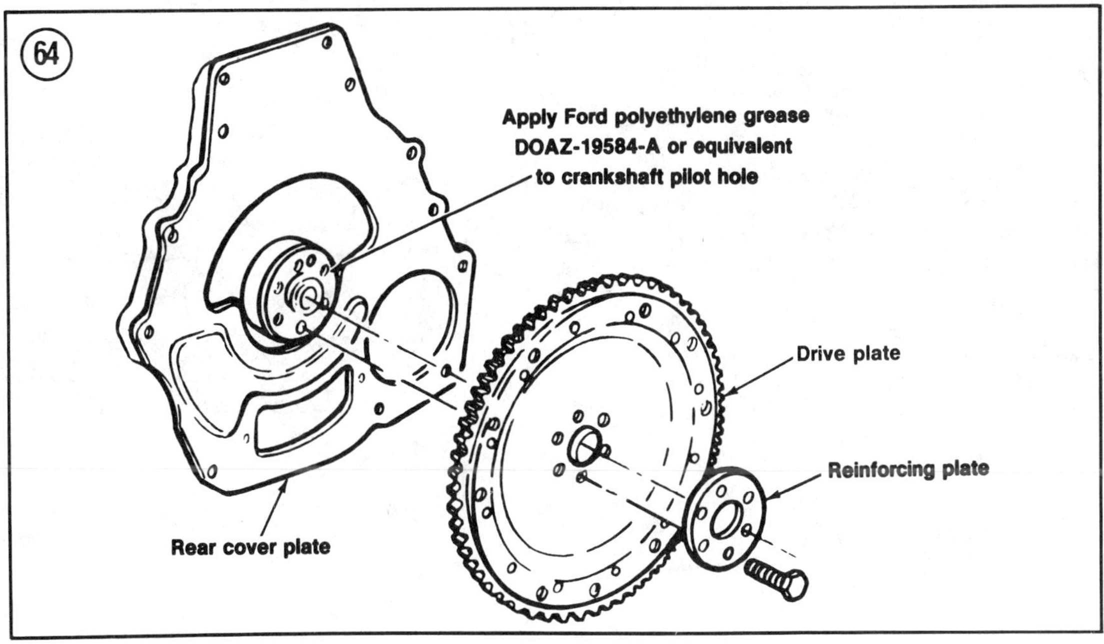

2. Examine the block for cracks. To confirm suspicions about possible leak areas, use a mixture of 1 part kerosene and 2 parts engine oil. Coat the suspected area with this solution, then wipe dry and immediately apply a solution of zinc oxide dissolved in wood alcohol. If any discoloration appears in the treated area, the block is cracked and should be replaced.
3. Check flatness of the cylinder block deck or top surface. Place an accurate straightedge on the block. If there is any gap between the block and straightedge, measure it with a flat feeler gauge (**Figure 67**). Measure from end to end and from corner to corner. If gap exceeds 0.002 in. (0.05 mm), have the block resurfaced. Do not remove more than 0.010 in. (0.254 mm) from the surface.
4. Measure cylinder bores with a bore gauge for out-of-roundness or excessive wear as described in *Piston Clearance Check* in this chapter. If the cylinders exceed maximum tolerances, they must be rebored. Reboring is also necessary if the cylinder walls are badly scuffed or scored.

CAUTION
*If one cylinder is bored out, the others must be bored to the same diameter. Before boring, install all main bearing caps and tighten the cap bolts to specifications in **Table 2**.*

CORE PLUG REPLACEMENT

The condition of all core plugs in the block and cylinder head should be checked whenever the engine is out of the vehicle for service. If any signs of leakage or corrosion are found around one core plug, replace them all.

Cup type core plugs must be installed with the flanged edge facing outward. See **Figure 68**. Since the maximum diameter of this type of plug is at the outer edge of the flange, the plug must be installed with a properly designed tool (**Figure 68**). If driven into the bore with a tool which contacts the plug flange, damaged may occur to the sealing edge. This can result in leakage or a plug blow-out.

Removal/Installation

CAUTION
Do not drive core plugs into the engine casting. It will be impossible to retrieve them and they can restrict coolant circulation, resulting in serious engine damage.

1. Drill a hole in the center of the plug and pry out with an appropriate size drift or pin punch. Work carefully to avoid damage to the plug bore. On large core plugs, the use of a universal impact slide hammer is recommended.
2. Clean the plug bore thoroughly and inspect for any damage that might interfere with proper sealing of the new plug. If damage is evident, true the surface by boring for the next oversize plug.

NOTE
Oversize plugs can be identified by an "OS" stamped in the flat on the cup side of the plug.

3. Coat the inside diameter of the plug bore and the outer diameter of the new plug with sealer. Use an oil-resistant sealer if the plug is to be installed in an oil gallery or a water-resistant sealer for plugs installed in the water jacket.
4. Install the new core plug with an appropriate size core plug replacer tool (**Figure 68**), driver or socket. The sharp edge of the plug should be at least 0.02 in. (0.5 mm) inside the lead-in chamfer.
5. Repeat Steps 1-4 to replace each remaining core plug.

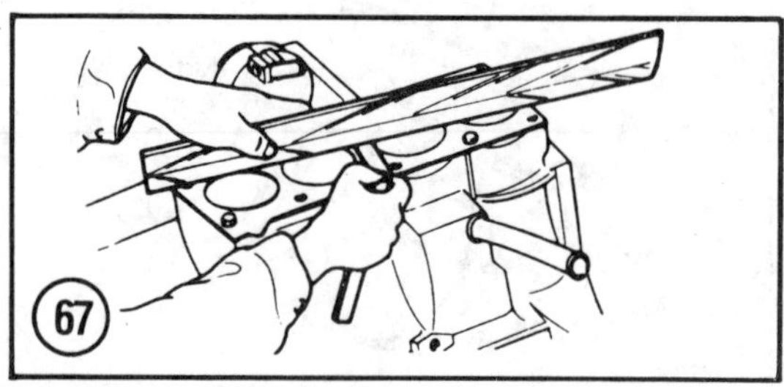

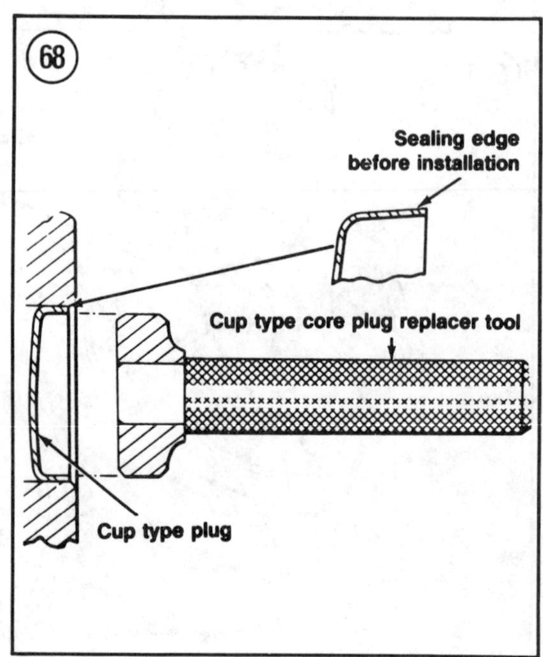

Table 1 2.3L OHC ENGINE SPECIFICATIONS

Engine type	Inline overhead cam 4-cylinder
Bore	3.780 in.
Stroke	3.126 in.
Displacement	140 cid
Firing order	1-3-4-2
Cylinder arrangement	1-2-3-4
Cylinder block	
Bore diameter	3.7795-3.7825 in.
Head gasket surface flatness	0.003 in. in any 6 in.; 0.006 in. overall
Out-of-round (maximum)	0.005 in.
Taper (maximum)	0.010 in.
Main bearing bore diameter	2.5902-2.5910 in.
Distributor shaft bearing bore diameter	0.5155-0.5170 in.
Valve system	
Valve guide bore diameter	0.3433-0.3443 in.
Valve seat width	
Intake	0.060-0.080 in.
Exhaust	0.070-0.090 in.
Valve seat angle	45°
Valve seat runout limit	0.0016 in.
Valve arrangement (front to rear)	E-I-E-I-E-I-E-I
Valve stem-to-guide clearance	
Intake	0.0010-0.0027 in.
Exhaust	0.0015-0.0032 in.
Service limit	0.0055 in. max.
Valve head diameter	
Intake	1.723-1.747 in.
Exhaust	1.490-1.510 in.
Valve face	
Runout limit	0.002 in. max.
Angle limit	44°
Valve stem diameter	
Standard	
Intake	0.3416-0.3423 in.
Exhaust	0.3411-0.3418 in.
0.015 in. oversize	
Intake	0.3566-0.3573 in.
Exhaust	0.3561-0.3568 in.
0.030 in. oversize	
Intake	0.3716-0.3723 in.
Exhaust	0.3711-0.3718 in.
Valve spring load (damper removed)	
1986	
Closed	71-79 lb. @ 1.52 in.
Open	152-156 lb. @ 1.52 in.
1987	
Closed	296-327 N @ 38.61 mm
Open	570-630 N @ 28.45 mm
Valve spring free length	1.877 in.
Valve spring assembled height	1.49-1.55 in.
Valve spring out-of-square service limit	0.078 in.

(continued)

4

Table 1 2.3L OHC ENGINE SPECIFICATIONS (continued)

Camshaft	
Lobe lift (intake & exhaust)	
1986	0.2437 in.
1987	0.2381 in.
Valve lift @ zero lash	
Intake and exhaust	0.3900 in.
End play	0.001-0.007 in.
Service limit	0.003 in.
Journal-to-bearing clearance	0.001-0.003 in.
Service limit	0.006 in.
Journal diameter	1.7713-1.7720 in.
Journal runout limit	0.005 in. max.
Out-of-round limit	0.005 in. max.
Crankshaft	
Main bearing journal diameter	2.399-2.3982 in.
Out-of-round limit	0.0006 in.
Taper limit	0.0006 in. per inch max.
Journal runout limit	0.002 in. max.
Thrust bearing journal length	1.99-2.01 in.
Connecting rod journal	
Diameter	2.0462-2.0472 in.
Out-of-round limit	0.0006 in. max.
Taper limit	0.0006 in. per inch max.
Main bearing thrust face	
Runout limit	0.001 in. max.
End play	
Normal	0.004-0.008 in.
Service limit	0.012 in.
Main bearing clearance	
Desired	0.0008-0.0015 in.
Allowed	0.0008-0.0026 in.
Connecting rod	
Piston pin bore diameter	0.9123-0.9126 in.
Crankshaft bearing bore diameter	2.1720-2.1728 in.
Out-of-round limit	0.0004 in.
Taper limit	0.0004 in.
Length (center-to-center)	5.2031-5.2063 in.
Bearing clearance	
Desired	0.0008-0.0015 in.
Allowed	0.0008-0.0026 in.
Alignment	
Twist	0.024 in.
Bend	0.012 in.
Side clearance	
Standard	0.0035-0.0105 in.
Service limit	0.014 in.
Auxiliary shaft	
Bearing clearance-to-shaft	0.0006-0.0026 in.
End play	0.001-0.007 in.
Flywheel	
Clutch face runout limit	0.005 in.
Ring gear lateral runout	
Manual transmission	0.025 in.
Automatic transmission	0.060 in.

(continued)

Table 1 2.3L OHC ENGINE SPECIFICATIONS (continued)

Piston	
Diameter (red code)	3.7780-3.7786 in.
Piston-to-bore clearance (select fit)	0.0014-0.0022 in.
Pin bore diameter	0.9123-0.9126 in.
Ring groove width	
Compression	0.080-0.081 in.
Oil	0.189-0.190 in.
Piston pin	
Length	3.01-3.04 in.
Diameter	
Standard	0.9119-0.9124 in.
0.001 in. oversize	0.9130-0.9133 in.
0.003 in. oversize	0.9140-0.9143 in.
Piston-to-pin clearance	0.0002-0.0004 in.
Pin-to-rod clearance	Interference fit
Piston rings	
Ring width	
Compression	0.0770-0.0780 in.
Oil	Snug fit
Side clearance	
Compression	0.002-0.004 in.
Oil	Snug fit (0.006 in. max.)
Ring gap	
Compression	0.010-0.020 in.
Oil (steel rail)	0.015-0.055 in.
Oil pump	
Relief valve spring tension	15.2-17.2 lb. @ 1.20 in.
Drive shaft-to-housing bearing clearance	0.0015-0.0030 in.
Relief valve-to-bore clearance	0.0015-0.0030 in.
Rotor assembly end clearance	0.004 in. max.
Outer-race-to-housing clearance	0.001-0.003 in.

Table 2 2.3L OHC ENGINE TIGHTENING TORQUES

Fastener	ft.-lb.	N•m
Auxiliary shaft		
Gear bolt	28-40	38-54
Thrust plate bolt	6-9	8-12
Cover bolt	6-9	8-12
Belt tensioner		
Adjusting bolt	14-21	19-29
Pivot bolt	28-40	38-54
Camshaft		
Gear bolt	50-71	68-96
Thrust plate bolt	6-9	8-12
Connecting rod nut	1	1
Crankshaft pulley bolt	100-120	136-162
Cylinder head bolt	2	2
Crossmember		
To frame nuts	145-195	196-264
To mounting brackets	37-52	50-70
To transmission insulator	71-94	97-127
	(continued)	

Table 2 2.3L OHC ENGINE TIGHTENING TORQUES (continued)

Fastener	ft.-lb.	N·m
Distributor clamp bolt	14-21	19-29
EGR valve-to-spacer	14-21	19-29
EGR valve tube nut	18-28	25-35
Exhaust manifold		
Attaching bolts	3	3
Inlet pipe	18-26	25-35
Flywheel-to-crankshaft	56-64	73-87
Front cover bolt	6-9	8-12
Intake manifold	13-18	18-24
Main bearing cap bolt	4	4
Oil pump pickup tube	15-22	19-29
Oil pump mounting bolt	15-22	19-29
Oil pan		
Drain plug	15-25	20-34
To block	7.5-10	10-13.5
To transmission	30-40	40-54
Oil filter insert-to-block	20-25	28-35
Timing belt cover		
Inner	14-21	19-29
Outer	6-9	8-12
Thermactor check valve	17-20	24-27
Valve cover	6-8	7-11
Water jacket drain plug	23-28	32-37
Standard torque values		
Grade 5 fasteners		
1/4-20	8	11
1/4-28	8	11
5/16-18	17	23
5/16-24	20	27
3/8-16	30	40
3/8-24	35	47
7/16-14	50	68
7/16-20	55	75
1/2-13	75	100
1/2-20	85	115
9/16-12	105	142
9/16-18	115	156

(continued)

Table 2 2.3L OHC ENGINE TIGHTENING TORQUES (continued)

Fastener	ft.-lb.	N•m
Grade 6 fasteners		
1/4-20	10.5	14
1/4-28	12.5	17
5/16-18	22.5	31
5/16-24	25	54
3/8-16	40	34
3/8-24	45	61
7/16-14	65	88
7/16-20	70	95
1/2-13	100	136
1/2-20	110	149
9/16-12	135	183
9/16-18	150	203

1. Tighten in 2 steps:
   a. Step 1 25-30 ft.-lb. (34-41 N•m)
   b. Step 2 30-36 ft.-lb. (41-49 N•m)
2. Tighten in 2 steps:
   a. Step 1 50-60 ft.-lb. (68-81 N•m)
   b. Step 2 80-90 ft.-lb. (108-122 N•m)
3. Tighten in 2 steps:
   a. 1986: Step 1 5-7 ft.-lb. (7-9 N•m); Step 2 16-23 ft.-lb. (22-31 N•m)
   b. 1987: Step 1 178-204 in.-lb. (20-30 N•m); Step 2 20-30 ft.-lb. (27-40.5 N•m)
4. Tighten in 2 steps:
   a. 1986: Step 1 50-60 ft.-lb. (68-81 N•m); Step 2 80-90 ft.-lb. (108-122 N•m)
   b. 1987: Step 1 50-60 ft.-lb. (68-81 N•m); Step 2 75-85 ft.-lb. (102-115 N•m)

CHAPTER FIVE

V6 ENGINE

A carburetted 2.8L (171 cid) V6 engine is optional on 1986 models; a fuel injected 3.0L (183 cid) V6 is optional on 1987 and the base engine on 1988 models. Both engines are a lightweight cast iron design with 60 degree block inclination. The 2.8L has a 3.65 in. bore and 2.70 in. stroke; the 3.0L has a 3.50 in. bore and a 3.14 in. stroke. The cylinders are numbered from front to rear: 1-2-3 on the passenger's side bank and 4-5-6 on the driver's side bank.

Valve arrangement of the 2.8L V6 from front to rear is I-E-E-I-E-I on the passenger's side bank and I-E-I-E-E-I on the driver's side bank. Valve arrangement of the 3.0L V6 from front to rear is I-E-I-E-I-E on the passenger's side bank and E-I-E-I-E-I on the driver's side bank. The cylinder firing order of both engines is 1-4-2-5-3-6. Mechanical (2.8L) or hydraulic (3.0L) valve lifters and pushrods operate the rocker arms and valves. Lash adjustment is required at specified intervals (2.8L only) and during assembly when some component in the valve train has been replaced (2.8L and 3.0L).

The crankshaft is supported by 4 main bearings, with the No. 3 bearing taking the end thrust.

The 2.8L V6 uses a gear-driven camshaft; the 3.0L V6 camshaft is chain-driven. Both are supported by 4 bearings and located above the crankshaft between the 2 cylinder banks. The oil pump is located on the bottom rear of the block and is driven by the distributor through an intermediate shaft. Specifications (**Table 1** and **Table 2**) and tightening torques (**Table 3** and **Table 4**) are at the end of the chapter.

ENGINE IDENTIFICATION

An engine identification label is attached to the right rocker arm cover. This label contains the engine calibration number, build date, plant code and engine code. The data on the label identifies each engine. The change level and engine code number tell is parts are unique to particular engines. This data should be used when ordering replacement parts to assure that the correct parts are furnished.

The 2.8L engine code is S; the 3.0L engine code is U. The engine code is the 8th digit/letter of the vehicle identification number (VIN). The VIN is the official identification for title and vehicle registration. The VIN is stamped on a metal vehicle identification plate attached to the top left of the instrument panel (**Figure 1**).

ENGINE SERVICE

Access to the V6 Aerostar engines is extremely limited. The engine fills the engine compartment and reaching many components such as the PCV valve is difficult at best without removing the engine from the vehicle. The small engine compartment panel underneath the instrument panel in the passenger compartment does not provide as much access as the traditional engine cover found in full-size vans.

The engine is removed and installed from the bottom of the vehicle and requires removal of the suspension. While many of the tasks detailed in this chapter can be performed with the engine in the vehicle, progress will be slow and require the use of an extensive selection of metric tools, including a variety of long and short socket extensions.

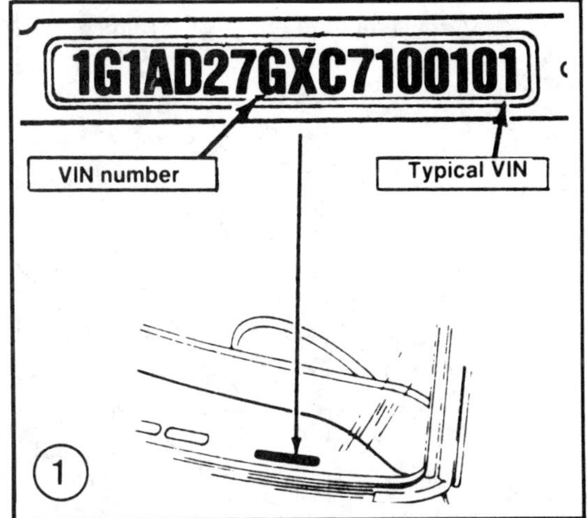

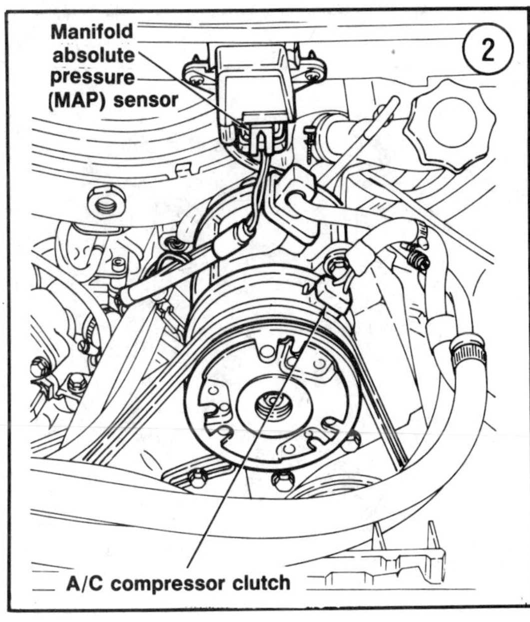

Before attempting any procedure, you should study the engine compartment and this chapter, then make a determination whether engine removal will make the task easier and faster. In most cases, the choice will depend upon your skill level as an owner/mechanic. Whatever the choice, expect that many service procedures will require more time than you first think, and be prepared to work slowly and patiently. You may even find it more convenient to perform some of the steps from underneath the engine, even though the procedure does not specify raising the engine.

2.8L V6 ENGINE REMOVAL/INSTALLATION

WARNING
The engine is heavy, awkward to handle and has sharp edges. It may shift or drop suddenly during removal. To prevent serious injury, always observe the following precautions.

1. Never place any part of your body where a moving or falling engine may trap, cut or crush you.

2. If you must push the engine during removal, use a board or similar tool to keep your hands out of danger.

3. Be sure the hoist is designed to lift engines and has enough load capacity for your engine.

4. Be sure the hoist is securely attached to safe lifting points on the engine.

5. The engine should not be difficult to lift with a proper hoist. If it is, stop lifting, lower the engine back onto its mounts and make sure the engine has been completely separated from the vehicle.

WARNING
Before opening any fuel system connection on a fuel injected engine, relieve system pressure as described in Chapter Six.

1. Raise and support the hood.
2. Disconnect the negative battery cable.
3. Drain the cooling system. See Chapter Seven.
4. Remove the air cleaner assembly and intake duct. See Chapter Six.
5. Unclamp and disconnect the upper and lower radiator hoses at the radiator. Remove the fan shroud. See Chapter Seven.
6. Unplug the MAP sensor electrical connector **(Figure 2).**

WARNING
The air conditioning system contains pressurized refrigerant which can cause frostbite if it touches skin and blindness if it touches the eyes. If discharged near an open flame, the refrigerant forms poisonous gas. Never disconnect air conditioning system lines unless the system has been discharged and evacuated by a professional.

7. If equipped with air conditioning, unplug the compressor clutch switch connector (**Figure 2**). Loosen the idler pulley adjustment bolt to release drive belt tension. Remove the belt from the compressor clutch pulley. Remove the compressor from its mounting bracket and place to one side out of the way without disconnecting any refrigerant lines.
8. Label and disconnect the following electrical connectors and vacuum lines:
   a. Idle speed control (ISC) motor (**Figure 3**).
   b. Coolant and water temperature sensors (**Figure 3**).
   c. EGR valve and valve position sensor (**Figure 3**).
   d. Alternator (**Figure 4**).
   e. Throttle position sensor (**Figure 5**).
   f. Canister purge solenoid valve (**Figure 5**).
   g. Choke cap (**Figure 5**).
   h. Carburetor bowl vent valve (**Figure 5**).
9. Remove the wiring harness from the engine compartment.

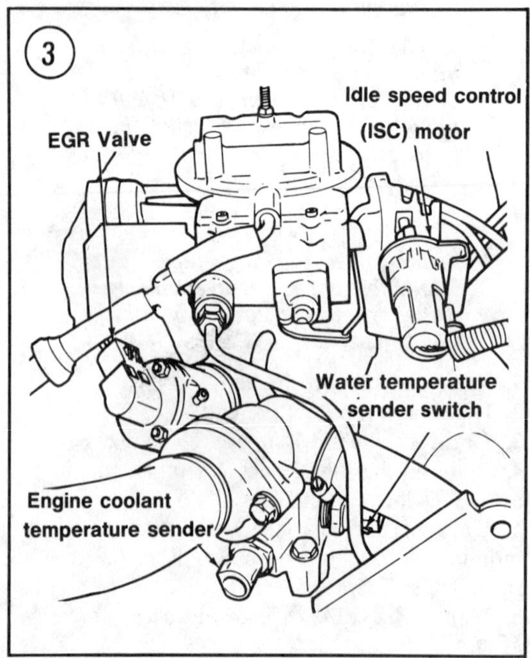

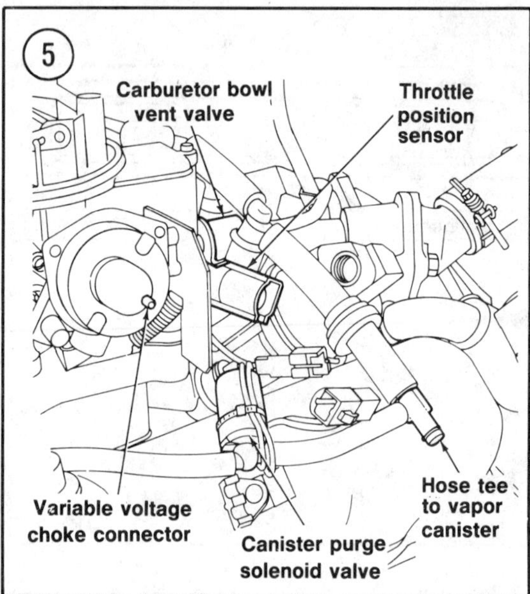

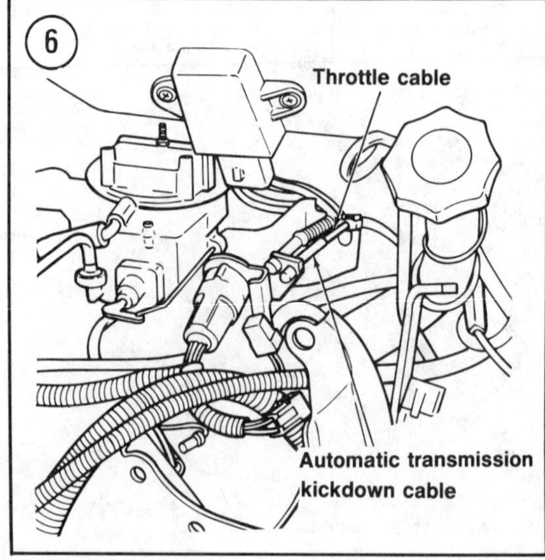

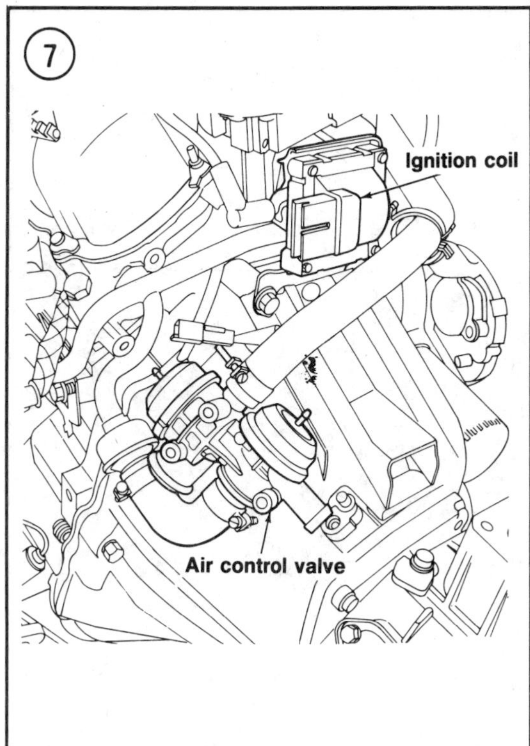

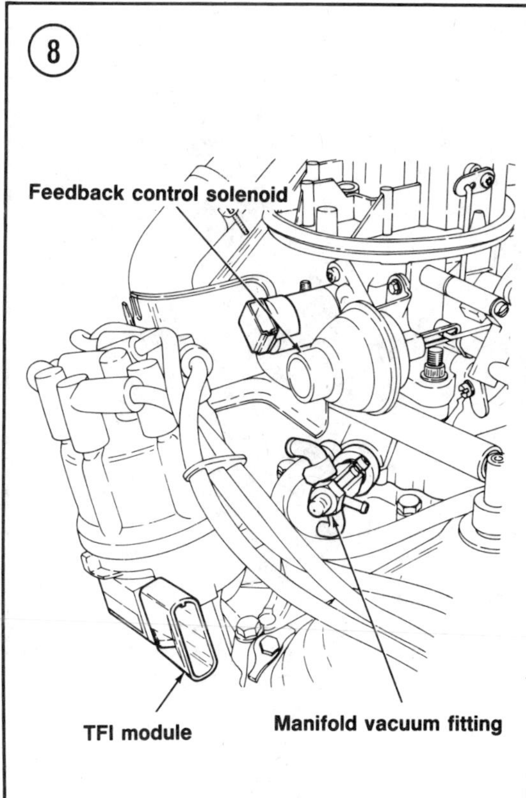

10. Working in the passenger compartment:
   a. Remove the engine cover from underneath the instrument panel.
   b. Unbolt and remove the throttle cable and transmission kickdown linkage bracket. (See **Figure 6**).
   c. Unplug the connectors at the ignition coil (**Figure 7**).
   d. Unclamp and disconnect the air control valve hose to the catalytic converter (**Figure 7**).
   e. Carefully disconnect the TFI module connector at the distributor (**Figure 8**).
   f. Unplug the feedback control solenoid at the rear of the carburetor (**Figure 8**).
   g. Label and disconnect all hoses at the manifold vacuum fitting (**Figure 8**).
   h. Remove the brake booster vacuum hose from its retaining clip.

11. Manual transmission—Remove the shift lever. See Chapter Nine.

12. Securely block the rear wheels so the vehicle will not roll in either direction.

13. Loosen the front wheel lug nuts, then raise the front of the vehicle with a jack and place it on jackstands.

14. Remove the wheel/tire assemblies.

15. Automatic transmission—Disconnect the oil cooler lines at the radiator. If equipped with quick-disconnect fittings, see *Quick-disconnect Fittings* in Chapter Six.

16. Unbolt and disconnect the intermediate steering column shaft from the steering gear. See **Figure 9**.

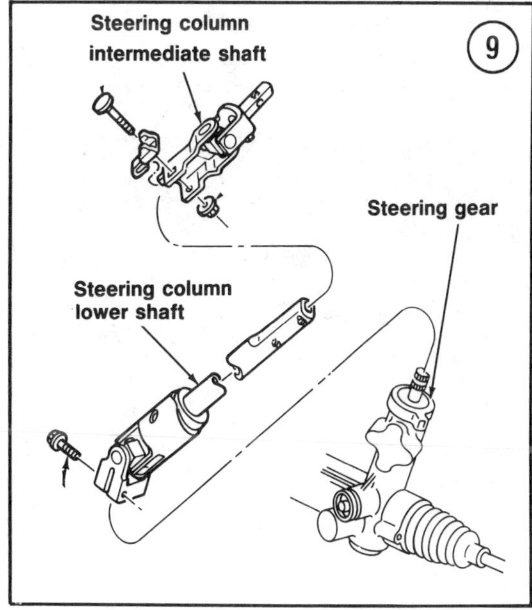

5

17. Unplug the elbow connector at the oil pressure sender (**Figure 10**).
18. Disconnect the fuel pump inlet and return lines (**Figure 10**). Plug the lines and cap the fittings to prevent leakage.
19. Unbolt and remove the ground strap at the engine (**Figure 11**). Disconnect the starter feed and ground cables from the starter motor (**Figure 11**), then rotate the cables out of the crossmember.
20. Manual transmission—Disconnect the slave cylinder hydraulic line. See Chapter Nine.
21. Unplug the exhaust gas oxygen sensor connector at the left exhaust manifold. See **Figure 12**.
22. Unplug the lead at the knock sensor located in the engine block above the starter. See **Figure 12**.
23. Disconnect the catalytic converter at the exhaust manifold. Remove the exhaust pipe and catalytic converter. See Chapter Six.
24. Disconnect all electrical connectors at the transmission. See Chapter Nine.
25. Automatic transmission—Disconnect the selector and kickdown cables at the transmission. See Chapter Nine.
26. Remove the drive shaft. See Chapter Eleven.
27. Disconnect the stabilizer bar at the lower control arm. See Chapter Ten.
28. Disconnect the front brake lines at the frame brackets.

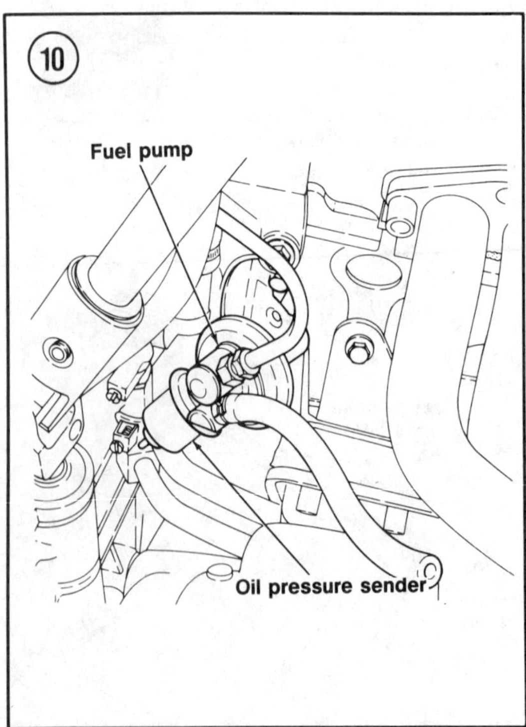

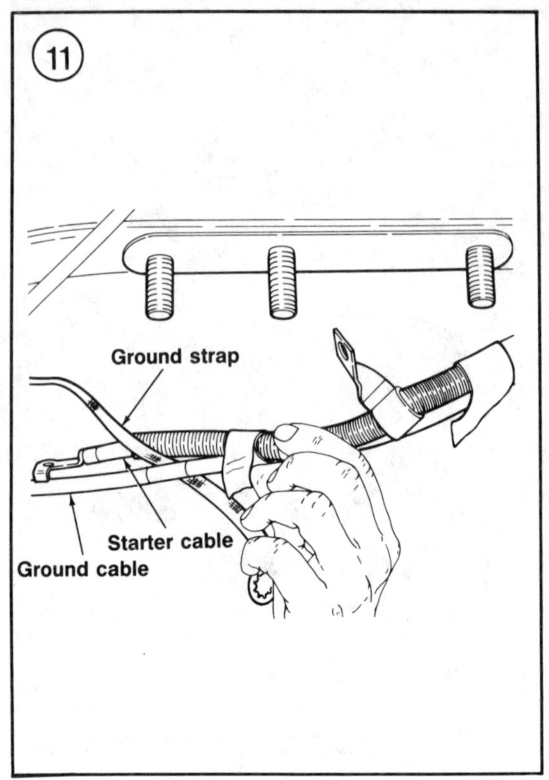

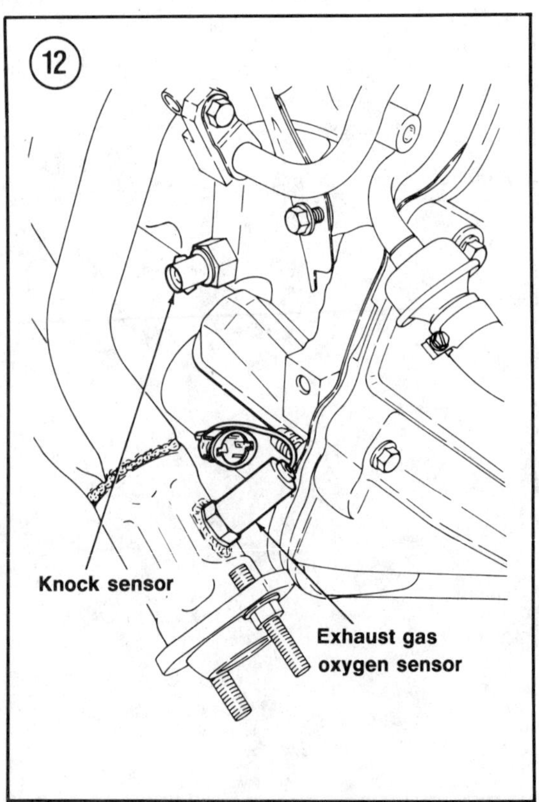

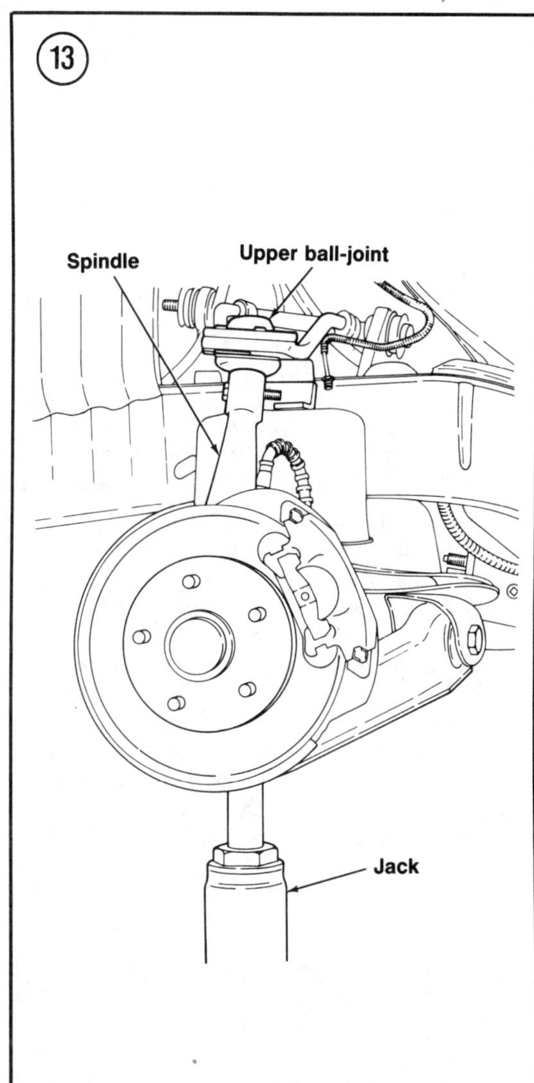

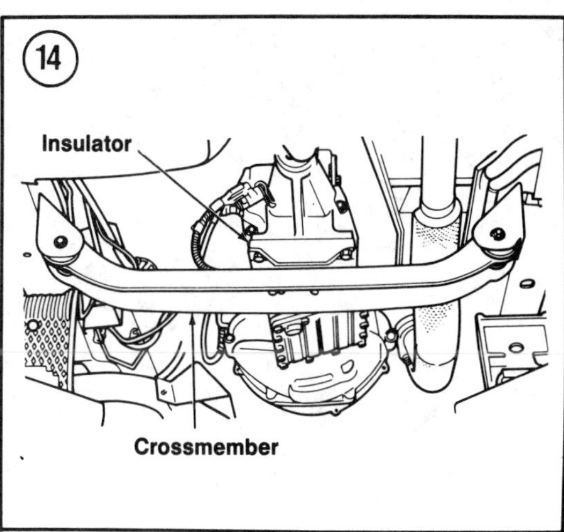

29. Place a jack under the lower control arm and raise the jack enough to apply tension to the control arm.
30. Remove the bolt and nut holding the spindle to the upper control arm ball-joint (**Figure 13**). Lower the jack until the spindle and ball-joint separate.
31. Install safety chains around the lower control arm and spring seat.
32. Repeat Steps 29-31 to disconnect the other lower control arm from the ball-joint.
33. Position a jack under the transmission. Raise the transmission enough to unbolt the insulator at the crossmember, then remove the nuts holding the crossmember to the frame. See **Figure 14**. Remove the crossmember from under the vehicle.
34. Remove the transmission. See Chapter Nine.
35. Position a suitable support table under the engine and crossmember assembly. Ford recommends the use of Rotunda table part No. 109-0002.
36. Slowly lower the vehicle until the crossmember rests on the support table. Position suitable wooden blocks under the front crossmember and rear of the engine block to keep the assembly level, then install safety chains around the table and crossmember.
37. Remove the fasteners holding the engine and crossmember assembly to the frame on each side of the vehicle. See **Figure 15**.

NOTE
At this point, there should be no hoses, wires or linkages connecting the engine to the body. Recheck to be sure nothing will hamper engine removal and that all accessories, hoses, tubes and wires are positioned out of the way.

38. Slowly raise the vehicle until it clears the engine and crossmember assembly on the support table (**Figure 16**). Roll the support table with the engine and crossmember assembly out from underneath the vehicle.
39. Attach an engine hoist chain or sling to the engine lifting bracket eyes.
40. Power steering—Disconnect the hydraulic fluid hoses at the power steering pump. Plug the lines and cap the fittings to prevent leakage.
41. Apply tension to the hoist chain or sling, then remove the nuts holding the engine to the crossmember assembly. Lift the engine up and off the crossmember assembly (**Figure 17**).
42. Once the engine is clear of the crossmember assembly, lower it to a suitable support or engine stand. Fasten the engine in the support or engine

stand, then disconnect the hoist and lifting chain or sling. Inspect the rubber motor mounts and insulators for wear or damage. If these conditions exist, replace the mounts or insulators before reinstalling the engine.

43. Engine installation is the reverse of removal, plus the following:

a. Tighten all fasteners to specifications (**Table 1**).
b. Fill the engine with an oil recommended in Chapter Three.
c. Fill the cooling system. See Chapter Seven.
d. Adjust the drive belts. See Chapter Seven.

3.0L V6 ENGINE REMOVAL/INSTALLATION

WARNING

The engine is heavy, awkward to handle and has sharp edges. It may shift or drop suddenly during removal. To prevent serious injury, always observe the following precautions.

1. Never place any part of your body where a moving or falling engine may trap, cut or crush you.

2. If you must push the engine during removal, use a board or similar tool to keep your hands out of danger.

3. Be sure the hoist is designed to lift engines and has enough load capacity for your engine.

4. Be sure the hoist is securely attached to safe lifting points on the engine.

5. The engine should not be difficult to lift with a proper hoist. If it is, stop lifting, lower the engine back onto its mounts and make sure the engine has been completely separated from the vehicle.

WARNING

Before opening any fuel system connection on a fuel injected engine, relieve system pressure as described in Chapter Six.

1. Raise and support the hood.
2. Disconnect the negative battery cable.
3. Drain the cooling system. Unclamp and disconnect the upper and lower radiator hoses at the radiator. See Chapter Seven.
4. Remove the air cleaner assembly and intake duct. See Chapter Six.
5. Unclamp the air cleaner resonator hose at the air cleaner housing and disconnect the hose (**Figure 18**). Unclamp and disconnect the resonator hose at the air intake throttle body (A, **Figure 19**). Remove resonator and hose assembly.

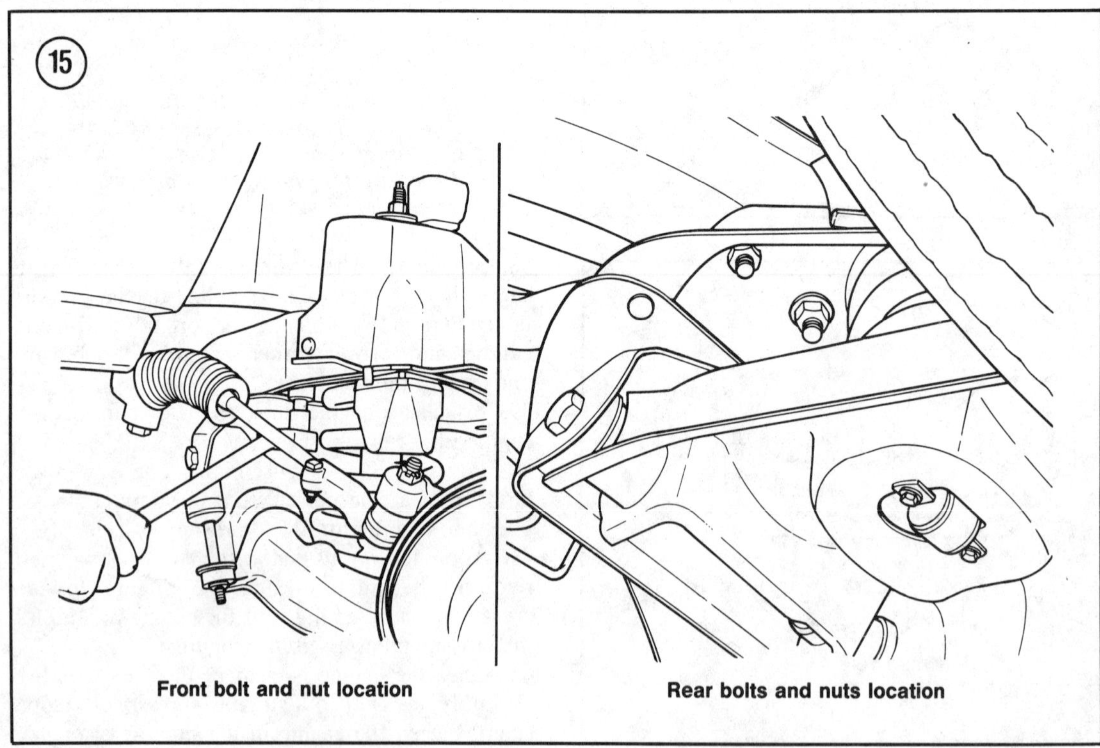

Front bolt and nut location

Rear bolts and nuts location

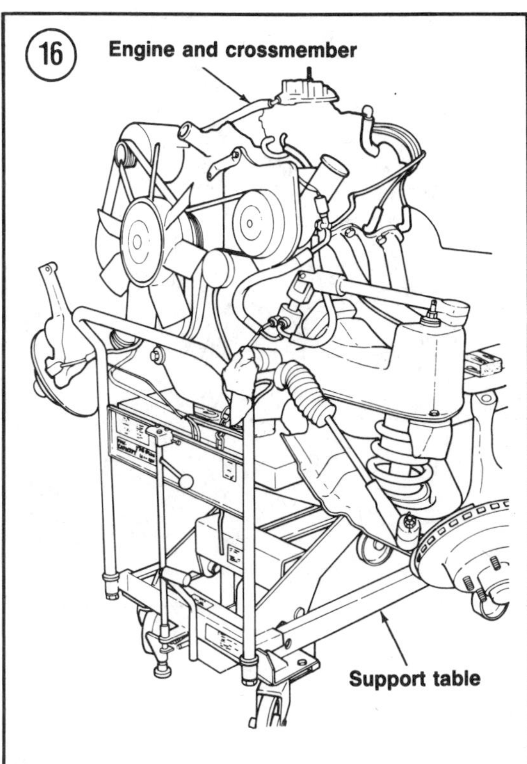

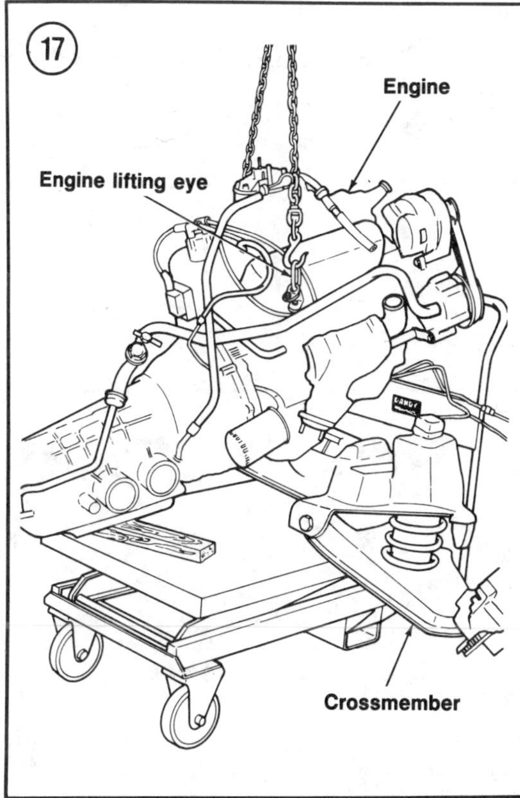

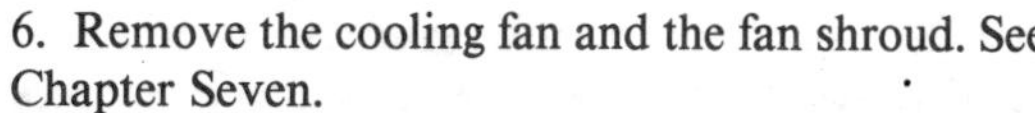

6. Remove the cooling fan and the fan shroud. See Chapter Seven.
7. Unplug the MAP sensor electrical connector (B, **Figure 19**) and disconnect the vacuum line.
8. Remove the shroud covering the throttle linkage (C, **Figure 19**). Disconnect the throttle linkage at the air intake throttle body.
9. Loosen the idler arm retaining bolts (**Figure 20**).

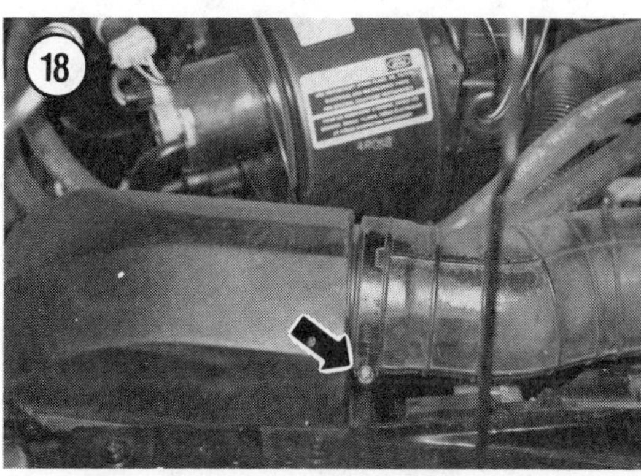

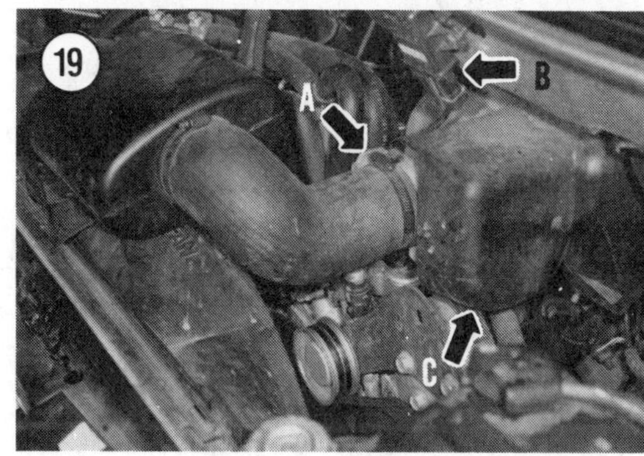

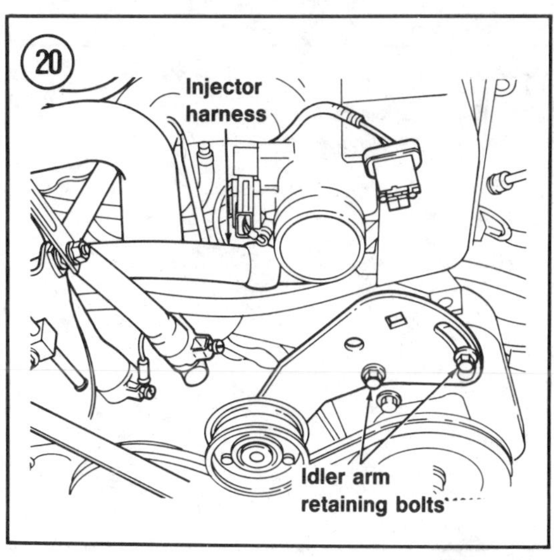

10. Pull the fuel injector harness forward to provide access to the engine coolant temperature sender and sensor (**Figure 21**). Unplug both connectors.
11. Disconnect the hoses from both sides of the canister purge solenoid.
12. If equipped with power steering, unplug the pump pressure switch (**Figure 22**).
13. Identify the heater inlet and outlet hoses (**Figure 23**) by marking them with chalk, then disconnect the hoses from the engine side of the ballast tube.
14. Disconnect the PCV breather tube at the air cleaner and rocker cover. Remove the tube from the engine compartment.
15. Remove the radiator. See Chapter Seven.
16. Loosen the alternator and remove the drive belt.

WARNING
The air conditioning system contains pressurized refrigerant which can cause frostbite if it touches skin and blindness if it touches the eyes. If discharged near an open flame, the refrigerant forms poisonous gas. Never disconnect air conditioning system lines unless the system has been discharged and evacuated by a professional.

17. If equipped with air conditioning, unplug the compressor clutch switch connector. Remove the compressor from its mounting bracket and place to one side out of the way without disconnecting any refrigerant lines.
18. Unbolt the oil fill tube from the alternator bracket (**Figure 24**).
19. Automatic transmission—Remove the bolt holding the dipstick tube to the top of the

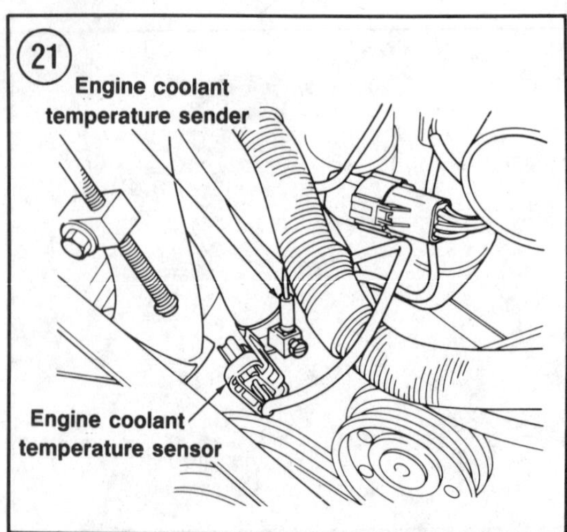

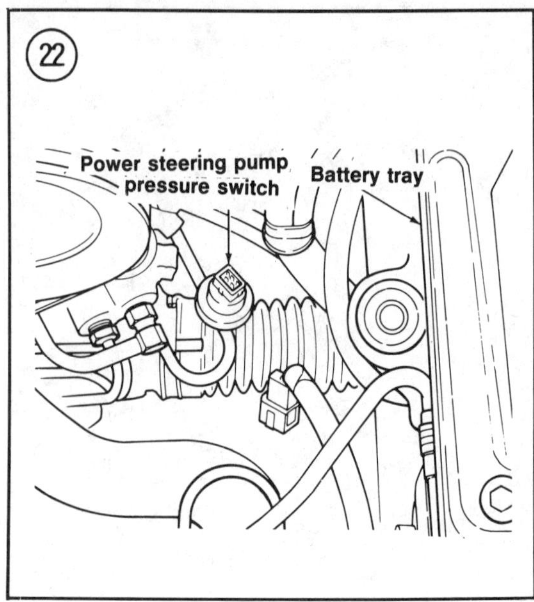

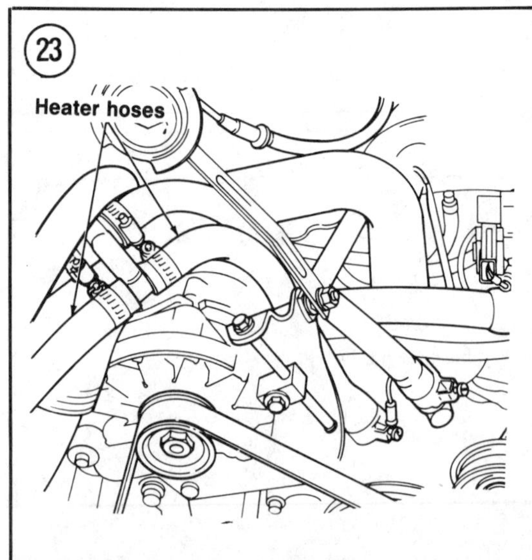

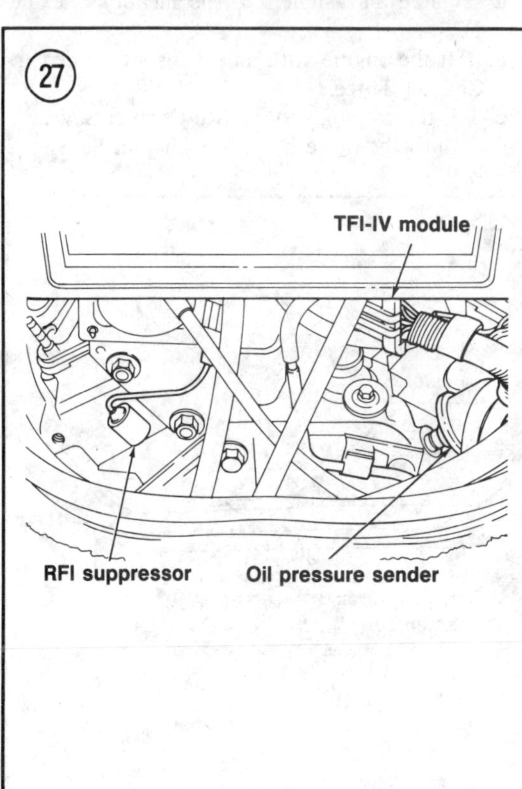

manifold. Carefully pull the dipstick tube out from the top of the vehicle.

20. Unplug the alternator electrical connectors (**Figure 25**).

21. Disconnect the vacuum brake booster hose at the booster unit.

22. Remove the bolt holding the steering gear shaft to the intermediate shaft (**Figure 26**).

23. Working inside the passenger compartment:

a. Remove the engine cover from under the instrument panel.

b. Disconnect the RFI suppressor (**Figure 27**).

c. Carefully disconnect the TFI-IV module connector at the distributor (**Figure 27**).

d. Unplug the oil pressure sender lead (**Figure 27**).

24. Manual transmission—Remove the shift lever. See Chapter Nine.

25. Securely block the rear wheels so the vehicle will not roll in either direction.

26. Loosen the front wheel lug nuts, then raise the front of the vehicle with a jack and place it on jackstands.

27. Remove the wheel/tire assemblies.

28. Disconnect the fuel line quick-disconnect fittings at the fuel sender (**Figure 28**). See *Quick-disconnect Fittings* in Chapter Six.

29. Disconnect the low oil level sensor from the oil pan (**Figure 29**).

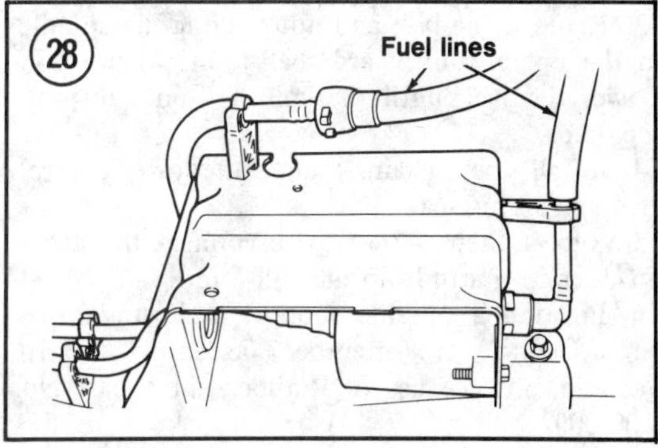

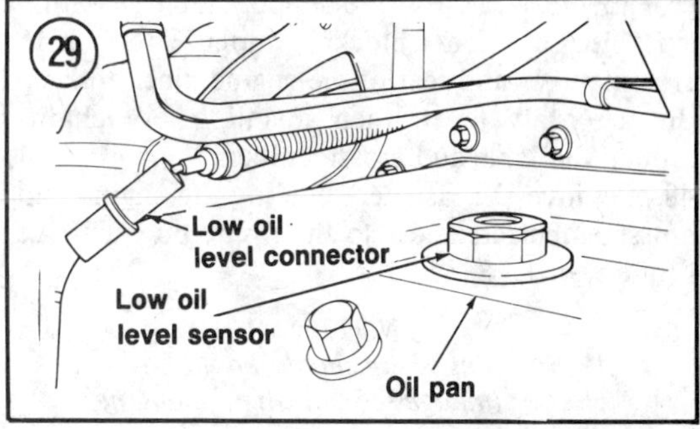

5

30. Remove the drive shaft. See Chapter Eleven.
31. Remove the starter motor. See Chapter Eight.
32. Manual transmission—Disconnect the slave cylinder hydraulic line. See Chapter Nine.
33. Disconnect all electrical connectors at the transmission. See Chapter Nine.
34. Unplug the exhaust gas oxygen sensor connector at the left exhaust manifold.
35. Disconnect the catalytic converter at the exhaust manifold. Remove the exhaust pipe and catalytic converter. See Chapter Six.
36. Automatic transmission—Disconnect the selector and kickdown cables at the transmission. See Chapter Nine.
37. Position a jack under the transmission. Raise the transmission enough to unbolt the insulator at the crossmember, then remove the nuts holding the crossmember to the frame. See **Figure 30**. Remove the crossmember from under the vehicle.
38. Remove the transmission. See Chapter Nine.
39. Disconnect the 2 engine ground straps located just behind the power steering pump on the cylinder head and just above the exhaust manifold and inlet pipe connection.
40. Disconnect the stabilizer bar at the lower control arm. See Chapter Ten.
41. Disconnect the front brake lines at the frame brackets.
42. Place a jack under the lower control arm and raise the jack enough to apply tension to the control arm.
43. Remove the bolt and nut holding the spindle to the upper control arm ball-joint (**Figure 13**). Lower the jack until the spindle and ball-joint separate.
44. Install safety chains around the lower control arm and spring seat.
45. Repeat Steps 42-44 to disconnect the other lower control arm from the ball-joint.
46. Position a suitable support table under the engine and crossmember assembly. Ford recommends the use of Rotunda table part No. 109-0002.
47. Slowly lower the vehicle until the crossmember rests on the support table. Position suitable wooden blocks under the front crossmember and rear of the engine block to keep the assembly level, then install safety chains around the table and crossmember.
48. Remove the fasteners holding the engine and crossmember assembly to the frame on each side of the vehicle. See **Figure 15**.

NOTE
At this point, there should be no hoses, wires or linkages connecting the engine to the body. Recheck to be sure nothing will hamper engine removal and that all accessories, hoses, tubes and wires are positioned out of the way.

49. Slowly raise the vehicle until it clears the engine and crossmember assembly on the support table (**Figure 16**). Make sure the A/C compressor and wiring harness do not interfere at this point. Roll the support table with the engine and crossmember assembly out from underneath the vehicle.
50. Attach an engine hoist chain or sling to the engine lifting bracket eyes.
51. Apply tension to the hoist chain or sling, then remove the nuts holding the engine to the crossmember assembly. Lift the engine up and off the crossmember assembly (**Figure 17**).
52. Once the engine is clear of the crossmember assembly, lower it to a suitable support or engine stand. Fasten the engine in the support or engine stand, then disconnect the hoist and lifting chain or sling. Inspect the rubber motor mounts and insulators for wear or damage. If these conditions exist, replace the mounts or insulators before reinstalling the engine.
53. Engine installation is the reverse of removal, plus the following:

a. Tighten all fasteners to specifications (**Table 1**).
b. Fill the engine with an oil recommended in Chapter Three.
c. Fill the cooling system. See Chapter Seven.
d. Adjust the drive belts. See Chapter Seven.

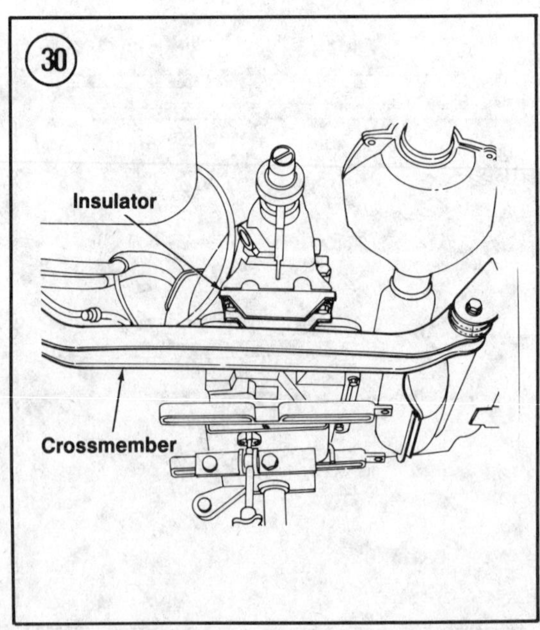

DISASSEMBLY CHECKLISTS

To use the checklists, remove and inspect each part in the order mentioned. To reassemble, go through the checklists backwards, installing the parts in order. Each major part is covered in its own section in this chapter, unless otherwise noted.

Decarbonizing or Valve Service

1. Remove the rocker arm cover.
2. Remove the intake and exhaust manifolds.
3. Remove the rocker arms.
4. Remove the cylinder head.
5. Have valves removed and inspected. Have valve guides and seats inspected, repairing or replacing as required.
6. Assemble by reversing Steps 1-4.

Valve and Ring Service

1. Perform Steps 1-5 of *Decarbonizing or Valve Service.*
2. Remove the oil pan and oil pump.
3. Remove the pistons with connecting rods.
4. Remove the piston rings. It is not necessary to separate the pistons from the connecting rods unless a piston, connecting rod or piston pin needs repair or replacement.
5. Assemble by reversing Steps 1-4.

General Overhaul

1. Remove the engine. Remove the clutch (Chapter Nine) from manual transmission vehicles.
2. Remove the flywheel (manual) or drive plate (automatic).
3. Remove the mount brackets and oil pressure sending unit from the engine.
4. If available, mount the engine on an engine stand. These can be rented from equipment rental dealers. The stand is not absolutely necessary, but it will make the job much easier.
5. Remove the following accessories or components from the engine, if present:
   a. Alternator and mounting bracket.
   b. Power steering pump and mounting bracket.
   c. Spark plug wires and distributor cap.
   d. Fuel lines.
   e. Oil filter.
6. Check the engine for signs of coolant or oil leaks.
7. Clean the outside of the engine.
8. Remove the distributor. See Chapter Eight.
9. Remove all hoses and tubes connected to the engine.
10. Remove the fuel pump (2.8L only). See Chapter Six.
11. Remove the intake and exhaust manifolds.
12. Remove the thermostat housing and water pump. See Chapter Seven.
13. Remove the rocker arm covers and rocker arms.
14. Remove the crankshaft pulley and front cover. Remove the timing gears and timing chain (3.0L).
15. Remove the cylinder heads.
16. Remove the camshaft sprocket and camshaft.
17. Remove the oil pan and oil pump.
18. Remove the pistons and connecting rods.
19. Remove the crankshaft and main bearings.
20. Inspect the cylinder block.
21. Assemble by reversing Steps 1-19.

5

ROCKER ARM COVERS REMOVAL/INSTALLATION (2.8L V6)

1. Remove the air cleaner assembly. See Chapter Six.
2. Disconnect the spark plug cables at the plugs and remove the plug cable retainers from their bracket on the cover.
3. On the right cover:
   a. Disconnect the PCV valve.
   b. Remove the 2 screws holding the TPS sensor connector to the carburetor choke air deflector shield. Remove the air deflector shield.
   c. Remove the automatic transmission dipstick tube bracket, if so equipped.
   d. Move the Thermactor air diverter and air bypass valves away from the cover.

WARNING
The air conditioning system contains pressurized refrigerant which can cause frostbite if it touches skin and blindness if it touches the eyes. If discharged near an open flame, the refrigerant forms poisonous gas. Never disconnect air conditioning system lines unless the system has been discharged and evacuated by a professional.

   e. Unbolt and remove the air conditioning compressor, if so equipped, without disconnecting any refrigerant lines. Place compressor to one side out of the way.
4. On the left cover:
   a. Disconnect the automatic transmission kickdown rod at the carburetor, if so equipped.
   b. Remove the oil filler tube.

c. Disconnect the power brake booster vacuum hose.
d. Disconnect the canister purge solenoid vacuum line, if so equipped.

5. Remove the cover attaching screws and load distribution washers. Note washer location for correct reinstallation.

NOTE
If the cover refuses to come free in Step 6, bump the end with a rubber mallet. If this does not break the gasket seal, carefully pry the cover loose with a screwdriver. Use caution to prevent distorting the cover sealing flange.

6. Tap the rocker arm cover with a plastic mallet to break the gasket seal. Remove the rocker arm cover and gasket. Discard the gasket.
7. Clean any gasket residue from the cylinder head and rocker arm cover with degreaser and a putty knife.

NOTE
An oil leak will develop if a new gasket is not used in Step 8 or if the load distribution washers are not properly installed.

8. Install rocker arm cover with a new gasket. Install attaching screws with load distribution washers. See **Figure 31**. Tighten attaching screws to specifications (**Table 3**).
9. Reverse Steps 1-4 to complete installation. Run the engine at fast idle and check for oil leaks.

ROCKER ARM COVERS REMOVAL/INSTALLATION (3.0L V6)

Refer to **Figure 32** for this procedure.

1. Remove the air cleaner assembly. See Chapter Six.
2. Disconnect the spark plug cables at the plugs and remove the plug cable retainers from the 3 attaching studs on the cover.
3. On the right cover:
   a. Disconnect the PCV valve.
   b. Drain the cooling system (Chapter Seven) and disconnect the heater hoses at the engine and ballast tube.
4. On the left cover:
   a. Disconnect the closure system hose.
   b. Remove the oil filler tube.
5. Remove the cover attaching screws and studs. Note the location of the studs used to hold the spark plug cable retainers for reinstallation reference.

NOTE
If the cover refuses to come free in Step 6, bump the end with a rubber mallet. If this does not break the gasket seal, carefully pry the cover loose with a screwdriver. Use caution to prevent distorting the cover sealing flange.

6. Tap the rocker arm cover with a plastic mallet to break the gasket seal. Remove the rocker arm cover and gasket. Discard the gasket.

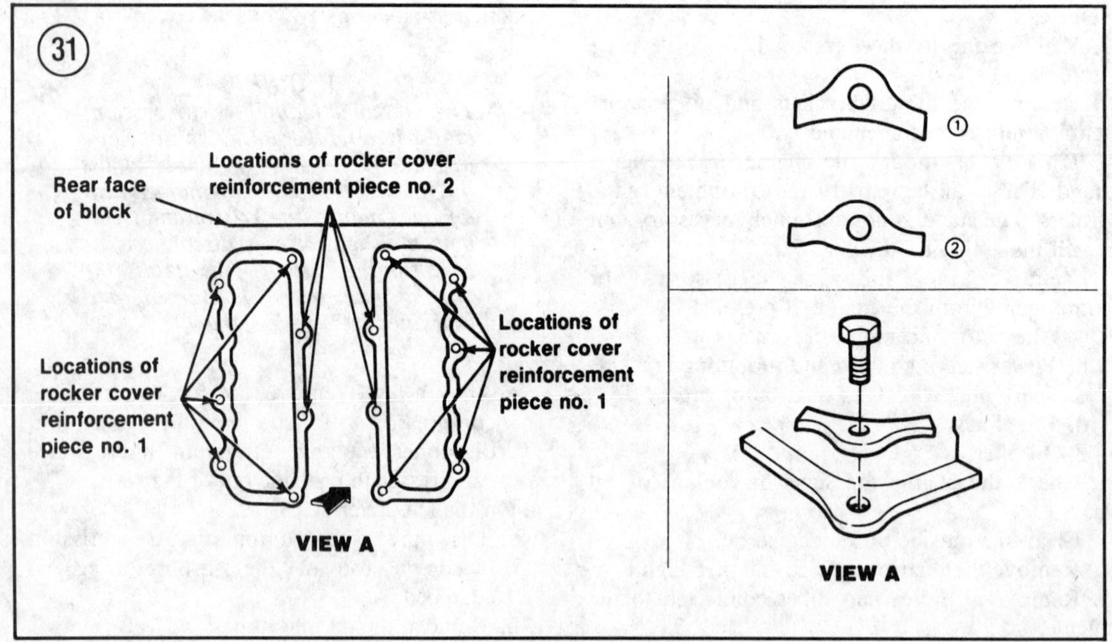

7. Clean any gasket residue from the cylinder head and rocker arm cover with degreaser and a putty knife.

NOTE
An oil leak will develop if a new gasket is not used in Step 8.

8. Run a 1/8 in. bead of RTV sealant at the cylinder head-to-intake manifold rail step (2 per rail). Install a new gasket on the cylinder head rail. If necessary, install locating or guide pins to align and hold gasket in place, then remove the pins after the rocker arm cover is in place.

9. Carefully position the rocker arm cover on the cylinder head and gasket. Install the attaching screws and studs. Make sure studs are properly located to hold spark plug cable retainers. Tighten the valve cover fasteners to specifications (**Table 4**).

10. Reverse Steps 1-4 to complete installation. Run the engine at fast idle and check for oil leaks.

Intake Manifold Removal/Installation

1. Disconnect the negative battery cable.
2. Drain the cooling system. See Chapter Seven.

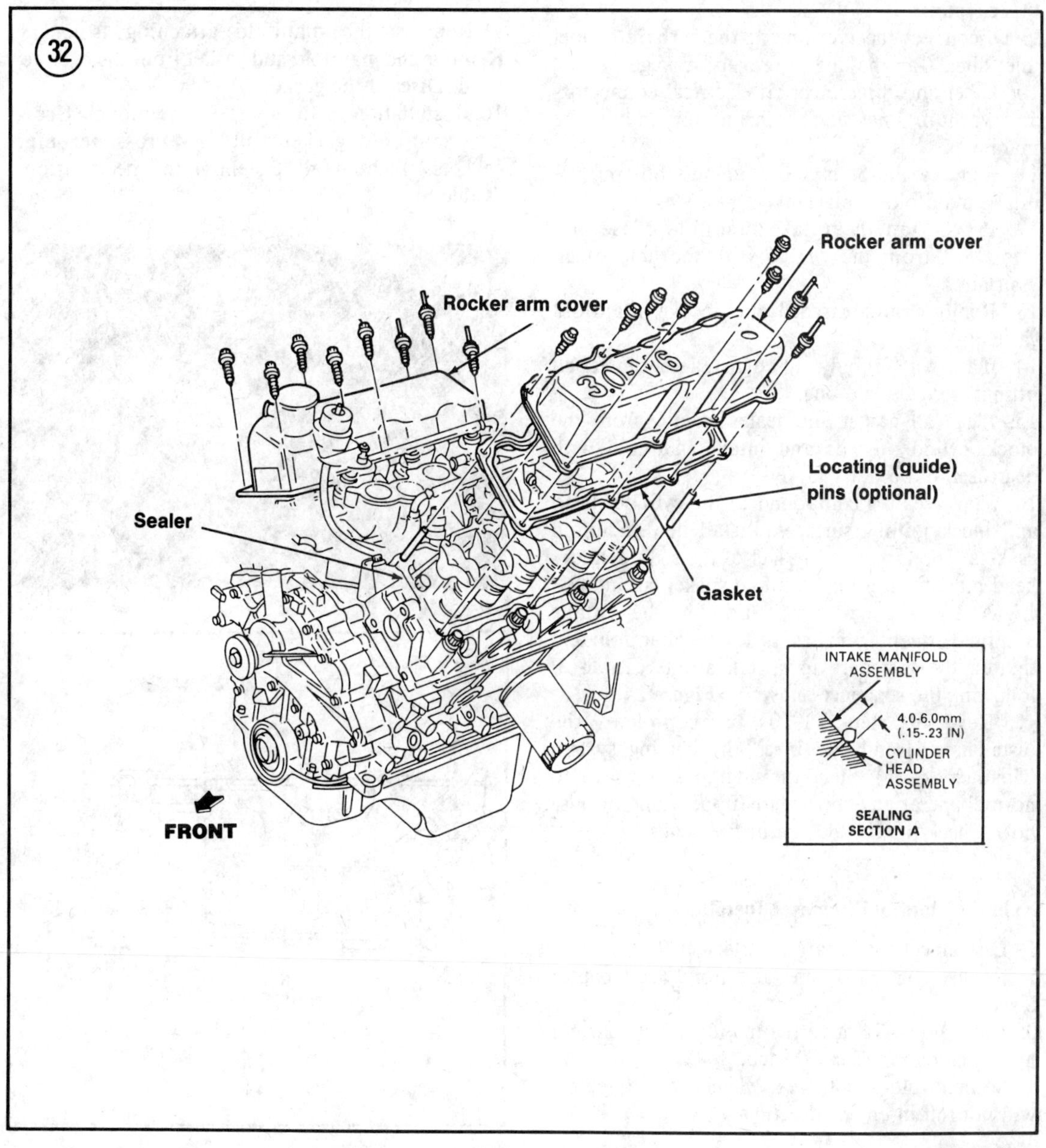

3. Remove the air cleaner assembly. See Chapter Six.
4. Disconnect the carburetor throttle cable. If equipped with an automatic transmission, disconnect the transmission kickdown rod. Unbolt and remove the throttle cable from the left cylinder head.
5. Unclamp and remove the upper radiator hose at the water outlet (**Figure 33**).
6. Unclamp and disconnect the bypass hose between the intake manifold and thermostat housing rear cover.
7. Remove the distributor. See Chapter Eight.
8. Remove the rocker arm covers as described in this chapter.
9. Disconnect the fuel line at the carburetor fuel inlet filter. Cap the line to prevent leakage.
10. Label and disconnect all electrical connectors and vacuum lines at the carburetor and intake manifold.
11. Remove the bolts and stud nuts holding the intake manifold in place.
12. Pry or tap the intake manifold loose and remove it from the engine with the help of an assistant.
13. Remove and discard the intake manifold gaskets.
14. If a new manifold is to be installed, transfer all fittings from the old one.
15. Clean all gasket and sealer residue from the block, cylinder heads and intake manifold with degreaser and a putty knife.
16. Apply sealing compound to the cylinder head and block joining surfaces. Install new manifold gaskets. The tab on the gasket of the right cylinder head must fit into the manifold gasket cutout.
17. Apply sealing compound on the intake manifold attaching bosses. Install the manifold and tighten the fasteners to specifications (**Table 3**) following the sequence shown in **Figure 34**.
18. Reverse Steps 1-10 to complete the installation. Refill and bleed the cooling system (Chapter Seven). Start the engine and warm to normal operating temperature (upper radiator hose hot). Check for coolant, oil or fuel leaks.

Exhaust Manifold Removal/Installation

1. Disconnect the negative battery cable.
2. Remove the air cleaner assembly. See Chapter Six.
3. Right side—Remove the manifold heat shroud nuts. Remove the heat shroud.
4. Securely block both rear wheels so the vehicle will not roll in either direction.
5. Raise the front of the vehicle with a jack and place it on jackstands.
6. Disconnect the crossover pipe at the exhaust manifold. See **Figure 35** (typical).
7. Unplug the exhaust gas oxygen sensor connector at the left manifold.
8. If equipped with a Thermactor system, remove the upstream crossover pipe and any other components that will interfere with manifold removal.

NOTE
You may find it easier to remove the jackstands and lower the vehicle to the ground to perform Step 9.

9. Remove the manifold attaching fasteners. Remove the manifold and gasket from the cylinder head. Discard the gasket.
10. Installation is the reverse of removal. Use a new manifold gasket and new crossover pipe gaskets. Tighten all fasteners to specifications (**Table 3**).

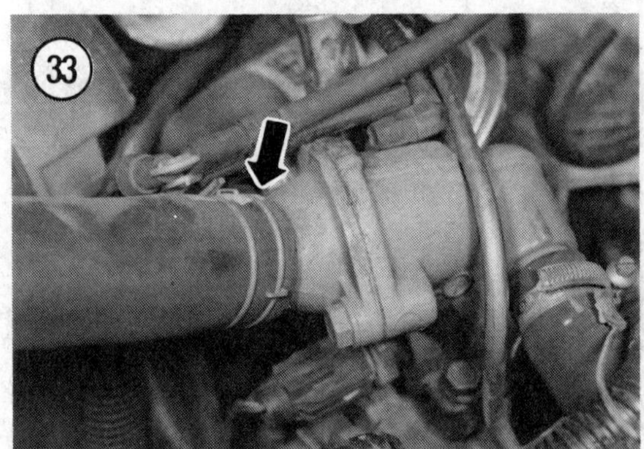

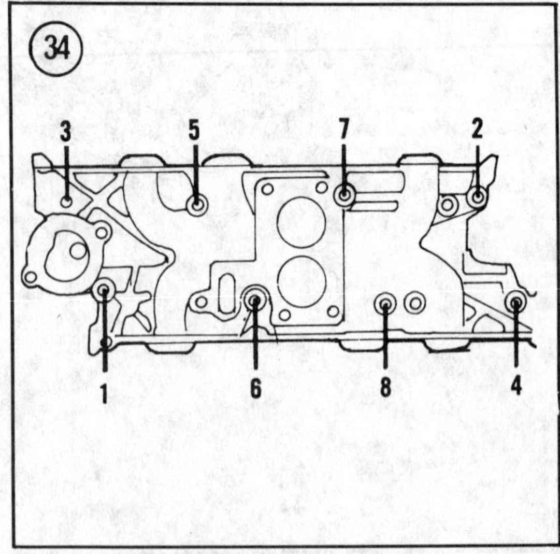

INTAKE AND EXHAUST MANIFOLDS (3.0L ENGINE)

Intake Manifold Removal/Installation

1. Remove the air intake throttle body. See *Multi-point Fuel Injection (3.0L EFI)* Chapter Six.
2. Remove the fuel injector wiring harness from the engine.
3. Unclamp and disconnect the upper radiator hose and water outlet heater hose at the intake manifold.
4. Remove the distributor. See Chapter Eight.
5. Remove the rocker arm covers as described in this chapter.

CAUTION
The head bolts are an external Torx-head design. Use the proper Torx driver in Step 6 to prevent damage to the bolt heads.

6. Unbolt and remove the intake manifold with the help of an assistant. If necessary, carefully pry the manifold from the cylinder heads and block rails.
7. Remove and discard the intake manifold side gaskets and end seals. Clean all RTV or gasket residue from the intake manifold and cylinder head mating surfaces with lacquer thinner.
8. If a new manifold is to be installed, transfer the thermostat housing, thermostat, all sending units and fittings from the old one. Use an electrically conductive sealer on sending unit threads. Coat a new thermostat housing gasket with Ford Perfect Seal (part No. B5A-19554-AZ) or equivalent water-resistant sealer.
9. Apply silicone rubber sealer part No. D6AZ-19562-A or equivalent to the joints where the cylinder block and head intersect. See **Figure 36**.
10. Install the front and rear manifold seals (**Figure 36**). Press their locating tabs into the holes in the block mating surface.

11. Install the manifold side gaskets (**Figure 37**). Interlock the gaskets with the seal tabs and align the gasket and cylinder head bolt holes and repeat Step 9.
12. Install a pair of suitable guide pins in the block to help position the manifold without smearing the sealer applied in Step 9 and Step 11 and creating a sealant void. Guide pins can be made by cutting the heads off a pair of spare intake manifold bolts, filing the rough edges and cutting screwdriver slots in the ends.
13. With the help of an assistant, carefully lower the intake manifold onto the cylinder block and cylinder heads. Check the front and rear seal alignment with a finger; if seals are not in position, remove the manifold and reposition the seals correctlv.
14. Remove the guide pins and install the manifold fasteners finger-tight. Tighten manifold fasteners to specifications (**Table 4**) following the sequence shown in **Figure 38**.
15. Reverse Step 1-5 to complete installation. Refill and bleed the cooling system (Chapter Seven). Start the engine and warm to normal operating temperature (upper radiator hose hot). Check for coolant, oil or fuel leaks.

5

Exhaust Manifold Removal/Installation

Left manifold

Refer to **Figure 39** for this procedure.

1. Disconnect the negative battery cable.
2. Unbolt and remove the dipstick tube bracket.
3. Disconnect the power steering pressure and return hoses, if so equipped. Plug the hoses and cap the pump fittings to prevent leakage and the entry of contaminants.
4. Securely block both rear wheels so the vehicle will not roll in either direction.
5. Raise the front of the vehicle with a jack and place it on jackstands.
6. Disconnect the crossover pipe at the exhaust manifold. See **Figure 35** (typical).

NOTE
You may find it easier to remove the jackstands and lower the vehicle to the ground to perform Step 7.

7. Unbolt and remove the exhaust manifold.
8. Clean the mating surfaces on the manifold, exhaust crossover pipe and cylinder head.
9. Installation is the reverse of removal. Lightly lubricate bolt and stud threads with engine oil before installing manifold. Tighten all fasteners to specifications (**Table 4**).

Right manifold

Refer to **Figure 40** for this procedure.

1. Disconnect the negative battery cable.
2. Drain the cooling system. See Chapter Seven.
3. Unbolt and remove the heater hose support bracket.
4. Unclamp and disconnect the heater hoses.
5. Securely block both rear wheels so the vehicle will not roll in either direction.
6. Raise the front of the vehicle with a jack and place it on jackstands.
7. Disconnect the crossover pipe at the exhaust manifold. See **Figure 35** (typical).

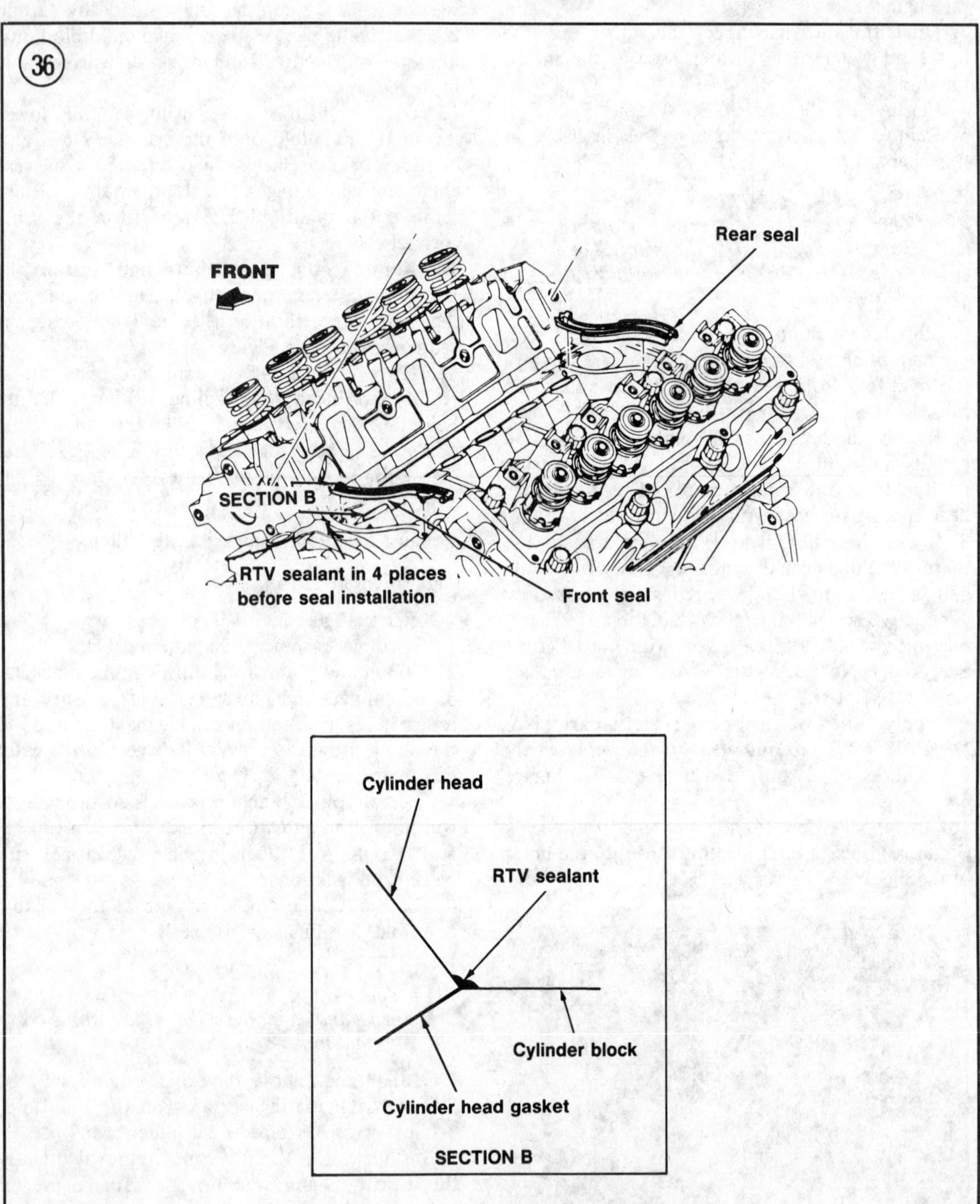

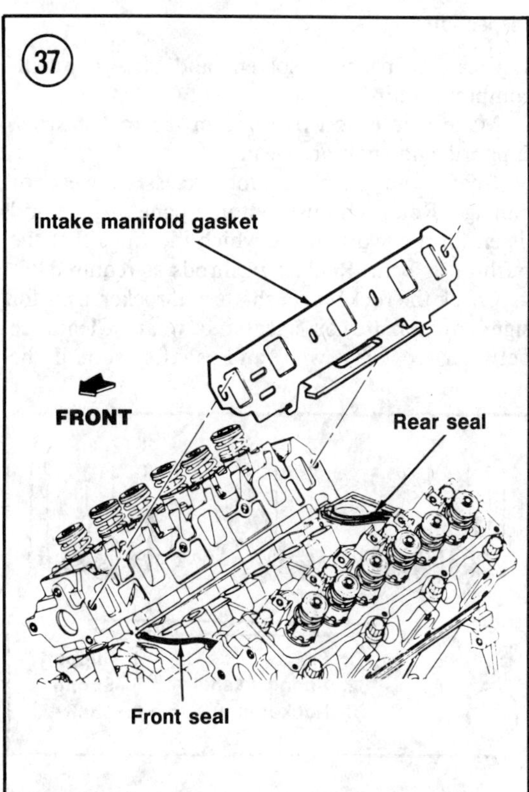

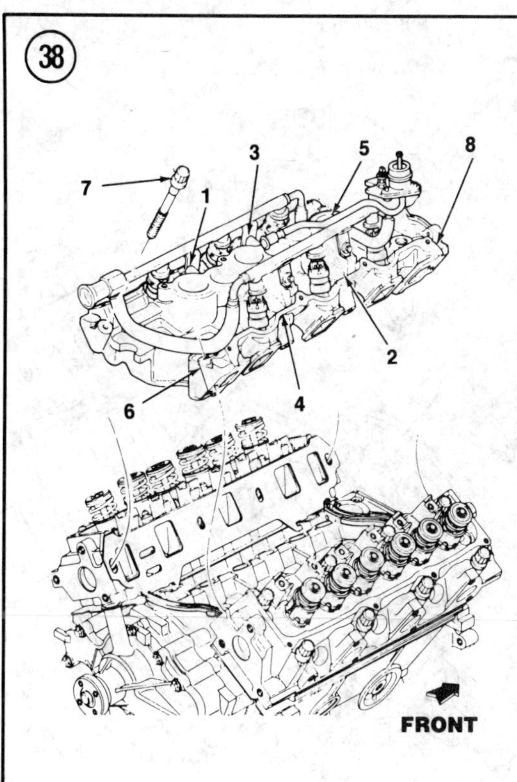

NOTE
You may find it easier to remove the jackstands and lower the vehicle to the ground to perform Step 8.

8. Unbolt and remove the exhaust manifold.
9. Clean the mating surfaces on the manifold, exhaust crossover pipe and cylinder head.
10. Installation is the reverse of removal. Lightly lubricate all bolt and stud threads with engine oil before installing manifold. Tighten all fasteners to specifications (**Table 4**). Refill and bleed the cooling system (Chapter Seven).

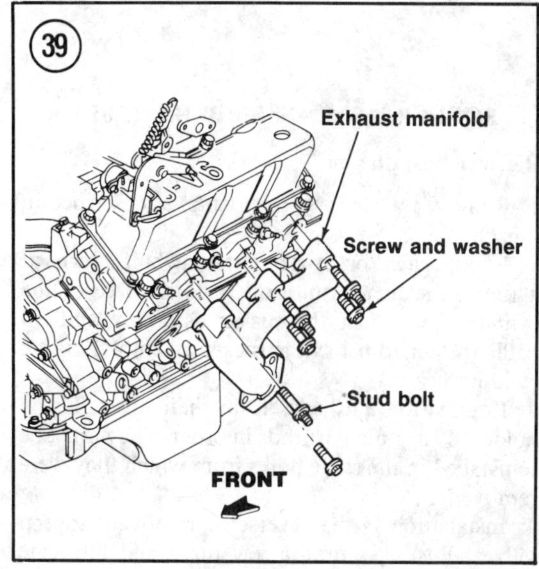

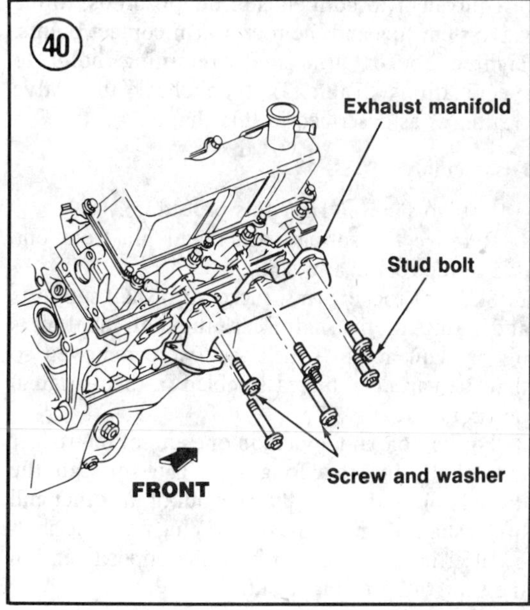

5

MANIFOLD INSPECTION

Intake and Exhaust Manifolds

1. Check the intake and exhaust manifolds for cracks or distortion. Replace as required.
2. Check the sealing surfaces for nicks or burrs. Small burrs may be removed with an oilstone.
3. Place a straightedge across the mainfold sealing surfaces and measure any gap between the straightedge and sealing surface with a flat feeler gauge. Measure from end to end and diagonally. If the sealing surface is not flat within 0.006 in. (0.15 mm) per foot of manifold length, replace the manifold.

ROCKER ARM ASSEMBLIES (2.8L)

Removal/Installation

1. Remove the rocker arm cover(s) as described in this chapter.
2. Loosen each rocker arm retaining bolt 2 turns at a time in sequence until all bolts are free of the cylinder head. Lift the rocker assembly and oil baffle (mounted below the rocker assembly) off the cylinder head.
3. Remove the pushrods from their bores. Use a holder to keep the pushrods in order. They must be reinstalled in the same bores from which they were removed.
4. Installation is the reverse of removal. Loosen valve adjusting screws a few turns and lubricate entire assembly with engine oil. Apply Lubriplate or equivalent to both ends of the pushrods, to the valve stem tips and the rocker arm contact points. Tighten rocker arm shaft retaining bolts to specifications (**Table 3**), then check the valve clearances as described in this chapter.

Disassembly

Refer to **Figure 41** for this procedure.

1. Remove the spring washer and pin from one end of the rocker arm shaft.
2. Slide the rocker arms, rocker arm shaft supports and springs off the shaft. Mark the individual parts in the sequence in which they were removed so that the parts can be reassembled in their original positions.
3. Drill a hole in the plug in one end of the rocker arm shaft. Insert a long steel rod through the drilled hole and knock the plug out of the other end of the shaft. Remove the drilled plug from the shaft by inserting the steel rod from the opposite end of the shaft and driving it out.

Inspection

1. Clean all parts in solvent and blow dry with compressed air.
2. Make sure all oil passages in the rocker arms, supports and shaft are clean.
3. Check the pushrods for excessive wear or damage. Roll each pushrod on a pane of glass and listen for a clicking noise which indicates that the pushrod is bent. Replace pushrods as required.
4. Check the rocker arm shafts and rocker arms for signs of seizure or excessive wear. Clearance between rocker arms and shafts should be

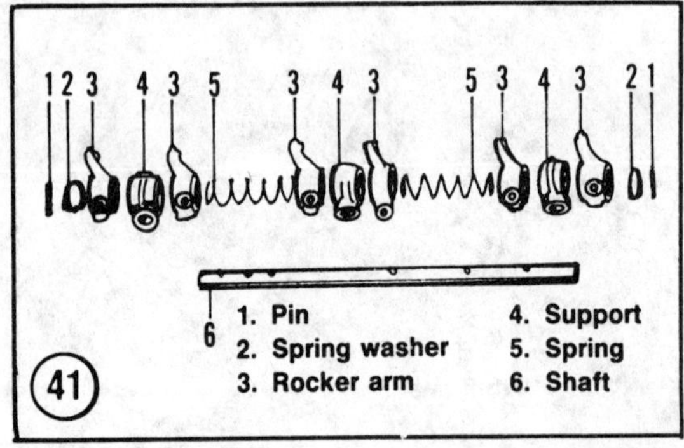

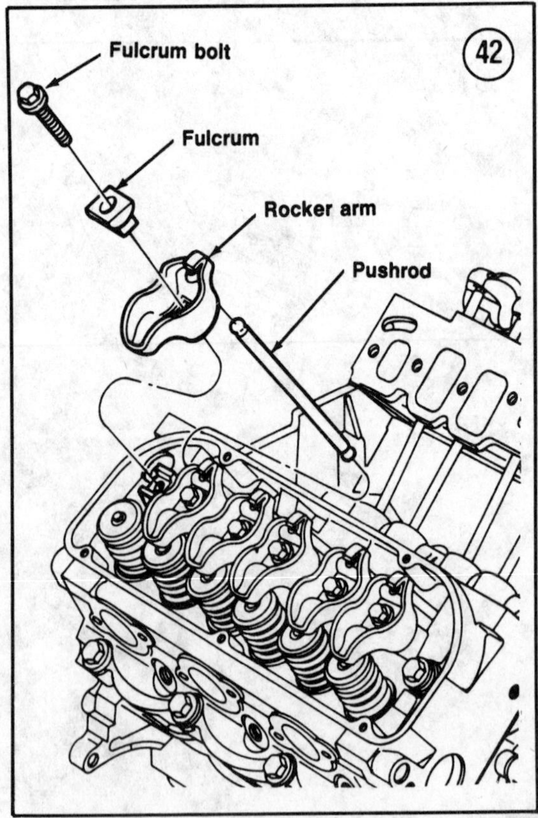

0.001-0.0035 in. Maximum permissible clearance is 0.006 in. as measured with a flat feeler gauge.
5. Check valve stem contact surfaces on each rocker arm for wear. Replace worn rocker arms. Do not try to smooth rocker arm bores or contact surfaces.

Assembly

Refer to **Figure 41** for this procedure.
1. Tap new plugs into the ends of the rocker arm shaft.
2. Lubricate all parts with clean engine oil.
3. Position the rocker arm shaft with the notch on the front face of the shaft pointing downward.
4. Install a spring washer and pin in one end of the rocker arm shaft, then install the rocker arms, supports and springs in their original positions.
5. Install the pin and spring washer in the opposite end of the rocker shaft.
6. Lubricate each rocker arm pad with Lubriplate.

ROCKER ARM ASSEMBLIES (3.0L)

The 3.0L V6 uses individual rocker arms which move on their own fulcrum seats. It is not necessary to remove individual rocker arms for pushrod replacement. Simply loosen the fulcrum bolt and move the arm away from the pushrod.

Removal/Installation

Refer to **Figure 42** and use the following procedure for complete rocker arm service.
1. Remove the rocker arm cover(s) as described in this chapter.
2. Remove the fulcrum bolt, fulcrum seat and rocker arm from each valve.
3. Remove the pushrods, if necessary.

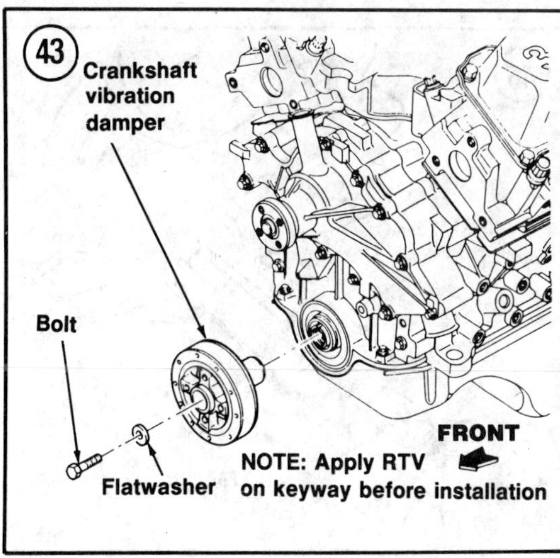

4. Place each rocker arm and pushrod set in a separate container or use a rack to keep them separated for reinstallation in the same position from which they were removed.
5. Installation is the reverse of removal. Wipe the tip of each valve stem, the cylinder head pushrod guide, each rocker arm fulcrum seat and seat socket with polyethylene grease (Ford part No. D0AZ-19584-A) or equivalent. Tighten each fulcrum bolt to specifications (**Table 4**). If valve train components have been replaced, check the valve clearance as described in this chapter.

Inspection

1. Clean all parts with solvent and use compressed air to blow out the oil passages in the pushrods.
2. Check each rocker arm, fulcrum seat and pushrod for scuffing, pitting or excessive wear.
3. Check pushrods for straightness by rolling them across a flat, even surface such as a pane of glass. Replace pushrods that do not roll smoothly.

CRANKSHAFT PULLEY AND DAMPER

Removal/Installation (2.8L V6)

1. Remove the alternator drive belt.
2. Remove the crankshaft pulley attaching bolts. Remove the pulley.
3. Remove the vibration damper bolt. Remove the damper with a suitable puller.
4. Installation is the reverse of removal. Tighten all fasteners to specifications (**Table 3**).

Removal/Installation (3.0L V6)

Refer to **Figure 43** for this procedure.
1. Loosen the accessory drive belts (Chapter Seven).
2. Loosen the right front wheel lug nuts. Raise the vehicle with a jack and place it on jackstands. Remove the right front wheel/tire assembly.
3. Working through the wheel well, remove the 4 pulley attaching bolts. Disengage the drive belt from the pulley and remove the pulley.
4. Remove the vibration damper bolt. Remove the damper with damper remover part No. T58P-6316-D and adapter part No. T82L-6316-B or equivalent.
5. Installation is the reverse of removal. Coat crankshaft damper sealing surface with clean engine oil. Apply RTV sealant to the crankshaft keyway before reinstalling the damper with tool part No. T82L-6316-A. Tighten all fasteners to specifications (**Table 4**).

FRONT COVER AND TIMING GEARS (2.8L V6)

Front Cover Removal/Installation

1. Remove the oil pan as described in this chapter.
2. Drain the cooling system. See Chapter Seven.

WARNING
The air conditioning system contains pressurized refrigerant which can cause frostbite if it touches skin and blindness if it touches the eyes. If discharged near an open flame, the refrigerant forms poisonous gas. Never disconnect air conditioning system lines unless the system has been discharged and evacuated by a professional.

3. On air conditioned models, remove the compressor and mounting bracket without disconnecting any refrigerant lines. Move compressor out of the way.
4. If equipped with power steering, remove the power steering pump and mounting bracket without disconnecting any hydraulic lines. Move the pump and bracket to one side out of the way.
5. Remove the alternator and Thermactor pump.
6. Remove the fan from the fan clutch assembly.
7. Remove the water pump. See Chapter Seven.
8. Remove the crankshaft pulley as described in this chapter.
9. Remove the front cover bolts. Tap cover lightly with a plastic mallet to break the gasket seal. Remove the cover.
10. Remove the 2 front cover plate screws (**Figure 44**). Remove the front cover plate and gasket.
11. Remove the 2 guide sleeves from the block (**Figure 45**). Remove and discard the O-ring on each sleeve.
12. Clean the block, cover plate and cover mating surfaces of all gasket and sealant residue.
13. Apply sealing compound to the mating surfaces on the block and rear of the cover plate.
14. Install guide sleeves with new O-rings. Chamfered end of sleeve must face front cover.
15. Position a new gasket and the cover plate on the block. Temporarily install 4 front cover screws to hold the gasket and plate in place.
16. Install and tighten the cover plate screws, then remove the 4 cover screws installed in Step 15.
17. Coat the front cover gasket surface with sealing compound and position a new gasket on the front cover.
18. Install front cover to block. Start all cover screws and then insert cover aligning tool part No. T74P-6019-A or equivalent in oil seal. Tighten cover screws to specifications (**Table 3**).
19. Reverse Steps 1-8 to complete installation. Fill and bleed the cooling system (Chapter Seven). Start the engine and run at fast idle to check for coolant and oil leaks.

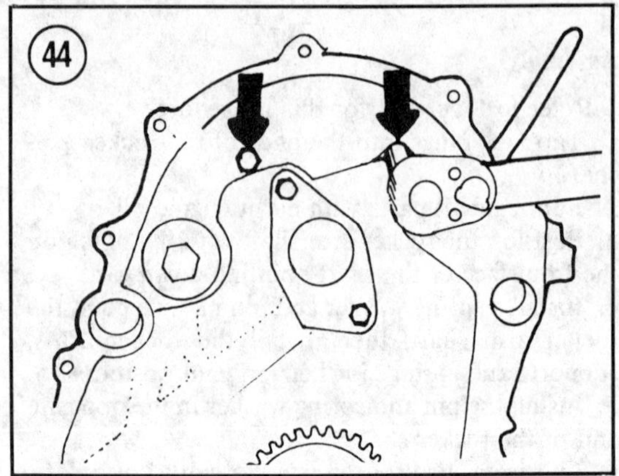

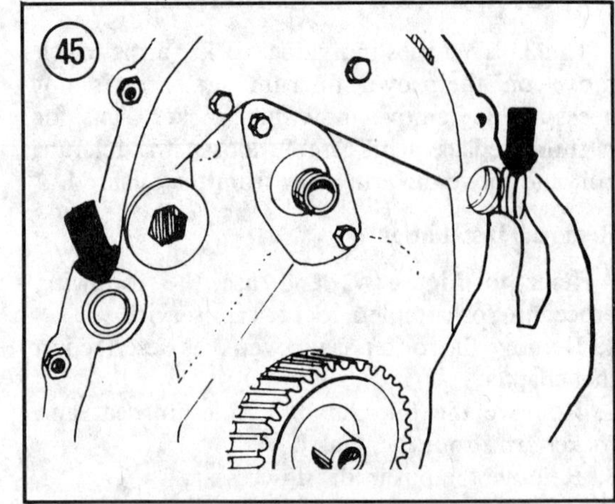

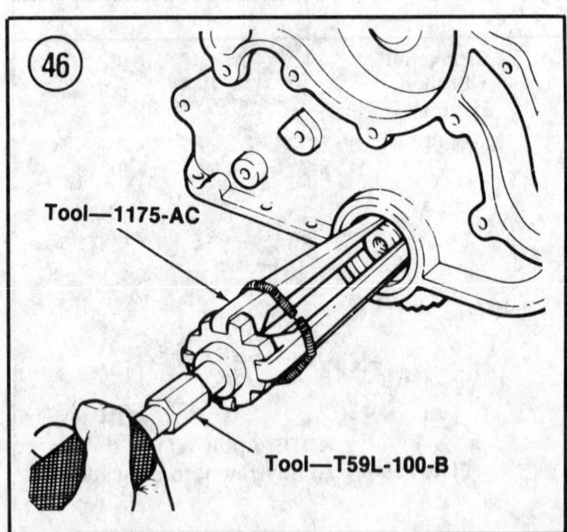

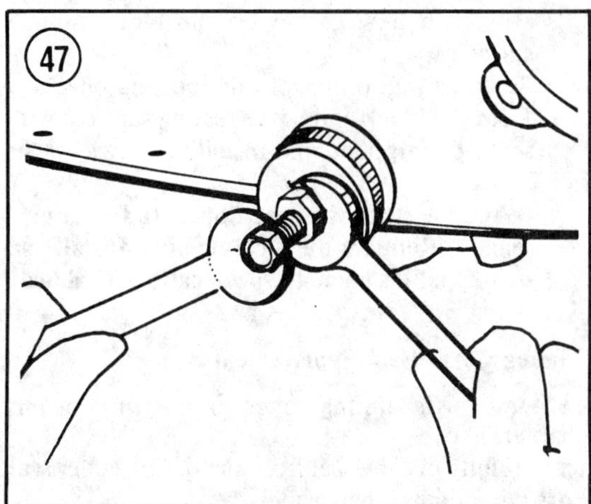

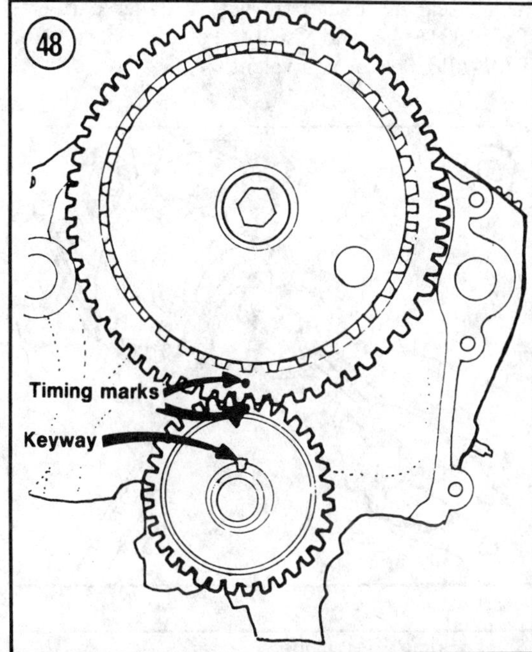

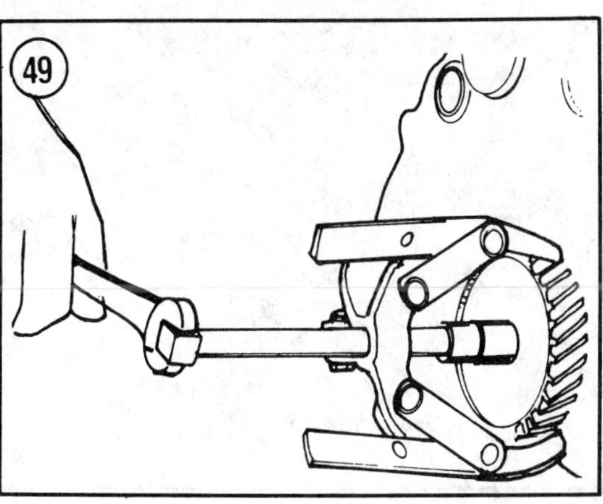

Front Cover Seal Replacement (In-vehicle Replacement)

1. Drain the cooling system and remove the radiator. See Chapter Seven.
2. Remove the crankshaft pulley as described in this chapter.
3. Remove the front cover seal with seal remover part No. 1175-AC and a suitable slide hammer. See **Figure 46**.
4. Wipe the outer diameter of a new seal with Lubriplate or equivalent.
5. Position new seal in cover recess and install with seal installer part No. T74P-6700-A. See **Figure 47**.

Front Cover Seal Replacement (Front Cover Removed)

1. Support the front cover to prevent cover damage.
2. Drive old seal out with front cover aligning tool part No. T74P-6019-A or equivalent.
3. Wipe the outer diameter of a new seal with Lubriplate or equivalent.
4. Position new seal in cover recess and install with aligning tool part No. T74P-6019-A or equivalent.

Timing Gear Removal

1. Remove the front cover as described in this chapter.
2. Check the camshaft end play as described in this chapter. Replace the thrust plate and spacer rings, if necessary, to obtain the proper end play. See **Table 1**.
3. Temporarily install the crankshaft damper bolt and rotate the crankshaft until the timing gear marks are aligned. See **Figure 48**. Remove the damper bolt.
4. Remove the camshaft sprocket retaining bolt and washer, then slide the sprocket off the camshaft and remove the camshaft key.
5. Remove the crankshaft gear with a puller as shown in **Figure 49**. Remove the crankshaft key.

Timing Gear Installation

1. Install the camshaft key. Align the camshaft sprocket keyway with the camshaft key and slide the sprocket onto the camshaft until it seats tightly against the camshaft spacer.
2. Install the crankshaft key. Align the crankshaft sprocket keyway with the crankshaft key and

position the sprocket on the crankshaft. The timing marks should align as shown in **Figure 48**.
3. Install a suitable gear or sprocket installer and draw the crankshaft gear into place (**Figure 50**).
4. Install the front cover as described in this chapter.

TIMING COVER, SEAL, SPROCKETS AND TIMING CHAIN (3.0L V6)

Timing Cover Removal/Installation

Refer to **Figure 51** for this procedure.
1. Remove the idler pulley and bracket assembly as shown in **Figure 52**.
2. Remove the drive and accessory belts.
3. Remove the crankshaft pulley and damper as described in this chapter.
4. Disconnect the lower radiator hose at the water pump.
5. Remove the oil pan-to-timing cover bolts.
6. Unbolt and remove the front cover.
7. Installation is the reverse of removal, plus the following:
   a. Carefully cut out and remove the exposed part of the oil pan gasket. Use this portion as a template to cut a similar part from a new oil pan gasket.
   b. Coat the gasket surface of the oil pan with sealing compound part No. B5A-19554-A or equivalent.
   c. Position the cut portion of the new oil pan gasket on the pan sealing surface. Apply sealing compound to the corners where the new part of the gasket mates with the old gasket.
   d. Install a new gasket on the block mating surface.
   e. Install a seal protector and locating pins.
   f. Coat the block and cover sealing surfaces with sealing compound and install the cover on the block.
   g. Wipe the threads of the upper stud with pipe sealant. Remove the locating pins. Install and tighten all fasteners to specifications (**Table 4**).

Timing Cover Seal Replacement

1. Remove the timing cover as described in this chapter.
2. Carefully pry the seal from the timing cover seal bore with a small flat-blade screwdriver.
3. Wipe the lip of a new seal with clean engine oil. Install seal in cover bore with installer part No. T82L-6316-A and seal replacer part No. T70P-6B070-A or equivalent.

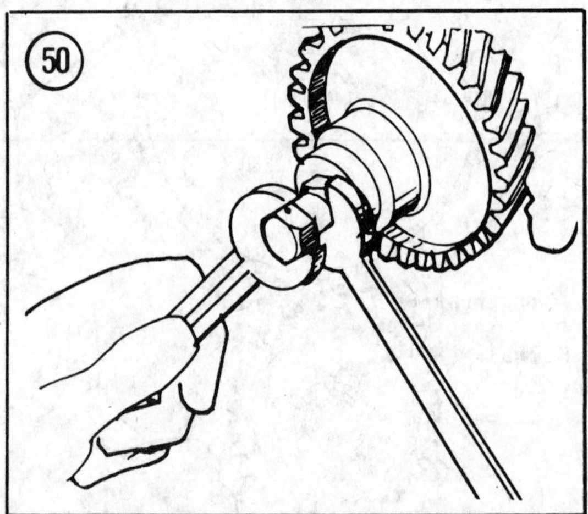

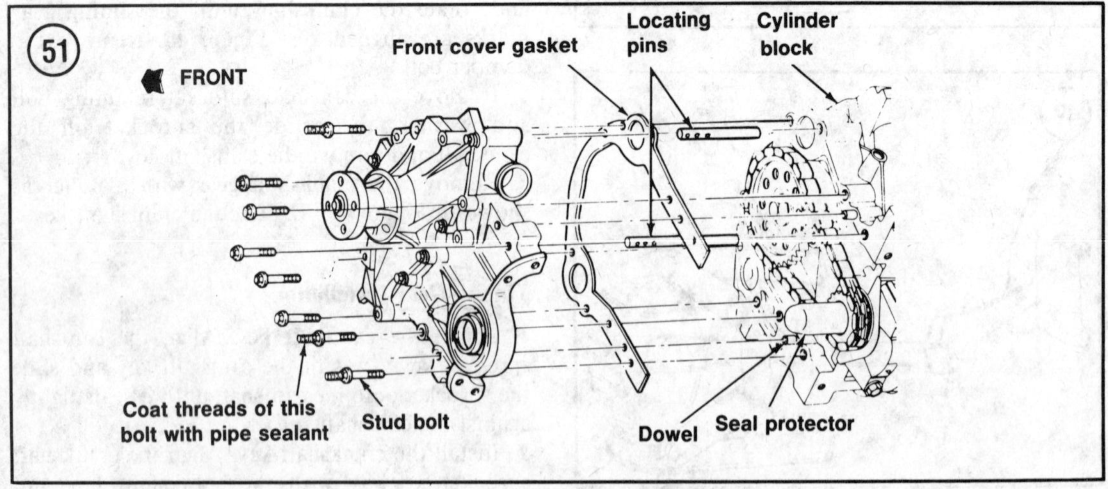

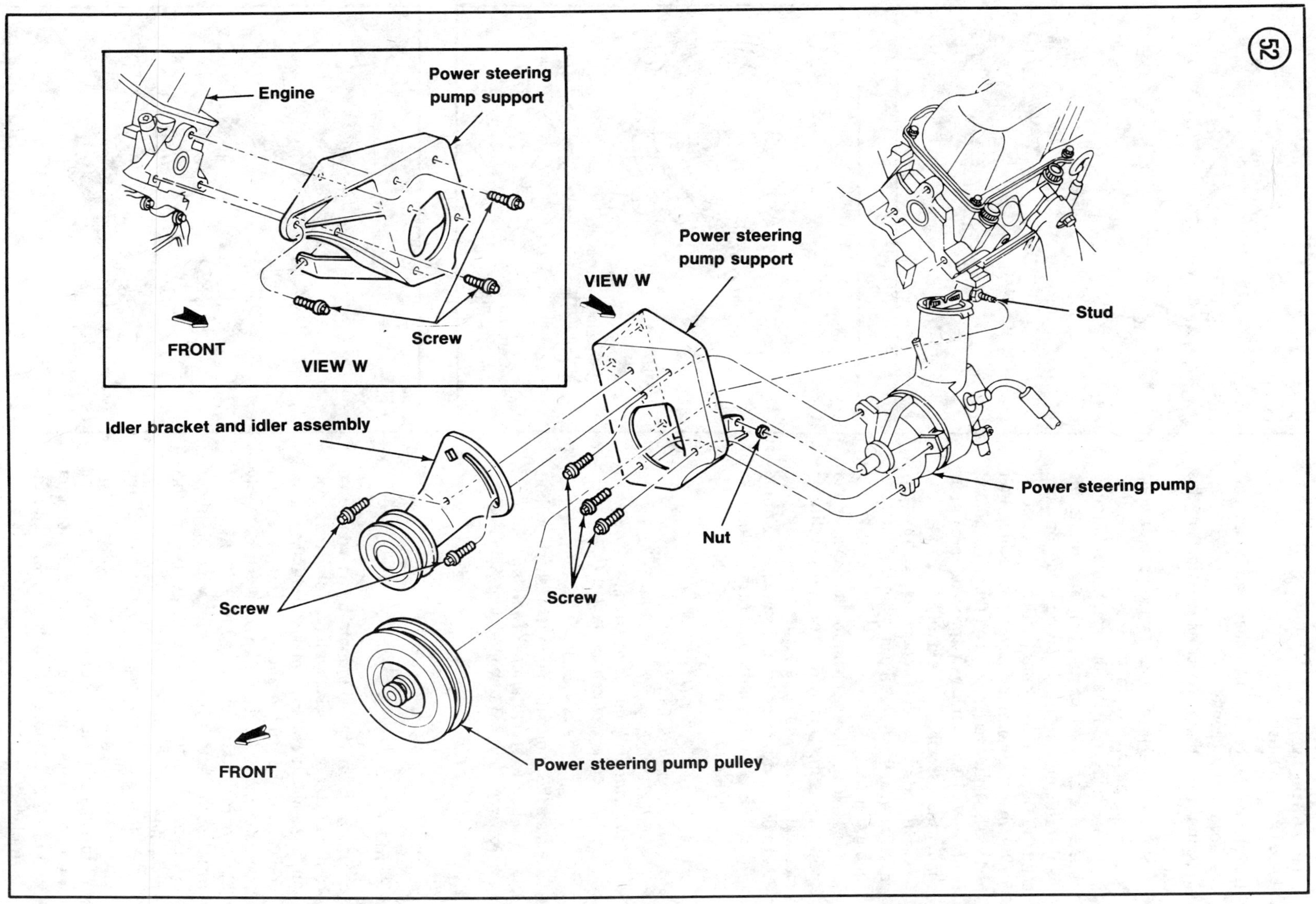
52
Engine
Power steering pump support
FRONT
VIEW W
Screw
Power steering pump support
VIEW W
Stud
Idler bracket and idler assembly
Power steering pump
Nut
Screw
Screw
FRONT
Power steering pump pulley

5

Timing Chain and Sprocket Removal/Installation

1. Remove the crankshaft pulley and damper as described in this chapter.
2. Remove the timing cover as described in this chapter.
3. Stuff a clean shop cloth into the oil pan opening to prevent the entry of contaminants.
4. Temporarily reinstall the crankshaft damper bolt. Place a socket on the bolt and rotate the crankshaft until the No. 1 piston is at top dead center (TDC) and the timing marks are aligned.
5. Remove the camshaft sprocket attaching bolt and washer. Slide the sprocket off the camshaft and remove with the crankshaft sprocket and timing chain as an assembly. See **Figure 53**.
6. Clean and check all components. Remove any gasket residue from the oil pan, cylinder block and timing cover.
7. Assemble the timing chain to the camshaft and crankshaft sprockets with the sprocket timing marks aligned as shown in **Figure 54**.
8. Install the timing chain and sprocket assembly to the camshaft and crankshaft. Recheck to make sure the timing marks are properly aligned.

NOTE
The camshaft sprocket bolt contains a drilled passage for timing chain lubrication. If bolt is replaced, be sure to install a replacement bolt with the drilled passage.

9. Install the camshaft sprocket washer and bolt. Tighten bolt to specifications (**Table 4**).
10. Reverse Steps 1-3 to complete installation.

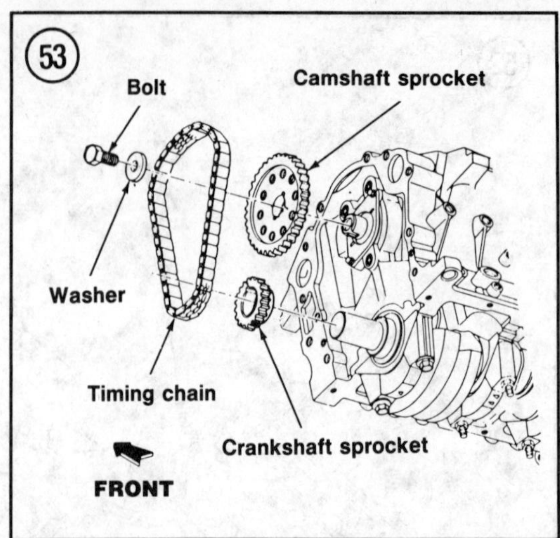

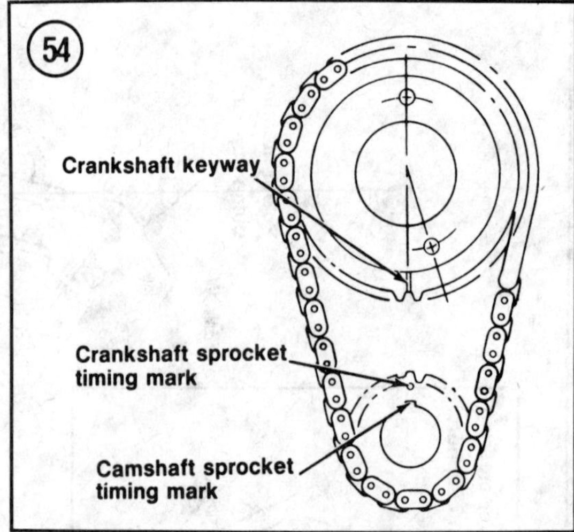

CAMSHAFT

End Play

Prying against the aluminum-nylon composite camshaft gear or sprocket with the valve train load on the camshaft can result in damage to the gear or sprocket. If the valve train is installed when end play is checked, loosen the rocker shaft assembly (2.8L) or rocker arm fulcrum bolts (3.0L) enough to free the camshaft, then readjust the valve clearance as described in this chapter after performing this procedure.

1. Push the camshaft as far to the rear of the engine as it will go.
2. Install a dial indicator on the front of the engine with its plunger touching the camshaft sprocket bolt or washer. **Figure 55** shows the 2.8L; the 3.0L is similar.

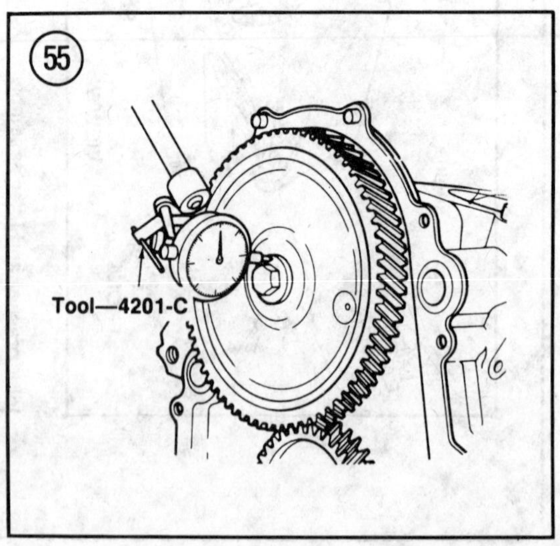

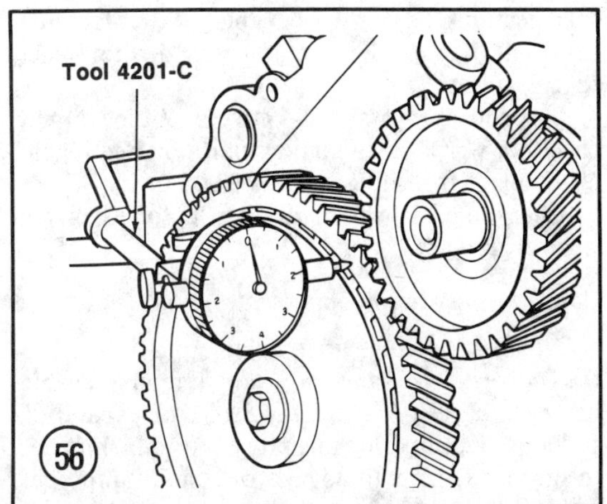

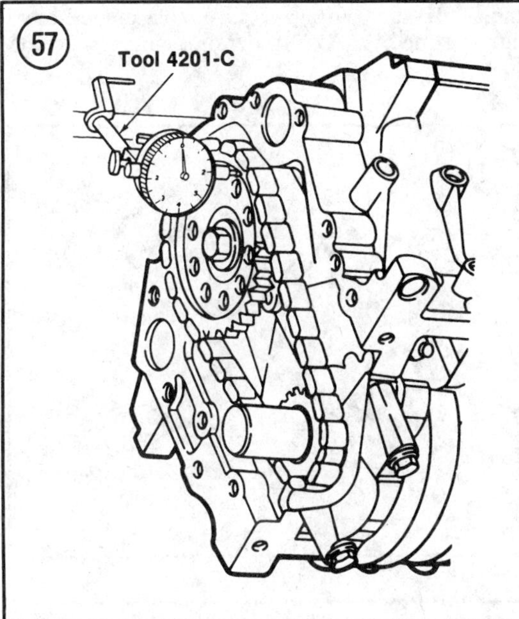

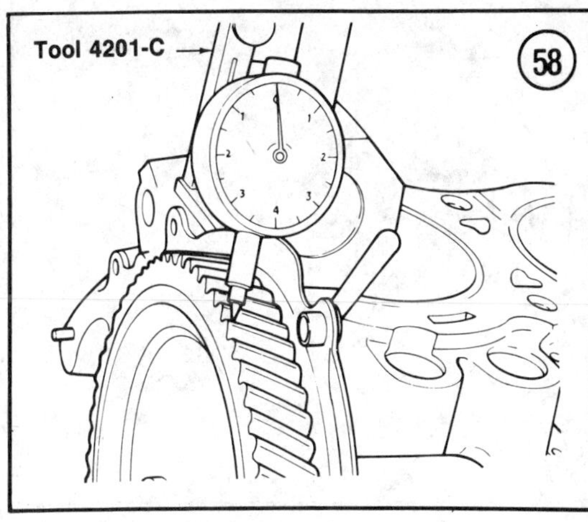

3. Set the indicator gauge at zero and pry the camshaft as far forward as possible with a large screwdriver, then release it.

4. Compare the dial indicator reading with specifications (**Table 1**). If the reading exceeds specifications, replace the camshaft thrust plate and spacer.

Timing Gear or Sprocket Runout

1. Install a dial indicator on the front of the engine with its plunger touching the camshaft gear or sprocket as shown in **Figure 56** (2.8L) or **Figure 57** (3.0L).
2. Hold the camshaft gear or sprocket against the thrust plate and set the dial indicator to zero.
3. Rotate the crankshaft through one complete revolution of the camshaft while holding the camshaft gear against the thrust plate.
4. If camshaft gear reading exceeds 0.005 in., check for burrs or contamination on or between the camshaft and gear pilot diameter or the mating flanges, then recheck the runout.
5. If reading still exceeds specifications, replace the timing gear.

Timing Gear Backlash (2.8L)

1. Install a dial indicator on the front of the engine with its plunger touching the camshaft sprocket as shown in **Figure 58**.
2. Rotate the camshaft gear against the dial indicator pointer as far as possible without turning the crankshaft gear.
3. If gear teeth backlash exceeds 0.004-0.010 in., replace the camshaft and crankshaft gears.

Camshaft Removal/Installation

2.8L engine

1. Remove the rocker arm covers, rocker arm assemblies, intake manifold and front cover as described in this chapter.
2. Check camshaft end play as described in this chapter.

NOTE
If the tappets are stuck in their bores, use tool part No. T52T-6500-DJD or T52T-6500-D to rotate the tappet back and forth. This will break the varnish or gum seal that is holding the tappet in place and allow its removal.

3. Remove the valve tappets with a pencil-type magnet. Place them in a rack in order of removal for reinstallation in their original location.
4. Remove the oil pump, fuel pump and distributor.

5. Remove the camshaft thrust plate and spacer.
6. Carefully withdraw the camshaft from the front of the engine with a rotating motion to avoid damage to the bearings.
7. Installation is the reverse of removal. Coat the camshaft with heavy engine oil before reinstalling in the block. Check end play as described in this chapter before tightening the rocker arms in place. Check valve clearance as described in this chapter.

3.0L engine

1. Remove the engine from the vehicle as described in this chapter.
2. Remove the timing cover and intake manifold as described in this chapter.

NOTE
If the tappets are stuck in their bores, use tool part No. T70L-6500-A or equivalent to rotate the tappet back and forth. This will break the varnish or gum seal that is holding the tappet in place and allow its removal.

3. Remove the valve tappets with a pencil-type magnet. Place them in a rack in order of removal for reinstallation in their original location.
4. Check camshaft end play as described in this chapter.
5. Remove the oil pump and distributor.
6. Remove the timing chain and sprockets as described in this chapter.
7. Remove the camshaft thrust plate and spacer.
8. Carefully withdraw the camshaft from the front of the engine with a rotating motion to avoid damage to the bearings.
9. Installation is the reverse of removal. Coat the camshaft with heavy engine oil before reinstalling in the block. Check end play as described in this chapter before tightening the rocker arms in place. Check valve clearance as described in this chapter.

Inspection

1. Check the journals and lobes for signs of wear or scoring. Lobe pitting in the toe area is not sufficient reason for replacement, unless the lobe lift loss is excessive.
2. Check each valve tappet for signs of wear, pitting or scoring. Replace as required.

NOTE
If you do not have precision measuring equipment, have Step 3 and Step 4 done by a machine shop.

3. Measure the camshaft journal diameters with a micrometer (**Figure 59**) and compare to specifications (**Table 1** or **Table 2**). Replace the camshaft if one or more journals do not meet specifications.
4. Suspend the camshaft between V-blocks and check for warpage with a dial indicator. See **Figure 60**. Replace if reading exceeds 0.005 in.
5. Check the distributor drive gear for excessive wear or damage.

Camshaft Bearing Replacement

Camshaft bearings are available pre-finished to the correct size and are not interchangeable between bores. A special puller and expanding collet are required for this procedure, which is not recommended for the owner/mechanic. Improper use of the special tools or use of the wrong expanding collet can result in severe bearing damage. If the bearings require replacement, have the job done by a Ford dealer or qualified machine shop.

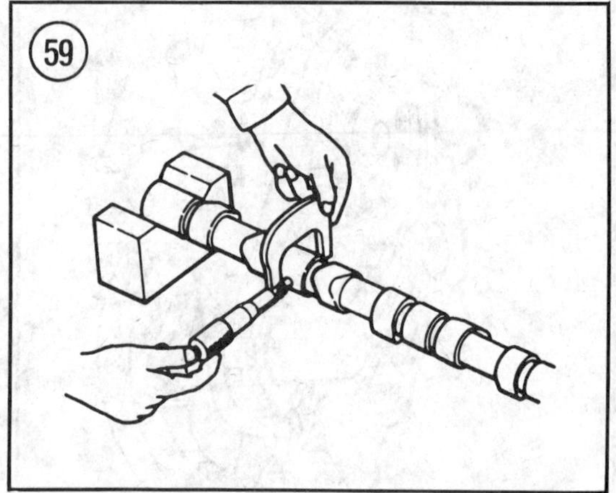

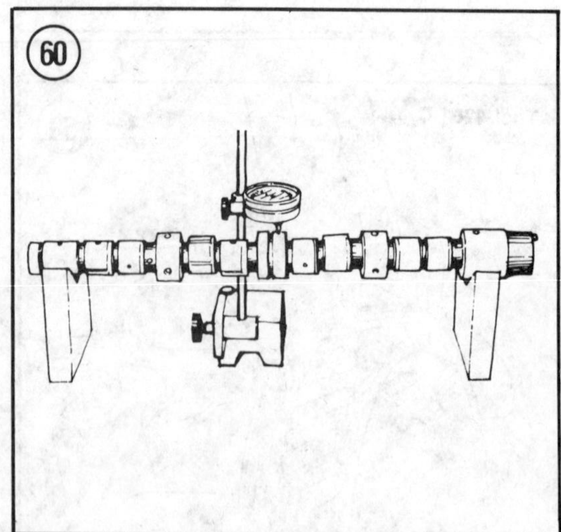

Camshaft Rear Bearing Bore Plug Removal/Installation

If the engine is removed from the vehicle, replacement of the camshaft rear bearing bore plug is accomplished by drilling a small hole in the plug, inserting a screwdriver or pin punch and prying the plug from the engine block. If the engine is installed in the vehicle, the following procedure should be used.

1. Remove the transmission. See Chapter Nine.
2. Remove the clutch components (manual transmission) or torque converter (automatic transmission) and housing. See Chapter Nine.
3. Remove the flywheel as described in this chapter.
4. Remove the engine rear cover plate, then remove the bore plug as described above.
5. Installation is the reverse of removal. Install the bore plug with a hollow drift of suitable diameter. See **Figure 61**.

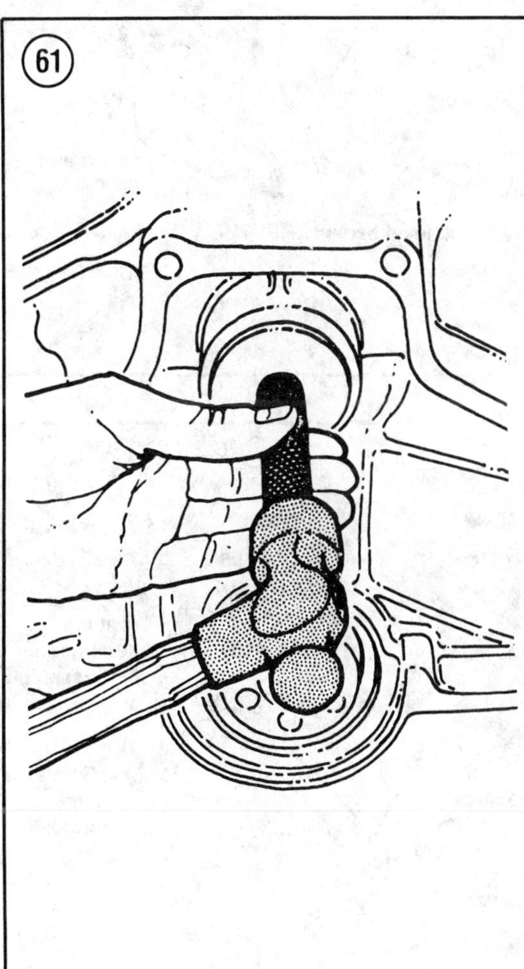

OIL PAN

Removal

1. Disconnect the negative battery cable.
2. 3.0L—Unbolt and remove the crankcase dipstick tube.
3. Securely block both rear wheels so the vehicle will not roll in either direction.
4. Raise the front of the vehicle with a jack and place it on jackstands.
5. Remove the starter motor. See Chapter Eight.
6. Drain the crankcase. See Chapter Three. If equipped with a low-oil level sensor, unplug the sensor connector.
7. 2.8L—Remove the nuts holding the front engine mounts to the crossmember. Position a floor jack with wooden block under the oil pan. Raise the engine enough to insert wooden blocks between the engine mount insulators and the No. 2 crossmember, then lower the engine onto the block and remove the jack.
8. 3.0L—Remove the lower engine/flywheel dust cover from the torque converter housing. Loosen the transmission attaching bolts and carefully pry the transmission to the rear 1/4 in.
9. Remove the oil pan attaching bolts. Lower the oil pan and remove from under the vehicle.
10. Remove and discard the oil pan gasket (3.0L) or 2-piece gasket with front and rear seals (2.8L).

Inspection

1. Remove all gasket residue from the oil pan flanges and crankcase side rails with degreaser and a putty knife.
2. Clean the pan thoroughly in solvent.
3. Check the pan for cracks, pinholes or damaged drain plug threads.
4. Check the pan for dents or warped gasket surfaces. Straighten or replace the oil pan as required.

Installation (2.8L V6)

1. Coat the block side rails with an oil-resistant sealer and position the 2 side gaskets on the oil pan flanges.
2. Install the front and rear seals on the block.
3. Carefully place the oil pan in position, make sure the gaskets and seals are not misaligned and install a pan attaching bolt finger-tight on each side of the block.
4. Install the remaining bolts and tighten all to specifications (**Table 3**). Work from the center outward in both directions.

Installation (3.0L V6)

Refer to **Figure 62** for this procedure.

1. Run a 1/5 in. bead of silicone sealer part No. D6AZ-19562-A or equivalent at the junction of the rear main bearing cap and cylinder block. Run another similar bead at the junction of the timing cover and cylinder block.
2. Fit a new oil pan gasket in the oil pan and hold in place with gasket and seat contact adhesive part No. D7AZ-19B508-A or equivalent.
3. Carefully place the oil pan in position and install a pan attaching bolt with washer finger-tight on each side of the block.
4. Install the remaining bolts with washers and tighten all to specifications **(Table 4)**. Work from the center outward in both directions.

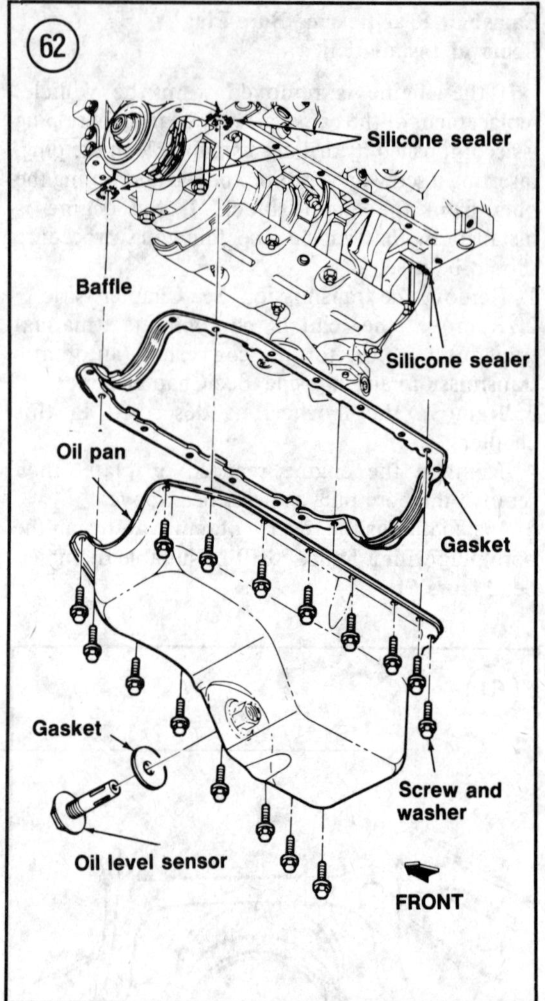

OIL PUMP

The oil pump is attached to the rear main bearing cap and is serviced as an assembly. The pump can be disassembled and clearances measured but if any component requires replacement, the pump is discarded and a new one installed.

Removal/Installation

Refer to **Figure 63** (typical) for this procedure.

1. Remove the oil pan as described in this chapter.
2. 3.0L—Unbolt and remove the baffle **(Figure 62)**.
3. 2.8L—Remove the fastener holding the inlet tube assembly and oil pickup screen to the block.
4. Remove the fasteners holding the oil pump to the block. Remove the oil pump.
5. Remove the oil pump intermediate shaft from the block.
6. Before reinstalling the pump, fill it with engine oil and rotate the pump intermediate shaft to distributor oil throughout the pump.
7. Install the pump intermediate shaft in the engine block until firmly seated.
8. Install the oil pump to the block and tighten the fasteners to specifications **(Table 3** or **Table 4)**.
9. 3.0L—Reinstall the baffle.
10. Install the oil pan as described in this chapter.

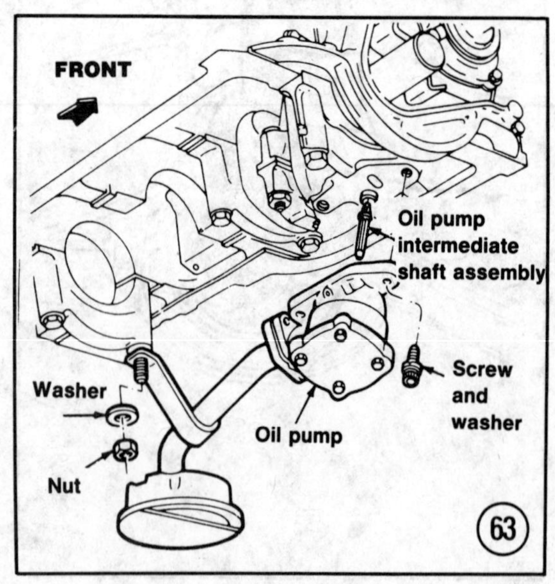

Disassembly/Assembly

Refer to **Figure 64** for this procedure.

1. Remove the oil inlet tube from the pump.
2. Remove and discard the gasket.
3. Remove the cover attaching screws and separate the cover from the pump body.
4. Remove the inner rotor and shaft, then the outer race.

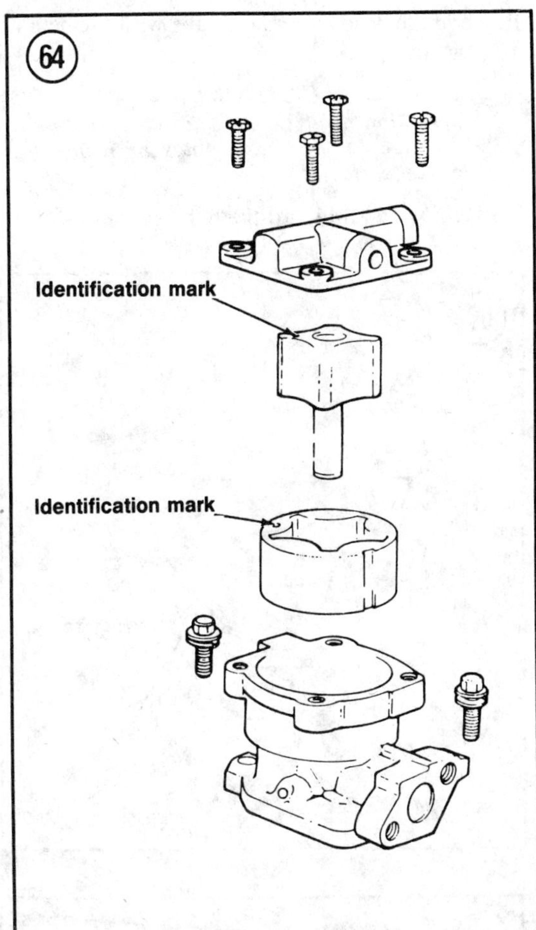

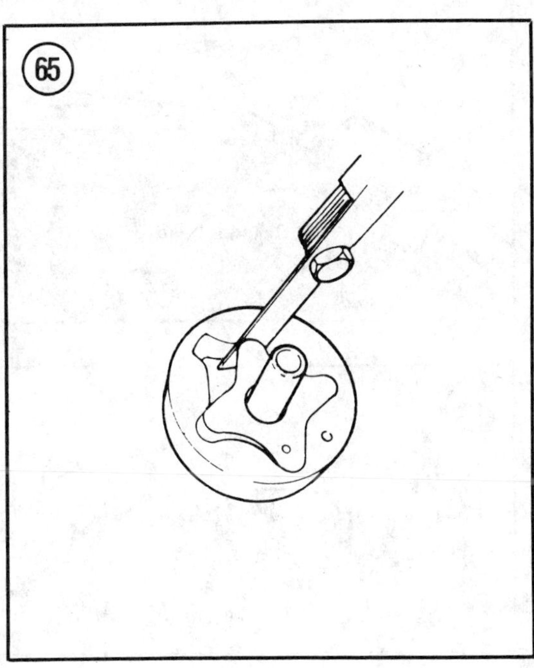

5. Assembly is the reverse of disassembly. Make sure the identification marks on the inner rotor and outer race align. Install the oil tube with a new gasket.

Cleaning and Inspection

1. Wash all components with solvent and a brush. Blow dry with compressed air, if available.
2. Check the inside of the pump housing, the outer race and rotor for signs of scoring or excessive wear.
3. Check the pump cover mating surface for excessive wear, scoring or grooving.
4. Install rotor assembly in outer race and measure the inner rotor tip clearance with a flat feeler gauge as shown in **Figure 65**. Compare to specifications (**Table 1** or **Table 2**).
5. Install the inner rotor and outer race in the pump body. Place a straightedge across the pump housing and measure the gap between the straightedge and inner rotor and the straightedge and outer race. See **Figure 66**. This is rotor end play and must not exceed 0.005 in.
6. Measure the outer diameter of the inner rotor shaft and the inner diameter of the housing bearing. Subtract the inner diameter from the outer diameter to obtain the drive shaft-to-housing clearance.
7. Check for a worn or collapsed relief valve spring. Make sure the relief valve piston is not scored and operates in the bore without binding.

5

CYLINDER HEAD

Cylinder head removal with the engine in the vehicle is a difficult and time-consuming job and involves working from the engine compartment and passenger compartment through the engine cover. While the procedures below assume the engine is in the vehicle, you may want to consider removing the engine for this service.

Removal (2.8L Engine)

1. Disconnect the negative battery cable.
2. Drain the cooling system. See Chapter Seven.
3. Remove the air cleaner assembly. See Chapter Six.
4. Disconnect the throttle linkage at the carburetor and remove the bracket.
5. Remove the distributor (Chapter Eight).
6. Unclamp and disconnect the upper radiator hose and bypass hose from the thermostat housing and intake manifold.
7. Remove the rocker arm covers as described in this chapter.

8. Remove the carburetor. See Chapter Six.
9. Remove the intake manifold as described in this chapter.
10. Remove the appropriate exhaust manifold as described in this chapter.
11. Remove the rocker arm assemblies and pushrods as described in this chapter.
12. Loosen the cylinder head bolts, working from the center of the head to the end in each direction.
13. Remove the head bolts. Tap the end of the head with a plastic mallet to break the gasket seal. Remove the head from the engine with the help of an assistant.

CAUTION
Place the head on its side to prevent damage to the spark plugs or head gasket surface.

14. Remove and discard the head gasket.

Removal (3.0L Engine)

1. Disconnect the negative battery cable.
2. Drain the cooling system. See Chapter Seven.
3. Remove the air cleaner outlet tube. See Chapter Six.
4. Remove the intake manifold as described in this chapter.
5. Loosen the accessory drive belt idler and remove the drive belt.
6A. Left-hand head—Remove alternator adjusting arm.
6B. Right-hand head—Remove accessory drive belt idler.
7. If equipped with power steering, unbolt and remove the pump and bracket assembly. Place to one side out of the way without disconnecting any hydraulic lines.
8A. Left-hand head—Remove ignition coil bracket and crankcase dipstick tube.
8B. Right-hand head—Remove the throttle cable support bracket and ground strap.
9. Remove the appropriate exhaust manifold as described in this chapter.
10. Remove the rocker arm cover(s).
11. Loosen the rocker arm fulcrum bolts enough to swivel the rocker arms off the pushrods. Remove the pushrods.
12. Loosen the cylinder head bolts, working from the center of the head to the end in each direction.
13. Remove the head bolts. Tap the end of the head with a plastic mallet to break the gasket seal. Remove the head from the engine with the help of an assistant.

CAUTION
Place the head on its side to prevent damage to the spark plugs or head gasket surface.

14. Remove and discard the head gasket.

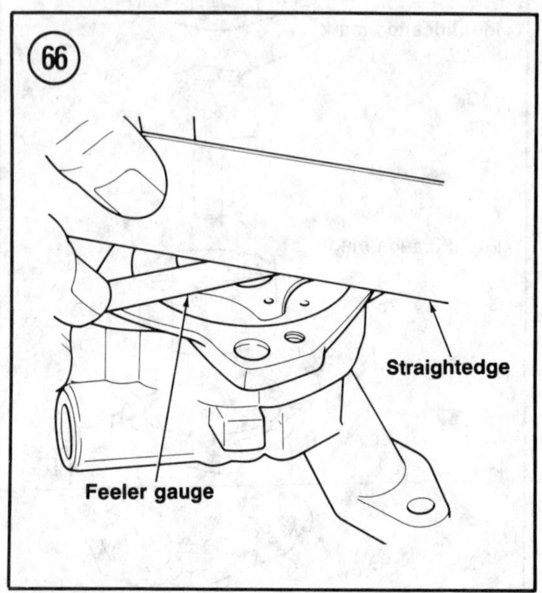

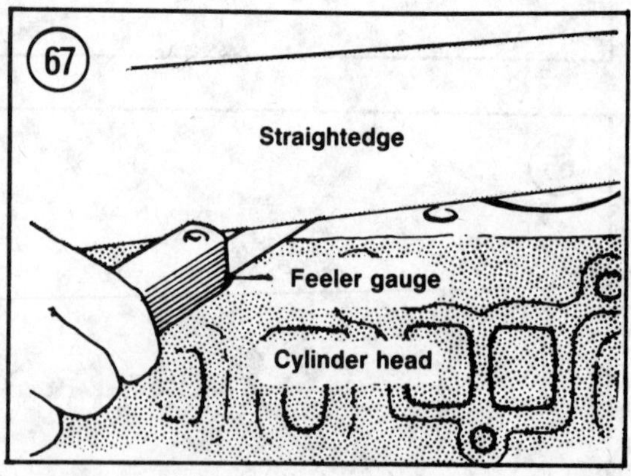

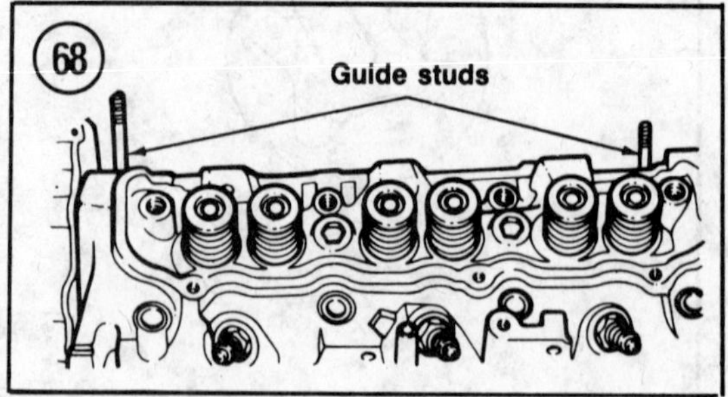

Decarbonizing

1. Without removing the valves, remove all deposits from the combustion chambers, intake ports and exhaust ports. Use a fine wire brush dipped in solvent or make a scraper from hardwood. Be careful not to scratch or gouge the combustion chambers.
2. After all carbon is removed from the combustion chambers and ports, clean the entire head in solvent.
3. Clean away all carbon on the piston tops. Do not remove the carbon ridge at the top of the cylinder bore.
4. Clean the bolt holes. Use a cleaning solvent to remove dirt and grease.

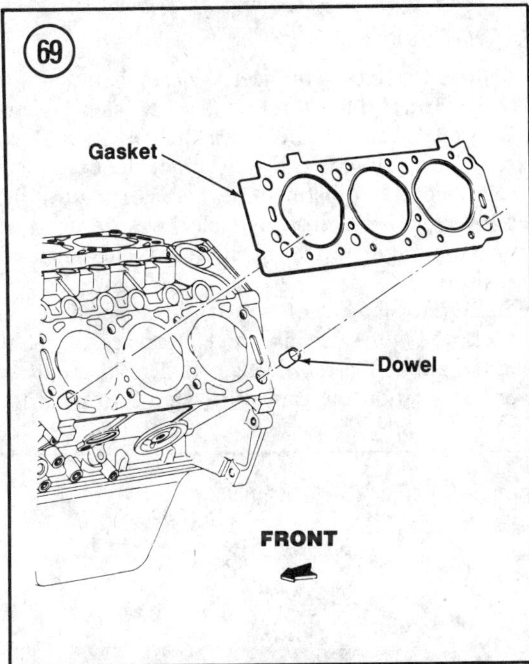

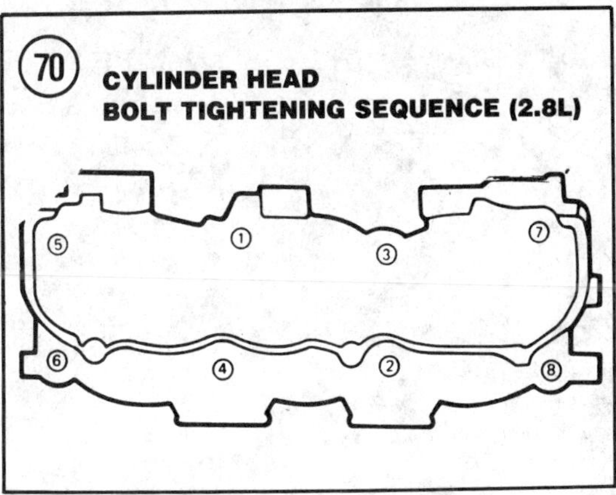

Inspection

1. Check the cylinder head for signs of oil or water leaks before cleaning.
2. Clean the cylinder head thoroughly in solvent. While cleaning, look for cracks or other visible signs of damage. Look for corrosion or foreign material in the oil and water passages.
3. Clean the passages with a stiff spiral brush, then blow them out with compressed air.
4. Check the cylinder head studs for damage and replace if necessary.
5. Check the flatness of the cylinder head-to-block surface with a straightedge and feeler gauge (**Figure 67**). Measure diagonally, as well as end to end. Maximum permissible head warp is 0.003 in. for any 6 in. length of the head surface or 0.006 in. overall. If cylinder head warpage is excessive, have the head milled by a dealer or competent machine shop. If more than 0.010 in. must be removed from the head, replace it.

Installation (All Engines)

1. Be sure the cylinder head, engine block mating surfaces and cylinder bores are clean and free of deposits, sealant or other debris. Check all visible oil passages in the cylinder head and engine block for cleanliness.
2. 2.8L—Fabricate guide studs from old cylinder head bolts by removing their heads and cutting screwdriver slots in the tops. Install a guide stud at the front and rear of the block as shown in **Figure 68**.

NOTE
Head gaskets are not interchangeable. The gasket is marked FRONT and TOP for correct positioning.

3. Install a new cylinder head gasket on the guide studs (2.8L) or the block mounting dowels (3.0L). See **Figure 69** (typical).
4. With the help of an assistant, position the cylinder head on the block.
5. If old head bolts are being reinstalled, coat threads with engine oil (new bolts have a preservative coating). Install the head bolts in their mounting holes and insert through the head gasket into the engine block. Remove the guide studs (2.8L) and install head bolts in their place.
6. Tighten the cylinder head bolts to specifications (**Table 3** or **Table 4**) following the sequence shown in **Figure 70** (2.8L) or **Figure 71** (3.0L).
7. Reverse Steps 1-11 of *Removal* to complete installation.

5

VALVES AND VALVE SEATS

Servicing the valves, guides and valve seats requires special knowledge and expensive machine tools. A general practice among those who do their own service is to remove the cylinder head, perform all disassembly except valve removal and take the head to a dealer or machine shop for inspection and service. Since the cost is low relative to the required effort and equipment, this is usually the best approach, even for experienced mechanics.

Valve Clearance Adjustment

Stem-to-rocker arm clearance must be within specifications. If valve clearance is excessive, the valve opens late and closes early, resulting in a rough engine idle. Overly tight clearance lets the valve open early and close too late, causing valve bounce and damage to the camshaft lobe.

2.8L engine

The 2.8L V6 uses mechanical valve lifters. Valve clearance should be checked and adjusted at the intervals specified in Chapter Three or whenever any valve train component is replaced. Valve clearance is checked with the engine cold. Intake valve clearance is 0.014 in. Exhaust valve clearance is 0.016 in. Valve arrangement (front to rear) is I-E-E-I-E-I on the left bank and I-E-I-E-E-I on the right bank.

1. Remove the rocker arm covers as described in this chapter.
2. Connect a remote starter button to the starter relay according to manufacturer's instructions.
3. Holding a finger on the No. 5 intake valve adjusting screw, turn the engine over with the remote starter button until the intake valve just starts to open. This positions the camshaft properly to adjust the No. 1 cylinder valves.

CAUTION
Insert feeler gauge at front or rear edge of valve tip and move it in the opposite direction to check clearance. Inserting the feeler gauge at the outer edge of the valve tip and moving it toward the carburetor will give a false feeling of insufficient clearance, resulting in unnecessary adjustment.

4. Insert a 0.014 in. feeler gauge between the rocker arm and the No. 1 intake valve stem (**Figure 72**). The gauge should enter the gap with slight resistance and have a light to moderate drag when removed. If adjustment is necessary, turn the self-locking adjusting screw clockwise to decrease or counterclockwise to increase clearance as required.
5. Repeat Step 4 with a 0.016 in. feeler gauge to check the No. 1 exhaust valve clearance.
6. To adjust the remaining cylinders in the firing order, position the cam as in Step 3 to open the

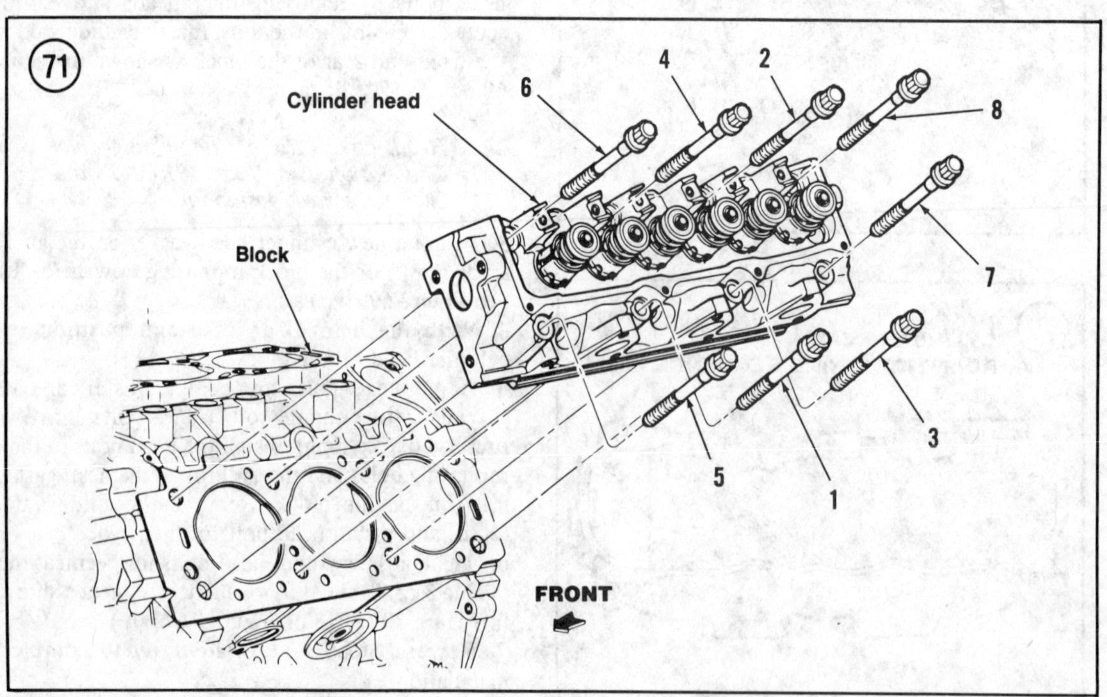

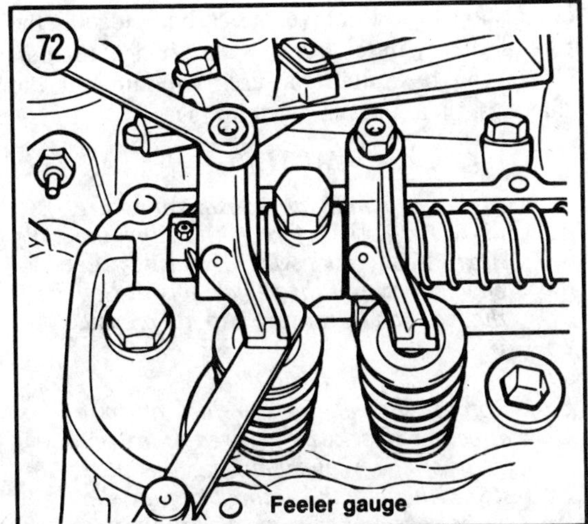

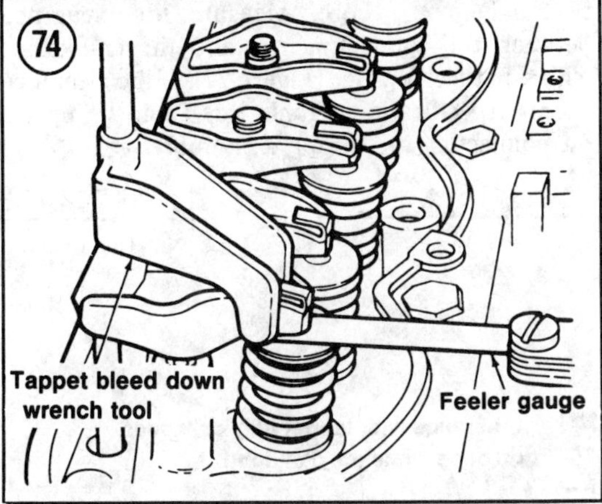

intake valves in the order specified and adjust the corresponding valves.

a. No. 3 intake valve starts to open—adjust both No. 4 valves.
b. No. 6 intake valve starts to open—adjust both No. 2 valves.
c. No. 1 intake valve starts to open—adjust both No. 5 valves.
d. No. 4 intake valve starts to open—adjust both No. 3 valves.
e. No. 2 intake valve starts to open—adjust both No. 6 valves.

7. Reinstall the rocker arm covers.

3.0L engine

A positive stop rocker arm bolt eliminates valve clearance adjustment on the 3.0L engine. However, valve train wear can be compensated for by installing a 0.060 in. longer or shorter pushrod, as required. Whenever any component in the valve train is replaced, the following procedure should be performed to determine if pushrod replacement is necessary.

1. Rotate the crankshaft until the No. 1 piston is at top dead center (TDC) on its compression stroke. Both No. 1 cylinder valves will be closed, the timing pointer and crankshaft damper marks will align and the crankshaft and camshaft timing marks will align as shown in **Figure 73**.

2. Install Ford tool part No. T70P-6513-A on the rocker arm of the No. 1 intake valve. See **Figure 74**. Slowly apply pressure to bleed the lifter down completely, hold lifter down with tool and check the clearance between the valve stem and rocker

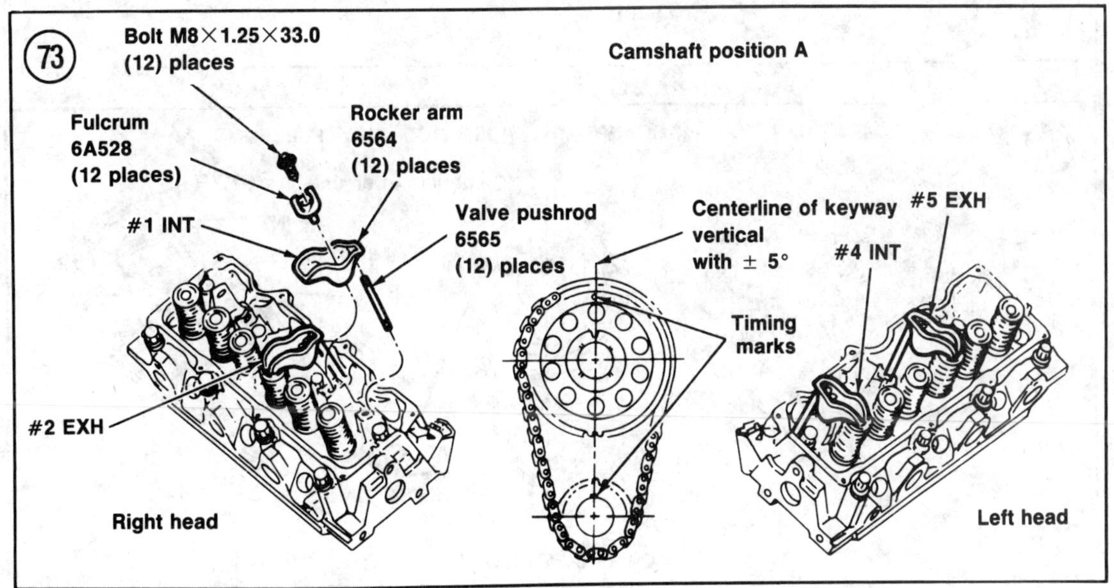

5

arm with a flat feeler gauge. See **Figure 75**. Write down the clearance and repeat for each valve listed: No. 2 exhaust, No. 4 intake and No. 5 exhaust.

3. Rotate the crankshaft 360° to position the crankshaft and camshaft sprocket timing marks as shown in **Figure 76**. Repeat Step 2 to check clearance of the following valves: No. 1 exhaust, No. 2 intake, No. 3 intake and exhaust, No. 4 exhaust, No. 5 intake and No. 6 intake and exhaust.

4. The allowable tappet gap clearance is 0.088-0.189 in. If clearance of any valve is less than 0.088 in., install a shorter pushrod. If greater than 0.189 in., install a longer pushrod. See your Ford dealer for pushrod selection.

PISTON/CONNECTING ROD ASSEMBLY

Piston/Connecting Rod Removal

1. Remove the cylinder head and oil pan as described in this chapter.

2. Rotate the crankshaft until one piston is at bottom dead center. Pack the cylinder bore with clean shop rags. Remove the carbon ridge at the top of the cylinder bores with a ridge reamer. These can be rented for use. Vacuum out the shavings, then remove the shop rages.

WARNING

Make sure manual transmissions are in NEUTRAL before performing the next step. Otherwise, rotating the engine may roll the vehicle forward off the jackstands, causing it to fall on you.

CAUTION

Rotate the engine in its normal direction (clockwise, viewed from the front of the vehicle) during the next step. Otherwise the timing belt may slip on its cogs and change valve timing.

3. Rotate the crankshaft until the connecting rod is centered in the bore. Measure the clearance between the connecting rod and the crankshaft with a flat feeler gauge (**Figure 77**). If the clearance exceeds specifications (**Table 1** or **Table 2**), replace the connecting rod during reassembly.

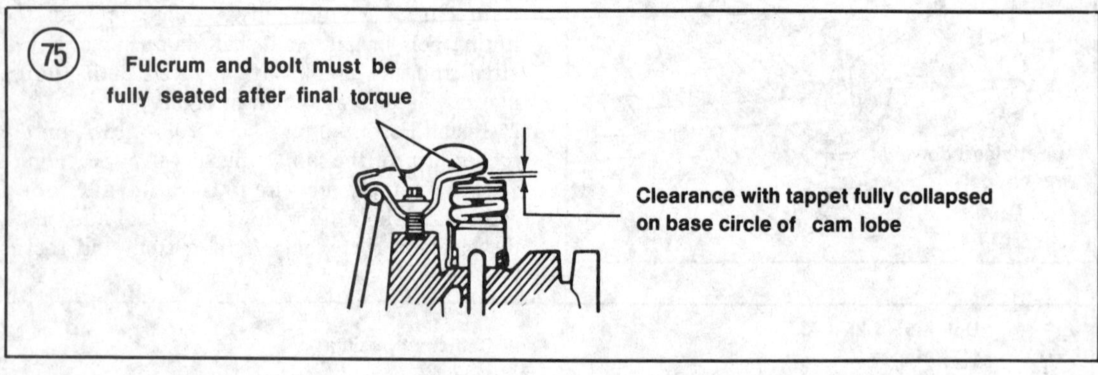

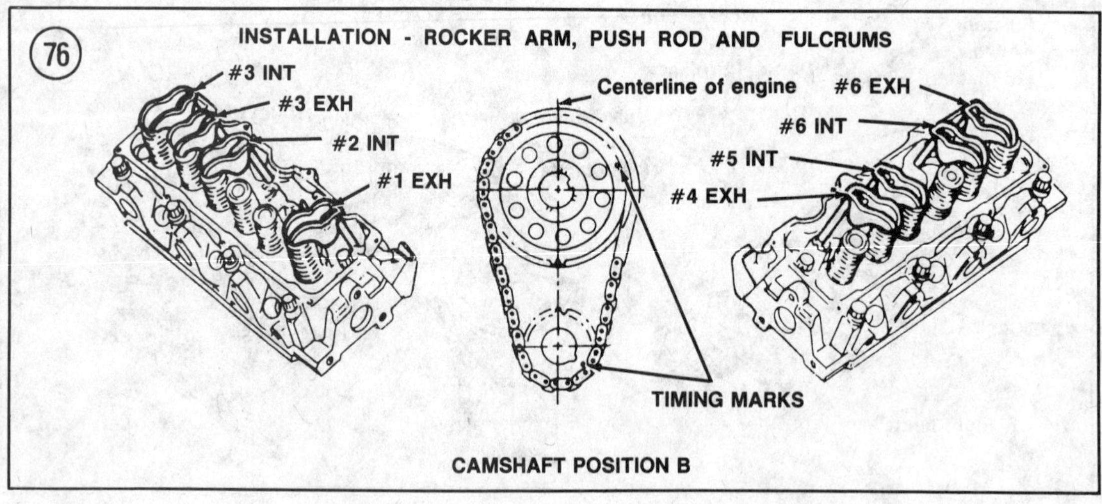

4. Remove the nuts holding the connecting rod cap. Lift off the cap, together with the lower bearing insert.

NOTE
If the connecting rod caps are difficult to remove, tap the studs with a wooden hammer handle.

5. Use the wooden hammer handle to push the piston and connecting rod from the bore.

NOTE
*Mark the cylinder number on the top of each piston with quick-drying paint. Check the cylinder numbers or identification marks on the connecting rod and cap. If they are not visible, make your own (**Figure 78**).*

6. Remove the piston rings with a ring remover (**Figure 79**).

7. Repeat Steps 2-6 for all remaining connecting rods.

Piston Pin Removal/Installation

The piston pins are press-fitted to the connecting rods and hand-fitted to the pistons. Removal requires the use of a press and support stand. This is a job for a dealer or machine shop equipped to fit the pistons to the pins, ream the pin bushings to the correct diameter and install the pistons and pins on the connecting rods.

Piston Clearance Check

Unless you have precision measuring equipment and know how to use it properly, have this procedure done by a machine shop.

1. Measure the piston diameter with a micrometer (**Figure 80**) at the piston pin centerline height, 90° to the piston pin axis.

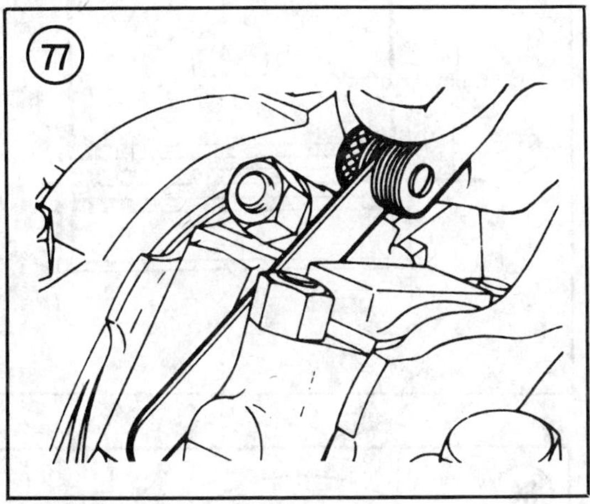

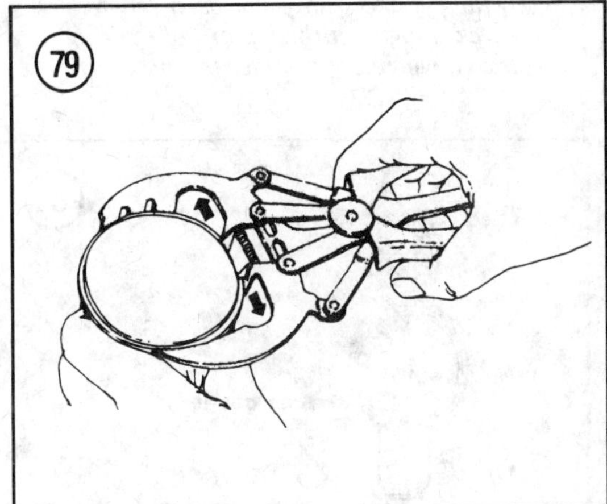

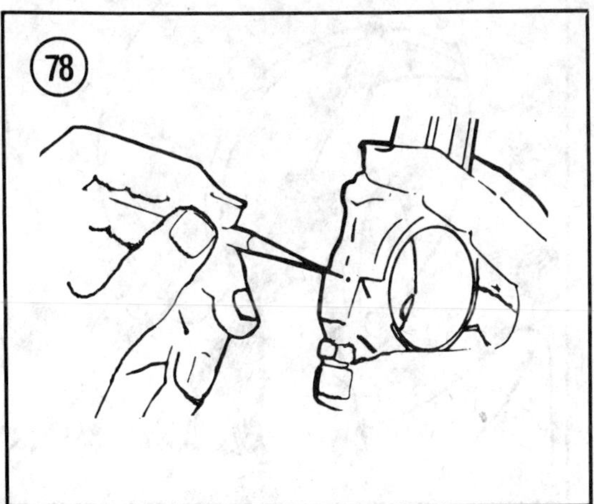

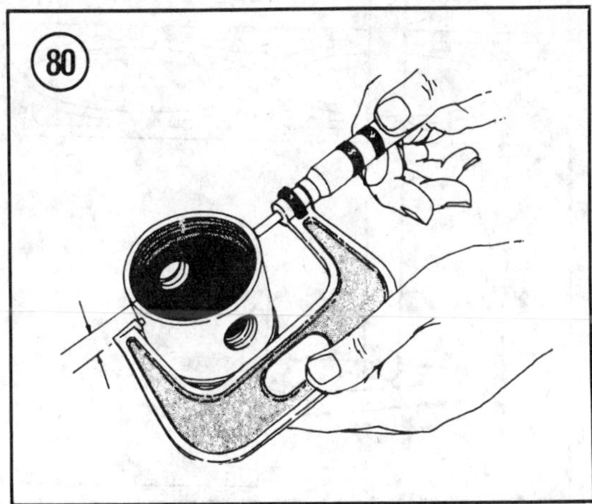

5

2. Measure the cylinder bore diameter with a bore gauge (**Figure 81**). **Figure 82** shows the points of normal cylinder wear. If dimension A exceeds dimension B by more than 0.003 in., the cylinder must be rebored and a new piston/ring assembly installed.

3. Subtract the piston diameter from the largest cylinder bore reading. If it exceeds the specifications in **Table 1** or **Table 2**, the cylinder must be rebored and an oversized piston installed.

NOTE
Obtain the new piston and measure it to determine the correct cylinder bore oversize dimension.

Piston Ring Fit/Installation

1. Check the ring gap of each piston ring. To do this, position the ring at the bottom of the ring travel area and square it by tapping gently with an inverted piston. See **Figure 83**.

NOTE
If the cylinders have not been rebored, check the gap at the bottom of the ring travel, where the cylinder is least worn.

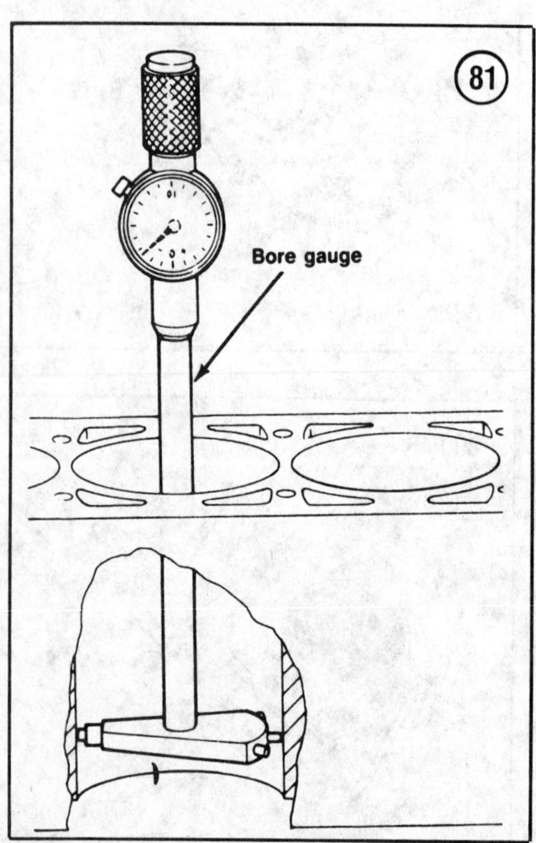

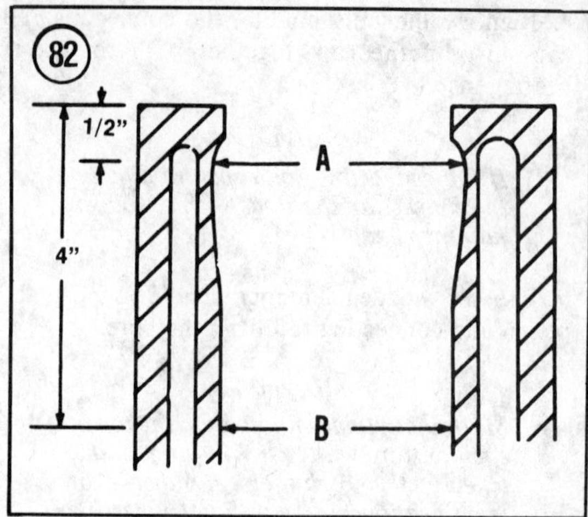

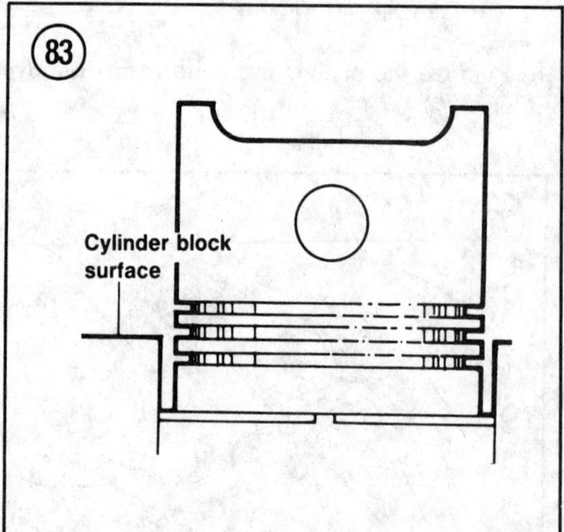

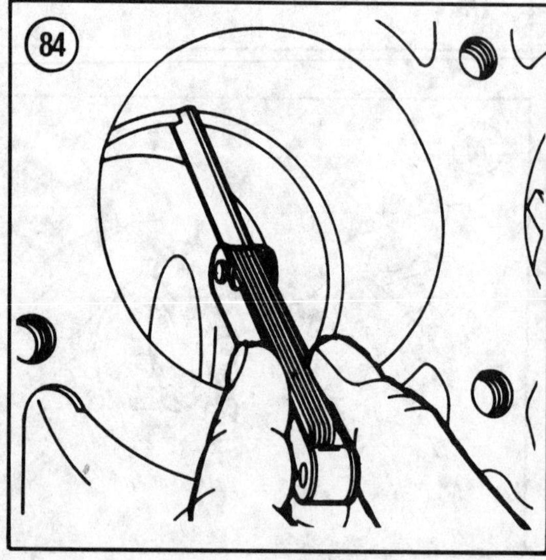

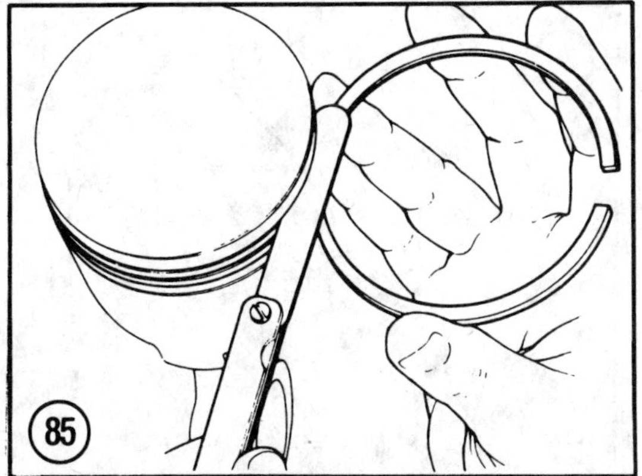

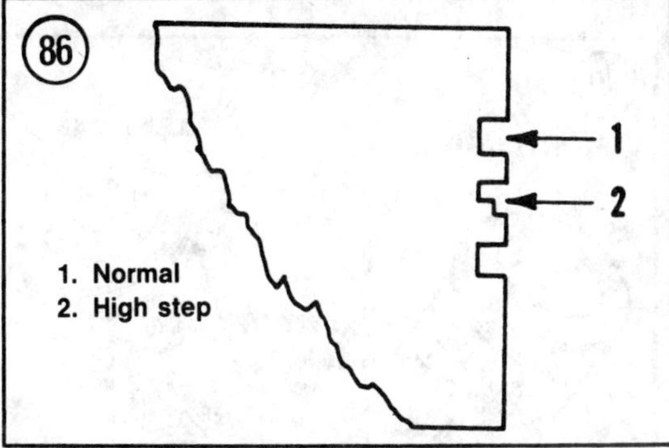

1. Normal
2. High step

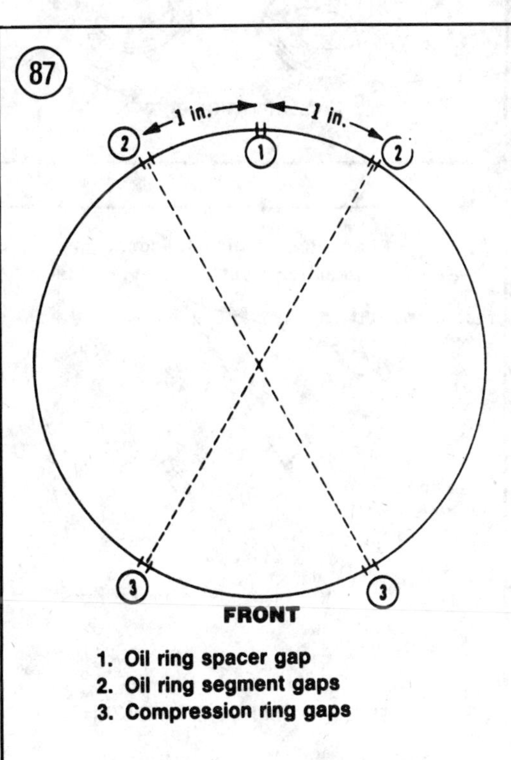

FRONT

1. Oil ring spacer gap
2. Oil ring segment gaps
3. Compression ring gaps

2. Measure the ring gap with a feeler gauge as shown in **Figure 84**. Compare with specifications in **Table 1** or **Table 2**. If the measurement is not within specifications, the rings must be replaced as a set. Check gap of new rings as well. If the gap is too small, file the ends of the ring to correct it.
3. Check the side clearance of the rings as shown in **Figure 85**. Place the feeler gauge alongside the ring all the way into the groove. The feeler gauge should slide all the way around the piston without binding. Any wear that occurs will form a step at the inner portion of the ring groove's lower edge. If large steps are discernible (**Figure 86**), replace the piston. Compare the inserted feeler gauge size with the specifications in **Table 1** or **Table 2**. If the measurement is not within specifications, either the rings or the ring grooves are worn. Inspect and replace as required.
4. Using a ring expander tool (**Figure 79**), carefully install the oil control ring, then the compression rings. Oil rings consists of 3 segments. The wavy segment goes between the flat segments to act as a spacer. Upper and lower flat segments are interchangeable. The second compression ring is tapered. The top of each compression ring is marked and must face upward.
5. Position the ring gaps as shown in **Figure 87**.

Connecting Rod Inspection

Have the connecting rods checked for straightness by a dealer or machine shop. When installing new connecting rods, have them checked for misalignment before installing the piston and piston pin. Connecting rods can spring out of alignment during shipping or handling.

Connecting Rod Bearing Clearance Measurement

1. Place the connecting rods and upper bearing halves on the proper connecting rod journals.
2. Cut a piece of Plastigage the width of the bearing. Place the Plastigage on the journal, then install the lower bearing half end cap.

NOTE
Do not place Plastigage over the journal oil hole.

3. Tighten the connecting rod cap to specifications (**Table 3** or **Table 4**). Do not rotate the crankshaft while the Plastigage is in place.
4. Remove the connecting rod caps. Bearing clearance is determined by comparing the width of

the flattened Plastigage to the markings on the envelope (**Figure 88**). If the clearance is excessive, the crankshaft must be reground and undersize bearings installed.

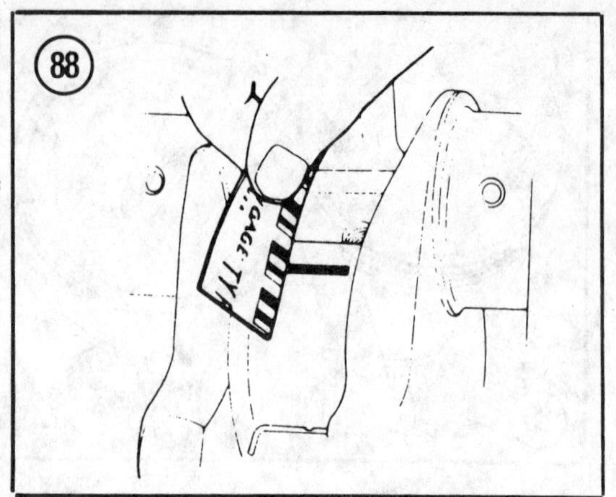

Piston/Connecting Rod Installation

Connecting rods and bearing caps are numbered from 1 to 3 in the passenger's side bank and from 4 to 6 in the driver's side bank. The numbers on the rod and cap must be on the same side when installed in the cylinder. When switching a connecting rod from one block or cylinder to another, always fit new bearings and number the rod and cap to correspond with the new cylinder number.

1. Make sure the pistons are correctly installed on the connecting rods, if they were separated. See **Figure 89** (2.8L) or **Figure 90** (3.0L).
2. Make sure the ring gaps are positioned as shown in **Figure 87**.
3. Slip short pieces of hose over the connecting rod studs to prevent them from nicking the crankshaft. Tape will work if you do not have the right diameter hose, but it is more difficult to remove.
4. Immerse the entire piston in clean engine oil. Coat the cylinder wall with oil.

CAUTION
Use extreme care in Step 5 to prevent the connecting rod from nicking the crankshaft journal.

5. Install the piston/connecting rod assembly in its cylinder with a piston ring compressor. The piston crown notch should face toward the front of the engine. See **Figure 91**. Tap lightly with a wooden hammer handle to insert the piston. Make sure that the piston number painted on top before removal corresponds to the cylinder number, counting from the camshaft belt end of the engine.
6. Clean the connecting rod bearings carefully, including the back sides. Coat the journals and bearings with clean engine oil. Place the bearings in the connecting rod and cap.
7. Turn the crankshaft throw to the bottom of its stroke. Push the piston downward until the connecting rod and bearing fit into place against the crankpin. Remove the protective hose or tape and lightly lubricate the connecting rod bolt threads with SAE 30W engine oil.
8. Install the connecting rod cap. Make sure the rod and cap marks align. Install the cap nuts finger-tight.

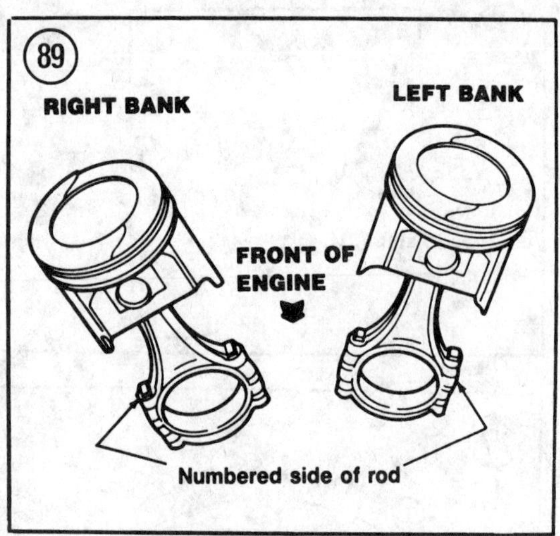

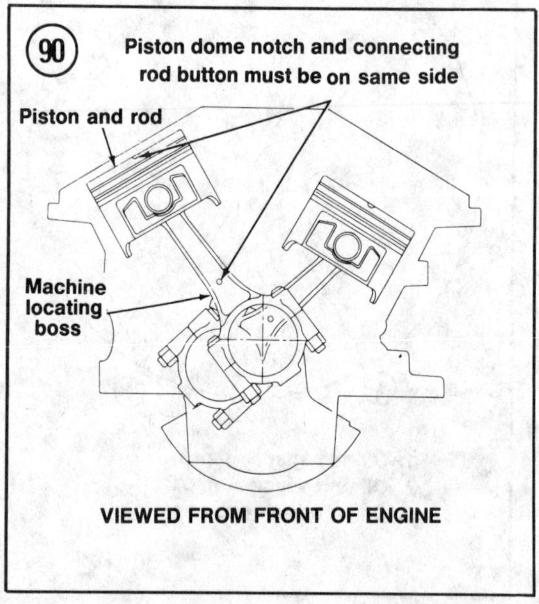

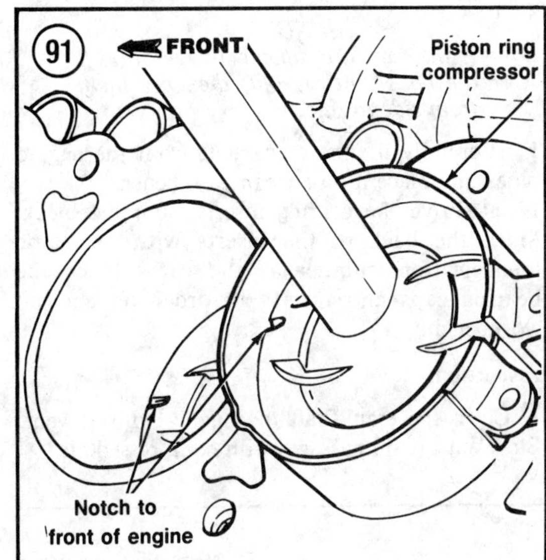

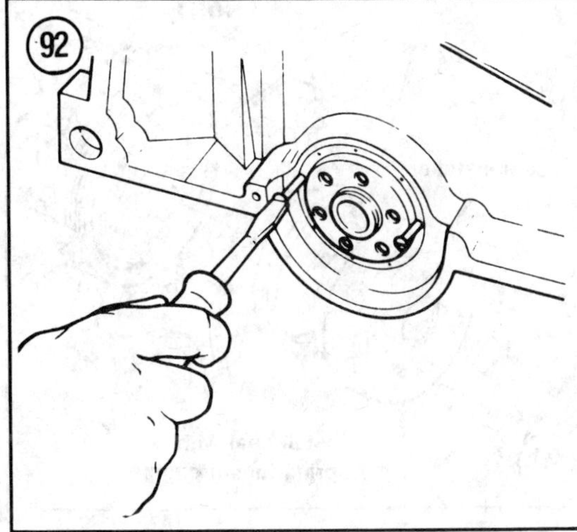

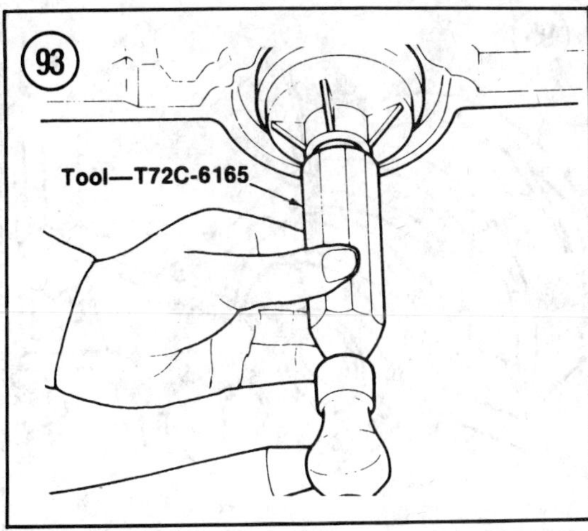

9. Repeat Steps 4-8 for each remaining piston/connecting rod assembly.
10. Tighten the cap nuts to specifications (**Table 3** or **Table 4**).
11. Check the connecting rod big-end play as described under *Piston/Connecting Rod Removal* in this chapter.

REAR MAIN OIL SEAL REPLACEMENT

2.8L Engine

1. Remove the engine as described in this chapter.
2. Remove the flywheel (manual) or drive plate (automatic) from the rear of the crankshaft as described in this chapter.
3. Remove the flywheel housing and rear plate.
4. Punch a hole on each side of the rear oil seal just above the bearing cap-to-cylinder block split line.
5. Install a sheet metal screw in each hole (**Figure 92**). Place small wooden blocks against the cylinder block and pry against the screws with a pair of large screwdrivers to remove the seal. Work slowly and carefully to avoid any possible damage to the crankshaft seal surface.
6. Clean the oil seal recess in the block and main bearing cap.
7. Wipe the seal-to-block surface of the new seal with engine oil. Lubricate the crankshaft and seal contact surfaces with Lubriplate or equivalent.
8. Install the seal in the recess and drive it in place with tool part No. T72C-6165. See **Figure 93**.
9. Reverse Steps 1-3 to complete installation.

3.0L Engine

1. Remove the engine as described in this chapter.
2. Remove the flywheel (manual) or drive plate (automatic) from the rear of the crankshaft as described in this chapter.
3. Remove the flywheel housing and rear plate.
4. Punch a single hole in the metal surface of the seal between the lip and engine block with a sharp awl.
5. Thread jet plug remover part No. T77L-9533-B or equivalent in the punched hole. Carefully remove the seal. Work slowly and carefully to avoid any possible damage to the crankshaft seal surface.
6. Clean the oil seal recess in the block and main bearing cap.
7. Wipe the seal-to-block surface of the new seal with engine oil. Lubricate the crankshaft and seal contact surfaces with clean engine oil.

8. Install new seal on installer part No. T82L-6701-A or equivalent. See **Figure 94**. Place tool and seal in position. Alternately tighten the tool bolts until the seal is seated within 0.005 in. (0.127 mm) of the rear face of the block.
9. Remove the seal installer tool and reinstall the flywheel or drive plate as described in this chapter.

CRANKSHAFT

End Play Measurement

1. Pry the crankshaft toward the rear of the engine as far as possible with a large screwdriver.
2. Install a dial indicator on the engine block so that its contact point rests against the crankshaft flange. The indicator axis should be parallel to the crankshaft axis. See **Figure 95**.
3. Set the indicator dial to zero. Pry the crankshaft to the front of the engine with the screwdriver.
4. Compare the dial indicator reading to specifications (**Table 1** or **Table 2**). If the end play is less than specified, check the No. 3 main bearing surfaces for scratches, nicks, burrs or dirt. If end play is excessive, replace the No. 3 main bearing.

Removal

Refer to **Figure 96** (typical) for this procedure.
1. Remove the engine as described in this chapter.
2. Remove the timing chain cover, timing chain and sprockets as described in this chapter.
3. Remove the spark plug wires from the spark plugs, then remove the spark plugs from the cylinder head.
4. Remove the flywheel (manual) or drive plate (automatic) from the rear of the crankshaft as described in this chapter, then remove the engine rear cover plate.
5. Remove the oil pan and oil pump as described in this chapter.
6. Rotate the crankshaft to position one connecting rod at the bottom of its stroke.
7. Remove the connecting rod bearing cap and bearing. Move the piston/rod assembly away from the crankshaft.
8. Repeat Step 6 and Step 7 for each piston/rod assembly.
9. Check the caps for identification numbers or marks. If none are visible, clean the caps with a wire brush. If marks still cannot be seen, make your own with quick-drying paint.
10. Unbolt and remove the main bearing caps and bearing inserts. Mark the back of the inserts with the same identification number as the caps.

NOTE
If the caps are difficult to remove, lift the bolts partway out, then pry them from side to side.

11. Carefully lift the crankshaft from the engine block and place it on a clean workbench.
12. Remove the bearing inserts from the block. Mark the back of the inserts with the same identification number as the caps. Place the bearing caps and inserts in order on a clean workbench.

Inspection

1. Clean the crankshaft thoroughly with solvent. Blow out the oil passages with compressed air.

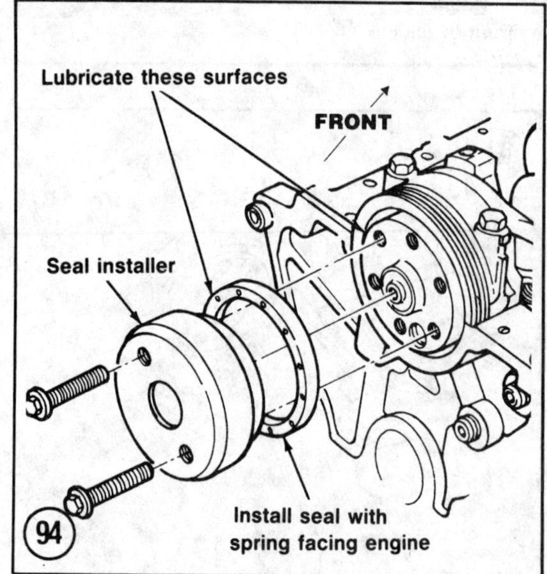

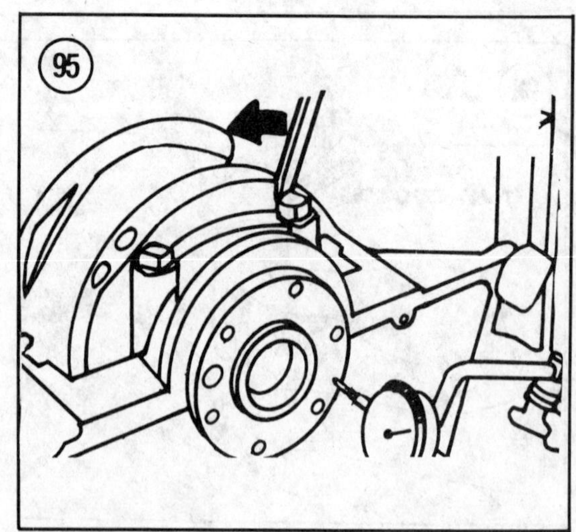

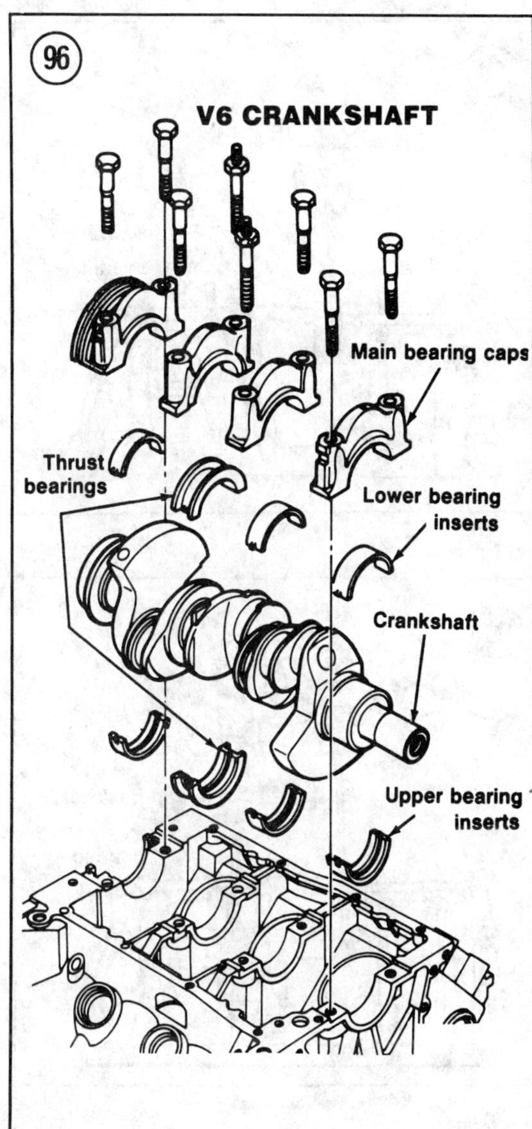

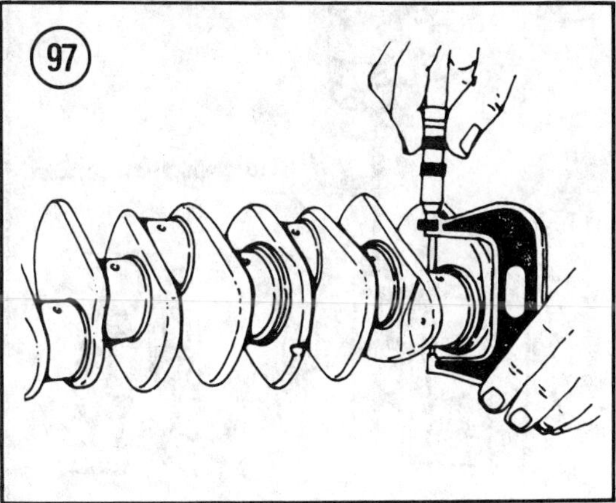

NOTE

If you do not have precision measuring equipment, have a machine shop perform Step 2.

2. Check the crankpins and main bearing journals for wear, scoring or cracks. Check all journals against specifications (**Table 1** or **Table 2**) for out-of-roundness and taper. See **Figure 97**. Have the crankshaft reground, if necessary, and install undersize bearings.

Main Bearing Clearance Measurement

Main bearing clearance is measured with Plastigage in the same manner as the connecting rod bearing clearance described in this chapter. If wear exceeds that specified in **Table 1** or **Table 2**, a 0.001 or 0.002 in. undersize bearing may be used on one-half of the journal in combination with the standard bearing on the other half. If undersize bearings are used on more than one journal, the undersize bearing should be installed in the cylinder block, non in the main bearing cap. If this does not produce the correct crankshaft-to-main bearing clearance, the crankshaft should be reground by a dealer or a competent machine shop and undersize main bearings installed.

Installation

Refer to **Figure 96** for this procedure.

1. With the main bearings removed from the bearing caps and cylinder block, clean the main bearing bores in the block, the main bearing caps and main bearing inserts with lacquer thinner to remove all contamination.
2. If the old main bearings are being reinstalled, be sure they are reinstalled in the main bearing caps and cylinder block bores from which they were removed. If new bearings (or undersize bearings) are being installed, be sure they are installed in the proper locations.
3. Make sure the bearing locating tangs are correctly positioned in the cylinder block and bearing cap notches.
4. Coat the main bearing surfaces and the crankshaft journals with a thick coat of clean, heavy engine oil.
5. Carefully place the crankshaft in the main bearings installed in the cylinder block, taking care not to damage the sides of the No. 3 (thrust) bearing.

6. Install all main bearing caps, except the No. 3 cap. Make sure the arrows on the top of the caps face toward the front of the engine.

NOTE

Check cap bolts for thread damage before reuse. If damaged, replace the bolts.

7. Lubricate the threads of all cap bolts with SAE 30W engine oil. Install the cap bolts and tighten to specifications (**Table 2**).
8. Install the No. 3 bearing cap and tighten the bolts finger-tight.
9. Use a large screwdriver or pry bar to force the crankshaft forward against the thrust surface of the upper half of the No. 3 bearing. See **Figure 98**.
10. Hold the crankshaft in this position and pry the thrust cap toward the rear of the engine (**Figure 99**) to align the thrust surfaces of both bearing halves.
11. Hold the crankshaft in the forward position and tighten the bearing caps to specifications (**Table 3** or **Table 4**). See **Figure 100**.
12. Rotate the crankshaft during tightening to make sure it turns smoothly without binding at the flywheel rim. If not, remove the bearing caps and crankshaft and check that the bearings are clean and properly installed. Make absolutely certain that bearings are the correct size, especially if the crankshaft has been reground. Never use undersize bearings (except as specified under *Main Bearing Clearance Measurement* in this chapter) if the crankshaft has not been reground.
13. Reinstall the connecting rods and caps on the crankshaft.
14. Reverse Steps 1-5 of the removal procedure to complete installation.

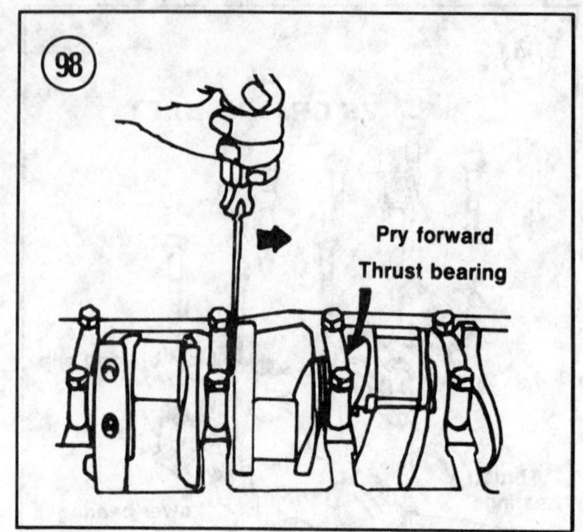

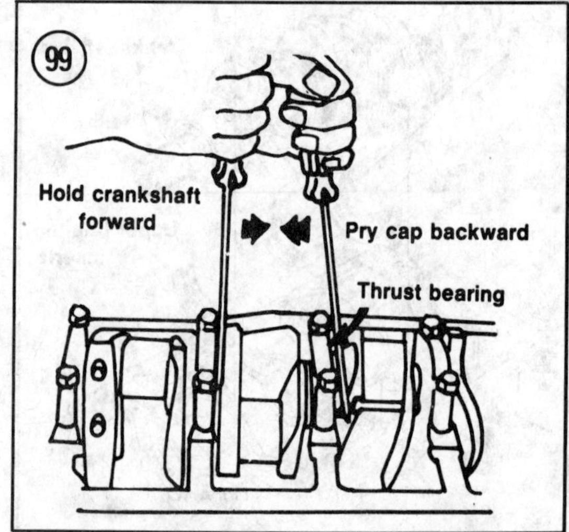

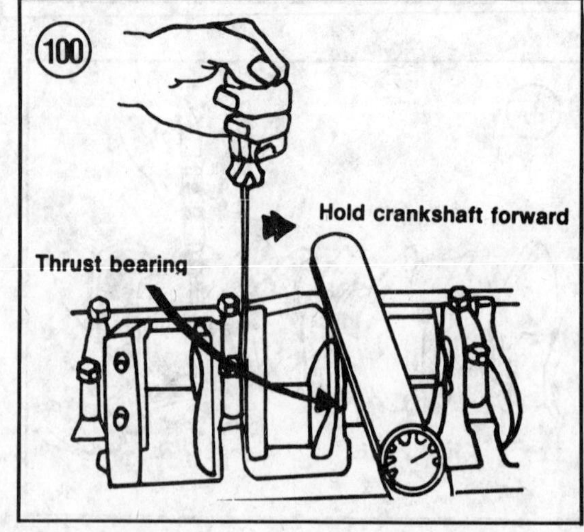

FLYWHEEL OR DRIVE PLATE

Removal/Installation

Refer to **Figure 101** (typical) for this procedure.

1. Remove the engine as described in this chapter.
2. Remove the clutch on manual transmission vehicles. See Chapter Nine.
3. Remove the 6 bolts holding the flywheel or drive plate to the crankshaft. Remove the flywheel or drive plate.
4. Installation is the reverse of removal. Gradually tighten the flywheel/drive plate bolts to specifications (**Table 3** or **Table 4**) in a diagonal pattern. Wipe all oil, grease and other contamination from the flywheel surface before reinstalling the clutch on manual transmission vehicles.

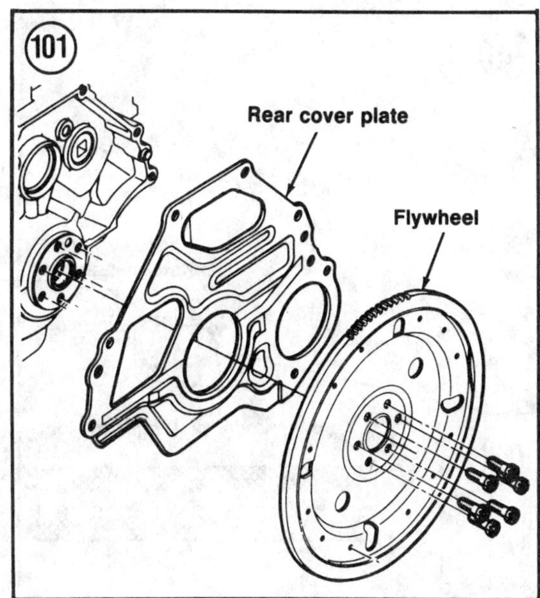

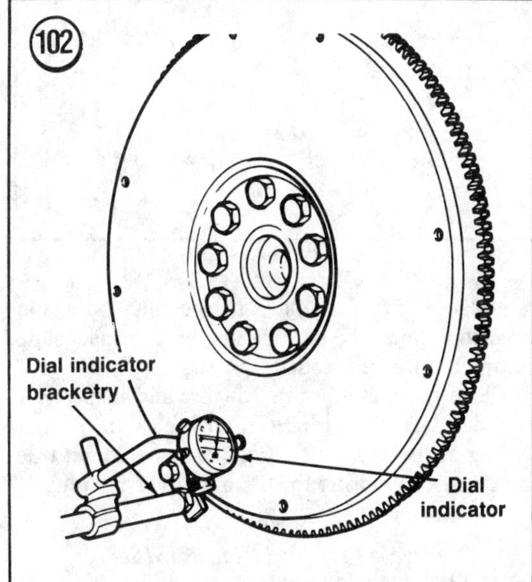

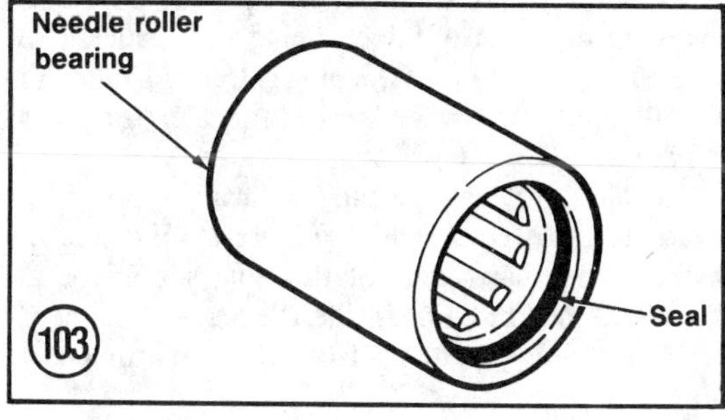

Inspection

1. Visually check the flywheel or drive plate surfaces for cracks, deep scoring, excessive wear, heat discoloration and checking. If the surface is glazed or slightly scratched, have the flywheel/drive plate resurfaced by a machine shop. Replace the flywheel if damage is severe or if more than 0.045 in. (1.143 mm) must be removed to restore the surface.
2. Measure flywheel/drive plate runout with a dial indicator. See **Figure 102**. Replace the drive plate or resurface the flywheel if runout exceeds 0.005 in.

NOTE
The ring gear is an integral part of the drive plate on automatic transmission models. If defective, the entire assembly must be replaced.

3. Inspect the flywheel ring gear teeth. If the teeth are chipped, broken or excessively worn, check the starter motor drive teeth for similar wear or damage. Have a new ring gear shrunk onto the flywheel by a machine shop.

PILOT BEARING

Engines fitted to manual transmissions are equipped with a sealed roller bearing clutch pilot inside the rear end of the crankshaft. See **Figure 103**.

1. Remove the clutch and transmission. See Chapter Nine.
2. Remove the bearing with tool part No. T58L-101-A and a slide hammer.
3. Wipe crankshaft pilot bearing bore with a light coat of Ford Multi-purpose Long-life Lubricant (part No. C1AZ-19590-B) or equivalent.
4. Install the new bearing with tool part No. T71P-7137-C.

CYLINDER BLOCK

Cleaning and Inspection

1. Clean the block thoroughly with solvent. Remove any RTV sealant residue from the machined surfaces. Check all core plugs for leaks and replace any that are suspect. See *Core Plug Replacement* in this chapter. Remove any plugs that seal oil passages. Check oil and coolant passages for sludge, dirt and corrosion while cleaning. If the passages are very dirty, have the block boiled out by a machine shop. Blow out all passages with compressed air. Check the threads in the head bolt holes to be sure they are clean. If dirty, use a tap to true up the threads and remove any deposits.

2. Examine the block for cracks. To confirm suspicions about possible leak areas, use a mixture of 1 part kerosene and 2 parts engine oil. Coat the suspected area with this solution, then wipe dry and immediately apply a solution of zinc oxide dissolved in wood alcohol. If any discoloration appears in the treated area, the block is cracked and should be replaced.
3. Check flatness of the cylinder block deck or top surface. Place an accurate straightedge on the block. If there is any gap between the block and straightedge, measure it with a flat feeler gauge. Measure from end to end and from corner to corner. If gap exceeds 0.002 in. (0.05 mm), have the block resurfaced. Do not remove more than 0.010 in. (0.254 mm) from the surface.
4. Measure cylinder bores with a bore gauge for out-of-roundness or excessive wear as described in *Piston Clearance Check* in this chapter. If the cylinders exceed maximum tolerances, they must be rebored. Reboring is also necessary if the cylinder walls are badly scuffed or scored.

CAUTION
*If one cylinder is bored out, the others must be bored to the same diameter. Before boring, install all main bearing caps and tighten the cap bolts to specifications in **Table 2**.*

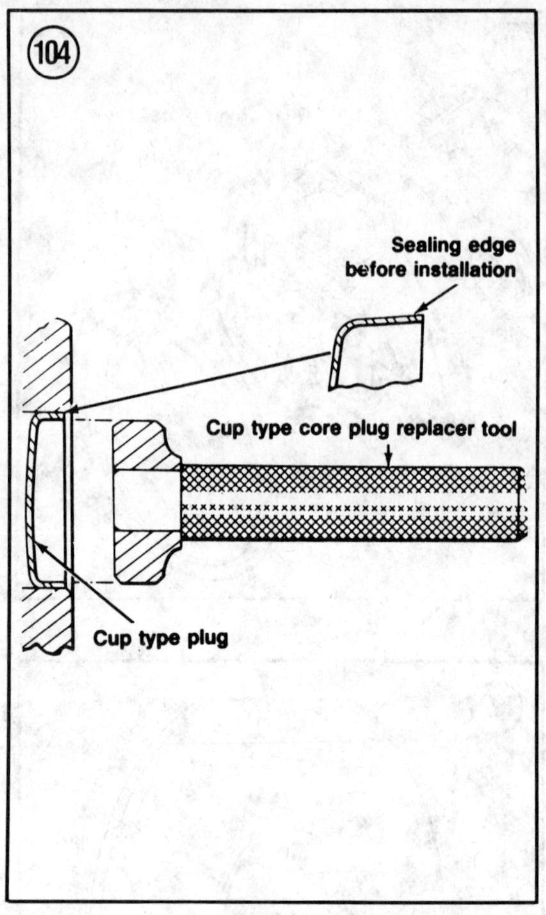

CORE PLUG REPLACEMENT

The condition of all core plugs in the block and cylinder head should be checked whenever the engine is out of the vehicle for service. If any signs of leakage or corrosion are found around one core plug, replace them all.

Cup type core plugs must be installed with the flanged edge facing outward. See **Figure 104**. Since the maximum diameter of this type of plug is at the outer edge of the flange, the plug must be installed with a properly designed tool (**Figure 104**). If driven into the bore with a tool which contacts the plug flange, damaged may occur to the sealing edge. This can result in leakage or a plug blow-out.

Removal/Installation

CAUTION
Do not drive core plugs into the engine casting. It will be impossible to retrieve them and they can restrict coolant circulation, resulting in serious engine damage.

1. Drill a hole in the center of the plug and pry out with an appropriate size drift or pin punch. Work carefully to avoid damage to the plug bore. On large core plugs, the use of a universal impact slide hammer is recommended.
2. Clean the plug bore thoroughly and inspect for any damage that might interfere with proper sealing of the new plug. If damage is evident, true the surface by boring for the next oversize plug.

NOTE
Oversize plugs can be identified by an "OS" stamped in the flat on the cup side of the plug.

3. Coat the inside diameter of the plug bore and the outer diameter of the new plug with sealer. Use an oil-resistant sealer if the plug is to be installed in an oil gallery or a water-resistant sealer for plugs installed in the water jacket.
4. Install the new core plug with an appropriate size core plug replacer tool (**Figure 104**), driver or socket. The sharp edge of the plug should be at least 0.02 in. (0.5 mm) inside the lead-in chamfer.
5. Repeat Steps 1-4 to replace each remaining core plug.

Table 1 2.8L V6 ENGINE SPECIFICATIONS

Engine type	60° V6
Bore	3.65 in.
Stroke	2.70 in.
Displacement	2800 cc
Firing order	1-4-2-5-3-6
Cylinder arrangement	
Passenger side	1-3-5
Driver side	2-4-6
Cylinder block	
Bore diameter	3.6614-3.6630 in.
Head gasket surface flatness	0.003 in. in any 6 in.; 0.006 in. overall
Out-of-round (maximum)	0.005 in.
Taper (maximum)	0.010 in.
Main bearing bore diameter	2.3866-2.3874 in.
Distributor shaft bearing bore diameter	0.4534-0.4549 in.
Valve system	
Valve guide bore diameter	0.3174-0.3184 in.
Valve seat width	
Intake & exhaust	0.060-0.079 in.
Valve seat angle	45°
Valve seat runout limit	0.0015 in.
Valve arrangement (front to rear	
Left side	IE-EI-EI
Right side	IE-IE-EI
Valve stem-to-guide clearance	
Intake	0.0008-0.0025 in.
Exhaust	0.0018-0.0035 in.
Service limit	0.0055 in. max.
Valve head diameter	
Intake	1.562-1.577 in.
Exhaust	1.261-1.276 in.
Valve face	
Runout limit	0.002 in. max.
Angle limit	44°
Valve stem diameter	
Standard	
Intake	0.3159-0.3157 in.
Exhaust	0.3149-0.3156 in.
0.008 in. oversize	
Intake	0.3239-0.3245 in.
Exhaust	0.3228-0.3235 in.
0.016 in. oversize	
Intake	0.3318-0.3324 in.
Exhaust	0.3307-0.3314 in.
0.032 in. oversize	
Intake	0.3475-0.3481 in.
Exhaust	0.3461-0.3468 in.
Valve spring load	
Closed	60-68 lb. @ 1.585 in.
Open	138-149 lb. @ 1.222 in.
Valve spring free length	1.91 in.
Valve spring assembled height	1 37/64-1 39/64 in.

(continued)

Table 1 2.8L V6 ENGINE SPECIFICATIONS (continued)

Valve spring out-of-square	
Service limit	0.078 in.
Rocker arm	
Shaft diameter	0.7799-0.7811 in.
Bore diameter	0.7830-0.7842 in.
Ratio	1.46:1
Pushrod runout	0.020 in.
Valve lifter	
Diameter	0.8736-0.8741 in.
Clearance-to-bore	0.0009-0.0024 in.
Service limit	0.005 in.
Valve lash (cold)	
Intake	0.014 in.
Exhaust	0.016 in.
Camshaft	
Lobe lift (intake & exhaust)	0.2555 in.
Valve lift @ zero lash	
Intake and exhaust	0.3730 in.
End play	0.0008-0.004 in.
Service limit	0.009 in.
Journal-to-bearing clearance	0.001-0.0026 in.
Service limit	0.006 in.
Gear backlash	0.006-0.010 in.
Journal diameter	
No. 1	1.7285-1.7293 in.
No. 2	1.7135-1.7143 in.
No. 3	1.6985-1.6992 in.
No. 4	1.6835-1.6842 in.
Journal runout limit	0.005 in. max.
Out-of-round limit	0.0003 in. max.
Crankshaft	
Main bearing journal diameter	2.2433-2.2441 in.
Out-of-round limit	0.0006 in.
Taper limit	0.0006 in. per inch max.
Journal runout limit	0.002 in. max.
Thrust bearing journal length	1.039-1.041 in.
Connecting rod journal	
Diameter	2.1252-2.1260 in.
Out-of-round limit	0.0006 in. max.
Taper limit	0.0006 in. per inch max.
Main bearing thrust face	
Runout limit	0.001 in. max.
End play	
Normal	0.004-0.008 in.
Service limit	0.012 in.
Main bearing clearance	
Desired	0.0008-0.0015 in.
Allowed	0.0005-0.0019 in.
Connecting rod	
Piston pin bore diameter	0.9450-0.9452 in.
Crankshaft bearing bore diameter	2.2370-2.2378 in.
Out-of-round limit	0.0004 in.
Taper limit	0.0004 in.
Length (center-to-center)	5.1386-5.1413 in.

(continued)

Table 1 2.8L V6 ENGINE SPECIFICATIONS (continued)

Bearing clearance	
Desired	0.0006-0.0016 in.
Allowed	0.0005-0.0022 in.
Alignment	
Twist	0.006 in.
Bend	0.002 in.
Side clearance	
Standard	0.004-0.011 in.
Service limit	0.014 in.
Flywheel	
Clutch face runout limit	0.005 in.
Ring gear lateral runout	
Manual transmission	0.025 in.
Automatic transmission	0.060 in.
Piston	
Diameter	
Red code	3.6605-3.6615 in.
0.020 oversize	3.6802-3.6812 in.
Pin-to-bore clearance	0.0011-0.0019 in.
Pin bore diameter	0.9450-0.9452 in.
Ring groove width	
Compression	
Top	0.0803-0.0811 in.
Bottom	0.1197-0.1205 in.
Oil	0.1579-0.1587 in.
Piston pin	
Length	2.835-2.866 in.
Diameter	
Standard	0.9446-0.9450 in.
Piston-to-pin clearance	0.0003-0.0006 in.
Pin-to-rod clearance	Interference fit
Piston rings	
Ring width	
Compression	
Top	0.0780-0.0783 in.
Bottom	0.1172-0.1177 in.
Side clearance	
Compression	0.0020-0.0033 in.
Oil	Snug fit (0.006 in. max.)
Ring gap	
Compression	0.015-0.023 in.
Oil (steel rail)	0.015-0.055 in.
Oil pump	
Relief valve spring tension	13.6-14.7 lb. @ 1.39 in.
Drive shaft-to-housing bearing clearance	0.0015-0.0030 in.
Relief valve-to-bore clearance	0.0015-0.0030 in.
Rotor assembly end clearance	0.004 in. max.
Outer-race-to-housing clearance	0.001-0.003 in.

Table 2 3.0L V6 ENGINE SPECIFICATIONS

Engine type	60° V6
Bore	3.50 in.
Stroke	3.15 in.
Displacement	3000 cc
Firing order	1-4-2-5-3-6
Cylinder arrangement	
Passenger side	1-3-5
Driver side	2-4-6
Cylinder block	
Bore diameter	3.504 in.
Head gasket surface flatness	0.003 in. in any 6 in.; 0.006 in. overall
Out-of-round (maximum)	0.001 in.
Taper (maximum)	0.002 in.
Main bearing bore diameter	2.712-2.713 in.
Valve system	
Valve guide bore diameter	0.3443-0.3433 in.
Valve seat width	
Intake & exhaust	0.06-0.08 in.
Valve seat angle	45°
Valve seat runout limit	0.003 in.
Bore diameter (insert counterbore diameter)	
Intake	1.8532-1.8542 in.
Exhaust	1.5645 in.
Gasket surface flatness	0.007 in.
Valve stem-to-guide clearance	
Intake	0.001-0.0027 in.
Exhaust	0.0015-0.0032 in.
Valve head diameter	
Intake	1.57 in.
Exhaust	1.30 in.
Valve face	
Runout limit	0.002 in. max.
Angle limit	44°
Valve stem diameter	
Standard	
Intake	0.3134-0.3126 in.
Exhaust	0.3129-0.3121 in.
Valve spring load	
Closed	73 lb. @ 1.54 in.
Open	185 lb. @ 1.11 in.
Valve spring assembled height	1.85 in.
Rocker arm ratio	1.61:1
Valve lifter	
Diameter	0.874 in.
Clearance-to-bore	0.0007-0.0027 in.
Service limit	0.005 in.
Collapsed tappet gap	
Intake and exhaust	0.088-0.189 in.
Camshaft	
Lobe lift (intake & exhaust)	0.260 in.
Valve lift @ zero lash	
Intake and exhaust	0.419 in.

(continued)

Table 2 3.0L V6 ENGINE SPECIFICATIONS (continued)

End play	1
Journal-to-bearing clearance	0.001-0.003 in.
Journal diameter	2.0074-2.0084 in.
Journal runout limit	0.002 in. max.
Out-of-round limit	0.001 in. max.
Crankshaft	
Main bearing journal diameter	2.5190-2.5198 in.
Out-of-round limit	0.0003 in.
Taper limit	0.0003 in. per inch max.
Journal runout limit	0.002 in. max.
End play	0.004-0.008 in.
Thrust bearing journal length	1.0148-1.067 in.
Connecting rod journal	
Diameter	2.1253-2.1261 in.
Out-of-round limit	0.0003 in. max.; 0.0006 in. total
Taper limit	0.0006 in. per inch max.
Main bearing thrust face	
Runout limit	0.001 in. max.
Main bearing clearance	
Desired	0.001-0.0014 in.
Allowed	0.0005-0.0023 in.
Connecting rod	
Piston pin bore diameter	0.9096-0.9112 in.
Crankshaft bearing bore diameter	2.250-2.251 in.
Length (center-to-center)	5.530-5.533 in.
Bearing clearance	
Desired	0.001-0.0014 in.
Allowed	0.00086-0.0027 in.
Alignment	
Twist	0.003 in. per in.
Bend	0.0016 in. per in.
Side clearance	
Standard	0.006-0.014 in.
Service limit	0.014 in. max.
Flywheel ring gear lateral runout	
Automatic transmission	0.070 in.
Piston	
Diameter	
Red code	3.5024-3.5031 in.
Blue code	3.5035-3.5041 in.
Yellow code	3.5045-3.5051 in.
Selection guide	
Piston bore diameter	
3.5043-3.5053 in.	Red code
3.5053-3.5063 in.	Blue code
3.5063-3.5073 in.	Yellow code
Pin-to-piston clearance	0.005-0.0012 in.
Pin-to-rod clearance	Press fit
Ring groove width	
Compression	0.0602-0.0612 in.
Oil	0.1587-0.1596 in.
Piston pin	
Length	3.012-3.039 in.
Diameter	0.9119-0.9124

(continued)

Table 2 3.0L V6 ENGINE SPECIFICATIONS (continued)

Piston rings	
Ring width	
Compression	0.0575-0.0587 in.
Side clearance	
Compression	0.0016-0.0037 in.
Ring gap	
Compression	0.01-0.02 in.
Oil (steel rail)	0.010-0.049 in.
Oil pump	
Relief valve spring tension	9.1-10.1 lb. @ 1.11 in.
Drive shaft-to-housing clearance	0.0019-0.0005 in.
Relief valve-to-bore clearance	0.0017-0.0029 in.
Pump gear backlash	0.008-0.12 in. max.
Pump gear radial clearance	0.0055-0.002 in.
Pump gear height clearance	0.0055-0.002 in.
Idler shaft-to-idler gear clearance	0.0017-0.0004 in.

1. 1986-1987 engines have no end play specification; the camshaft restrained by spring. An end play specification of 0.003 in. is provided by Ford for 1988 engines.

Table 3 2.8L V6 ENGINE TIGHTENING TORQUES

Fastener	ft.-lb.	N·m
Alternator		
Mounting bracket		
To block	29-40	40-55
To head		
M8	14-22	20-30
M10	29-40	40-55
Adjustment arm	60-70	70-95
Pivot bolt	45-61	61-82
Air conditioning pulley-to-crankshaft pulley	19-28	26-38
Camshaft		
Gear bolt	30-36	41-49
Thrust plate bolt	13-16	17-21
Connecting rod nut	19-24	26-33
Crankshaft pulley bolt	85-96	115-130
Cylinder head bolt	1	1
Carburetor spacer-to-intake manifold	14-22	20-30
EGR valve-to-spacer	14-22	20-30
Exhaust gas sensor-to-manifold	28-32	39-43
Exhaust manifold	20-30	27-40
Fan-to-fan clutch	6-8	8-11
Fan clutch-to-water pump hub	15-25	21-34
Flywheel-to-crankshaft	47-52	64-70
Front cover bolt	13-16	17-21
Front plate bolt	10-13	13-17
Fuel pump mounting bolt	15-18	21-25

(continued)

Table 3 2.8L V6 ENGINE TIGHTENING TORQUES (continued)

Fastener	ft.-lb.	N•m
Heat shroud		
To exhaust manifold	14-22	20-30
Outer-to-inner shroud	3-5	5-7
Intake manifold	[2]	[2]
Knock sensor-to-block	30-40	40-54
Main bearing cap bolt	65-75	88-102
Oil pump		
Pickup tube-to-pump	6-10	9-13
Pickup tube support	12-15	17-21
Case bolts	6-10	9-13
Oil pan		
Drain plug	15-21	20-28
To block	5-8	7-10
Oil filter adapter-to-block	15-30	20-40
Rocker arm shaft support bolt	43-50	59-67
Timing pointer-to-front cover	5-7	7-9
Thermactor pump		
Pivot bolt	30-40	40-55
Adjusting arm	30-40	40-55
Tube-to-exhaust manifold	14-22	20-30
Pulley	12-18	17-25
Valve cover	3-5	4-7
Water jacket drain plug	14-18	20-25
Water outlet	12-15	17-21
Water pump		
To front cover	7-9	9-12
Pulley	14-22	20-30
Standard torque values		
Grade 5 fasteners		
1/4-20	8	11
1/4-28	8	11
5/16-18	17	23
5/16-24	20	27
3/8-16	30	40
3/8-24	35	47
7/16-14	50	68
7/16-20	55	75
1/2-13	75	100
1/2-20	85	115
9/16-12	105	142
9/16-18	115	156

(continued)

Table 3 2.8L V6 ENGINE TIGHTENING TORQUES (continued)

Fastener	ft.-lb.	N•m
Grade 6 fasteners		
1/4-20	10.5	14
1/4-28	12.5	17
5/16-18	22.5	31
5/16-24	25	54
3/8-16	40	34
3/8-24	45	61
7/16-14	65	88
7/16-20	70	95
1/2-13	100	136
1/2-20	110	149
9/16-12	135	183
9/16-18	150	203

1. Tighten in 3 steps:
   a. Step 1 29-40 ft.-lb. (39-54 N•m)
   b. Step 2 40-51 ft.-lb. (54-69 N•m)
   c. Step 3 70-85 ft.-lb. (95-115 N•m)
2. Tighten in 5 steps:
   a. Step 1 Hand start and snug nuts
   b. Step 2 3-6 ft.-lb. (4-8 N•m)
   c. Step 3 6-11 ft.-lb. (8-15 N•m)
   d. Step 4 11-15 ft.-lb. (15-21 N•m)
   e. Step 5 15-18 ft.-lb. (21-25 N•m)

Table 4 3.0L V6 ENGINE TIGHTENING TORQUES

Fastener	ft.-lb.	N•m
Air conditioning compressor		
Front brace	15-22	20-30
All others	30-45	41-61
Alternator pivot bolt	45-57	61-75
Camshaft sprocket	40-51	55-70
Connecting rod nut	1	1
Crankshaft pulley bolt	20-28	26-38
Crankshaft damper bolt	141-169	190-230
Cylinder head bolt	2	2
Distributor hold-down bolt	20-29	27-40
Engine bracket reinforcement brace-to-engine bracket		
Nut	60-80	80-107
Bolt	35-50	47-67
Fuel rail-to-intake manifold	6	8
Exhaust manifold	15-22	20-30
Flywheel-to-crankshaft	54-64	73-87
Front cover bolt	15-22	20-30
Heater tube-to-intake manifold	15-22	20-30
Idler		
Bracket-to-alternator bolt	24-34	33-46
Top bracket bolt	30-40	40-55
Front lower attaching bolt	30-40	40-55
Front upper attaching bolt	52-70	70-95
Intake manifold	3	3
Low oil level sensor	26-35	34-47.5

(continued)

Table 4 3.0L V6 ENGINE TIGHTENING TORQUES (continued)

Fastener	ft.-lb.	N•m
Main bearing cap bolt	65-81	88-110
Oil inlet tube		
To main bearing cap	30-40	40-54
To block	15-22	20-30
Oil pan	7-8	9-12
Oil filter adapter-to-block	18-22	25-30
Power steering		
With A/C		
Lower brace bolt	18-24	24-32
All others	30-45	40-62
Without A/C (all)	30-45	40-62
Rocker arm fulcrum-to-head	4	4
Thermostat housing	15-22	20-30
Valve cover	7-8	9-12
Water pump	6-8	8-12
Standard torque values		
Grade 5 fasteners		
1/4-20	8	11
1/4-28	8	11
5/16-18	17	23
5/16-24	20	27
3/8-16	30	40
3/8-24	35	47
7/16-14	50	68
7/16-20	55	75
1/2-13	75	100
1/2-20	85	115
9/16-12	105	142
9/16-18	115	156
Grade 6 fasteners		
1/4-20	10.5	14
1/4-28	12.5	17
5/16-18	22.5	31
5/16-24	25	54
3/8-16	40	34
3/8-24	45	61
7/16-14	65	88
7/16-20	70	95
1/2-13	100	136
1/2-20	110	149
9/16-12	135	183
9/16-18	150	203

1. Tighten in 3 steps:
   a. Step 1 20-28 ft.-lb. (26-38 N•m)
   b. Step 2 Back nuts off @ least 2 full turns
   c. Step 3 20-25 ft.-lb. (26-34 N•m)
2. Tighten in 2 steps:
   a. Step 1 48-54 ft.-lb. (65-75 N•m)
   b. Step 2 63-80 ft.-lb. (85-110 N•m)
3. Tighten in 2 steps:
   a. Step 1 11 ft.-lb. (15 N•m)
   b. Step 2 18 ft.-lb. (24 N•m)
4. Tighten in 2 steps:
   a. Step 1 5-11 ft.-lb. (7-15 N•m)
   b. Step 2 18-25 ft.-lb. (25-34 N•m)

5

CHAPTER SIX

FUEL, EXHAUST AND EMISSION CONTROL SYSTEMS

This chapter consists of service procedures for the air cleaner, carburetor, electronic fuel injection (EFI) unit, fuel pump, fuel tank and lines, exhaust system and fuel-related emission controls.

Table 1 (tightening torques) is at the end of the chapter.

The fuel system consists of a rear-mounted fuel tank connected by a fuel line to a mechanical fuel pump (carburetted models) or electric fuel pump (fuel injected models). The pump delivers fuel through a fuel filter to the carburetor or injectors.

Various systems are used to remove harmful pollutants from the exhaust gases before they are released into the atmosphere. These systems include a positive crankcase ventilation (PCV) system to return blowby gas and other vapors to the combustion chambers for further burning. An evaporative emission control system holds and stores fuel vapor from the fuel system so that it will eventually be burned in the combustion chambers instead of being vented into the atmosphere. A Thermactor air injection system on 1986 engines injects fresh air into the exhaust system to promote further burning of pollutants. An exhaust gas recirculation (EGR) system lowers the combustion chamber temperatures by metering a small amount of exhaust gas into the intake manifold. The catalytic converter promotes more complete burning of gases in the exhaust system.

All engines except the 1986 2.8L V6 use a multi-point fuel injection system. The 2-barrel Motorcraft 2150 carburetor is used on 1986 2.8L V6 engines. All engines use the EEC-IV ignition system. The EEC-IV system is designed to control emissions while providing maximum fuel economy, driveability and performance. A microprocessor reads inputs from a variety of sensors, compares the data against an internal program and sends controlling output signals to various components in order to maintain a proper air-fuel ratio and ignition timing.

The EEC-IV microprocessor contains a memory to store trouble codes when one or more EEC-IV system components malfunctions. Any malfunction of the EEC-IV system should be diagnosed and serviced by a dealer or qualified garage with the necessary special tools and test equipment.

With the exception of the fuel tank and carburetor, the repair of all systems discussed in this chapter is by replacement of major parts. The carburetor is considered a part of the emission control system. Due to strict emission regulation requirements, the only adjustments that can be performed on the carburetor by an amateur mechanic are curb idle and fast idle settings. The idle mixture and other adjustments are either permanently pre-set at the factory or require the use of tools and special test equipment not available outside a Ford dealership or other competent garage.

AIR CLEANER SYSTEM

Description

A dry air cleaner containing a replaceable air filter element is standard on all engines. The filter element can be changed without removing the air cleaner housing from the engine.

Carburetted Engines

The air cleaner is attached to the top of the carburetor on 1986 2.8L V6 engines. Various sensors, switches and a vacuum-operated control valve or door in the air cleaner snorkel control intake air temperature. The air cleaner furnishes temperature-regulated air to the carburetor to reduce emissions and improve driveability. The air cleaner duct/valve assembly is connected to a fresh air inlet tube and a hot air tube/shroud assembly surrounding the exhaust manifold. Air flow from these 2 sources is controlled by a valve in the snorkel. This valve is operated by a vacuum motor mounted on the snorkel. The door and motor are connected by mechanical linkage inside the snorkel. A temperature sensor inside the air cleaner housing modulates vacuum to the motor according to air cleaner air temperature. **Figure 1** shows the major components of the carburetted air cleaner assembly.

EFI Engines

The air cleaner on EFI engines furnishes clean air to the intake air throttle body through a resonator assembly that acts like a plenum. EFI engines do not require temperature-regulated air. This makes the EFI air cleaner system less complex, as there are no sensors, control valves or hot air tube/shroud to contend with. **Figure 2** (I4) and **Figure 3** (V6) show the major components of the EFI air cleaner assembly.

Heated Air Inlet System Operation (Carburetted Engine)

When the engine is first started, the air cleaner draws hot air from near the exhaust manifold through the hot air tube (A, **Figure 4**). As the engine warms up, the duct door changes position to partially block off air from the hot air tube. Once the air cleaner temperature reaches a specified value, the duct door closes off the hot air hose completely (B, **Figure 4**). This allows the air cleaner to draw intake air through the fresh air inlet tube.

Filter Replacement

See *Air Cleaner Filter,* Chapter Three.

Air Cleaner Removal/Installation

2.3L EFI engine

Refer to **Figure 2** for this procedure.

1. Unclamp and disconnect the resonator inlet and outlet tubes at the air cleaner cover (**Figure 5**) and upper intake manifold.
2. Unbolt and remove the resonator assembly with the inlet and outlet tubes attached. See **Figure 6**.
3. Remove the screws holding the air cleaner cover. Remove the cover and filter element.
4. Reach underneath the air cleaner tray and remove the 3 nuts holding the housing in place.
5. Remove the air cleaner housing from the engine compartment.
6. Installation is the reverse of removal. Make sure the duct tube adapter is properly installed between the air cleaner housing and the RH fender apron.

2.8L V6 engine

Refer to **Figure 1** for this procedure.

1. Disconnect the fresh air tube at the duct and valve assembly. Remove the fresh air tube from the engine compartment.
2. Disconnect the vacuum line at the duct and valve assembly vacuum motor. See A, **Figure 7**.
3. Disconnect the hot air tube at the duct and valve assembly.
4. Unplug the air charge temperature sensor connector. See B, **Figure 7**.
5. Disconnect the PVC hose at the air cleaner housing.
6. Reach underneath the cowl and remove the air cleaner cover wing nut. Remove the cover and filter element.
7. Lift the air cleaner housing up enough to clear the carburetor air horn and remove it from the engine compartment. Place on a clean flat surface to prevent damage to the duct/valve or hot air tube.
8. Check the carburetor air horn mounting gasket. If not found on the air horn, it may be attached to the underside of the air cleaner housing.
9. Installation is the reverse of removal. If the old mounting gasket is damaged or missing, install a new gasket to prevent a vacuum leak. The gasket should be installed with its adhesive side facing the

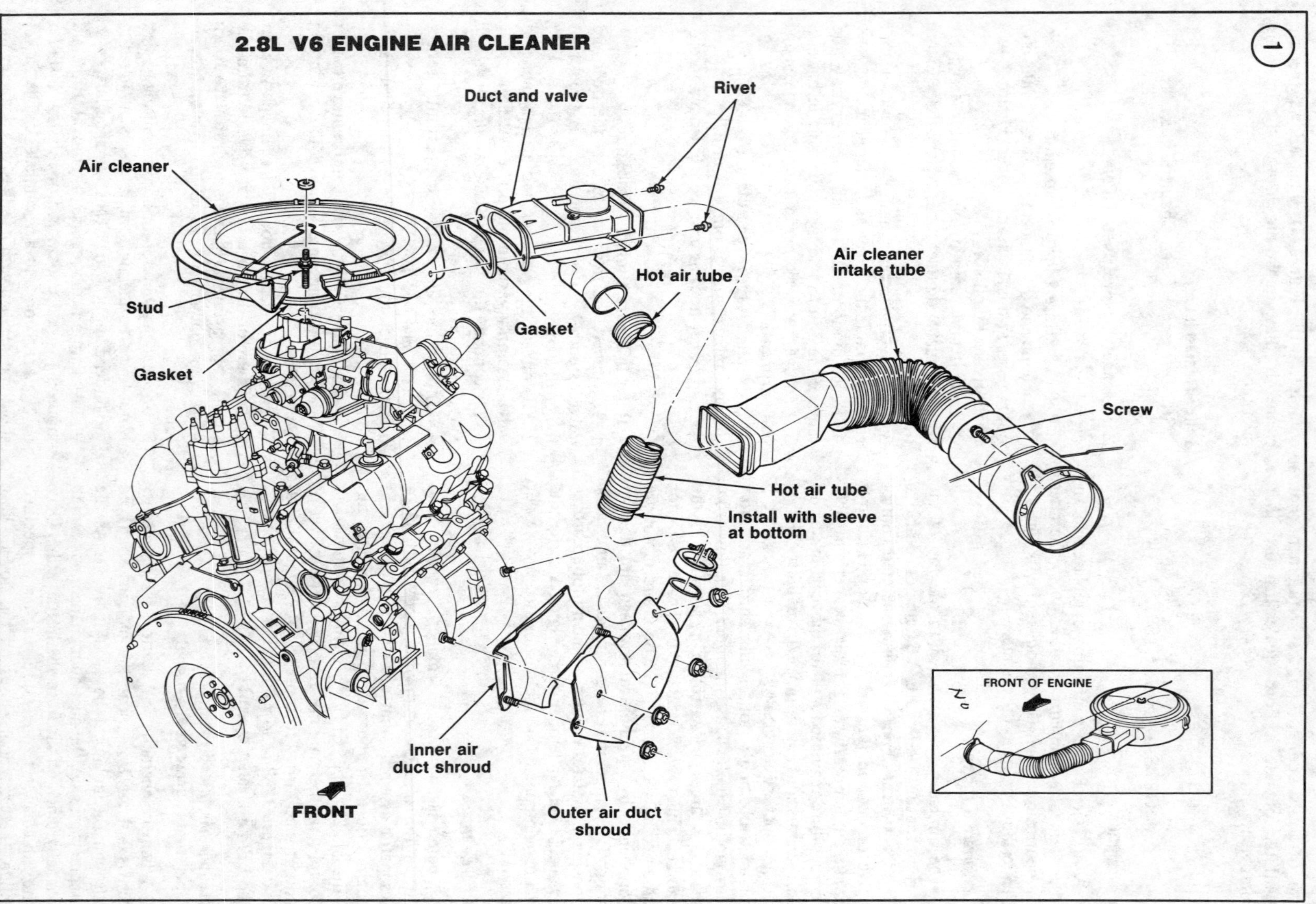
1
2.8L V6 ENGINE AIR CLEANER
Duct and valve
Rivet
Air cleaner
Air cleaner intake tube
Hot air tube
Stud
Gasket
Gasket
Screw
Hot air tube
Install with sleeve at bottom
FRONT OF ENGINE
Inner air duct shroud
FRONT
Outer air duct shroud

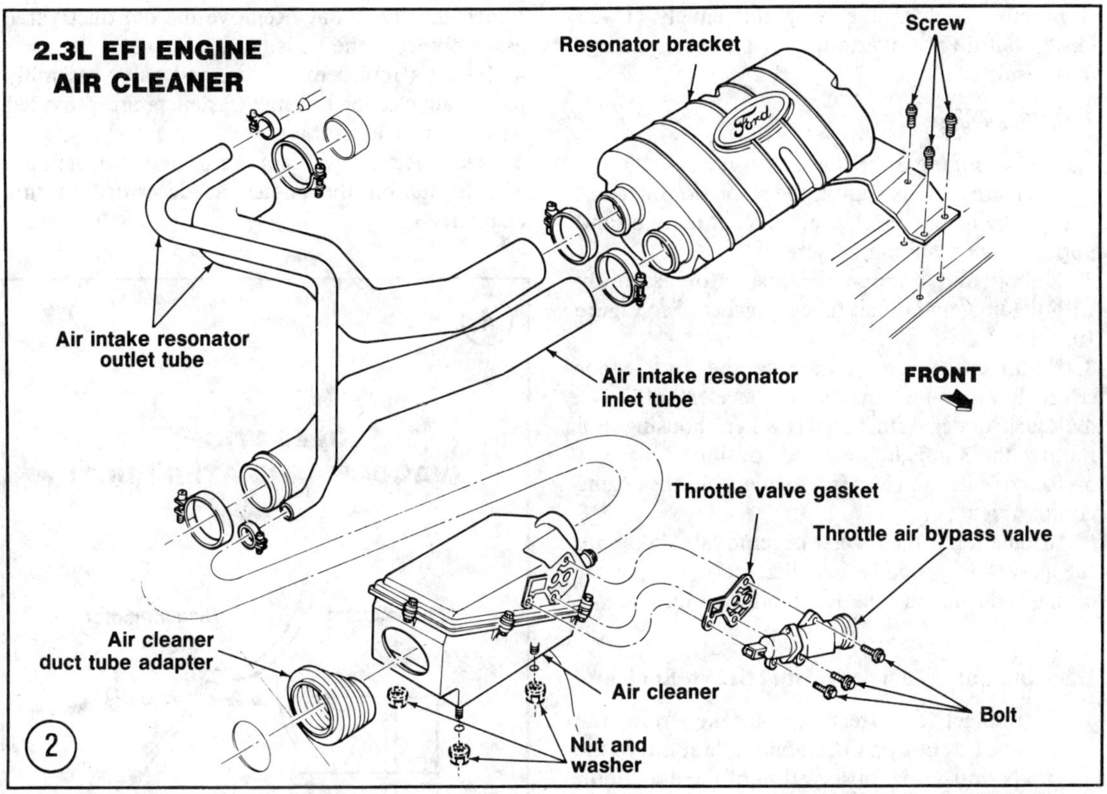

2.3L EFI ENGINE
AIR CLEANER
Resonator bracket
Screw
Air intake resonator
outlet tube
Air intake resonator
inlet tube
FRONT
Throttle valve gasket
Throttle air bypass valve
Air cleaner
duct tube adapter
Air cleaner
Bolt
Nut and
washer
2

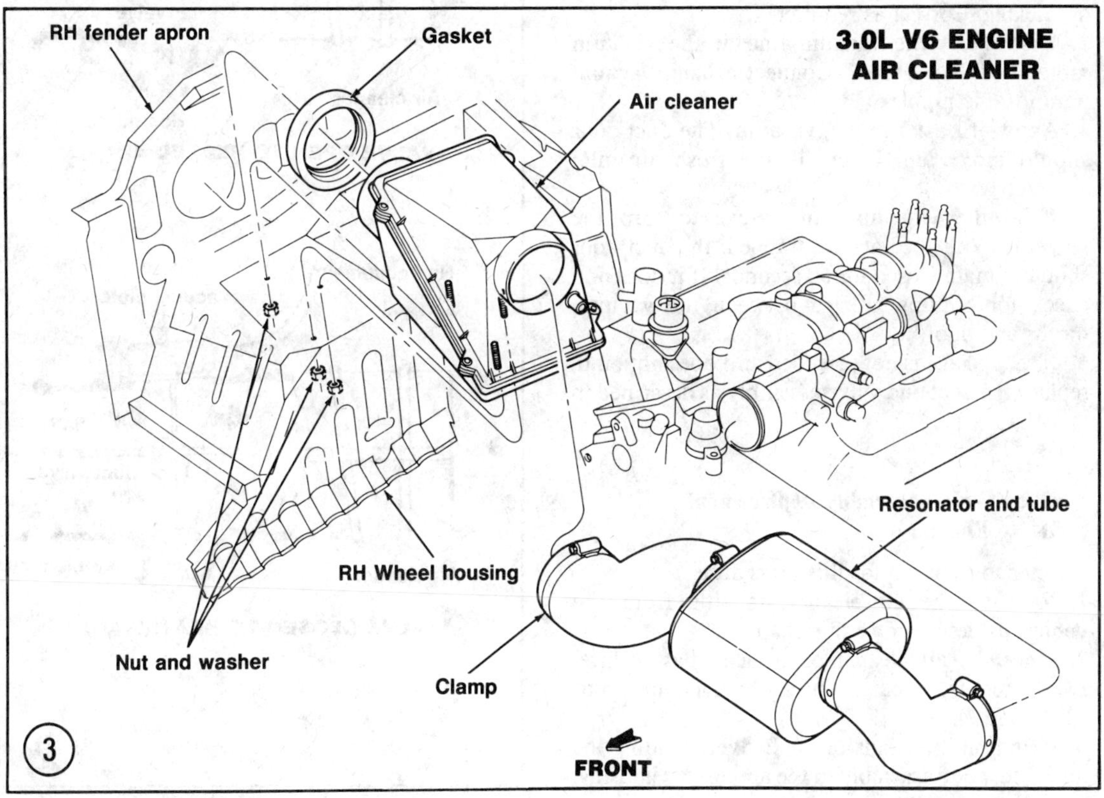

RH fender apron
Gasket
3.0L V6 ENGINE
AIR CLEANER
Air cleaner
Resonator and tube
RH Wheel housing
Nut and washer
Clamp
FRONT
3

carburetor. Tighten the wing nut snugly (15-25 in.-lb.) but do not overtorque or air horn warpage may result.

3.0L V6 engine

Refer to **Figure 3** for this procedure.

1. Unclamp and disconnect the resonator inlet and outlet tube at the air cleaner cover (**Figure 8**) and upper intake manifold (**Figure 9**).
2. Unbolt and remove the resonator assembly with the inlet and outlet tubes attached. See **Figure 10**.
3. Remove the screws holding the air cleaner cover. Remove the cover and filter element.
4. Reach underneath the RH wheel housing and remove the 3 nuts holding the housing in place.
5. Remove the air cleaner housing from the engine compartment.
6. Installation is the reverse of removal. Make sure the gasket is properly installed between the air cleaner housing and the RH fender apron.

Duct and Valve Function Test (2.8L V6 Engine)

1. Disconnect the fresh air intake from the duct/valve assembly and carefully fold it out of the way to permit visual observation of the duct door.
2. Depress door with a finger to check for binding or sticking. Correct as required.
3. Disconnect the vacuum line at the vacuum motor. See B, **Figure 7**. Connect a hand vacuum pump to the nipple.
4. Apply at least 7 in. Hg vacuum. The duct door should move and block off the fresh air inlet completely.
5. Bend the vacuum pump hose to trap the vacuum. With the vacuum trapped, the duct door should remain closed for 60 seconds. If it does not, check for binding linkage between the vacuum motor and door.
6. If the linkage is not corroded and does not bind, replace the duct and valve assembly as described in this chapter.

Duct and Valve Assembly Replacement (2.8L V6 Engine)

Refer to **Figure 3** for this procedure.

1. Remove the air cleaner housing from the vehicle as described in this chapter.
2. Place the air cleaner on a clean flat surface. Disconnect the vacuum line at the vacuum motor (B, **Figure 7**).
3. Grind off the heads of the 2 rivets holding the duct and valve assembly to the air cleaner housing. Punch the rivets out. Remove the old duct/valve assembly from the housing.
4. Install a replacement duct and valve assembly to the air cleaner housing (fasteners are provided with the new assembly).
5. Reconnect the vacuum motor line. Reinstall the air cleaner on the engine as described in this chapter.

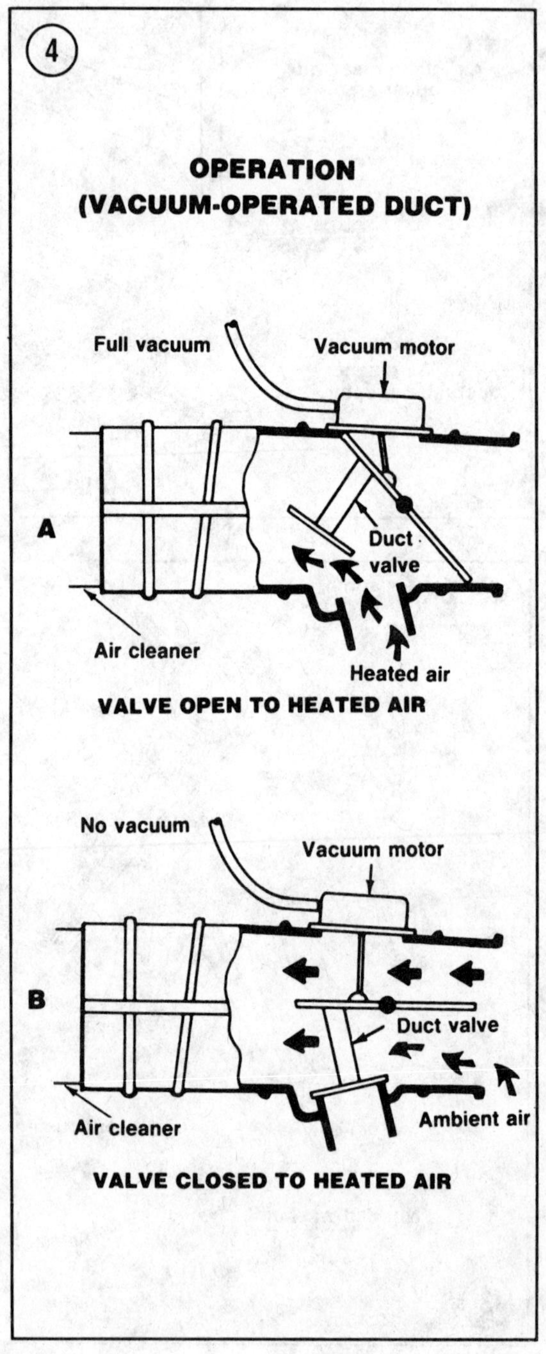

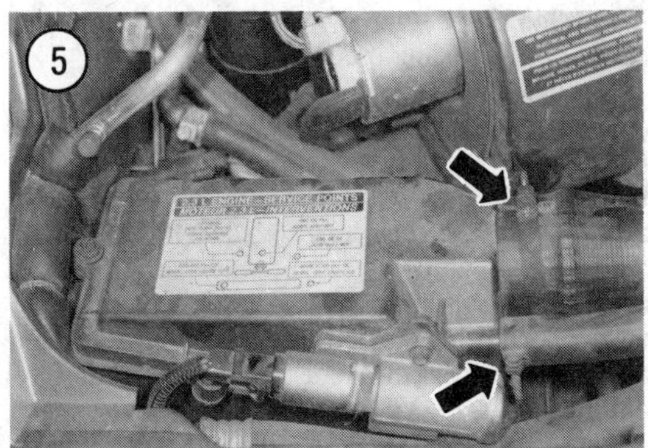

FUEL QUALITY

Gasoline blended with alcohol is widely available, although it is not legally required to be labeled as such in many states. A mixture of 10 percent ethyl alcohol and 90 percent unleaded gasoline is called gasohol.

Fuels with an alcohol content tend to absorb moisture from the air. When the moisture content of the fuel reaches approximately one percent, it combines with the alcohol and separates from the fuel. This water-alcohol mixture settles at the bottom of the fuel tank where the fuel pickup carries it into the fuel line to the carburetor or fuel injectors.

The greatest problem with gasohol is its cleaning effect on service station storage tanks, as well as the vehicle's fuel tank. As a result of this cleaning action, a combination of rust, a jelly-like sludge and metallic particles pass into the automotive fuel system. These substances cause reduced fuel flow through the filter and will eventually plug the carburetor or injector passageways.

Some methods of blending alcohol with gasoline now make use of cosolvents as a suspension agent to prevent the water-alcohol from separating from the gasoline. Regardless of the method used, however, alcohol mixed with gasoline in any

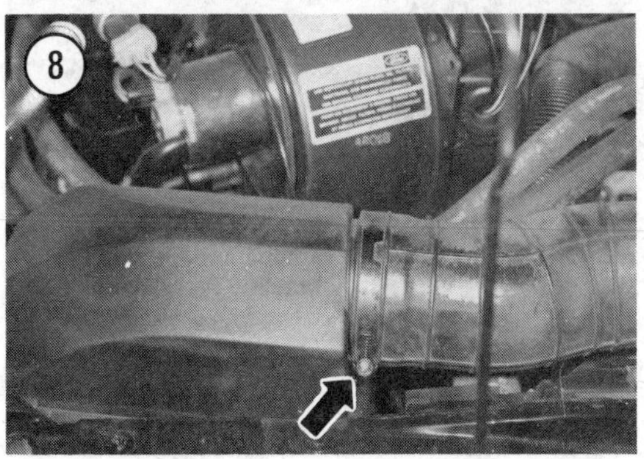

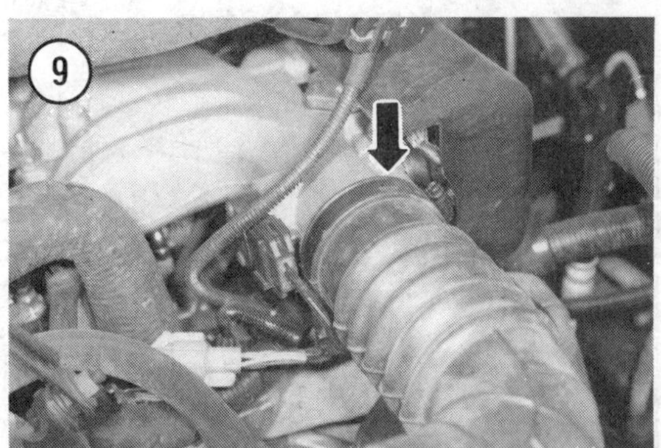

manner can cause numerous and serious problems with an automotive fuel system, including:

a. Corrosion formation on the inside of fuel tanks, steel fuel lines, fuel pumps, carburetors and fuel injectors.
b. Deterioration of the plastic liner used in some fuel tanks, resulting in eventual plugging of the in-tank filter.
c. Deterioration and failure of synthetic rubber or plastic materials such as O-ring seals, diaphragms, inlet needle tips, accelerator pump cups and gaskets.
d. Premature failure of fuel line hoses.
e. Hot weather driveability problems.

The problem of gasoline blended with alcohol has become so prevalent around the United States that Miller Tools (32615 Park Lane, Garden City, MI 48135) and Kent-Moore (28635 Mound Road, Warren, MI 48092) now offer Alcohol Detection Kits (Miller part No. C-4846; Kent-Moore part No. J-34353) so that owners can determine the quality of fuel being used.

The detection procedure is performed with water as a reacting agent. However, if cosolvents have been used as a suspension agent in alcohol blending, the test will not show the presence of alcohol unless ethylene glycol (automotive antifreeze) is used instead of water as a reacting agent. It is suggested that a gasoline sample be tested twice using the detection kit: first with water and then with ethylene glycol (automotive antifreeze).

The procedure cannot differentiate between types of alcohol (ethanol, methanol, etc.) nor is it considered to be absolutely accurate from a scientific standpoint, but it is accurate enough to determine whether or not there is enough alcohol in the fuel to cause the user to take precautions. Maintaining a close watch on the quality of fuel used can save hundreds of dollars in engine and fuel system repairs.

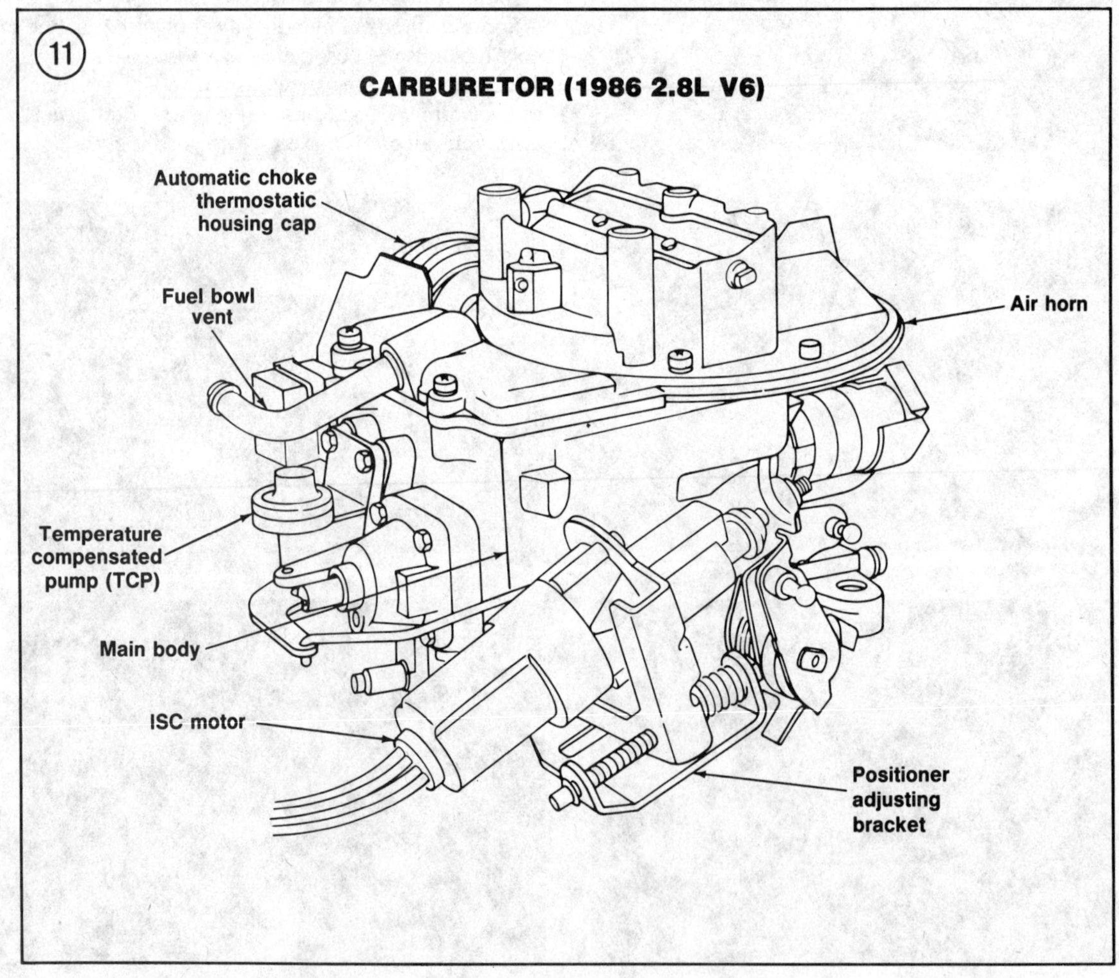

CARBURETOR

The 1986 2.8L V6 uses a Motorcraft 2150 2-barrel feedback carburetor (**Figure 11**).

WARNING
Tampering with a sealed carburetor is a violation of Federal law. Choke, idle mixture and other sealed adjustments can legally be made only under specified circumstances. Adjustment of these systems should be left to a Ford dealer.

Removal and installation procedures are provided for the carburetors. Carburetor specifications vary with point of first sale and engine/transmission application. This means that specifications will differ according to whether the engine is a Federal (49-state), California or high altitude model. The necessary specifications are provided on instruction sheets accompanying overhaul kits, along with specific procedures required for proper adjustment. Such instruction sheets also incorporate any recent changes authorized by the factory in adjustment specifications.

Model Identification

A carburetor identification tag (**Figure 12**) is attached to the carburetor by one of the air horn screws. The basic part number is 9510. To obtain the correct carburetor overhaul kit and/or replacement parts, the part number prefix, suffix and design change information must be used. Write down all information on the identification tag and give it to the parts department of any Ford dealer or auto parts store.

(12)

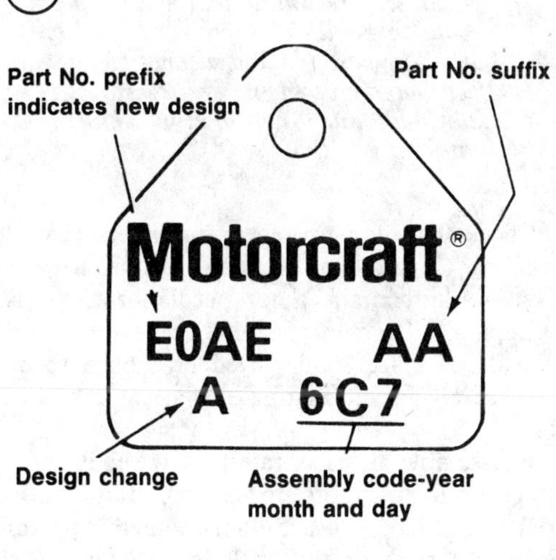

Carburetor Removal/Installation

1. Disconnect the negative battery cable.
2. Remove the air cleaner as described in this chapter.
3. Disconnect the throttle cable at the throttle lever. Disconnect the cruise control cable and/or automatic transmission detent cable, if so equipped.
4. Label and disconnect all vacuum lines and electrical connectors.
5. Hold the fuel filter with a suitable open-end wrench and use a second wrench to break the fuel line fitting nut loose at the filter. Disconnect the fuel line from the filter. Plug the line to prevent leakage.
6. Remove the carburetor retaining nuts. Remove the carburetor from the intake manifold.
7. Remove the carburetor mounting gasket spacer/insulator.
8. Stuff a clean shop cloth in the intake manifold opening to prevent the entry of contamination.
9. Installation is the reverse of removal. If the gasket spacer/insulator is damaged, install a new one. Tighten attaching fasteners in a clockwise pattern to prevent carburetor base warpage. Tighten to 14-16 f.t-lb. (20-21 N•m).

Preparation for Overhaul

Before removing and disassembling any carburetor, be sure you have the proper overhaul kit, a sufficient quantity of fresh carburetor cleaner and the proper tools. Work slowly and carefully, follow the disassembly/assembly procedures, refer to the exploded drawing of your carburetor when necessary and do not apply excessive force at any time.

It is not necessary to disassemble the carburetor linkage or remove linkage adjusting screws when overhauling a carburetor. Solenoids, dashpots and other diaphragm-operated assist devices attached to the carburetor body should be removed, as carburetor cleaner will damage them. Wipe such parts with a cloth to remove road film, grease and other contamination.

Use carburetor legs to prevent throttle plate damage while working on the carburetor. If legs are not available, thread a nut on each of four 2 1/4 in. bolts. Install each bolt in a flange hole and thread another nut on the bolt. These will hold the bolts securely to the carburetor and serve the same purpose as legs.

WARNING
Tampering with a sealed carburetor is a violation of Federal law. Choke, idle mixture and other sealed adjustments can legally be made only under specified circumstances. Adjustment of these systems should be left to a Ford dealer.

The carburetors use on the vehicles covered in this manual have riveted choke housings and plug seals over the idle mixture needles in accordance with Federal regulations. These adjustments are factory-set and should not be changed by the home mechanic. If the engine will not run properly after the carburetor is cleaned, reassembled and installed, it is advisable to install a rebuilt carburetor.

Cleaning and Inspection

Dirt, varnish, gum or other contamination in or on the carburetor are often the cause of unsatisfactory performance. Gaskets and accelerating pump cups may swell or leak, resulting in carburetion problems. Efficient carburetion depends upon careful cleaning, inspection and proper installation of new parts. All parts provided in the carburetor overhaul kit (except the idle mixture needle) should be installed when overhauling the carburetor.

Wash all parts except the choke cap, diaphragms, dashpots, solenoids and other vacuum or electrically operated assist devices in a cleaning solvent. Immersion-type carburetor cleaners are often used to remove dirt, gum and varnish from carburetor parts, but the use of such cleaners can remove the sealing compound (dichromate finish) applied to the carburetor castings at the factory to prevent porosity. Cleaning with an aerosol type cleaner or with solvent and a brush will do the job without damage to the sealing compound.

If a commercial cleaning solvent is used, suspend the air horn in the cleaner to prevent the solution from reaching the riveted choke cap and housing. Do not leave any parts in the cleaning solution longer than necessary to avoid removal of the sealing compound.

Rinse parts cleaned in solvent with kerosene. Blow all parts dry with compressed air. Wipe all parts which cannot be immersed in solvent or gasoline with a soft cloth slightly moistened with solvent, then with a clean, dry cloth.

Force compressed air through all passages in the carburetor.

CAUTION
Do not use a wire brush to clean any part. Do not use a drill or wire to clean out any opening or passage in the carburetor. A drill or wire may enlarge the hole or passage and change the calibration.

Check the choke and throttle plate shafts for grooves, wear or excessive looseness or binding. Inspect the choke and throttle plates for nicked edges or burrs which prevent proper closure. Choke and throttle plates are positioned during production and should not be removed unless damaged.

Clean all gasket residue from the air horn, main body and throttle body sealing surfaces with a putty knife. Since carburetor castings are aluminum, a sharp instrument should not be used to clean the gasket residue or damage to the carburetor assemblies may result.

Inspect all components for cracks or warpage. Check floats for wear on the lip and hinge pin. Check hinge pin holes in air horn, bowl cover or float bowl for wear and elongation.

Check composition floats for fuel absorption by gently squeezing and applying fingernail pressure. If moisture appears, replace the float.

Replace the float if the arm needle contact surface is grooved. If the float or floats are serviceable, gently polish the needle contact surface of the arm with crocus cloth or steel wool. Replace the float if the shaft is worn.

NOTE
Some gasolines contain additives that will cause the viton tip on the fuel inlet needle to swell. This problem is also caused by gasoline and alcohol blends. If carburetor problems are traced to a deformed inlet needle tip, change brands of gasoline used.

Check the viton tip of the fuel inlet needle for swelling or distortion. Discard the needle if the overhaul kit contains a new needle for assembly.

Replace all screws and nuts that have stripped threads. Replace all distorted or broken springs. Inspect all gasket mating surfaces for nicks or burrs.

Reassemble all parts carefully. It should not be necessary to apply force to any parts. If force seems to be required, you are doing something wrong. Stop and refer to the exploded drawing of the carburetor (**Figure 13**).

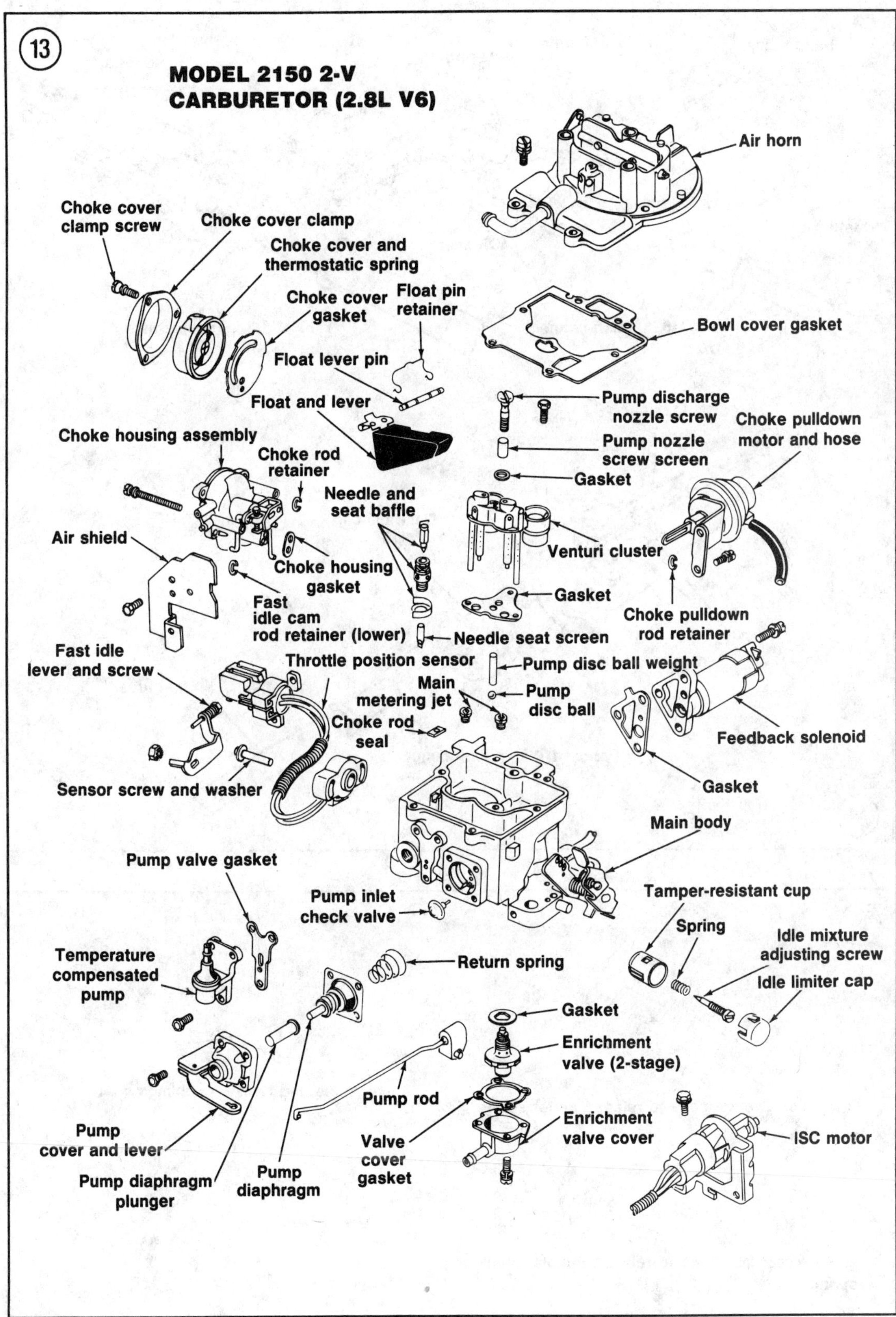
13
MODEL 2150 2-V
CARBURETOR (2.8L V6)
Air horn
Choke cover clamp screw
Choke cover clamp
Choke cover and thermostatic spring
Choke cover gasket
Float pin retainer
Bowl cover gasket
Float lever pin
Float and lever
Pump discharge nozzle screw
Choke pulldown motor and hose
Choke housing assembly
Pump nozzle screw screen
Choke rod retainer
Gasket
Needle and seat baffle
Air shield
Venturi cluster
Choke housing gasket
Gasket
Fast idle cam rod retainer (lower)
Choke pulldown rod retainer
Needle seat screen
Fast idle lever and screw
Throttle position sensor
Pump disc ball weight
Main metering jet
Pump disc ball
Choke rod seal
Feedback solenoid
Sensor screw and washer
Gasket
Main body
Pump valve gasket
Tamper-resistant cup
Pump inlet check valve
Spring
Idle mixture adjusting screw
Temperature compensated pump
Return spring
Idle limiter cap
Gasket
Enrichment valve (2-stage)
Pump rod
Enrichment valve cover
Pump cover and lever
Valve cover gasket
ISC motor
Pump diaphragm plunger
Pump diaphragm

6

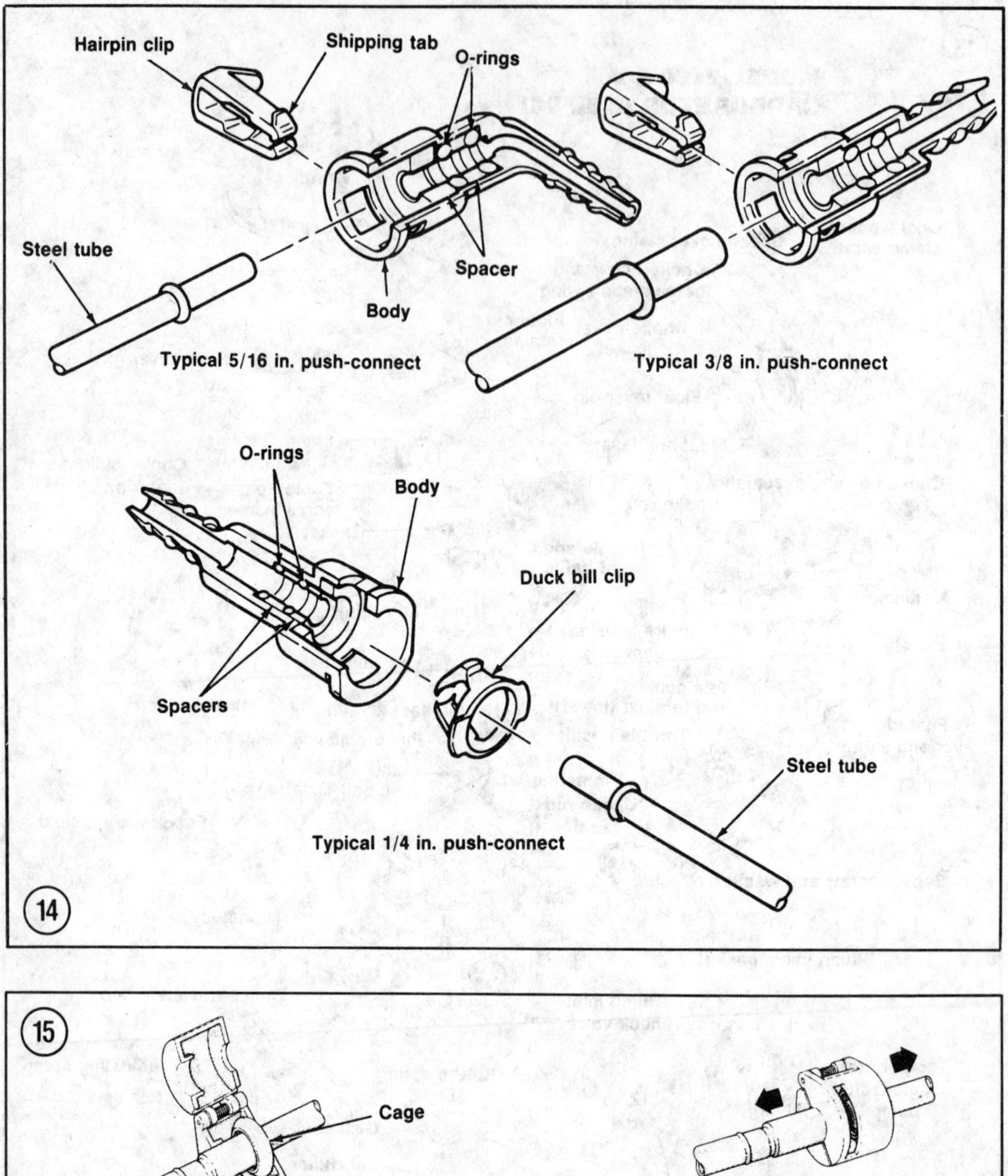

Hairpin clip
Shipping tab
O-rings
Steel tube
Spacer
Body
Typical 5/16 in. push-connect
Typical 3/8 in. push-connect

O-rings
Body
Duck bill clip
Spacers
Steel tube
Typical 1/4 in. push-connect

14

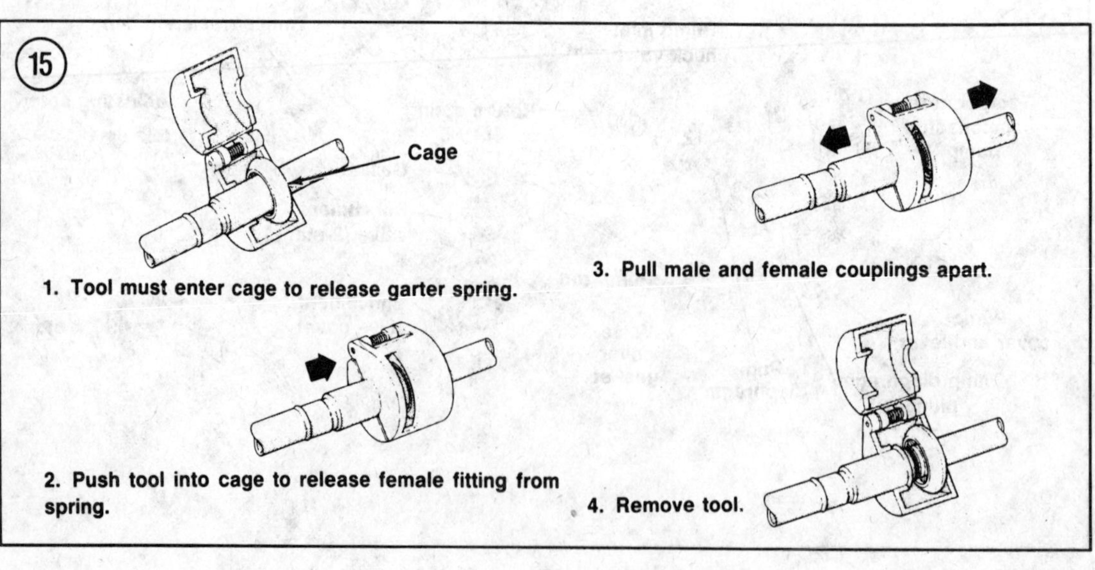

1. Tool must enter cage to release garter spring.

2. Push tool into cage to release female fitting from spring.

3. Pull male and female couplings apart.

4. Remove tool.

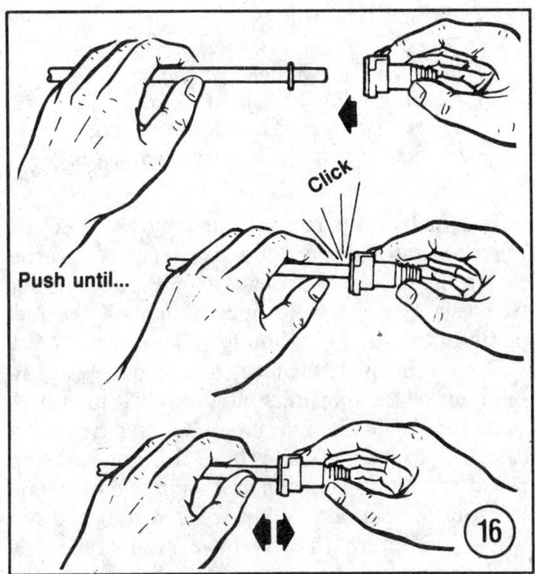

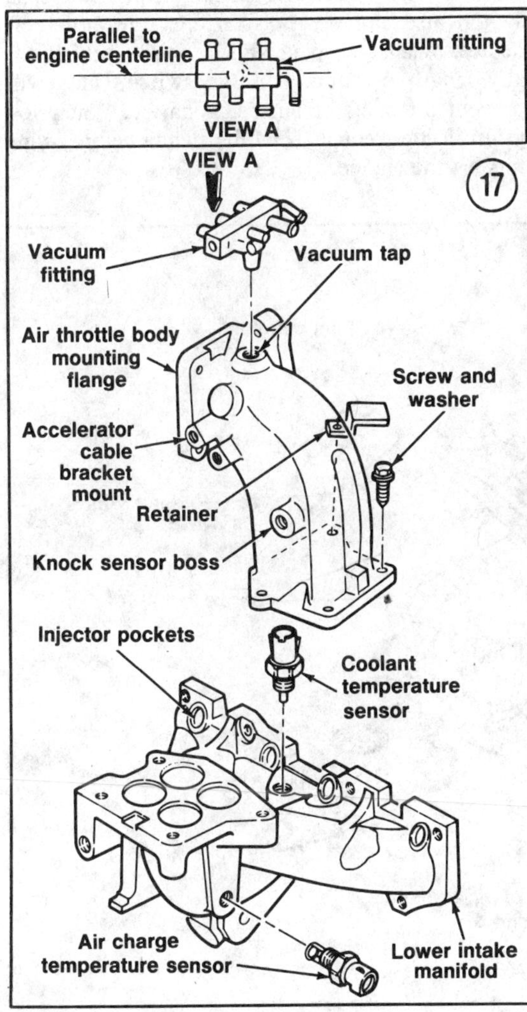

QUICK-DISCONNECT FITTINGS

Two types of quick-disconnect fuel line fittings are used on all fuel injected vehicles covered in this manual: a push-connect and a spring lock coupling.

The push-connect fitting is used to connect steel tubing to nylon fuel hose. Two styles are used: the duck bill clip and the hairpin clip (**Figure 14**). To disengage the duck bill clip, align the slot on tool part No. T82L-9500-AH with either clip tab (90° from the fitting slots) and insert. To disengage the hairpin clip, bend the shipping tab down to clear the connector body. Spread the ends of the clip enough to disengage the fitting body and push them into the fitting. Grasp the top of the clip and work it free of the fitting body. Ford recommends that a new clip be used when reconnecting the fitting.

The spring lock coupling is used to connect two lengths of steel tubing. It contains a garter spring inside a circular cage, with 2 O-rings used to seal the 2 halves of the coupling. When the flared end of the female fitting is inserted into the cage, it slides under the garter spring, which prevents it from pulling out. This type of fitting also is used on air conditioning system and cooling system connections and some automatic transmission oil cooler connections. All can be separated using the same general procedure, but the specific special tool for that type coupling should be used.

O-ring and garter spring condition is critical on this connection and should be checked each time a connection is opened. Special replacement O-rings and garter springs are available at Ford dealerships. If the garter spring is damaged or missing, it can be replaced with the use of a small hooked wire.

The spring lock coupling requires the use of tool part No. T81P-19623-G (3/8 in. to 1/2 in.) or part No. T81P-19623-G1 (3/8 in. to 3/8 in.). Refer to **Figure 15** to disconnect a spring lock coupling with the coupling tool. Refer to **Figure 16** to reconnect the coupling.

MULTI-POINT FUEL INJECTION (2.3L EFI)

A multi-point fuel injection system is used on all 2.3L 4-cylinder engines. A 2-piece fuel charging assembly consists of the upper intake manifold with air intake throttle body, the lower intake manifold (**Figure 17**) and a fuel supply manifold containing an injector for each cylinder, each positioned above an intake valve (**Figure 18**). All injectors simultaneously spray a predetermined amount of fuel into the intake air stream once every crankshaft revolution.

Airflow to the engine is controlled by the air intake throttle body positioned between the air cleaner resonator and the upper intake manifold. Signals from the throttle position sensor mounted on the throttle body and the air bypass valve assembly on the air cleaner cover are combined with other sensor inputs by the electronic engine control (EEC-IV) microprocessor. The microprocessor determines how much fuel is required to maintain a prescribed air-fuel ratio for proper engine operation at the time, then operates the fuel injectors. Since the microprocessor controls the quantity and duration of fuel flow, the only adjustment on the fuel charging assembly is a minimum idle airflow screw on the air intake throttle body. Adjustment of this screw should be left to a dealer or qualified fuel injection specialist with the proper test equipment.

Fuel is delivered to the fuel manifold by an electric fuel pump system. Early 1986 2.3L engines use a 2-pump system: a low-pressure boost pump inside the fuel tank and a high-pressure pump mounted on the frame rail. The 3.0L V6 and 1986 1/2 and later 2.3L engines use a single high-pressure pump inside the fuel tank.

WARNING
The fuel system will remain under pressure even though the engine is not running. Before opening any fuel system connections, you must relieve the fuel system pressure as described in this chapter.

The fuel pump is controlled by the EEC-IV microprocessor through a power relay. An inertia switch connected in series with the pump power feed acts as a safety feature to shut off the fuel pump in case of a collision or rollover.

The inertia switch is located on the toeboard to the right of the transmission hump (**Figure 19**). A button is provided on the switch to reset the unit in case it is tripped. If the vehicle will not start and run after a minor collision or if it ran fine when you left it in the parking lot but will not start and run when you return (it may have been tapped by someone else in the parking lot), try resetting the inertia switch before summoning help. The inertia switch also can serve as an effective anti-theft device. When you park and leave the vehicle for any length of time, trip the switch. This will prevent the engine from being started. When you return to the vehicle, reset the switch before trying to start the engine.

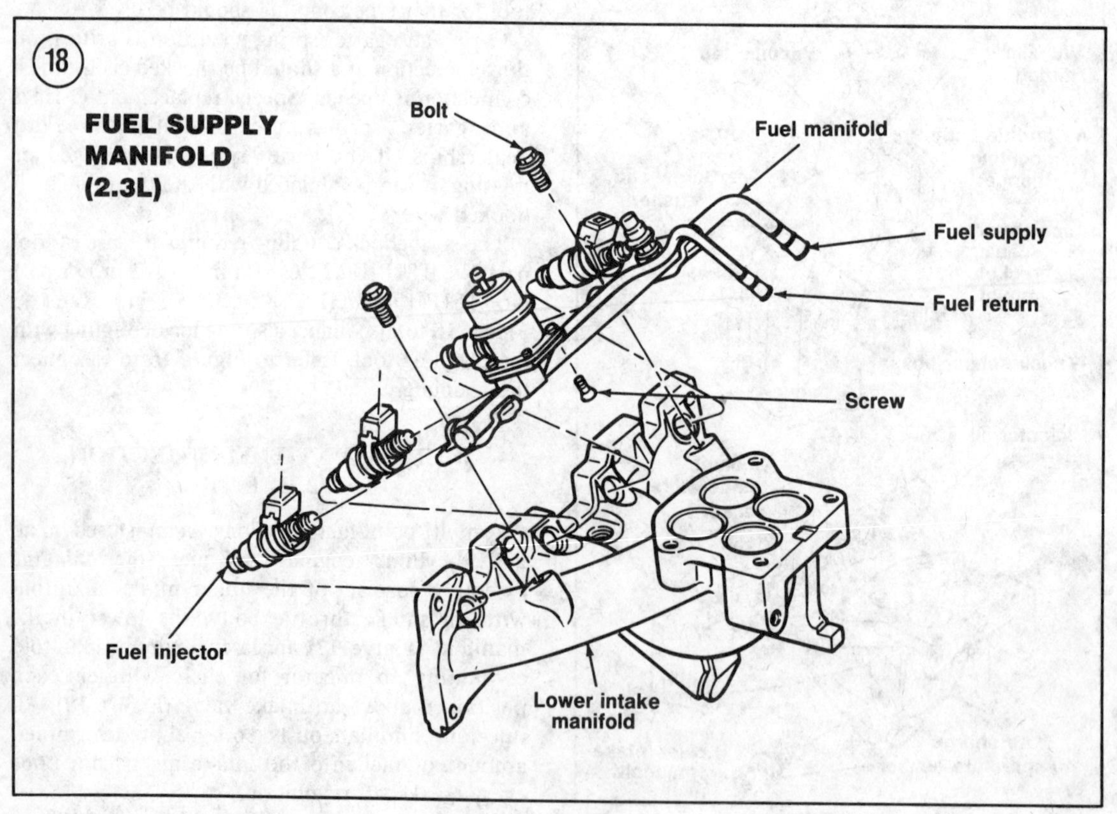

Since the EFI system is electronically controlled, no attempt should be made to adjust the idle speed with the idle airflow screw. Owner service should be limited to replacement only. If the EFI system is not working properly, take the vehicle to a dealer for diagnosis and adjustment.

NOTE
Some gasolines may cause injector clogging problems. When used as directed, Chevron Techron additive or Ford Injector and Fuel System Cleaner (part No. E6AZ-19579-A) will prevent this from happening.

Relieving System Pressure

Before opening any fuel connection on a 2.3L EFI system, the fuel pressure must be relieved.

1. Disconnect the negative battery cable.
2. Remove the fuel tank filler cap to release any pressure in the tank.
3. Locate the Schrader pressure relief valve on the fuel injection manifold (**Figure 20**) or in the flexible fuel supply line about 12 inches from its point of connection to the engine. Remove the valve cap.

NOTE
If the proper gauge is not available, disconnect the vacuum line at the pressure regulator. Connect a hand vacuum pump to the regulator fitting, then draw and hold 25 in. Hg vacuum to release pressure into the tank through the return line.

4. Connect fuel injection pressure gauge (part No. T80L-9974-A) to the pressure relief valve and bleed off the pressure.
5. Remove the pressure gauge and reinstall the relief valve cap.

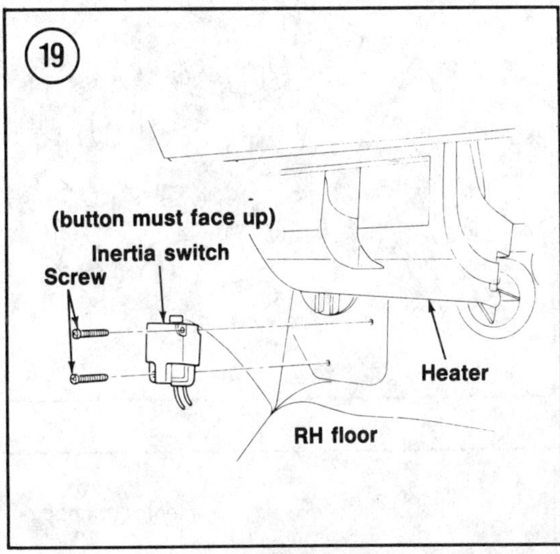

Fuel Supply Manifold Removal/Installation

Fuel supply manifold removal requires that the upper intake manifold be removed. This procedure also includes removal of the lower intake manifold, as it involves only one additional step. The lower manifold does not have to be removed to service the fuel supply manifold. Refer to **Figure 17** and **Figure 18** for this procedure.

1. Relieve fuel system pressure as described in this chapter.
2. Drain the cooling system. See Chapter Seven.
3. Unplug the following electrical connectors:
   a. Throttle position sensor at the air intake throttle body.
   b. Knock sensor at the upper intake manifold.
   c. Injector wiring harness at the main engine harness and water temperature indicator sensor.
   d. Air charge temperature sensor at the intake manifold.
   e. Coolant temperature sensor at the intake manifold.
4. Label and disconnect the vacuum lines at the upper intake manifold vacuum tree, EGR valve and fuel pressure regulator.
5. Remove the throttle linkage shield (**Figure 20**).
6. Disconnect the throttle linkage and speed control cables at the air intake throttle body. Unbolt the accelerator cable from its bracket and place cable out of the way.
7. Disconnect the air intake, air bypass and crankcase vent hoses.
8. Disconnect the PCV hose from its fitting underneath the upper intake manifold.
9. Unclamp and disconnect the coolant bypass line at the lower intake manifold.

6

10. Unbolt and remove the upper intake manifold and air intake throttle body as an assembly from the lower intake manifold. See **Figure 21**.
11. Unbolt the engine oil dipstick tube (**Figure 22**).
12. Disconnect the fuel supply and return quick-disconnect fittings as described in this chapter.
13. Unplug the electrical connectors at the fuel injectors (**Figure 23**) and place harness out of the way.
14. Unbolt and remove the fuel supply manifold with injectors (**Figure 18**).
15. Remove the bolts holding the lower intake manifold to the cylinder head (**Figure 24**). Remove the manifold, engine lifting eye bracket and gasket. Discard the gasket.
16. Clean all gasket residue from the upper and lower intake manifolds and mating surfaces.
17. Installation is the reverse of removal. Use a new gasket and tighten lower manifold fasteners to specifications (**Table 1**) following the sequence shown in **Figure 25**. Use a new gasket between the upper and lower intake manifold. Tighten bolts to specifications (**Table 1**) in a crisscross pattern. Tighten all other fasteners to specifications (**Table 1**).

Fuel Injector Removal/Installation

1. Remove the fuel supply manifold as described in this chapter.
2. Grasp the injector by its body and rock from side to side while pulling upward and out of its port in the fuel supply manifold.
3. Check the condition of the two O-rings (**Figure 26**). Replace as required (it is a good idea to replace them regardless of condition).
4. Check the condition of the little plastic "hat" and washer that protects the injector pintle. See **Figure 26**. If hat is not found on the injector, check the injector port in the intake manifold. Replace as required.
5. If new O-rings are installed, lubricate lightly with engine oil before sliding them into place on the injector.
6. Position injector over the manifold port and push into place with a light twisting motion.
7. Reinstall the fuel supply manifold as described in this chapter.

MULTI-POINT FUEL INJECTION (3.0L EFI)

A multi-point fuel injection system is used on all 3.0L V6 engines. A fuel rail assembly is installed between the upper and lower intake manifolds.

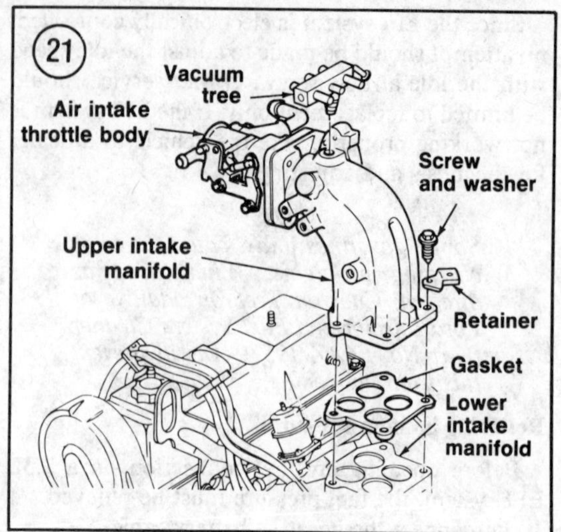

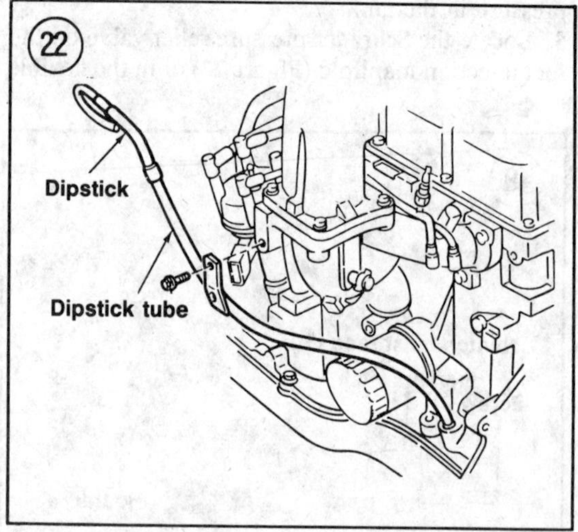

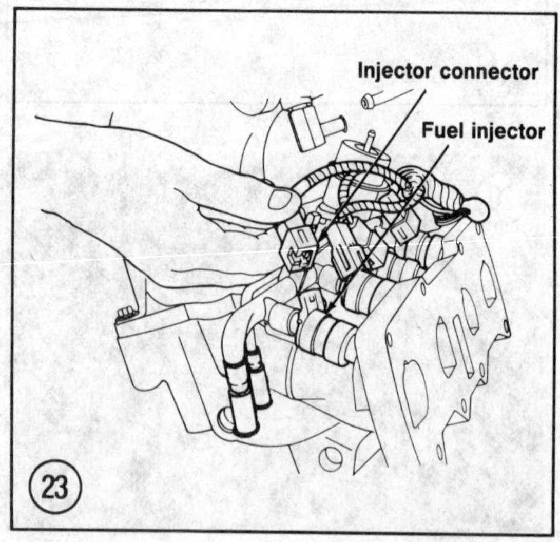

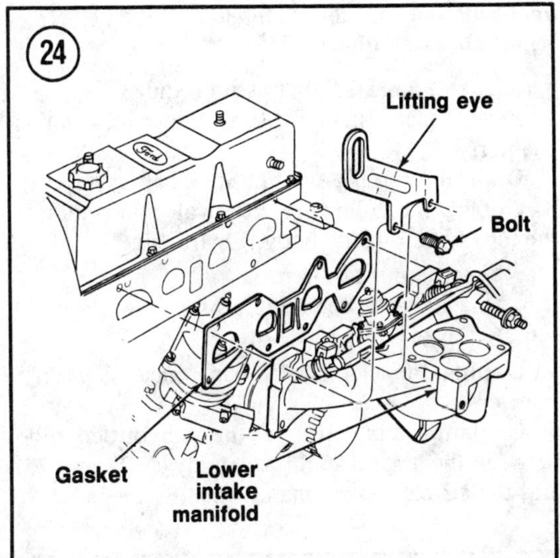

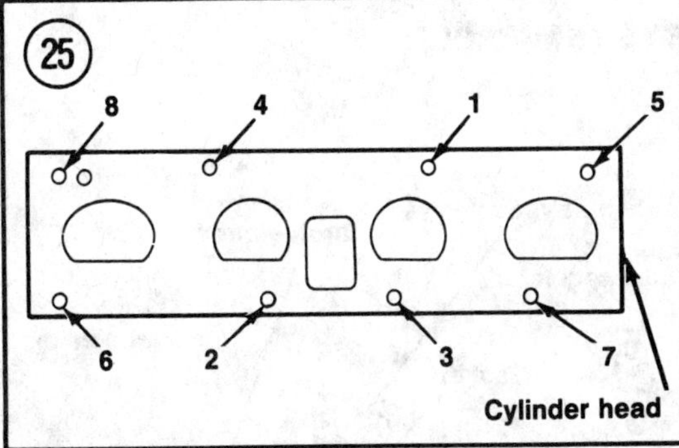

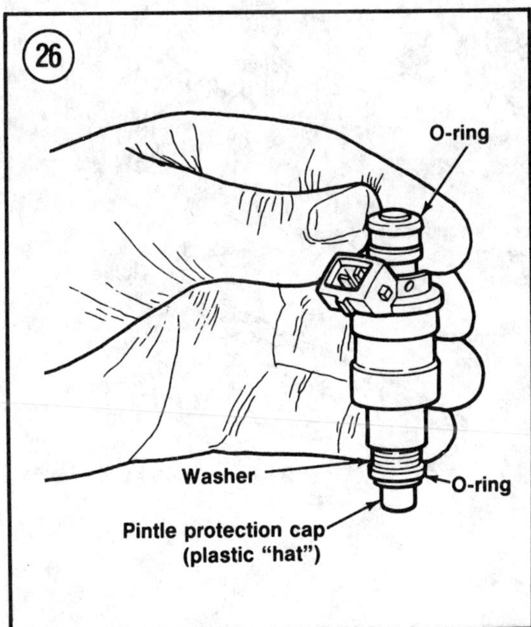

The fuel rail contains an injector for each cylinder positioned above an intake valve. **Figure 27** shows these components and their relationship. The injectors operate in 2 groups of 3 injectors. Each group sprays a predetermined amount of fuel into the intake air stream once every other crankshaft revolution.

Airflow to the engine is controlled by the air intake throttle body. The throttle body is an integral part of the upper intake manifold. Signals from the throttle position sensor mounted on the air intake throttle body and the air bypass valve assembly on the upper intake manifold (**Figure 28**) are combined with other sensor inputs by the electronic engine control (EEC-IV) microprocessor. The microprocessor determines how much fuel is required to maintain a prescribed air-fuel ratio for proper engine operation at the time, then operates the fuel injectors. Since the microprocessor controls the quantity and duration of fuel flow, the only adjustment on the fuel injection system is a minimum idle airflow screw on the air intake throttle body. Adjustment of this screw should be left to a dealer or qualified fuel injection specialist with the proper test equipment.

6

Fuel is delivered to the fuel rail by a single high-pressure pump inside the fuel tank.

WARNING

The fuel system will remain under pressure even though the engine is not running. Before opening any fuel system connections, you must relieve the fuel system pressure as described in this chapter.

The fuel pump is controlled by the EEC-IV microprocessor through a power relay. An inertia switch connected in series with the pump power feed acts as a safety feature to shut off the fuel pump in case of a collision or rollover.

The inertia switch is located in the engine compartment. A red button is provided on top of the switch to reset the unit in case it is tripped. If the vehicle will not start and run after a minor collision or if it ran fine when you left it in the parking lot but will not start and run when you return (it may have been tapped by someone else in the parking lot), try resetting the inertia switch before summoning help. The inertia switch also can serve as an effective anti-theft device. When you park and leave the vehicle for any length of time, trip the switch. This will prevent the engine from being started. When you return to the vehicle, reset the switch before trying to start the engine.

Since the EFI system is electronically controlled, no attempt should be made to adjust the idle speed with the idle airflow screw. Owner service should be limited to replacement only. If the EFI system is not working properly, take the vehicle to a dealer for diagnosis and adjustment.

NOTE
Some gasolines may cause injector clogging problems. When used as directed, Chevron Techron additive or Ford Injector and Fuel System Cleaner (part No. E6AZ-19579-A) will prevent this from happening.

Relieving System Pressure

See *Multi-point fuel injection (2.3L EFI)* in this chapter.

Fuel Rail and Injector Manifold Removal/Installation

Refer to **Figure 27** for this procedure.

1. Relieve fuel system pressure as described in this chapter.
2. Drain the cooling system. See Chapter Seven.
3. Unplug the following electrical connectors at the air intake throttle body (**Figure 28**):
   a. Throttle position sensor.
   b. Air charge temperature sensor.
   c. Air bypass valve.
4. Unplug the electrical wiring harness at the injectors.
5. Unclamp and remove the air outlet tube between the air intake throttle body (A, **Figure 29**) and the air cleaner resonator.

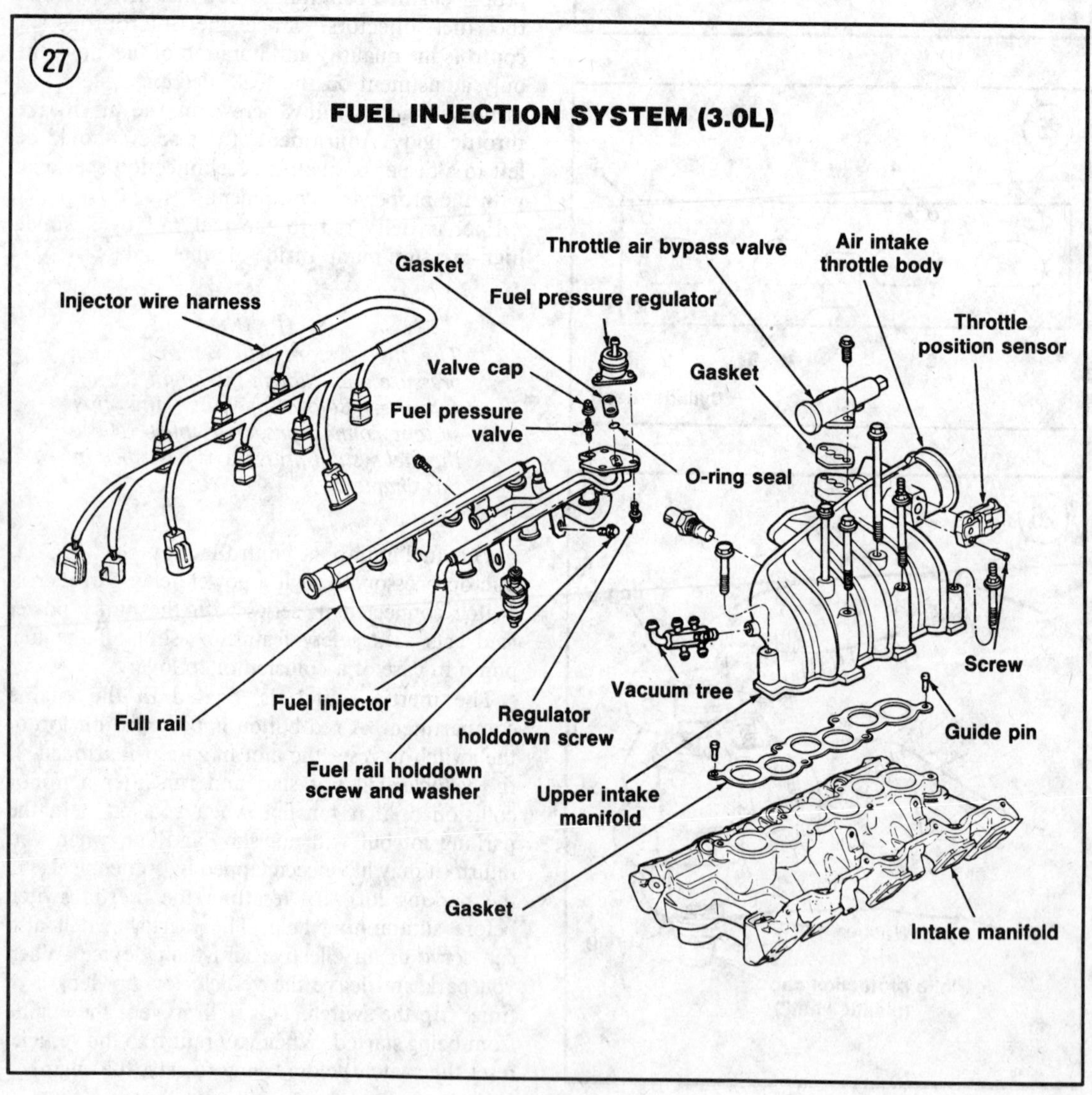

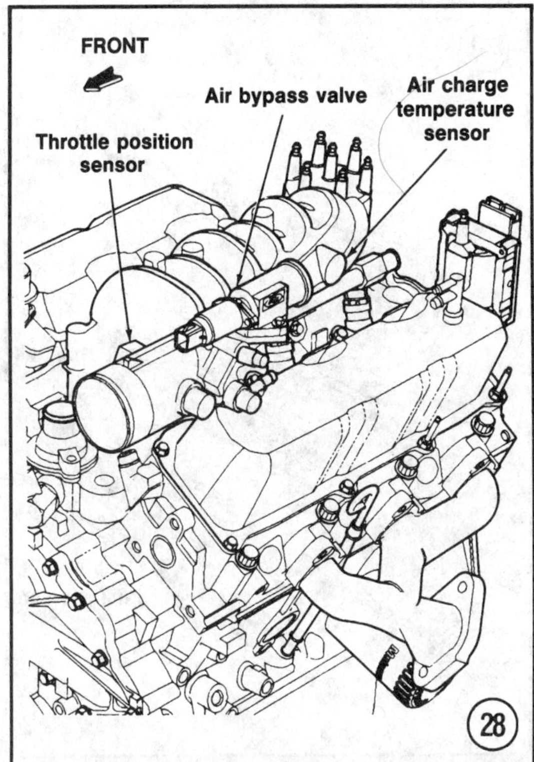

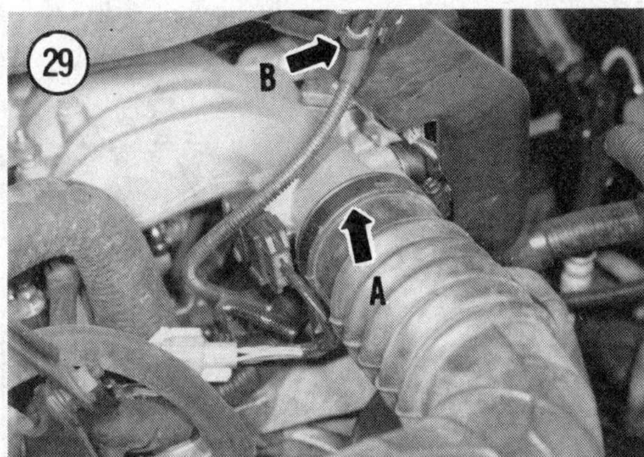

6. Remove the snow shield covering the throttle linkage (B, **Figure 29**). Three push retainers hold the shield to the power steering pump and accelerator cable brackets.

7. Disconnect and remove the throttle and speed control cables at the throttle mounting bracket and lever. See **Figure 30**. Disconnect the transmission TV linkage at the throttle lever, if so equipped.

8. Label and disconnect all vacuum lines at the intake manifold.

9. Loosen and remove the air intake throttle body mounting bolts. Remove the air intake throttle body assembly from the lower intake manifold. See **Figure 31**. Remove and discard the gasket.

10. Disconnect the fuel supply and return quick-disconnect fittings as described in this chapter.

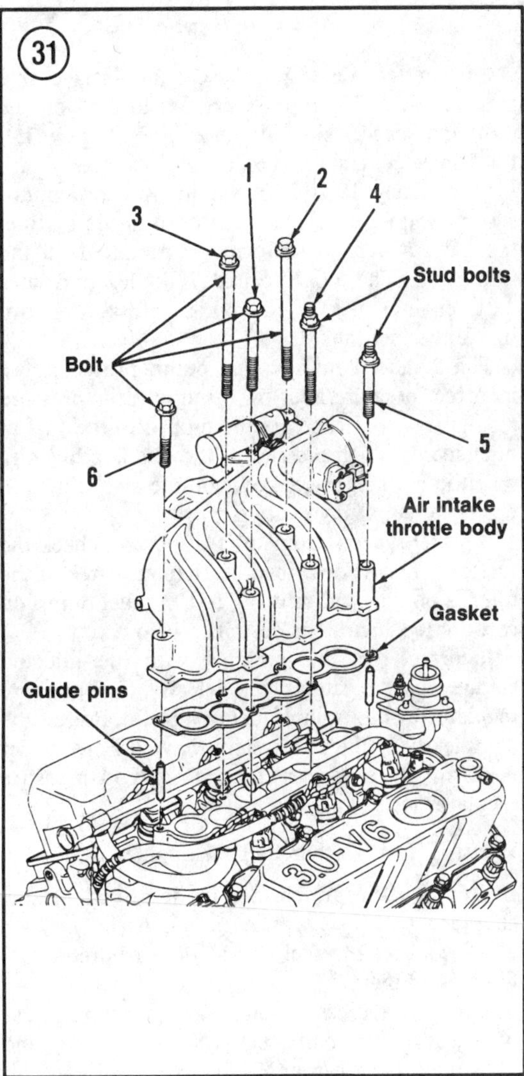

11. Unplug the electrical connectors at the fuel injectors (**Figure 32**) and place harness out of the way.
12. Unbolt and remove the fuel rail with injectors (**Figure 33**).
13. Clean all gasket residue from the upper and lower intake manifolds and mating surfaces.
14. Installation is the reverse of removal. Use a new gasket and tighten air intake throttle body fasteners to specifications (**Table 1**) following the sequence shown in **Figure 31**. Tighten all other fasteners to specifications (**Table 1**).

Fuel Injector Removal/Installation

See *Multi-point Fuel Injection (2.3L EFI)* in this chapter.

FUEL PUMP

Carburetted V6 engines use a non-serviceable mechanical fuel pump (**Figure 34**) located on the right (passenger) side of the engine (**Figure 35**). Fuel injected engines use an electric fuel pump system. Early 1986 2.3L engines use a 2-pump system: a low-pressure boost pump inside the fuel tank and a high-pressure pump mounted on the frame rail. The 3.0L V6 and 1986 1/2 and later 2.3L engines use a single high-pressure pump inside the fuel tank.

The 2 most common fuel pump problems are incorrect pressure and low volume. Low pressure results in a too-lean mixture and too little fuel at high speeds. High pressure will cause flooding and result in poor mileage. Low volume also results in too little fuel at high speeds.

If a fuel system problem is suspected, check the fuel filter first as described in Chapter Three. If the filter is not clogged or dirty, test the fuel pump on carburetted engines as described below.

Incorrect fuel line pressure with fuel-injected engines may be caused by a defective fuel pressure regulator or the in-tank fuel pump. Because of the complexity of the EFI system, have a Ford dealer perform the necessary fuel pump and pressure regulator tests.

Pressure Test (Carburetted V6 Engine)

1. Remove the air cleaner as described in this chapter.
2. Disconnect the fuel line at the carburetor fuel filter. See **Figure 35**.
3. Connect a pressure gauge and a flexible hose with a restrictor clamp between the fuel line and filter inlet, as shown in **Figure 36**.

32

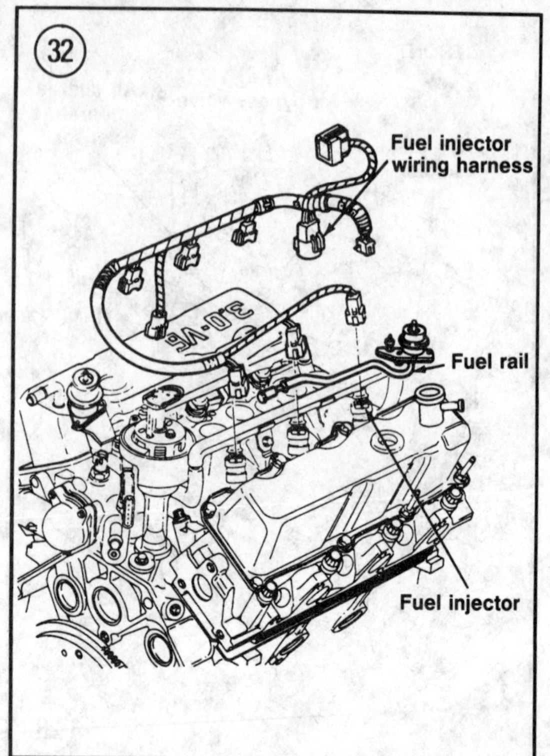

33

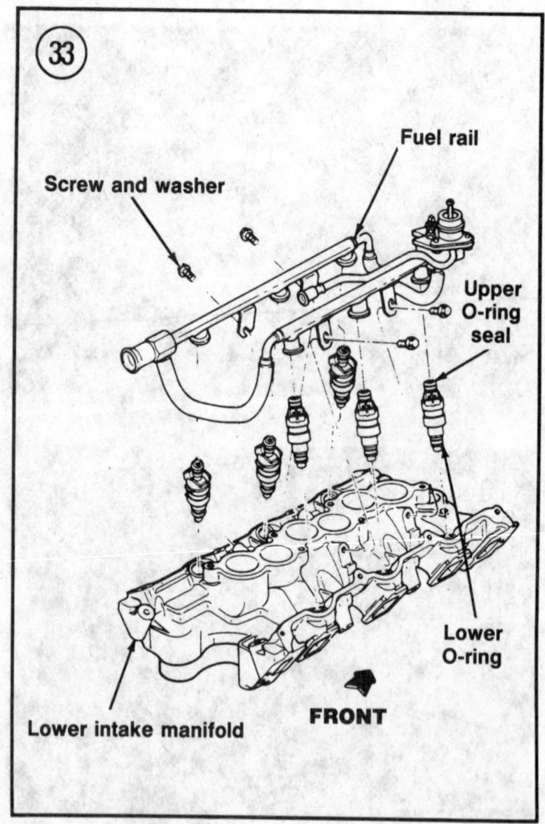

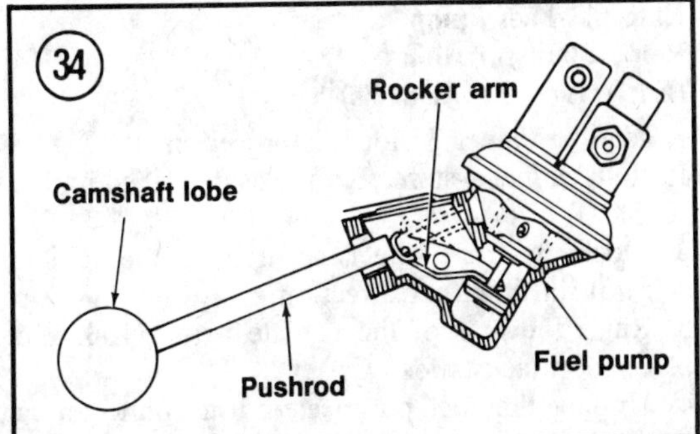

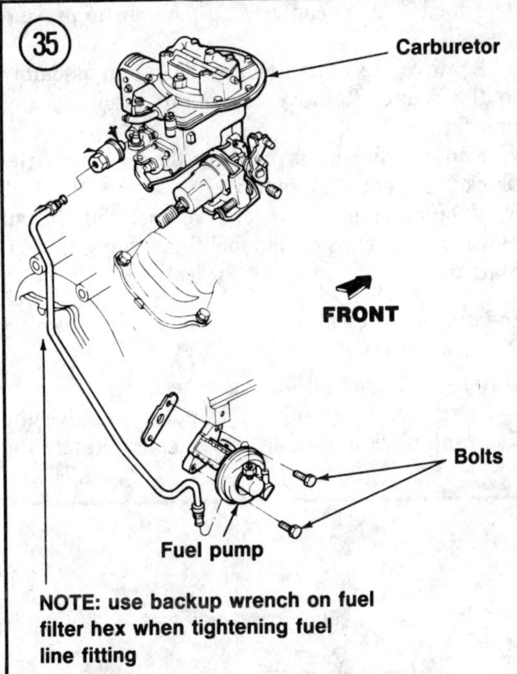

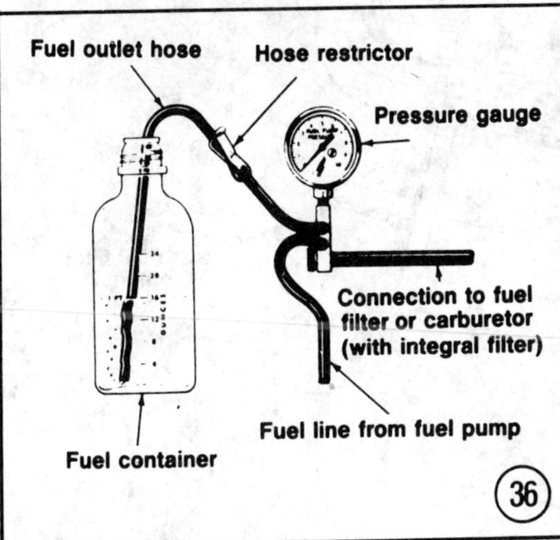

4. Place the other end of the line in a clean quart-size container.
5. Start the engine and let it idle. Vent the fuel system into the container by opening and closing the restrictor.
6. Let the pressure stabilize and read the gauge. It should read between 4 1/2 and 6 1/2 psi.
7. Slowly increase the idle speed and watch the gauge. The pressure should not vary considerably at different engine speeds.
8. If the pump pressure is not within specifications in Step 6 or if it varies considerably in Step 7, replace the pump.
9. Shut the engine off. Disconnect the pressure gauge and restrictor. Reconnect the fuel line to the carburetor fuel filter.

Flow Test (Carburetted V6 Engine)

1. Perform Steps 1-4 of *Pressure Test (Carburetted Engine)* described above.
2. Disconnect the high tension lead at the center of the ignition coil and ground it with a jumper wire.
3. Crank the engine 10 revolutions and check the fuel in the container. If little or no fuel has accumulated, the pump is inoperative and must be replaced.
4. If the pump appears capable of delivering sufficient fuel, reconnect the coil high tension lead. Start the engine and let it run.
5. Open the hose restrictor for 30 seconds, then close the restrictor.
6. Check the container. It should be approximately 1/2 full. If not, replace the fuel pump.
7. Shut the engine off. Disconnect the pressure gauge and restrictor. Reconnect the fuel line to the carburetor fuel filter.

Replacement (Carburetted V6 Engine)

Refer to **Figure 35** as required for this procedure.
1. Disconnect the negative battery cable.
2. Use 2 open-end wrenches to loosen and remove the fuel line nuts at the pump inlet and outlet fittings. If fuel hoses are used, remove the clamps and pull the hoses from the fittings. Cap the lines to prevent leakage.
3. Loosen the pump mounting bolts 2 full turns. Rap the pump sharply with your hand or a rubber mallet to break the gasket seal.
4. Hold the pump while an assistant rotates the engine by turning the ignition key ON and OFF quickly to bring the camshaft eccentric near its low point. When this is reached, tension on the fuel pump will be noticeably reduced.

5. Remove the pump mounting bolts, fuel pump and gasket. Discard the gasket.
6. Clean all gasket residue from the engine mounting flange with a putty knife. If reinstalling the same pump, clean gasket residue from the pump mounting pad.
7. If the pushrod came out with the pump, check its length. If less than 6.10 in., install a new pushrod. Lubricate the pushrod with clean engine oil and install in the engine.
8. Check rubber hoses between fuel lines and pump. If cracked, hardened or frayed, install new lengths of fuel hose before installing the pump.
9. Install a new gasket to the pump mounting pad and insert the bolts through the pump flanges to hold the gasket in place.
10. Install the fuel pump and gasket to the engine block and thread the bolts into the mounting pad. Tighten the bolts to specifications **(Table 1)**.
11. Connect the fuel line to the pump outlet fitting using a backup wrench to hold the pump fitting while tightening the fuel line fitting to specifications (**Table 1**).
12. Install a new hose clamp and connect the pump inlet line. Tighten hose clamp securely.
13. Reconnect the negative battery cable.
14. Start the engine and let it run for 2 minutes. Stop the engine and check for fuel leaks at the pump base and inlet/outlet connections.

External Fuel Pump Removal/Installation (Early 1986 EFI Models)

Refer to **Figure 37** for this procedure.

1. Relieve fuel system pressure as described in this chapter.
2. Block the front wheels securely so the vehicle will not roll in either direction.
3. Raise the rear of the vehicle with a jack and place it on jackstands.
4. Unplug the fuel pump electrical connector at the body harness.
5. Disconnect the fuel inlet and outlet lines as described in this chapter. Cap the lines to prevent leakage.
6. Remove the bolts holding the pump assembly to the frame. Remove the pump assembly and bracket.
7. Remove the bolts holding the pump to the bracket. Remove the pump.
8. Installation is the reverse of removal. Install new retaining clips on the fuel line fittings, if used. Start the engine and check for leaks.

In-tank Fuel Pump Removal/Installation

Refer to **Figure 38** for this procedure.

To replace the in-tank fuel pump, remove the fuel tank as described in this chapter. Rotate the

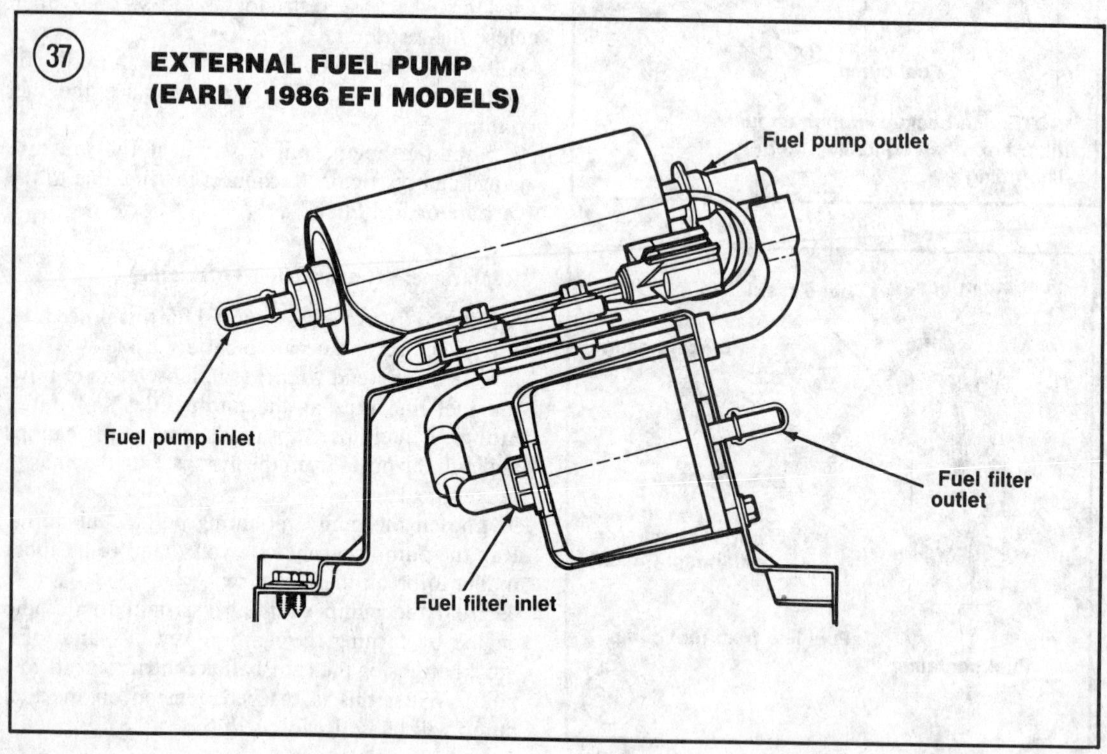

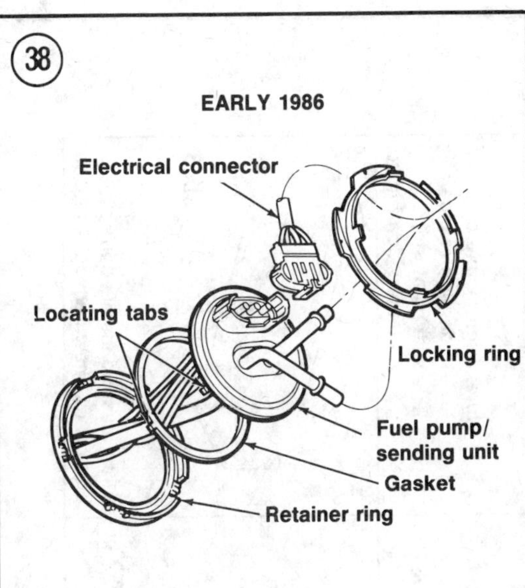

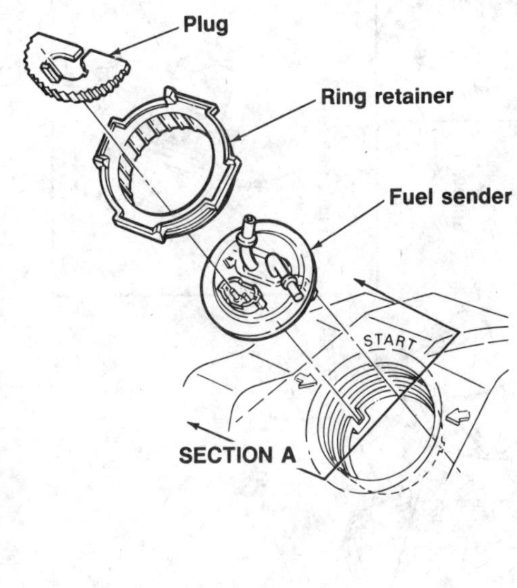

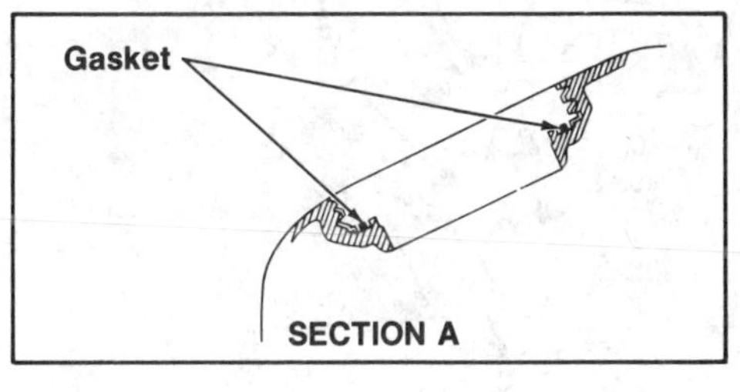

locking ring in a counterclockwise direction with Ford tool part No. T74P-9275-A or equivalent and remove the fuel pump/sending unit or fuel pump from the tank. Installation is the reverse of removal.

FUEL TANK AND LINES

The fuel tank is located underneath the left center of the vehicle. Two metal straps attached to the underbody hold the tank in place. A fuel tank shield is used on all model. **Figure 39** (typical) shows the fuel tank and method of attachment.

WARNING
Before opening any fuel injection system connections, relieve system pressure as described in this chapter.

Fuel Tank Removal/Installation

Refer to **Figure 39** for this procedure.

1. Relieve fuel system pressure as described in this chapter.

NOTE
Tanks used with fuel injection systems contain reservoirs and baffles which can prevent siphon or pump tubes from reaching the bottom of the tank. Once the tank appears to be empty in Step 2, it is a good idea to reorient the siphon/pump tube in several different positions to make sure all fuel has been removed.

2. Remove the fuel tank filler cap. Insert a hand-operated pump or siphon device through the filler neck and into the tank. Remove as much fuel as possible with the pump or siphon.

WARNING
Never store gasoline in an open container, since it is an extreme fire hazard. Store gasoline in a sealed metal container away from heat, sparks and flame.

3. Securely block both front wheels so the vehicle will not roll in either direction.
4. Raise the vehicle with a jack and place it on jackstands.
5. Support the fuel tank with a jack. Unclamp and disconnect the filler pipe neck and vent hoses.
6. Unbolt and remove the rear strap, then the front strap.
7. Disconnect all fuel lines and electrical connectors at the fuel tank.
8. Remove the fuel tank from the vehicle.
9. Installation is the reverse of removal. Replace any hoses as required with fuel line hose.

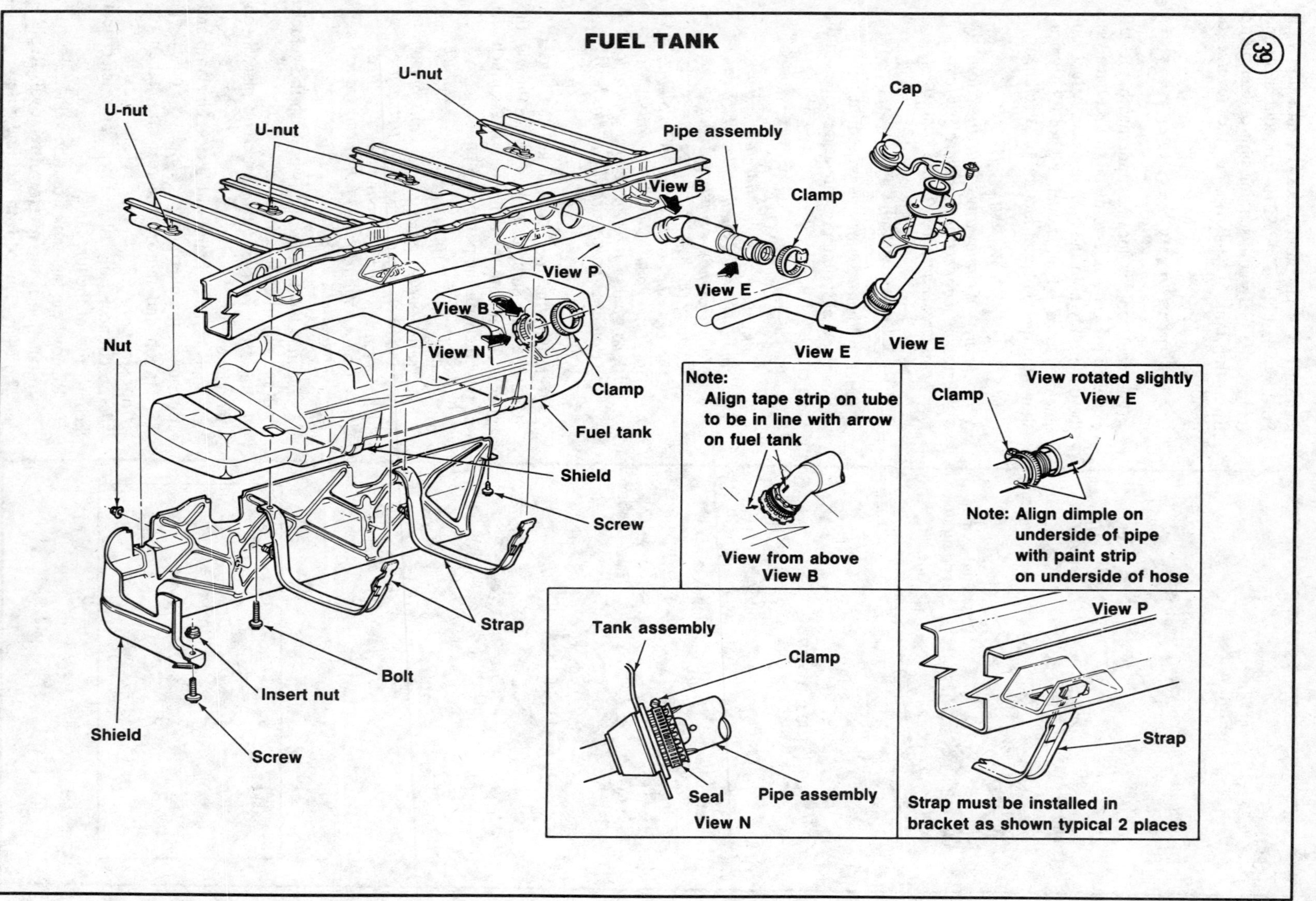
39
FUEL TANK
U-nut
U-nut
U-nut
Pipe assembly
Cap
View B
Clamp
View P
View E
View B
View N
Nut
View E
View E
Clamp
Fuel tank
Shield
Screw
Strap
Bolt
Insert nut
Shield
Screw
Note:
Align tape strip on tube to be in line with arrow on fuel tank
View from above
View B
View rotated slightly
View E
Clamp
Note: Align dimple on underside of pipe with paint strip on underside of hose
Tank assembly
Clamp
Seal
Pipe assembly
View N
View P
Strap
Strap must be installed in bracket as shown typical 2 places

Repairing Metal Fuel Tank Leaks

Fuel tank leaks can be repaired by soldering.

WARNING
The fuel tank is capable of exploding and killing anyone nearby. Always observe the following precautions when repairing a tank.

1. Have the tank steam-cleaned *inside* and *outside.*
2. Fill the tank with inert gas such as nitrogen or carbon dioxide, or fill the tank *completely* with water. Gasoline residue on the tank walls can form a highly explosive vapor if allowed to mix with air.
3. Have a dry chemical (Class B) fire extinguisher close by.
4. Whenever the tank is cleaned, the fuel meter on the top of the tank should be removed and the strainer screen cleaned with compressed air.
5. After making the necessary repairs, pour the water out, put about one quart of gasoline in the tank and slosh it around. Pour the gasoline out, blow the tank dry with compressed air and reinstall in the vehicle.

Fuel Lines

The fuel tank and lines are part of the evaporative emission control system. The rubber hoses (carburetted engine) and nylon tubing (fuel injected engines) used in this system are manufactured of special fuel-resistant materials. Regular hose or tubing should never be used as a replacement.

Unlike steel fuel lines, nylon fuel tubing can be quickly damaged by excessive heat or sparks caused by welding or grinding operations. When such operations must be performed near the fuel tubing, Ford Motor Company recommends that the fuel tubing be removed from the vehicle.

Nylon fuel tubing and push-connect fittings cannot be repaired by using hoses and clamps as a means of splicing a damaged or leaking section. Ford supplies approved service parts to safely correct any problems with nylon fuel lines.

6

EXHAUST SYSTEM

All models are fitted with a single muffler or resonator assembly, a single catalytic converter and connecting pipes. **Figure 40** shows the components

(40) **4-CYLINDER EXHAUST SYSTEM**

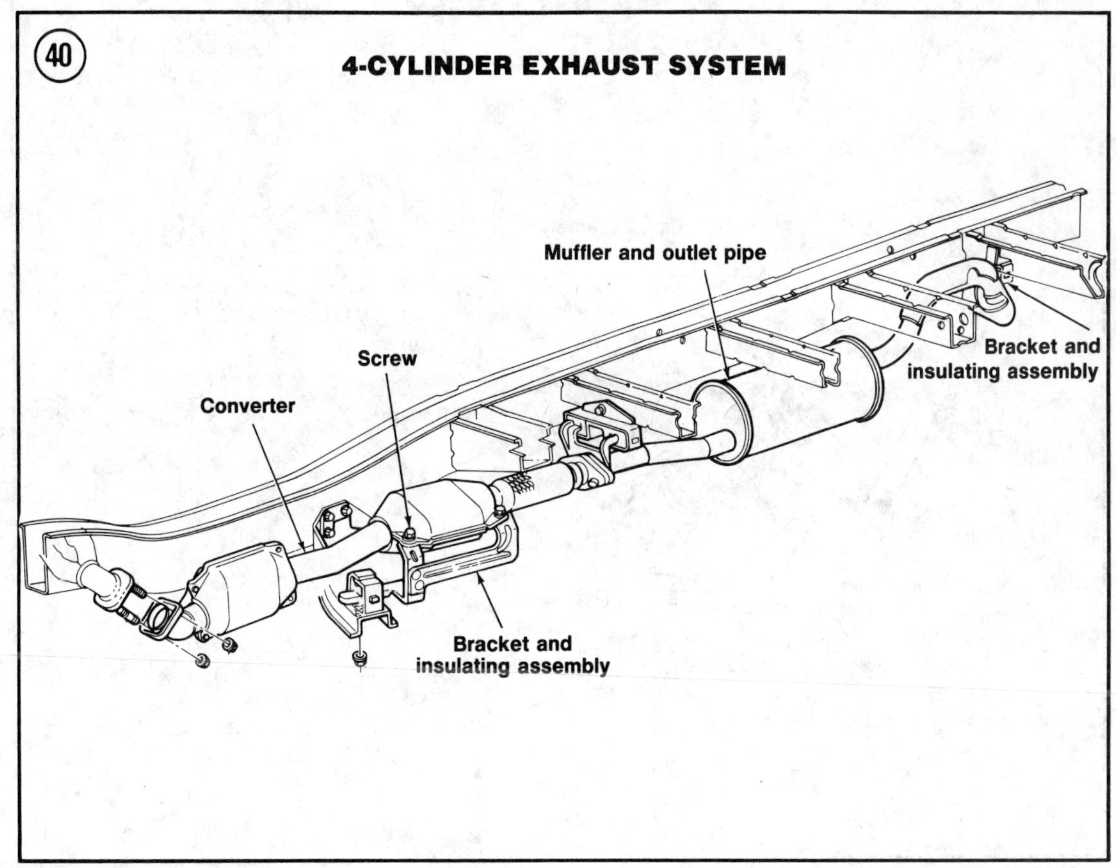

of the 4-cylinder system. **Figure 41** shows the converter-to-exhaust manifold components; the rear part of the system is the same as that used with the 4-cylinder engine.

The exhaust system should be free of corrosion, leaks, binding, grounding or excessive vibration. Loose, broken or misaligned clamps, shields, brackets or pipes should be serviced as necessary to keep the exhaust system in a safe operating condition. See **Figure 42** (typical). Pay particular attention to the condition of heat shields designed to protect the underbody from excessive heat.

Removal/Installation

WARNING
The exhaust system is extremely hot under normal operating conditions. To avoid the possibility of a bad burn, it is advisable to work on the system only when it is cool. Be especially careful around the catalytic converter. It reaches temperatures of 600° F or greater after only a brief period of engine operation.

1. Prior to removal, soak all bolts, nuts and pipe joints with a penetrating oil such as WD-40. See **Figure 43** (typical).
2. Undo the required clamps and hanger brackets.
3. Replace the worn, damaged or corroded component(s).
4. Align the exhaust components. Start at the front of the system and tighten all fasteners securely.
5. Make sure there is adequate clearance between the exhaust system components and any pipes, hoses or other components that might be adversely affected by heat. There should also be sufficient clearance between the exhaust system and body/frame members to permit normal component movement without contact to prevent exhaust system rattle or noise.

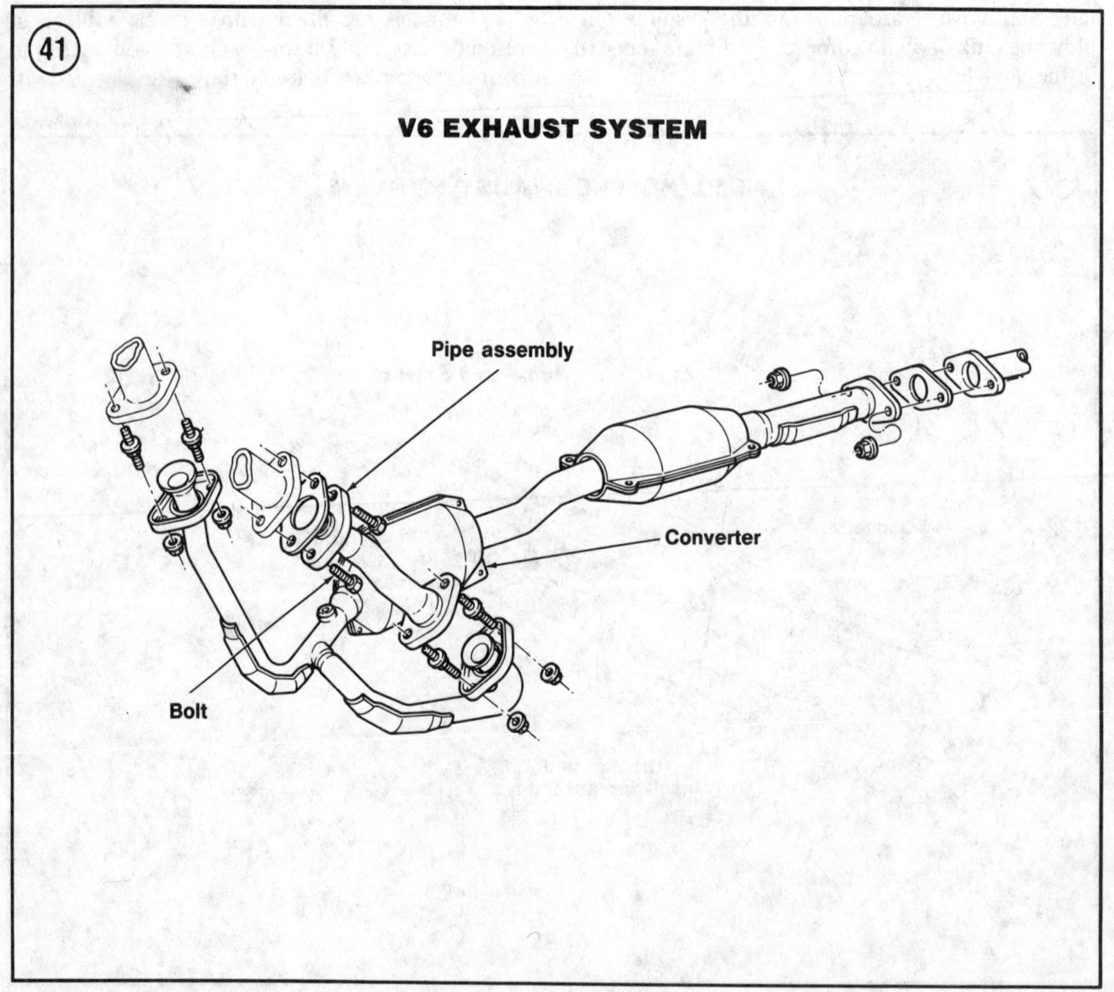

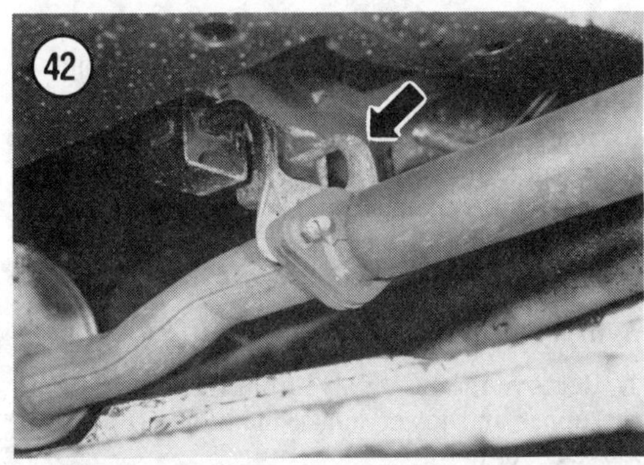

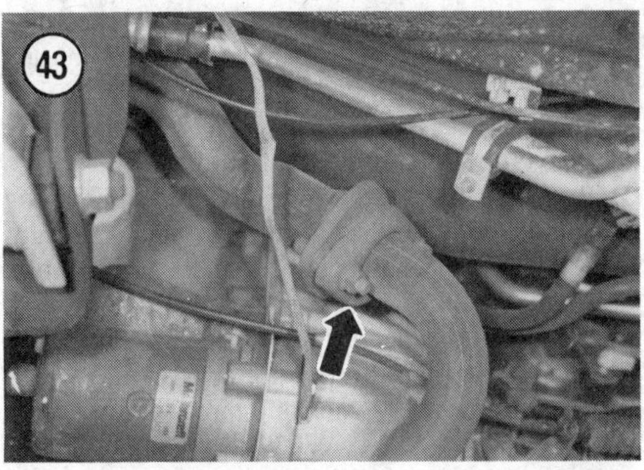

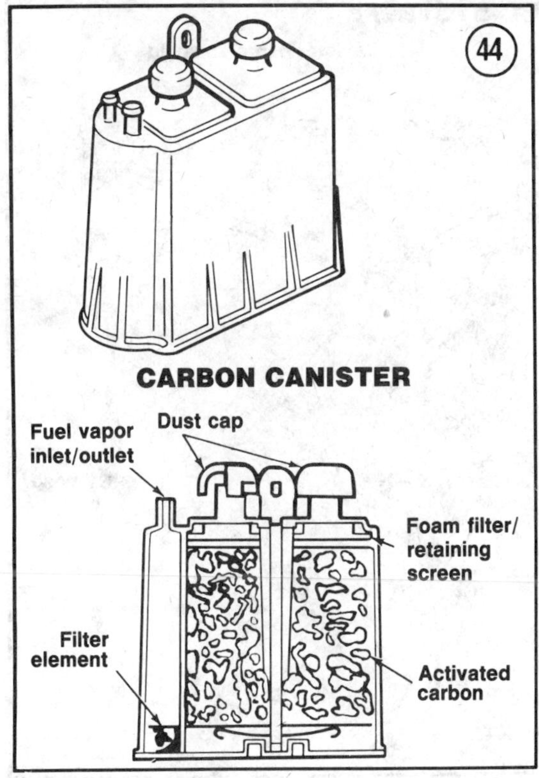

EMISSION CONTROL SYSTEMS

All vehicles covered in this manual have a number of systems designed to minimize harmful emissions. Owner service to emission control systems is described in detail in this chapter and Chapter Three. Other service on vehicles equipped with EEC-IV engine control systems is not recommended. Most of the components are non-adjustable and non-repairable. In many cases, expensive tools and test equipment, as well as considerable knowledge and experience, are required.

Evaporative Emission Control (EEC) System

This system is used on all models to prevent gasoline vapors from escaping into the atmosphere. Fuel vapors from the fuel tank pass through a vent restrictor to a carbon canister. Vapors from the carburetor float bowl are vented directly to the canister on 1986 2.8L V6 engines.

The carbon contained within the canister (**Figure 44**) absorbs and stores the vapors when the engine is stopped. When the engine is running, manifold vacuum draws the vapors from the canister into the engine for burning. Instead of being released into the atmosphere, the fuel vapors become part of the normal combustion process.

There is no scheduled maintenance of the EEC system. Physical damage, leaks and missing components are the most common causes of evaporative system failures. **Figure 45** shows a typical 4-cylinder EEC system. The V6 EEC system is shown in **Figure 46**.

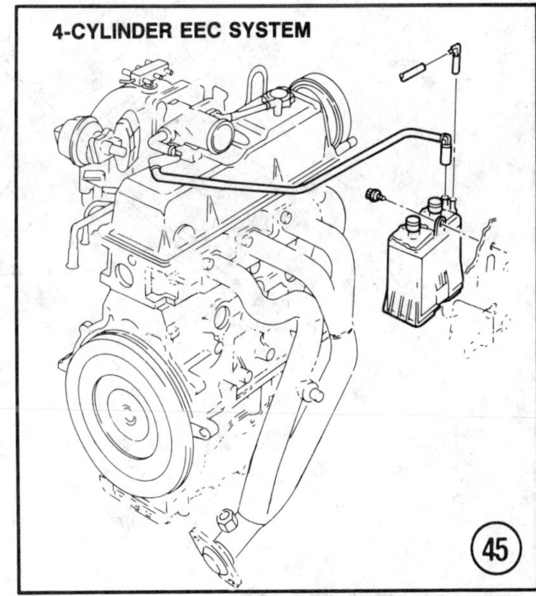

System inspection

1. Check the vapor lines for cracks or loose connections. Replace or tighten as necessary.
2. Check for a deformed fuel tank. Make sure the tank is not cracked and does not leak gasoline.
3. Inspect the canister for cracks or other damage.
4. Check the vapor hoses and tubes to make sure they slope downhill from the carburetor or throttle body to the canister.
5. Check the fuel filler cap for a damaged gasket.

CAUTION
Any damage or contamination which prevents the filler cap pressure-vacuum valve from working properly can result in deformation of the fuel tank.

Positive Crankcase Ventilation (PCV) System

A closed crankcase ventilation system is used to recycle crankcase vapors into the combustion chambers for burning. A vent hose connects the air cleaner to the valve cover. This provides a positive flow of air through the crankcase. Fresh air and crankcase vapors are drawn into the intake manifold through a PCV valve. The valve contains a spring-loaded plunger and is installed in the valve cover of V6 engines (**Figure 47**) or in a line between the upper and lower intake manifolds of 4-cylinder engines. The 4-cylinder PCV valve is located in the line at a point close to the distributor.

The PCV system should be inspected and the PCV valve and air cleaner crankcase vent filter replaced at intervals specified in Chapter Three.

System check

1. Remove the PCV valve from the hose between the upper and lower intake manifolds (I4) or the valve cover (V6).
2. Start the engine and run at idle.
3. Place a thumb over the valve end to check for vacuum. If there is no vacuum, check for plugged hoses.
4. Shake the PCV valve. If the check needle inside the valve does not rattle, replace the valve.
5. Reinstall the PCV valve and disconnect the crankcase inlet hose at the air cleaner. Vacuum should be felt when a finger is placed over the hose.
6. If no vacuum is felt in Step 5, check for a plugged hose or vacuum leak in the PCV system.
7. Check all system hoses for cracks, brittleness or loose connections. Tighten and replace as required.

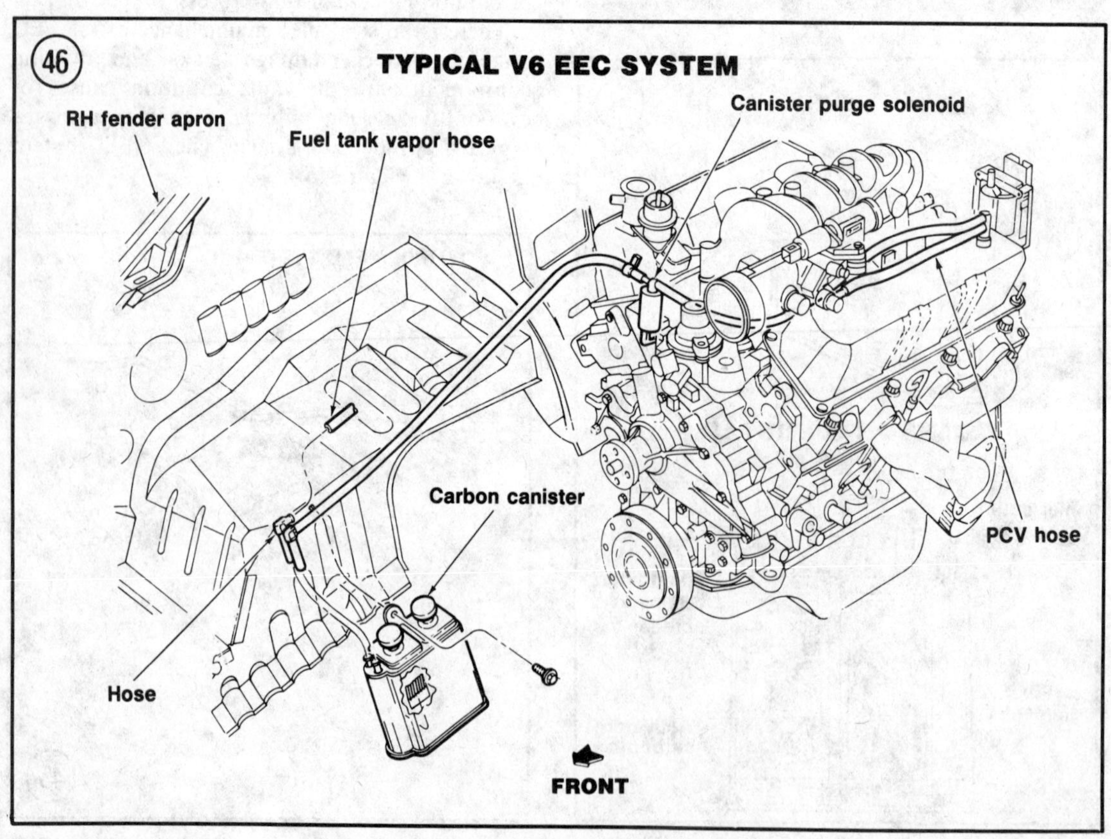

System Maintenance

1. Remove the PCV system components from the engine (PCV valve, hoses, tubes, elbows and grommets).
2. Clean rubber hoses by pushing a cleaning brush through them. Wash hoses in petroleum base solvent, then blow dry with compressed air. Replace any hoses which show obvious signs of deterioration.
3. Make sure all hoses, fittings and connections are free of obstructions. Check grommets for signs of deterioration and replace as required. Reinstall all components removed in Step 1.

Thermactor System

A conventional Thermactor system is used on 1986 engines. On 1987 and later engines, a Thermactor system is not required to meet emission standards. The Thermactor system consists of a belt-driven air pump, air management valve, check valves, air injection tube/manifold and connecting hoses.

The Thermactor system injects fresh air into the exhaust manifold whenever the engine is running. The fresh air combines with the hot exhaust gases to create a more complete oxidation or burning of the gases, reducing carbon monoxide and hydrocarbon emissions. Intake air is drawn through a centrifugal filter fan at the front of the pump. This air is sent from the pump to the air management valve, which directs it to the air injection manifold(s) or dumps it into the atmosphere, according to system application and engine operating conditions. The check valves prevent hot exhaust gases from reversing their flow in the system and causing pump damage.

Rough idling or poor performance can be caused by a leaking air management valve vacuum line. Backfiring can be caused by a defective air management valve or its connections. If there is no air flow to the exhaust ports, HC/CO emission levels will be excessive.

Air pump operation

The air pump can be distinguished from the alternator by the centrifugal filter fan located on the rotor shaft/drive hub. The pump located on the front of the engine below the alternator and is serviced by replacement only. It should not be disassembled.

NOTE
There is a small vent hole at the top front of some pump housings. Do not mistake it for a lubrication point. Air pumps require no lubrication.

Air pumps are not noiseless in operation. Pump noise is normal and rises in pitch as engine speed increases. Three types of pump noise may be noticed:

a. A chirp or squeak is often heard intermittently at low engine speeds. It is usually caused by the pump vanes rubbing in the housing bore, but may also be caused by drive belt slippage if the pump seizes.
b. A rolling sound heard at all speeds is caused by the bearings. This sound is also normal, but can indicate bearing failure if it reaches an objectionable level.
c. A continuous knocking noise indicates definite bearing failure. The pump must be replaced.

Air pump functional check

1. Check and adjust the drive belt tension, if required. See Chapter Seven.
2. Inspect all system hoses for cracking, burning or loose connections. Replace hoses or tighten connections as necessary.
3. Start the engine. Disconnect the pump output hose. There should be air flow. If not, replace the pump.
4. Gradually increase engine speed to approximately 1,500 rpm. If air flow does not increase, replace the pump.
5. Reconnect the hoses. Increase engine speed to 2,000 rpm. Release the throttle quickly. If a backfire occurs, the air bypass valve is not operating properly or is defective. Replace the air bypass valve.
6. Disconnect the check valve line and remove the check valve.
7. Blow through both ends of the valve. Suck air through both ends. The valve should pass air in only one direction. If it passes air in both

directions or does not pass air in either direction, install a new check valve.

Further air management system testing should be left to a dealer.

Exhaust Gas Recirculation (EGR) System

This system is used on 4-cylinder and 2.8L V6 engines. It recirculates a small amount of exhaust gas into the incoming air-fuel mixture through an electronic EGR valve at engine speeds above idle. This lowers the combustion temperature and reduces oxides of nitrogen (NOx) emissions.

The EGR valve on 2.3L EFI engines is mounted on an adapter attached to the upper intake manifold (**Figure 48**) and connected to the exhaust manifold by a metal tube. The 2.8L V6 EGR valve is mounted on the intake manifold to the rear of the carburetor.

An EGR valve position sensor attached to the valve sends a voltage signal to the EEC-IV microprocessor. Since the unit is completely sealed, valve movement cannot be seen. The EGR valve and sensor can be serviced separately.

EGR system testing should be left to a dealer. Correct system operation is dependent on a variety of factors. Proper functioning of the electronic EGR valve depends upon the EEC-IV microprocessor. The testing of this system is best left to a qualified technician.

Catalytic Converter

The catalytic converter is mounted in the exhaust system between the manifold exhaust pipe and the muffler. The converter reduces carbon monoxide and unburned hydrocarbon pollutants in the exhaust gases. This process changes the harmful pollutants into harmless carbon dioxide and water. Oxides of nitrogen are reduced to pure nitrogen and oxygen. The converter contains a monolithic honeycomb coated with a catalytic material containing platinum and palladium. The converter requires no maintenance other than the use of unleaded gasoline and replacement of the heat shield, if damaged. If it becomes necessary to replace the converter, see *Exhaust System* in this chapter.

Oxygen Sensor

An oxygen sensor is installed in the exhaust manifold or manifold pipe (**Figure 49**) on all vehicles equipped with the EEC-IV system. Some 1986 and 1987 vehicles use a heated exhaust gas oxygen sensor (HEGO). This can be identified by its 3-wire electrical lead; a non-heated sensor has a single wire. An oxygen sensor does not function until it has reached a certain temperature. The HEGO receives power from the EEC-IV microprocessor to heat it more rapidly, allowing it to function sooner.

The oxygen sensor has a permanently attached pig-tail and connector which should not be removed from the unit. Care is required in handling an oxygen sensor to assure proper operation. Keep the inline electrical connector and louvered end of the sensor free of grease or other contaminants and do not attempt to clean it with any type of solvent. Use of only a few tankfuls of leaded gasoline will destroy the sensor's sensitivity and result in driveability problems and poor gas

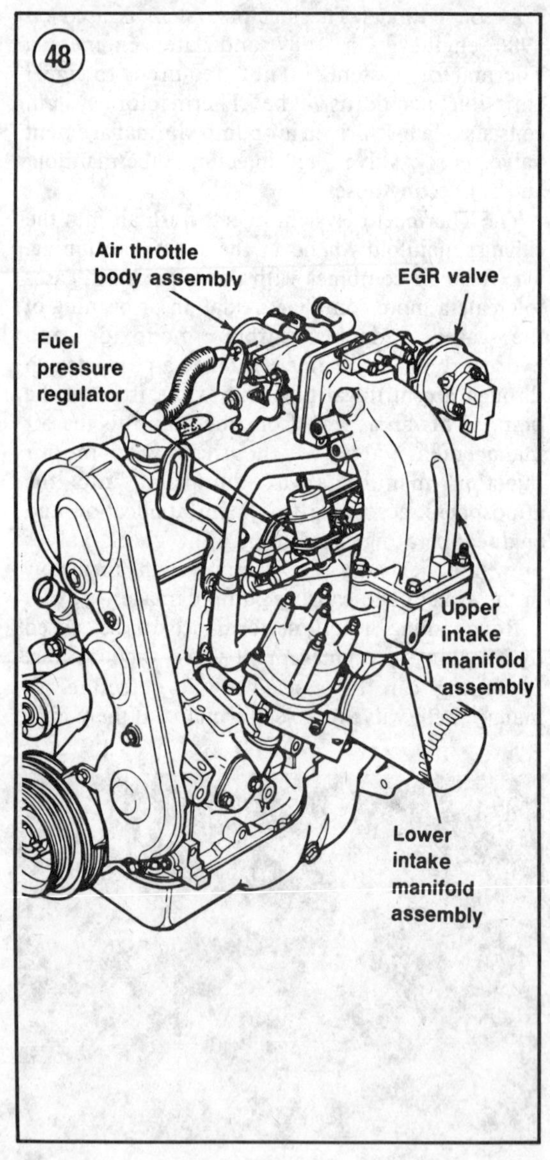

mileage. Any attempt to measure the output voltage with a voltmeter also will permanently damage an oxygen sensor.

It may be difficult to remove the sensor if engine temperature is under 120° F (48° C). Use of excessive force can cause thread damage in the exhaust manifold. Use the following procedure to replace a damaged sensor or transfer the sensor to a new manifold.

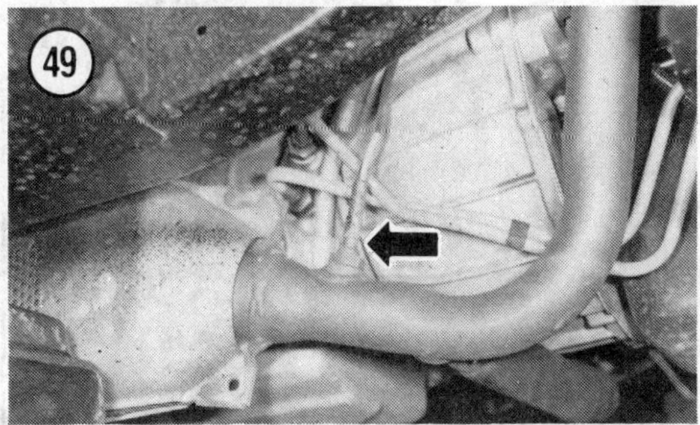

1. Securely block both rear wheels so the vehicle will not roll in either direction.
2. Raise the front of the vehicle with a jack and place it onjackstands.
3. Locate the sensor in the exhaust manifold pipe (**Figure 49**), then unplug the sensor electrical connector at the wiring harness.
4. Remove the sensor with an appropriate size open-end wrench.

NOTE
If the sensor does not unscrew easily, spray the sensor thread area with a penetrating lubricant and let soak for 5 minutes, then try removing it.

5. If installing the same sensor, wipe its threads with an electrically conductive anti-seize compound. New sensors are pre-coated.
6. Thread the sensor in place by hand and tighten to 30 ft.-lb. (41 N•m).
7. Reconnect the sensor electrical connector to the wiring harness.

Table 1 is on the following page.

Table 1 TIGHTENING TORQUES

Fastener	in.-lb.	ft.-lb.	N·m
Carburetor attaching nuts		14-16	20-21
Converter-to-muffler		18-26	25-35
Fuel pump			
Attaching bolts		14-21	19-29
Fuel line-to-outlet fitting		15-18	20-24
Fuel tank			
Attaching bolts		35-45	47-61
Shield nuts		6-8	8-11
Filler pipe clamps	26-35		3-4
Inlet pipe-to-manifold		25-34	34-46
2.3L EFI system			
Accelerator cable bracket		10-15	13.5-20.5
Air bypass valve		6.0-8.5	8.0-11.5
Air supply tube clamps	15-23		1.7-2.6
EGR tube		18-28	25-35
Engine oil dipstick bracket		15-22	20-30
Fuel supply manifold-to-fuel charging assembly		15-22	19-29
Lower intake manifold		15-22	19-29
Pressure regulator	26-40		3.0-4.5
Pressure relief valve		4.1-7.0	5.5-9.5
Throttle body		12-15	16-20
Throttle position sensor	14-15		1.6-1.8
Upper intake manifold		15-22	20-30
Vacuum tree		12-18	16-24
Water bypass line	12-20		1.4-2.2
3.0L V6 EFI system			
Air bypass valve	71-97		8-11
Air intake throttle body		15-22	20-30
Air supply tube clamps	17-26		2-3
Lower intake manifold		20-28	26-38
Fuel rail		6-8	8-12
Pressure regulator	27-40		3.0-4.5
Pressure relief valve	48-84		6-10

CHAPTER SEVEN

COOLING, HEATING AND AIR CONDITIONING SYSTEMS

7

All vehicles covered in this manual use a pressurized cooling system (15 psi) sealed with a pressure-type radiator cap. The higher operating pressure of the system increases the efficiency of the radiator by raising the boiling point of the coolant.

The cooling system consists of the radiator, water pump, cooling fan, thermostat, coolant recovery tank, temperature sensors and connecting hoses. The crossflow radiator is mounted on the engine compartment front body support panel.

The heater is a hot water type which circulates coolant through a small radiator (heater core) under the instrument panel.

The air conditioning system is a cycling clutch (intermittent) fixed-orifice refrigerant type and uses outside air at all times. The chapter includes service procedures for the radiator, thermostat, water pump, cooling fan, heater and air conditioner. Cooling system flushing procedures are also described. **Tables 1-3** are at the end of the chapter.

COOLING SYSTEM

All vehicles use a crossflow radiator (**Figure 1**) mounted on the engine compartment front body support panel. The crossflow radiator is constructed in a tube and slit-fin-core arrangement for crossflow of the coolant. The header tanks on each side of the radiator provide uniform distribution of the coolant to the crossflow tubes. The outlet port (lower hose connection) connects to the water pump inlet port. The inlet port (upper hose connection) connects to the water housing outlet or thermostat housing elbow. The left header tank contains the transmission oil cooler on automatic transmission models.

A coolant recovery system is incorporated in all cooling systems. This consists of a translucent plastic overflow reservoir connected to the radiator filler neck by a hose (**Figure 2**). The reservoir is installed underneath the battery tray and cannot be seen in many engine compartments because of the many hoses, lines and wires. Unlike other coolant recovery systems, coolant level is checked and coolant added directly to the radiator.

When coolant in the radiator expands to the overflow point, it passes through the filler neck and into the plastic reservoir. Once the coolant in the radiator cools down, it contracts. The vacuum created pulls coolant from the reservoir back into the radiator. This system prevents the radiator from boiling over. By remaining filled to capacity, cooling efficiency is maintained at all times.

The recommended coolant is a 50/50 mixture of ethylene glycol antifreeze and low mineral content water, which provides a lower freezing point and higher boiling point than water alone.

The water pump circulates the coolant through the cooling system when the engine is running. When the engine is cold, the coolant is trapped inside the engine water jacket by the thermostat, which is located in the mouth of the hose leading to the radiator inlet tank. The thermostat remains closed until the coolant heats up to operating temperature. It then opens and the coolant flows through the hose into the radiator inlet tank. The coolant passes through the radiator tubes to the outlet tank, where it flows through the radiator outlet hose to the water pump inlet to start the cycle over again.

The cooling fan draws air through the radiator and removes excess heat from the coolant. A viscous fan drive clutch (thermostatic) fan is used. The viscous clutch fan contains a silicone-filled coupling that automatically increases or decreases fan speed according to temperature to provide proper engine cooling under all conditions.

All models have a shroud attached to the radiator to funnel air through the radiator more efficiently.

COOLING SYSTEM CHECKS

1. Visually inspect the cooling system and heater hoses for signs of cracking, checking, excessive swelling or leakage. Restrictions in the cooling system may cause the radiator hoses to collapse, expand, vibrate or thump. An upper radiator hose relief valve is on the radiator cap.

2. Check that all supporting or protective hose brackets or straps are properly positioned and that the hoses are correctly supported in the bracket or restrained by the strap.

3. Inspect the front and rear of the radiator core and tanks, all seams and the radiator draincock for signs of seepage or leaks.

4. Make sure all hose connections are tight and in good condition. See **Figure 3** (typical). Check the hoses carefully at their clamps for cuts or weakness. Overtightening strap-type clamps can cut the outer surface of a hose and weaken it.

5. Remove the radiator pressure cap. Check the rubber cap seal surfaces for tears or cracks (**Figure 4**). Check for a bent or distorted cap. Raise the vacuum valve and rubber seal and rinse the cap under warm tap water to flush away any loose rust or dirt particles.

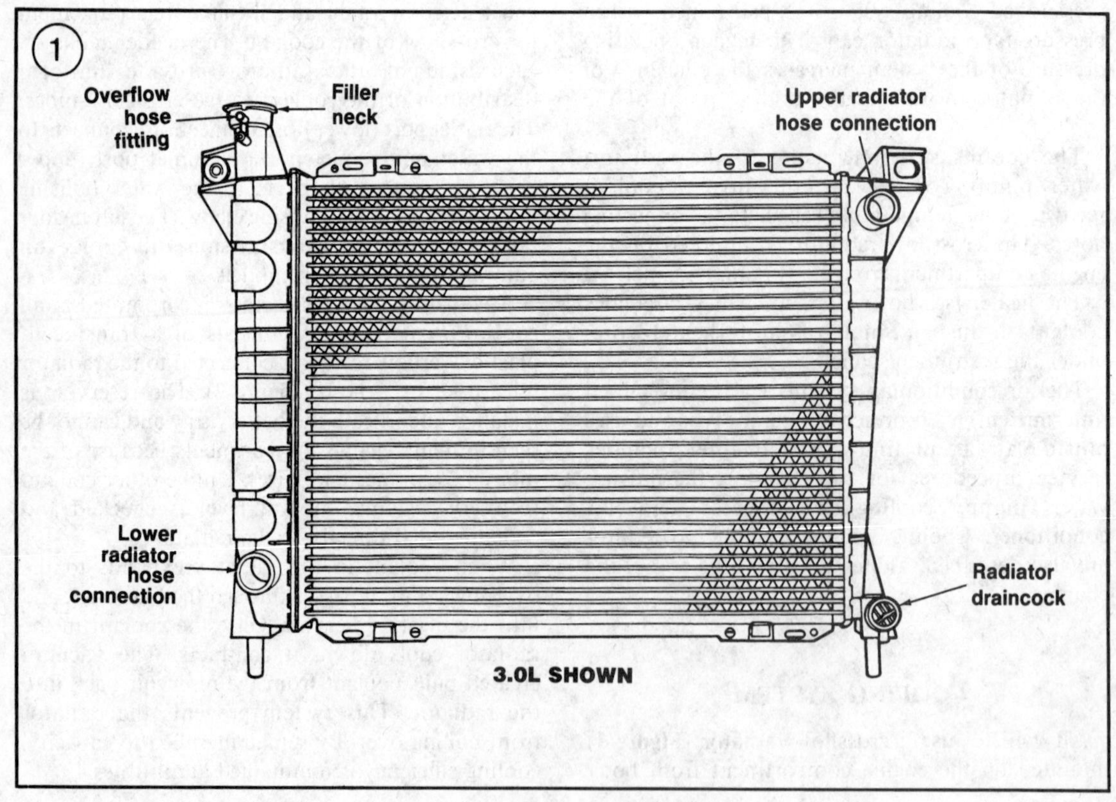

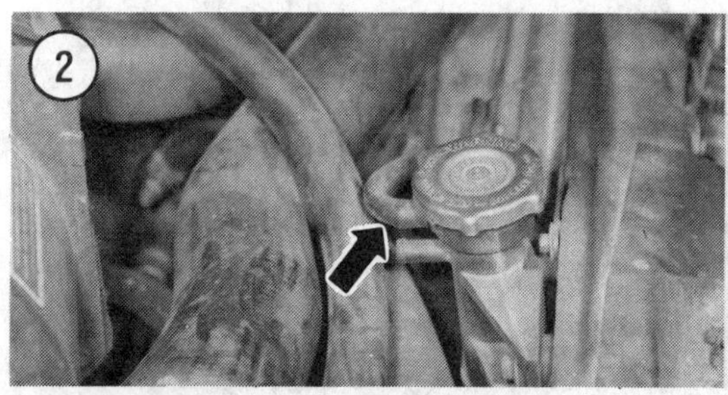

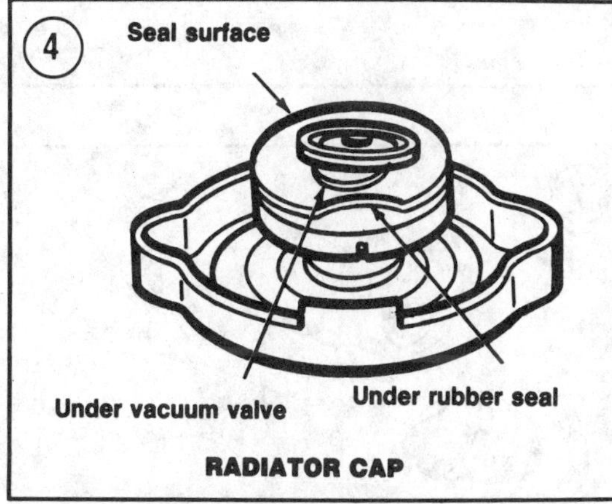

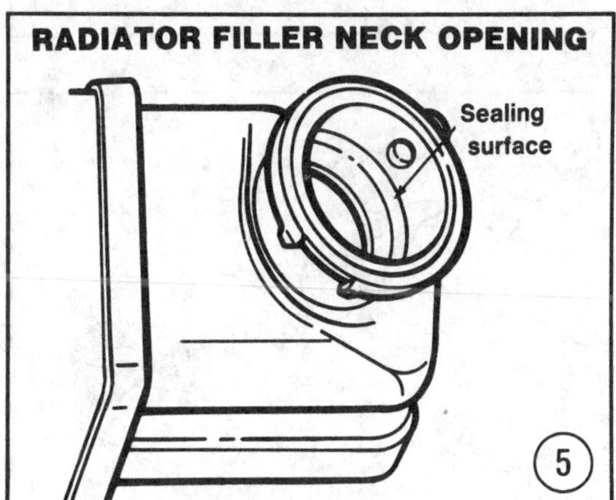

6. Inspect the filler neck seat and sealing surface (**Figure 5**) for nicks, dents, distortion or contamination. Wipe the sealing surface with a clean cloth to remove any rust or dirt. Install the cap properly.

7. Start the engine and warm to normal operating temperature. Shut the engine off and carefully feel the radiator. Crossflow radiators should be hot along the left side and warm along the right side with an even temperature rise from right to left. Any cold spots indicate obstructed or clogged radiator sections.

8. Restart the engine and squeeze the upper radiator hose to check water pump operation. If a pressure surge is felt, the water pump is functioning properly. If not, check for a plugged vent hole in the pump.

9. Visually check the area underneath the water pump for signs of leakage or corrosion. A defective water pump will usually leak through the vent hole at the bottom of the pump. The leakage will generally leave a white or greenish-white residue on the front of the block. If such residue is found, service the water pump at the first available opportunity.

10. Check the crankcase oil dipstick for signs of coolant in the engine oil. On automatic transmission models, check the coolant for signs of transmission fluid leaking from the oil cooler. Check the transmission lines which connect to the oil cooler.

11. If a cooling system suffers from overheating and none of the above steps point to the cause, perform the following diagnosis:

a. Remove the water pump. Remove the rear cover of the pump and check internal passages with a penlight.
b. Remove the thermostat as described in this chapter and check for restrictions in the crossover passage at the front of the intake manifold with a penlight.
c. Remove the cylinder head(s) and check for restrictions in the coolant passages of the block with a penlight. All water jacket passages in the block can be inspected in this manner, so never assume the block is restricted unless you can visually determine that a restriction exists.
d. If none of these steps locate a restriction, the cylinder head(s) is most likely at fault.

Coolant passages in the head are very complex and are not as easily checked visually as those in the block or water pump. If the coolant passages in a cylinder head are blocked, they are most likely blocked in more than one place. Check the head(s) for a dark blue or black area, which results from overheating. If no discoloration is found, check the coolant passages visually with a penlight as best you can, then probe all accessible passages with a length of wire that is flexible enough to negotiate sharp turns. Since it may not be possible to satisfactorily inspect all of the coolant passages in this way, try to determine if any of the passages have rough or ragged internal surfaces. Even if no direct evidence of blockage can be found, a suspect cylinder head should be replaced and the new head checked in the same manner before installation.

COOLING SYSTEM LEAKAGE TEST

If the cooling system requires frequent topping up, it probably has a leak. Small cooling system leaks are not easy to locate; the hot coolant evaporates as fast as it leaks out, preventing the formation of tell-tale rusty or grayish-white stains.

A pressure test of the cooling system will usually help to pinpoint the source of the leak. This test requires a reliable pressure tester (**Figure 6**) and can be performed quickly and economically by your dealer or a radiator shop. The test should be performed if frequent additions of coolant are necessary to keep the cooling system topped up and your radiator is known to be in good condition.

1. Remove the radiator cap.
2. Dip the cap in water and attach a cooling system pressure tester, using the adapter supplied with the tester. See **Figure** 7 (typical).
3. **Pump the pressure to 15 psi. The cap relief valve should open at between 10.7-15 psi. If not, replace the cap.**
4. **Pump the pressure to 10 psi. If pressure drops rapidly below 8.5 psi, replace the cap.**
5. Wipe the filler neck sealing surface on the radiator with a clean dry cloth. Make sure the coolant is within 1-1 1/2 in. of the cap seal seat in the filler neck.
6. Install the radiator cap and disconnect the overflow line at the filler neck nipple. See **Figure 2** (typical). Connect the pressure tester to the nipple and pump it up. If the radiator cap does not hold pressure at 8.5 psi and reliéve it above 10.7 psi, the radiator cap seal is defective.
7. Remove the radiator cap and reconnect the overflow line. Connect the pressure tester to the filler neck (**Figure 8**). Pump the pressure to 12.8 psi. If it drops below 10 psi, check all system components for signs of leakage.

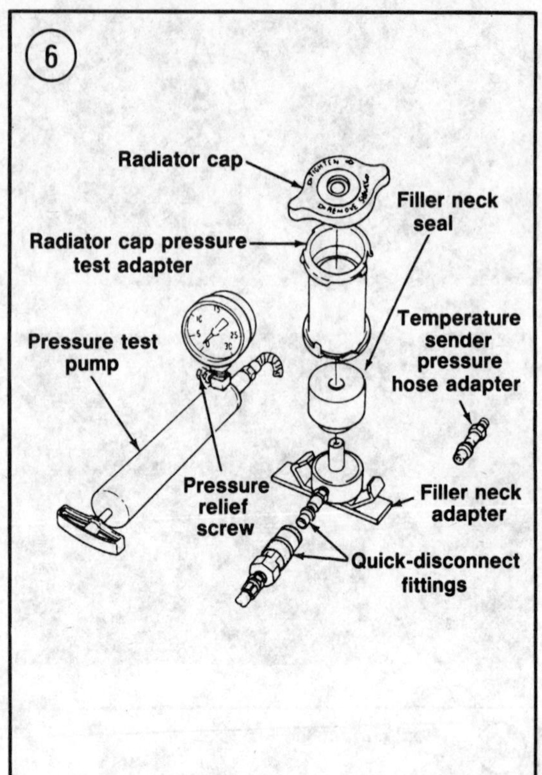

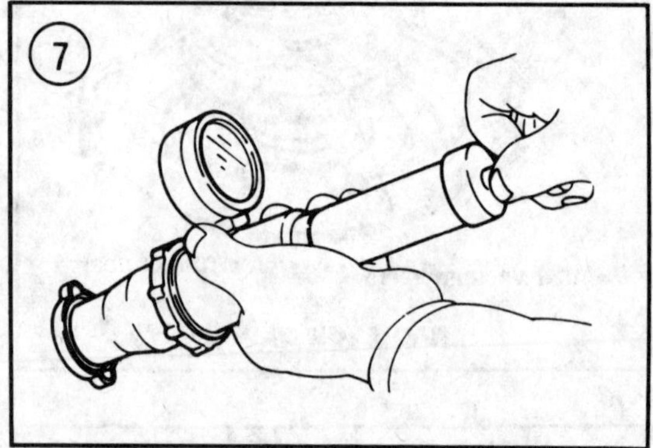

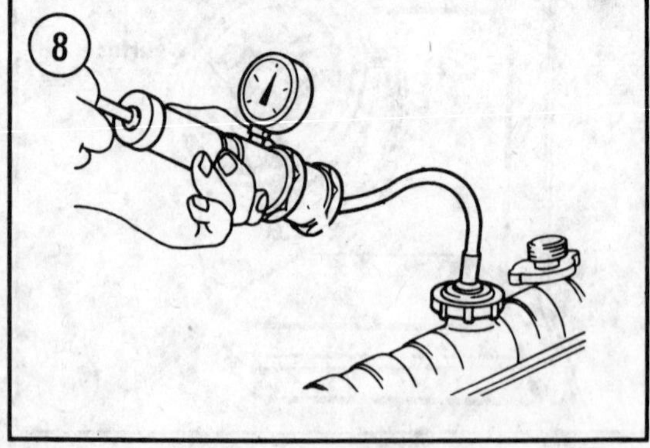

WARNING
Pressure builds up quickly in Step 8. Do not let it exceed 15 psi.

8. If the system will not hold at least 10 psi in Step 7 but no external leaks can be found, remove the tester but do not install the radiator cap. Start and run the engine until the upper radiator hose is hot. Reconnect the tester and pump the pressure to 12.8 psi.
   a. If the tester needle fluctuates, the head gasket is probably leaking.
   b. If the tester needle holds steady, rapidly open and close the throttle several times while an assistant checks for an abnormal amount of coolant or steam coming out of the tail pipe. This is caused by a defective head gasket or an engine block or cylinder head that is cracked.
   c. If the tester needle holds steady and the system does not emit coolant or steam in Step b, there may be an internal leak. Shut the engine off and remove the crankcase dipstick. Check the dipstick for signs of water mixed with the oil (milky-looking oil). If found, the engine must be removed and disassembled to locate and correct the leakage.

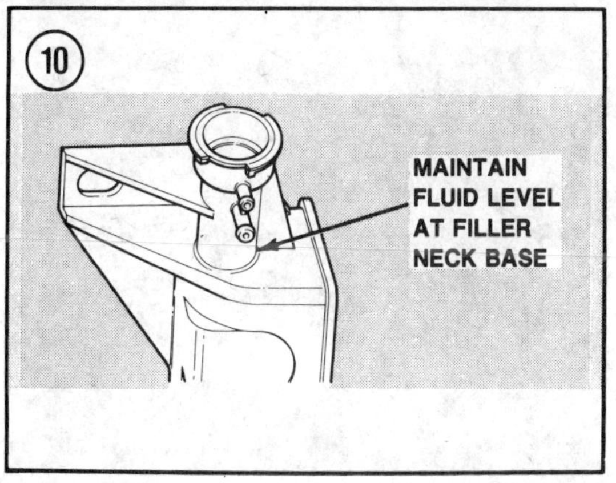

If the cooling system passes a pressure test but continues to lose coolant, check for an exhaust leak into the cooling system.

1. Drain the coolant until the level is just above the top of the cylinder head(s).
2. Disconnect the upper radiator hose and remove the thermostat and water pump drive belt.

CAUTION
Do not run the engine with the water pump belt disconnected for more than 30 seconds or the engine may overheat.

3. Add sufficient coolant to bring the level within 1/2 in. of the top of the thermostat housing.
4. Start the engine and open the throttle several times while observing the coolant. If the level rises noticeably or if bubbles appear in the coolant, exhaust gases are probably leaking into the cooling system. This probably means that the cylinder head gasket is defective.
5. **Reinstall the thermostat and drive belt. Reconnect the upper radiator hose to the thermostat housing.**
6. **Add the coolant drained in Step 1 and adjust the drive belt tension.**

COOLANT LEVEL CHECK

Always check coolant level with the engine and radiator cold. Coolant expands as it is heated and checking a hot or warm system will not give a true level reading.

Cooling systems equipped with a coolant recovery feature are generally checked at the reservoir instead of the radiator, but on the Aerostar, coolant level must be checked at the radiator. Remove the radiator cap (**Figure 9**). Add coolant as required to bring the level in the radiator at a point level with the filler neck base. See **Figure 10**. Install the radiator cap.

COOLING SYSTEM FLUSHING

The recommended coolant is a 50/50 mixture of ethylene glycol antifreeze and water. Ford recommends that only an antifreeze containing a silicate inhibitor and meeting Ford specification ESE-M97B44-A be used. Ford Cooling System Fluid (part No. E2FZ-19549-A) and Prestone II are recommended coolants which meet this specification.

Recommended coolants are designed to prevent corrosion of aluminum components used in late-model engines and cooling systems. The use of antifreeze without the silicate inhibitor which does not meet Ford specifications may cause a thermo-chemical reaction resulting in serious radiator and engine damage.

7

The radiator should be drained, flushed and refilled at the intervals specified in Chapter Three. The heater core is flushed separately after the cooling system is serviced. After initial filling, the coolant level may drop by as much as one quart after engine operation due to the displacement of entrapped air.

CAUTION
Under no circumstances should a chemical flushing agent be used. Flush the cooling system with clear water only.

1. Coolant can stain concrete and harm plants. Park the vehicle over a gutter or similar area.
2. Remove the air cleaner assembly. See Chapter Six.
3. Loosen the radiator cap to its first detent and release the system pressure, then turn the cap to its second detent and remove it.
4. Attach a tube to the draincock at the bottom of the radiator tank (**Figure 11**) to minimize coolant loss and splash. Open the draincock and let the cooling system drain into a suitable container.
5. Remove the engine block drain plug. Let the engine block drain.
6. Loosen the clamp on the lower radiator hose at the radiator. Disconnect the hose from the radiator and drain any remaining fluid in the hose into the container.
7. Remove the thermostat as described in this chapter. Temporarily reinstall the thermostat housing.
8. Disconnect the top radiator hose from the radiator.
9. Insert a garden hose into the top radiator hose. Run water into the top hose until clear water flows from the bottom hose.
10. Insert the garden hose into the hose fitting at the bottom of the radiator. Run water into the radiator until clear water flows from the top fitting, then turn the water off.
11. Close the radiator draincock and install the engine drain plug.
12. Disconnect the heater core outlet hose at the water pump. Disconnect the inlet hose at the engine block. See **Figure 12** (I4), **Figure 13** (2.8L V6) or **Figure 14** (3.0L V6). Let any coolant in the hoses drain.

NOTE
Some 1988 3.0L V6 engines use a molded heater hose assembly that connects to the heater tubes with quick-disconnect fittings. ***Figure 15*** *shows the hoses disconnected. Other 1985-on heater hose fittings on the I4 and 2.8L V6 engine may also use the same fittings. Quick-disconnect fittings require the use of heater hose tool part No. T85T-18539-AH to disconnect the hoses from the heater tubes, heater core or engine fittings. See* ***Figure 16****. New O-rings should be installed whenever the fittings are disconnected.*

13. Connect a garden hose to the heater inlet hose. This does not have to be a positive fit, as long as most of the water enters the heater hose. Run water into the heater hose until clear water flows from the other heater hose.
14. If equipped with the optional rear heater, a water valve is installed in the heater inlet hose. Connect a hand vacuum pump to the vacuum fitting and apply 6-8 in. Hg vacuum to check valve operation. Make sure that it closes without water leakage. Disconnect the vacuum pump (the valve should open) and reconnect the vacuum line.
15. Reconnect the outlet hose to the water pump and the inlet hose to the engine block.
16. Reconnect the upper and lower radiator hose. Reinstall the thermostat.
17. Slowly pour 4 quarts (I4) or 8 quarts (V6) of a 50/50 mixture of Ford Cooling System Fluid or equivalent and water into the radiator.
18. Add sufficient coolant mixture to bring the fluid level to the base of the filler neck. Do not install the radiator cap yet.
19. Wait several minutes for the coolant mixture to flow throughout the crossflow radiator and for any trapped air to bubble out.
20. Install the radiator cap to its first detent. This prevents spillage yet lets air escape from the radiator.
21. Set the heater temperature and mode selection levers to the maximum heat position.
22. Reinstall the air cleaner assembly. See Chapter Six.

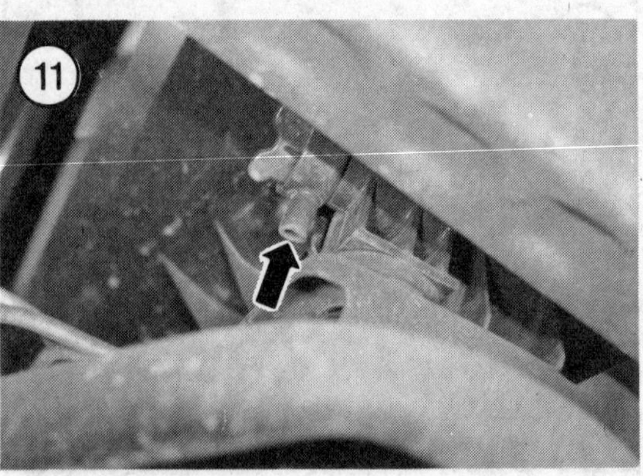

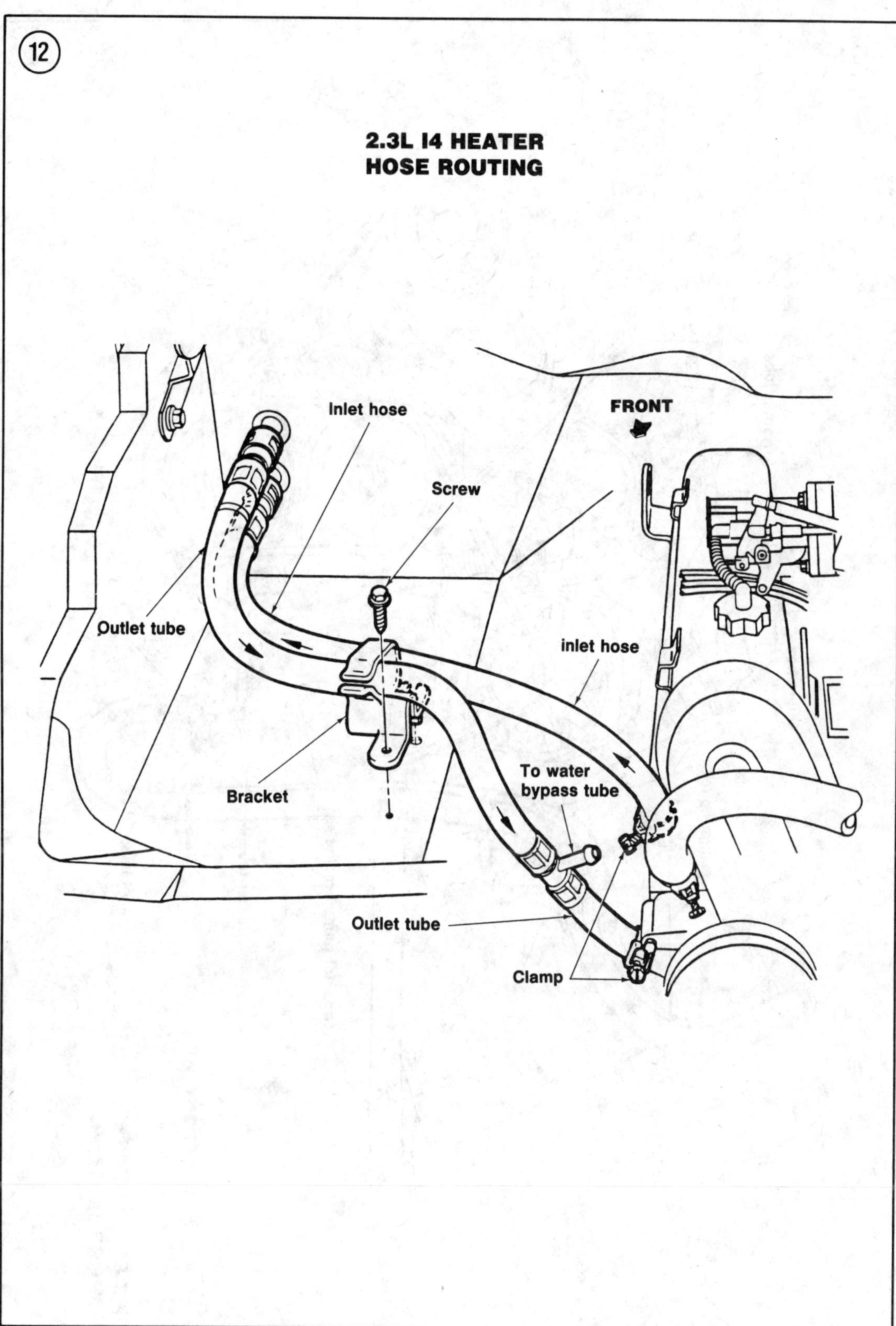
12
2.3L I4 HEATER
HOSE ROUTING
Inlet hose
FRONT
Screw
Outlet tube
inlet hose
To water
bypass tube
Bracket
Outlet tube
Clamp

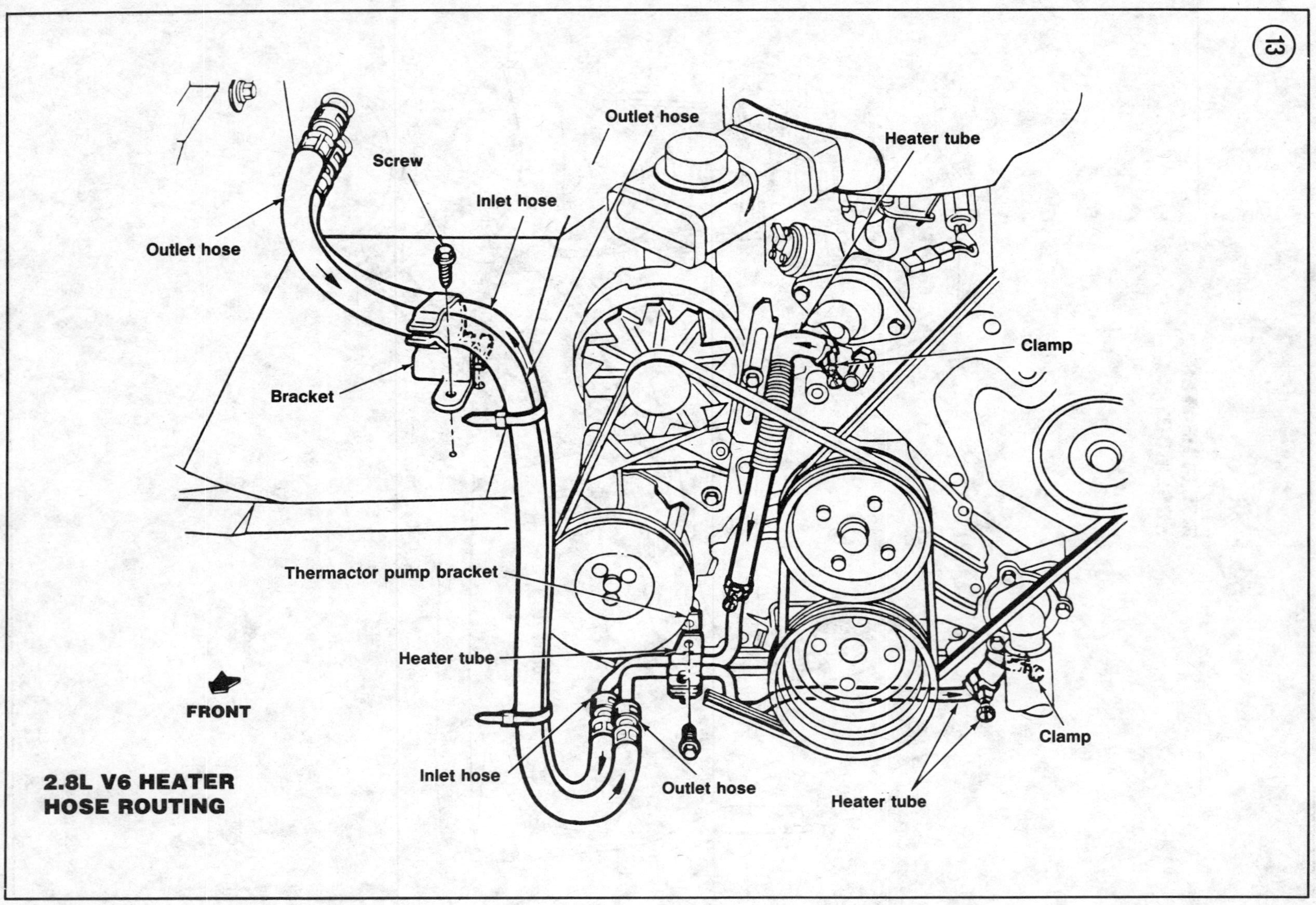

2.8L V6 HEATER HOSE ROUTING

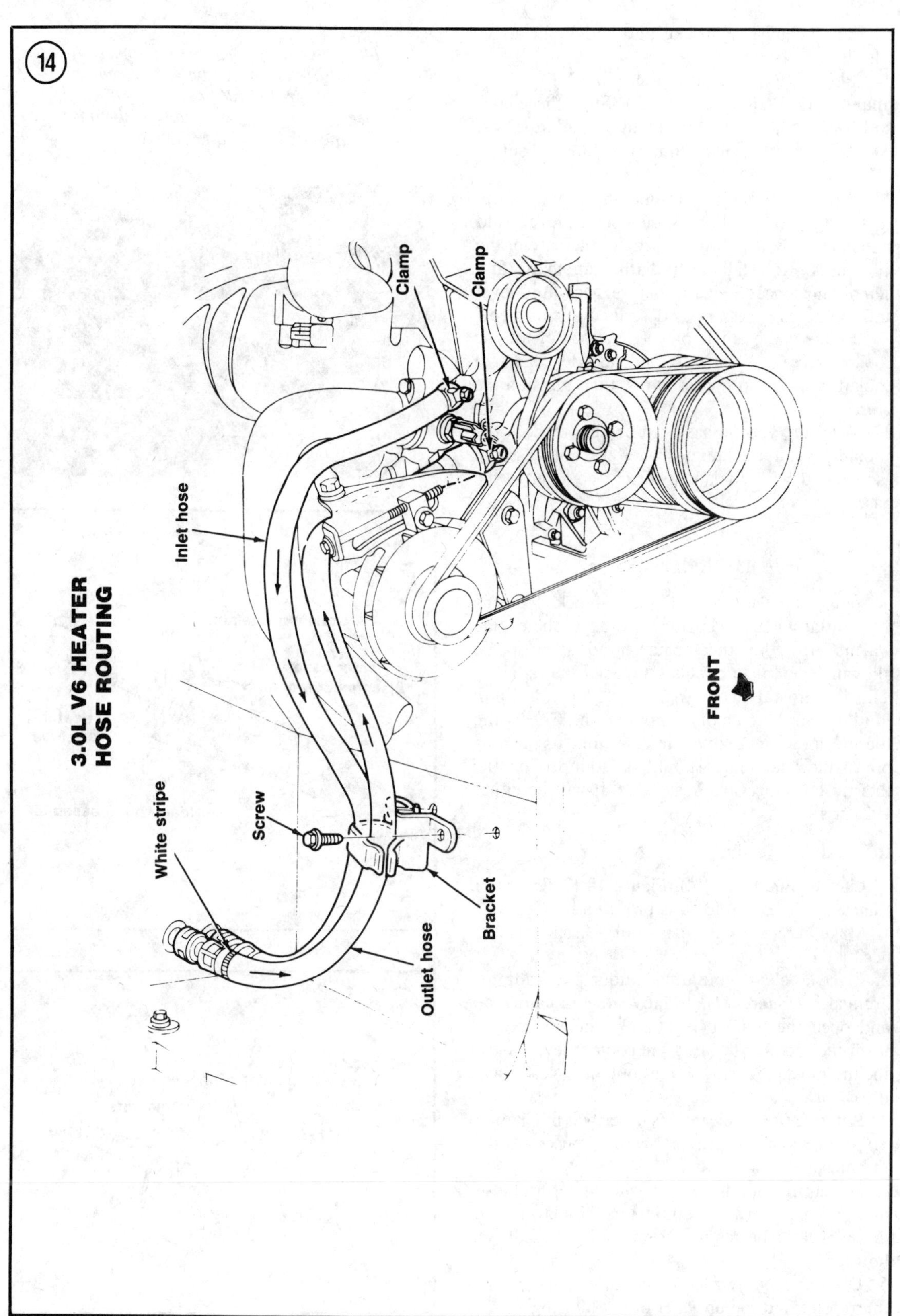
14
3.0L V6 HEATER
HOSE ROUTING
Clamp
Clamp
Inlet hose
FRONT
White stripe
Screw
Bracket
Outlet hose

23. Set the parking brake and block the drive wheels.
24. Place the transmission in NEUTRAL (manual) or PARK (automatic). Start the engine and run at a fast idle until the upper radiator hose is hot. Return the engine to normal idle and shut it off.
25. Wrap a thick cloth around the radiator cap. Remove the cap and check the coolant level. Add sufficient coolant to bring it back to the base of the filler neck. Reinstall the radiator cap to its first detent and repeat Step 19, then recheck fluid level and top up as necessary as described in this step.
26. Remove the small plug from the top of the coolant recovery reservoir and add 1.1 quart of coolant mixture to the reservoir, then reinstall the plug.
27. After the vehicle has been driven, recheck the coolant level in the radiator when it is cold. Top up as required with coolant to bring the level to the base of the filler neck.

THERMOSTAT

Coolant flow to the radiator is blocked by the thermostat when the engine is cold. As the engine warms up, the thermostat gradually opens, allowing coolant to circulate through the radiator. The thermostat heat range used depends upon model year and engine application. Check the thermostat when removed to determine its opening point; the heat range should be stamped on the thermostat flange. In most cases, it will be either 192° or 197° F.

Removal and Testing

Refer to **Figure 17** (I4), **Figure 18** (2.8L V6) or **Figure 19** (3.0L V6) for this procedure.
1. Make sure the engine is cool. Disconnect the negative battery cable.
2. Place a clean container under the radiator draincock (**Figure 11**). Remove the radiator cap and open the draincock. Drain sufficient coolant from the radiator to bring the coolant level below the thermostat housing. If the coolant is clean, save it for reuse.
3. Remove the air cleaner as described in Chapter Six, if necessary to provide working access to the thermostat housing.
4. Unclamp and disconnect the upper radiator hose at the thermostat housing. Unclamp and disconnect the heater hose from the I4 and 2.8L V6 housing.
5. Disconnect any electrical connectors at the thermostat housing or water outlet housing.

NOTE
The thermostat housing on some installations may be obscured by vacuum or hydraulic lines. In such cases, either work around or disconnect the lines as required in Step 6.

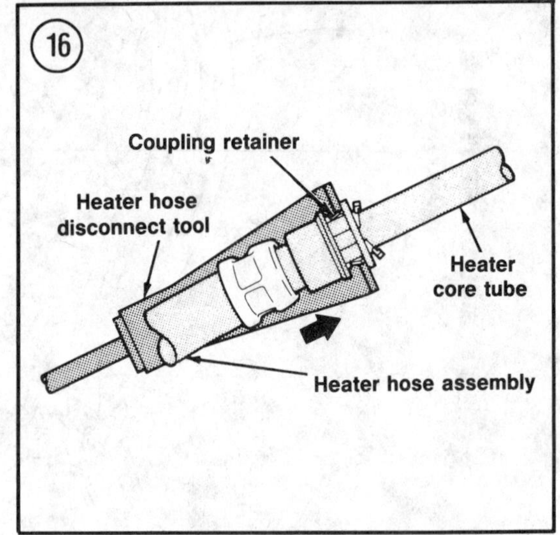

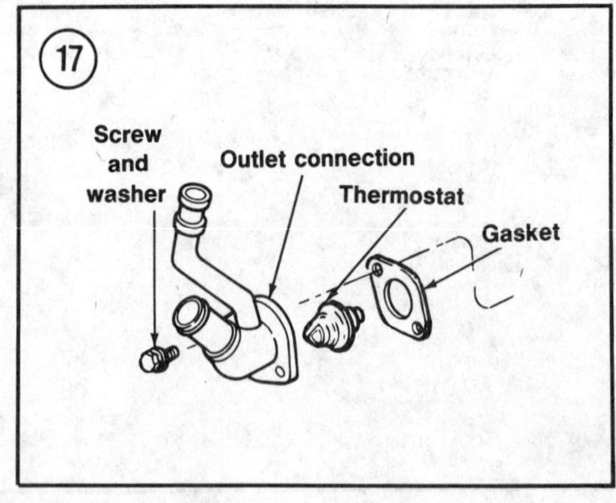

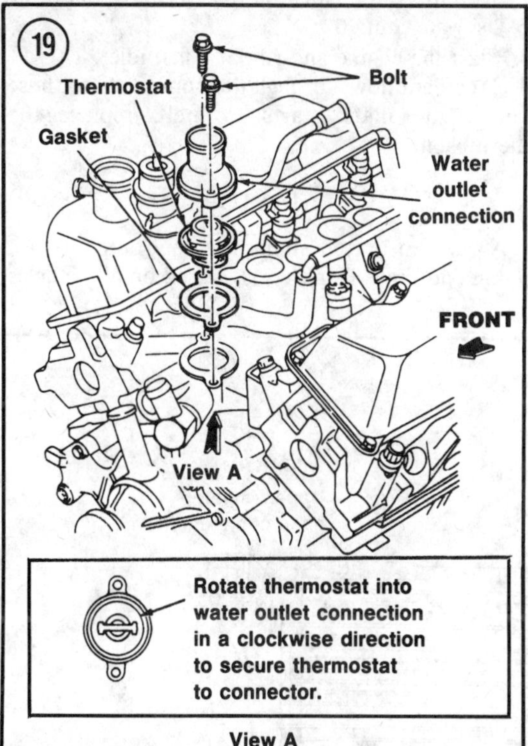

6. Remove the thermostat or water outlet housing bolts. Lift the cover clear of the cylinder head (I4) or intake manifold (V6).

7. Remove the thermostat from the cylinder head (I4) or intake manifold (V6). Remove and discard the gasket.

8. Prepare a container of coolant mixed 1 part antifreeze to 3 parts water and suspend a thermometer in the container (**Figure 20**). Heat the solution 25° F above the heat range stamped on the thermostat flange. Submerge the thermostat in the container of coolant and agitate the solution thoroughly. Replace the thermostat if the valve does not open fully (1/8 in.).

NOTE
Support the thermostat with wire so it does not touch the sides or bottom of the pan.

9. Cool the solution 25° F below the temperature stamped on the thermostat flange. Replace the thermostat if the valve does not return to within 0.003 in. of being completely closed.

10. Let the thermostat cool to room temperature. Hold it close to a light bulb and check for leakage. If light can be seen around the valve, the thermostat is defective.

Installation

Refer to **Figure 17** (I4), **Figure 18** (2.8L V6) or **Figure 19** (3.0L V6) for this procedure.

1. If a new thermostat is being installed, test it as described in this chapter.

2. Stuff a clean shop cloth in the cylinder head (I4) or intake manifold (V6) to prevent gasket residue from entering the engine. Clean all gasket and RTV sealant residue from the mating surfaces with a putty knife.

3. Install the thermostat in the cylinder head (I4) or intake manifold (V6). The copper element should face toward the engine and the thermostat flange must fit in the recess provided. See **Figure 19** for proper installation of 3.0L V6 thermostat.

4. Install a new gasket, coated on both sides with sealer.

5. Install the thermostat or water outlet housing cover. Tighten the attaching bolts to 15-22 ft.-lb. (20-30 N•m).

6. Reinstall the upper radiator hose to the thermostat or water outlet housing and tighten the clamp securely. Reinstall the heater hose on I4 and 2.8L V6 engines.

7. Reinstall the air cleaner, if removed.
8. Reconnect any vacuum lines, hydraulic lines or electrical connectors disconnected during removal.
9. Refill the cooling system to the specified level as described in this chapter.
10. Reconnect the negative battery cable.
11. Start the engine and check for leaks. Check coolant level and top up if required.

In-vehicle Testing

Thermostat operation can be tested without removing it from the engine. This procedure requires the use of 2 thermostat sticks available from auto parts stores. A thermostat stick looks like a carpenter's pencil and is made of a chemically impregnated wax material which melts at a specific temperature.

This technique can be used to determine the thermostat's operation by marking the thermostat housing with 188° F or 206° F sticks, depending upon the problem. As the coolant reaches 188° F, the mark made by that stick will melt. The mark made by the 206° F stick will not melt until the coolant increases to that temperature.

Overheated engine

1. Carefully remove the radiator cap to relieve the cooling system pressure.
2. Rub the 206° F stick on the thermostat housing cover/water outlet.
3. Start the engine and run at a fast idle.
4. If no coolant flows through the upper radiator hose by the time the mark starts to melt, replace the thermostat.

Slow engine warmup

1. Carefully remove the radiator cap to relieve the cooling system pressure.
2. Rub the 188° F stick on the thermostat housing cover/water outlet.
3. Start the engine and run at a fast idle.
4. If coolant flows through the upper radiator hose before the mark starts to melt, replace the thermostat.

RADIATOR

A vacuum brazed aluminum core radiator with nylon end tanks (**Figure 21**) is used on all vehicles

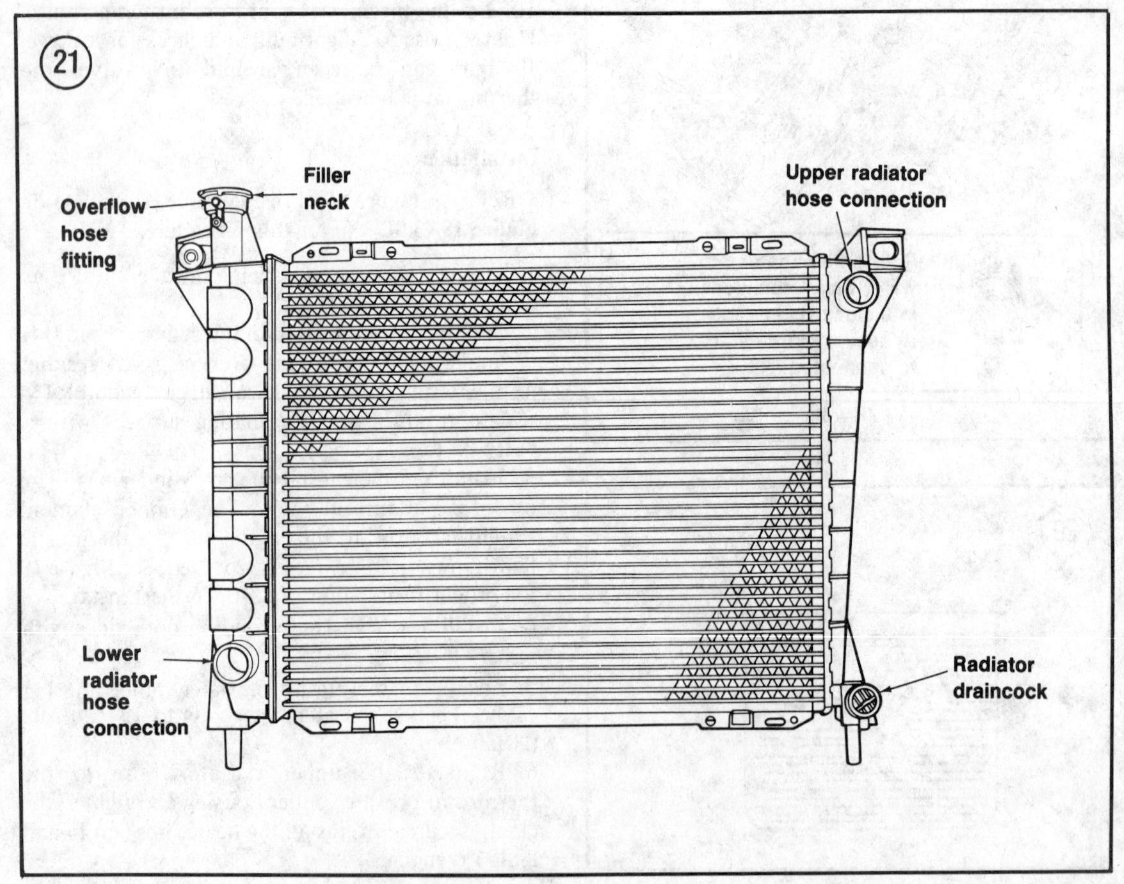

(instead of a copper/brass core radiator with metal header tanks). Work carefully when removing or installing hoses to a nylon end tank. If excessive pressure is applied, the fitting may crack or break. If this happens, the radiator must be removed and the end tank replaced.

Removal/Installation

Refer to **Figure 22** (I4), **Figure 23** (2.8L V6) or **Figure 24** (3.0L V6) for this procedure.

1. Make sure that the engine is cool enough to touch comfortably.
2. Coolant can stain concrete and harm plants. Park the vehicle over a gutter or similar area. Place a clean container under the draincock.
3. Remove the radiator cap and open the draincock at the bottom of the radiator. See **Figure 11** (typical).
4. Disconnect the overflow tube at the radiator filler neck nipple (**Figure 2**).
5. Remove the 2 screws holding the upper part of the fan shroud or the fingerguard. Lift the shroud from its lower retaining clips, move shroud back and drape it over the fan.
6. Disconnect the upper and lower hoses at the radiator.

NOTE
On some installations, it may be necessary to disconnect the lower radiator hose and oil cooler line from underneath the vehicle.

7. If equipped with an automatic transmission cooler, disconnect the 2 cooler lines at the radiator fittings. Cap the fittings and lines to prevent leakage.
8. Remove the 2 fasteners holding the radiator to its support assembly.
9. Tilt the radiator back as required, then lift it up and out of the lower mounting pads. Remove the radiator from the vehicle.
10. Lift the shroud off the fan and remove it from the engine compartment.
11. Remove the lower radiator support pads and/or insulators (if used) and inspect for wear or damage. Replace as required.
12. Installation is the reverse of removal. Make sure the lower support pads and/or insulators (if

7

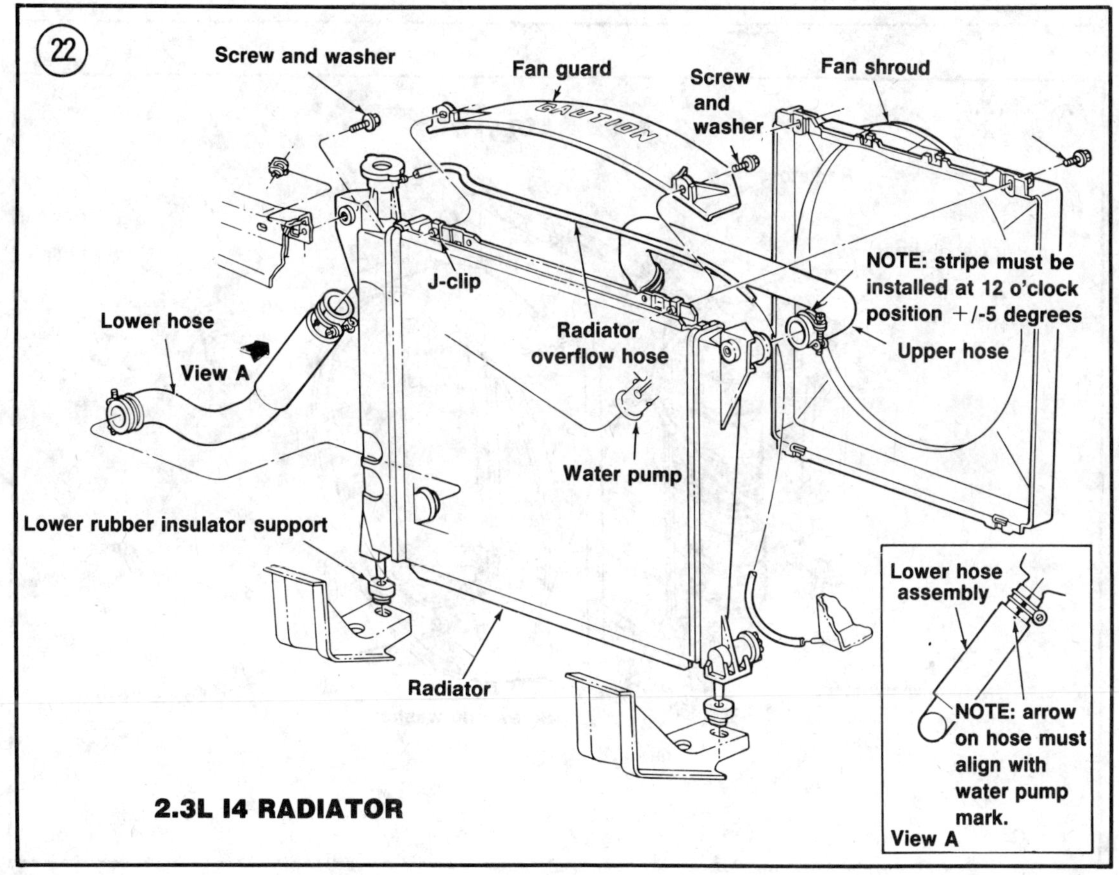

2.3L I4 RADIATOR

23

2.8L V6 RADIATOR

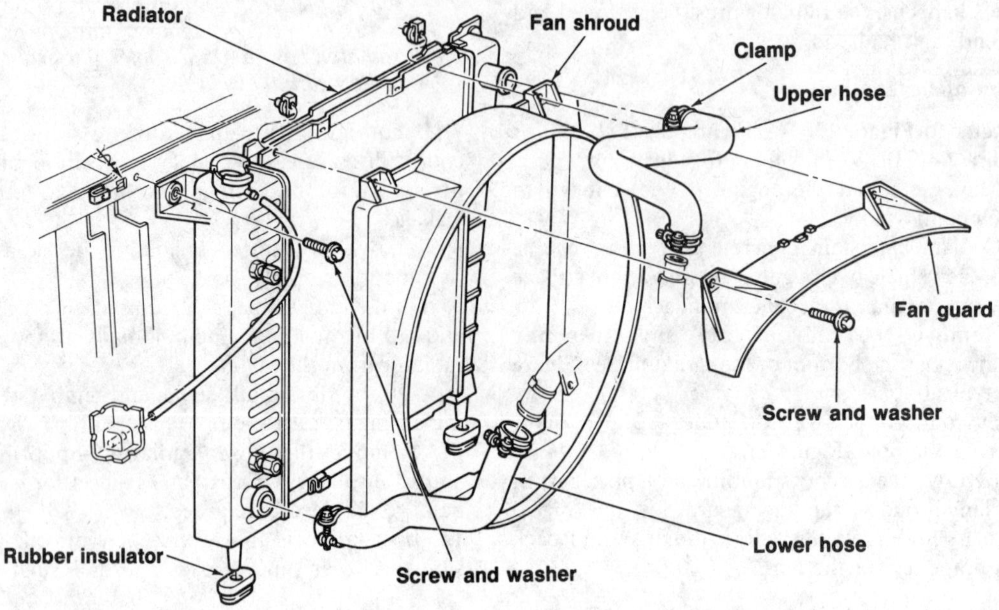

24

3.0L V6 RADIATOR

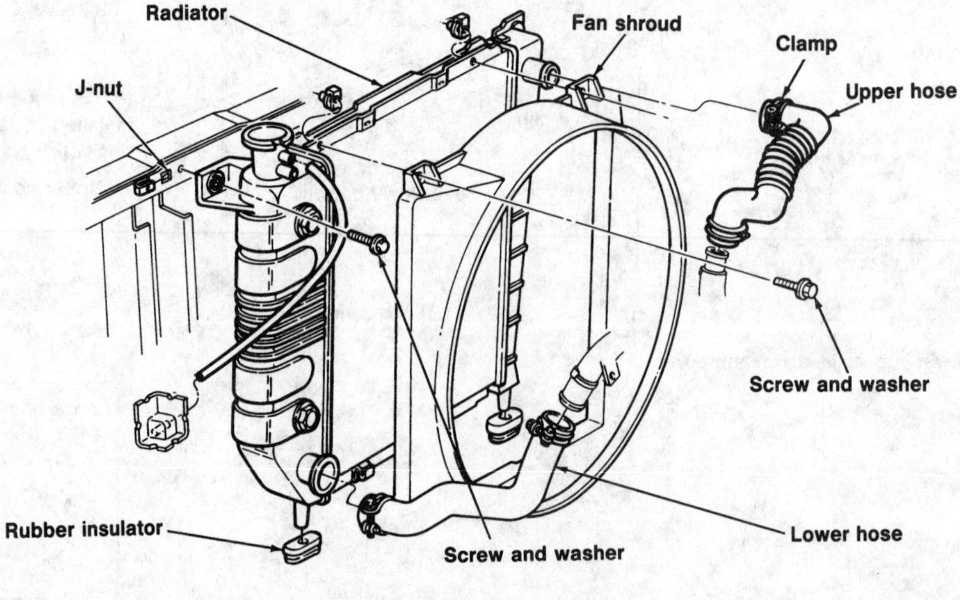

used) are properly positioned and engage the radiator as it is lowered into place. Tighten all fasteners to specifications (**Table 1**). Reconnect the negative battery cable and pour the drained coolant into the radiator filler neck. If the coolant is dirty or rusty, discard and install new coolant as described in *Cooling System Flushing* in this chapter.

End Tank Replacement

The aluminum tube radiator core is fitted with molded glass-filled nylon end tanks which incorporate radiator and fan shroud mounting brackets. Each end tank is attached to the core header by cinched metal tabs. A high temperature rubber gasket between the tank and header acts as a seal. **Figure 25** shows the major components of the radiator assembly.

NOTE
A small section of the header side may bend as the tabs are opened in the following procedure. A slight deformation of the header side is not harmful, as long as the tabs are opened just enough to permit tank removal. Such deformation will generally return to a normal position once the tabs are recrimped when the tank is reinstalled.

1. Remove the radiator as described in this chapter.
2. Insert a screwdriver tip between the tank and the end of the header tab, as shown in **Figure 26**. Carefully pry each tab away from the tank edge (except those under the inlet, outlet and/or filler neck) just enough for tank removal. Do not overbend the tabs or they may break off. If more than 3 tabs are broken on one side of the header or more than 2 adjacent tabs are broken, replace the core.
3. Carefully lift the tank enough to slide it out from underneath the remaining tabs that are still cinched. Remove the rubber gasket from the header and discard it. A new gasket must be installed whenever the tank and header are separated.
4. Clean the header and gasket groove to remove all contamination and gasket residue. Clean the sealing edge of the end tank.

7

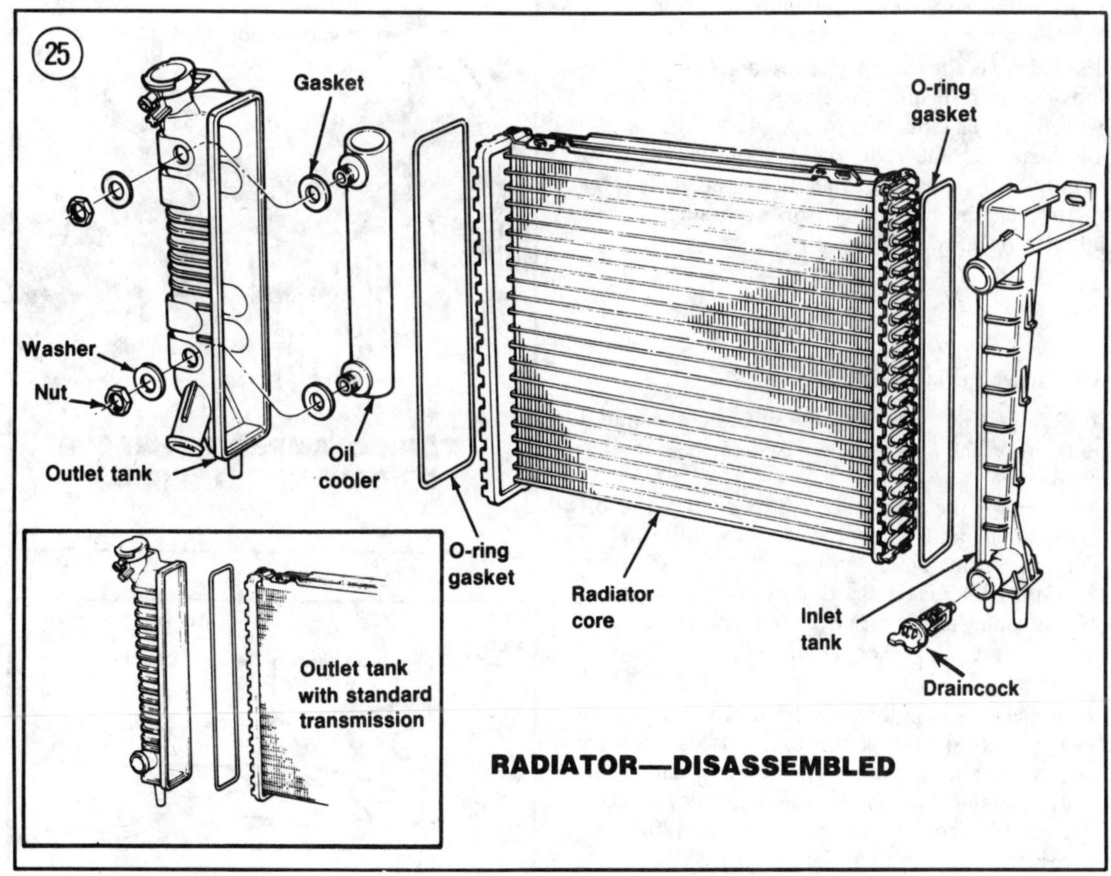

RADIATOR—DISASSEMBLED

5. Check the tank flange and header gasket surface for signs of leakage. Clean or repair the surfaces as required to remove any dirt, burrs or bumps.
6. If the outlet tank of an automatic transmission model is being replaced, transfer the oil cooler to the new tank as described in this chapter.
7. Dip a new tank gasket in coolant and install in the core header grooves. Make sure the gasket does not twist when the tank is reinstalled.
8. Fit the tank to the core header with the top and bottom of the new tank aligned with the other tank.
9. Install 2 Barbee No. 200 crimp clamps or equivalent on the header as shown in **Figure 27** and tighten just enough to compress the new gasket.
10. Fit a hex nut on a pair of locking pliers as shown in **Figure 28**. Close and lock the plier jaws. Turn the adjusting screw to fit the jaws around the shank of a 13/32 in. drill bit (**Figure 29**). Tighten the hex nut to lock the jaws in place. Remove the drill bit.
11. Using the pliers prepared in Step 10, crimp 4 cinch tabs to secure the tank to the core header.
12. Clamp the remaining tabs using the same procedure as in Step 11. Some tabs will be blocked by the clamps.
13. Remove the crimp clamps and squeeze the tabs that were behind the clamps down into place with the other tabs.
14. Leak test the radiator at 20 psi (138 kPa). Minor seal leaks can usually be corrected by recrimping the header tabs on both sides of the apparent leak.

Oil Cooler Replacement

1. Remove the radiator and separate the outlet tank from the core header as described in this chapter.
2. Remove the nuts and washers from the oil cooler inlet and outlet connections. Lift the oil cooler from the outlet tank.
3. If the cooler is damaged or defective, discard it. If the cooler is to be reused, remove and discard the neoprene gaskets from the inlet/outlet connections.
4. Replacement is the reverse of removal. Install new gaskets on the cooler to be used. Start the cooler retaining nuts by hand, then apply water-resistant sealer to the exposed threads. Tighten the cooler nuts to 15 ft.-lb. (20 N•m); excessive torque can cut the cooler gaskets.

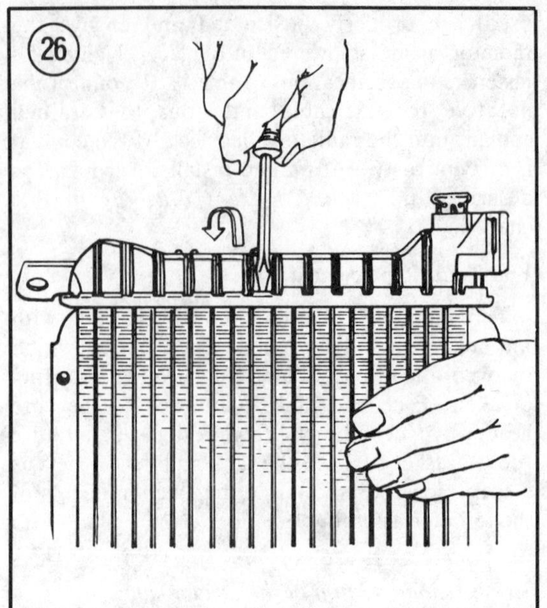

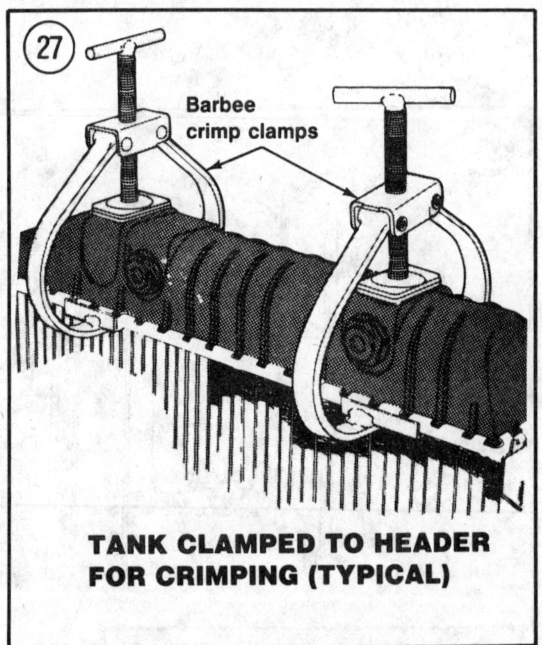

TANK CLAMPED TO HEADER FOR CRIMPING (TYPICAL)

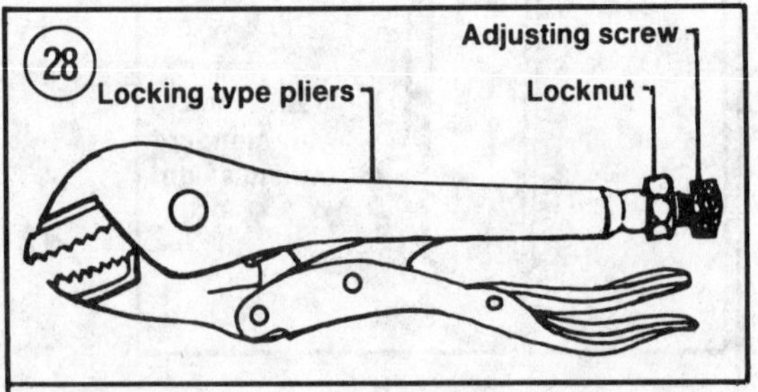

Draincock Replacement

1. Remove the radiator as described in this chapter.
2. Turn the draincock until fully open and pull the stem from the radiator tank and draincock body. See **Figure 30**.
3. Squeeze the sides of the draincock body together with pliers and remove from the inlet tank opening.
4. To reinstall, squeeze the sides of the draincock body together with pliers and insert in the inlet tank opening until it locks in place.
5. Fit the stem into the body opening and push until the stem tabs engage with the draincock body. Turn the draincock stem until it is fully closed.
6. Reinstall the radiator as described in this chapter.

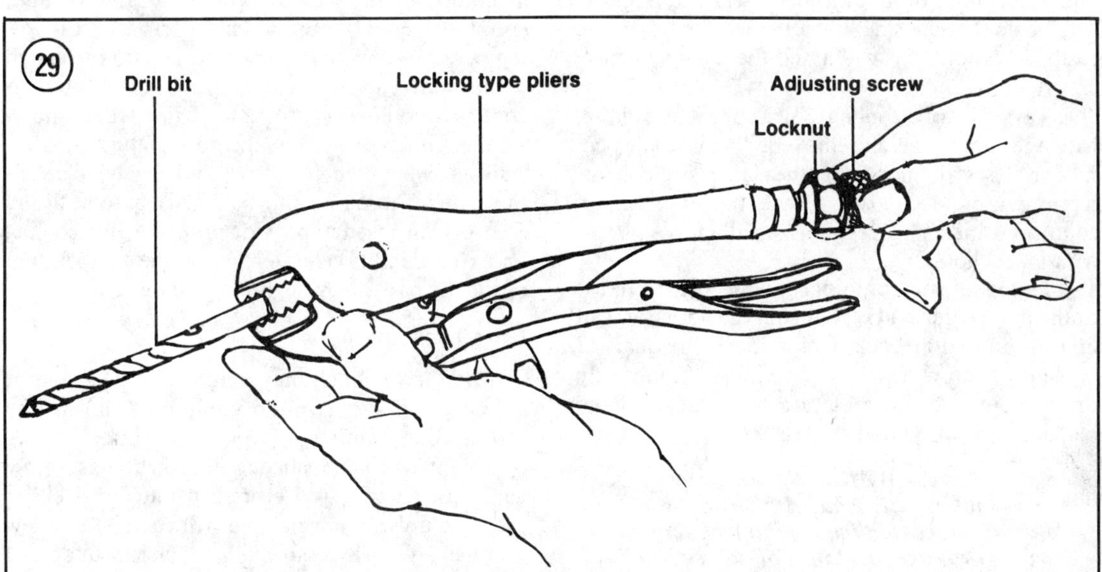

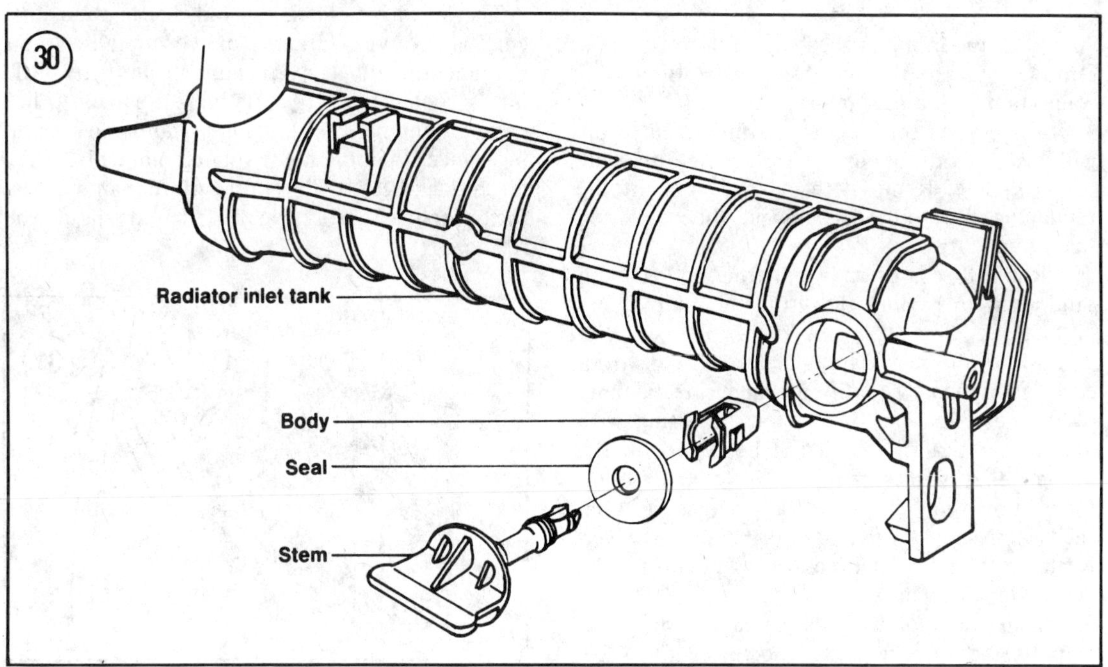

7

Radiator and Heater Hose Replacement

Hose life is rated by manufacturers at 2 years. It is a good idea to replace *all* cooling system hoses at this interval, even if they appear to be good. This will prevent an unnecessary and inconvenient roadside breakdown and possible engine damage resulting from a ruptured hose and subsequent overheating.

Replace any hoses that are cracked, brittle, mildewed or very soft or spongy. If a hose is in doubtful condition, but not definitely bad, replace it to be on the safe side. Even though the hoses are easily accessible, this will avoid the inconvenience of a roadside repair.

Always replace a cooling system or radiator hose with the same type as removed. Plain or pleated rubber hoses do not have the same strength as reinforced molded hoses. Check the hose clamp condition and, if necessary, install new clamps with a new hose.

1. Place a clean container under the radiator draincock (**Figure 11**). Remove the radiator cap and open the draincock. Drain about one quart of coolant when replacing an upper hose. Completely drain the coolant to replace a lower hose. If the coolant is clean, save it for reuse.

WARNING
Coolant is poisonous. Its sweet taste may attract children or animals. Store the drained coolant in a sealed container, inaccesible to children or pets.

2. Loosen the clamp at each end of the hose to be removed. Grasp the hose and twist it off the connection with a pulling motion.
3. If the hose is corroded to the fitting, cut it off with a sharp knife about one inch beyond the end of the fitting. Remove the clamp and slit the remaining piece of hose lengthwise, then peel it off the fitting.
4. Clean all corrosion from the fitting with sandpaper, then rinse the fitting to remove any particles.
5. Position the new clamps at least 1/4 in. from each end of the new hose. Wipe the inside diameter of the hose and the outside of the fitting with dishwasher liquid. Install the hose end on the fitting with a twisting motion.
6. Position the clamps for easy access. Tighten each clamp snugly with a screwdriver or nut driver. Recheck them for tightness after operating the vehicle for a few days.
7. Fill the radiator with the coolant removed in Step 1. Start the engine and operate it for a few minutes, checking for signs of leakage around the connection. Recheck the coolant level and top up, if necessary.

COOLING FAN

All engines are fitted with a fan drive clutch (**Figure 31**). The fan drive clutch incorporates a temperature-controlled fluid or viscous coupling that permits use of a powerful fan without great power loss or noise. In this design, the fan blade assembly is attached to a clutch housing or fluid coupling containing a silicone-base oil. A temperature-sensitive bi-metallic coil on the clutch opens and closes a valve inside the clutch to control fluid flow according to engine temperature. As the temperature rises, the flow of fluid causes a resistance between the drive and driven plate in the clutch, engaging the fan. This automatically controls fan speed to provide proper engine cooling under all conditions according to the temperature of the air passing through the radiator core.

Fan Clutch Diagnosis

A fan drive clutch may make noise whenever it is engaged for maximum cooling or during the initial few minutes of operation after setting overnight when the silicone fluid in the assembly has settled and must be redistributed. In either case, the noise is normal and will cease after a few minutes. If an excessive noise persists under all high speed engine operation, an internal failure has locked up the clutch assembly.

The fan drive clutch can fail due to fluid loss, control valve failure or bi-metallic coil malfunction. When overheating occurs with little or no coolant loss, try rotating the fan on a hot engine (engine OFF). There should be some resistance when the fan is rotated manually. If the fan rotates freely without drag more than 5 times, the clutch assembly has failed and should be replaced.

Removal/Installation

On some installations, the fan is more easily removed from underneath the vehicle. The following generalized procedures can be used to remove any fan installation. Before attempting the procedure, however, it is a good idea to follow it visually while looking at the engine compartment.

CAUTION
When correctly installed, lateral movement of up to 1/4 in. measured at the fan tip is normal and results from the type of bearing used. Excessively loose, bent or damaged fans should not be reused, as any distortion will affect fan balance and operation. Damaged fans cannot be properly repaired and should be discarded.

Viscous Clutch/Fan Removal/Installation (I4 Engine)

Refer to **Figure 32** (typical) for this procedure.

1. Disconnect the negative battery cable.
2. Remove the radiator shroud and/or raise the front of the vehicle with a jack and place it on jackstands. If vehicle must be raised, be sure to block the rear wheels to prevent it from rolling in either direction.
3. Check the fan mounting system to see if the drive belt tension should be relieved. If so, loosen the alternator adjusting and pivot bolts to relieve the drive belt tension.

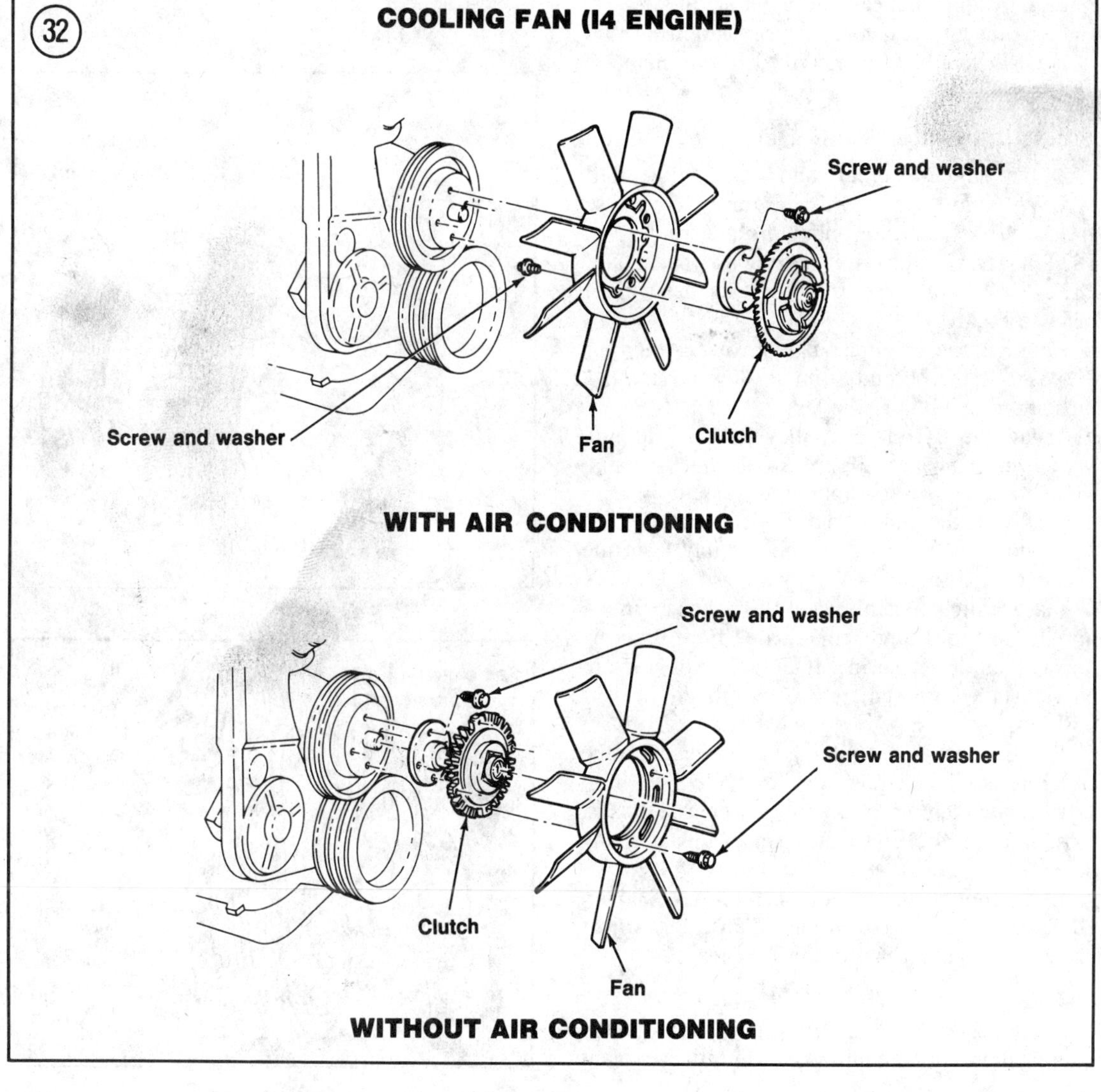

7

4. Scribe balance marks on the fan clutch and water pump hub for proper alignment during installation.
5. Remove the attaching fasteners holding the fan clutch hub to the water pump hub. Remove the fan clutch assembly from the vehicle.
6. Remove the fasteners holding the fan to the drive coupling. Separate the fan and coupling.
7. Place clutch assembly on work bench in an upright position to prevent silicone from draining into the fan drive bearing. If clutch is not going to be reinstalled immediately, store in an upright position.
8. Check the fan blade carefully for cracks, breaks, loose rivets or broken welds. Replace the fan if any defect is noted.
9. Installation is the reverse of removal. Check fan drive clutch flange-to-water pump hub for proper mating. Align balance marks made in Step 4. Tighten attaching fasteners to specifications (**Table 1**). Adjust drive belts as described in this chapter.

Viscous Clutch/Fan Removal/Installation (V6 Engine)

The fan clutch assembly and water pump shaft have *left-hand* threads (must be turned clockwise to loosen). A special pulley holder (part No. T83T-6312-A) and nut wrench (part No. T83T-6312-B) are required for this procedure. Refer to **Figure 33**.

1. Remove the 2 upper fan shroud attaching screws. Lift the shroud from its lower retaining clips and drape it over the fan.
2. Install the fan clutch pulley holder and nut wrench as shown in **Figure 34**. Rotate the nut wrench *clockwise* while holding the assembly from moving with the pulley holder.
3. Remove the fan and clutch assembly from the engine compartment.
4. Place clutch assembly on work bench in an upright position to prevent silicone from draining into the fan drive bearing. If clutch is not going to be reinstalled immediately, store in an upright position.
5. Remove the screws holding the fan blade to the clutch assembly. Remove the fan blade.
6. Check the fan blade carefully for cracks, breaks, loose rivets or broken welds. Replace the fan if any defect is noted.
7. Installation is the reverse of removal. Tighten all fasteners to specifications (**Table 1**). Adjust drive belts as described in this chapter.

WATER PUMP

A water pump may warn of impending failure by making noise. If the pump seal is defective, coolant may leak from behind the pump pulley. The water pump can be replaced on all models without discharging the air conditioning system. The pump is serviced as an assembly.

Removal/Installation (4-Cylinder Engine)

The water pump can be replaced without discharging the air conditioning system. A provision for wrench clearance has been made in the timing belt outer cover. Only the outer cover must be removed to replace the water pump. The pump is serviced as an assembly. Refer to **Figure 35** for this procedure.

1. Disconnect the negative battery cable.
2. Drain the cooling system as described in this chapter.
3. Remove the 2 screws holding the fan shroud to the radiator. Drape the shroud over the cooling fan.

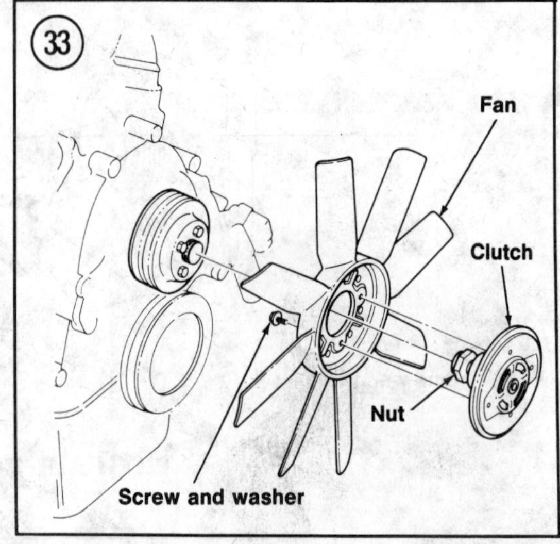

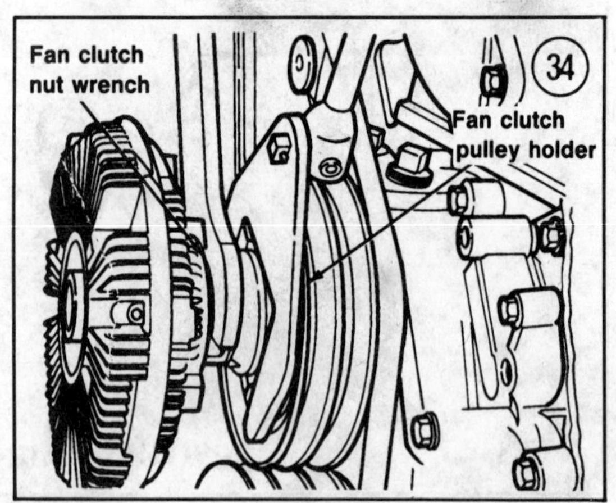

4. Remove the fasteners holding the fan assembly to the water pump shaft. Remove the fan and shroud.
5. Loosen all accessory units and remove the drive belts.
6. Remove the water pump pulley.
7. Remove the heater hose at the water pump.
8. Remove the bolts holding the outer timing belt cover. Remove the cover.
9. Unclamp and disconnect the lower radiator hose at the water pump.
10. Remove the 3 water pump retaining bolts. Remove the water pump and gasket from the cylinder block. Discard the gasket.
11. Remove all gasket residue from the block mounting surface (and water pump, if it is to be reinstalled).
12. Installation is the reverse of removal, plus the following.
   a. Use a new gasket and coat with contact adhesive part No. D7AZ-19B508-A or equivalent.
   b. Coat all pump bolt threads with Pipe Sealant with Teflon (part No. D8AZ-19554-A) or equivalent).
   c. Tighten all fasteners to specifications (**Table 1**).

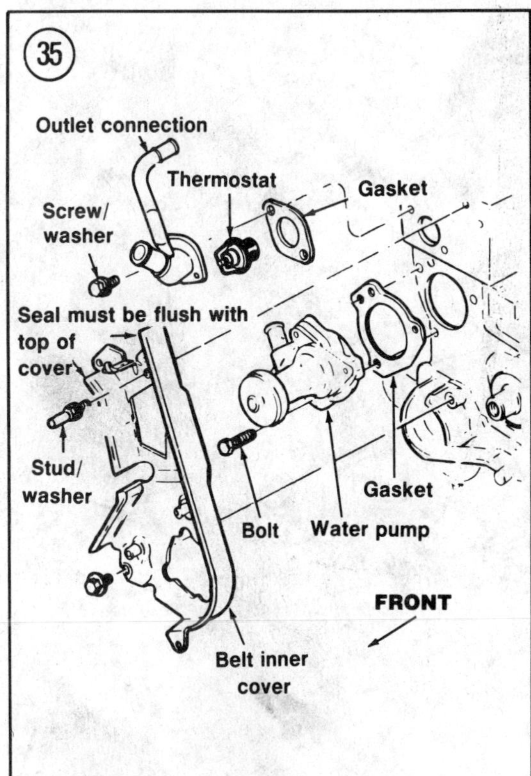

   d. Refill the cooling system as described in this chapter.
   e. Adjust the drive belts as described in this chapter.*2.8L V6 engine*

Removal/Installation (2.8L V6 Engine)

1. Disconnect the negative battery cable.
2. Drain the cooling system as described in this chapter.
3. Disconnect the lower radiator hose and heater return hose at the water pump.
4. Remove the fan clutch assembly as described in this chapter.
5. Remove the alternator and drive belt. If equipped with air conditioning, also remove the alternator bracket. See Chapter Eight.
6. Remove the water pump pulley.
7. Remove the water pump retaining bolts. Remove the water pump and gasket from the cylinder block. Discard the gasket.
8. Remove all gasket residue from the block mounting surface (and water pump, if it is to be reinstalled).
9. Installation is the reverse of removal, plus the following.
   a. Use a new gasket and coat with contact adhesive part No. D7AZ-19B508-A or equivalent.
   b. Coat all pump bolt threads with Pipe Sealant with Teflon (part No. D8AZ-19554-A) or equivalent.
   c. Tighten all fasteners to specifications (**Table 1**).
   d. Refill the cooling system as described in this chapter.
   e. Adjust the drive belts as described in this chapter.

3.0L V6 engine

1. Disconnect the negative battery cable.
2. Drain the cooling system as described in this chapter.
3. Loosen the accessory drive belt idler and remove the drive belts as described in this chapter.
4. Unbolt and remove the idler bracket from the engine.
5. Disconnect the heater hose at the water pump.
6. Remove the fan clutch assembly as described in this chapter.
7. Remove the 4 pulley-to-pump hub bolts. The pulley must be removed with the pump because of insufficient clearance.

8. Remove the bolts holding the water pump to the front cover (**Figure 36**). Remove the water pump with pulley and gasket from the engine compartment. Discard the gasket.
9. Remove all gasket residue from the block mounting surface (and water pump, if it is to be reinstalled).
10. Installation is the reverse of removal, plus the following.
   a. Use a new gasket and coat with contact adhesive part No. D7AZ-19B508-A or equivalent.
   b. Coat the threads of the pump bolt that goes into the engine block water jacket with Pipe Sealant with Teflon (part No. D8AZ-19554-A) or equivalent. Lightly wipe all other bolt threads with engine oil.
   c. Tighten all fasteners to specifications (**Table 1**).
   d. Refill the cooling system as described in this chapter.
   e. Adjust the drive belts as described in this chapter.

DRIVE BELTS

All vehicles use V-ribbed drive belts. These belts should be inspected at regular intervals (Chapter Three) to make sure they are in good condition and are properly tensioned. Worn, frayed, cracked or glazed belts should be replaced immediately. The components to which they direct power are essential to the safe and reliable operation of the vehicle. If correct adjustment is maintained on all belts, they will usually all give the same service life. For this reason and because of the cost involved in replacing an inner belt (requiring the removal of all outer belts), it is a good idea to replace all belts as a set. The added expense is small compared to the cost of replacing the belts individually and eliminates the possibility of a breakdown on the road which could cost far more in time and money. more in time and money.

A V-ribbed drive belt should be correctly tensioned at all times. If loose, the belt will not permit the driven components to operate at maximum efficiency. The belt will also wear

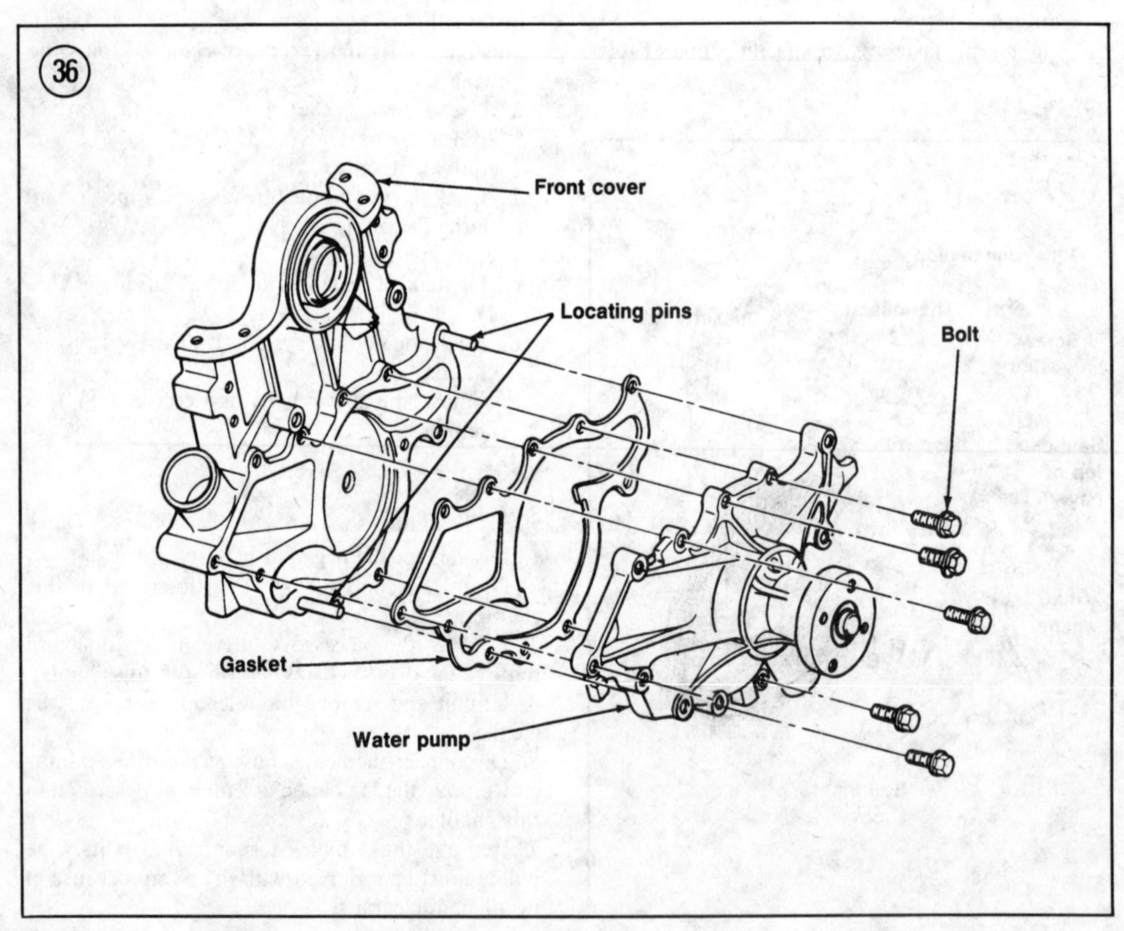

rapidly because of the increased friction caused by slipping. Belts that are too tight will be overstressed and prone to premature failure. An excessively tight belt will also overstress the accessory unit's bearings, resulting in their premature failure.

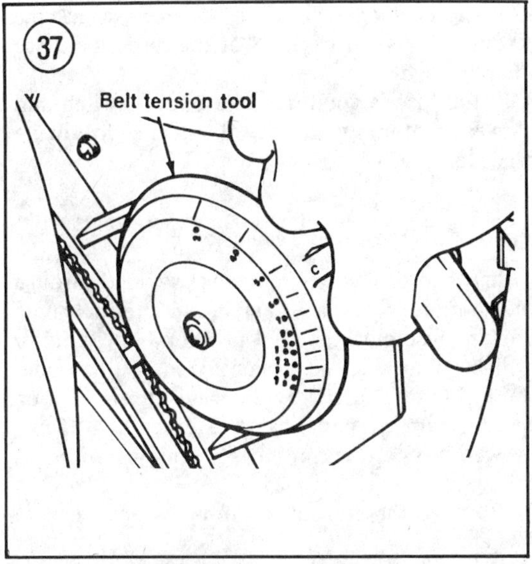

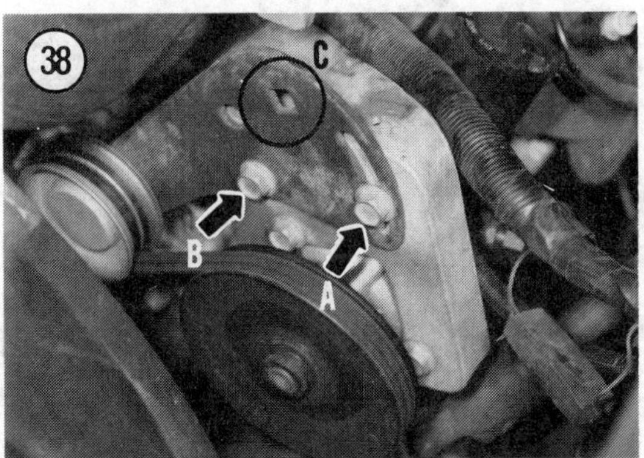

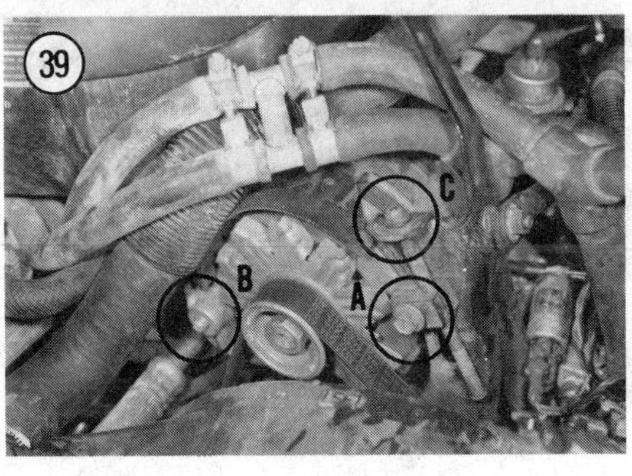

Tension Adjustment

The tension of V-ribbed drive belts cannot be checked by the belt deflection method. Tension must be checked with a belt tension gauge (**Figure 37**) (part No. T63L-8620-A or equivalent). On some single drive belt models, adjustment is made at the alternator; others are adjusted with an idler. On dual drive belt models, one belt is adjusted with an idler and the other belt is adjusted with an accessory unit. Some vehicles have one fixed idler and a second one that is adjustable. Drive belt specifications are provided in **Table 2**.

1. Install the gauge on the drive belt (**Figure 37**) and check tension according to the gauge manufacturer's instructions. Compare to the specifications in **Table 2**.

2A. With idler—If adjustment is required, loosen the idler adjustment and pivot bolts. See A and B, **Figure 38** (typical). insert a suitable breaker bar in the bracket slot (C, **Figure 38**) and apply pressure counterclockwise to tighten or clockwise to loosen the belt. When tension is correct, tighten the pivot and adjustment bolts.

2B. Without idler—If adjustment is required, loosen the accessory adjustment and pivot bolts. See A and B, **Figure 39** (typical). If accessory bracket is provided with a jackscrew (C, **Figure 39**), loosen or tighten jackscrew as required. On other accessory units, carefully move the accessory unit toward or away from the engine as required until correct tension is obtained. Tighten the adjustment bolt, release pressure on the accessory unit, then tighten the pivot bolt.

CAUTION

Do not pry on the accessory unit to reposition it. Most adjustment brackets have a slot provided for use of a breaker bar as a pry tool. To move the accessory, insert a suitable breaker bar in the bracket slot and reposition the unit as required.

3. Recheck belt tension. If necessary, repeat the procedure to obtain the correct tension.

Removal (Standard Drive Belt)

Vehicles equipped with dual drive belts may require removal of one drive belt before the other belt can be removed. Depending upon the positioning of the accessory unit, some steps of this procedure may have to be performed from underneath the vehicle. With some installations, it may be more convenient to remove the fan assembly before proceeding.

1. Loosen the idler or accessory pivot and adjustment bolts.
2. Move the idler or accessory unit toward the engine until there is enough slack in the outer belt to permit its removal from the pulleys. Remove the belt from the pulleys and lift it over the fan.
3. Repeat Step 2 to remove the inner belt.
4. Install the new inner belt over the fan and fit in the grooves of the appropriate pulleys.
5. Pry the idler or accessory unit away from the engine with a breaker bar inserted in the proper slot until its belt appears to be correctly tensioned and tighten the adjustment bolt, then the pivot bolt.

CAUTION

Do not pry on the accessory unit to reposition it. Most adjustment brackets have a slot provided for use of a breaker bar as a pry tool. To move the accessory, insert a suitable breaker bar in the bracket slot and reposition the unit as required.

6. If the outer belt was removed, repeat Step 4 and Step 5 to tension each remaining drive belt.
7. Recheck belt tension with the tension gauge. If necessary, repeat the procedure to obtain the correct tension.

HEATER SYSTEM

The heater system is a blend-air design and consists of a blower air inlet and a heater/defroster assembly to provide heating, ventilation and windshield defogging. Vent, heat and defrost functions are controlled by the heater/defroster assembly. The blower motor and blower air inlet are connected to the front of the cowl in the engine compartment. See A, **Figure 40** or A, **Figure 41**. A vacuum reservoir is used with 1986 models. See B, **Figure 40** or B, **Figure 41**. The heater/defroster is fastened to the rear of the firewall in the passenger compartment. Mounting gaskets on both components prevent air, water and noise from entering the passenger compartment.

The system is controlled by a cable and vacuum line connected between the instrument panel control assembly and the heater/modular ducting. Access to the blower motor and resistor block for testing and service is provided in the engine compartment.

This section covers the heater on non-air conditioned models only. Repair of the integral heater on air conditioned models requires special skills and tools and should be left to a dealer or competent repair shop.

Troubleshooting

1. If the heater does not produce heat, make sure the engine will warm up in a reasonable amount of time. If the thermostat sticks in the open position, the engine will not completely warm up. Since hot engine coolant provides heat for the heater, a defective thermostat may be the problem.
2. If the heater blower does not work, check the 30-ampere fuse in cavity 8 of the fuse block. See Chapter Eight.
3. If the fuse is good, test the blower switch and blower motor as described in the following procedures.

Blower Motor Switch Testing

Power to the blower motor is provided through the ignition switch, a 30-ampere fuse in the cavity 8 of the fuse block and a 4-position blower motor switch. Blower speed is controlled in all modes (OFF, LO, MED, HI) by the 4-position switch on the instrument panel control assembly. If the blower motor does not run, test the switch as follows:

1. Remove the control assembly as described in this chapter.

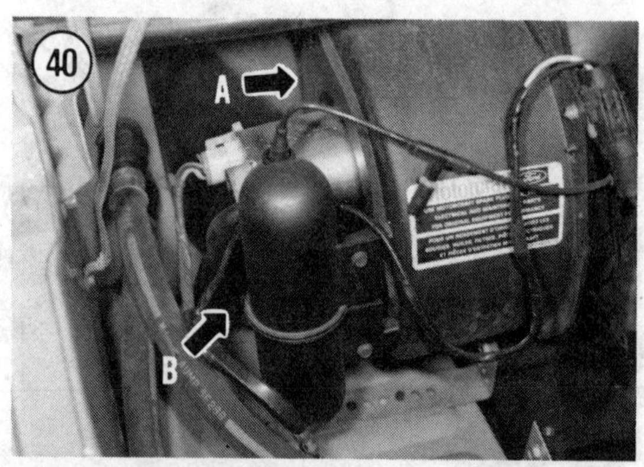

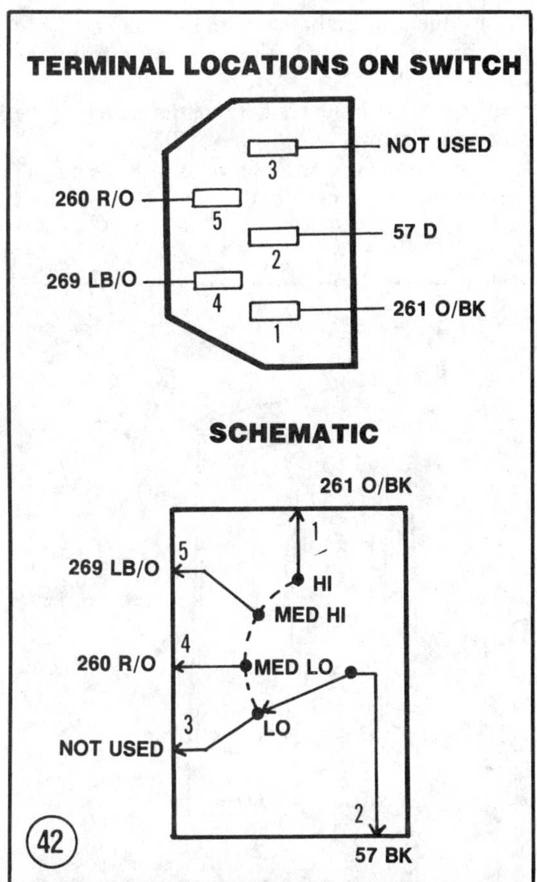

2. Refer to **Figure 42** and connect a self-powered test lamp or ohmmeter to the switch terminals as indicated in the following steps. Move the switch through all positions.

3. To test low speed, check terminals 2 and 3. A good switch will indicate continuity only in the low position.

4. To test medium low speed, check terminals 2 and 5. A good switch will indicate continuity only in the medium low position.

5. To test medium high speed, check terminals 2 and 4. A good switch will indicate continuity only in the medium high position.

6. To test high speed, check terminals 1 and 2. A good switch will indicate continuity only in the high position.

7. If the switch fails to perform as described in Steps 3-6, replace it as described in this chapter.

Blower Motor Voltage Test

1. Set the temperature selector on the control assembly at a point midway between COOL and WARM.

2. Set the function control lever in the VENT position.

3. Block the drive wheels, set the parking brake and start the engine.

4. Probe the blower motor connector (**Figure 43** or A, **Figure 44**) with a voltmeter and measure and record the voltage drop as an assistant moves the blower switch through each position. Compare with specifications in **Table 3**.

Blower Motor Current Draw Test

1. Set the temperature selector on the control assembly at a point midway between COOL and WARM.

2. Set the function control lever in the VENT position.

3. Unplug the blower motor connector (**Figure 43** or A, **Figure 44**).

4. Connect an ammeter between the right (positive) terminal on the motor and its corresponding terminal in the connector. Install a jumper wire between the left (ground) motor and connector terminals.

5. Block the drive wheels, set the parking brake and start the engine.

6. Measure and record the current draw as an assistant moves the blower switch through each position. Compare with specifications in **Table 3**.

7. Disconnect the ammeter and reconnect the blower motor connector.

Blower Switch Replacement

Refer to **Figure 45** for this procedure.

1. Disconnect the negative battery cable.
2. Carefully pry the switch knob off with a screwdriver.
3. Remove the control assembly as described in this chapter but do not disconnect the cables.
4. Lift the connector snap-lock retainer with a screwdriver, then pull the connector from the switch terminals.
5. Remove the fasteners holding the switch to the control assembly.
6. Align the pin on the new switch with the hole in the mounting bracket and install the fasteners securely.

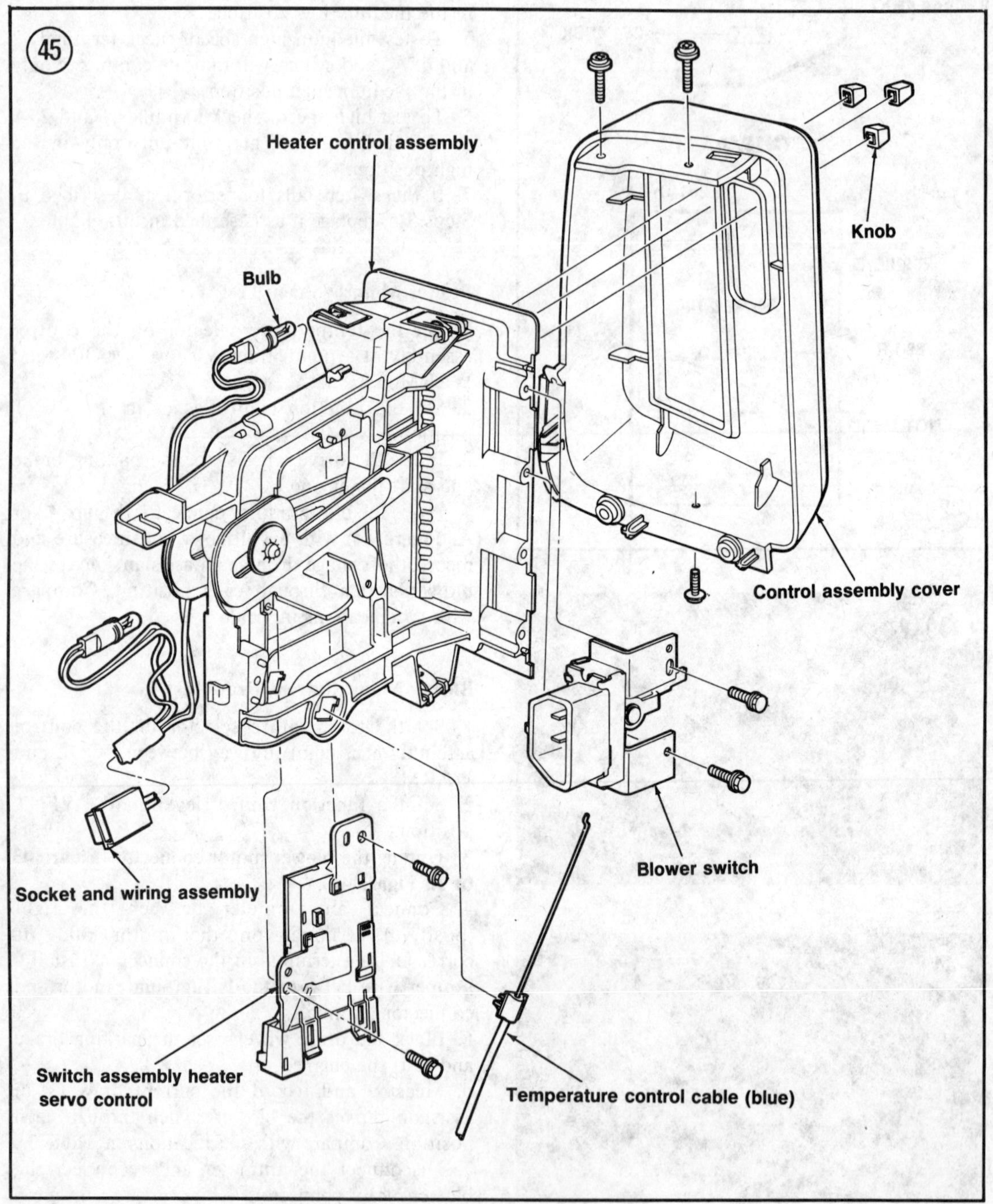

7. Push the knob on the switch shaft as far as it will go. Reconnect the wiring harness connector.
8. Reinstall the control assembly as described in this chapter. Test the new switch for proper blower motor operation.

Control Assembly Removal/Installation

Refer to **Figure 46** for this procedure.

1. Disconnect the negative battery cable.
2. Remove the instrument cluster. See *Instruments* in Chapter Eight.
3. Remove the 3 screws holding the control assembly to the instrument panel.
4. Pull the control assembly out far enough to unplug the electrical connectors.
5. Disconnect the vacuum harness from the function lever selector valve.
6. Unsnap and remove the blue temperature control cable. See **Figure 45**.
7. Installation is the reverse of removal.

Blower Motor Removal/Installation

Refer to **Figure 47** (typical) for this procedure.

1. Disconnect the negative battery cable.
2. Remove the air cleaner assembly or the air inlet duct as required. See Chapter Six.
3. If vacuum reservoir is attached to blower motor (**Figure 40**), unbolt and remove the reservoir.
4. Unplug the wiring connectors at the blower motor (**Figure 43**) and resistor block (C, **Figure 41**). Lift the connector snap-lock retainer with a screwdriver, then pull the connector from the terminals.
5. Disconnect the cooling tube (D, **Figure 41**) at the blower motor.
6. Remove the 3 screws holding the blower motor to the heater blower assembly.
7. Hold the cooling tube to one side and remove the blower motor from the heater blower assembly.
8. If a new motor is to be installed, remove the blower wheel hub clamp from the motor shaft. Pull the wheel from the motor shaft.
9. Installation is the reverse of removal.

7

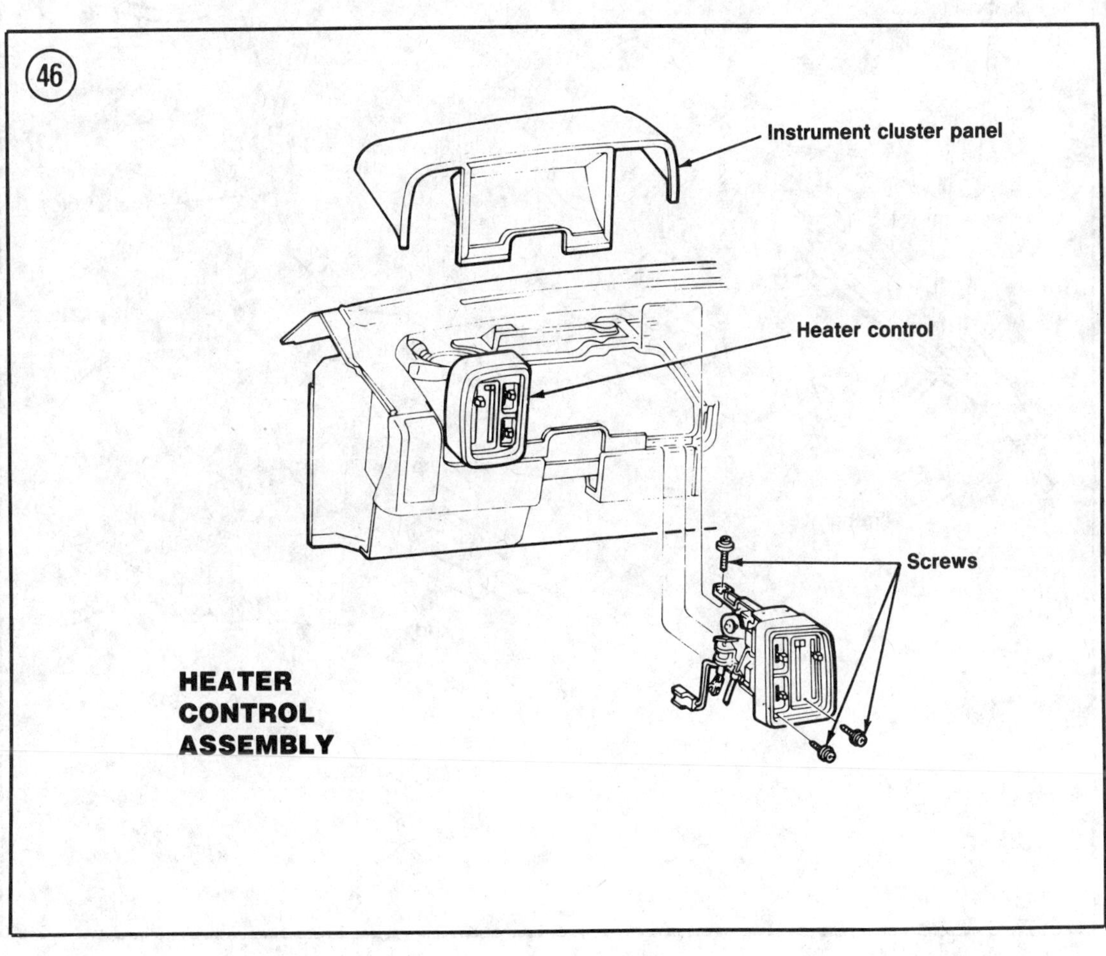

HEATER CONTROL ASSEMBLY

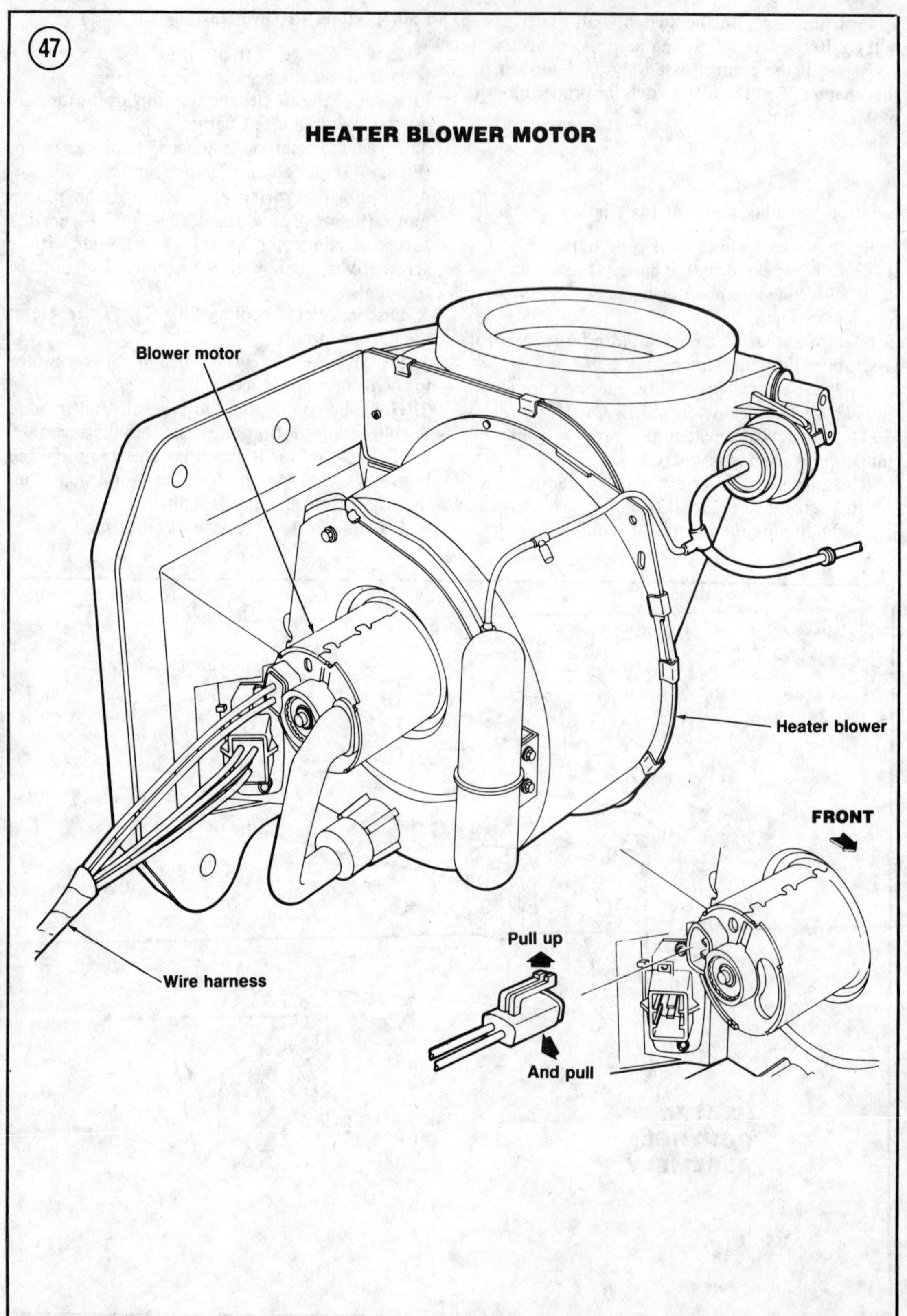
47
HEATER BLOWER MOTOR
Blower motor
Heater blower
FRONT
Pull up
Wire harness
And pull

AIR CONDITIONING

A cycling clutch, fixed-orifice tube design (**Figure 48**) is used on all vehicles. Spring-lock push-connect fittings similar to those used in the fuel system (see Chapter Six) require the use of a spring-lock coupling tool set (part No. D81L-19703-A) for removal.

This section covers the maintenance and minor repairs that can prevent or correct common air conditioning problems. Major repairs require special training and equipment and should be left to a dealer or air conditioning expert.

System Operation

There are 5 basic components common to the air conditioning system used with all vehicles.

a. Compressor.
b. Condenser.
c. Accumulator/drier.
d. Fixed-orifice tube.
e. Evaporator.

For practical purposes, the cycle begins at the compressor. See **Figure 48**. The refrigerant enters the low-pressure side of the compressor in a warm low-pressure vapor state. It is compressed to a high-pressure hot vapor and pumped out of the high-pressure side to the condenser.

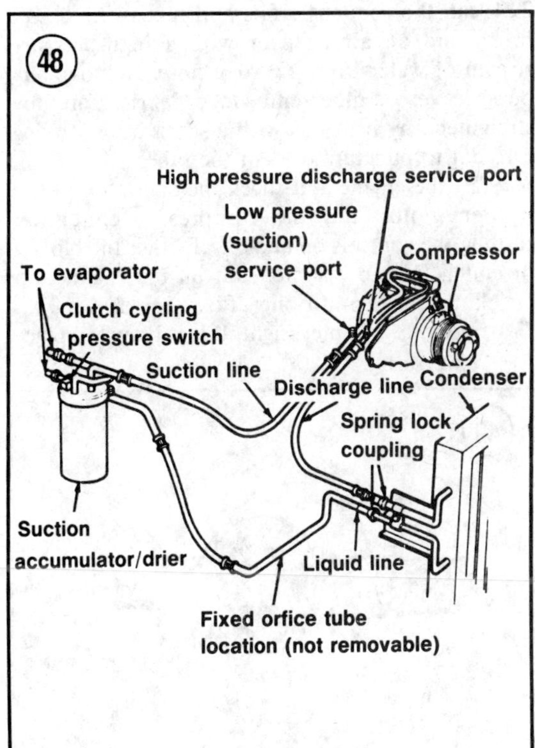

Air flow through the condenser removes heat from the refrigerant and transfers the heat to the outside air. As the heat is removed, the refrigerant condenses to a warm high-pressure liquid.

The refrigerant than flows through a line containing a fixed orifice tube to the evaporator, where it removes heat from the passenger compartment air that is blown across the evaporator's fins and tubes. Refrigerant flow continues to the accumulator/drier, where moisture is removed and impurities are filtered out. The refrigerant is stored in the accumulator/drier until it is needed. From the accumulator/drier, the refrigerant then returns to the compressor as a warm low-pressure liquid and the cycle begins again.

Compressor

The compressor is located on the drive belt end of the engine, like the alternator, and is driven by a V-ribbed belt. The large pulley on the front of the compressor contains an electromagnetic clutch. This activates and operates the compressor when the air conditioning is switched on.

Condenser

The condenser is mounted in front of the radiator. Air passing through the condenser tubes and fins removes heat from the refrigerant in the same manner it removes heat from the engine coolant as it passes through the radiator. The cooling fan also pulls air through the condenser.

Accumulator/drier

The accumulator/drier is a small tank-like unit connected to the evaporator outlet tube and hosuing the cycling clutch pressure switch. See B, **Figure 44**. The switch controls evaporator core pressure to prevent evaporator icing and blocked air flow. This cycling operation will cause occasional slight changes in engine speed and power under certain operating conditions, but this should be considered normal.

Fixed-orifice Tube

This is a restrictor located in the condenser liquid line. Filter screens on each end of the tube body strain the liquid refrigerant passing through the orifice. The fixed-orifice tube is non-serviceable and must be replaced as a unit if defective.

Evaporator

The evaporator is located in the passenger compartment as a part of the blower motor assembly. Warm air is blown across the fins and tubes, where it is cooled and dried, then ducted into the passenger compartment.

Vacuum Tank

The 1986 air conditioning system incorporates a vacuum supply tank (B, **Figure 40**) to store vacuum for use whenever manifold vacuum decreases, as during heavy acceleration. This assures a steady supply of vacuum for continuous use, regardless of engine operating condition.

REFRIGERANT

The air conditioning system uses a refrigerant called dichlorodifluoromethane, or R-12.

WARNING
Refrigerant creates freezing temperatures when it evaporates. This can cause frostbite if it touches the skin, and blindness if it touches the eyes. If discharged near an open flame, R-12 creates poisonous gas. If the refrigerant can is hooked up to the pressure side of the compressor, it may explode. Always wear safety goggles and gloves when working with R-12.

ROUTINE MAINTENANCE

Basic maintenance of the air conditioning system is easy. At least once a month, even in cold weather, start your engine, turn on the air conditioner and operate it at each of the control settings. Operate the air conditioner for about 10 minutes, with the engine running at about 1,500 rpm. This will ensure that the compressor seal does not deform from sitting in the same position for a long period of time. If deformation occurs, the seal is likely to leak.

The efficiency of the air conditioning system also depends in great part on the efficiency of the cooling system. If the cooling system is dirty or low on coolant, it may be impossible to operate the air conditioner without the engine overheating. Inspect the coolant. If necessary, flush and refill the cooling system as described in this chapter.

NOTE
Do not install a bug screen on vehicles with air conditioning. The screen reduces air flow and thus affects air conditioner efficiency. During hot weather, a bug screen can cause the engine to overheat.

Use an air hose and a soft brush to clean the radiator and condenser fins and tubes. Remove any bugs, leaves or other embedded debris.

Check drive belt tension as described in this chapter.

If the condition of the cooling system thermostat is in doubt, test it as described in this chapter.

Once you are sure the cooling system is in good condition, the air conditioning system can be inspected.

Inspection

1. Clean all lines, fittings and system components with solvent and a clean rag. Pay particular attention to the fittings; oily dirt around connections almost certainly indicates a leak. Oil from the compressor will migrate through the system to the leak. Carefully tighten threaded connections, but do not overtighten and strip the threads. If the leak persists, it will soon be apparent as oily dirt will continue to accumulate.

NOTE
*Some fittings in the air conditioning system use spring-lock couplings (**Figure 49**) in which the flared end of the one fitting slips behind a garter spring inside the other fitting cage. The spring and cage prevent the coupling from disengaging. Due to the design of this coupling, no attempt should be made to tighten it. If the fitting is leaking, have it replaced by a dealer or air conditioning expert.*

2. Clean the condenser fins and tubes with a soft brush and an air hose or with a high-pressure stream of water from a garden hose. Remove any bugs, leaves or other embedded debris. Carefully straighten any bent fins with a screwdriver, taking care not to puncture or dent the tubes.

3. Start the engine and check the operation of the blower motor and the compressor clutch by turning the controls on and off. If either the blower or clutch fails to operate, shut off the engine and check the air conditioner fuse. See *Fuses and Fusible Links*, Chapter Eight. If it is blown, replace

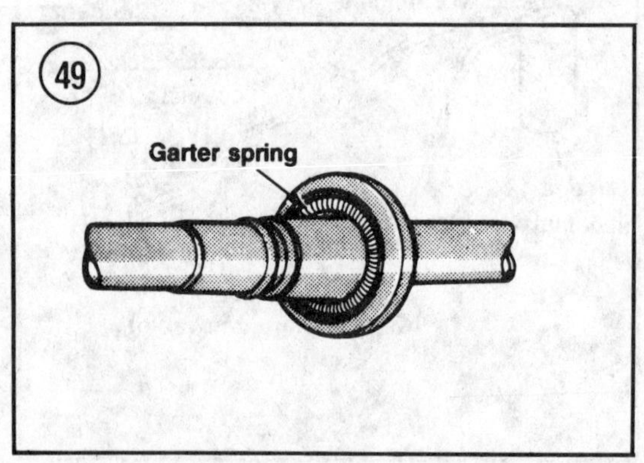

it. If not, remove and clean the fuse holder contacts. Then check the clutch and blower operation again. If they still will not operate, take the vehicle to a dealer or air conditioning specialist.

Troubleshooting

If the air conditioner fails to blow cold air, the following steps can help locate the problem.

1. First, stop the vehicle and look at the control settings. One of the most common air conditioning problems occurs when the temperature is set for maximum cold and the blower is set on LOW. This promotes ice buildup on the evaporator fins and tubes, particularly in humid weather. Eventually, the evaporator will have iced over completely and restricted air flow. Turn the blower on HI and place a hand over an air outlet. If the blower is running but there is little or no air flowing through the outlet, the evaporator will ice over completely and restrict air flow. Leave the blower on HI and turn the temperature control off or to its warmest setting and wait. It will take 10-15 minutes for the ice to start melting.
2. If the blower is not running, the fuse may be blown, there may be a loose wiring connection or the blower motor may be burned out. First, check the fuse block for a blown or incorrectly seated fuse, then check the wiring for loose connections.
3. If the blower runs but not on high speed, check for a blown fusible link in the electrical wiring between the junction terminal and air conditioner relay.
4. Shut off the engine and inspect the compressor drive belt. If worn or loose, replace or tighten as required as described in this.
5. Start the engine. Check the compressor clutch by turning the air conditioner on and off. If the clutch does not activate, its fuse may be blown or the evaporator temperature-limiting switches may be defective. If the fuse is defective, replace it. If the fuse is not the problem, have the system checked by a dealer or an air conditioning specialist.
6. If the system appears to be operating as it should, but air flow into the passenger compartment is not cold, check the condenser for debris that could block air flow. Recheck the cooling system as described in this chapter. If the preceding steps have not solved the problem, take the vehicle to a dealer or air conditioning shop for service.

Tables are on the following page.

Table 1 TIGHTENING TORQUES

Fastener	ft.-lb.	N•m
Alternator		
I4		
Adjustment bolt	24-34	32-46
Pivot bolt	45-57	61-77
V6		
Adjustment bolt	24-49	33-66
Pivot bolt	30-40	40-55
Fan drive clutch		
I4	12-18	16-25
V6	30-100	41-135
Radiator		
Attaching fasteners	12-20	17-27
Transmission cooler line		
Fitting to radiator	18-21	25-28
Oil line nut to fitting	12-18	17-24
Thermostat housing bolts	12-15	17-20
Water pump		
I4	14-21	19-29
2.8L V6	7-9	9-12
3.0L V6	6-8	8-12

Table 2 STANDARD DRIVE BELT TENSION

Belt	Tension in lbs. New	Used*	Allowable minimum
I4	150-190	140-160	90
V6			
Alternator only	120-160	110-130	70
Alternator and air conditioning	150-190	140-160	90
Power steering	100-140	80-100	60

* A belt is considered used after one complete revolution on the engine pulleys.

Table 3 BLOWER MOTOR CURRENT DRAW AND VOLTAGE DROP

Switch position	Amperes	Volts
Off	0	0
Low	3.2	4.1-5.6
Medium low	6.0	6.4-7.9
Medium high	9.5	8.7-10.2
High	13.5	11.3-12.8

CHAPTER EIGHT

ELECTRICAL SYSTEM

All vehicles covered in this manual are equipped with a 12-volt, negative-ground electrical system. Many electrical problems can be traced to a simple cause such as a blown fuse, a loose or corroded connection, a loose alternator drive belt or a frayed wire. While these are easily corrected problems which may not appear important, they can quickly lead to serious difficulty if allowed to go uncorrected.

Complete overhaul of electrical components such as the alternator, distributor or starter motor is neither practical nor economical. In many cases, the necessary bushings, bearings or other worn parts are not available for individual replacement.

If tests indicate a unit with problems other than those discussed in this chapter, replace it with a new or rebuilt unit. Make certain, however, that the new or rebuilt part to be installed is an exact replacement for the defective one removed. Also make sure to isolate and correct the cause of the failure before installing a replacement. For example, an uncorrected short in an alternator circuit will most likely burn out a new alternator as quickly as it damaged the old one. If in doubt, always consult an expert.

This chapter provides service procedures for the battery, charging system, starter, ignition system, lights, switches, turn indicators, horn, windshield wipers and washers, fuses and fusible links.

Table 1 and **Table 2** are at the end of the chapter.

BATTERY

The battery is the single most important component in the automotive electrical system. It is also the one most frequently neglected. In addition to checking and correcting the battery electrolyte level in unsealed batteries on a weekly basis (Chapter Three), the battery should be cleaned and inspected at periodic intervals.

New vehicles are factory-equipped with a lightweight, low-maintenance battery of vent cap design which requires electrolyte level inspections only at the start of each winter season or every 15,000 miles. A sealed maintenance-free battery is optional and may be used for replacement.

When a standard vent cap battery is used as a replacement, it should be checked periodically for electrolyte level, state of charge and corrosion. During hot weather periods, frequent checks are recommended. If the electrolyte level is below the bottom of the vent well in one or more cells, add distilled water as required. To assure proper mixing of the water and acid, operate the engine immediately after adding water. *Never* add battery acid instead of water—this will shorten the battery's life.

Maintenance-free batteries do not permit or require the addition of water. The battery case is completely sealed except for small vent holes in the top. The vent holes are provided to allow battery gases to escape. This type of battery should be kept in an upright position, as tipping the case more than 45° in any direction may allow electrolyte to escape through the vent holes.

Care and Inspection

1. Loosen the bolts in the negative terminal clamp enough so the clamp can be spread apart. Lift the negative clamp straight up to remove it from the battery post. After removing the negative clamp, remove the positive clamp in the same manner. See A and B, **Figure 1**.

CAUTION

*If the cable clamp will not come off the battery post easily when the clamp bolt is loosened, use a battery terminal puller as shown in **Figure 2**. Hitting the clamp or trying to pry it off the post can cause internal damage to the battery.*

2. Remove the 2 battery hold-down clamp nuts (**Figure 3**). Remove the hold-down clamp.
3. Attach a battery carrier or carrier strap and lift the battery from the engine compartment. See **Figure 4**.
4. Check the entire battery case for cracks or other damage.
5. If the battery has removable vent caps, cover the vent holes in each cap with small pieces of masking tape.

NOTE

Keep cleaning solution out of the battery cells in Step 6 or the electrolyte will be seriously weakened.

6. Scrub the top of the battery with a stiff bristle brush, using a baking soda and water solution (**Figure 5**). Rinse the battery case with clear water and wipe dry with a clean cloth or paper towels. Remove the masking tape from the filler cap vent holes, if so equipped.
7. Inspect the battery tray in the engine compartment for corrosion. Remove and clean if necessary with the baking soda and water solution. Rinse with clear water and wipe dry, then reinstall.

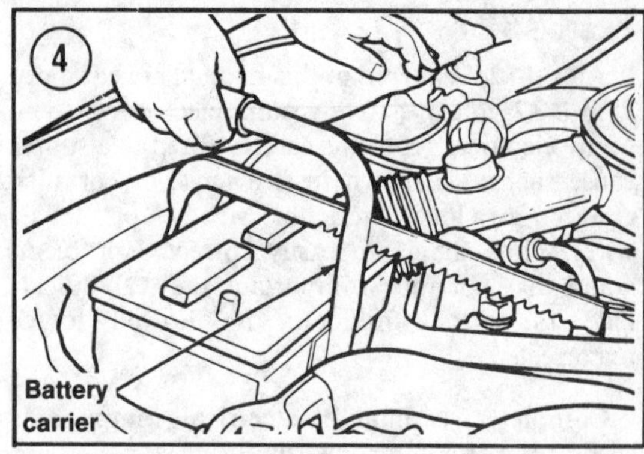

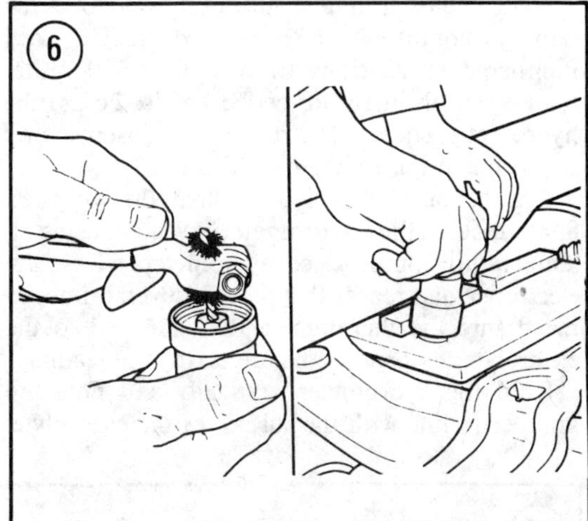

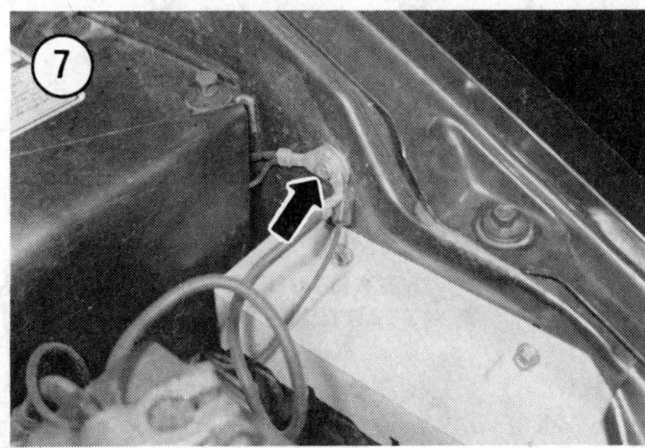

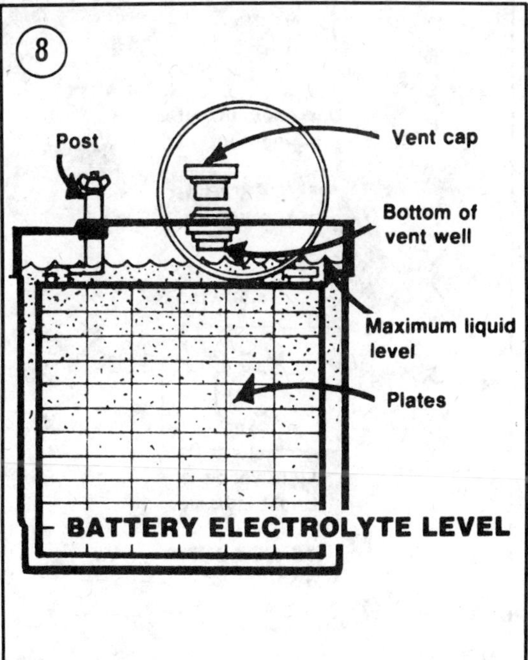

8. Clean the battery cable clamps with a stiff wire brush or one of the many tools made for this purpose (**Figure 6**). The same tool is used for cleaning the threaded battery posts (**Figure 6**).
9. Reposition the battery on the battery tray and remove the carrier or strap. Install the hold-down clamp legs in the slots on the battery tray, then fit the clamp over the legs and install the attaching nuts. Tighten the nuts only enough to keep the battery case from moving; overtightening them can crack the battery case.
10. Reinstall the positive battery cable, then the negative battery cable. Some models use a ground connection at the fender apron (**Figure 7**). If so equipped, be sure the connection is clean and tight.

CAUTION
Be sure the battery cables are connected to their proper terminals. Connecting the battery backwards will reverse the polarity and can damage the alternator.

11. Tighten the battery cable connections to 60-90 in.-lb. (6.7-10 Nm). Tightening the connections more than this can cause damage to the battery case. Coat the connections with a petroleum jelly such as Vaseline or a light mineral grease.
12. If the battery has removable filler caps, check the electrolyte level. The electrolyte should cover the battery plates by at least 1/4 in. (6 mm). See **Figure 8**. Top up with distilled water to the bottom of the fill ring in each cell, if necessary.

Testing Maintenance-free Batteries

Sealed maintenance-free batteries require different testing procedures. A maintenance-free battery case generally contains a visual test indicator (**Figure 9**). This test indicator is a built-in

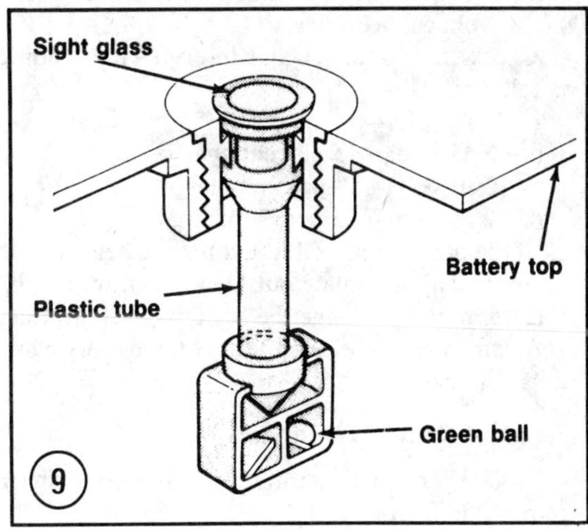

hydrometer installed in one cell. It provides visual information on battery condition for testing only and should not be used as a basis for determining whether the battery is properly charged or discharged, good or bad.

To use the test indicator, make sure the battery is level and the test indicator sight glass is clean. If necessary, wipe the sight glass with a paper towel moistened with water. A penlight often is useful under dim lighting conditions to determine the indicator color. Look down into the sight glass and refer to **Figure 10**. If the dot appears green in color, the battery has a sufficient charge for testing. If it appears dark, black or red, charge the battery before testing. A clear or light yellow appearance indicates that the battery should be replaced and the charging system checked. Do not charge, test or jump start the battery when the sight glass appears light yellow in color.

Open Circuit Voltage Test (Maintenance-free Batteries)

This procedure applies to sealed batteries without removable filler caps. The use of a digital voltmeter capable of reading to 1/100 volt is recommended to read open circuit voltage accurately. The relationship between open circuit voltage (OCV) and battery specific gravity is a direct one. To determine the state of charge or specific gravity of a maintenance-free battery, perform the test below and refer to **Table 1**.

1. The battery surface charge must be removed if the vehicle has just been driven. Turn the headlights on for 20 seconds.
2. Turn the headlights off and wait a minimum of 5 minutes to allow battery voltage to stabilize.
3. Connect a digital voltmeter across the negative and positive battery terminals to determine open circuit voltage. See **Figure 11**.
4. Check the voltmeter and interpret the reading as follows:
   a. 12.60 volts—full charge.
   b. 12.45 volts—75 percent charge.
   c. 12.30 volts—50 percent charge.
   d. 12.15 volts—25 percent charge.
5. If the battery open circuit voltage is below 12.45 volts at an approximate outside temperature of 70° F (21°degrees C), charge the battery for 20 minutes at 35 amps and repeat the test. If the battery again fails the test, replace it.

Unsealed Battery Testing

This procedure applies to batteries with removable filler caps.

Hydrometer testing is the best way to check battery condition. Use a hydrometer with numbered graduations from 1.100-1.300 rather than one with just color-coded bands. To use the hydrometer, squeeze the rubber ball, insert the tip in a cell and release the ball (**Figure 12**).

Draw enough electolyte to float the weighted float inside the hydrometer. When using a temperature-compensated hydrometer, release the electrolyte and repeat this process several times to make sure the thermometer has adjusted to the electrolyte temperature before taking the reading.

Hold the hydrometer vertically and note the number in line with the surface of the electrolyte.

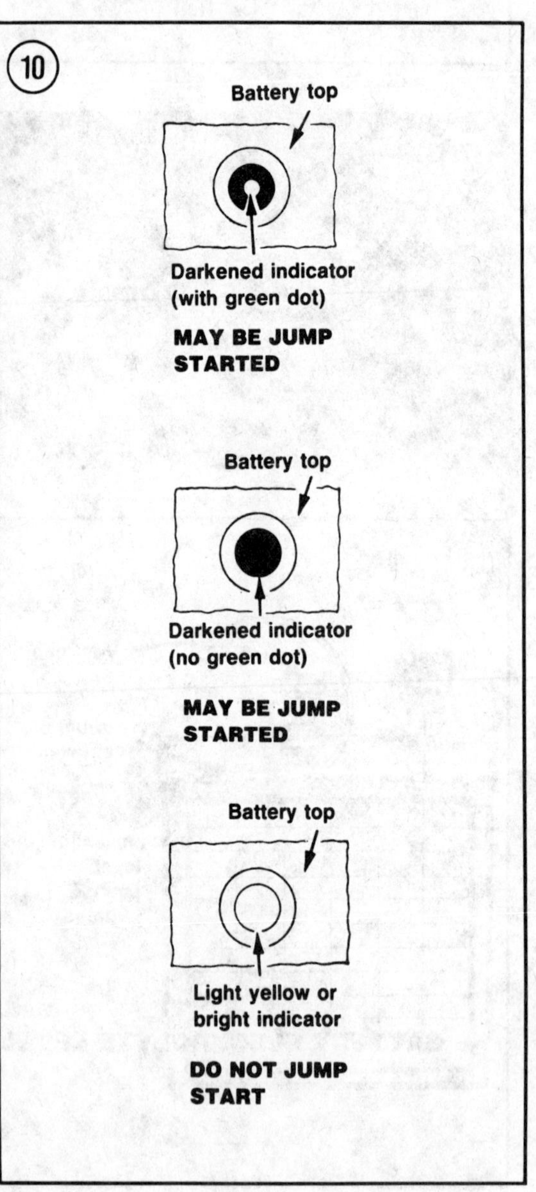

This is the specific gravity for the cell. Return the electrolyte to the cell from which it came.

The specific gravity of the electrolyte in each battery cell is an excellent indicator of that cell's condition. A fully charged cell will read 1.260 or more at 80° F (27°degrees C). If the cells test below 1.220, the battery must be recharged. Charging is also necessary if the specific gravity varies more than 0.050 from cell to cell.

NOTE

If a temperature-compensated hydro meter is not used, add 0.004 to the specific gravity reading for every 10° above 80° F (27° C). For every 10° below 80° F (27° C), subtract 0.004.

Safety Precautions

When working with batteries, use extreme care to avoid spilling or splashing the electrolyte. This solution contains sulfuric acid, which can ruin clothing and cause serious chemical burns. If any electrolyte is spilled or splashed on clothing or skin, immediately neutralize with a solution of baking soda and water, then flush with an abundance of clean water.

WARNING

Electrolyte splashed into the eyes is extremely dangerous. Safety glasses should always be worn while working with batteries. If electrolyte is splashed into the eyes, call a physician immediately, force the eyes open and flood with cool, clean water for approximately 15 minutes.

If electrolyte is spilled or splashed onto any surface, it should be immediately neutralized with baking soda and water solution and then rinsed with clean water.

While batteries are being charged, highly explosive hydrogen gas forms in each cell. Some of this gas escapes through filler cap openings (unsealed battery) or vent openings (sealed battery) and may form an explosive atmosphere in and around the battery. This condition can persist for several hours. Sparks, an open flame or a lighted cigarette can ignite this gas, causing an internal battery explosion and possible serious personal injury.

Take the following precautions to prevent an explosion:

1. Do not smoke or permit any open flame near any battery being charged or which has been recently charged.
2. Do not disconnect live circuits at battery terminals, since a spark usually occurs when a live circuit is broken. Take care when connecting or disconnecting any battery charger. Be sure its power switch is off before making or breaking connections. Poor connections are a common cause of electrical arcs which cause explosions.

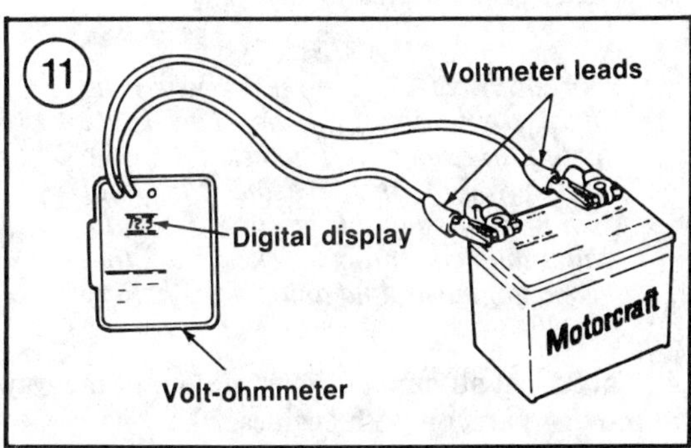

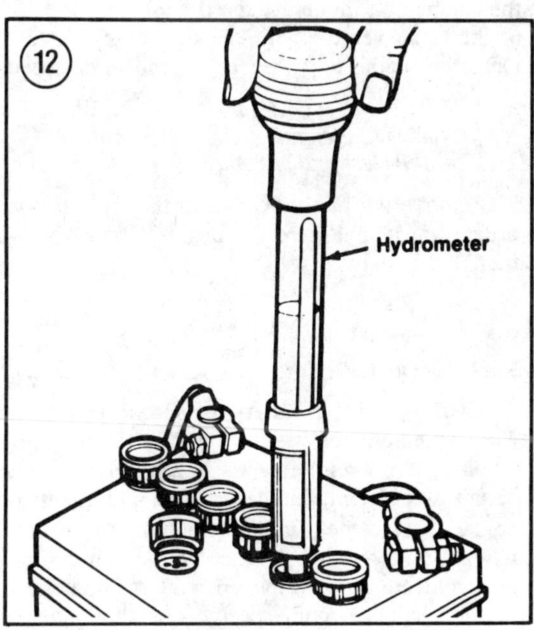

Charging

A good state of charge should be maintained in batteries used for starting. Check the battery with a voltmeter as shown in **Figure 11**. Any battery that cannot deliver at least 9.6 volts under a starting load should be recharged. If recharging does not bring it up to strength or if it does not hold the charge, replace the battery.

A cold battery will not accept a charge readily. If the temperature is below 40° F (5° C), the battery should be allowed to warm up to room temperature before charging.

The battery does not have to be removed from the vehicle for charging. Just make certain that the area is well-ventilated, the battery cables are disconnected and there is no chance of sparks or flames occuring near the battery.

WARNING
Charging batteries give off highly explosive hydrogen gas. If this explodes, it may spray battery acid over a wide area.

Disconnect the negative battery cable first, then the positive cable. On unsealed batteries, make sure the electrolyte is fully topped up. Remove the vent caps and place a folded paper towel over the vent openings to absorb any electrolyte that may spew as the battery charges.

Connect the charger to the battery—negative to negative, positive to positive. If the charger output is variable, select a high setting (30-40 amps), set the voltage selector to 12 volts and plug the charger in. Let the battery charge for 30 minutes,then reduce the charge rate to 5-10 amps.

Once the battery starts to accept a charge, the charge rate should be reduced to a level that will prevent excessive gassing and electrolyte spewing. This is especially important with sealed batteries, as excessive gassing will reduce the amount of electrolyte (which cannot be replaced) in the battery cells.

The length of time required to recharge a battery depends upon its size, state of charge and temperature. Generally speaking, the current input time should equal the battery amp-hour rating. For example, a 45 AH battery will require a 9-amp charging rate for 5 hours (9X5=45) or a 15-amp charging rate for 3 hours (15X3=45). On unsealed batteries, check charging progress with the hydrometer. **Table 2** gives approximate state of charge according to specific gravity.

Jump Starting

If the battery becomes severely discharged on the road, it is possible to start and run a vehicle by jump starting it from another battery. If the proper procedure is not followed, however, jump starting can be dangerous.

Before jump starting an unsealed battery when temperatures are 32° F (0° C) or lower, check the condition of the electrolyte. If it is not visible or if it appears to be frozen, do *not* attempt to jump start the battery, as the battery may explode or rupture. Do *not* jump start sealed batteries when the temperature is 32° F (0° C) or lower.

WARNING
Use extreme caution when connecting a booster battery to one that is discharged to avoid personal injury or damage to the vehicle.

1. Position the 2 vehicles so that the jumper cables will reach between batteries, but the vehicles do not touch. Set the parking brake on each vehicle.

CAUTION
Do not disconnect the battery of the vehicle to be started. This could damage the electronic ignition module or vehicle electrical system.

2. Turn on the heater blower of the vehicle to be started to remove any transient voltage. Make sure all other switches and lights are turned OFF.
3. Connect the jumper cables in the order and sequence shown in **Figure 13**.

WARNING
An electrical arc may occur when the final connection is made. This could cause an explosion if it occurs near the battery. For this reason, the final connection should be made to the alternator mounting bracket or another good engine ground and not the battery itself.

4. Check that all jumper cables are out of the way of moving parts on both engines.
5. Start the vehicle with the good battery and run the engine at a moderate speed.
6. Start the vehicle with the discharged battery. Once the engine starts, run it at a moderate speed.

CAUTION
Racing the engine may cause damage to the electrical system.

7. Remove the jumper cables in the exact reverse order shown in **Figure 13**. Begin at point No. 4, then 3, 2 and 1.

Replacement Batteries

When replacing a battery, be sure to install one with sufficient power to handle the engine's cranking requirements. As a general rule, the battery's cold cranking capacity should equal the engine displacement in cubic inches. For example, a 302 cid V8 requires a battery with a minimum of 300 cold cranking amps. In winter climates, the battery's cold cranking specification should exceed the engine displacement by 50 percent, as battery efficiency can be reduced during cold weather.

Battery Cables

Poor terminal connections will cause excessive resistance. Defective cable insulation can cause partial short circuits. Both conditions may result in an abnormal voltage drop in the starter motor cable. When this happens, the resulting hard-start condition will place further strain on the battery. Cable condition and terminal connections should be checked periodically.

IAR CHARGING SYSTEM

The integral alternator/regulator (IAR) charging system consists of the alternator with integral voltage regulator, battery, ignition switch, ammeter or charge indicator light, fusible link and connecting wiring.

A drive belt driven by the engine crankshaft pulley turns the alternator, which produces electrical energy to charge the battery. As engine speed varies, the voltage output of the alternator varies. The regulator maintains the voltage to the electrical system within safe limits. The ammeter or charge indicator light signals when charging is not taking place.

Complete troubleshooting of the charging system requires test equipment and skills which the average home mechanic does not possess. However, there are basic tests which can be done to pinpoint most problems.

Charging system troubles are generally caused by a defective alternator, voltage regulator, battery or a blown fuse. They may also be caused by something as simple as incorrect drive belt tension.

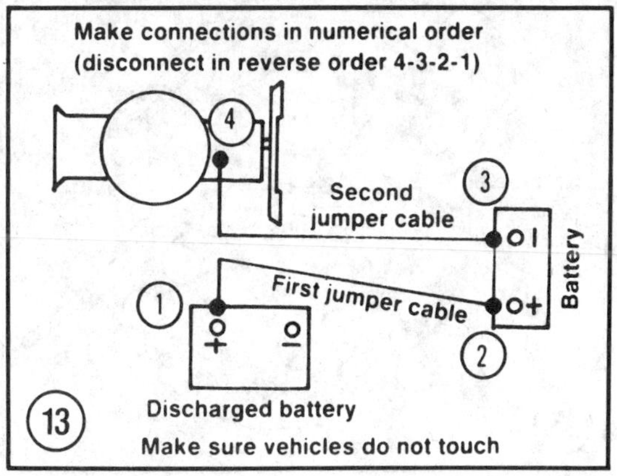

Make connections in numerical order
(disconnect in reverse order 4-3-2-1)
Second jumper cable
First jumper cable
Battery
Discharged battery
Make sure vehicles do not touch
13

The following are symptoms of problems you may encounter:

1. *Battery dies frequently, even though the ammeter indicates no discharge*—This can be caused by a drive belt that is slightly loose. Grasp the alternator pulley with both hands and try to turn it. If the pulley can be turned without moving the belt, the drive belt is too loose. As a rule, keep the belt tight enough so that it can be deflected only about 1/2 in. under moderate thumb pressure applied between the pulleys. The battery may also be at fault; test the battery condition as described in this chapter.
2. *Ammeter needle does not move when ignition switch is turned ON*—This may indicate a defective ignition switch, battery, voltage regulator or ammeter. Try to start the engine. If it doesn't start, check the ignition switch and battery.
   a. If equipped with an ammeter and the engine starts, remove and test the ammeter.
   b. If equipped with an indicator light and the engine starts, check for a blown bulb.
   c. If the problem persists, the alternator brushes may not be making contact. Perform the *Charging System Test* in this section.
3. *Ammeter needle fluctuates between "Charge" and "Discharge"*—This usually indicates that the charging system is working intermittently. Check drive belt tension first, then check all electrical connections in the charging circuit. As a last resort, check the alternator.
4. *Battery requires frequent addition of water or lamps require frequent replacement*—The alternator is probably overcharging the battery.
5. *Excessive noise from the alternator*—Check for loose mounting brackets and bolts. The problem may also be worn bearings or (in some cases) lack of lubrication. If an alternator whines, a shorted diode may be the problem.

Preliminary Testing

The first indication of charging system trouble is usually a slow engine cranking speed during starting or headlights that dim as engine speed decreases. This will often occur long before the charge warning light or ammeter indicates that there is a potential problem. When charging system trouble is first suspected, perform the following checks.

1. Check the alternator drive belt for correct tension (Chapter Seven).
2. Check the battery to make sure it is in satisfactory condition and fully charged and that all connections are clean and tight.

3. Check all connections at the alternator to make sure they are clean and tight.

NOTE
If locating the fusible link in Step 4 proves difficult in some engine compartments, connect a voltmeter between a good engine ground and the alternator BAT terminal. If the meter shows no voltage reading, the fusible link is probably burned out and should be replaced.

4. Check the fusible link located in the line between the starter solenoid and the alternator. If burned, determine the cause and correct it, then install a new fusible link.

If there are still indications that the charging system is not performing as it should after each of the above points has been carefully checked and any unsatisfactory conditions corrected, perform a *Charging System Test* as described in this chapter.

Charging System Test

A voltmeter with a 0-20 volt scale, an ohmmeter, a jumper wire, 2 blade terminals and an engine tachometer are required for an accurate charging system test.

1. Check the alternator drive belt tension. See Chapter Seven.
2. Check the battery terminals and cables for corrosion and/or loose connections. Clean and tighten as necessary.
3. Check all wiring connections between the alternator and engine.
4. Connect the positive voltmeter lead to the positive battery cable clamp. Connect the negative voltmeter lead to the negative battery cable clamp. See **Figure 11**. Make sure the ignition and all accessories are off.
5. Record the voltage displayed on the voltmeter scale. This is the battery or base voltage.
6. Connect a tachometer to the engine according to manufacturer's instructions.
7. Start the engine and bring its speed up to about 1,500 rpm. The voltmeter reading should increase from that recorded in Step 5, but not by more than 2 volts.
8. If the voltage increase is within specifications in Step 7, perform the *Load Test*. If the voltage increase is greater than 2 volts, perform the *Over-voltage Test*. If the voltage does not increase, perform the *Under-voltage Test*.

Load Test

1. With the engine running, turn the headlights on high beam and the heater or air conditioning blower on HIGH speed.
2. Increase the engine speed to about 2,000 rpm. If the voltmeter does not read a minimum of 0.5 volt more than the base voltage, perform the *Under-voltage Test.*Over-voltage Test.

Over-voltage Test

Refer to **Figure 14** for this procedure.

1. With the ignition ON (engine OFF), connect the negative voltmeter lead to the rear housing of the alternator. Conenct the positive voltmeter lead first

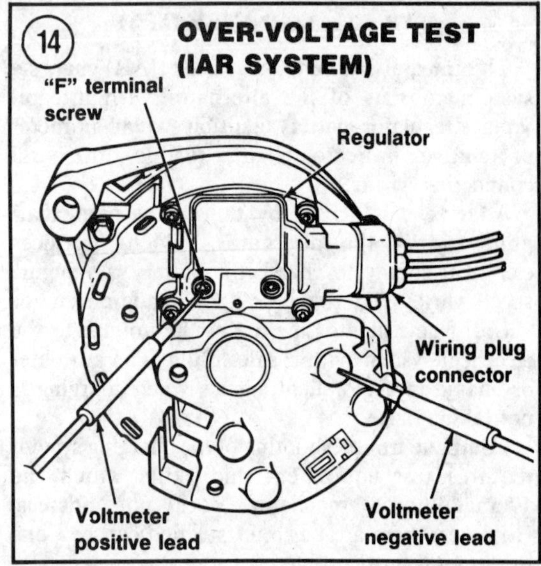

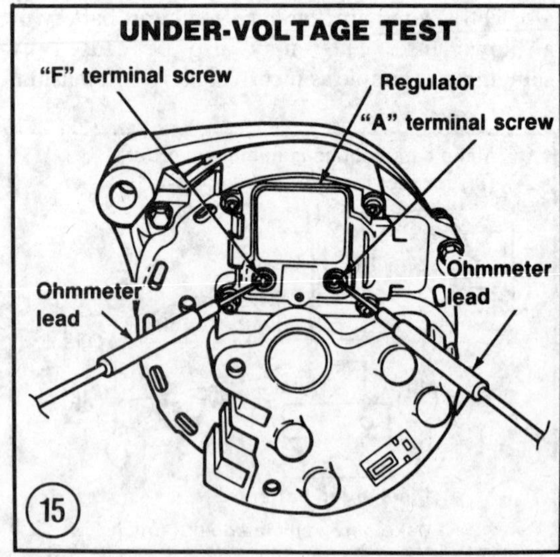

to the alternator output connection at the starter relay, then to the A screw head on the regulator. If the difference in readings exceeds 0.5 volt, there is excessive resistance (such as a break or bad connection) in the A wire circuit. Locate and correct as required.
2. Check for loose regulator-to-alternator ground screws. Tighten regulator ground screws to 15-26 in.-lb. (1.7-2.8 N•m).

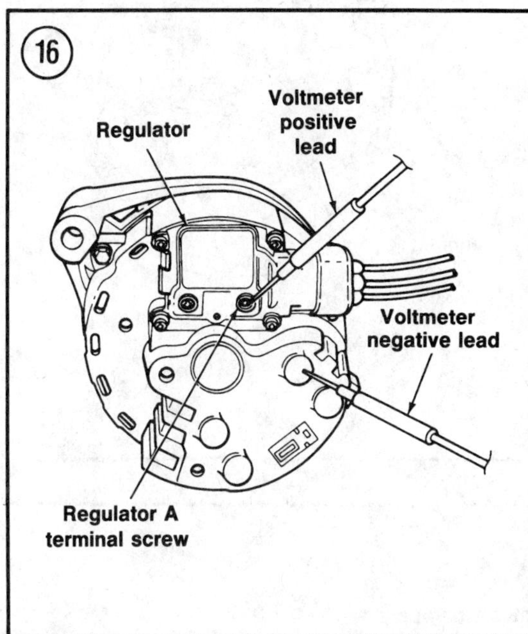

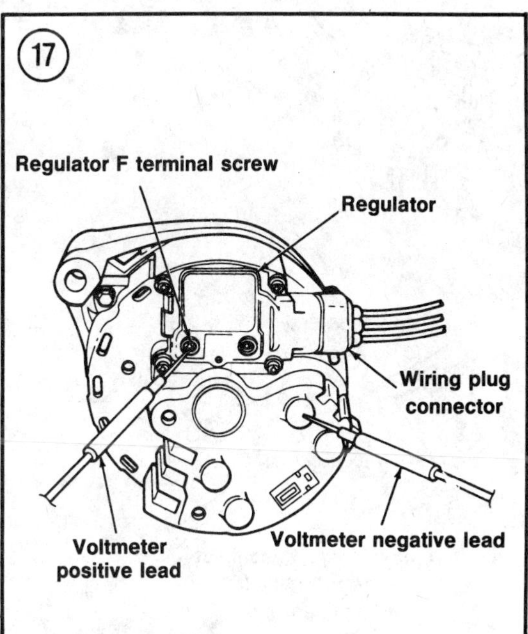

3. If the voltage increase still exceeds 2 volts, connect the negative voltmeter lead to the alternator rear housing. With the ignition OFF, connect the positive voltmeter lead first to the regulator A screw head, then to the F screw head.
4. If the voltage reading is the same at both screw heads in Step 3, replace the regulator. If the reading differs, remove the alternator and take it to a dealer for further testing and service.

Under-voltage Test

1. With the engine off, disconnect the regulator wiring plug and connect an ohmmeter between the regulator A and F terminal screws (**Figure 15**). The meter should read more than 2.4 ohms. If it reads less than 2.4 ohms, remove the alternator and have a dealer check for a shorted rotor or field circuit.
2. If the meter reads more than 2.4 ohms, reconnect the regulator wiring plug. Connect the negative voltmeter lead to the alternator rear housing. Touch the positive voltmeter lead to the regulator A terminal screw. See **Figure 16**. If the meter does not read battery voltage, there is an open in the A wire circuit. Locate and correct as required, then perform the *Load Test*.
3. If the voltmeter reads battery voltage in Step 2, connect the negative voltmeter lead to the alternator rear housing. With the ignition switch OFF, touch the positive voltmeter lead to the regulator F terminal screw. See **Figure 17**. If the meter does not read battery voltage, there is an open in the field circuit. Locate and correct as required, then perform the *Load Test*.
4. If the voltmeter reads battery voltage in Step 3, connect the negative voltmeter lead to the alternator rear housing. Turn the ignition switch ON (engine OFF) and touch the positive voltmeter lead to the regulator F terminal screw. See **Figure 17**. If the meter reading is 1.5 volts or less, proceed to Step 6.
5. If the meter reading in Step 4 exceeds 1.5 volts, perform the *I Circuit Test*. If this test is satisfactory, replace the regulator and perform the *Load Test*.
6. Disconnect the alternator wiring plug. Connect 12-gauge jumper wires between the alternator BAT (+) terminal blades and the corresponding wiring connector terminals. See **Figure 18**. Perform the *Load Test* but with the positive voltmeter lead connected to one of the jumper wire terminals. If the reading exceeds battery voltage by 0.5 volt, repair or replace the alternator-to-starter relay wiring.

7. If the reading in Step 6 does not increase more than 0.5 volt above battery voltage, connect a third jumper wire between the alternator rear housing and the regulator F terminal screw. See **Figure 19**. Perform the *Load Test* with the positive voltmeter lead connected to one of the BAT (+) jumper wire terminals as in Step 6. If the voltage now increases more than 0.5 volt above battery voltage, replace the regulator.

8. If the reading in Step 7 does not increase more than 0.5 volt, remove the alternator and take it to a dealer for further testing and service.

I Circuit Test

1. Disconnect the regulator wiring plug. Connect a jumper wire between the regulator A terminal and the wiring plug A terminal. Connect another jumper wire between the regulator F screw and the rear of the alternator housing. See **Figure 20**.

2. Start the engine and let it idle. Connect the negative voltmeter lead to the negative battery terminal and the positive voltmeter lead to the wiring plug S terminal, then the I terminal while noting the readings. The voltage at the S terminal should be about one-half that shown at the I terminal.

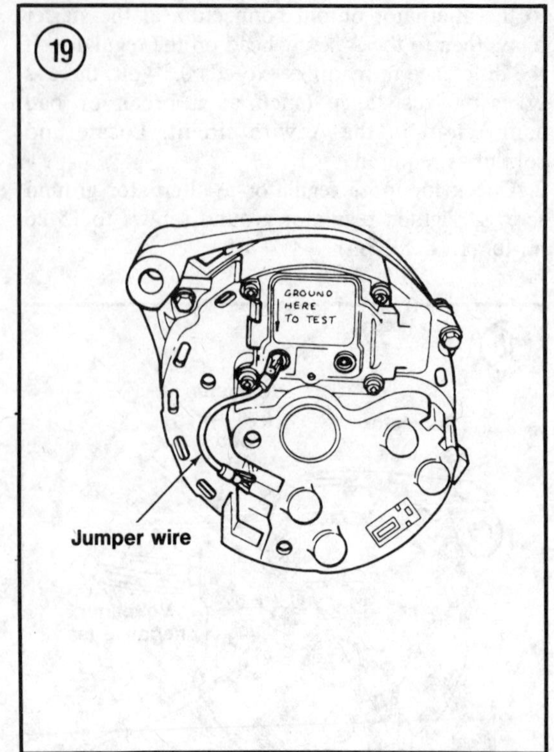

18

Alternator wiring plug

Jumper wire

B+ terminal

1986 only

F

S

A

I

Use jumper wire to connect A and F terminals at regulator plug

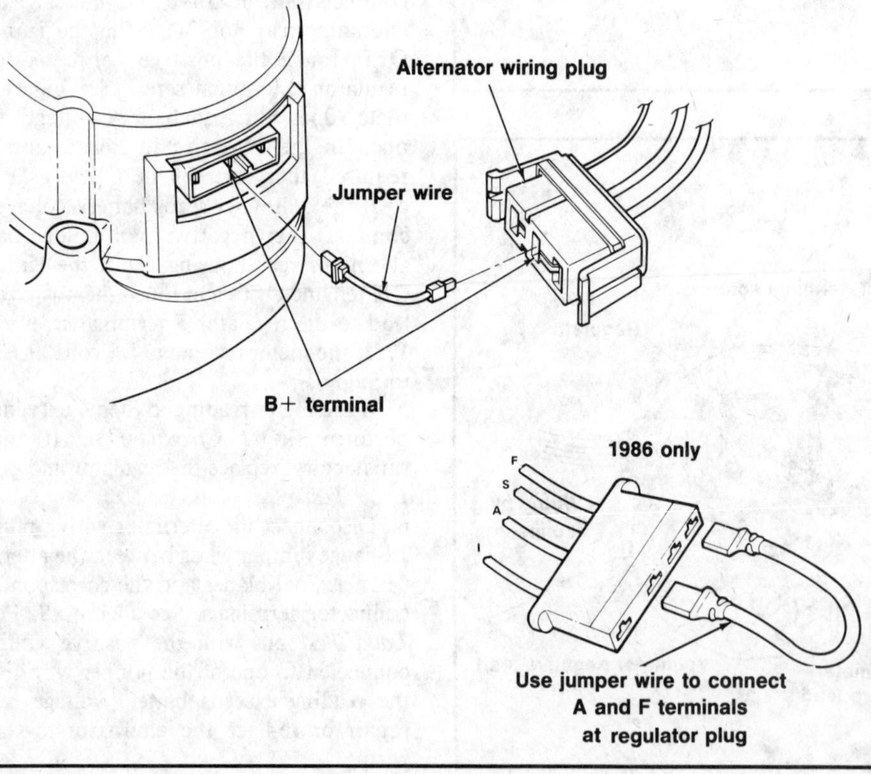

Field Circuit Drain Test

1. With the ignition switch OFF, connect the voltmeter negative lead to the alternator rear housing. Connect the positive lead to the regulator F terminal screw (**Figure 17**). If battery voltage is shown, the system is working properly.

2. If less than battery voltage is shown in Step 1, unplug the regulator connector and insert the voltmeter positive lead in the I terminal of the plug (**Figure 21**). If voltage is indicated, locate and correct the problem in the circuit between the regulator plug and the ignition switch.

3. If no voltage was shown in Step 1, insert the voltmeter positive lead in the regulator plug S terminal. If voltage is indicated, locate and correct the problem in the regulator plug S wire circuit. If no voltage is shown, replace the alternator rectifier assembly.

Constant Current Drain Test (Without Trip Computer)

1. Make sure all electrical circuits are off. Connect a 12-volt test lamp across the battery terminals. The lamp should light. Disconnect the test lamp, then disconnect the positive battery cable.

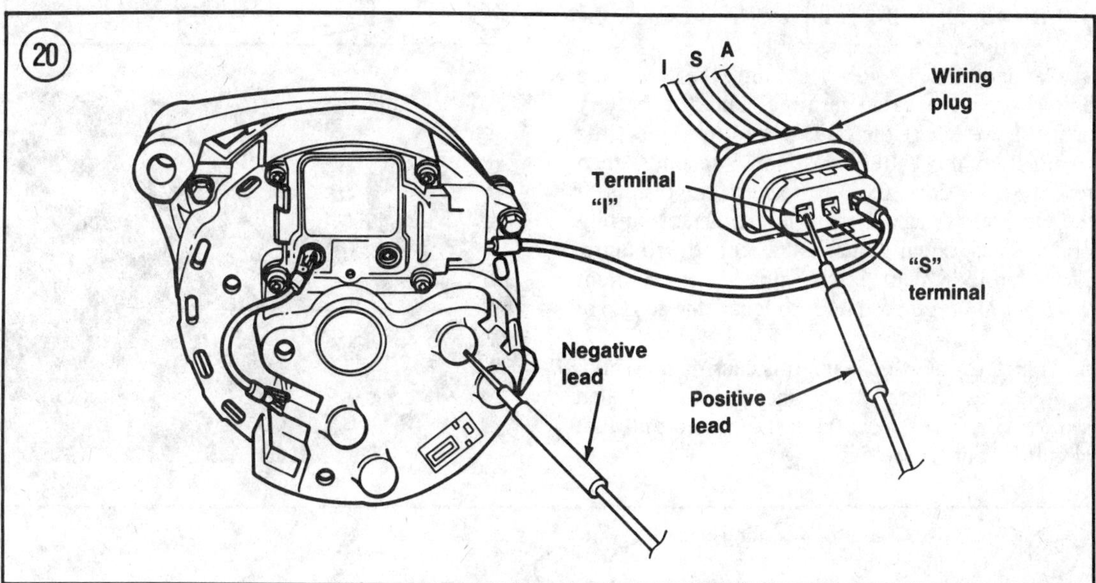

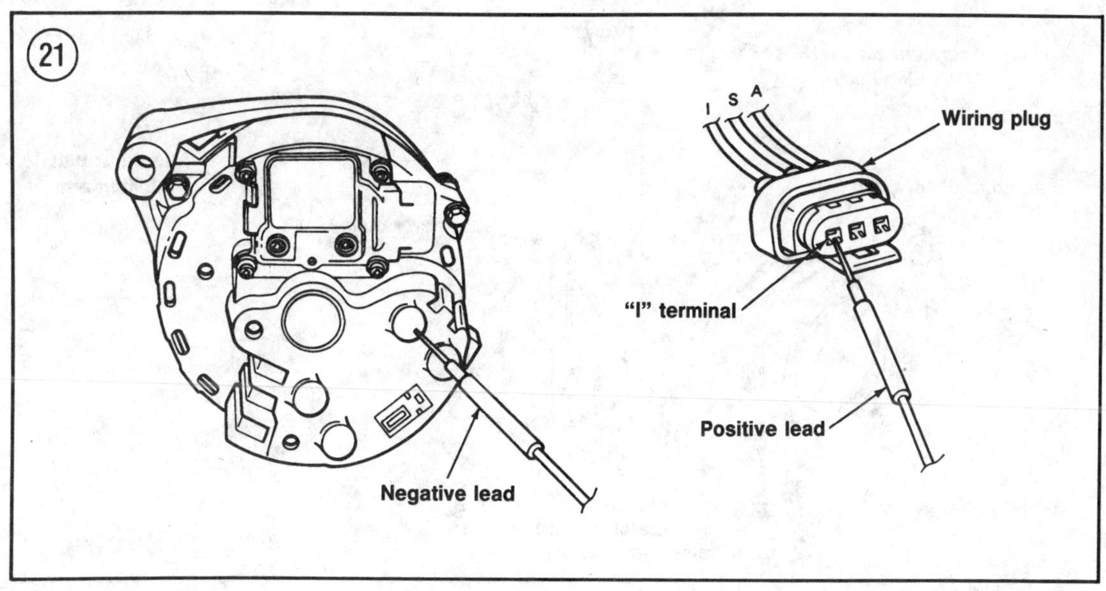

8

WARNING
If the next step is done improperly, the battery may explode and spray sulfuric acid. Be sure to follow the correct sequence.

2. Connect a test lamp between the battery positive cable and positive terminal as follows:
   a. Disconnect the negative cable from the battery.
   b. Disconnect the positive cable from the battery. Connect the test lamp between the positive cable and positive terminal as shown in **Figure 22**.
   c. Reconnect the negative cable to the battery. Do not allow the positive cable to touch the positive terminal or any metal.
3. Connect the 12-volt test lamp between the battery positive cable terminal and the battery post, **Figure 22**. If the lamp glows, reconnect the terminal to the battery post for 5 seconds, then repeat Step 2 and Step 3 to recheck the results. If the lamp glows again, there is a constant current drain. Check circuits such as the underhood lamp, cargo compartment lamp, glove compartment lamp or vanity mirror lamps to locate the source of the drain.
4. To determine which circuit is causing the drain, remove and reinstall fuses one at a time. When removing a fuse makes the test lamp go out, that circuit is causing the drain.

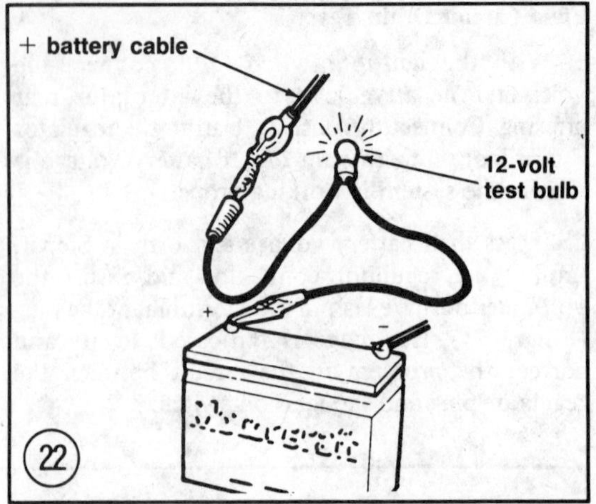

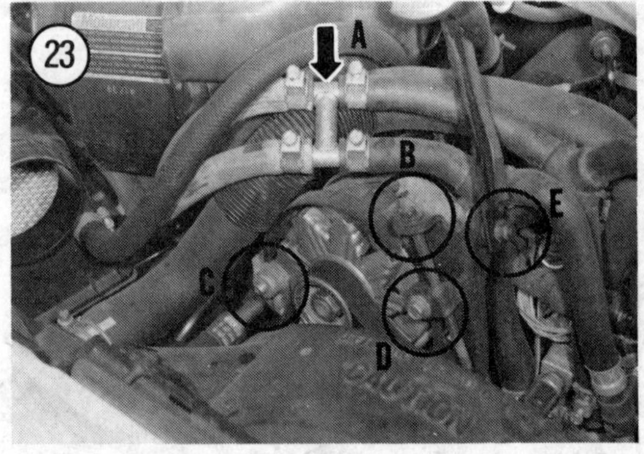

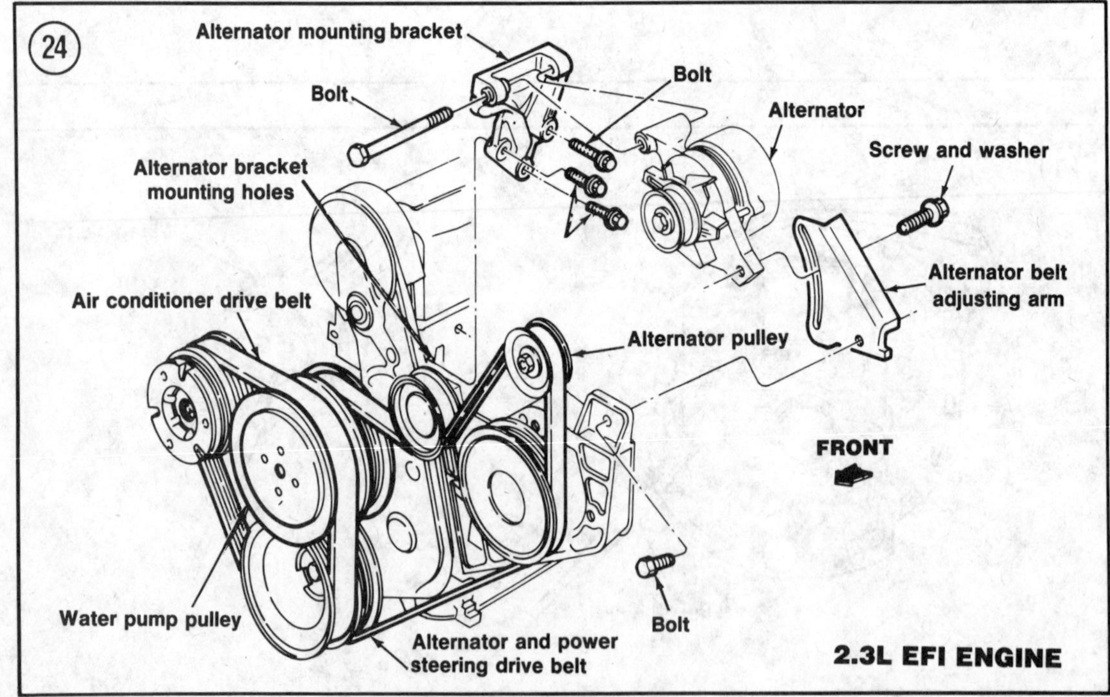

Constant Current Drain Test (With Trip Computer)

1. Make sure all electrical circuits are off. Disconnect either battery cable and connect a digital ammeter (set at its highest current scale) between the cable terminal and battery post.

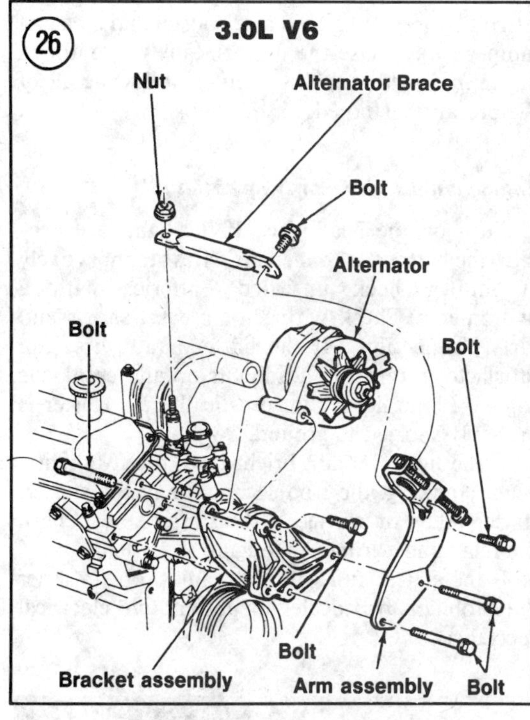

2. Reset the ammeter to its lowest current scale and wait about one minute for the meter to stabilize.
   a. If the ammeter shows a current drain of less than 0.05 ampere, the drain is caused by the trip computer and is normal.
   b. If the current drain exceeds 0.05 ampere, check circuits such as the underhood lamp, cargo compartment lamp, glove compartment lamp or vanity mirror lamps to locate the source of the drain.

3. To determine which circuit is causing the drain, remove and reinstall fuses one at a time. When removing a fuse makes the test lamp go out, that circuit is causing the drain.

Alternator Removal/Installation

This procedure is generalized to cover all applications. Not all steps will be required by every installation. Exact steps required will depend upon the engine and other accessory units installed. Access to the alternator is very limited in all engine compartments. See **Figure 23** (typical). Work slowly and carefully to avoid personal injury. Refer to **Figure 24** (I4), **Figure 25** (2.8L V6) or **Figure 26** (3.0L V6) for this procedure.

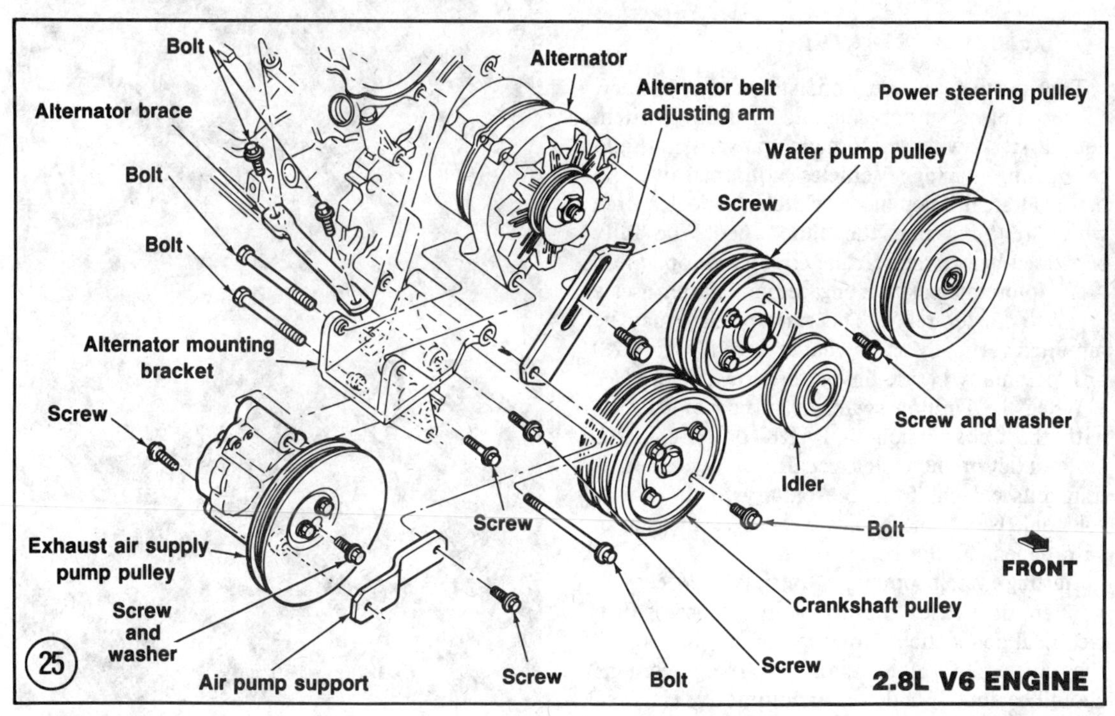

pulley

1. Disconnect the negative battery cable.
2. Drain about 2 quarts from the cooling system and disconnect the upper radiator.
3. On 3.0L V6 engines, disconnect the heater hose assembly at the metal H-fitting. See A, **Figure 23**.
4. Unplug the 2 wiring connectors at the rear of the alternator. See **Figure 27** (typical).
5. Loosen the adjusting bolt (B, **Figure 23**), if so equipped.
6. Loosen the pivot bolt (C, **Figure 23**) and remove the adjusting bolt (D, **Figure 23**).
7. Remove the pivot bolt (C, **Figure 23**), move the alternator towards the engine and disengage the drive belt from the alternator pulley.
8. If necessary, unbolt and remove the adjusting arm to provide sufficient access for alternator removal. On 3.0L V6 engines, the oil fill tube brace must be unbolted from the adjusting arm. See E, **Figure 23**.
9. Installation is the reverse of removal. Make sure the alternator connectors are properly installed before reconnecting the negative battery cable. Adjust the belt tension (Chapter Seven), then tighten the pivot bolt to 45-57 ft.-lb. (61-77 N•m) on I4 engines, 30-40 ft.-lb. (40-55 N•m) on 2.8L V6 engines or 45-61 ft.-lb. on 3.0L V6 engines. Tighten the adjusting bolt to 24-34 ft.-lb. (32-46 N•m) on I4 engines, 24-49 ft.-lb. (33-66 N•m) on 2.8L V6 engines or 24-33 ft.-lb. (32-46 N•m) on 3.0L V6 engines. Tighten the adjusting arm bolts to 30-40 ft.-lb. (40-55 N•m).

STARTER

The starting system consists of the battery, starter motor, starter solenoid, ignition switch, neutral start switch (automatic transmission) and connecting wiring. Vehicles equipped with a manual transmission have a clutch interlock switch which requires that the clutch pedal be fully depressed before the starting circuit will operate.

A Motorcraft positive engagement starter uses a separate starter relay. The starter relay may be mounted vertically on the fender apron (**Figure 28**) or horizontally beside the battery tray (**Figure 29**).

When the ignition switch is turned to START with the transmission in PARK or NEUTRAL (automatic) or the clutch pedal fully depressed, it transmits current from the battery to the starter solenoid, which mechanically engages the starter with the engine flywheel.

Starting system problems are relatively easy to find. In most cases, the trouble is a loose or dirty electrical connection. However, any repairs inside the unit itself (other than brush replacement) should be done by a dealer or automotive electrical shop. Installation of a professionally rebuilt unit is generally less expensive and thus more practical than trying to rebuild a starter motor at home.

On-vehicle Testing

Three of these procedures require a fully charged 12 volt battery to be used as a booster and a pair of jumper cables. Use the jumper cables as outlined in *Jump Starting* in this chapter, following all of the precautions noted.

Engine cranks very slowly or not at all

1. Turn on the headlights. If the lights are very dim, the battery or connecting wires are most likely at fault. Check unsealed batteries with a hydrometer. Check wiring for breaks, shorts and dirty connections. If the battery and wires are satisfactory, turn the headlights on and crank the engine. If the lights dim drastically, the starter is probably shorted to ground.
2. If the lights remain bright or dim only slightly when cranking, the trouble may be in the starter, starter relay, or wiring. If the starter spins, check the relay and wiring to the ignition switch.
3. If the starter still will not crank properly, refer the problem to a dealer or automotive electrical specialist.

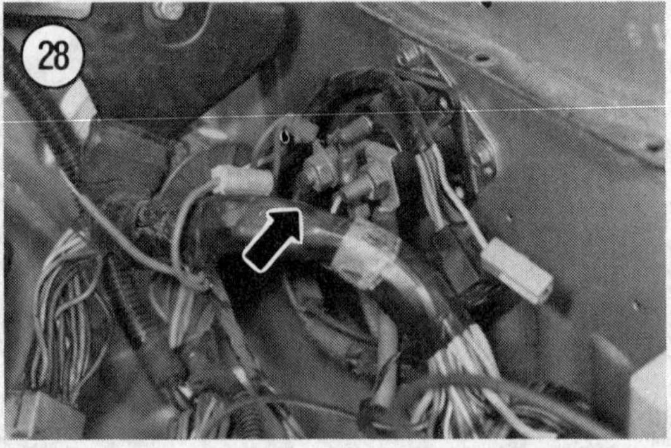

Slow cranking starter

1. Connect the jumper cables. Listen to the starter cranking speed as the engine is started. If the cranking speed sounds normal, check the battery for loose or corroded connections or a low charge. Clean and tighten the connections as required. Recharge the battery if necessary.
2. If cranking speed does not sound normal, clean and tighten all starter relay connections and the battery ground on the frame and/or engine.
3. Repeat Step 1. If the cranking speed is still too slow, replace the starter.

Starter relay clicks, starter does not crank

1. Clean and tighten all starter and relay connections. Make sure the terminal eyelets are securely fastened to the wire strands and are not corroded.
2. Remove the battery terminal clamps. Clean the clamps and battery posts. Reinstall the clamps and tighten securely.

3. If the starter does not crank, connect the 12 volt booster battery to the vehicle's battery with the jumper cables. If the starter still does not crank, replace it.

Starter relay chatters (no click), starter does not crank

1. Check the red/blue wire connection at the starter solenoid. Clean and tighten if necessary.
2. Check the relay mounting screws for a good, tight ground.
3. Place the transmission in PARK (automatic) or NEUTRAL (manual).
4. Disconnect the red/blue wire at the starter relay. Connect a jumper wire between this relay connector and the positive battery terminal.

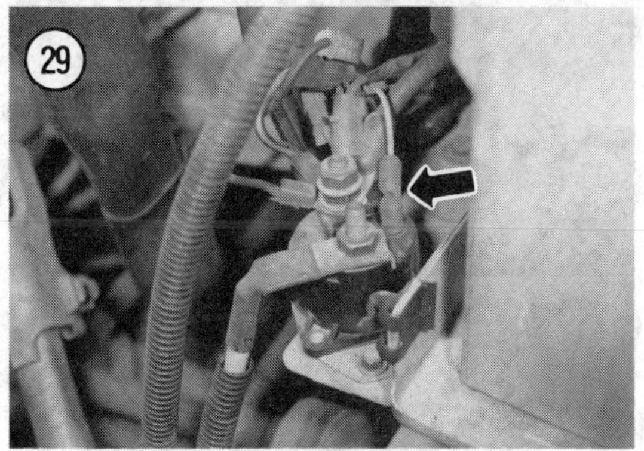

5. Connect the 12 volt booster battery to the vehicle's battery with the jumper cables. Try starting the engine (depress the clutch on manual transmission vehicles with a clutch interlock switch).
6. If the engine starts, check the ignition switch, neutral start switch or clutch interlock switch and the system wiring for an open circuit or a loose connection. If the engine does not start, replace the starter relay.

Starter spins but does not crank

1. Remove the starter as described in this chapter.
2. Check the starter pinion gear. If the teeth are chipped or worn, inspect the flywheel ring gear for the same problem. Replace the starter and/or ring gear as required.
3. If the pinion gear is in good condition, disassemble the starter and check the armature shaft for corrosion. See *Brush Replacement* in this chapter for disassembly procedure.
4. If there is no corrosion, the starter drive assembly is slipping. Replace the starter with a new or rebuilt unit.

Starter will not disengage when ignition switch is released

This problem is usually caused by a sticking solenoid but the pinion may jam on the flywheel ring gear of high-mileage vehicles. If equipped with a manual transmission, the pinion can often be temporarily freed by rocking the vehicle in high gear.

Loud grinding noises when starter runs

This can be caused by improper meshing of the starter pinion and flywheel ring gear or by a broken overrunning clutch mechanism.
1. Remove the starter as described in this chapter.
2. Check the starter pinion gear. If the teeth are chipped or worn, inspect the flywheel ring gear for the same problem. Replace the starter and/or ring gear as required.
3. If the pinion gear is in good condition, disassemble the starter and check the overrunning clutch mechanism. See *Brush Replacement* in this chapter for disassembly procedure.

Starter Relay Replacement

Two slightly different types of starter relays may be used. Refer to **Figure 30** as required for this procedure.

1. Disconnect the negative battery cable.
2. Disconnect the ignition switch and coil wires from the relay terminals.
3. Remove the nuts holding the starter and battery cables to the relay. Disconnect the cables.
4. Remove the screws holding the relay to the fender apron and remove the relay.
5. Installation is the reverse of removal.

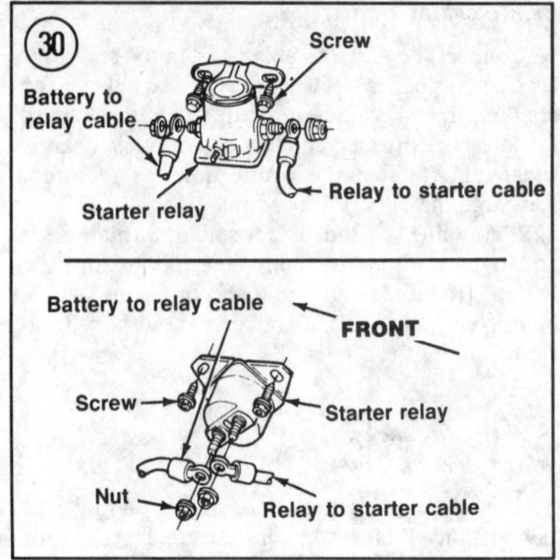

Starter Removal/Installation (All Engines)

Refer to **Figure 31** (typical) for this procedure.
1. Disconnect the negative battery cable.
2. Set the parking brake and place the transmission in PARK or 1st gear.
3. Securely block the rear wheels so the vehicle will not roll in either direction.
4. Raise the front of the vehicle with a jack and place it on jackstands.
5. Remove any starter motor brace or heat shield that will interfere with starter motor removal.
6. Remove the starter motor mounting bolts (A, **Figure 32**) and let the starter drop down out of position. Retrieve any mounting shims that may fall out.
7. Disconnect the starter cable (**Figure 33**). Remove the starter motor.
8. Installation is the reverse of removal. Reinstall any shims that were removed to assure proper pinion-to-flywheel mesh. Be sure to reinstall cable bracket and ground wire under the appropriate starter mounting bolt. See B, **Figure 32**. Tighten the mounting bolts to 15-20 ft.-lb. (20-27 N•m) on all engines.

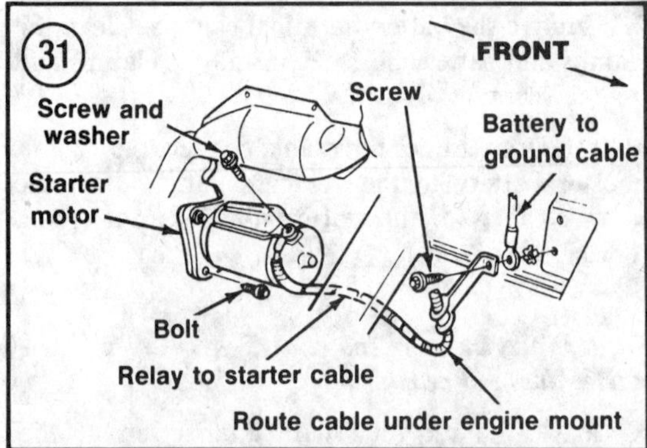

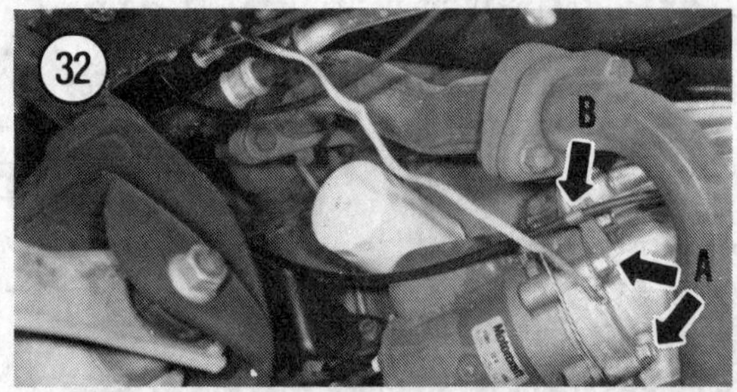

Starter Brush Replacement

Brush replacement requires partial diassembly of the starter. Always replace brushes in complete sets. Refer to **Figure 34** for this procedure.
1. Remove the 2 through-bolts from the starter frame.
2. Remove the brush end plate, bushing, insulator and brush holder.
3. Remove the brush springs and brushes from the brush holder.
4. Inspect the brushes. Replace all brushes if any are worn to 1/4 in. or less in length.
5. Inspect the plastic brush holder for cracks or broken mounting pads.
6. To replace ground brushes, remove the brush lead attaching rivets from the starter frame. Take

out the brushes and install new ones with new rivets.

7. To replace the field coil brushes, cut the insulated brush leads as close as possible to the field coil connections. Attach new brush leads with the clips provided in the replacement brush kit. Crimp each clip to hold the brush lead to the field coil connection and solder the connection together with rosin core solder and a 300-watt soldering iron.

8. Install the brush holder. Insert brushes in holder and install brush springs.

NOTE

Position the brush leads in their brush holder slots correctly to prevent a potential ground.

9. Install the brush insulator, bushing and end plate. The end plate boss must engage in the frame slot.

10. Install and tighten the through-bolts to 55-75 in.-lb. (6-8 N•m).

11. Connect the starter to a battery to check its operation, then install it as described in this chapter.

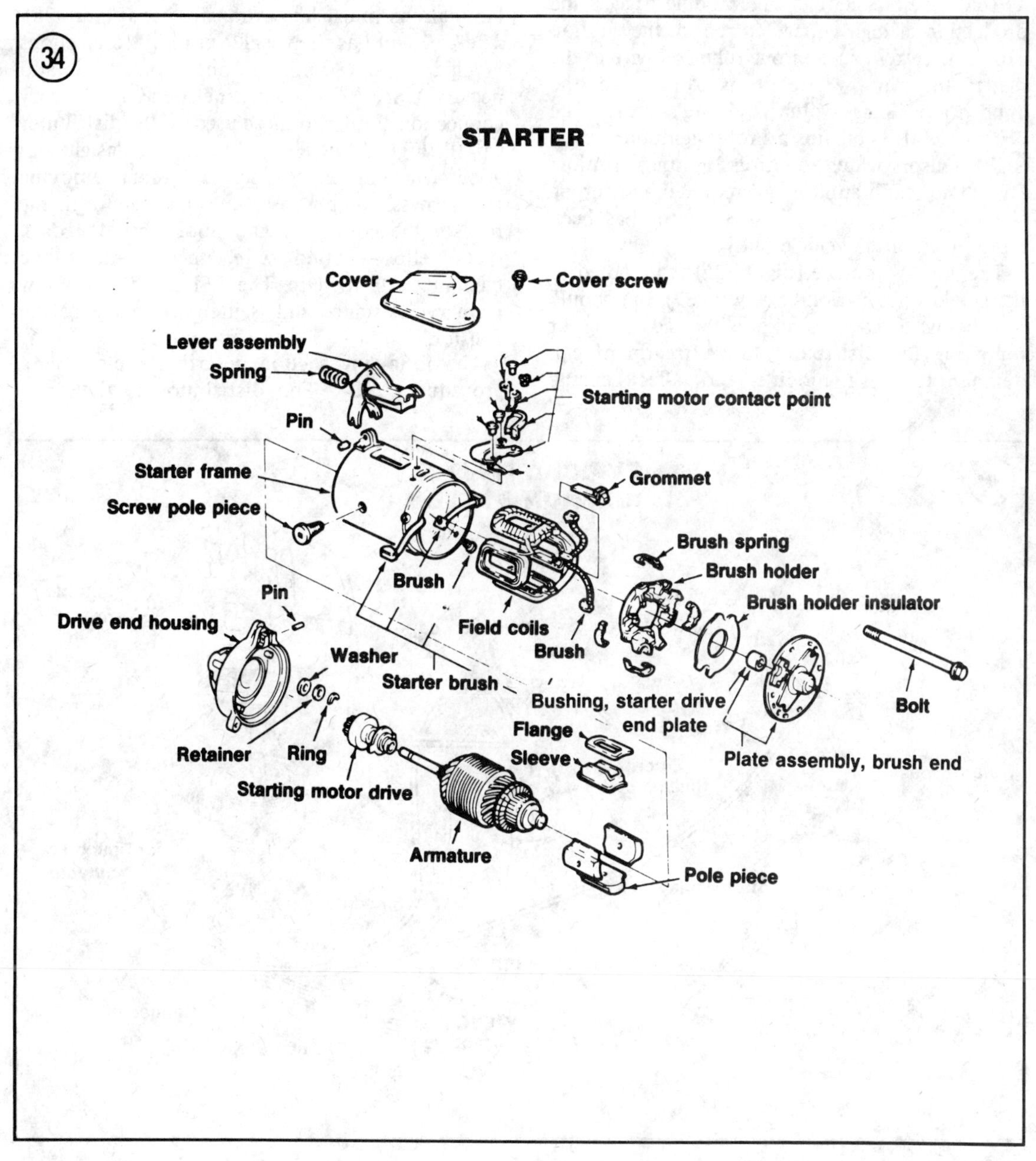

TFI-IV IGNITION SYSTEM

All engines use a Thick Film Integrated (TFI) ignition system with a universal distributor and E-core ignition coil. See **Figure 35** (typical). The major difference between engines and model year is the type of rotor used. The TFI-IV ignition is a part of a fourth-generation electronic engine control system (EEC-IV). The TFI-IV distributor has no centrifugal or vacuum advance mechanism (the advance function is incorporated in the EEC-IV module). A Hall switch in the distributor induces a magnetic signal which is sent to the TFI-IV ignition module. The module triggers the production of high voltage current in the ignition coil. This current runs through the coil wire to the distributor cap, where it is routed to the appropriate spark plug by the rotor. The distributor also contains a Profile Ignition Pickup (PIP) sensor which controls ignition timing. Distributor calibration is not required and timing is required only when the distributor has been removed from the vehicle.

The TFI-IV module (**Figure 36**) is mounted to the side of the distributor (**Figure 37**), but should not be used as a handle when adjusting or removing the distributor. Such treatment can damage the TFI module and affect engine operation. If the plastic TFI module separates from the metal base plate next to the connector, a no-start or intermittent run condition will result. A visual inspection usually can determine if this has happened. If so, remove the module as described in this section and coat the base plate with a 1/32 in. thick coat of silicone compound (part No. D7AZ-19A331-A) or equivalent. Reinstall the module to the distributor and tighten the mounting screws to 15-35 in.-lb. (1.7-4.0 N•m).

The TFI ignition coil also is a new design, much smaller than previous coils used. Instead of being oil-filled, it is potted in plastic and has external laminations much like a transformer (**Figure 38**). The TFI coil has the usual 2 primary connections labeled "plus" and "minus" (positive and negative). See A, **Figure 39**. It also has a secondary connection similar to those used on the distributor cap (B, **Figure 39**). The coil harness is designed to allow a tachometer connection without removing the harness. Simply insert an aligator clip in the rear of the connector and hook onto the dark green/yellow dotted wire, then connect the tachometer to the clip. The TFI coil has very low primary resistance and is used without a ballast resistor.

The following section describes replacement procedures only. The distributor is the only

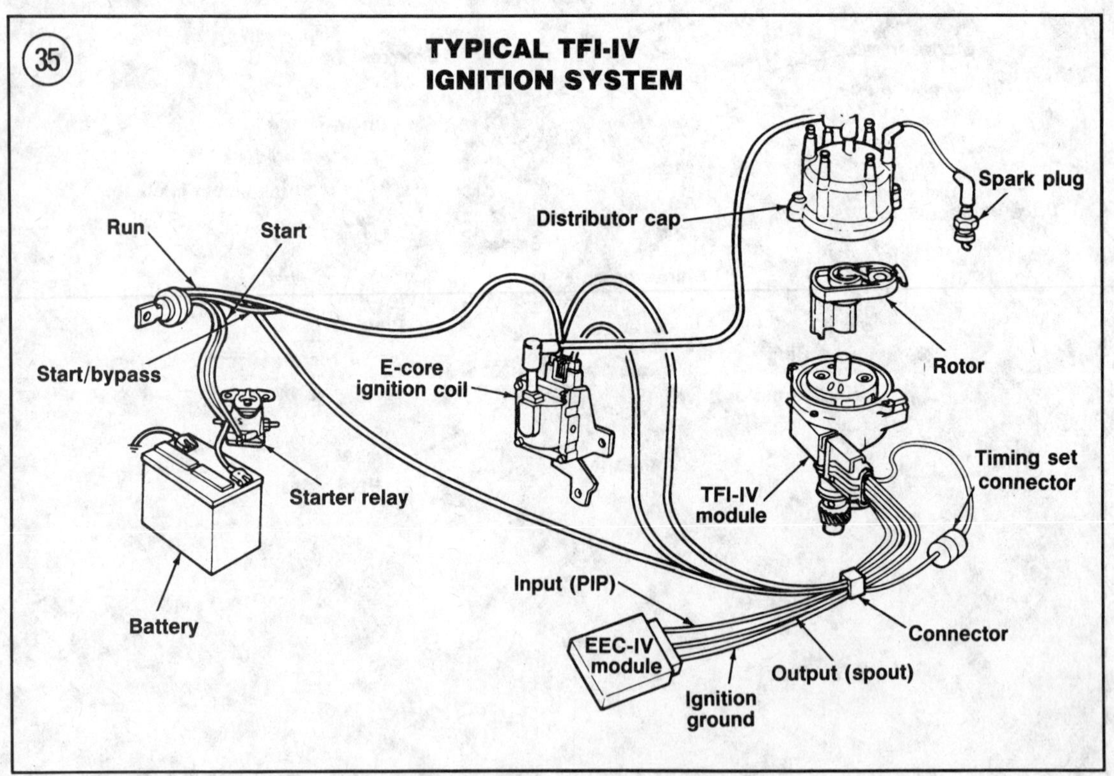

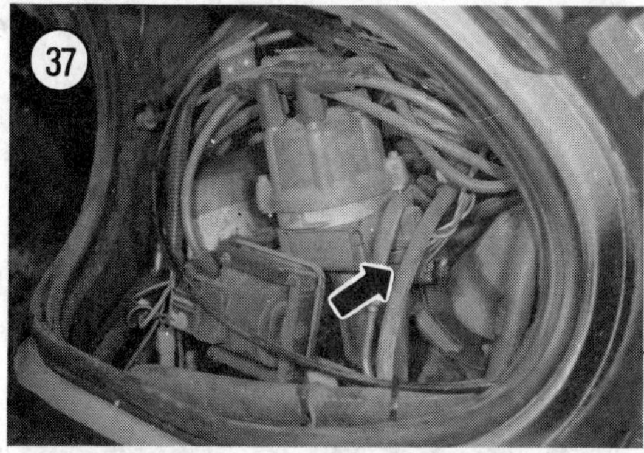

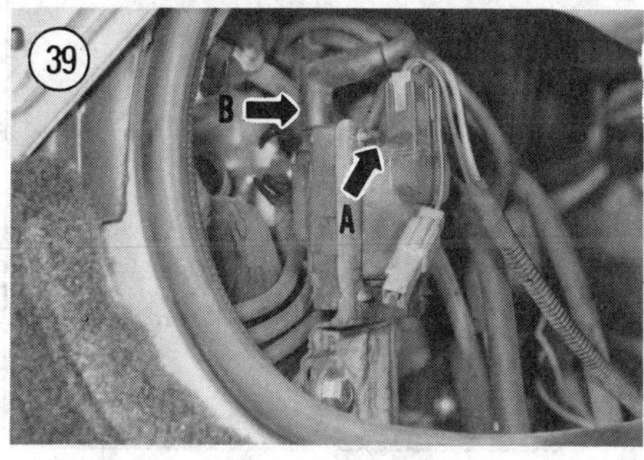

repairable ignition component; work on it should be entrusted to a dealer or qualified specialist.

Distributor Removal/Installation

The V6 distributor is mounted vertically at the rear of the engine block and is serviced from inside the vehicle by removing the engine cover panel. The I4 distributor is mounted at the lower front of the engine on the driver's side and is serviced from under the hood. Distributor removal on all engines is a slow and time-consuming task because of the limited access and large amount of wiring, hoses, etc. surrounding it. See **Figure 37** (typical). The coil is mounted near the distributor on all engines.

1. Disconnect the negative battery cable.
2. V6 engine—Remove the engine cover panel inside the passenger compartment.
3. Turn the engine over by hand until the No. 1 cylinder is at top dead center on its compression stroke. The timing mark and pointer will align and the distributor rotor will point to the No. 1 terminal in the distributor cap.
4. Disconnect the distributor wiring connectors.
5. Mark the position of the distributor cap No. 1 spark plug tower on the distributor base for reinstallation reference.
6. Remove the distributor cap with wires attached. Position it to one side to provide access for distributor removal.
7. Remove the distributor hold-down bolt and clamp. Remove the distributor from the engine.
8. Align the rotor tip with the mark scribed in Step 5, then rotate the distributor shaft just enough to align the leading edge of a Hall switch vane with the vane switch stator.
9. Insert the distributor in the engine and rotate as required to realign leading edge of vane to the vane switch with the rotor pointing to the No. 1 spark plug terminal in the distributor cap. When the distributor engages the camshaft gear (V6) or auxiliary shaft gear (I4), the rotor will turn slightly and the distributor will seat fully.
10. Install the hold-down clamp and bolt but do not tighten the bolt at this time.
11. Connect the distributor wiring connectors.
12. Start the engine and set base timing as described in Chapter Three.

TFI-IV Module Removal/Installation

1. Remove the distributor from the engine as described in this chapter.

8

2. Place the distributor on a clean workbench and remove the 2 hex-head module attaching screws (**Figure 40**).

CAUTION
Do not try to remove the module without working it off the connector terminals in the distributor base. The terminals will break and you will have to install a new distributor.

3. Carefully pull on the module with a rocking motion to disengage its terminals from the distributor base connectors, then pull the right side of the module downward toward the distributor mounting flange and remove.

NOTE
The module base which mates against the distributor body is covered with silicone grease. Do not remove this grease from the module base or body mounting pad if the module is to be reinstalled. If a new module is to be installed, clean the body mounting pad and apply the packet of grease accompanying the new module to the module base in a uniform 1/32 in. thick layer before installation.

4. Installation is the reverse of removal. Tighten the module mounting screws to 15-35 in.-lb. (1.7-4.0 N•m).

TFI Coil Removal/Installation

1. Unclip and remove the primary lead connector (A, **Figure 39**).
2. Disconnect the coil secondary terminal lead (B, **Figure 39**).
3. Remove the attaching screws and coil from its mounting bracket.
4. Installation is the reverse of removal.

LIGHTING SYSTEM

Sealed Beam Headlights

Individual rectangular combination high/low sealed beam lamps are standard equipment on all models. Halogen lamps are optional.

CAUTION
Torx head fasteners are used extensively in the lighting assemblies of late-model vehicles. Do not try to remove such fasteners with a Phillips head screwdriver—use an appropriate Torx head driver to prevent damage to the fastener head.

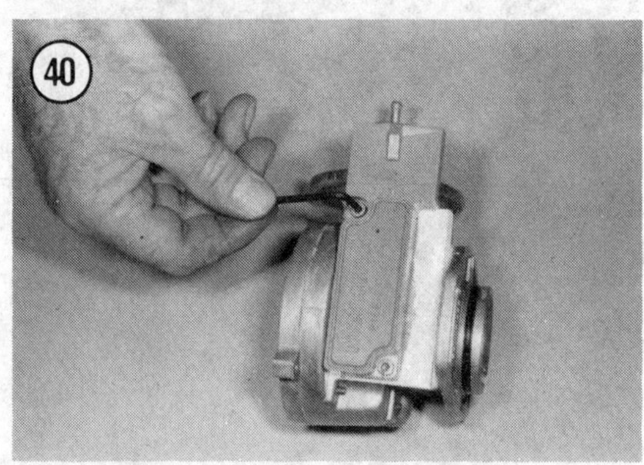
40

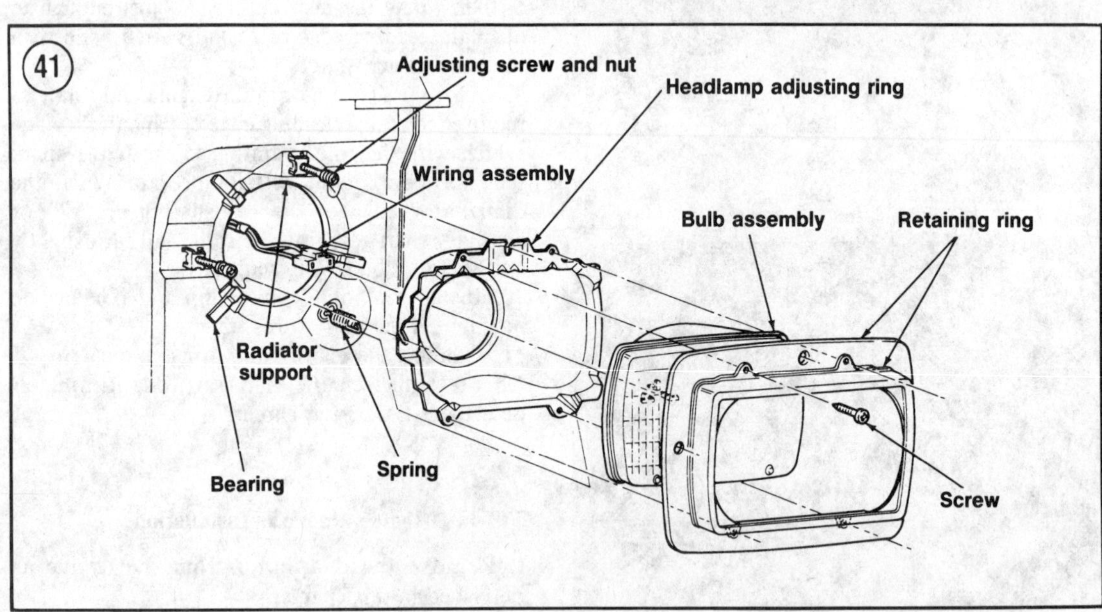

A good ground is necessary for proper exterior light operation. Always check for an unsatisfactory ground first when troubleshooting a dim lamp or one that fails to light. Do not overlook a loose ground strap between the engine and body dash panel—this can affect headlight as well as instrument gauge operation. Failure of one circuit in the bulb requires replacement of the entire sealed beam unit.

If both filaments in the lamp fail at the same time, the problem is generally a short in the wiring to that particular lamp. Check the fuse to make sure it is the correct amperage rating and replace it if it is not. Carefully inspect the wiring and connector for deterioration, chafing or other damage and correct as required.

Sealed Beam Headlight Replacement

Refer to **Figure 41** (typical) for this procedure.

1. Open and support the hood.
2. Disconnect the negative battery cable.

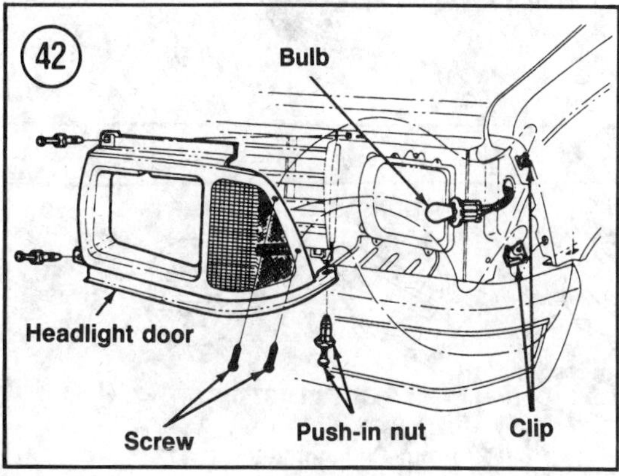

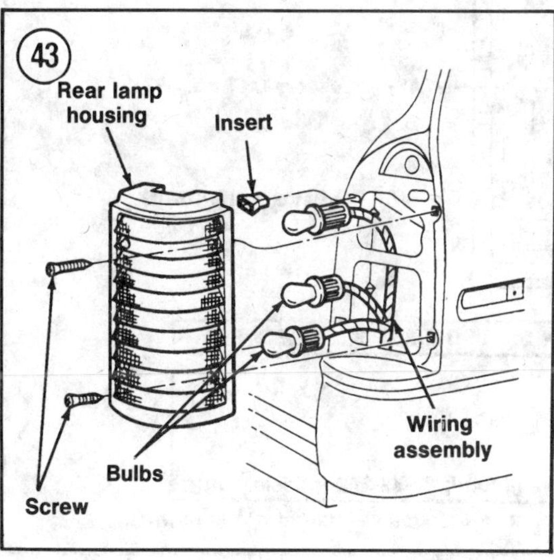

3. Remove the screws holding the headlight door in place. Remove the headlamp door. See **Figure 42**.

NOTE
Do not turn the headlight adjustment screws by mistake in Step 4. This will disturb the aim of the headlight beam and require readjustment by a dealer or certified station.

4. Remove the screws holding the retaining ring assembly. Remove retaining ring assembly from vehicle.
5. Rotate headlight as required to disengage it from the adjustment screws.
6. Carefully pull the headlight from the adjusting ring and unplug the wiring connector at the rear of the lamp. Remove the headlight from the vehicle.
7. Installation is the reverse of removal. Make sure the lugs on the lamp engage the recesses in the lamp adjusting ring. If the adjustment screws were disturbed, have the headlights adjusted by a dealer or certified station.

Front Park, Side Marker and Turn Signal Lamp Replacement

Refer to **Figure 42** for this procedure.

1. Disconnect the negative battery cable.
2. Remove the screws holding the headlamp door assembly. Remove the headlamp door assembly.
3. Pull bulb from socket. Push new bulb into socket.
4. Reinstall headlamp door assembly and reconnect negative battery cable.

Rear Lamp Replacement

Refer to **Figure 43** for this procedure.

1. Disconnect the negative battery cable.
2. Remove the 4 lamp housing screws and disengage lamp housing from fender.
3. Rotate sockets 1/4-turn and remove from lamp housing.
4. Pull defective bulb from its socket. Push new bulb into socket.
5. Reinstall sockets in lamp housing, rotating 1/4-turn to lock in place.
6. Position lamp housing on fender and reinstall attaching screws.
7. Reconnect the negative battery cable.

Dome Lamp Bulb Replacement

1. Disconnect the negative battery cable.
2. Carefully pry the lens from the dome lamp assembly.

3. Remove the bulb from the lamp housing retainers.
4. Installation is the reverse of removal.

Instrument Lights

The instrument cluster bezel must be removed to replace any lamp. See *Instruments* in this chapter.

IGNITION SWITCH

A blade-type terminal switch with one multiple connector is used. The switch is attached to the steering column with 2 shear bolts.

Removal

1. Disconnect the negative battery cable.
2. Insert the ignition key in the lock cylinder and turn it to the LOCK position.
3. If equipped with a tilt column, squeeze the upper extension shroud at the top and bottom to pop it free from the retaining plate. Remove the shroud.
4. Remove the screws holding the 2 trim shroud halves.
5. Disconnect the ignition switch connector. See **Figure 44**.
6. Drill out the 2 shear bolts, holding the switch in place with a 1/8 in. drill bit.
7. Use an EX-3 "Easy-out" tool to remove the 2 bolts.
8. Disengage the ignition switch from the actuator pin and remove it from the steering column.

44

Turn signal/
dimmer
switch
Hazard
warning
switch
Screw
Screw
To ignition
switch
Wiring harness

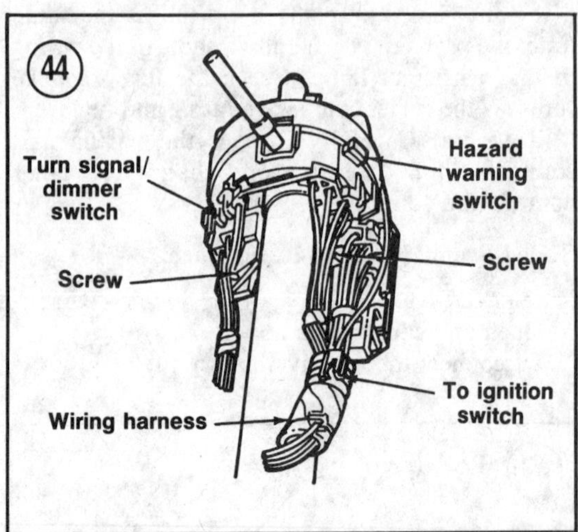

45

ACC
LOCK
OFF
RUN
START
Continuity test
(P1) Proof 1-CKT no. 977
(5) Start-CKT no. 32
(P2) Proof-CKT no. 208
(I1) Ignition-CKT no. 16
(I2) Ignition bypass-CKT no. 262
(A2) Accessory-CKT no. 687
(A1) Accessory-CKT no. 297
(BATT) Battery-CKT no. 37
P1
ST
32
P2
I1
16
A2
I2
262
A2
A1
297
BATT
A1
297
BATT
37

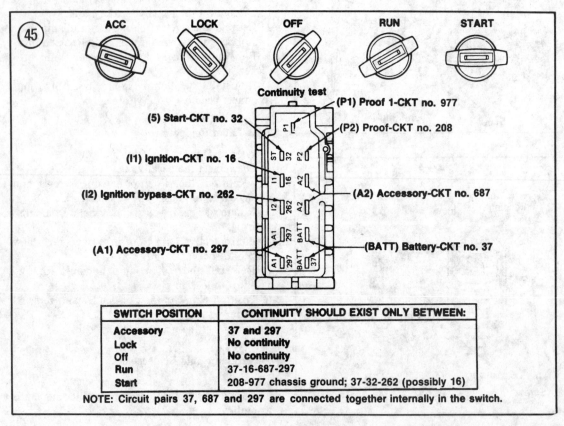

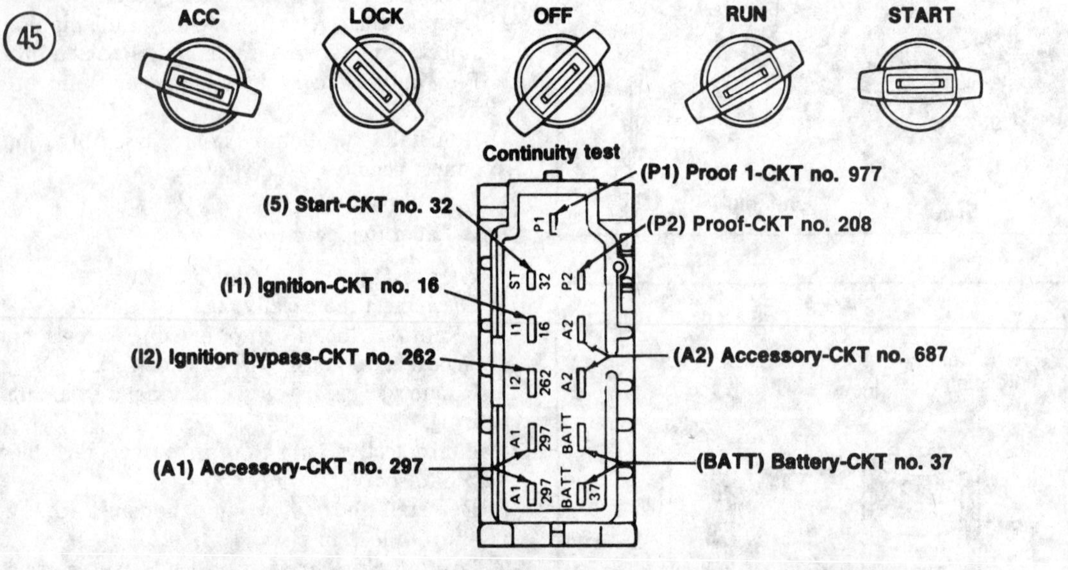

SWITCH POSITION	CONTINUITY SHOULD EXIST ONLY BETWEEN:
Accessory	37 and 297
Lock	No continuity
Off	No continuity
Run	37-16-687-297
Start	208-977 chassis ground; 37-32-262 (possibly 16)

NOTE: Circuit pairs 37, 687 and 297 are connected together internally in the switch.

Installation

1. Rotate the ignition key to the RUN position (about 90° clockwise from the LOCK position).
2. If reinstalling the old switch, make sure the carrier is in the RUN position (new switches are already properly positioned).
3. Align the switch holes with those in the lock cylinder housing. It may be necessary to make a minor adjustment in the lock cylinder position to align the actuator pin with the U-slot in the switch carrier.
4. Install new shear bolts. Operate the ignition switch to check for proper operation in all modes. Tighten bolts until their heads shear off.
5. Connect the wiring harness to the switch.
6. Reinstall the steering column trim shrouds.
7. Reconnect the negative battery cables.

Testing

Refer to **Figure 45** for this procedure.

1. Perform Steps 1-5 of *Ignition Switch Removal* as described in this chapter.
2. Identify the switch terminals according to **Figure 45**.
3. Connect an ohmmeter or self-powered test lamp across the terminals in the sequence shown in **Figure 45**. Continuity should exist as indicated in **Figure 45**. If any switch position fails the continuity test, replace the switch.

HEADLIGHT SWITCH

The 3-position rocker-type headlight switch is mounted in the upper left of the LH control pod on the instrument panel (**Figure 46**). It controls circuits to the headlights, parking/marker, taillights and license plate lamps. A rotating thumbwheel mounted on the lower edge of the instrument panel to the left of the steering column controls the interior and instrument panel lights. Removal of the control pod is required for headlight switch continuity testing.

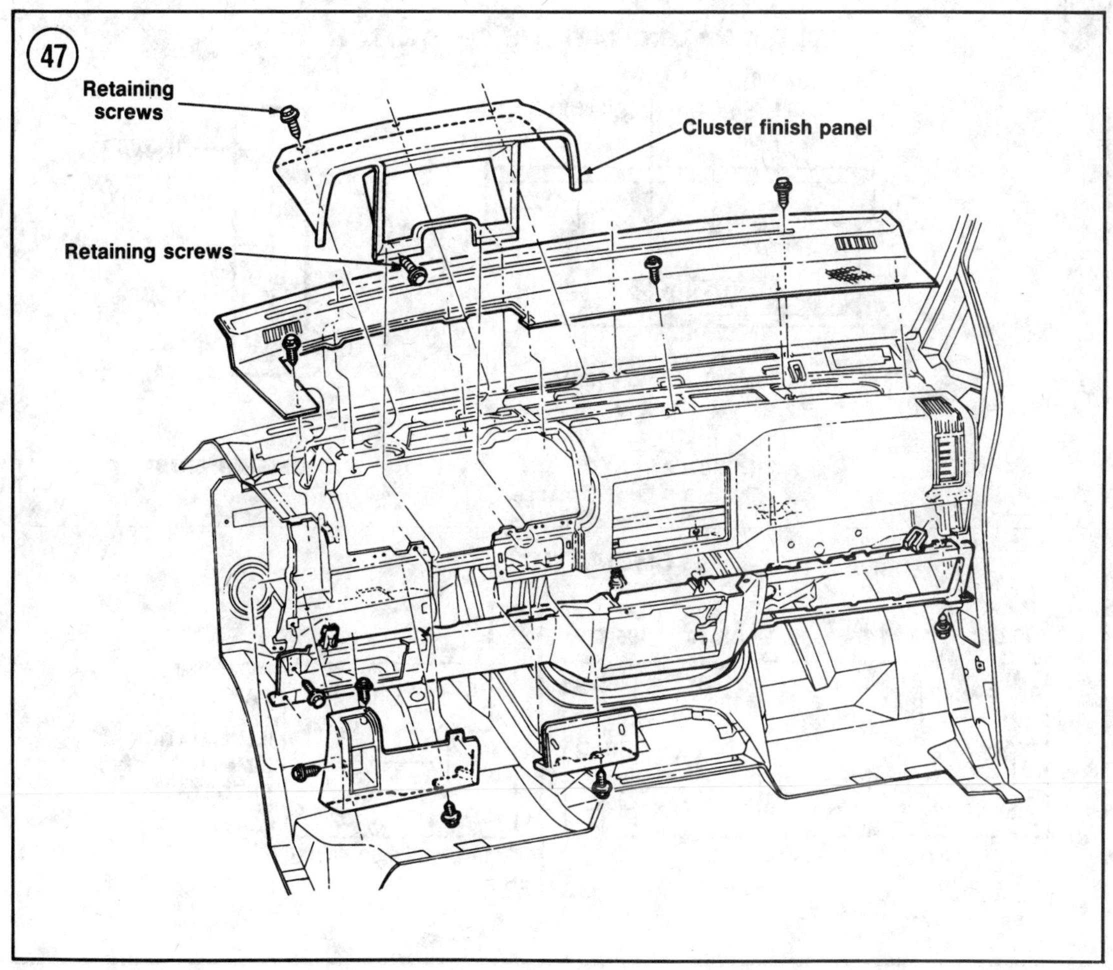

8

Removal/Installation

Refer to **Figure 46** and **Figure 47** for this procedure.

1. Disconnect the negative battery cable.
2. Remove the 5 screws holding the cluster finish panel to the instrument panel (**Figure 47**).
3. Remove the 3 screws holding the control pod to the instrument panel.
4. Pull the control pod out far enough to unplug the electrical connectors at the switches.
5. Remove the control pod from the instrument panel.
6. Remove the 2 headlight switch retaining screws. Remove the switch from the control pod.
7. If instrument cluster rheostat switch requires testing, it can be removed from the instrument panel by removing the 2 attaching screws and unplugging the wiring connector.
8. Installation is the reverse of removal.

LH control pod
Retaining screw
Retaining screws
Headlight switch
46

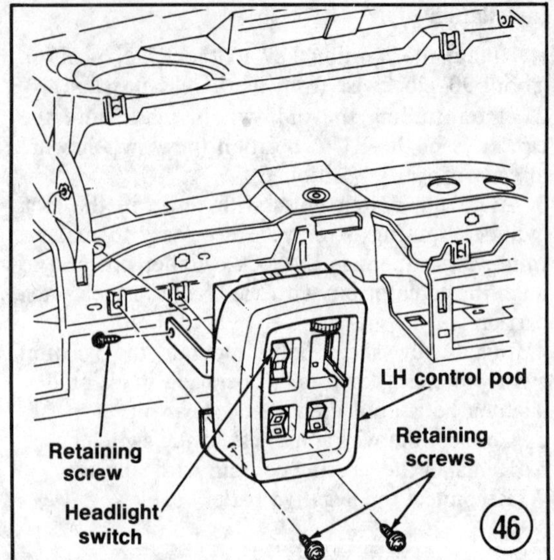

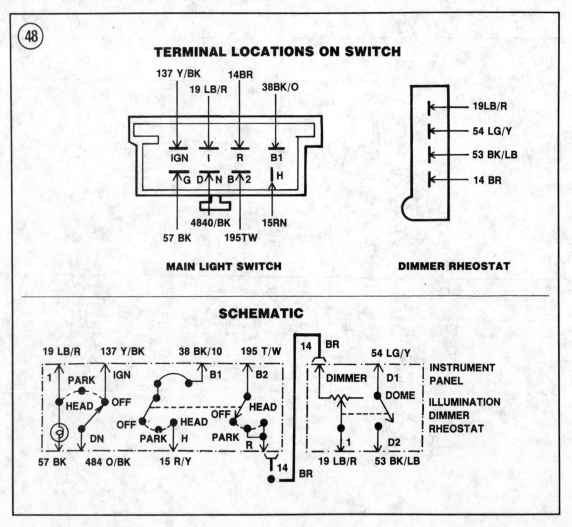

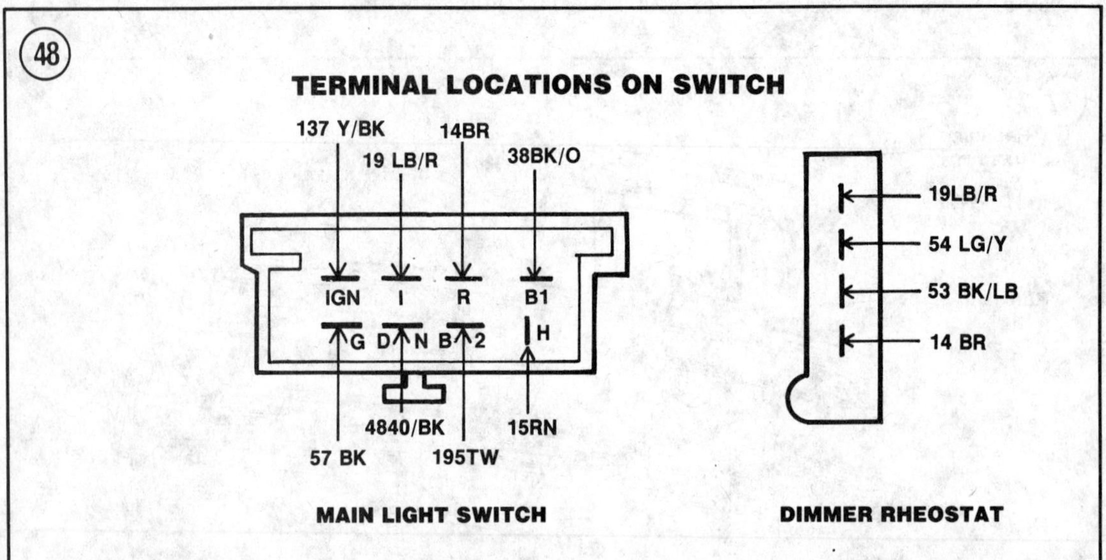

48
TERMINAL LOCATIONS ON SWITCH
137 Y/BK
14BR
19 LB/R
38BK/O
IGN
I
R
B1
G D N B 2
H
4840/BK
15RN
57 BK
195TW
MAIN LIGHT SWITCH
19LB/R
54 LG/Y
53 BK/LB
14 BR
DIMMER RHEOSTAT
SCHEMATIC
19 LB/R
137 Y/BK
38 BK/10
195 T/W
14
BR
54 LG/Y
1
PARK
IGN
B1
B2
DIMMER
D1
INSTRUMENT PANEL
HEAD
OFF
HEAD
DOME
OFF
OFF
HEAD
ILLUMINATION DIMMER RHEOSTAT
DN
PARK
H
PARK
R
1
D2
57 BK
484 O/BK
15 R/Y
14
BR
19 LB/R
53 BK/LB

Testing

With the switch removed, identify the terminals according to **Figure 48**. Connect an ohmmeter or self-powered test lamp to the terminals specified in the following steps and move the switch rocker through all positions.

1. Test the headlight circuit at terminals B1 and H. There should be continuity only in the HEADLIGHT position.
2. Test the parking light circuit at terminals B2 and R. There should be continuity in both PARK and HEADLIGHT positions.
3. Test the ignition on, lamps off circuit at terminals DN and IGN. There should be continuity only in the OFF position.
4. Test the dimmer cluster circuit at terminals DN and I. There should be continuity in both PARK and HEADLIGHT positions.
5. Test the switch illumination circuit at terminals I and G. If there is not continuity at all times, replace the ISO symbol bulb.
6. Continuity should not exist between any other terminal combinations. Replace the switch if it fails to perform as indicated in any test step.

WIPER/WASHER SWITCH

All vehicles are equipped with a 2-speed wiper system. A 2-speed wiper system with interval control is optional. A slide-type wiper/washer switch is mounted on the LH control pod. A rocker-type wiper/washer switch mounted below it control the rear wiper, when so equipped. See **Figure 49**.

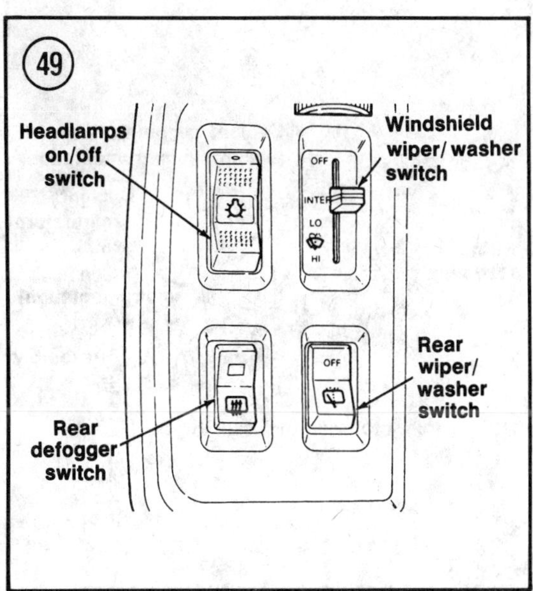

Removal/Installation

Refer to **Figure 46** and **Figure 47** for this procedure.

1. Disconnect the negative battery cable.
2. Remove the 5 screws holding the cluster finish panel to the instrument panel (**Figure 47**).
3. Remove the 3 screws holding the control pod to the instrument panel.
4. Pull the control pod out far enough to unplug the electrical connectors at the switches.
5. Remove the control pod from the instrument panel.
6. Remove the screws holding the wiper switch or switches to the control pod. Remove the switch or switches.
7. Installation is the reverse of removal.

Front Wiper/Washer Switch Test

1. Perform Steps 1-5 of *Removal/Installation* as described in this chapter.
2. Check the continuity between the switch terminals as shown in **Figure 50** with an ohmmeter. Move the switch lever while taking each reading.
3. If the switch does not show continuity as indicated in **Figure 50** or if there is poor continuity in any switch position, replace the switch.

Rear Wiper/Washer Switch Test

The rear wiper/washer switch is a 2-position rocker switch. It should show continuity in one position and no continuity in the other position. The washer function is tested by pushing and holding the bottom of the rocker switch to the overtravel position. There should be continuity in this position and no continuity in any other position.

COOLANT TEMPERATURE SWITCH

Vehicles with a standard cluster use a temperature warning lamp in the instrument panel. Those equipped with the optional electronic display cluster use an LCD display. Both types are controlled by a thermal switch which senses coolant temperature.

The switch is mounted in the rear of the engine block on I4 models (**Figure 51**), in the water outlet housing on 2.8L V6 engines (**Figure 52**) or at the front of the intake manifold on 3.0L V6 engines.

Testing

1. Disconnect the water temperature switch lead and ground it to the block with a jumper wire.

8

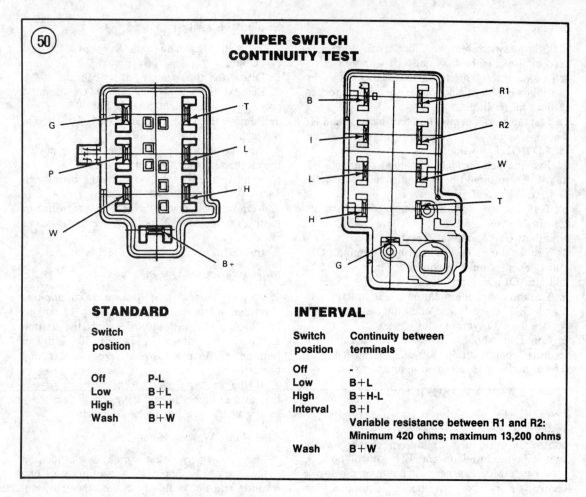

(50)

WIPER SWITCH CONTINUITY TEST

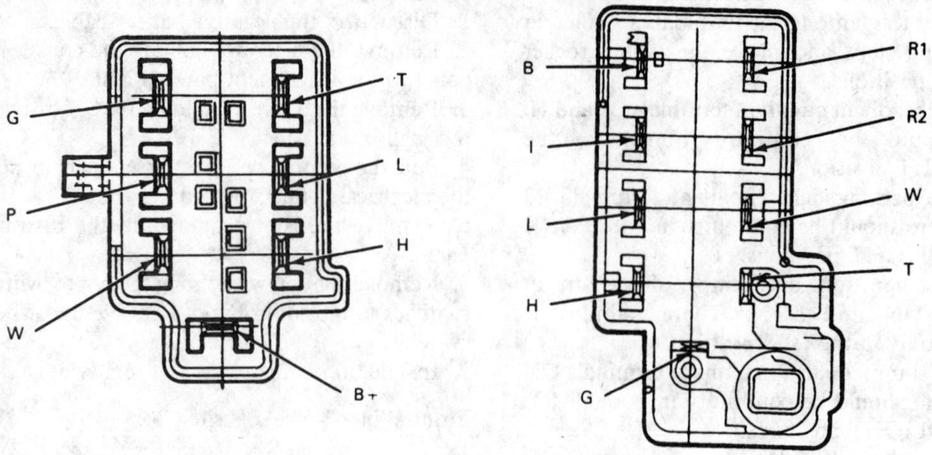

STANDARD

Switch position	
Off	P-L
Low	B+L
High	B+H
Wash	B+W

INTERVAL

Switch position	Continuity between terminals
Off	-
Low	B+L
High	B+H-L
Interval	B+I Variable resistance between R1 and R2: Minimum 420 ohms; maximum 13,200 ohms
Wash	B+W

(51)

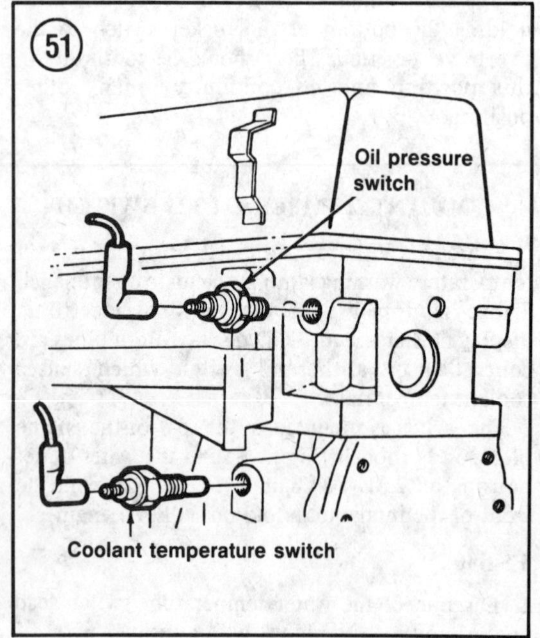

(52)

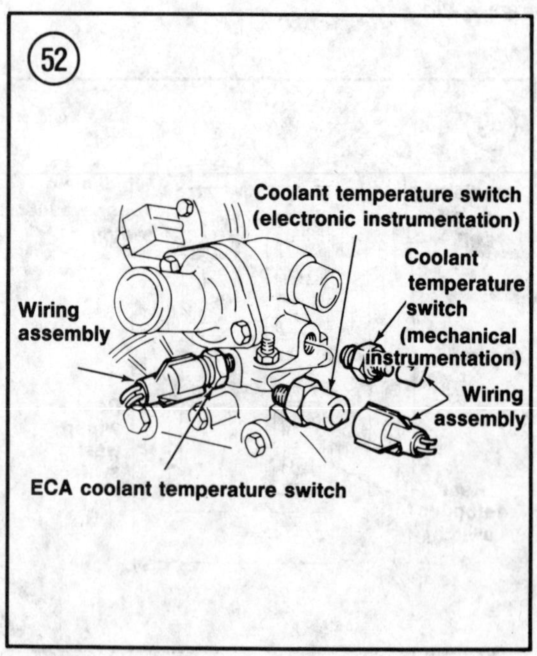

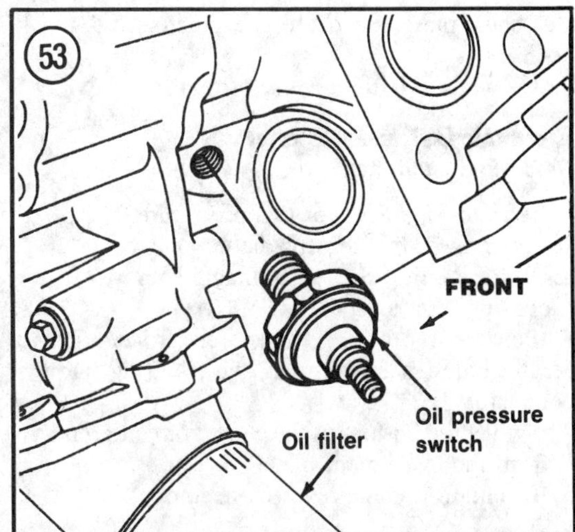

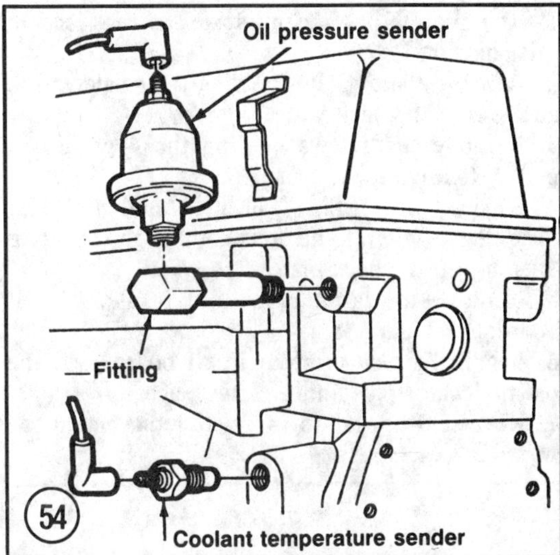

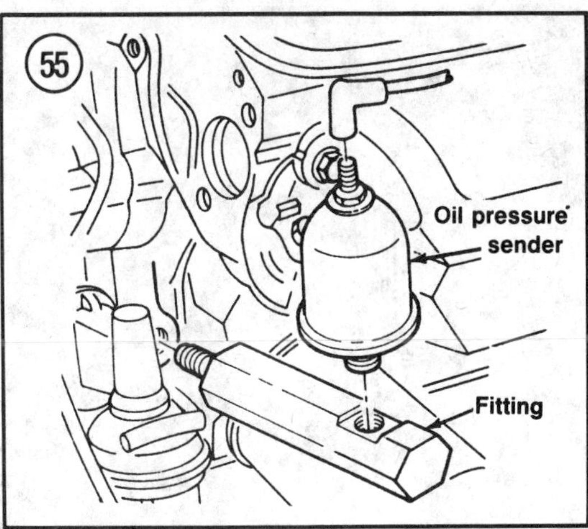

2. Turn the ignition switch to the RUN position. If the warning lamp or display does not come on, check for an open circuit in the wire between the ignition and temperature switches. Repair or replace as required.
3. If the lamp or display comes on in Step 2, check for an open circuit in the wire between the lamp or display unit and the ignition switch. Repair or replace as required.

Replacement

1. Remove the radiator cap to relieve any pressure in the cooling system. Partially drain the cooling system below the level of the cylinder head(s). See Chapter Seven.
2. Unplug the electrical lead at the switch. Remove the switch with a suitable open-end wrench.
3. Wrap a piece of Teflon tape around the threads of the new switch. Teflon paste or other electrically conductive water-resistant sealers can also be used.
4. Install and tighten the new switch to 8-18 ft.-lb. (11-24 N•m).
5. Reconnect the electrical lead to the switch terminal.
6. Refill the cooling system to the proper level. See Chapter Seven.
7. Start the engine. Check the switch operation. Check for leaks.

8

OIL PRESSURE SWITCH/SENDING UNIT

A single terminal switch is used on engines with an oil pressure indicator light. See **Figure 51** (I4) or **Figure 53** (all V6) for typical location.

Vehicles equipped with an oil pressure gauge or electronic display use a variable resistance sender. See **Figure 54** (I4) or **Figure 55** (all V6) for typical location.

Testing

The oil pressure sending unit fitted to engines with an oil pressure gauge or electronic display requires special equipment not commonly available to the home mechanic. Have the sending unit on such vehicles tested by a dealer.

To test the switch used on engines with an indicator light, turn the ignition switch ON but do not start the engine. The indicator light should come on. If it does not, disconnect the wire at the switch terminal and ground it with a jumper lead. If the indicator light comes on, replace the switch. If the light does not come on, check for a burned-out indicator bulb or an open circuit between the bulb and switch.

INSTRUMENTS

Two types of instrument clusters are used in Aerostar models. The conventional cluster with electromagnetic gauges uses a printed circuit board to supply current to the gauges and lamps. This is made of copper foil bonded to a polyester base such as Mylar. There is no approved procedure for in-vehicle testing of the printed circuit. Using a probe may pierce the printed circuit or burn the copper conductor. If no damage seems apparent, check each circuit with a test light or ohmmeter. If an open or short circuit is found, replace the printed circuit board. Instrument cluster bulbs can be replaced by removing the cluster assembly.

The electronic cluster contains 2 modules that provide the LCD displays. This cluster is serviced by module replacement and the owner/mechanic should not attempt to test the modules.

Conventional Instrument Cluster Removal/Installation

Refer to **Figure 56** for this procedure.

1. Disconnect the negative battery cable.
2. Remove the 7 screws holding the cluster housing to the panel. Remove the cluster housing.
3. Remove the 4 screws holding the cluster to the panel.
4. Pull the cluster out far enough to unplug the 2 wiring harness connectors from the back plate.
5. Disconnect the speedometer cable.
6. If access is required to the instruments, remove the 5 screws holding the cluster mask and lens to the back plate. Separate the cluster and mask assembly.
7. Installation is the reverse of removal.

Electronic Instrument Cluster Removal/Installation

Refer to **Figure 57** for this procedure.

1. Disconnect the negative battery cable.
2. Remove the cluster binnacle and 4 cluster mounting screws.
3. Pull the top of the cluster forward enough to reach behind it and unplug the 3 wiring harness connectors.
4. Swivel the bottom of the cluster out and remove it from the instrument panel.
5. Installation is the reverse of removal.

Printed Circuit Board Replacement (Conventional Cluster)

1. Remove the instrument cluster as described in this chapter.
2. Remove the 5 screws holding the cluster mask and lens to the back plate.
3. Remove the screws holding the 4 gauges in place. Remove the gauges.
4. Squeeze each of the 9 gauge terminal clips with needlenose pliers and push through the clip openings in the back plate.
5. Remove the lamp bulbs and printed circuit board. See **Figure 58**.
6. Install the new printed circuit board over the plastic locator pins and press in place.
7. Reverse Steps 1-5 to complete replacement.

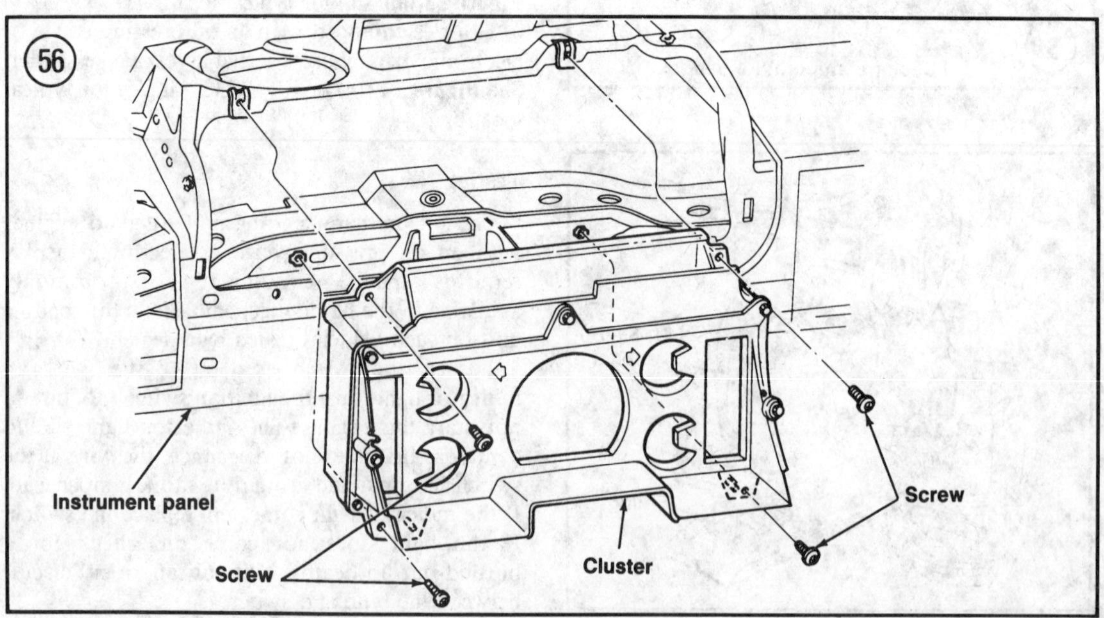

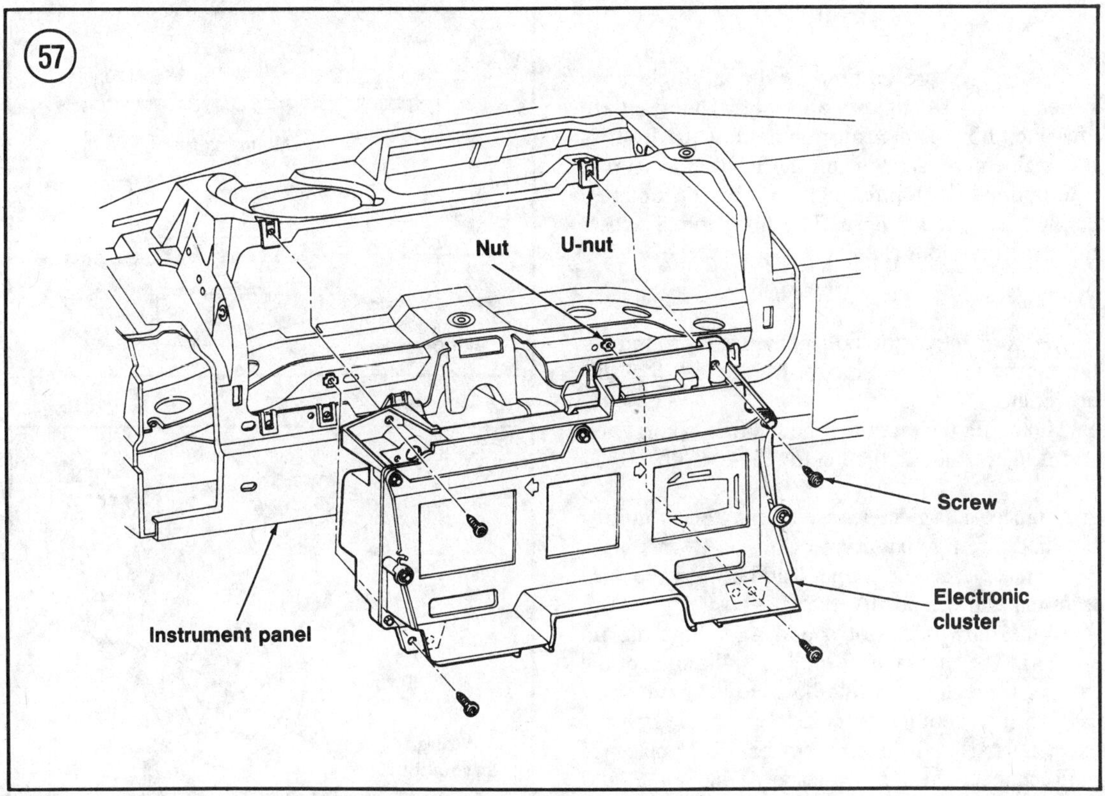

57

Nut
U-nut
Screw
Electronic cluster
Instrument panel

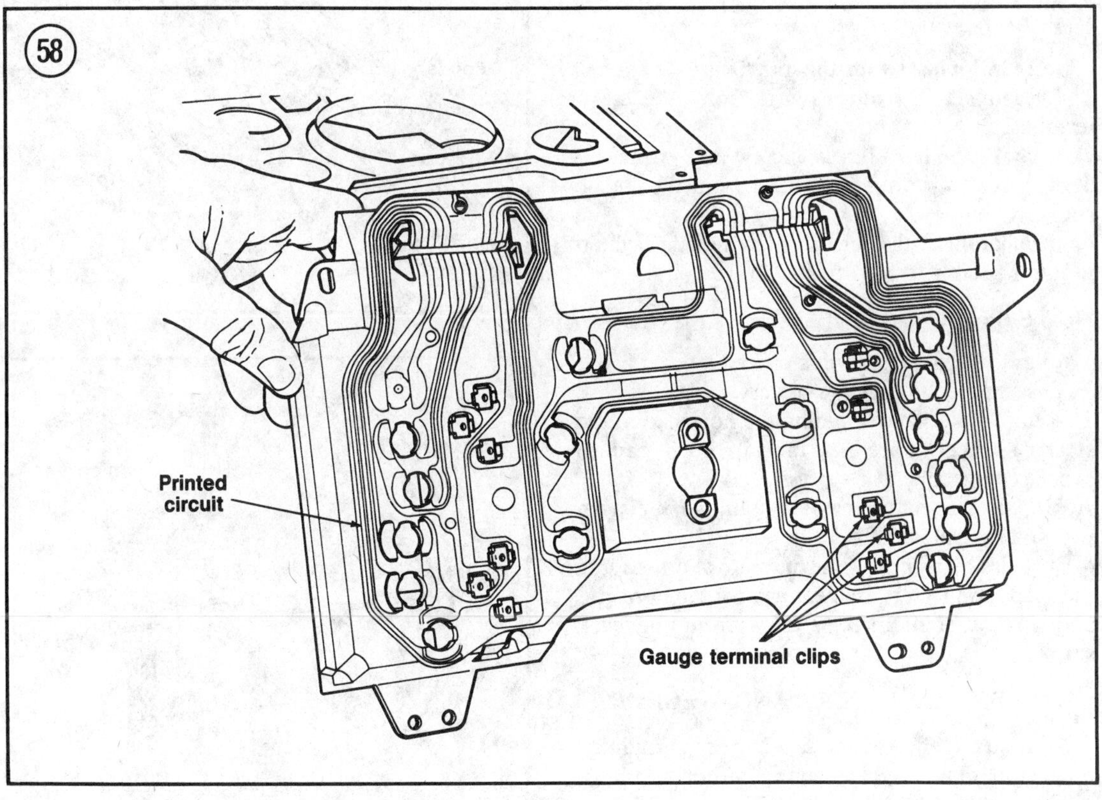

58

Printed circuit
Gauge terminal clips

HORN

All vehicles are equipped with a single horn system. Dual horns are optional. The standard low-pitch horn is bracket-mounted at the front of the engine compartment on the RH fender apron. The optional high-pitch horn is bracket-mounted below the standard horn. The horn switch closes the circuit without using a relay.

Testing

The horn mounting bolt provides a ground for the horn circuit. Refer to **Figure 59** for this procedure.

1. Make sure the mounting bolt is free of corrosion and is tight. If loose, tighten to 7.5-9.0 ft.-lb. (10-12 N•m).
2. Connect a jumper lead between the mounting bolt and negative battery post.
3. Connect a second jumper lead between the horn terminal and the positive battery post.
4. If the horn does not sound and there are no sparks at the battery post in Step 3, disconnect the jumper leads and turn the horn adjustment screw 1/4-3/8 turn counterclockwise. Crimp the housing extrusions around the screw to hold it in place.
5. Reconnect the jumper leads as in Step 2 and Step 3. If the horn does not sound, replace it.

Horn Replacement

Refer to **Figure 60** for this procedure.

1. Disconnect the horn wire from the horn terminal.
2. Remove the horn bracket screw and washer.
3. Remove the horn and bracket from the engine compartment.
4. Installation is the reverse of removal. Tighten mounting screw to 8-11 ft.-lb. (11-16 N•m).

Horn Switch Replacement

Refer to **Figure 61** for this procedure.

1. Disconnect the negative battery cable.
2. Remove the screws holding the horn pad to the steering wheel. Carefully unsnap horn pad to expose connectors.
3. Unplug the connectors and remove the horn pad and switch assembly.
4. Installation is the reverse of removal. Make sure the spade connectors are bent against the horn pad and do not point directly away from the back surface.

WINDSHIELD WIPERS AND WASHERS

All front wiper systems use a 2-speed permanent magnet, rotary type wiper motor with a

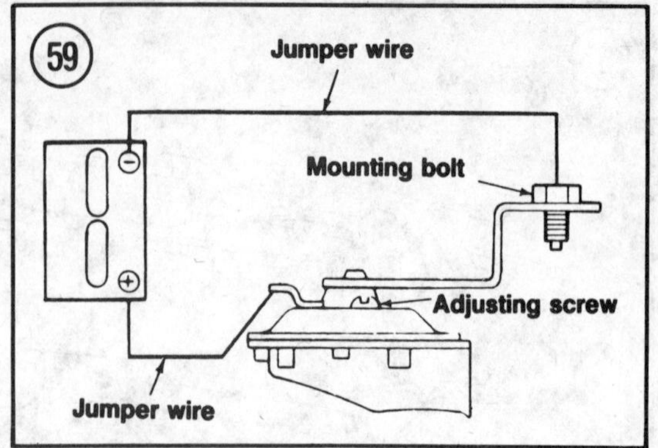

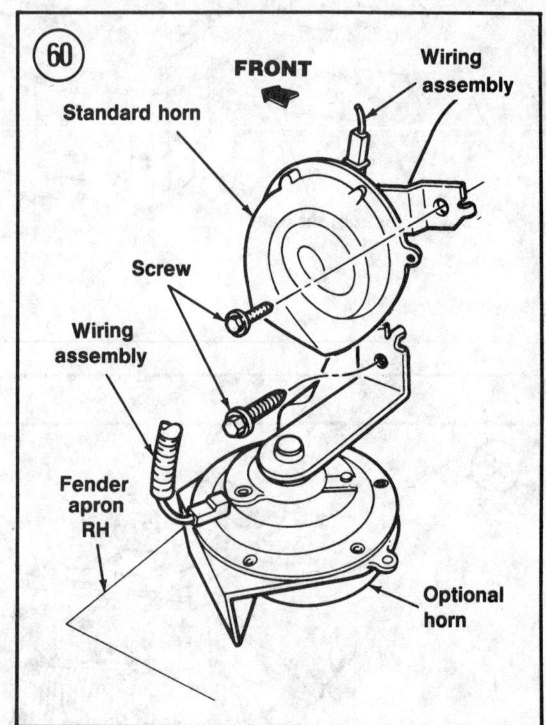

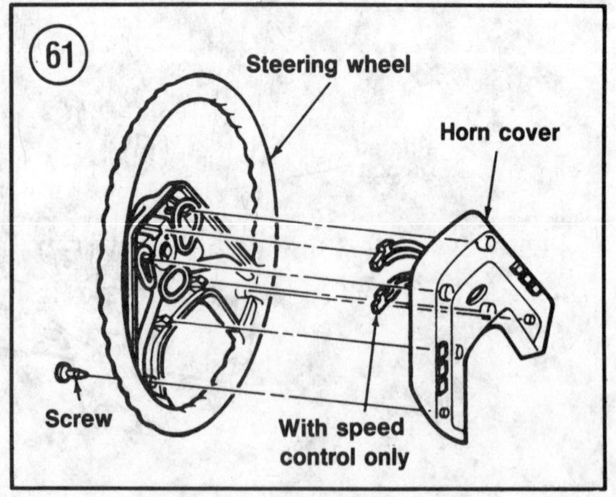

non-depressed park feature. The motor is located underneath the cowl grille. The washer reservoir contains an integral pump and is connected to the washer jets by a rubber hose. The reservoir is mounted either on the radiator support or fender apron and has a projecting neck for filling (**Figure 62**).

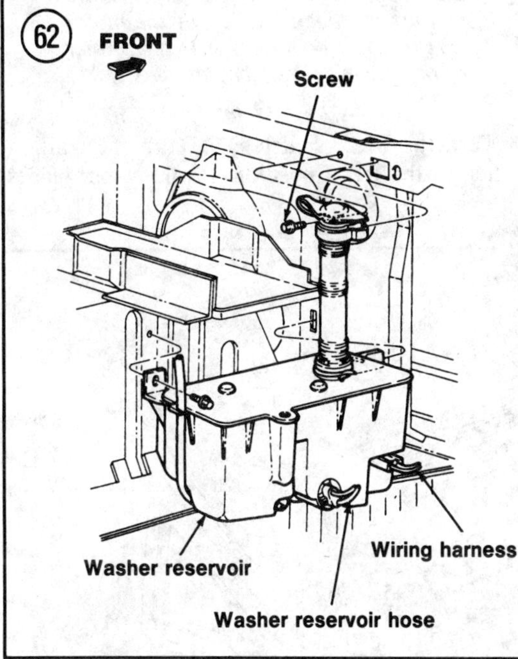

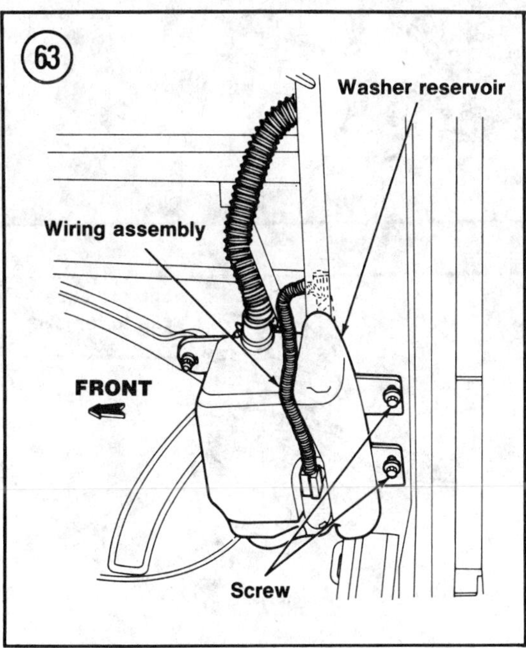

The rear wiper system uses a single speed wiper motor installed inside the liftgate. The rear washer reservoir is installed behind the right rear quarter trim panel (**Figure 63**).

Wiper Troubleshooting

1. If the wipers do not work, replace the 6-ampere circuit breaker in the fuse block cavity with one known to be good. See *Electrical Circuit Protection* in this chapter.
2. If the wipers still do not work with a known-good circuit breaker, connect a jumper lead from the wiper motor housing to the vehicle body and test for ground. Ground is supplied by a ground strap and the attaching screws. Check the screws and strap for a loose connection or corrosion. Clean or tighten as necessary.
3. If the wipers still do not work, check wiper switch continuity as described in this chapter.
4. If switch continuity is good, test the wiper motor current draw.

Front Wiper Motor Current Draw Test

Refer to **Figure 64** for this procedure.

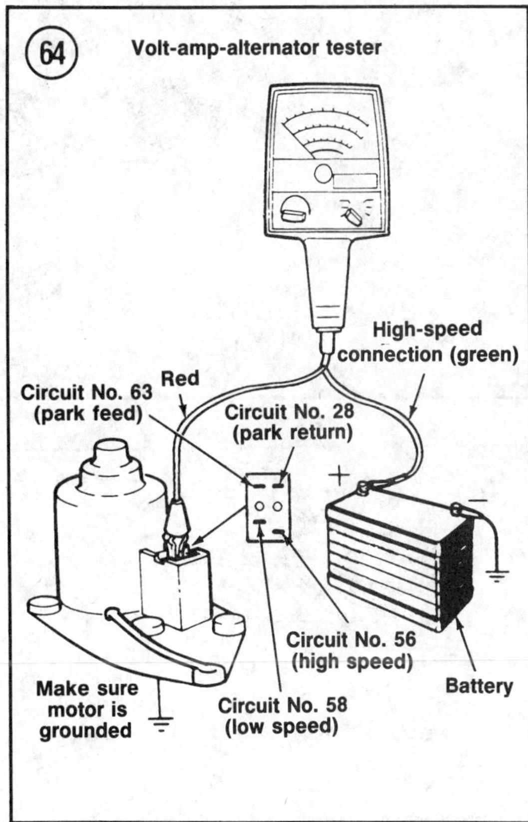

8

1. Disconnect the positive battery cable at the battery.
2. Remove the cowl vent grille (**Figure 65**).
3. Unclip and disconnect the linkage drive arm from the motor crank pin (**Figure 66**).
4. Unplug the electrical connector at the wiper motor.
5. Connect the volt-amp-alternator as shown in **Figure 64**. Alternately probe the low- and high-speed connections in the motor plug with the red test lead. If the current draw exceeds 3 amperes at either connection, replace the motor.

WARNING
To prevent a battery explosion, disconnect the negative cable, then reconnect the positive cable. The negative cable can be reconnected after the positive cable is tightened securely.

6. Remove the test equipment and reconnect all wiring.

Front Wiper Motor Replacement

CAUTION
The wiper motor contains ceramic permanent magnets. Handle the motor carefully and do not tap with a hammer or the magnets may be damaged.

1. Turn the wiper switch ON. Turn the ignition switch to the RUN position. As the wiper blades

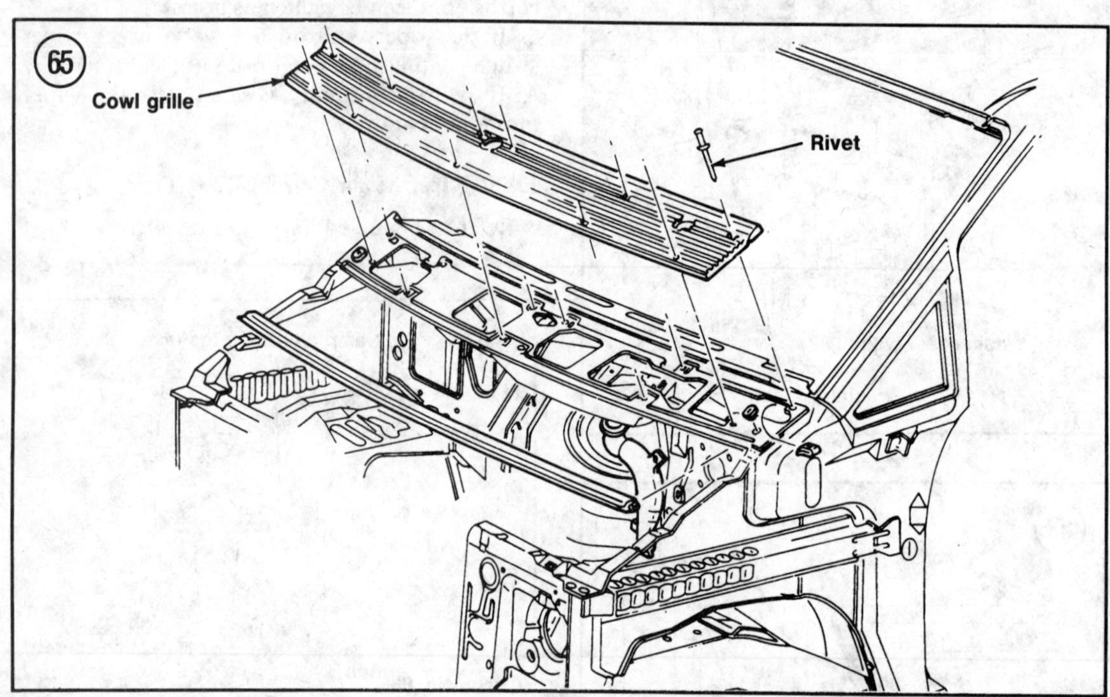

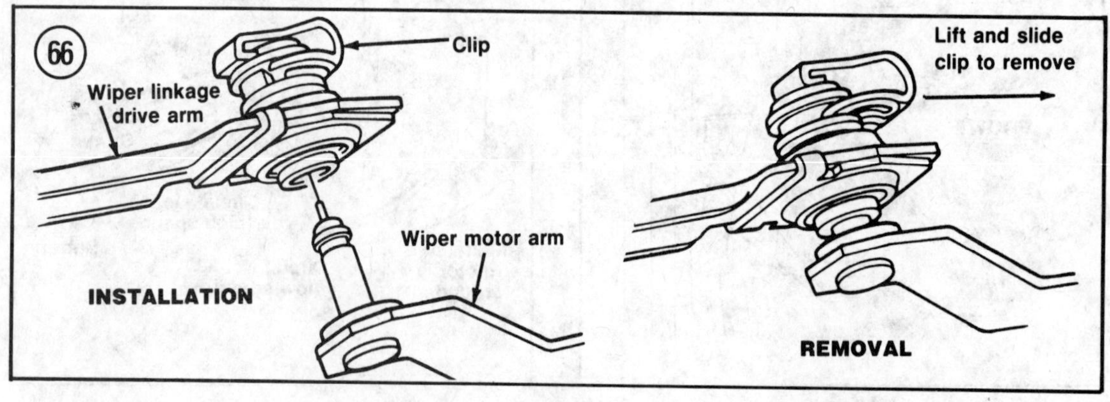

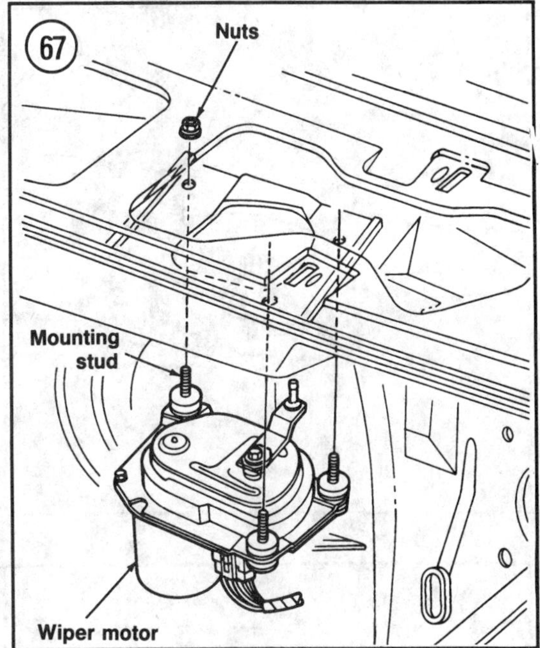

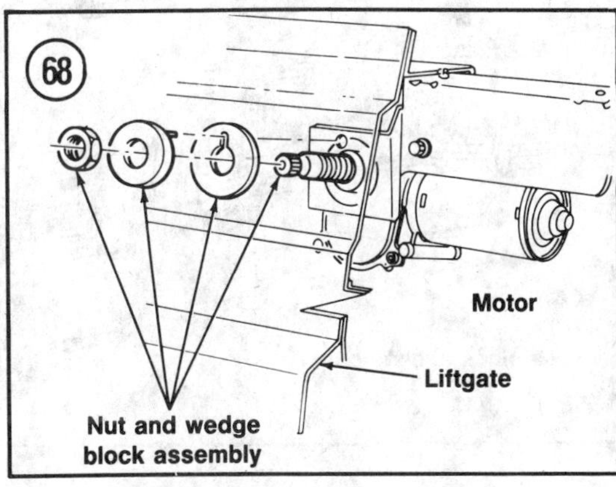

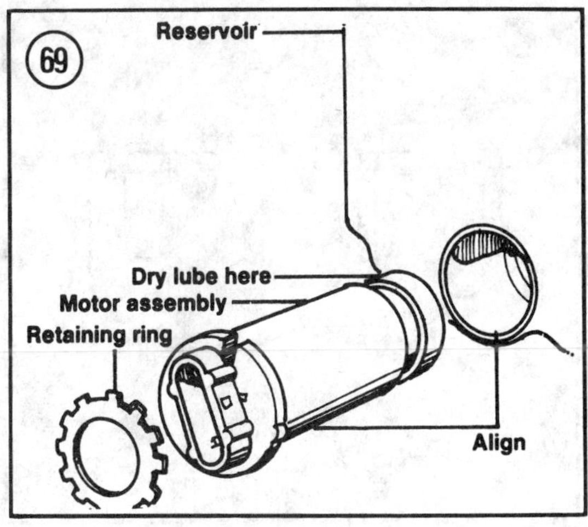

move to the mid-point of their travel, turn the ignition switch OFF.

2. Disconnect the negative battery cable.
3. Remove both wiper arm and blade assemblies.
4. Remove the cowl vent grille, if necessary to provide access.
5. Unclip and disconnect the linkage drive arm from the motor crank pin (**Figure 66**).
6. Unplug the electrical connector at the wiper motor.
7. Remove the 3 motor retaining nuts (**Figure 67**) Remove the motor from the cowl.
8. Installation is the reverse of removal. Tighten the attaching nuts snugly.

Rear Wiper Motor Replacement

1. Disconnect the negative battery cable.
2. Remove the wiper arm and blade assembly.
3. Remove the nut and wedge block from the motor shaft. See **Figure 68**.
4. Remove the liftgate trim panel.
5. Unplug the electrical connector at the motor.
6. Remove the fasteners holding the motor in place. Remove the motor.
7. Installation is the reverse of removal. Tighten the motor shaft nut to 5.0-5.8 ft.-lb. (6.8-7.9 N•m).

8

Washer Reservoir Replacement

The front washer reservoir is located under the battery tray. While it can be removed from underneath the vehicle, it is just as easy and much faster to remove the battery and battery tray, which is a good excuse to service the battery and tray as described in this chapter.

To remove the front washer reservoir, refer to **Figure 62**, and disconnect the fluid hoses and lock-tab wire connector. Remove the retaining screws and lower or lift the assembly from the engine compartment. Installation is the reverse of removal.

The rear washer reservoir is located behind the right rear quarter trim panel (**Figure 63**). After trim panel removal, disconnect the fluid hose and unplug the electrical connector.Remove the screws holding the reservoir to the quarter panel and floor, then remove the reservoir from the vehicle. Installation is the reverse of removal.

Washer Motor, Seal and ImpellerRemoval/Installation

1. Remove the washer reservoir as described in this chapter.
2. Pry out the retaining ring with a small flat-blade screwdriver (**Figure 69**).

3. Remove the motor, seal and impeller assembly by pulling it out with a pair of pliers (**Figure 70**).
4. Clean the inside of the reservoir thoroughly before installing a new motor assembly.
5. Lubricate the outer diameter of the seal with powdered graphite.
6. Align the motor end cap projection with the reservoir slot and press the assembly inward until the seal seats against the bottom of the motor cavity.
7. Hand press the retaining ring in place with a 12-point, 1-inch socket.
8. Install the reservoir assembly as described in this chapter. Fill with fluid and check operation. Check for leaks.

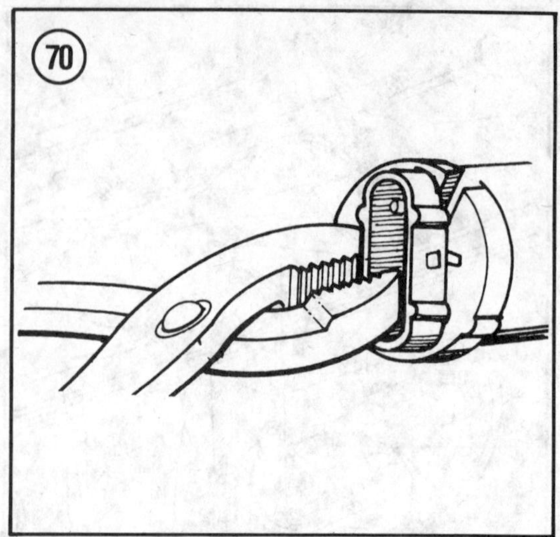

ELECTRICAL CIRCUIT PROTECTION

Electrical circuits are protected by a variety of devices: fuses, circuit breakers and fusible links.

Fuses

A fuse is a "safety valve" installed in an electrical circuit which "blows" (opens) the circuit when excessive current flows through the circuit. This protects the circuit and electrical components such as the alternator from damage.

The fuse block is located behind an access cover on the lower left edge of the instrument panel to the left of the steering column (**Figure 71**). Fuse and circuit breaker identification is provided on the fuse block.

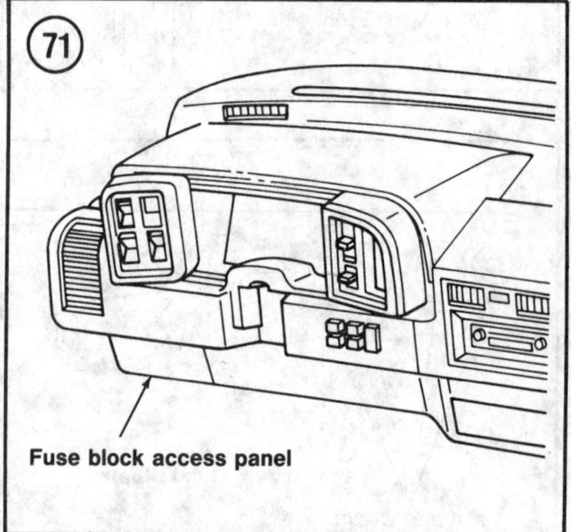

All models use mini-fuses. The mini-fuse is a flat design with 2 blades connected by a metal link encapsulated in plastic. When the fuse is installed, the end of each metal blade is exposed, allowing the fuse condition to be checked with test probes. The plastic is color-coded according to amperage value. Some colors make it difficult to determine whether the fuse is good or bad. **Figure 72** shows the difference between a good and a blown mini-fuse. Fuse and circuit breaker identifications for all models are shown in **Figure 73**.

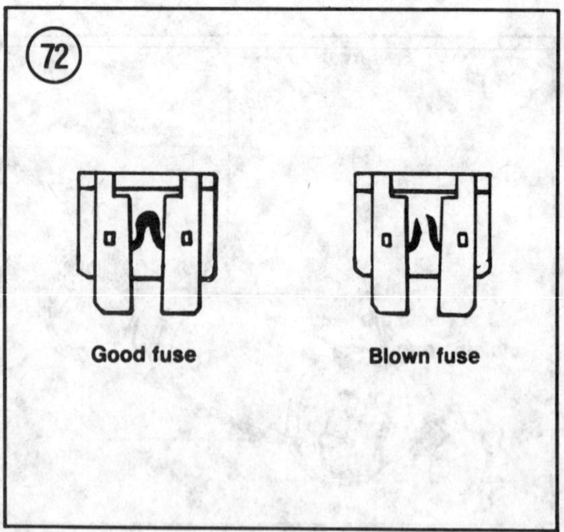

Whenever a failure occurs in any part of the electrical system, always check the fuse first to see if it is blown. Usually, the trouble is a short circuit in the wiring. This may be caused by worn-through insulation or by a wire that has worked its way loose and shorted to ground. Occasionally, the electrical overload which causes a fuse to blow may occur in a switch or motor.

A blown fuse should be treated as more than a minor annoyance; it should serve as a warning that something is wrong in the electrical system. Before replacing a fuse, determine what caused it to blow and correct the problem. Always carry several

FUSE PANEL

Position	Description	Color	Circuit Protected
1	15 Amp. Fuse	Light Blue	Stop Lamps, Emergency Warning Flasher
2	6 Amp. C.B.		Front Wiper/Washer
3	15 Amp. Fuse	Light Blue	Rear Lamps, Park Lamps, Marker Lamps, License Lamps, Trailer Lamps Relay
4	15 Amp. Fuse	Light Blue	Turn Signal Flasher, Back-Up Lamps, Illuminated Visor Vanity, Trailer Tow Turn Signal Relay, Illuminated Entry Module, Electronic Day/Night Mirror
5	20 Amp. Fuse	Yellow	Speed Control, Rear Wiper/Washer/Defrost, Washer Fluid Sensor, Warning Chime
6	Not Used		
7	15 Amp. Fuse	Light Blue	Courtesy Lamps, Dome Lamp, Glove Box Lamp, Radio Memory, Cargo Lamp, Trip Computer, Headlamps On Indicator, Footwell Lamp, Reading Lamps
8	30 Amp. Fuse	Light Green	Heater and A/C Motor Blower, Air Conditioning Clutch
9	20 Amp. Fuse	Yellow	Flash to Pass
10	15 Amp. Fuse	Light Blue	Radio/Tape Player, Amplifier
11	20 Amp. Fuse	—	Rear Cigar Lighter, Less Power Door Locks
	30 Amp. C.B.		Rear Cigar Lighter, Power Door Locks
12	5 Amp. Fuse	Tan	Automatic Transmission Floor Shift Illumination, Instrument Panel Illumination Lamps
13	20 Amp. C.B.		Power Windows
14	Not Used		
15	20 Amp. Fuse	Yellow	Front Cigar Lighter, Horns
16	10 Amp. Fuse	Red	Instrument Cluster, Speedometer, Electronic Cluster Day Illumination
17	10 Amp. Fuse	Red	Warning Lamps, Seat Belt Buzzer, Carburetor Circuits, Low Fuel Warning, Door Ajar

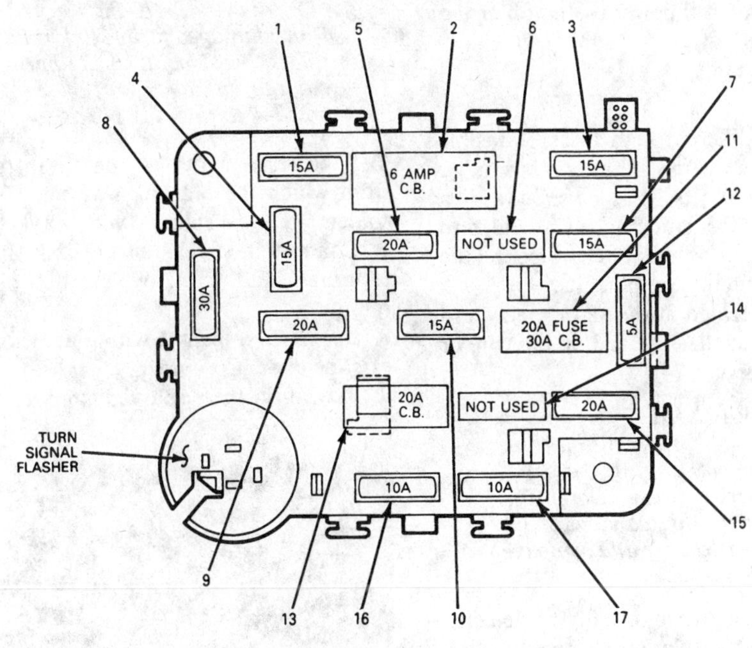

spare fuses of the proper amperage values in the glovebox. Never replace a fuse with one of higher amperage rating than that specified for use. Failure to follow these basic rules could result in heat or fire damage to major parts or loss of the entire vehicle.

Fuse Replacement

To replace a mini-fuse, grasp the plastic covered top and pull the fuse from the fuse block. Insert a new one of the same amperage value (color) in its place.

Circuit Breakers

Some circuits are protected by circuit breakers. These may be mounted in the fuse block, installed in the circuit itself or located within the switch assembly. A circuit breaker conducts current through an arm made of 2 different types of metal connected together. If too much current passes through this bimetal arm, it heats up and expands. One metal expands faster than the other, causing the arm to move and open the contacts to break the current flow. As the arm cools down, the metal contracts and the arm closes the contacts, allowing current to pass. Cycling inline circuit breakers will repeat this sequence as long as power is applied or until the condition is corrected. Non-cycling circuit breakers use a coil around the bimetal arm to hold it in an open position until power is shut off or the condition is corrected.

Fusible Links

Fusible links are different than fuses. A fusible link is a short length of wire several gauges smaller than the circuit it protects. It is covered with a thick non-flammable insulation and is intended to burn out if an overload occurs, thus protecting the wiring harness and circuit components.

Fusible links are located at the starter relay and can be identified by the flag molded on the wire or terminal insulator (**Figure 74**).

WARNING
Always replace a burned fusible link with a replacement bearing the same color code or wire gauge. Never use ordinary wire, as this can cause an overload, an electrical fire and complete loss of the vehicle.

Burned-out fusible links can usually be detected by melted or burned insulation. When the link appears to be good but the starter does not work, check the circuit for continuity with an ohmmeter or self-powered test lamp.

Fusible Link Replacement

Factory-installed fusible links are color-coded according to the link rating and have a molded flag at one end for easy identification. Service or replacement links are either black or green depending upon usage. Refer to **Figure 75** for this procedure.

1. Obtain the proper service fusible link. Make sure the replacement link is a duplicate of the one removed in terms of wire gauge, length and insulation. Do not substitute any other type or gauge of wire.
2. Disconnect the negative battery cable.
3. Disconnect the damaged fusible link and/or eyelet terminal from the component to which it is attached.

NOTE
Production fusible links have an eyelet terminal for a 5/16 in. stud on one end. When the terminal is not required, cut the fusible link off as close to the terminal as possible, then strip 1/8 in. of insulation from the cut end.

4. Cut the fusible link and the splice(s) from the wire(s) to which it will be connected.
5. Disconnect the feed part of the wiring and cut out the damaged portion as close as possible behind the splice in the harness.

NOTE
If the damaged fusible link is between 2 splices (weld point in the harness), cut out the damaged portion as close as possible to the weld points.

6. Splice and solder the new link to the wire(s) from which the old link was cut. Use rosin core solder. Wrap the splice(s) with vinyl electrical tape.
7. Connect the eyelet of the link (if any) to the terminal stud from which the old link was removed.
8. Install the repaired wiring as before, using the existing clips if provided.
9. Reconnect the negative battery cable.

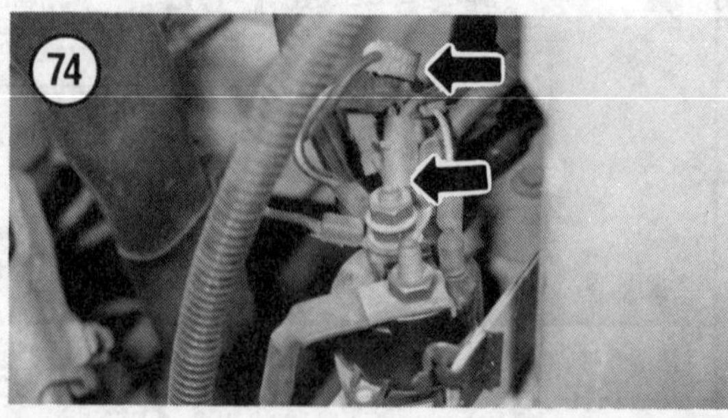
74

TURN SIGNALS

The turn signal flasher is located in the fuse block.

Testing

1. *One side flashes later than the other, or only one side operates*—Check for a burned-out bulb. Clean socket of any corrosion. Check for a badly grounded bulb. Check for breaks in the wiring.

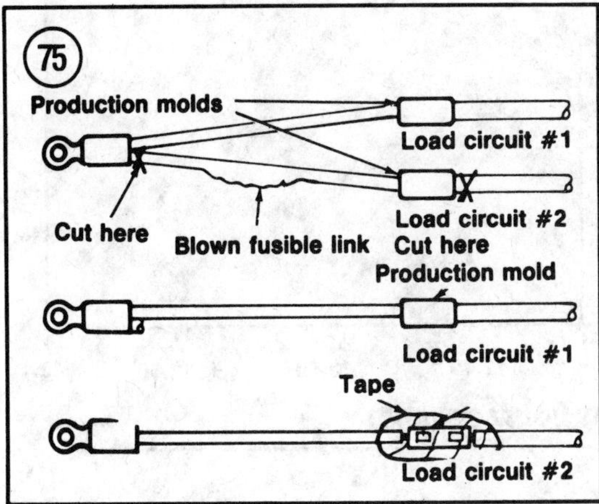

2. *Turn signals do not work at all*—Check the fuse in fuse block cavity 4 by operating the back-up lights. If the fuse is good, check the wiring for a break or poor connection. If the wiring is good, install a new turn signal flasher unit.
3. *Lights flash slowly or stay on*—Make sure the battery is fully charged. Check the fuse in fuse block cavity 4 for a poor contact. Check for a break or poor connection in the wiring. If none of these problems are found, replace the turn signal flasher.
4. *Lights flash too quickly*—Check for a burned-out bulb or disconnected wire. If none are found, replace the turn signal flasher.

HAZARD FLASHER

The hazard flasher is identical in appearance to the turn signal flasher. It is located in on the rear side of the fuse block.

Testing

1. Check the fuse in fuse block cavity 1 by operating the stop lights.
2. If the fuse is good and the turn signals operate on both sides, replace the hazard flasher.

8

Tables are on the following page.

Table 1 OPEN CIRCUIT VOLTAGE (STATE OF CHARGE)

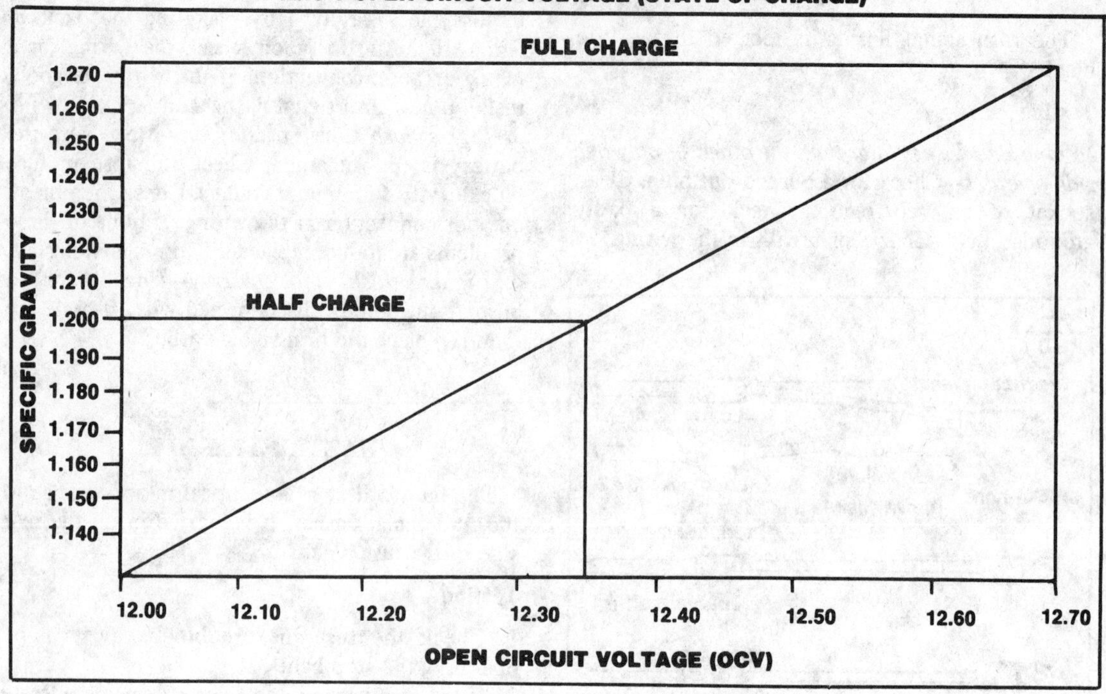

Table 2 BATTERY CHARGE PERCENTAGE

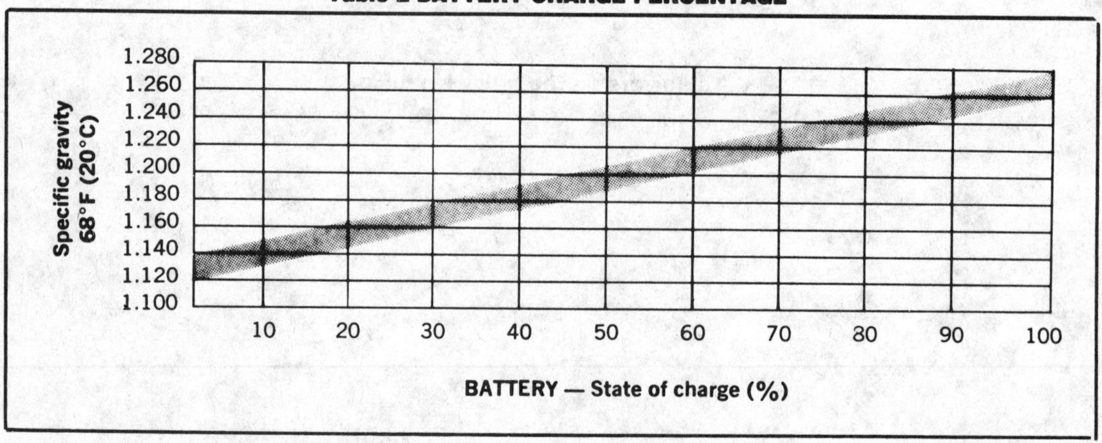

CHAPTER NINE

CLUTCH AND TRANSMISSION

A 5-speed Toyo Kogyo overdrive manual transmission (manufactured by Mazda) is the standard Aerostar transmission. A 4-speed automatic overdrive transmission is optional.

Power is transmitted from the engine to the transmission, then to the differential or rear end where it is sent to the axle shafts which turn the wheel hubs. Manual transmissions are connected to the engine by a hydraulic clutch; automatic transmissions are connected to the engine by a torque converter.

This chapter provides inspection, linkage adjustment, removal and installation procedures for the clutch, manual transmission and automatic transmission.

Transmission repair requires special skills and tools and should be left to a dealer or other qualified shop. The inspection procedures will tell you if professional service is necessary. **Table 1** is at the end of the chapter.

CLUTCH

Components

A hydraulic clutch system is used on all manual transmission models. The major components of the clutch system are the flywheel, clutch disc, clutch pressure plate/cover assembly, and clutch release or throwout bearing. The 1986-1987 system is shown in **Figure 1** (2.3L), **Figure 2** (2.8L V6) and **Figure 3** (3.0L V6). The 1988-on system is shown in **Figure 4**. The clutch operating system consists of the pedal/bracket assembly, fluid reservoir, master cylinder, slave cylinder and connecting tubing. See **Figure 5** (1986-1987) or **Figure 6** (1988-on).

The master cylinder changes mechanical movement of the clutch pedal into hydraulic fluid pressure. The slave cylinder mounted in the bellhousing on the transmission input shaft changes the hydraulic fluid pressure back to mechanical movement to operate the clutch release bearing. The hydraulic clutch system locates the clutch pedal and provides automatic clutch adjustment.

Parts Identification

Some clutch parts have 2 or more names. To prevent confusion, the following list gives part names used in this chapter and common synonyms.

a. Bellhousing—flywheel housing.
b. Clutch disc—driven plate, friction disc.
c. Clutch fork—release fork or arm, throw-out lever or arm, withdrawal lever.
d. Clutch plate—pressure plate, clutch cover.
e. Release bearing—throw-out bearing.

(1)

2.3L CLUTCH COMPONENTS

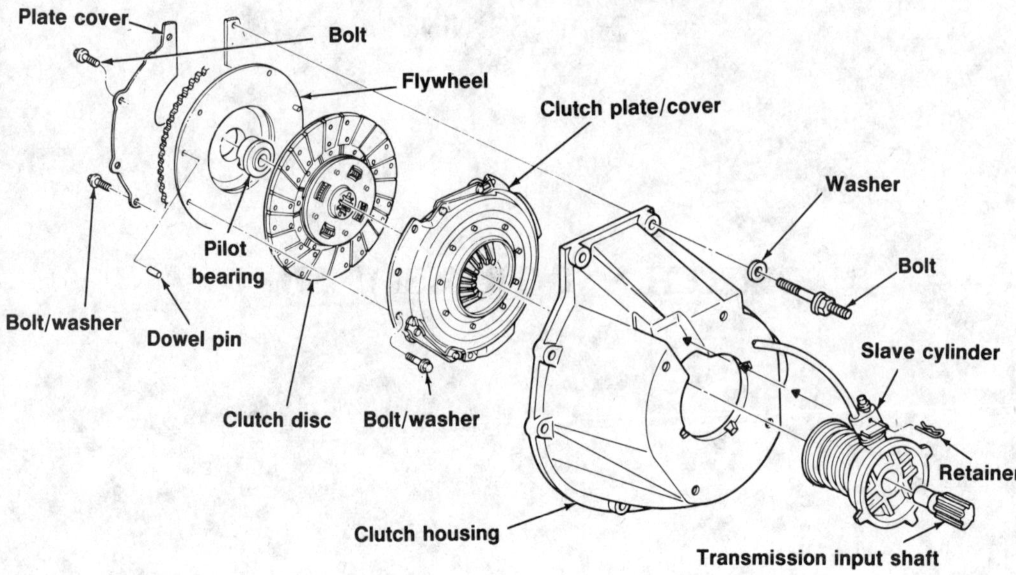

(2)

2.8L V6 CLUTCH COMPONENTS

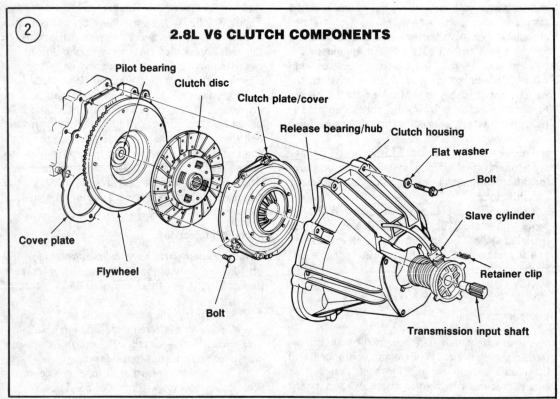

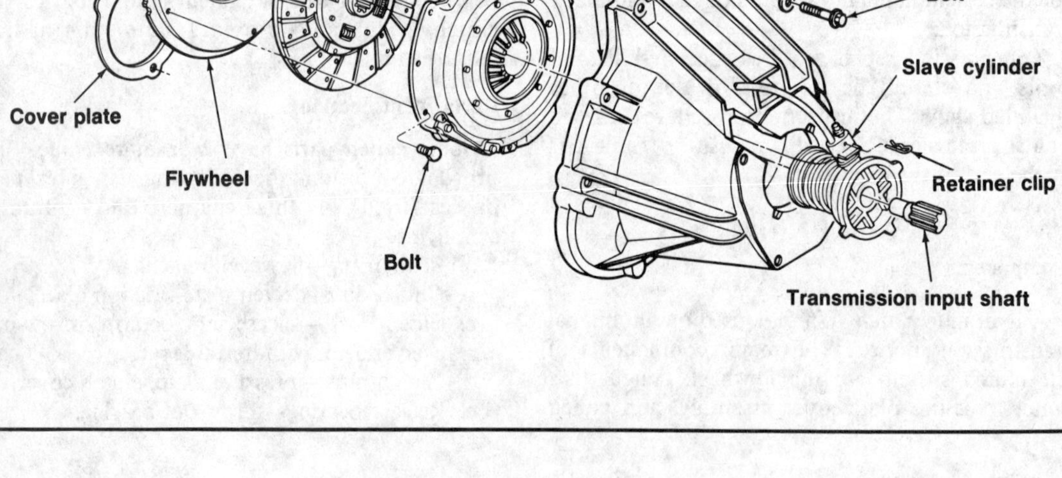

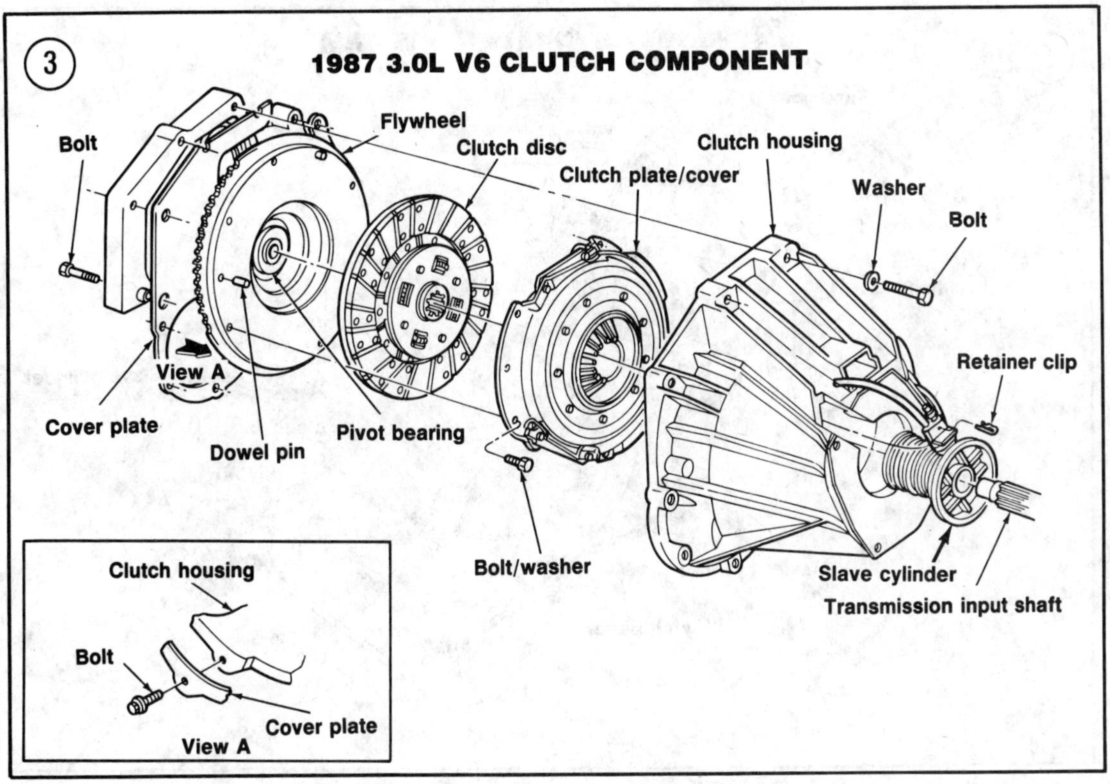

(3) **1987 3.0L V6 CLUTCH COMPONENT**

Flywheel
Bolt
Clutch disc
Clutch housing
Clutch plate/cover
Washer
Bolt
Retainer clip
View A
Cover plate
Pivot bearing
Dowel pin
Bolt/washer
Slave cylinder
Transmission input shaft
Clutch housing
Bolt
Cover plate
View A

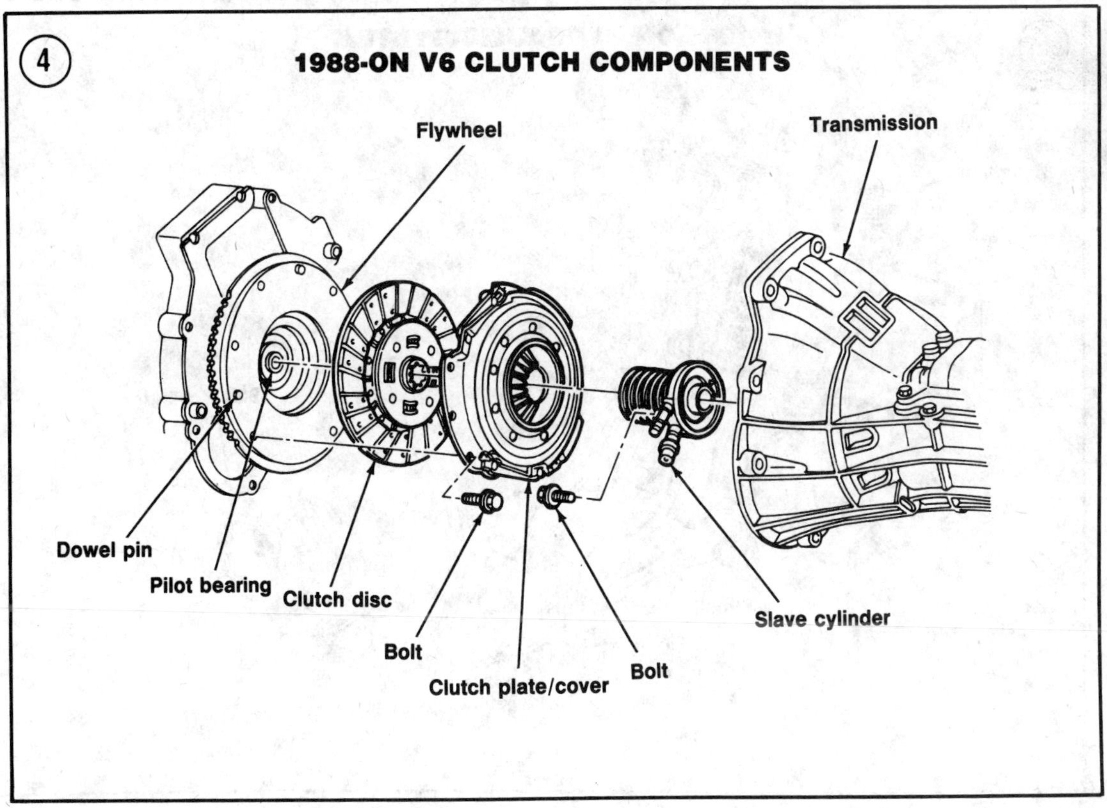

(4) **1988-ON V6 CLUTCH COMPONENTS**

Flywheel
Transmission
Dowel pin
Pilot bearing
Clutch disc
Slave cylinder
Bolt
Bolt
Clutch plate/cover

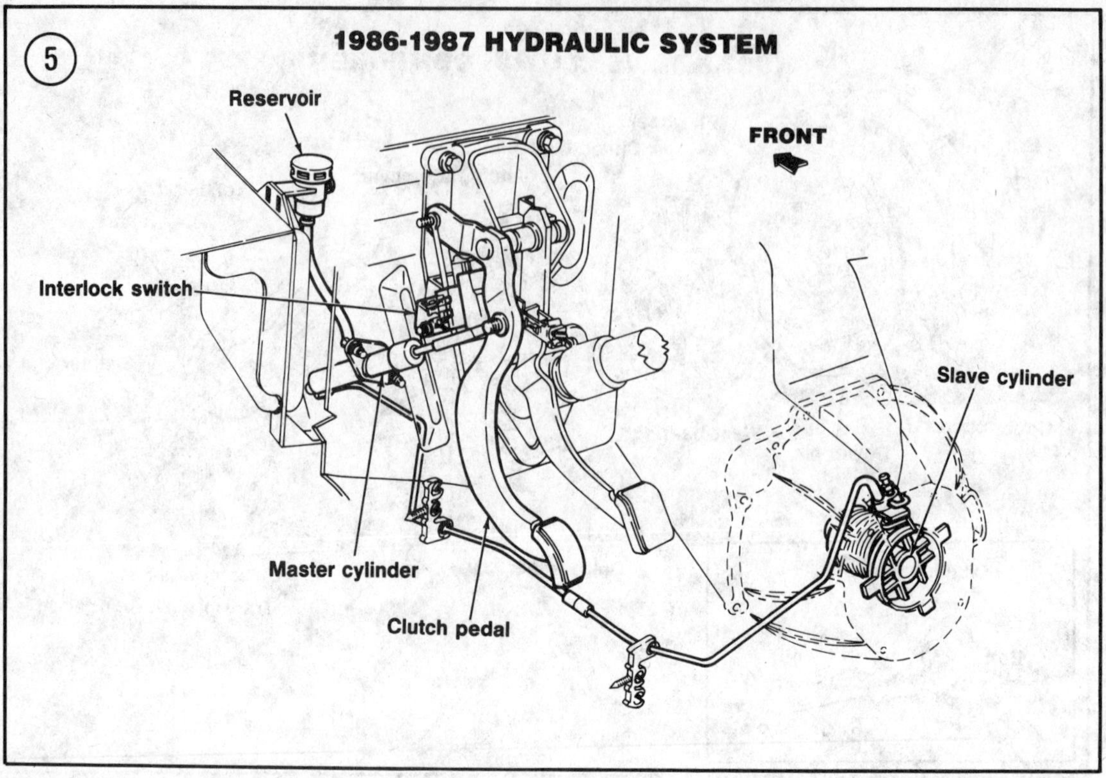

5

1986-1987 HYDRAULIC SYSTEM

Reservoir
FRONT
Interlock switch
Slave cylinder
Master cylinder
Clutch pedal

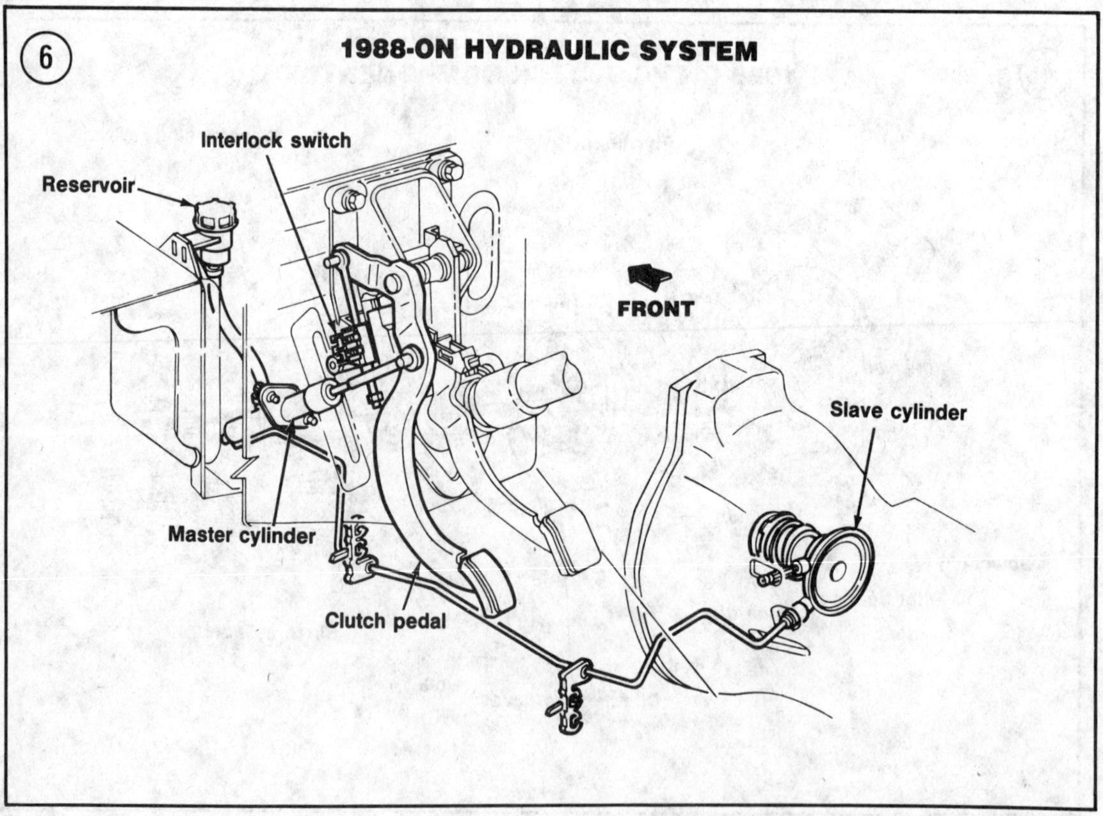

6

1988-ON HYDRAULIC SYSTEM

Interlock switch
Reservoir
FRONT
Slave cylinder
Master cylinder
Clutch pedal

CLUTCH HYDRAULIC SYSTEM (1986-1987)

The hydraulic portion of the clutch system is serviced as 3 complete assemblies (**Figure 5**): the master cylinder reservoir and nylon interconnecting line; the master cylinder and nylon interconnecting line; the slave cylinder and release bearing.

The clutch release bearing can be replaced as required. If the hydraulic system does not operate properly, determine whether the problem is in the master cylinder/reservoir assembly or the slave cylinder/release bearing assembly and replace the defective assembly as a unit.

Master Cylinder Reservoir Removal/Installation

Refer to **Figure 5** for this procedure.

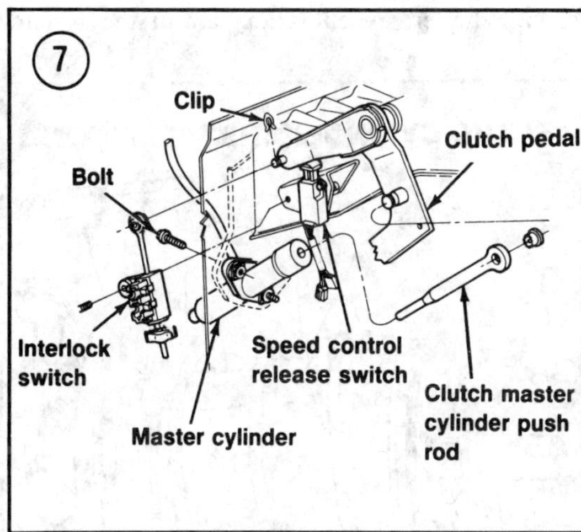

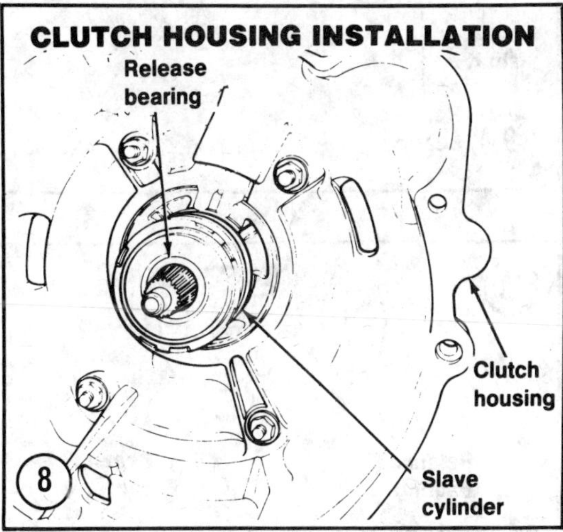

1. Slide the reservoir from its locating slots in the electrical cover box.
2. Disconnect the reservoir line at the master cylinder. Plug the line and cap the master cylinder fitting to prevent leakage and the entry of contamination.
3. Remove the reservoir from the engine compartment.
4. Installation is the reverse of removal. Bleed the hydraulic system as described in this chapter.

Master Cylinder Removal/Installation

Refer to **Figure 5** for this procedure.

1. Working in the cab, remove the retainer bushing holding the master cylinder pushrod to the clutch pedal and disconnect the pushrod from the pedal. See **Figure 7**.
2. Securely block both rear wheels to prevent the vehicle from rolling in either direction.
3. Raise the front of the vehicle with a jack and place it on jackstands.
4. Remove the clip holding the master cylinder line to the slave cylinder at the transmission bellhousing. Remove the line and fitting. Cap the line and bellhousing opening to prevent leakage and the entry of contamination.
5. Disconnect the hydraulic line from the underbody side rail clips.
6. Remove the jackstands and lower the vehicle to the ground.

7A. If the reservoir is to be removed with the master cylinder, slide the reservoir from its locating slots in the electrical cover box.

7B. If the reservoir is not to be removed with the master cylinder, disconnect the reservoir line at the master cylinder. Plug the line and cap the master cylinder fitting to prevent leakage and the entry of contamination.

8. Working in the engine compartment, unbolt and remove the master cylinder assembly (with reservoir, if it is to be removed) and hydraulic line.
9. Installation is the reverse of removal. Tighten master cylinder bolts to 15-20 ft.-lb. (21-27 N•m). Bleed the hydraulic system as described in this chapter.

Slave Cylinder Removal/Installation

Refer to **Figure 5** for this procedure.

1. Remove the transmission as described in this chapter.
2. Remove the nuts holding the clutch housing to the transmission. Remove the clutch housing. See **Figure 8**.

9

3. Remove the slave cylinder from the input shaft. See **Figure 9**.
4. Installation is the reverse of removal. Position the slave cylinder with its tower part facing the transmission and make sure it seats in the clutch housing notches. Bleed the hydraulic system as described in this chapter.

Clutch Release Bearing Replacement

Refer to **Figure 10** for this procedure.

1. Remove the clutch slave cylinder as described in this chapter.
2. Working carefully, bend back each of the 4 plastic retainers on the bearing carrier enough to remove the release bearing from the carrier.
3. Before reinstalling the bearing, use Ford Multi-purpose Long-life Lubricant (part No. C1AZ-19590-B) and fill the annular groove on the bearing, then wipe a thin coat of lubricant on the inside diameter of the bearing.
4. Align the bearing with the plastic carrier retainers and push the bearing into the carrier.
5. Reinstall the clutch slave cylinder as described in this chapter.

Bleeding the Hydraulic System

After long usage, brake fluid absorbs enough atmospheric moisture to significantly reduce its boiling point and make it prone to vapor lock under certain conditions. While no hard and fast rule exists for changing the fluid in the clutch hydraulic system, it should be checked at least annually by bleeding fluid from the slave cylinder and inspecting it for moisture. If moisture is present, the system should be drained, refilled and bled.

The hydraulic clutch system must also be bled whenever air enters it. This occurs when the clutch hydraulic line has been disconnected, when the fluid level in the master cylinder is low or when the master/slave cylinder is defective. Air in the system will compress, rather than transmit pedal pressure to the clutch operating parts, making shifting of gears very difficult.

This procedure requires handling brake fluid. Be careful not to get any brake fluid on painted surfaces. Two people are needed: one to operate the clutch pedal and the other to open and close the bleed valve.

Periodically check the brake fluid level in the clutch master cylinder during bleeding and top up as required. If the fluid level is allowed to drop too low, air will enter the hydraulic lines and the entire bleeding procedure will have to be repeated.

1. Clean all dirt and grease from the master cylinder reservoir and cap.
2. Remove the cap and diaphragm. Fill the reservoir to the top with DOT 3 brake fluid.
3. Securely block both rear wheels to prevent the vehicle from rolling in either direction.
4. Raise the front of the vehicle with a jack and place it on jackstands.
5. Fit an appropriate box end wrench over the slave cylinder bleed screw and then install a suitable length of transparent hose over the bleed screw to prevent fluid from entering the clutch housing. See **Figure 11**. Transparent hose allows you to see the air bubbles as they exit the bleed screw; if it is not available and regular hose must be used, place the end of the hose into a container of brake fluid and have an assistant watch for the air bubbles.
6. Loosen the slave cylinder bleed screw. Gravity will carry fluid from the master cylinder into the slave cylinder, expelling any air in the system.

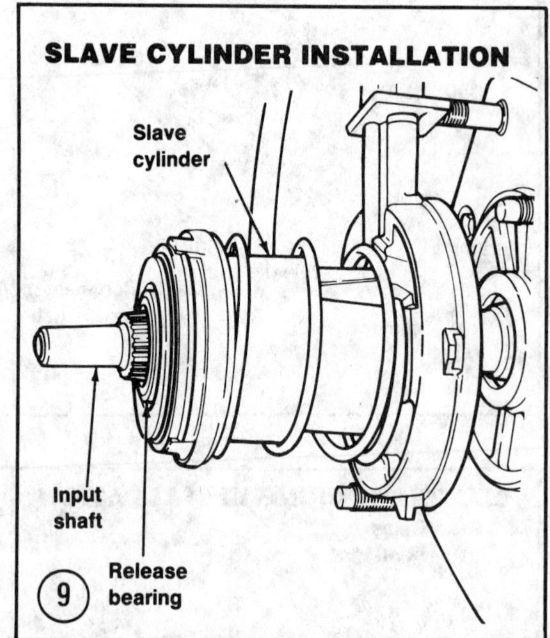

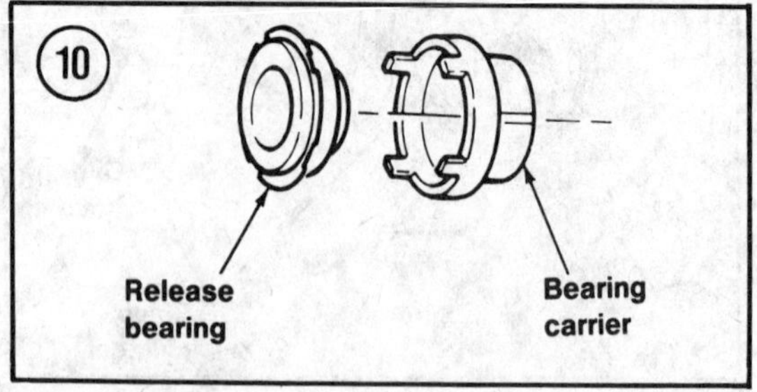

When a steady stream of fluid comes out of the bleed screw without air bubbles, tighten the screw.
7. Top up the reservoir until the fluid is level with the step inside the reservoir, then reinstall the cap and diaphragm.
8. Have an assistant slightly depress the clutch pedal while you crack the bleed screw. The assistant should continue depressing the pedal until it reaches the floorboard. At that time, tighten the bleed screw and then have the assistant remove foot pressure, allowing the pedal to return to normal position.
9. Repeat Step 7 and Step 8 as required until there is no evidence of air remaining in the hydraulic system.
10. When there is no sign of air remaining in the slave cylinder, have the assistant slowly depress the clutch pedal. Rap the side of the line between the slave and master cylinders several times. If there is any air remaining in the line, this will send it to the master cylinder where it will pass into the reservoir.
11. Remove the jackstands and lower the vehicle to the ground. Start the engine, depress the clutch pedal to the floorboard and move the shift lever into Reverse. If you hear a grating of gears at this time, there is still air remaining in the system and it will be necessary to return to Step 7 after raising the vehicle and placing it on jackstands.

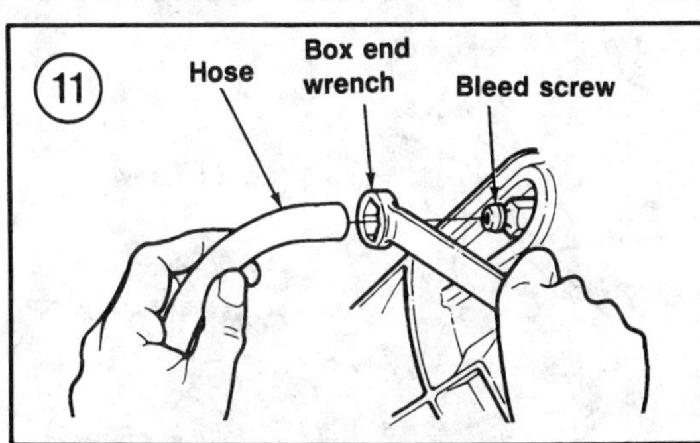

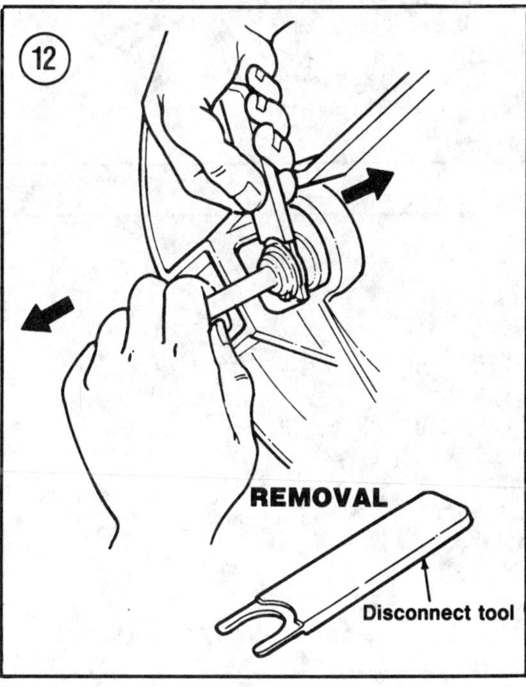

CLUTCH HYDRAULIC SYSTEM (1988-ON)

The hydraulic portion of the clutch system is serviced as 3 complete assemblies (**Figure 6**):
1. The master cylinder reservoir and nylon interconnecting line.
2. The master cylinder and nylon interconnecting line.
3. The slave cylinder and release bearing. The clutch release bearing can be replaced as required.
If the hydraulic system does not operate properly, determine whether the problem is in the master cylinder/reservoir assembly or the slave cylinder/release bearing assembly and replace the defective assembly as a unit.

Master Cylinder Reservoir Removal/Installation

Refer to **Figure 6** for this procedure.
1. Slide the reservoir from its locating slots in the electrical cover box.
2. Disconnect the reservoir line at the master cylinder. Plug the line and cap the master cylinder fitting to prevent leakage and the entry of contamination.
3. Remove the reservoir from the engine compartment.
4. Installation is the reverse of removal. Bleed the hydraulic system as described in this chapter.

Master Cylinder Removal/Installation

Refer to **Figure 6** for this procedure.
1. Working in the cab, remove the retainer bushing holding the master cylinder pushrod to the clutch pedal and disconnect the pushrod from the pedal. See **Figure 7**.
2. Securely block both rear wheels to prevent the vehicle from rolling in either direction.
3. Raise the front of the vehicle with a jack and place it on jackstands.
4. Disconnect the master cylinder line quick-release coupling at the slave cylinder in the transmission bellhousing with tool part No. T88T-70522-A. See **Figure 12**. Cap the line and

bellhousing opening to prevent leakage and the entry of contamination.

5. Disconnect the hydraulic line from the underbody side rail clips.

6. Remove the jackstands and lower the vehicle to the ground.

7A. If the reservoir is to be removed with the master cylinder, slide the reservoir from its locating slots in the electrical cover box.

7B. If the reservoir is not to be removed with the master cylinder, disconnect the reservoir line at the master cylinder. Plug the line and cap the master cylinder fitting to prevent leakage and the entry of contamination.

8. Working in the engine compartment, unbolt and remove the master cylinder assembly (with reservoir, if it is to be removed) and hydraulic line.

9. Installation is the reverse of removal. Tighten master cylinder bolts to 15-20 ft.lb. (21-27 N•m). Bleed the hydraulic system as described in this chapter.

Slave Cylinder Removal/Installation

Refer to **Figure 6** for this procedure.

1. Disconnect the master cylinder line quick-release coupling at the slave cylinder in the transmission bellhousing with tool part No. T88T-70522-A. See **Figure 12**. Cap the line and bellhousing opening to prevent leakage and the entry of contamination.

2. Remove the transmission as described in this chapter.

3. Unbolt the slave cylinder from the transmission bellhousing. See **Figure 13**.

4. Remove the slave cylinder from the input shaft. See **Figure 13**.

5. Installation is the reverse of removal. Position the slave cylinder with its bleed screw and coupling facing the left side of the transmission case. Tighten the mounting bolts to 13-19 ft.-lb. (18-26 N•m). Bleed the hydraulic system as described in this chapter.

Clutch Release Bearing Replacement

Refer to **Figure 14** for this procedure.

1. Remove the transmission as described in this chapter.

2. Rotate the release bearing and carrier assembly until you feel resistance, then continue rotating it until the preload spring pushes the bearing assembly off the slave cylinder.

3. Before reinstalling the bearing, lubricate both the bearing and bearing carrier bore with Ford Multi-purpose Long-life Lubricant (part No. C1AZ-19590-B) or equivalent.

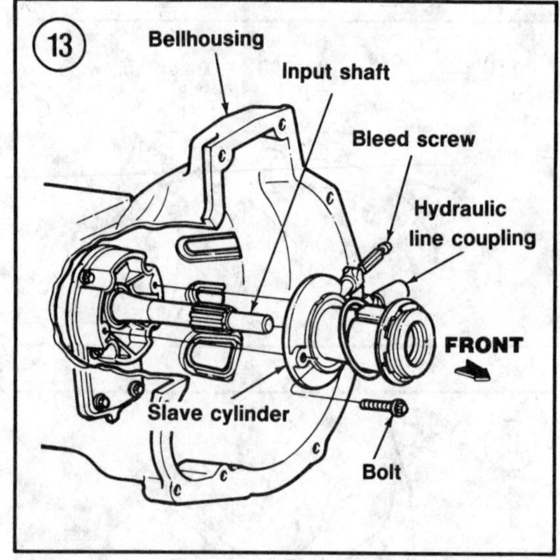

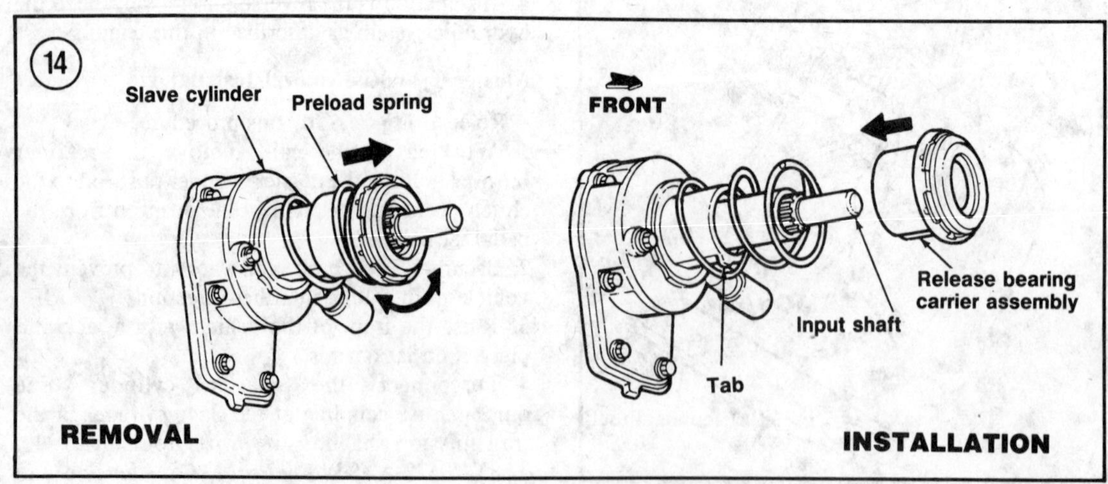

4. Position the bearing over the input shaft and push it into place.
5. Reinstall the transmission as described in this chapter.

Bleeding The Hydraulic System

See *Clutch Hydraulic System (1986-1987)* in this chapter.

CLUTCH

Removal

Refer to **Figures 1-4** as required for this procedure.

1. Working in the cab, remove the retainer bushing holding the master cylinder pushrod to the clutch pedal and disconnect the pushrod from the pedal. See **Figure 7**.

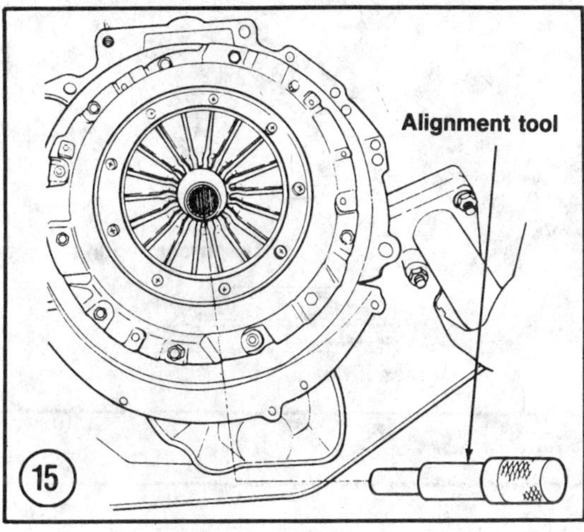

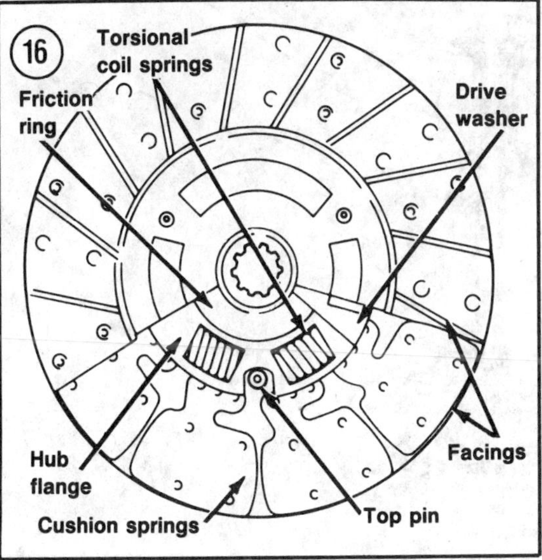

2. Securely block both rear wheels so the vehicle will not roll in either direction.
3. Raise the front of the vehicle with a jack and place it on jackstands.

4A. 1986-1987—Remove the clip holding the master cylinder line to the slave cylinder at the transmission bellhousing. Remove the line and fitting. Cap the line and bellhousing opening to prevent leakage and the entry of contamination.

4B. 1988-on—Disconnect the master cylinder line quick-release coupling at the slave cylinder in the transmission bellhousing with tool part No. T88T-70522-A. See **Figure 12**. Cap the line and bellhousing opening to prevent leakage and the entry of contamination.

5. Remove the starter motor. See Chapter Eight.
6. Support the engine and remove the transmission as described in this chapter.

NOTE

If clutch cover and flywheel are marked with a visible "X," omit Step 7.

7. Make alignment marks on the clutch cover and flywheel for reference during reassembly.
8. Insert alignment tool part No. T74P-7137-K or a suitable dummy shaft through the clutch disc hub. See **Figure 15**.

NOTE

An input shaft from a junk transmission can be used to make a dummy shaft. Inexpensive aligning bars can also be purchased from some auto parts stores. Some tool rental dealers and parts stores rent universal aligning bars which can be adapted.

9. Unbolt the clutch cover from the flywheel. Loosen the bolts in several stages using a diagonal pattern to prevent warping the cover.
10. Remove the pressure plate and disc from the flywheel.

Clutch Disc Inspection

Refer to **Figure 16** for this procedure.

1. Check the clutch disc for the following:
   a. Oil or grease on the facings.
   b. Glazed or warped facings.
   c. Loose or missing rivets.
   d. Facings worn to within 1/16 in. (2 mm) of any rivet (measure with a vernier caliper as shown in **Figure 17** or have the measurements made by a machine shop).
   e. Broken torsional coil or cushion springs (loose springs are considered normal).

9

f. Warped or distorted hub flange.
g. Missing stop pins.
h. Loose fit or rough movement on the transmission input shaft splines.

2. Remove small amounts of oil or grease with aerosol brake cleaner and dress the facings with a wire brush, if necessary. However, if the facings are soaked with oil or grease, replace the disc. The disc must also be replaced if any of the other defects is present or if the facings are partially worn and a new pressure plate is being installed.

Pressure Plate Inspection

Refer to **Figure 18** for this procedure.

1. Check the pressure plate for:
   a. Scoring.
   b. Overheating (blue-tinted areas).
   c. Burn marks.
   d. Cracks.
   e. Uneven mating surfaces.
2. Clean the mating surfaces with a cloth moistened in solvent to remove any oil film.
3. Check the diaphragm springs for wear or damage at the release bearing contact surface. Check for bent, excessively worn or broken spring fingers. Replace the pressure plate and cover assembly if any defects are found.
4. If the clutch trouble is still not apparent, take the pressure plate and disc to a competent machine shop. Have the disc and pressure plate checked for runout and the diaphragm springs checked for correct finger height. Do not attempt to dismantle the pressure plate or readjust the fingers yourself. This requires the proper tools and experience.

Release Bearing Inspection

Never reuse a release bearing unless necessary. When other clutch parts are worn, the bearing is probably worn. If it is necessary to reinstall the old bearing, do not wash it in solvent.

1. Remove the release bearing from the slave cylinder.
2. Wipe all dirt or oil from the bearing with a clean cloth.

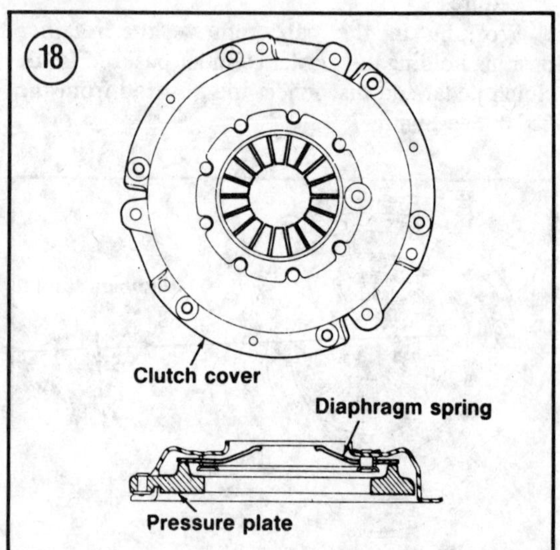

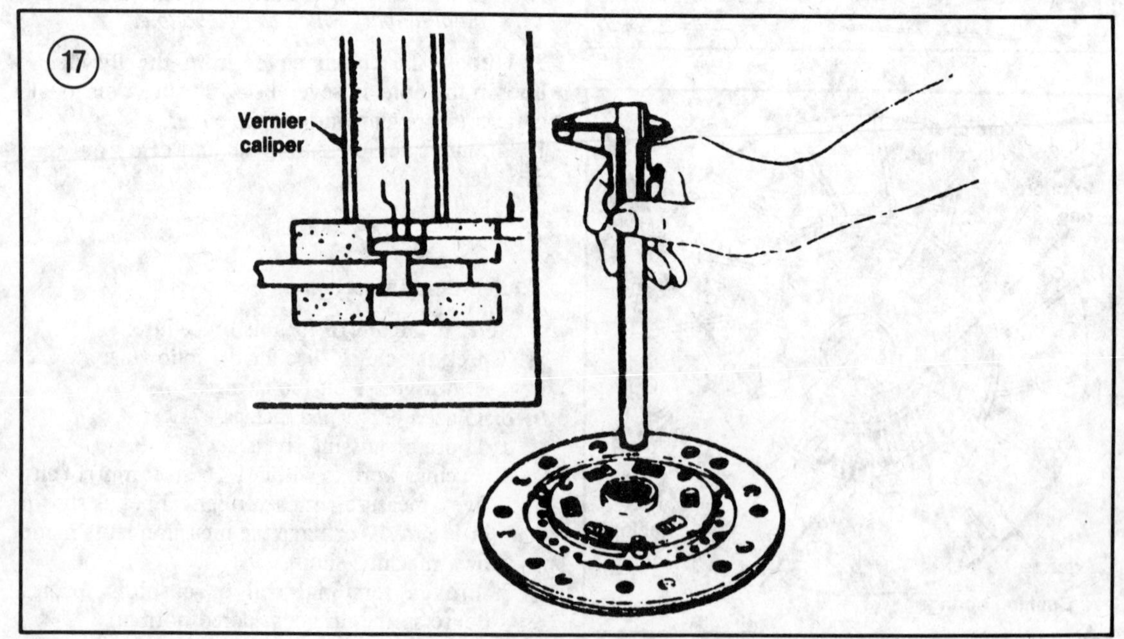

3. Hold the inner race from moving and rotate the outer race while applying a slight amount of pressure. Replace the bearing if rotation is noisy or rough.
4. Check the bearing assembly for burrs. If present, clean with fine crocus cloth, then check the transmission input shaft for scoring and polish out with crocus cloth.

Clutch Installation

Refer to **Figures 1-4** as required for this procedure.

1. Be sure your hands are clean and free of oil or grease.

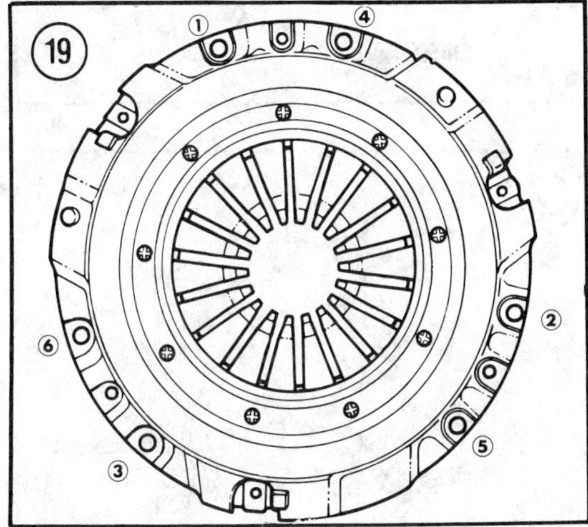

2. Make sure the disc facings, pressure plate and flywheel are free of oil, grease and other foreign material.
3. If installing a new clutch disc, lightly sand the friction surface of the flywheel and pressure plate with a medium-fine emery cloth. Sand across (not around) the surfaces until they are covered with fine scratches. This breaks the glaze and helps in seating a new clutch disc.
4. Place the clutch disc and cover plate in position on the flywheel. The side flywheel dowel pins must engage the holes in the clutch cover. Make sure the alignment marks on the cover and flywheel are aligned.
5. Start but do not tighten the cover bolts. Center the disc and pressure plate with alignment tool part No. T74P-7137-K or a suitable dummy shaft.
6. Gradually tighten the cover bolts to specifications (**Table 1**) following the sequence shown in **Figure 19**. Remove the alignment tool.
7. Install the transmission as described in this chapter.
8. Reconnect the hydraulic line to the slave cylinder as described in this chapter.
9. Reconnect the master cylinder pushrod to the clutch pedal.
10. Bleed the hydraulic system as described in this chapter.

Clutch Pedal Removal/Installation

Refer to **Figure 20** for this procedure.

9

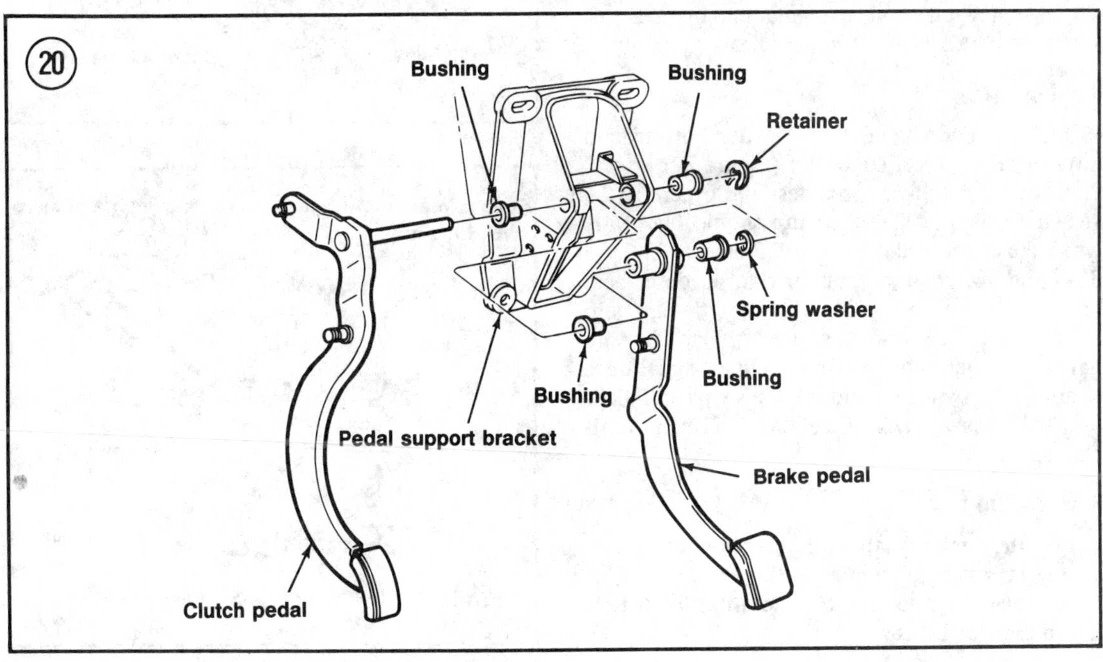

1. Working in the cab, remove the retainer bushing holding the master cylinder pushrod to the clutch pedal and disconnect the pushrod from the pedal. See **Figure 7**.
2. Remove the clutch interlock switch as described in this chapter.
3. Remove the EEC module on models where it interferes with pedal removal.
4. Remove the clutch pedal shaft retainer. Slide the pedal and shaft from the bracket. The brake pedal, inner bushings and spring washer will drop out of the bracket as the clutch pedal is removed.
5. Remove the outer bushings from the bracket. Check all bushings for wear or damage. Replace as required. Lubricate bushings with SAE 30W engine oil.
6. Install the 2 outer bushings in the bracket. Position the brake pedal, inner bushings and spring washer in the bracket, then insert the clutch pedal shaft through the bracket. Reinstall the shaft retainer.
7. Reverse Steps 1-3 to complete installation. Adjust the clutch interlock switch as described in this chapter.

Clutch Interlock Switch

All vehicles equipped with a manual transmission use a clutch interlock switch to prevent the engine from starting unless the clutch pedal is fully depressed.

The self-adjusting interlock switch is mounted on the brake/clutch pedal support bracket (**Figure 21**). It is connected across the ignition switch and starter motor relay coil to maintain an open circuit when the clutch pedal is in the released position.

Testing

1. Flex the retaining tab on the switch housing and unplug the electrical connector (**Figure 22**).
2. Connect a self-powered test lamp across the switch terminals. The test lamp should light only when the clutch pedal is fully depressed.
3. If the switch does not operate as described, remove the self-adjusting clip (**Figure 23**) and reposition it closer to the switch. Snap the clip halves together and operate the clutch pedal once to adjust the switch position. If the switch still does not operate properly, replace it as described in this chapter.

Replacement

1. Flex the retaining tab on the switch housing and unplug the electrical connector (**Figure 22**).
2. Remove the retaining clip holding the switch rod to the clutch pedal.

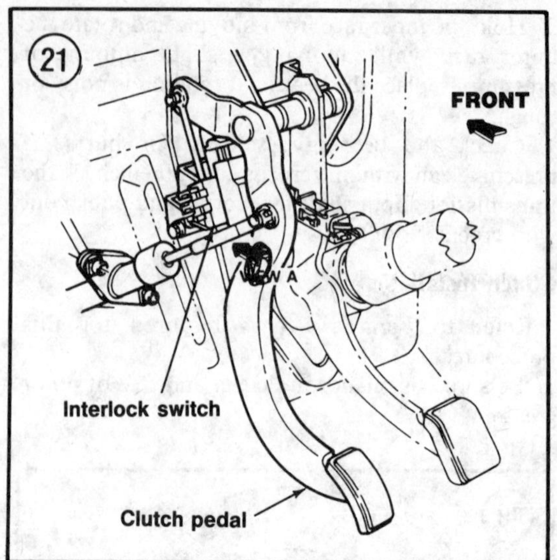

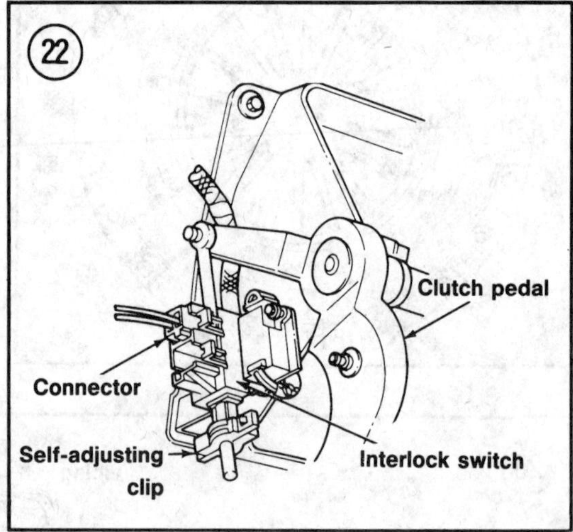

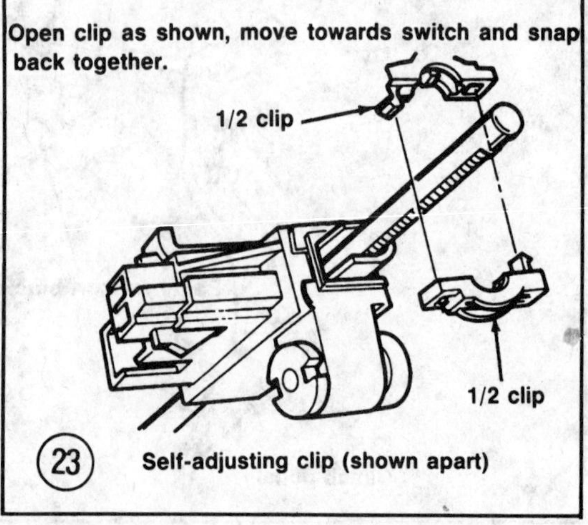

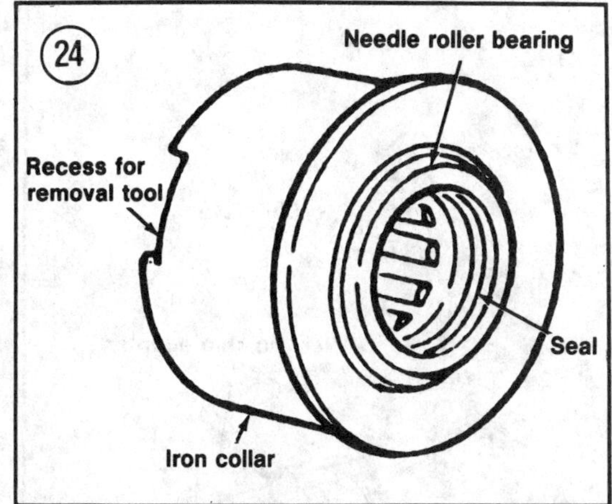

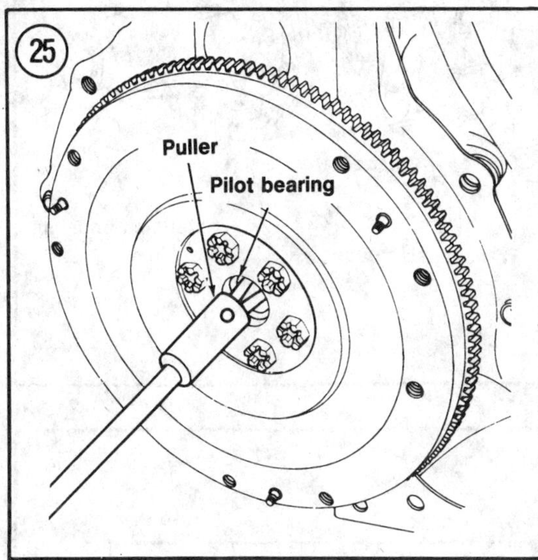

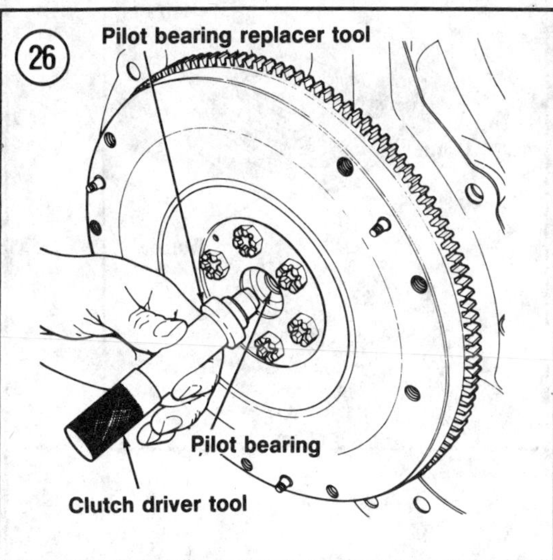

3. Remove the attaching screw from the stationary bracket.
4. Disengage the switch rod from the clutch pedal pivot and remove it from the vehicle.
5. Install the switch rod on the clutch pedal pivot with the switch positioned straight down.
6. Rotate the switch upward until the attaching screw hole is aligned with the stationary bracket hole.
7. Install the attaching screw and reconnect the electrical connector.
8. Depress the clutch pedal to the floor to adjust the switch.

Pilot Bearing

The transmission input shaft rides on a needle roller bearing and adaptor assembly (**Figure 24**) in the crankshaft bore. A glazed, worn or improperly lubricated pilot bearing will produce an objectionable squeal or chirping noise when the clutch is activated.

The pilot bearing is pressed in place and should not be loose. A bearing that has been removed should never be reinstalled. If removed for any reason, install a new bearing.

Check the bearing for misalignment, scoring, heat discoloration, insufficient lubrication and excessively worn or broken rollers. Check the bearing seal for signs of grease on the retainer or crankshaft. Replace the bearing if any of these conditions are evident.

9

Removal/Installation

The needle bearing and adaptor assembly cannot be serviced separately. The needle bearing and seal are prelubricated and require no additional lubricant when installed.

1. Remove the clutch as described in this chapter.
2. Attach a slide hammer to bearing remover part No. T58L-101-B or equivalent and remove the bearing. See **Figure 25.**
3. Clean the crankshaft bearing bore.
4. Install a new bearing (seal facing transmission) with installer part No. T74P-7137-A (2.8L V6) or part No. T74P-7137-C (all others). See **Figure 26.** Make sure the bearing is properly seated and is not cocked.
5. Reinstall the clutch as described in this chapter.

MANUAL TRANSMISSION

The standard Aerostar transmission is a 5-speed Toyo Kogyo (Mazda) overdrive unit. The gear shift lever is installed on the top front of the aluminum transmission case and connects to the transmission shift mechanism on the extension housing through a remote shift adapter (**Figure 27**).

Disassembly and assembly of this transmission requires a large number of special tools and considerable experience. If the transmission requires overhaul, remove it from the vehicle and take it to a dealer or transmission shop for service.

A service identification tag is located on the side of the transmission case. The information on this tag is used when ordering replacement parts.

Shift Lever/Boot Assembly Removal/Installation

Refer to **Figure 28** for this procedure.

1. Lift the carpet up around the shift lever boot and remove the 4 screws holding the boot to the floorpan.
2. Remove the 4 bolts holding the shift lever to the remote shift adapter. Remove the shift lever from the vehicle.
3. To reinstall, lubricate the end of the shift lever with Ford Multi-purpose Long-life Lubricant (part No. C1AZ-19590-B) or equivalent.
4. Install the lever in the remote shift adapter. Wipe the bolt threads with a suitable thread adhesive and tighten to 6-9 ft.-lb. (8-12 N•m).
5. Position the rubber boot on the floorpan. Install and tighten the boot attaching screws securely. Reposition the carpet around the boot.

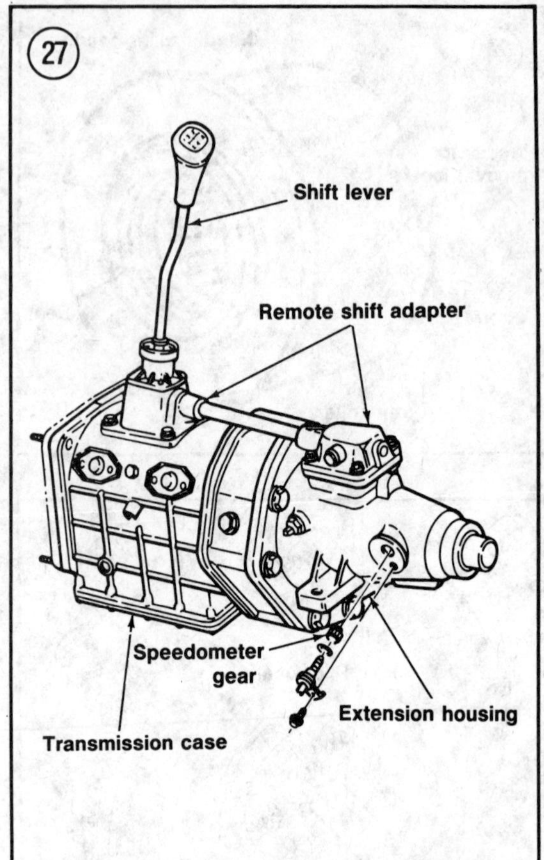

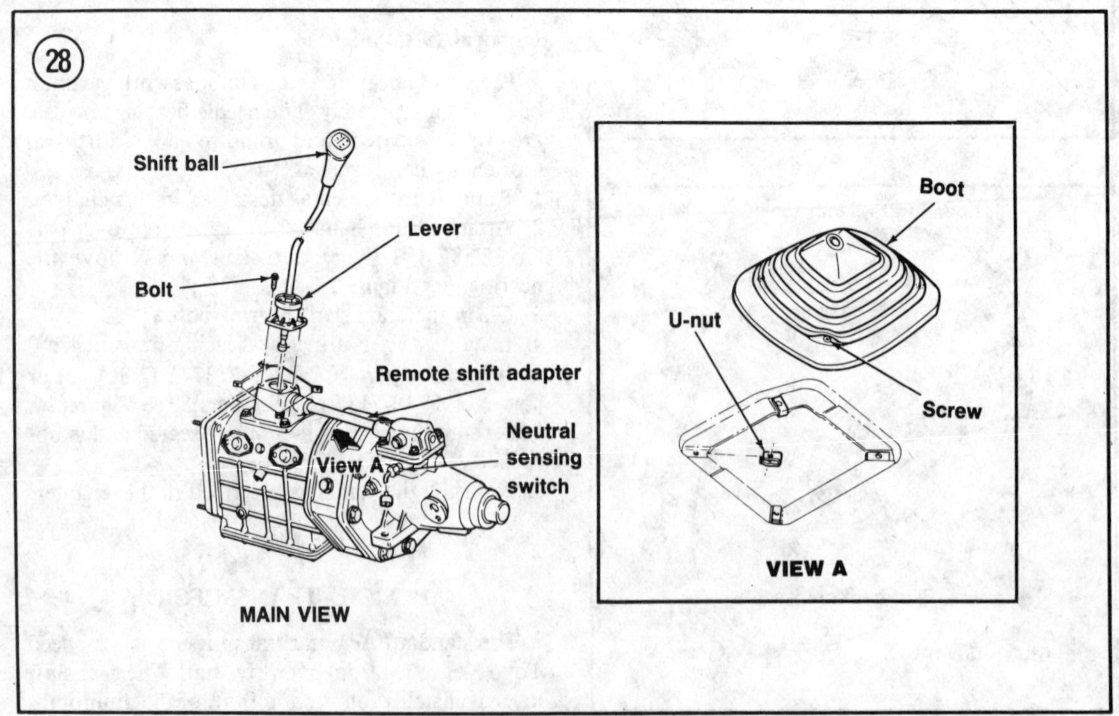

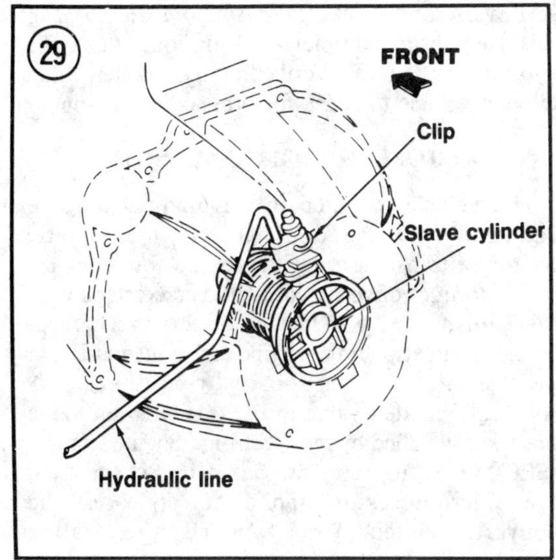

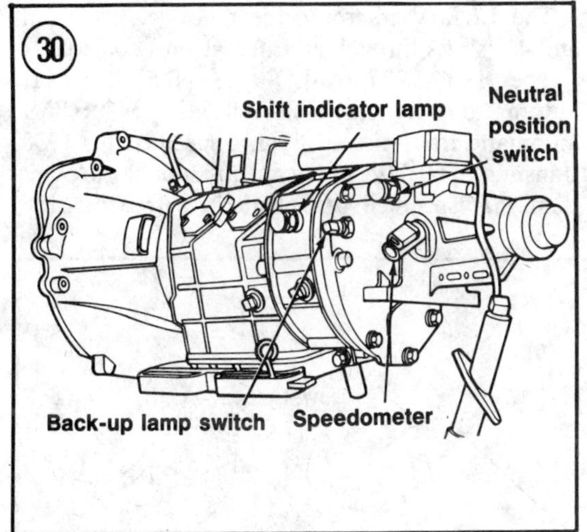

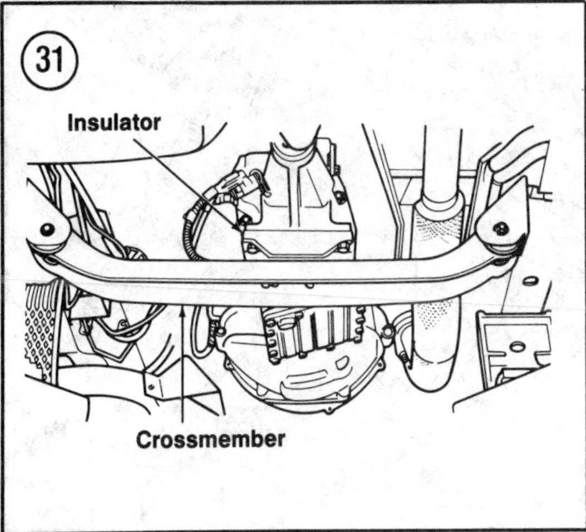

Transmission Removal

1. Disconnect the negative battery cable.
2. Place the transmission in neutral and remove the shift lever as described in this chapter.
3. Securely block both rear wheels so the vehicle will not roll in either direction.
4. Raise the front of the vehicle with a jack and place it on jackstands.
5. Remove the starter motor. See Chapter Eight.

6A. 1986-1987—Remove the clip holding the master cylinder line to the slave cylinder at the transmission bellhousing. Remove the line and fitting. Cap the line and bellhousing opening to prevent leakage and the entry of contamination. See **Figure 29**.

6B. 1988-on—Disconnect the master cylinder line quick-release coupling at the slave cylinder in the transmission bellhousing with tool part No. T88T-70522-A. See **Figure 12**. Cap the line and bellhousing opening to prevent leakage and the entry of contamination.

7. Unplug all electrical connectors from the transmission sending units. Disconnect the speedometer cable (conventional speedometer) or disconnect the electrical lead (electronic speedometer) from its fitting, as require. See **Figure 30**.
8. Remove the drive shaft and insert a suitable plug in the transmission extension housing to prevent leakage. See Chapter Eleven.
9. Remove the nuts holding the insulator to the crossmember. See **Figure 31**. Loosen the fasteners holding the crossmember insulators to the frame brackets.
10. Support the transmission with a transmission jack and secure in place with a safety chain. Raise the jack enough to take the transmission weight off the crossmember. Unbolt and remove the crossmember from the vehicle.
11. Support the rear of the engine with a hydraulic jack. Use a block of wood between the jack and engine to protect the oil pan.
12. Remove the bolts holding the transmission to the engine.

NOTE

Once the transmission is out of the vehicle, do not depress the clutch pedal or the clutch disc will fall out of position.

13. Pull the transmission to the rear until the input shaft clears the bell housing, then lower the transmission to the floor with the jack and remove it from under the vehicle.

9

Transmission Installation

1. Lightly lubricate the splined part of the transmission input shaft with Ford Multi-purpose Long-life Lubricant (part No. C1AZ-19590-B) or equivalent. Do not apply too much lubricant or the clutch disc can become contaminated during operation.
2. Raise the transmission on a jack until the input shaft splines are aligned with the clutch disc splines. Move the transmission forward to mate with the engine. Make sure the dowel pins in the engine block engage the matching holes in the clutch housing (**Figure 32**).
3. Install the transmission mounting bolts and lockwashers (only aluminum lockwashers should be used or galvanic corrosion will occur). Tighten bolts to specifications (**Table 1**).
4. Reinstall the insulator to the transmission and tighten fasteners to specifications (**Table 1**).
5. Align the crossmember in the frame brackets. Install and partially tighten the attaching fasteners.
6. Lower the transmission with the jack while indexing the insulator studs in the crossmember holes. Tighten the insulator-to-crossmember nuts to specifications (**Table 1**), then tighten the crossmember insulators-to-frame brackets to specifications (**Table 1**). See **Figure 33**.
7. Reverse Steps 1-8 of *Transmission Removal* in this chapter to complete installation. Bleed the hydraulic system as described in this chapter. Road test the vehicle to check for proper shift action.

AUTOMATIC TRANSMISSION

The vehicles covered in this manual may be equipped with the optional A4LD automatic overdrive transmission with lock-up converter.

The torque converter contains a converter clutch mechanism to provide a direct mechanical connection between the engine and transmission at predetermined speed/load conditions. A solenoid-operated valve in the transmission valve body is controlled by the Electronic Engine Control (EEC-IV) microprocessor. Based on sensor data, the microprocessor applies or releases the converter clutch. When applied, this feature reduces slippage losses in the converter, which translates into better fuel economy.

The EEC-IV microprocessor also controls 3-4 and 4-3 shifts through an internal shift solenoid.

The 1986-1987 A4LD uses DEXRON II automatic transmission fluid. MERCON automatic transmission fluid is specified for 1988 transmissions. Use of a transmission fluid other than that specified can result in a transmission

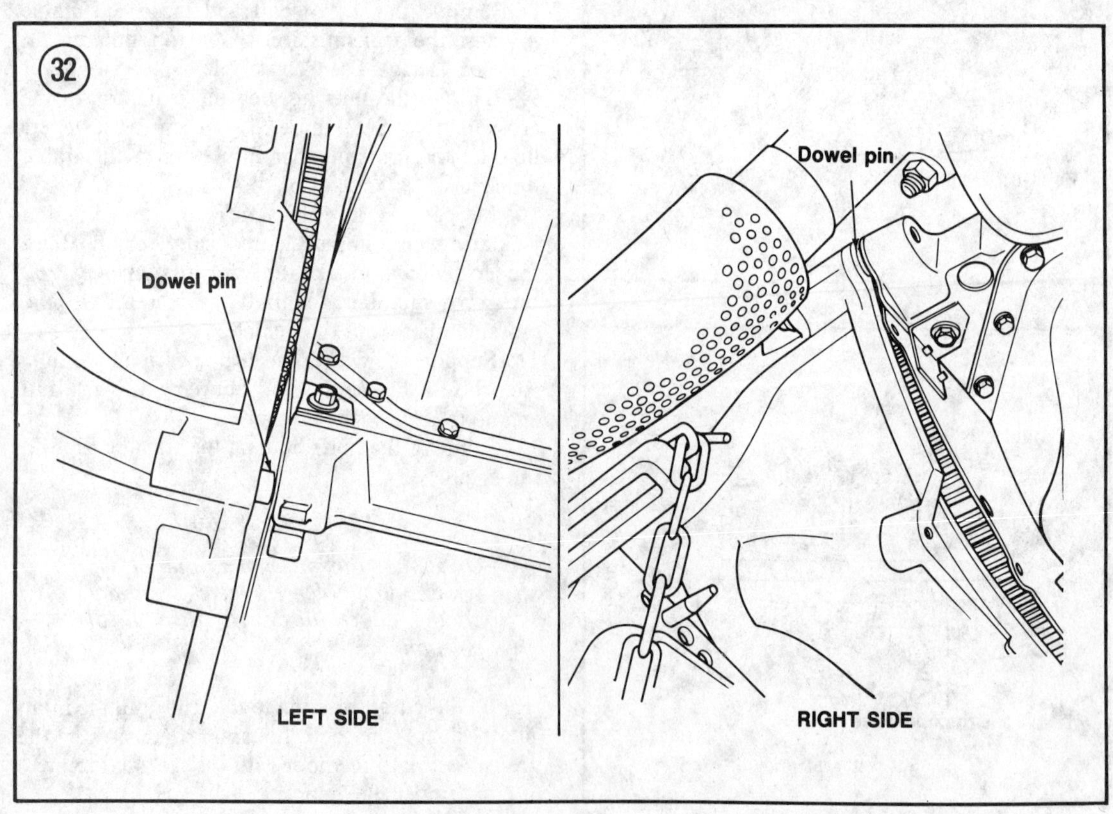

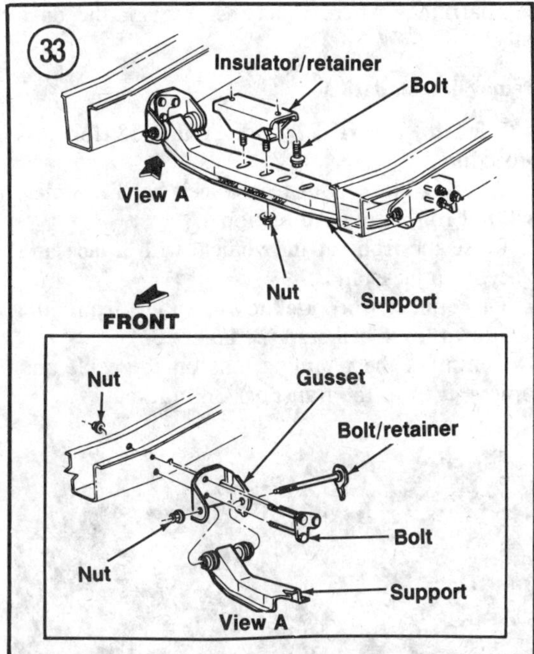

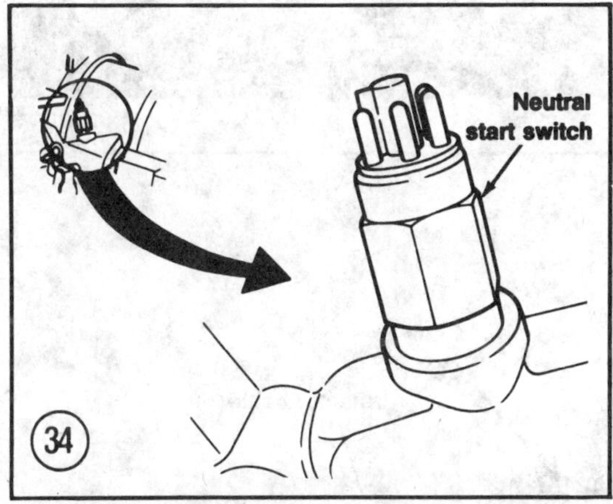

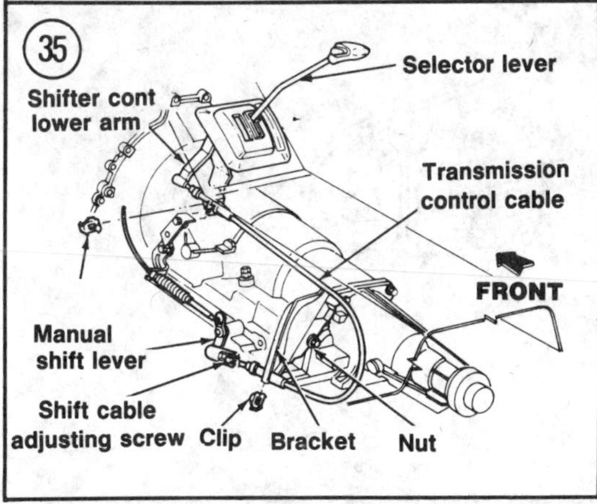

malfunction and/or premature failure. Fluid checking and changing procedures are described in Chapter Three.

This section includes checks and adjustment procedures to be performed with the transmission in the vehicle. Many problems can be corrected with the adjustment procedures provided here. Automatic transmission overhaul, however, requires professional skills, many special tools and extremely high standards of cleanliness. Although procedures for removal and installation are included in this chapter, disassembly and overhaul should be left to a dealer, or a competent automatic transmission repair shop.

Neutral Start Switch

The A4LD switch is serviced by replacement only.

Replacement

Refer to **Figure 34** for this procedure.

1. Set the parking brake. Securely block both rear wheels so the vehicle will not roll in either direction.
2. Raise the front of the vehicle with a jack and place it on jackstands.
3. Disconnect the electrical connector plug at the neutral start switch.

CAUTION
Ford recommends the use of a special thin-wall switch socket tool in Step 4 to prevent the possibility of crushing or puncturing the switch walls.

4. Unscrew and remove the switch with Ford tool part No. T74P-77247-A or equivalent.
5. Remove and discard the switch O-ring.
6. Installation is the reverse of removal. Use a new O-ring and tighten the switch to 7-10 ft.-lb. (10-14 N•m).

Manual Linkage Adjustment

Correct manual linkage adjustment is critical to the performance and service life of an automatic transmission. It positions the manual valve in the transmission to provide proper fluid pressure and direction to the various components. Improper adjustment can cause cross-leakage and result in premature transmission failure. Refer to **Figure 35** for this procedure.

1. Place the shift lever in the OVERDRIVE position (this is the small circle with the D inside it).
2. Securely block both rear wheels so the vehicle will not roll in either direction.

3. Raise the front of the vehicle with a jack and place it on jackstands.
4. Loosen the shift cable adjustment screw and disconnect the end fitting from the manual lever ball stud. See A, **Figure 36**.
5. Move the manual lever to the rear as far as possible, then bring it 3 detents forward to place it in the OVERDRIVE position.
6. Hold the shift lever against the rear stop and connect the end of the cable to the manual lever. Tighten the screw to 45-60 in.-lb. (5-7 N•m).
7. Have an assistant move the shift lever into the PARK position while you watch the control lever. It should move to the right when the shift lever is placed in PARK.
8. Remove the jackstands and lower the vehicle to the ground.
9. Start the engine and move the shift lever through all positions to make sure the transmission shifts properly. If it does not, repeat the procedure.

Kickdown Cable

The self-adjusting kickdown cable is routed through the dash panel and connected to the accelerator pedal near the pedal cable (**Figure 37**). The self-adjuster mechanism is attached to the kickdown cable at the point in the engine compartment where it passes through the dash panel.

Removal/Installation

Refer to **Figure 37** and **Figure 38** for this procedure.

1. Securely block both rear wheels so the vehicle will not roll in either direction.
2. Raise the front of the vehicle with a jack and place it on jackstands.
3. Disconnect the kickdown cable from the kickdown lever ball stud (B, **Figure 36**).
4. Compress the retaining tabs on the cable and remove it from the transmission bracket.

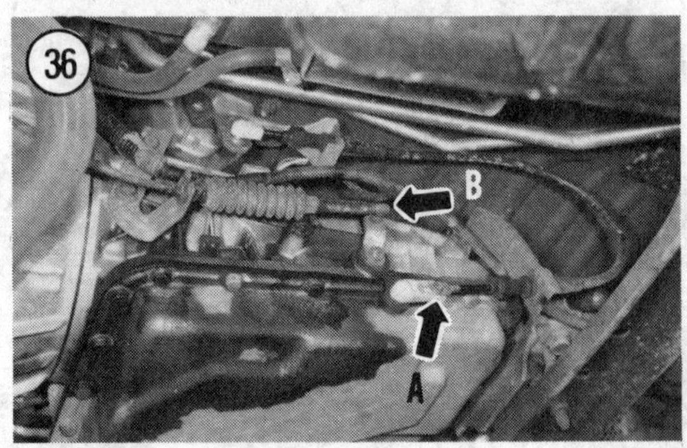

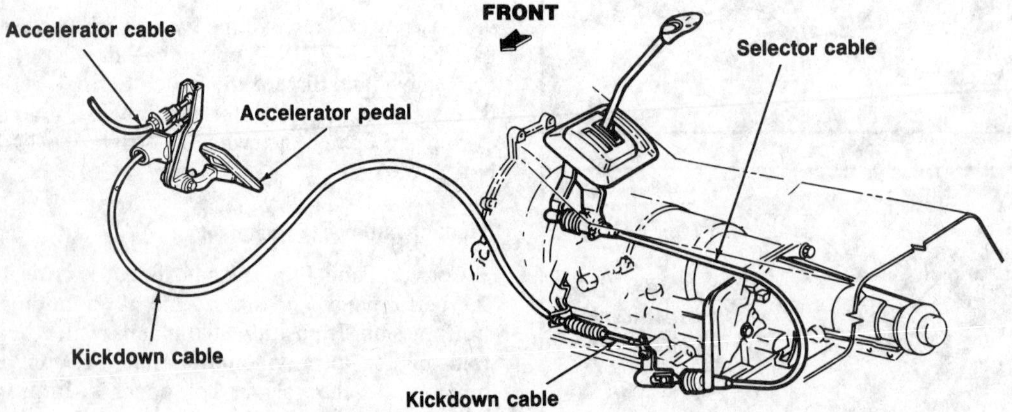

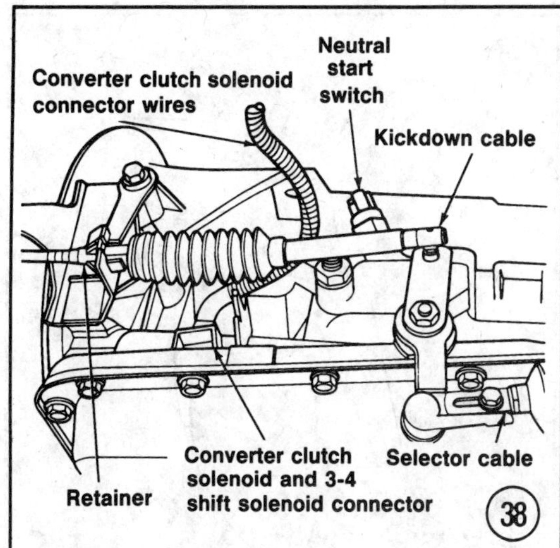

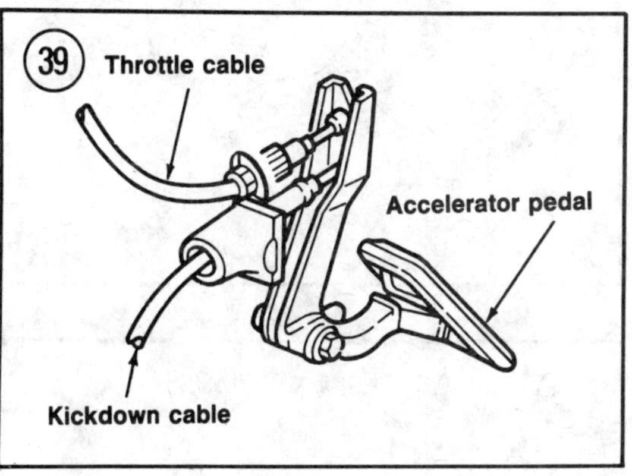

5. Remove the jackstands and lower the vehicle to the ground.
6. Working inside the cab, disconnect the kickdown cable from the accelerator pedal (**Figure 39**).
7. Compress the retaining tabs on the cable at the dash panel and pull the cable into the engine compartment, then remove it from the vehicle.
8. To reinstall, pry up the locking tab on the cable body (**Figure 40**). Depress the D-flat while pushing the cable conduit at the wiper cap back into the body. Once this is done, the cable will automatically adjust to its correct length the first time the accelerator pedal is fully depressed after installation.
9. Feed the accelerator end of the cable through the dash panel from the engine compartment. Make sure the retaining tabs are fully seated in the dash panel.
10. Working in the cab, connect the end of the cable to the accelerator pedal (**Figure 39**).
11. Raise the front of the vehicle with a jack and place it on jackstands.
12. Insert the cable through the transmission mounting bracket. Make sure the retaining tabs are fully seated in the bracket.
13. Connect the end of the cable to the kickdown lever ball stud (**Figure 38**).
14. Remove the jackstands and lower the vehicle to the ground.
15. Depress the accelerator pedal fully to adjust the cable.
16. Remove the wheel chocks.

9

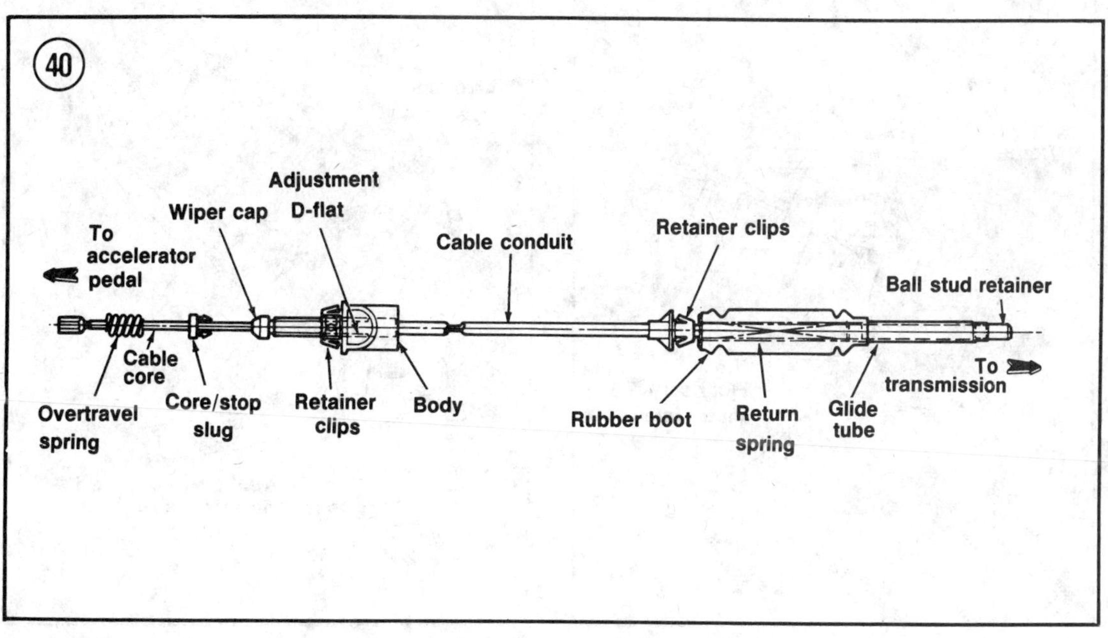

Selector Lever Removal/Installation

Refer to **Figure 41** for this procedure.

1. Securely block both rear wheels so the vehicle will not roll in either direction.
2. Raise the front of the vehicle with a jack and place it on jackstands.
3. Remove the cable retaining clip, then disconnect the cable from the selector lever.
4. Remove the jackstands and lower the vehicle to the ground.
5. Carefully pry the floor carpet center retainer free and remove it from the selector lever.
6. Remove the 4 bolts holding the selector lever assembly to the floorpan. Remove the selector lever assembly from the vehicle.
7. Installation is the reverse of removal. Recheck manual linkage adjustment as described in this chapter.

Transmission Removal

1. Disconnect the negative battery cable.
2. Securely block both rear wheels so the vehicle will not roll in either direction.
3. Raise the front of the vehicle with a jack and place it on jackstands.
4. Place a suitable container under the transmission and drain the fluid. See Chapter Three. Temporarily reinstall the oil pan.
5. Remove the converter access cover. On 2.3L models, it is on the bottom of the engine oil pan;

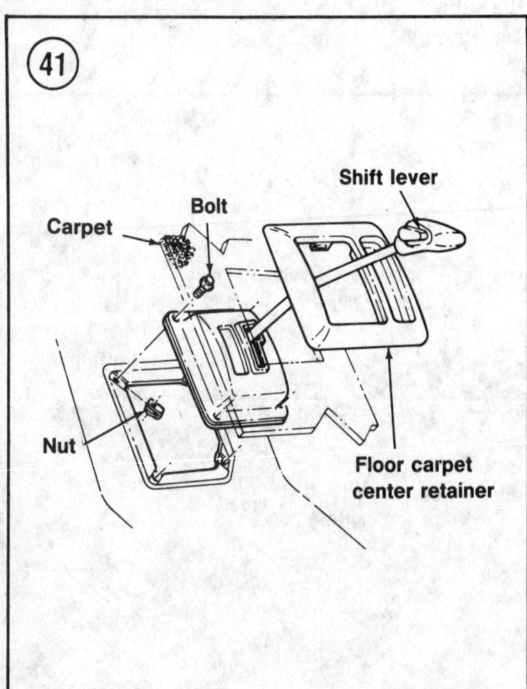

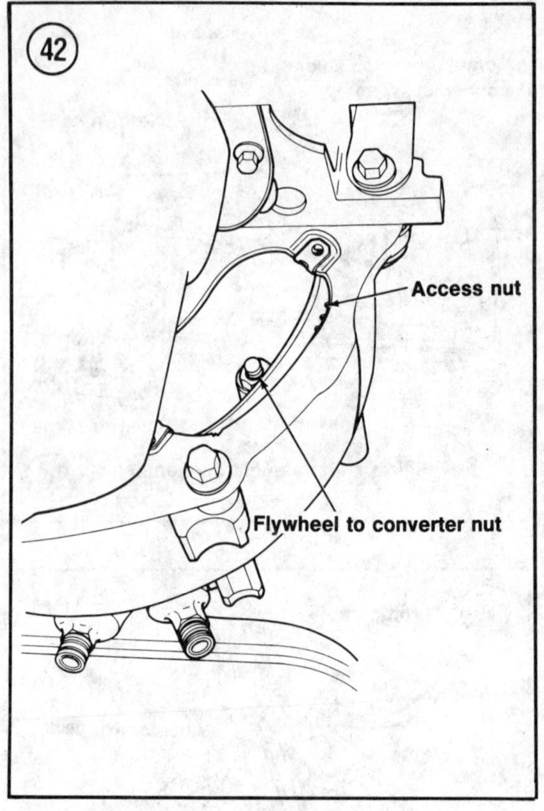

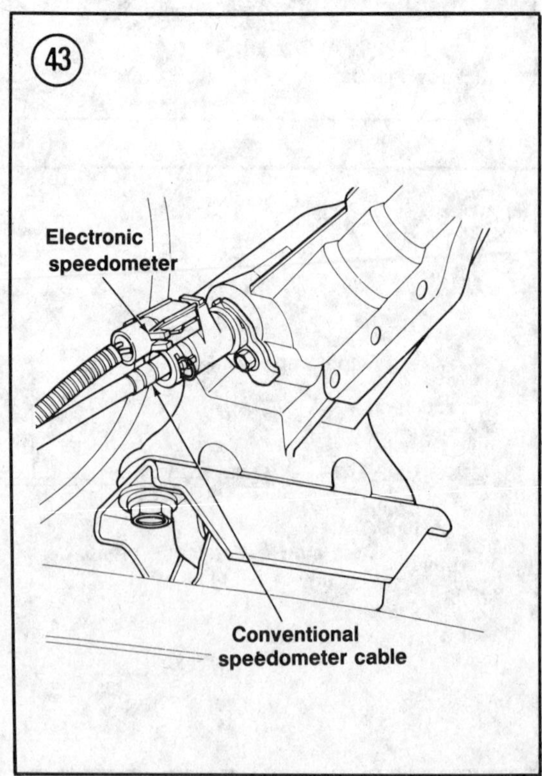

on V6 models, it is on the lower right side of the converter housing (**Figure 42**).

6. Place a 22 mm socket and breaker bar on the crankshaft pulley bolt and rotate the crankshaft pulley clockwise (as seen from the front of the engine) to provide access to a flywheel-to-converter nut (**Figure 42**). Remove the nut, then rotate the crankshaft a partial turn to align another nut for removal. Continue this procedure until all 4 nuts are removed.

7. Remove the drive shaft and insert a suitable plug in the transmission extension housing to prevent leakage. See Chapter Eleven.

8. If equipped with a conventional speedometer, disconnect the cable at the transmission. Unplug the electrical connector if equipped with an electronic speedometer. **Figure 43** shows both types of connections, but only one will be found on a given vehicle.

9. Unplug the electrical wires at the neutral start switch and converter clutch solenoid (**Figure 38**).

10. Disconnect the kickdown cable and remove it from its mounting bracket as described in this chapter.

11. Unplug the vacuum line at the vacuum modulator (**Figure 44**).

12. Remove the starter motor. See Chapter Eight.

13. Unbolt and remove the transmission dipstick tube.

14. Support the transmission with a transmission jack and secure in place with a safety chain. Raise the jack enough to take the transmission weight off the crossmember.

15. Remove the nuts holding the insulator to the crossmember. See **Figure 45**.

16. Loosen the fasteners holding the crossmember insulators to the frame bracket on each side of the vehicle. See **Figure 46**. Unbolt and remove the crossmember from the vehicle.

17. Support the rear of the engine with a hydraulic jack. Use a block of wood between the jack and engine to protect the oil pan.

18. Remove the bolts holding the converter housing to the engine.

19. Lower the jack just enough to provide access to the transmission oil cooler lines. Disconnect the lines at the transmission (**Figure 47**). Cap the lines and plug the fittings to prevent leakage and the entry of contamination.

20. Move the transmission back slightly and install a holding fixture or strap to prevent the torque converter from falling out.

21. Lower the transmission carefully and remove it from under the vehicle.

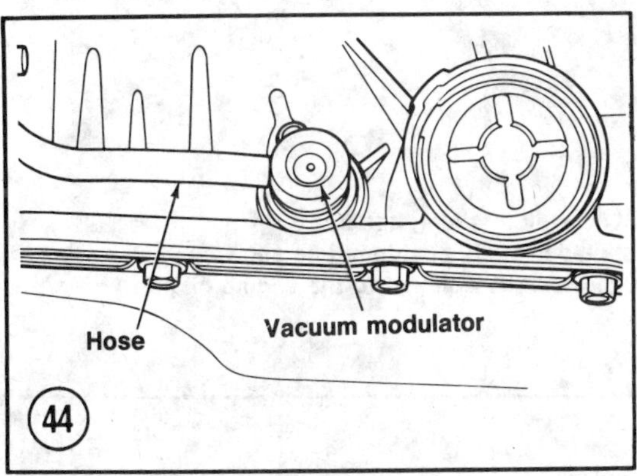

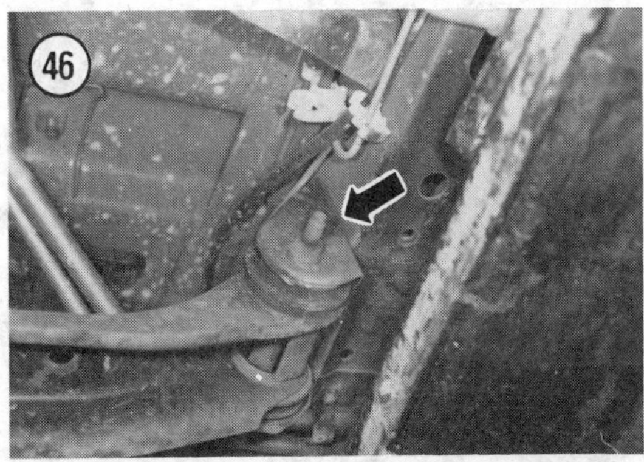

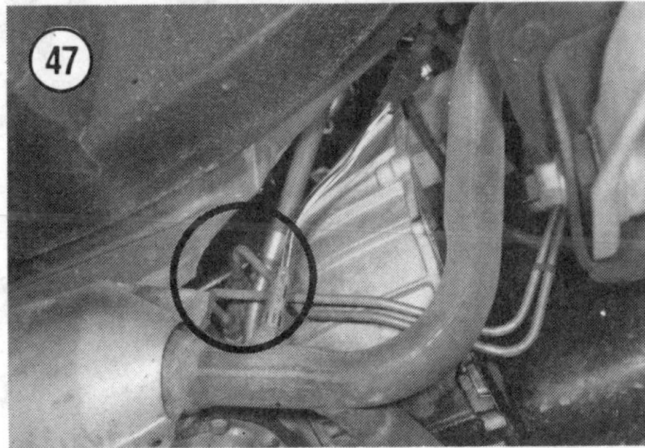

9

Transmission Installation

Installation is the reverse of removal, plus the following:

1. Make sure the converter hub is completely engaged in the pump gear.
2. Tighten the flywheel-to-converter bolts by hand, then retighten to specifications (**Table 1**) to ensure proper converter alignment.
3. Refer to **Figure 48** for correct installation of attaching fasteners.
4. Refer to **Figure 33** for correct installation of crossmember and insulator.
5. Tighten all fasteners to specifications (**Table 1**).
6. Fill the transmission with the required amount of DEXRON II (1986-1987) or MERCON (1988) automatic transmission fluid. See Chapter Three.
7. Check the fluid level (Chapter Three). Add or remove fluid as required.
8. Warm the engine to normal operating temperature, then recheck the fluid level and adjust as required.
9. Adjust the manual linkage and kickdown cable as described in this chapter.
10. Road test the vehicle. Make sure the transmission shifts smoothly, makes no abnormal noises and hold the vehicle when in PARK (parking brake should be applied). After road testing, check for fluid leaks.

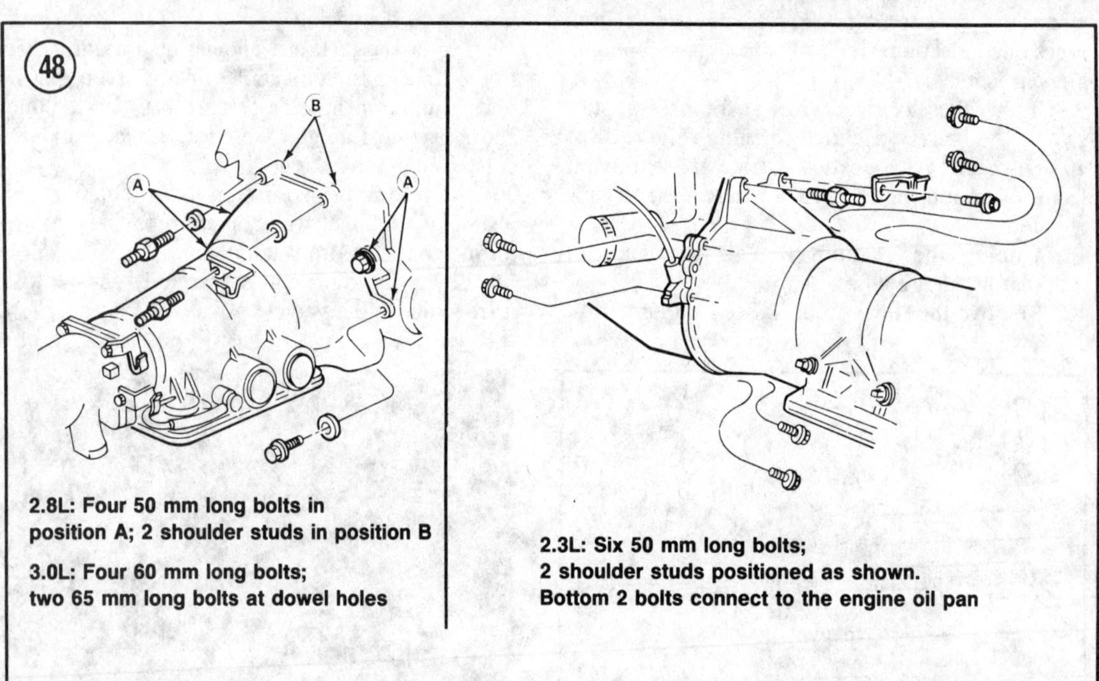

2.8L: Four 50 mm long bolts in position A; 2 shoulder studs in position B

3.0L: Four 60 mm long bolts; two 65 mm long bolts at dowel holes

2.3L: Six 50 mm long bolts; 2 shoulder studs positioned as shown. Bottom 2 bolts connect to the engine oil pan

Table 1 TIGHTENING TORQUES

Fastener	ft.-lb.	N•m
CLUTCH		
Clutch housing		
To engine	28-38	38-51
To transmission case	30-40	41-54
Drive shaft U-bolts	8-15	11-20
Insulator		
To crossmember	71-94	97-127
To Transmission	60-80	81-108
Master cylinder bolts	15-20	21-27
Pressure plate-to-flywheel	15-24	21-32
Starter-to-clutch housing	15-20	21-27
MANUAL TRANSMISSION		
Crossmember-to-frame gusset	37-52	50-71
Frame gusset-to-frame rail	95-125	128-170
Insulator		
To crossmember	71-94	97-127
To transmission	60-80	82-108
Drive shaft U-bolts	8-15	11-20
Clutch housing-to-engine block	28-38	38-51
Drain & fill plugs	18-29	25-39
AUTOMATIC TRANSMISSION		
Crossmember-to-frame gusset	37-52	50-71
Frame gusset-to-frame rail	95-125	128-170
Insulator		
To crossmember	71-94	97-127
To transmission	60-80	82-108
Drive shaft U-bolts	8-15	11-20
Oil cooler lines	18-23	24-31
Oil pan screws	8-10	11-14
Transmission-to-engine	28-38	38-51

CHAPTER TEN

FRONT SUSPENSION, WHEEL BEARINGS AND STEERING

All vehicles use an independent front suspension (**Figure 1**). The suspension consists of unequal length upper and lower control arms containing integral ball-joint assemblies and bushings, helical coil springs and cast front wheel spindles. Front wheel relationship is maintained by 2 tie rods connected between the rack-and-pinion steering gear and steering arms on the front wheel spindles.

Coil springs are mounted between the lower control arms and spring housings on the No. 1 crossmember assembly. Telescopic low pressure gas-filled shock absorbers mounted inside the coil springs provide ride control. The upper end of each shock absorber is attached to the upper spring seat in the No. 1 crossmember and is retained with rubber bushings and a nut. The lower shock absorber end is attached to the lower control arm. A spring steel stabilizer shaft controls front suspension side roll. The stabilizer ends are connected to the lower control arms by link bolts isolated by rubber grommets.

The upper control arm is connected to a pivot shaft arm, which is bolted to frame brackets. The brackets are bolted in turn through the body side rail to the No. 1 crossmember. The upper control arm connects to the wheel spindle through an integral ball-joint. Adjustment shims provided in the upper control arm permit caster and camber adjustments to be made.

Tightening torques (**Table 1**) are provided at the end of the chapter.

FRONT SUSPENSION

Shock Absorber Operational Check

Shock absorbers can be routinely checked while installed on the vehicle. Bounce the front of the vehicle up and down several times and release. Repeat this action with the rear of the vehicle. In either case, the vehicle should not continue to bounce more than twice. Excessive bouncing is an indication of worn shock absorbers. This test is not conclusive, since the spring stiffness of the vehicle makes it difficult to detect marginal shock absorbers.

If there is any doubt about their serviceability, remove the shock absorbers and perform the following procedure. If a shock absorber is found to be defective, replace both shocks on that end of the vehicle at the same time. If one shock absorber has failed because of physical damage, both should be replaced at the same time, even if the remaining shock appears to be satisfactory. If only one shock absorber is to be replaced, make sure that the replacement unit carries the same part number as the original shock absorber.

NOTE

Comparison of a used shock absorber believed to be good with a new shock absorber is not a valid test. The new shock absorber will tend to offer more resistance due to the greater friction of the new rod seal.

1. Inspect the shock absorber piston rod for bending, galling and abrasion. Discard the shock absorber if any of these conditions are noted.
2. Check the outside of the shock absorber for fluid leakage. A light film of fluid on the rod is normal, but severe leakage requires replacement.
3. Remove the shock absorber as described in this chapter. Secure the lower end of the shock absorber in a vise with protective jaws. If protective jaws are not available, place the shock between soft wooden blocks or wrap it in shop cloths before clamping it in the vise.
4. Compress and extend the piston rod as rapidly as possible and check the dampening action. The resistance should be smooth and uniform throughout each stroke, and the resistance felt during extension should be greater than during compression. Repeat this step with the other shock absorber. Both shock absorbers in a pair should feel the same.
5. If the damping action is erratic or resistance to rapid extension/compression is very low (or the same in both directions), replace the shock absorbers as a set.

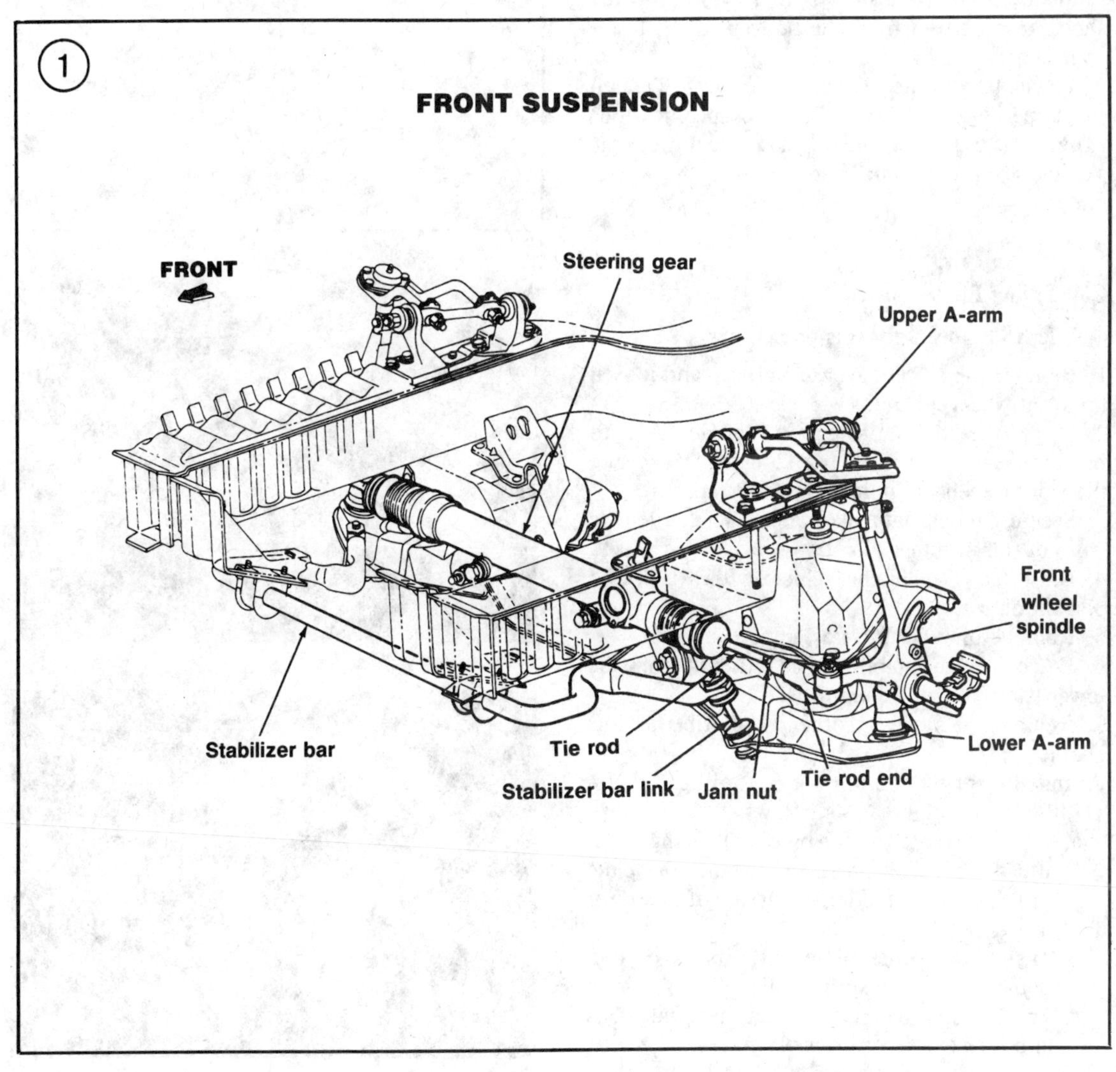

10

Shock Absorber Replacement

Always use new rubber insulators/bushings when installing new shock absorbers. Refer to **Figure 2** for this procedure.

1. Set the parking brake. Place the transmission in PARK or NEUTRAL.
2. Reach behind the wheel/tire assembly and clean the upper shock absorber threads. Oil the threads for ease in removal during Step 5.
3. Securely block both rear wheels so the vehicle will not roll in either direction.
4. Raise the front of the vehicle with a jack and place it on jackstands.
5. Hold the upper end of the shock absorber from turning with an open-end wrench. Remove the upper retaining nut with a second wrench. See **Figure 3**. Remove the retainer and rubber bushing.
6. Remove the 2 bolts holding the shock absorber to the lower control arm (**Figure 4**). Withdraw the shock absorber out from the bottom of the lower control arm.
7. Installation is the reverse of removal. Tighten the upper nut and lower bolts to specifications (**Table 1**). Remove the jackstands, lower the vehicle to the ground and remove the wheel chocks.

Coil Spring Replacement

Refer to **Figure 5** for this procedure.

1. Remove the wheel cover or hub cap and loosen the front wheel lug nuts.
2. Place the transmission in NEUTRAL to prevent the steering wheel from locking. Make sure the front wheels are pointing straight ahead.
3. Securely block both rear wheels so the vehicle will not roll in either direction.
4. Raise the front of the vehicle with a jack and place it on jackstands.
5. Remove the wheel/tire assembly.
6. Disconnect the stabilizer bar link bolt from the lower control arm (**Figure 6**).
7. Remove the shock absorber as described in this chapter.
8. Install spring compressor tool part No. D78P-5310-A (**Figure 7**) as follows:
   a. Place one plate with its pivot ball facing down into the coils of the spring. Rotate the plate until flush with the upper surface of the lower arm.
   b. Install the other plate with its pivot ball facing up into the spring coils.
   c. Fit the upper ball nut through the spring coils so nut rests in the upper plate.

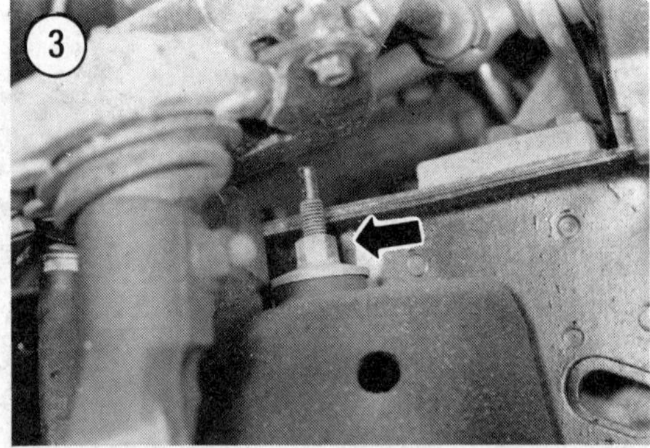

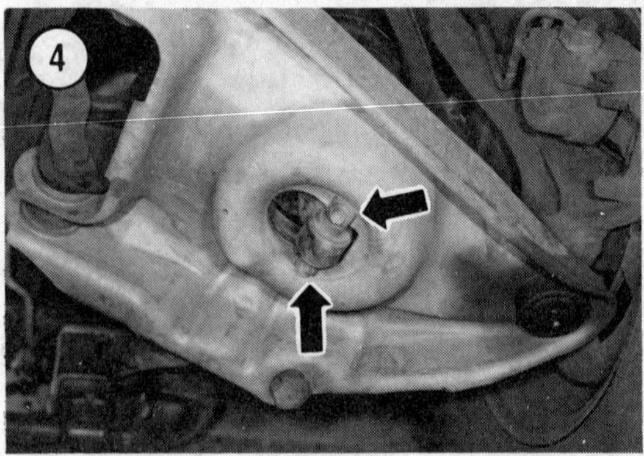

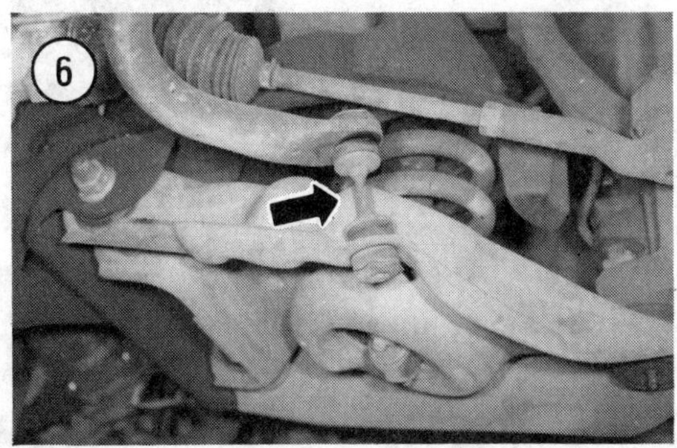

d. Insert the compression rod through the lower arm opening, upper and lower plates and engage the upper ball nut.

e. Install the securing pin through the upper ball nut and compression rod.

9. Rotate the upper plate until it contacts the upper spring seat, then back it off 1/2 turn.

10. Thread the lower ball nut and thrust washer on the end of the compression rod, then install the forcing nut.

11. Tighten the forcing nut until it compresses the spring enough to free it from the spring seat.

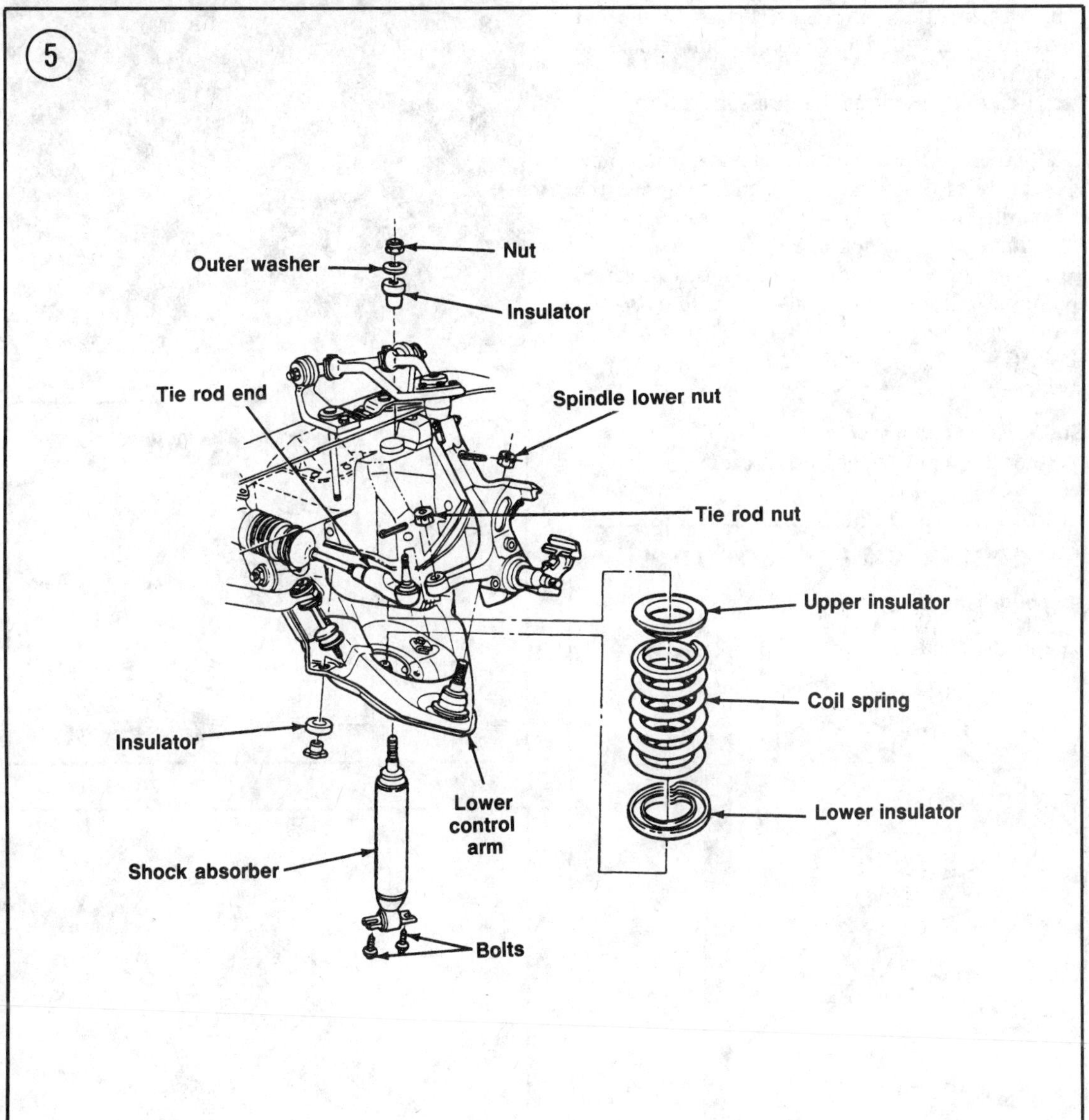

12. Loosen the 2 lower arm pivot bolts (**Figure 8**). Remove the cotter pin from the nut holding the lower ball-joint to the spindle. Loosen but do not remove the castellated nut.
13. Loosen the lower ball-joint with Pitman arm puller part No. T64P-3590-F or equivalent (**Figure 9**), then remove the tool.
14. Support the lower control arm with a hydraulic jack. Remove the castellated ball-joint nut. Lower the control arm and remove the spring.
15. If installing a new spring:
   a. Scribe the position of the upper and lower plates on the spring (**Figure 10**).
   b. Measure the compressed length of the old spring, then loosen the forcing nut enough to relieve spring tension.
   c. Remove the spring compressor tool from the old spring.
   d. Assemble the spring compressor on the new spring as described above and compress the spring until its height is the same as the dimension obtained in Step b.
16. Installation is the reverse of removal. Tighten the lower ball-joint nut to 80-120 ft.-lb. (108-163 N•m). Tighten the stabilizer link bolt nut to 12-18 ft.-lb. (18-24 N•m). Tighten all other fasteners to specifications (**Table 1**).

Stabilizer Bar Removal/Installation

Refer to **Figure 11** for this procedure.

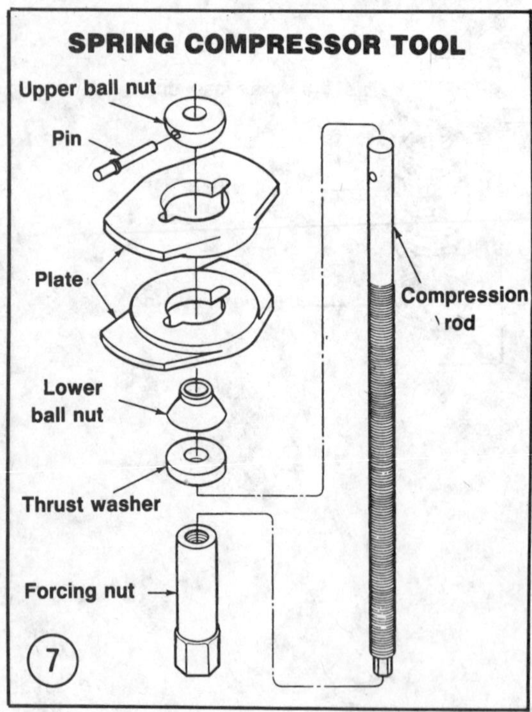

1. Securely block both rear wheels so the vehicle will not roll in either direction.
2. Raise the front of the vehicle with a jack and place it on jackstands.
3. Remove the nuts holding each end of the stabilizer bar to the lower control arm link (**Figure 6**). Remove the insulators and disconnect the bar from the links.
4. If necessary, remove the nut holding each link to its lower control arm. Remove the insulators and links from the control arms.

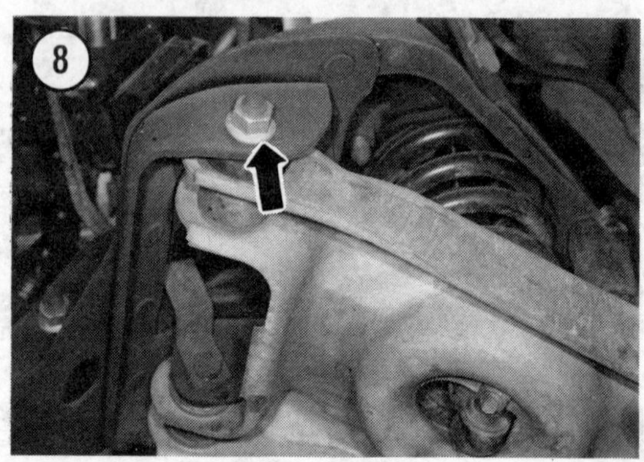

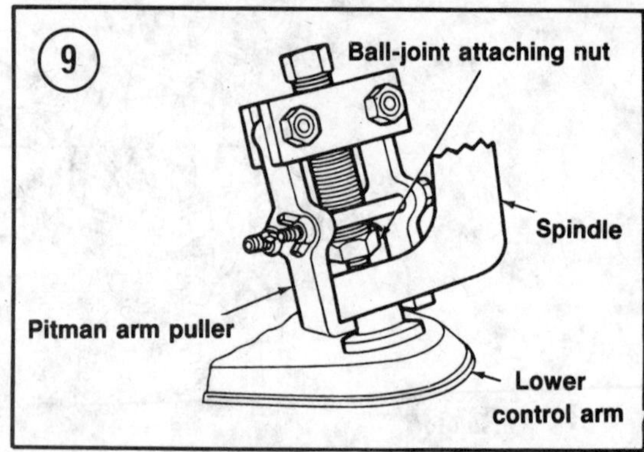

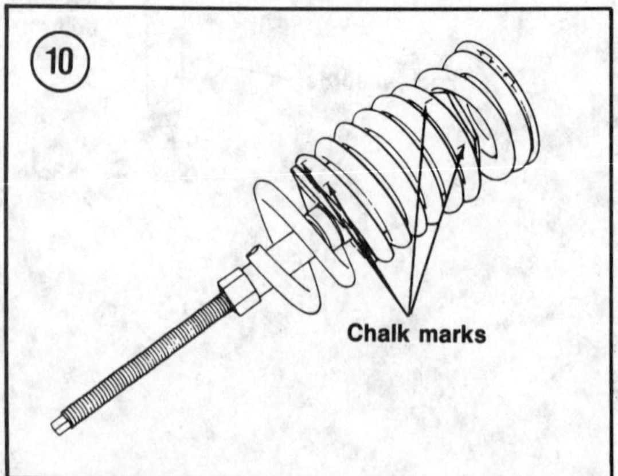

5. Unbolt and remove each mounting bracket from the frame. Remove the stabilizer bar.
6. If necessary, remove the insulators from the stabilizer bar and install new ones in the same positions as those removed.
7. Installation is the reverse of removal. Tighten all fasteners to specifications (**Table 1**).

Spindle Removal/Installation

Ford Motor Company recommends the use of a twin-post type hoist for this procedure. Refer to **Figure 12**.

1. Remove the wheel cover or hub cap and loosen the front wheel lug nuts.

11

FRONT
Insulator
Mounting bracket
Bolt
Stabilizer bar
Nut
Insulator
Stabilizer link
Insulator
Nut
Lower arm bushing and joint

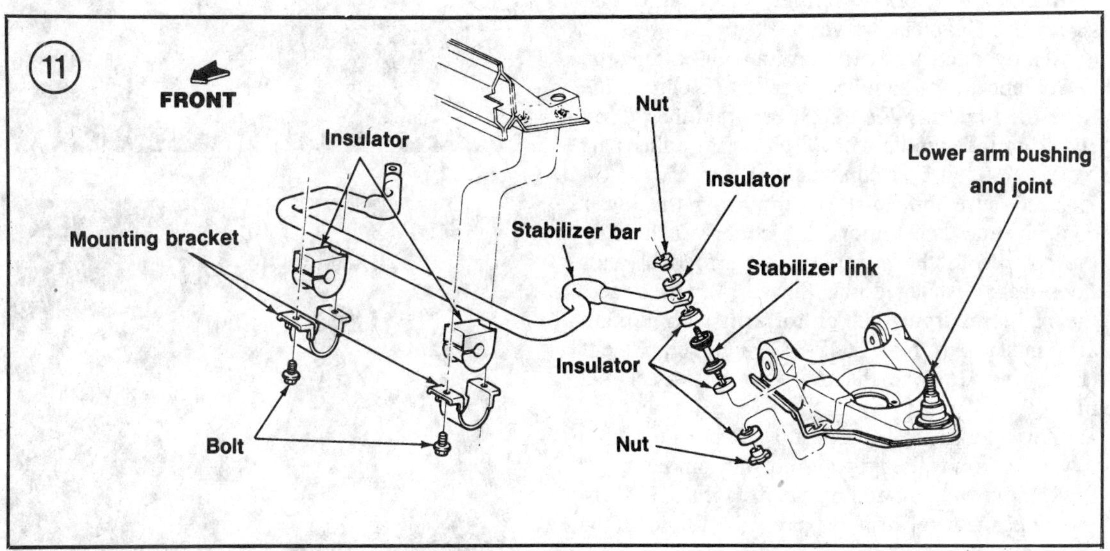

12

Nut
Insulator
Outer washer
Upper control arm
Tie rod end
Bolt
Nut
Cotter pin
Spindle
Nut
Stabilizer bar link
Insulator
Nut
Cotter pin
Nut
Shock absorber
Lower control arm
Bolts

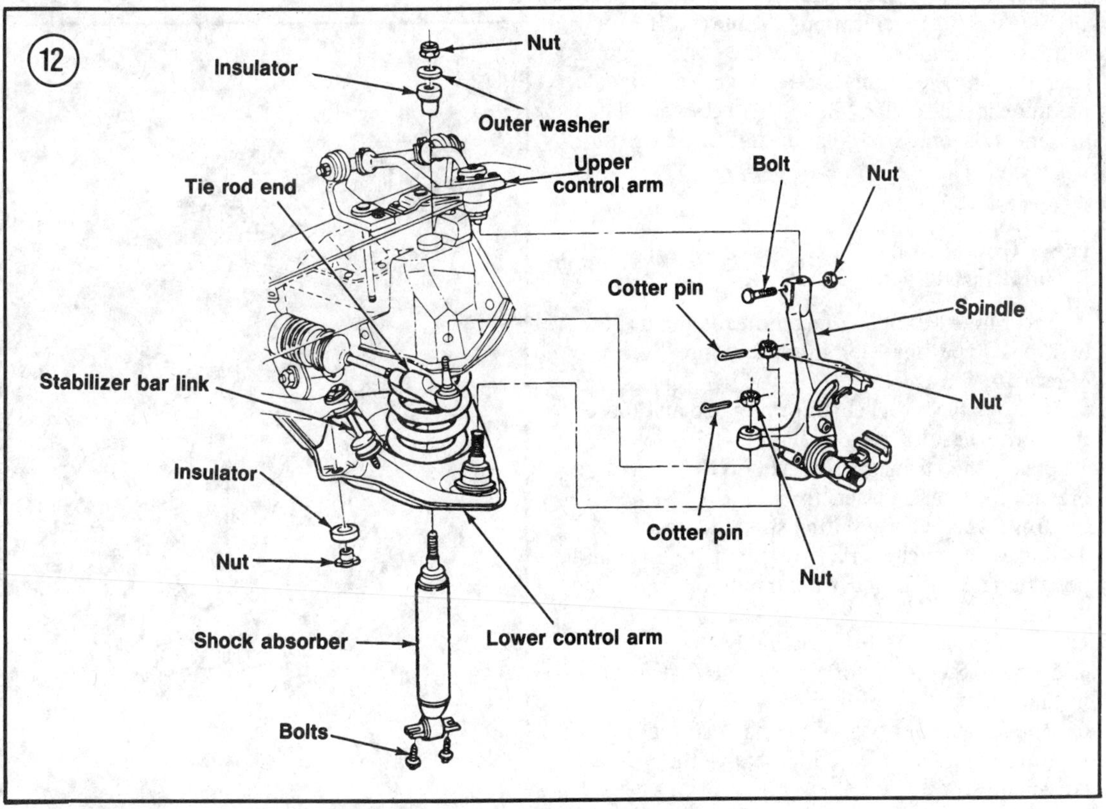

2. Place the transmission in NEUTRAL to prevent the steering wheel from locking. Make sure the front wheels are pointing straight ahead.
3. Raise the vehicle on a twin-post type hoist and position jackstands under the frame to support the vehicle.
4. Remove the wheel/tire assembly.
5. Remove the brake caliper, rotor and dust shield. See Chapter Twelve.
6. Remove the cotter pin from the nut holding the tie rod end to the spindle lower arm. Remove the castellated nut. See **Figure 13**. Separate the tie rod end from the spindle with Pitman arm puller part No. T64P-3590-F or equivalent (**Figure 9**).
7. Make sure the hoist is supporting the lower control arm, then remove the cotter pin holding the spindle to the lower control arm ball-joint. Loosen the castellated nut (**Figure 14**). Disconnect the ball-joint from the control arm with Pitman arm puller part No. T64P-3590-F or equivalent (**Figure 9**). Remove the tool and the castellated nut.
8. Slowly lower the front post of the hoist until the lower ball-joint disengages from the spindle.
9. Remove the bolt and nut holding the spindle to the upper control arm (**Figure 15**). Remove the spindle.
10. Installation is the reverse of removal. Tighten all fasteners to specifications (**Table 1**). If a new cotter pin cannot be installed in the castellated nut after the proper torque has been applied, tighten the nut enough to align the holes in the castellated nut and ball-joint stud, then install the cotter pin.

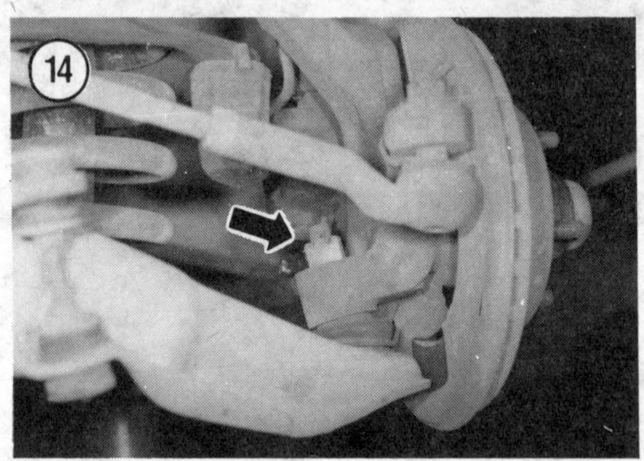

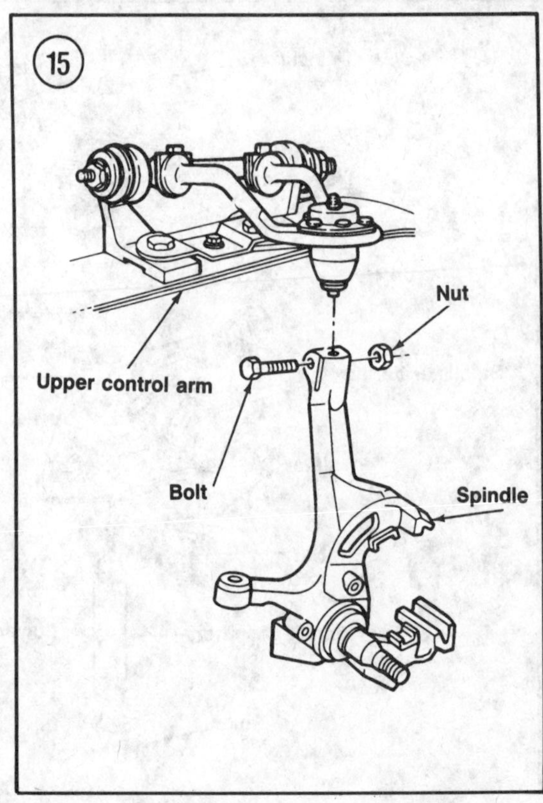

Lower Control Arm Removal/Installation

Ford Motor Company recommends the use of a twin-post type hoist for this procedure. Refer to **Figure 16**.

1. Remove the wheel cover or hub cap and loosen the front wheel lug nuts.
2. Place the transmission in NEUTRAL to prevent the steering wheel from locking. Make sure the front wheels are pointing straight ahead.
3. Raise the vehicle on a twin-post type hoist and position jackstands under the frame to support the vehicle.
4. Remove the wheel/tire assembly.
5. Perform Steps 6-14 of *Coil Spring Replacement* in this chapter.
6. Rotate the front post of the hoist so that it will support the vehicle underneath the No. 1 crossmember.

7. Unbolt and remove the lower control arm from the No. 1 crossmember. If lower control arm bushings require replacement, the entire lower control arm must be replaced.
8. Installation is the reverse of removal, plus the following:

a. Install the No. 1 crossmember bolts as shown in **Figure 16**. Do not tighten at this time.

b. After installing the coil spring, bring the vehicle to its normal ride position and torque the No. 1 crossmember fasteners to specifications (**Table 1**).

Upper Ball-joint/Control Arm Assembly Removal/Installation

Ford Motor Company recommends the use of a twin-post type hoist for this procedure. The upper control arm and ball-joint are serviced as an assembly. The adjustment arm and mounting brackets are also serviced as an assembly. Refer to **Figure 17** and **Figure 18** for this procedure.

1. Remove the coil spring as described in this chapter.
2. Remove the spindle as described in this chapter.
3. Unbolt and remove the cowl drain bracket and retainer plate.

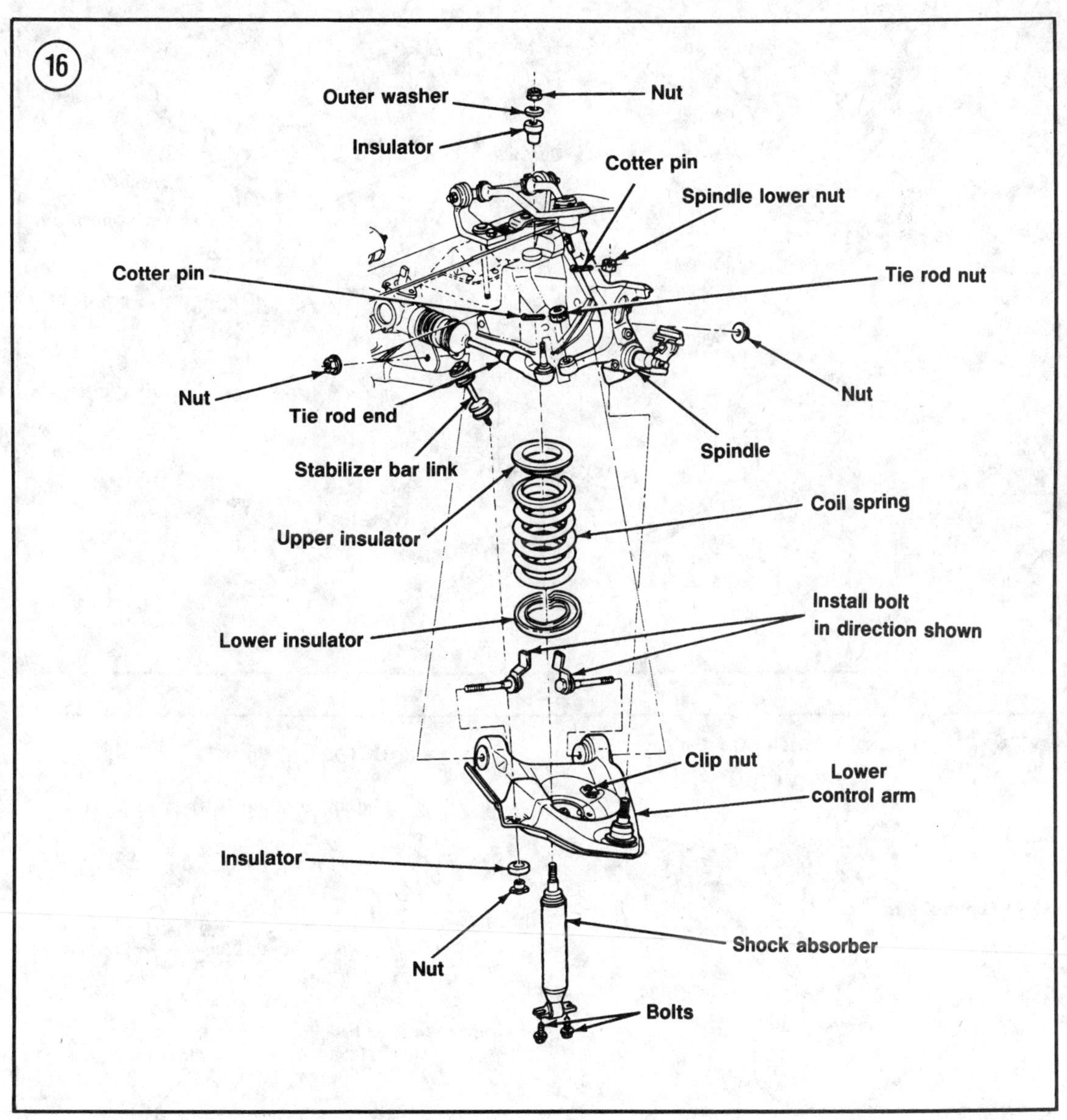

10

4. Mark the position of the control arm mounting brackets on the flat plate, then remove the screw/washer holding the front mounting bracket to the flat plate.
5. Working from under the rail, remove the nuts from the 3 bolts holding the 2 upper control arm mounting brackets to the body rail.
6. Rotate the upper control arm as required to remove the 3 bolts.
7. Remove the upper control arm, upper ball-joint and mounting bracket assembly with flat plate from the vehicle.
8. If necessary, replace the ball-joint boot seal.
9. If necessary, remove the nuts securing the upper control arm to the adjusting arm. Be sure to write down the number and position of any shim on the control arm studs. Remove the control arm from the adjusting arm.
10. The upper control arm and ball-joint are an assembly. If one or the other is defective, both must be replaced.
11. The adjusting arm and mounting brackets are an assembly. If one or the other is defective, both must be replaced.

17

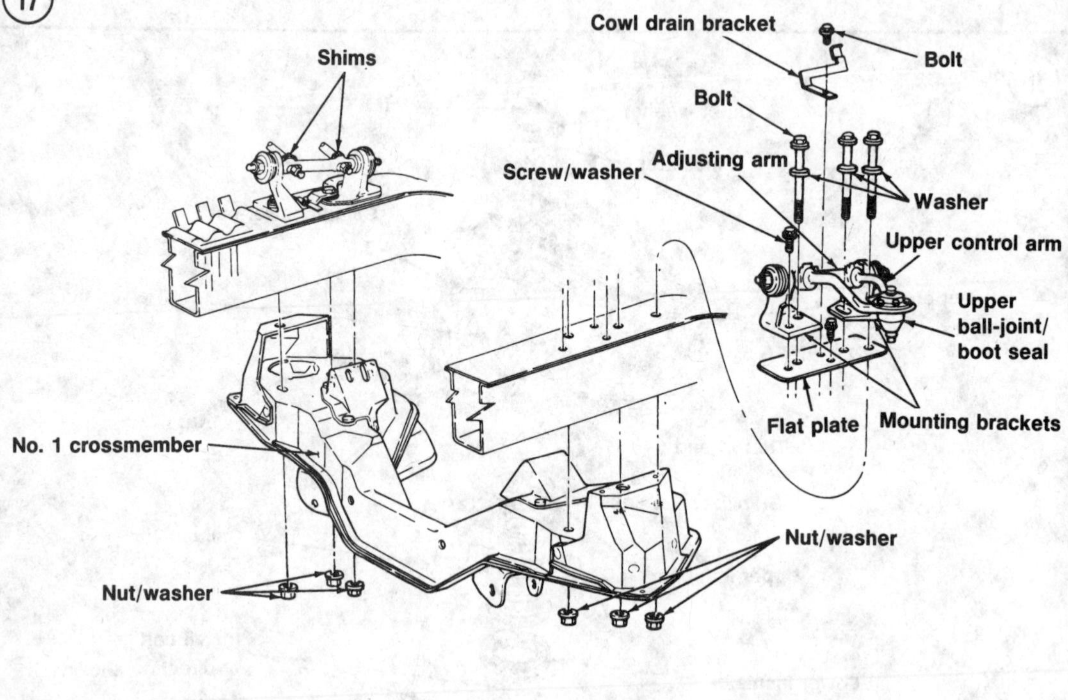

Cowl drain bracket
Bolt
Shims
Bolt
Adjusting arm
Screw/washer
Washer
Upper control arm
Upper ball-joint/ boot seal
Flat plate
Mounting brackets
No. 1 crossmember
Nut/washer
Nut/washer

18

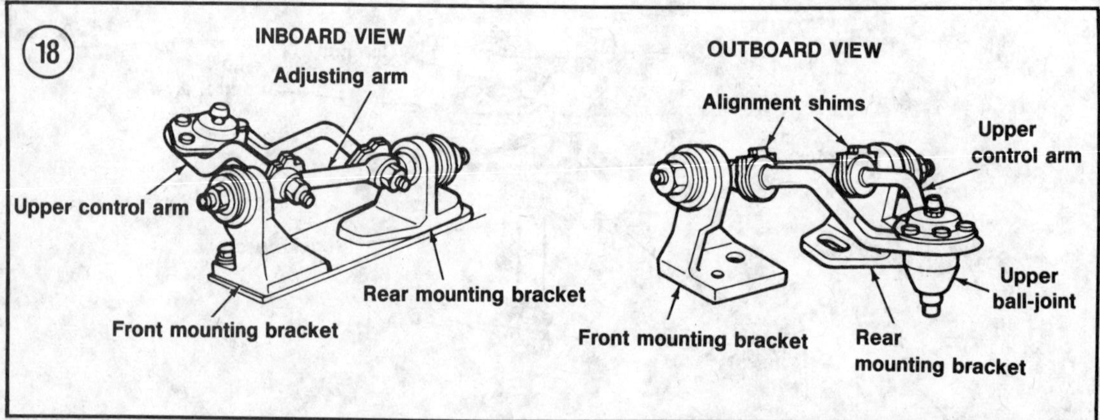

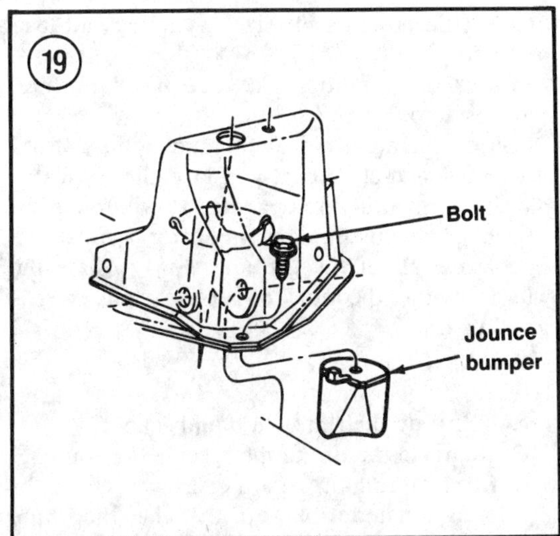

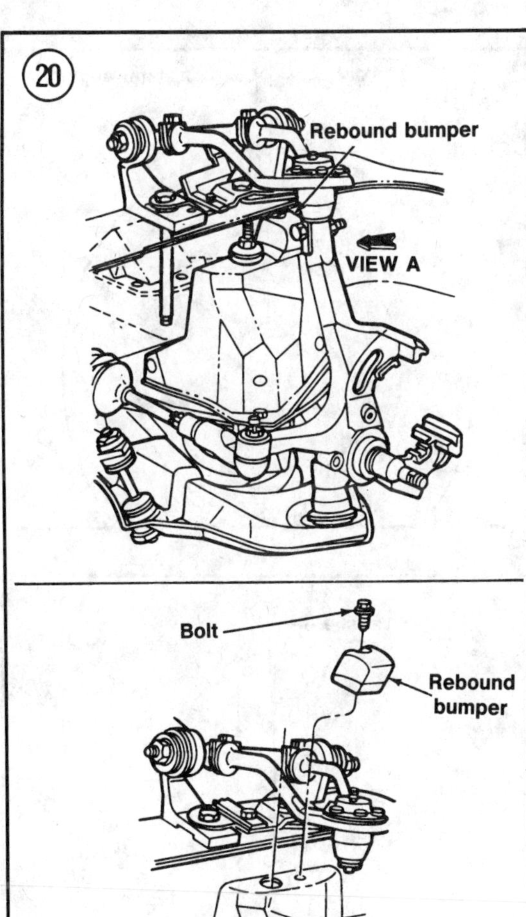

Upper Ball-joint/Control Arm Assembly/Installation

1. If the control arm was removed from the adjusting arm, install it. Be sure to retrun shims to their original locations. The shims control caster and camber.
2. Install the ball-joint boot seal (if removed).
3. Position the mounting bracket flat plate on the body rail. Tighten its mounting bolt to specifications (**Table 1**).
4. Position the mounting bracket/control arm assembly on the flat plate. Install the 3 long bolts/washers that secure the mounting brackets to the body rail. Move the assembly around until its bolt heads rest against the mounting bracket and the studs extend through the body rail.
5. Place the mounting brackets in the position marked during Step 4 of *Removal.*

WARNING
The torque setting in Step 6 is critical. The bolts and nuts must be tightened to the correct torque setting.

6. Install the nuts on the mounting bracket-to-body rail bolts. lTighten to specifications in **Table 1**. Be sure the mounting brackets do not move from their marked positions during tightening.
7. Bolt the front mounting bracket to the flat plate. Tighten the bolt to specifications.
8. Reverse Steps 1-3 of *Installation.*
9. Have wheel alignment checked by a dealer or front-end shop.

Jounce Bumper Removal/Installation

Refer to **Figure 19** for this procedure.

1. Unbolt and remove the jounce bumper from the No. 1 crossmember.
2. Installation is the reverse of removal. Tighten the bolt to 24-33 ft.-lb. (32-45 N•m).

Rebound Bumper Removal/Installation

Refer to **Figure 20** for this procedure.

1. Unbolt and remove the rebound bumper from the shock tower part of the No. 1 crossmember.
2. Installation is the reverse of removal. Tighten the bolt to 15-21 ft.-lb. (20-28 N•m).

WHEEL ALIGNMENT

Several suspension angles affect the running and steering of the front wheels. These angles must be properly aligned to prevent excessive wear, as well as to maintain directional stability and ease of steering. The angles are:

a. Caster.
b. Camber.
c. Toe.
d. Steering axis inclination.
e. Steering lock angles.

Steering axis inclination and steering lock angles are built in and cannot be adjusted. These angles are measured to check for bent suspension parts. Caster and camber should not be adjusted without the use of an alignment rack. Toe can be adjusted at home as described in this section, but the procedure given should be used only as a temporary measure to allow you to drive the vehicle to a dealer or alignment shop where accurate measurements can be made and set.

WARNING
Do not attempt to adjust alignment angles by bending or twisting suspension or steering linkage components.

Pre-Alignment Check

Adjustment of the steering and various suspension angles is affected by several factors. For this reason, steering and handling problems which may seem to be caused by misalignment can result from other factors which are easily corrected without expensive equipment. The following procedure should be carried out whenever steering, handling or tire wear problems exist. It should also be performed before having the alignment checked or prior to adjusting the toe setting.

1. Check tire pressure (with tires cold) and adjust to the specified pressure, if necessary. Both front tires should be the same size, ply rating and load range.
2. Check tire condition. See *Tire Wear Analysis*, Chapter Two.
3. Check the radial and lateral runout of both front tires with a dial indicator. Place the indicator plunger against the tire tread and slowly rotate the wheel. Then position the indicator against the outer sidewall of the tire and slowly rotate the wheel. If either the radial or lateral runout exceeds 0.080 inch:
   a. Deflate the tire.
   b. Rotate the tire 90° on the rim.
   c. Lubricate the rim with liquid soap.
   d. Reinflate the tire to the specified pressure.
   e. Recheck runout. If still excessive, check for foreign material between the wheel and hub. Clean as required and recheck.

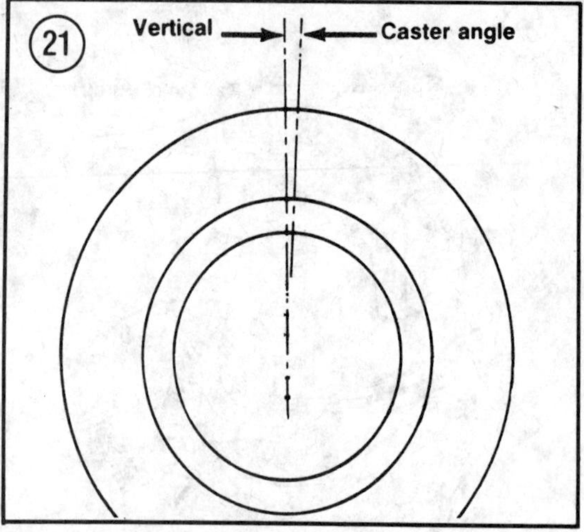

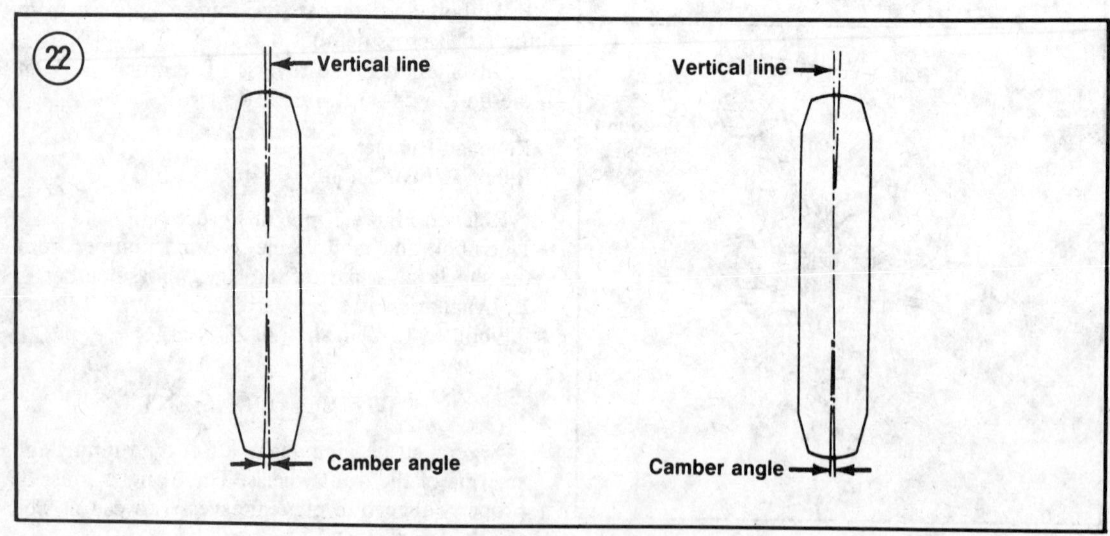

f. If runout is still too high, check for a bent wheel. If the wheel is not bent, the tire is defective.

4. Check all suspension components, steering components and linkage for wear, damage or improper adjustment. Replace if required as described in this chapter.
5. Check the steering gear rack mounting bolt torque. Retighten as required.
6. Make sure the suspension is properly lubricated. See Chapter Three.
7. Check brakes for proper operation. See Chapter Twelve.
8. Check the shock absorbers for proper operation as described in this section.
9. Check wheels and balance as required.
10. Check rear suspension for looseness.

Front tire wear problems can indicate alignment problems. These are covered under *Tire Wear Analysis*, Chapter Two.

Caster and Camber

Caster is the inclination from vertical of the line through the ball-joints (**Figure 21**). Positive caster shifts the wheel forward; negative caster shifts the wheel rearward. Caster causes the wheels to return to a straight-ahead position after a turn. It also prevents the wheels from wandering due to wind, potholes or uneven road surfaces.

Camber is the inclination of the wheel from vertical (**Figure 22**). With positive camber, the top of the tire leans outward. With negative camber, the top of the tire leans inward. Excessive camber causes tire wear. Negative camber wears the inside of the tire; positive camber wears the outside.

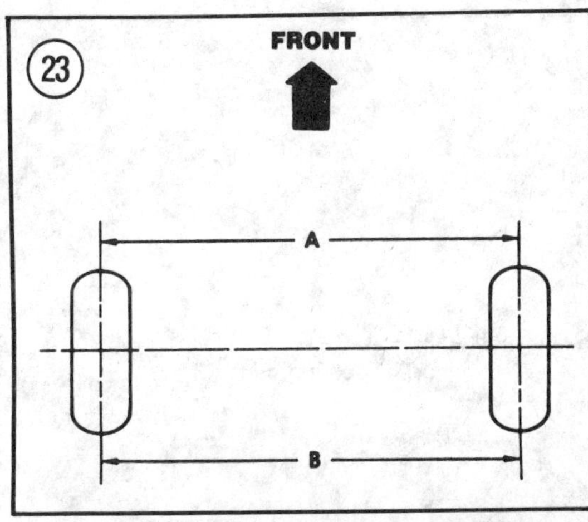

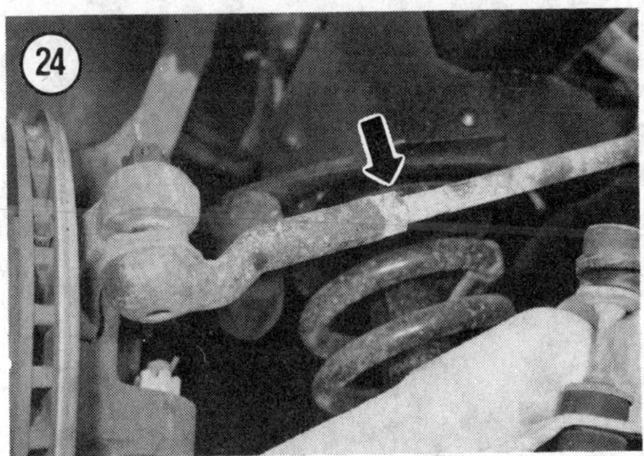

Toe

Since the front wheels tend to point outward when the vehicle is moving in a forward direction, the distance between the front edges of the tire (A, **Figure 23**) is generally slightly less than the distance between the rear edges (B, **Figure 23**) when the vehicle is at rest.

Toe Adjustment

Although toe adjustment requires only a simple homemade tool, it usually is not worth the trouble for home mechanics. Alignment shops include toe adjustment as part of the alignment procedure, so you probably will not save any money by doing it yourself. The procedure described here can be used for an initial toe setting after spindle or ball-joint replacement and allow you to drive the vehicle to a dealer or alignment shop.

1. With the steering wheel centered, roll the vehicle forward about 15 ft. on a smooth, level surface.
2. Mark the center of the tread at the front and rear of each tire.
3. Measure the distance between the forward chalk marks (A, **Figure 23**). Use 2 pieces of telescoping aluminum tubing. Telescope the tubing so each end contacts a chalk mark. Using a sharp center scribe, mark the small diameter tubing where it enters the large diameter tubing.
4. Measure between the rear chalk marks with the telescoping tubes. Make another mark on the small tube where it enters the large one. The distance between the 2 scribe marks is the toe-in and must be divided in half to determine the amount of toe at each wheel.
5. If toe-in is incorrect, remove the bellows seal clamps on the steering rack boots which cover each tie rod end and free the boots from the tie rod ends.
6. Loosen the tie rod end assembly jam nut (**Figure 24**) at each wheel.
7. Using locking pliers and a wrench, grasp the flats provided and rotate the rod assembly as

required until correct alignment (1/32 inch in) is obtained.

8. When alignment is correct, hold each tie rod end with the locking pliers and tighten its jam nut to 43-50 ft.-lb. (58-67 N•m). Reinstall bellows seal clamp.

Steering Axis Inclination

Steering axis inclination is the inward or outward lean of the line through the ball-joints. It is not adjustable on the vehicles covered in this manual but is measured to check for bent suspension parts.

Steering Lock Angles

When a vehicle turns, the inside wheel makes a smaller circle than the outside wheel. Because of this, the inside wheel turns at a greater angle than the outside wheel. These angles are not adjustable on the vehicles covered in this manual.

WHEEL BEARINGS

The front wheels use adjustable tapered roller bearings which must be cleaned, repacked with grease and adjusted at periodic intervals. A grease retainer at the inner end of the hub prevents lubricant from leaking onto the brake rotor. A retainer locknut and cotter pin hold the entire assembly on the spindle.

The rear wheel bearings are sealed and receive their lubrication from the oil carried in the rear differential. There is no adjustment required for the rear bearings.

Front Wheel Bearing Adjustment

Refer to **Figure 25** for this procedure.

1. Securely block both rear wheels so the vehicle will not roll in either direction.
2. Raise the front of the vehicle with a jack enough to lift the front wheels off the ground, then place it on jackstands.
3. Remove the wheel cover or hub cap.
4. Carefully pry the grease cap from the hub and wipe the grease from the end of the spindle.
5. Remove and discard the retainer nut cotter pin. Remove the nut lock retainer.
6. Loosen the adjusting nut 3 full turns. Lightly rap on the brake caliper housing with a soft-faced

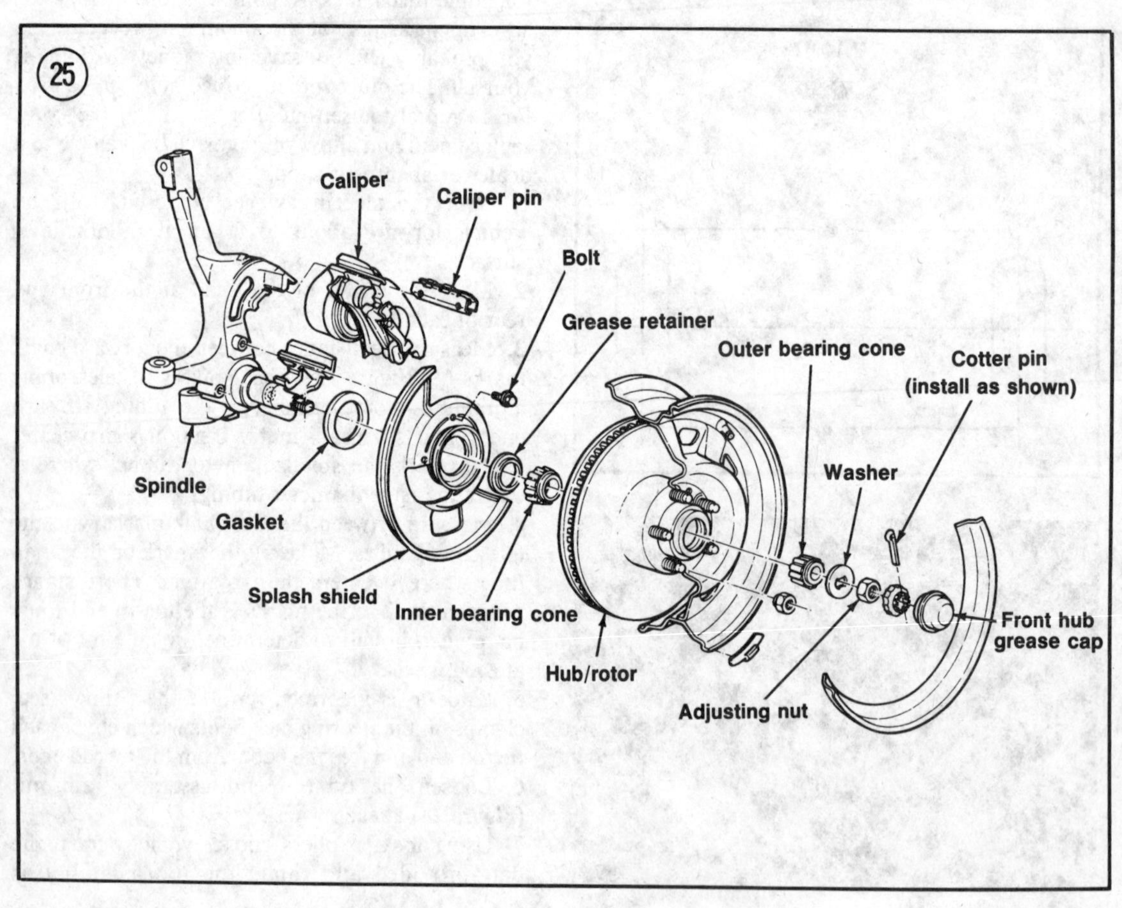

mallet to obtain running clearance between the rotor and brake pads.

7. Rotate the wheel in a forward direction while tightening the adjusting nut to 17-25 ft.-lb. (23-34 N•m). See **Figure 26**.

8. Back the adjusting nut off one full turn (**Figure 27**), then retighten the nut to 18-20 in.-lb. (2.0-2.3 N•m). See **Figure 26**.

9. Fit the nut lock retainer over the adjusting nut. If retainer castellations do not align with cotter pin hole in spindle, remove the retainer, rotate it and put it back on in a different position. Keep trying different positions until the holes align. Install a new cotter pin and bend the ends of the pin up around the retainer. See **Figure 28**.

reinstall the grease cap and wheel cover. If the wheel is still loose, its rotation is noisy or rough or the indicator reading is not within specifications, remove the bearings and cups to check for dirt, damage or excessive wear.

11. Lower the vehicle to the ground. Remove the jackstands and wheel chocks.

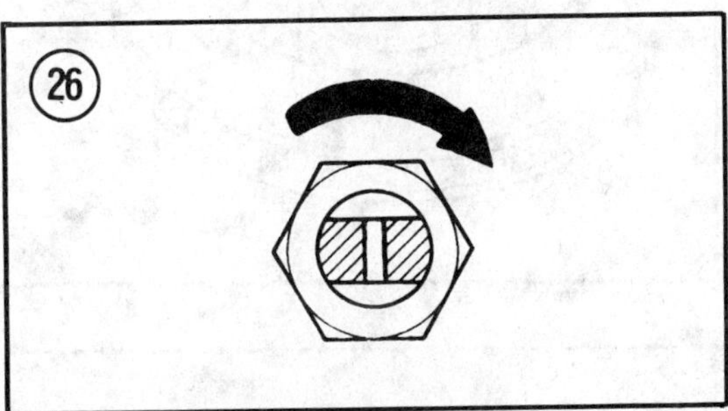
26

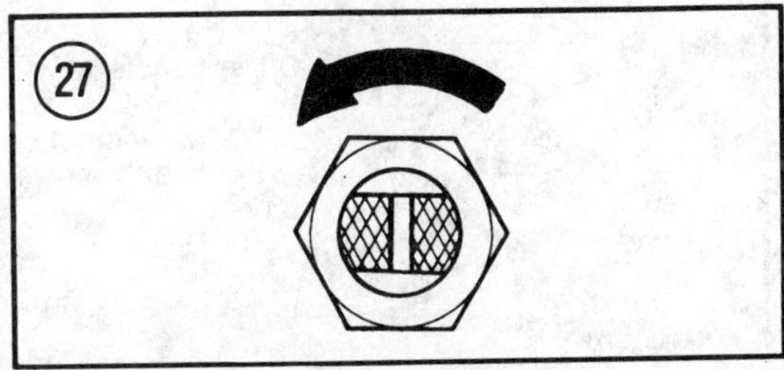
27

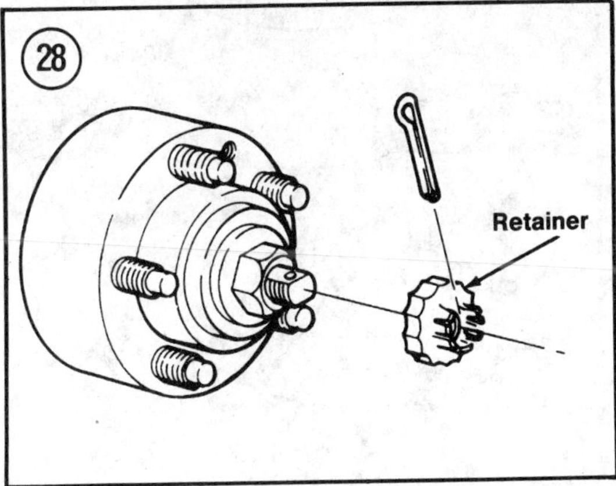

28

Front Wheel Bearing Replacement

If rough and noisy operation or looseness is not eliminated by adjustment, the wheel bearings should be removed, cleaned, inspected and repacked with the specified lubricant or replaced as required. A lithium-base grease such as Ford Multi-purpose Long-life Lubricant (part No. C1AZ-19590-B) or equivalent should be used. Do not use other types of grease, as they are not compatible and can result in premature bearing failure.

Refer to **Figure 25** for this procedure.

1. Remove the wheel cover or hub cap and loosen the front wheel lug nuts.
2. Securely block both rear wheels so the vehicle will not roll in either direction.
3. Raise the front of the vehicle with a jack enough to lift the front wheels off the ground, then place it on jackstands.
4. Remove the wheel/tire assemblies.
5. Remove the brake caliper. See Chapter Twelve.
6. Carefully pry the grease cap from the hub and wipe the grease from the end of the spindle.
7. Remove and discard the retainer nut cotter pin.
8. Remove the adjusting nut and washer from the spindle.
9. Grasp the brake rotor/hub assembly and pull it outward enough to loosen the outer wheel bearing. Remove the outer wheel bearing from the spindle.
10. Pull the brake rotor/hub assembly straight off the spindle to prevent damage to the inner bearings or spindle.
11. Remove and discard the grease seal. Remove the inner bearing assembly from the hub.

WARNING

Do not spin bearings with compressed air in Step 12; it is capable of rotating the bearings at speeds far in excess of those for which they were designed. The bearing could disintegrate, causing damage and injury.

12. Thoroughly clean the bearings, races and inside of the hub with solvent. Blow dry with compressed air.
13. Check the bearing rollers and cups for signs of wear, scoring, pitting, chipping, rust or a bluish tint that indicates overheating. If any of these defects are found, replace the bearings and cups as an assembly.

14. If cups require replacement, use push puller part N. T81P-1104-C and bearing cup puller part No. T77F-1102-A or equivalent as shown in **Figure 29** to remove the old cups.
15. Install new bearing cups using driver part No. T80T-4000-W or equivalent as shown in **Figure 30**.
16. Carefully clean the spindle with a cloth moistened in solvent.
17. Lightly grease the spindle at the outer and inner bearing seats, the shoulder and seal seat with Ford Multi-purpose Long-life Lubricant (part No. C1AZ-19590-B) or equivalent.
18. If installing the original bearings, thoroughly pack the bearing assemblies with Ford Multi-purpose Long-life Lubricant or equivalent. If a bearing packer is not available, work the lubricant in carefully by hand.
19. Lightly coat the inner cone with the same lubricant and install the inner bearing assembly in the inner cup.
20. Place a new seal in the hub. Cover with a flat plate or a block of wood and tap into place until the seal is flush with the hub. Wipe a thin coat of grease across the seal lip.
21. Install the rotor/hub assembly on the spindle, keeping the hub centered to prevent damage to the seal.
22. Install the outer wheel bearing assembly and flat washer on the spindle and seat in the rotor hub. Thread the adjusting nut in place finger-tight.
23. Adjust the wheel bearings as described in this chapter.
24. Reverse Steps 1-5 to complete installation.

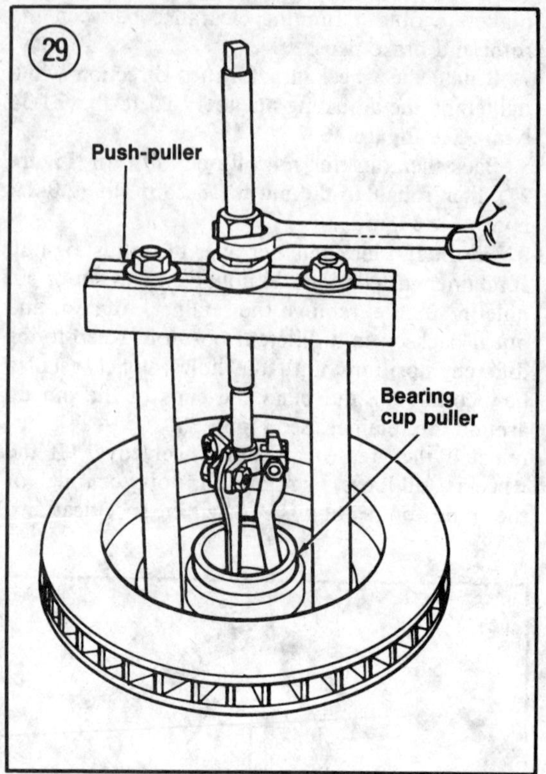

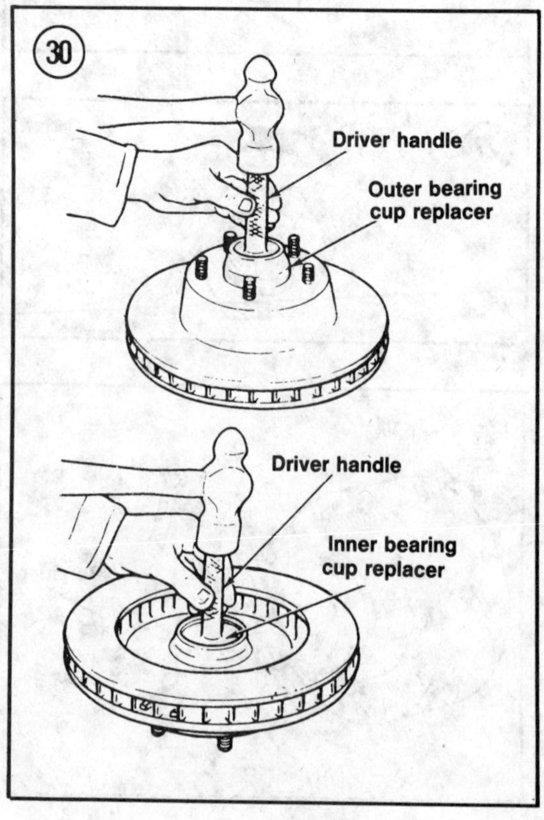

STEERING SYSTEM

Vehicles covered in this manual may be equipped with manual (non-power) or integral power rack-and-pinion steering. The steering gearbox transfers steering wheel movements to the tie rod ends through the integral rack-and-pinion assembly. The tie rods move the spindles to the desired steering angle. **Figure 31** shows the power steering system; **Figure 32** shows the manual steering system.

Tie Rod End Replacement

1. Securely block both rear wheels so the vehicle will not roll in either direction.

Refer to **Figure 31** or **Figure 32** for this procedure.

2. Raise the front of the vehicle with a jack and place it on jackstands.

3. Remove and discard the tie rod ball stud cotter pin. Remove the castellated nut (**Figure 33**) and disconnect the tie rod from the spindle with tool part No. 3290-C or equivalent.
4. Hold the tie rod flat with one wrench and loosen the jam nut with a second wrench. See **Figure 34**.
5. Hold the tie rod flat with locking pliers and unscrew the tie rod end from the tie rod, counting the number of complete turns required.
6. Clean the tie rod threads with a wire brush to remove all rust and contamination. Lubricate the threads with clean engine oil.

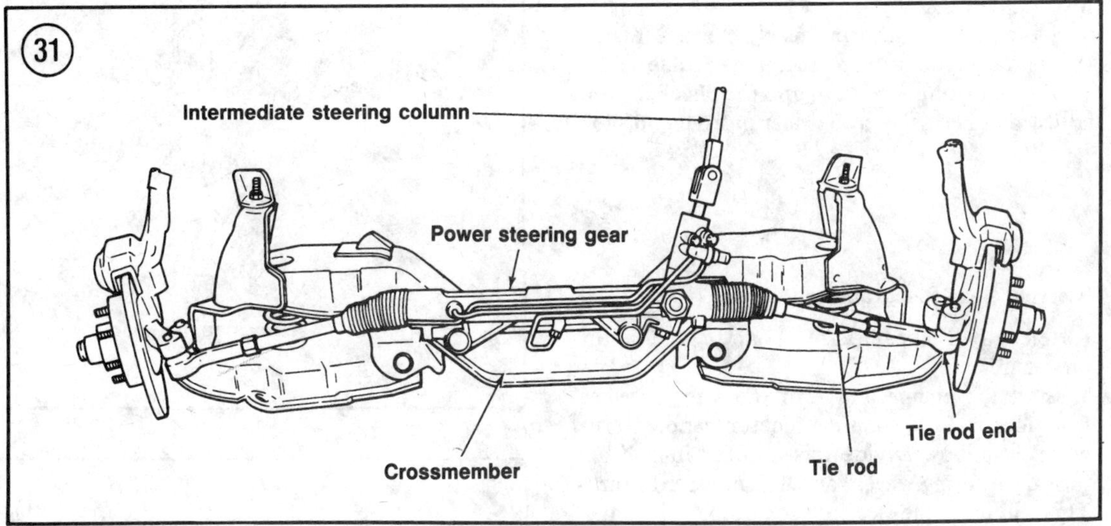

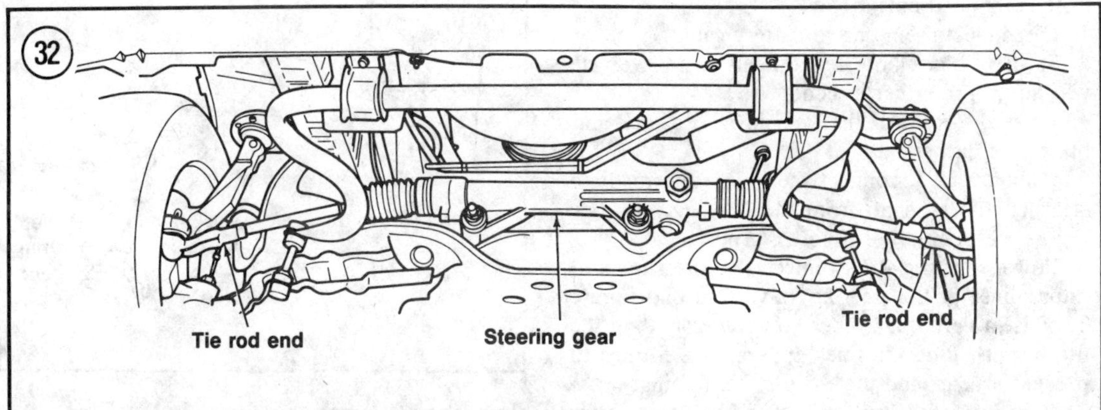

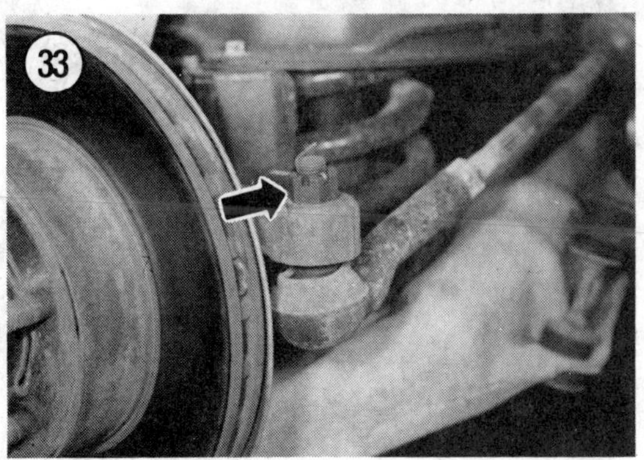

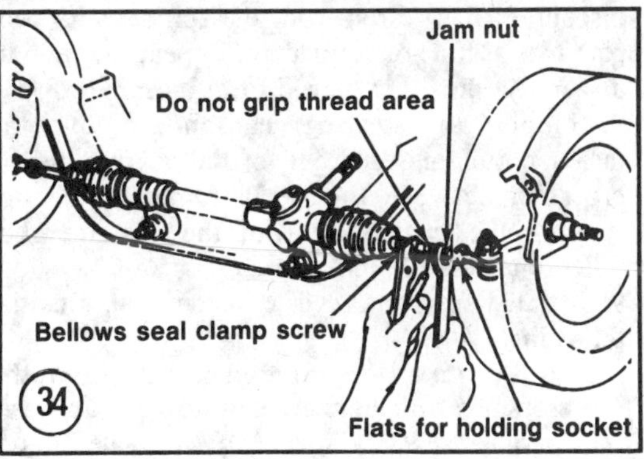

7. Thread the new tie rod end onto the tie rod the same number of turns required to remove the old one.
8. Fit the tie rod ball-stud through the spindle and install a new nut. Tighten the nut to specifications (**Table 1**). If cotter pin hole in nut does not align with hold in stud, tighten nut to align holes and install a new cotter pin.
9. Set toe as described in this chapter and tighten the tie rod jam nut to specifications (**Table 1**).
10. Have front end alignment checked and adjusted as necessary by a dealer or front end shop.

Steering Gear Removal/Installation

Refer to **Figure 31** or **Figure 32** for this procedure.

1. Start the engine and turn the steering wheel from lock-to-lock, counting the number of steering wheel rotations. Divide this number in half and turn the steering wheel back that number of turns. This will place the steering rack in the "on-center" position. Shut the engine off. Leave the ignition key in the ON position.
2. Disconnect the negative battery cable.
3. Securely block both rear wheels so the vehicle will not roll in either direction.
4. Raise the front of the vehicle with a jack and place it on jackstands.
5. Unbolt and disconnect the lower intermediate steering column shaft from the steering gear. See **Figure 35** (manual) or **Figure 36** (power).
6. Power steering—Disconnect the pressure and return lines at the steering valve housing (**Figure 37**). Use a flare nut wrench to avoid rounding the fitting nuts. Plug the lines and cap the fittings to prevent leakage and the entry of contamination.
7. Remove and discard the tie rod ball stud cotter pin. Remove the castellated nut (**Figure 33**) and disconnect the tie rod from the spindle with tool part No. 3290-C or equivalent. Repeat this step to disconnect the other tie rod from its spindle.
8. Support the steering gear and remove the fasteners holding each end of the gearbox to the crossmember. See **Figure 38** (typical). Do not remove the insulators from the crossmember unless they require replacement.
9. Installation is the reverse of removal, plus the following:
   a. If the insulators were removed from the crossmember, lubricate with rubber lubricant (part No. D9AZ-19583-A or equivalent) and

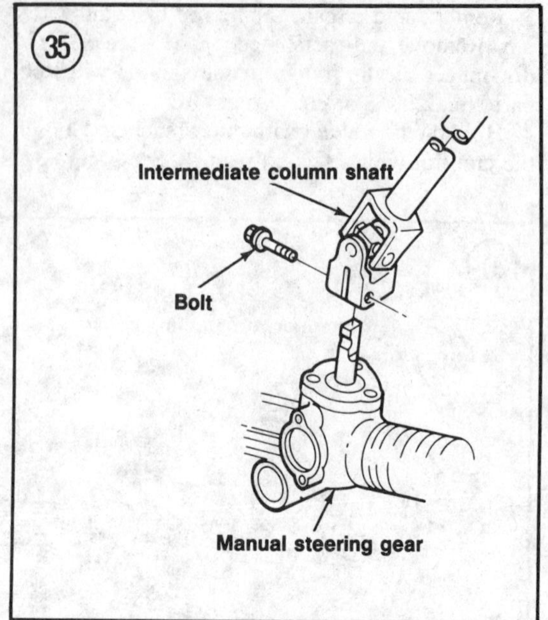

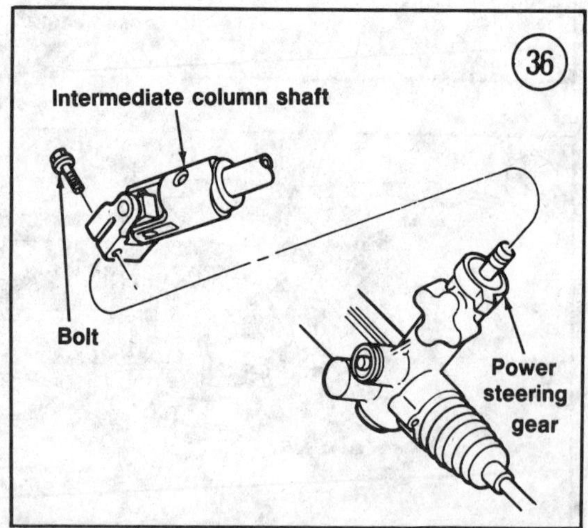

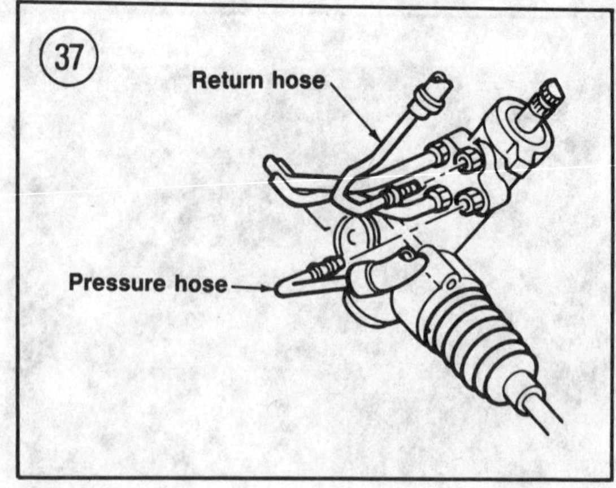

insert completely into the gear housing before installing the gearbox to the crossmember. There should be no gap between the gear boss face and insulator when properly installed. See **Figure 39**.

b. Tighten all fasteners to specifications (**Table 1**).

38

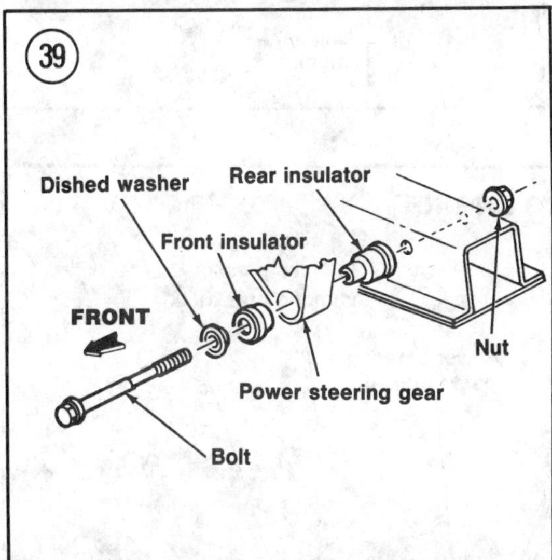

39

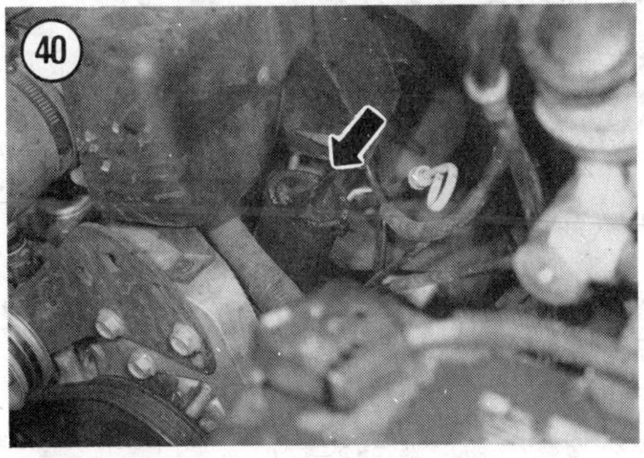

40

c. Power steering—Fill the power steering pump reservoir (**Figure 40**) with power steering fluid. Start the engine and run for several seconds, then recheck the fluid level and top up if necessary. Repeat this procedure until the fluid level remains constant after running the engine. With the engine running, turn the steering wheel lock-to-lock several times and recheck the fluid level. Top up if necessary, then shut the engine off.

d. Have front end alignment check and adjusted if necessary by a dealer or alignment shop.

2.3L Power Steering Pump Removal/Installation

Refer to **Figure 41** for this procedure.

1. Disconnect the fluid return hose at the power steering pump reservoir and drain the fluid in the hose into a suitable container.
2. Disconnect the pressure hose at the pump.
3. Loosen the alternator pivot and adjusting bolts. Move the alternator toward the engine to eliminate belt tension. Remove the drive belt from the power steering pump pulley.
4. Install pulley remover part No. T69L-10300-B on the pump pulley. Hold the pump from moving and turn the tool nut counterclockwise to remove the pulley.
5. Unbolt the pump from the bracket. Remove the pump from the engine compartment.
6. Installation is the reverse of removal, plus the following:
   a. Tighten pump bolts to 30-45 ft.-lb. (41-61 N•m).
   b. Install pulley with pulley replacer part No. T65P-3A733-C. Pull-off groove on pulley must face front of vehicle and pulley must be pressed in place on the shaft with a tolerance of flush to 0.010 in. (0.254 mm).
   c. Tighten alternator pivot bolt to 45-57 ft.-lb. (61-78 N•m) and adjusting bolt to 24-40 ft.-lb. (33-54 N•m).
   d. Fill the power steering pump reservoir with power steering fluid. Start the engine and run for several seconds, then recheck the fluid level and top up if necessary. Repeat this procedure until the fluid level remains constant after running the engine. With the engine running, turn the steering wheel lock-to-lock several times and recheck the fluid level. Top up if necessary, then shut the engine off.

41
Power steering pump
VIEW A
Pressure hose
VIEW B
Return hose
Power steering gear
Power steering pressure switch
MAIN VIEW
2.3L ENGINE
Power steering pump
Bolt
Support bracket
Power steering pressure switch
Pulley
Clamp
Pressure hose
Pulley pull-off groove must face front
Return hose
VIEW B
VIEW A
Support bracket
Bolt
Engine block

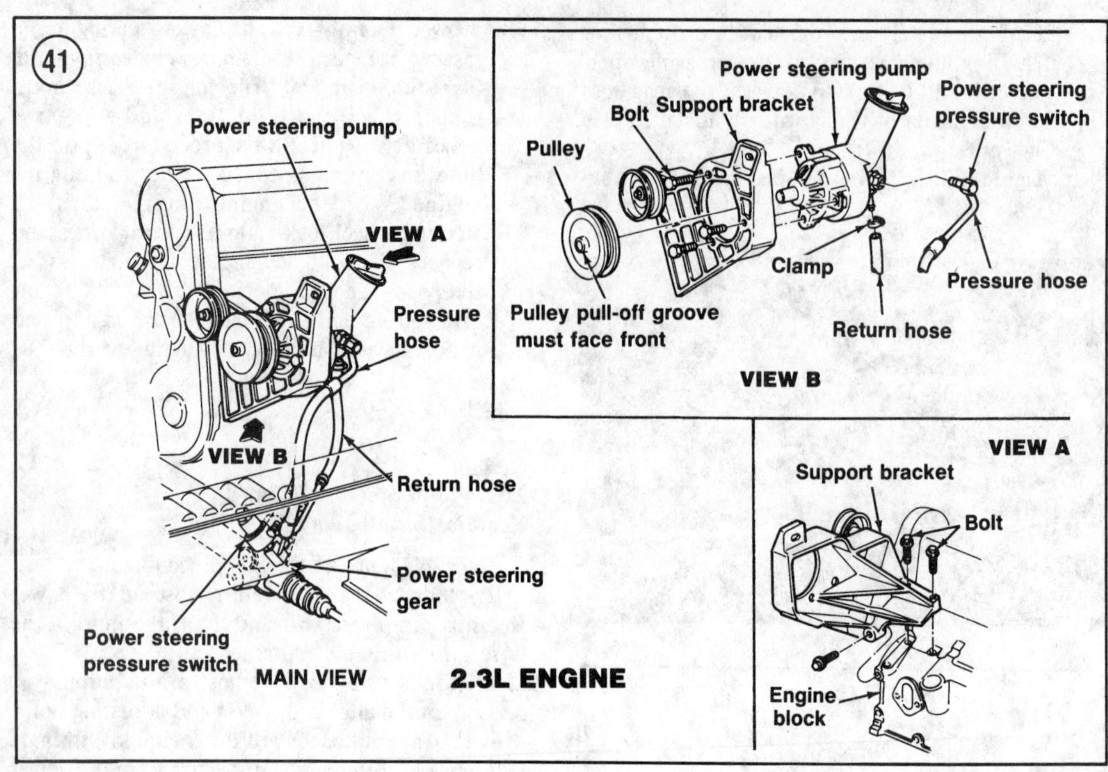

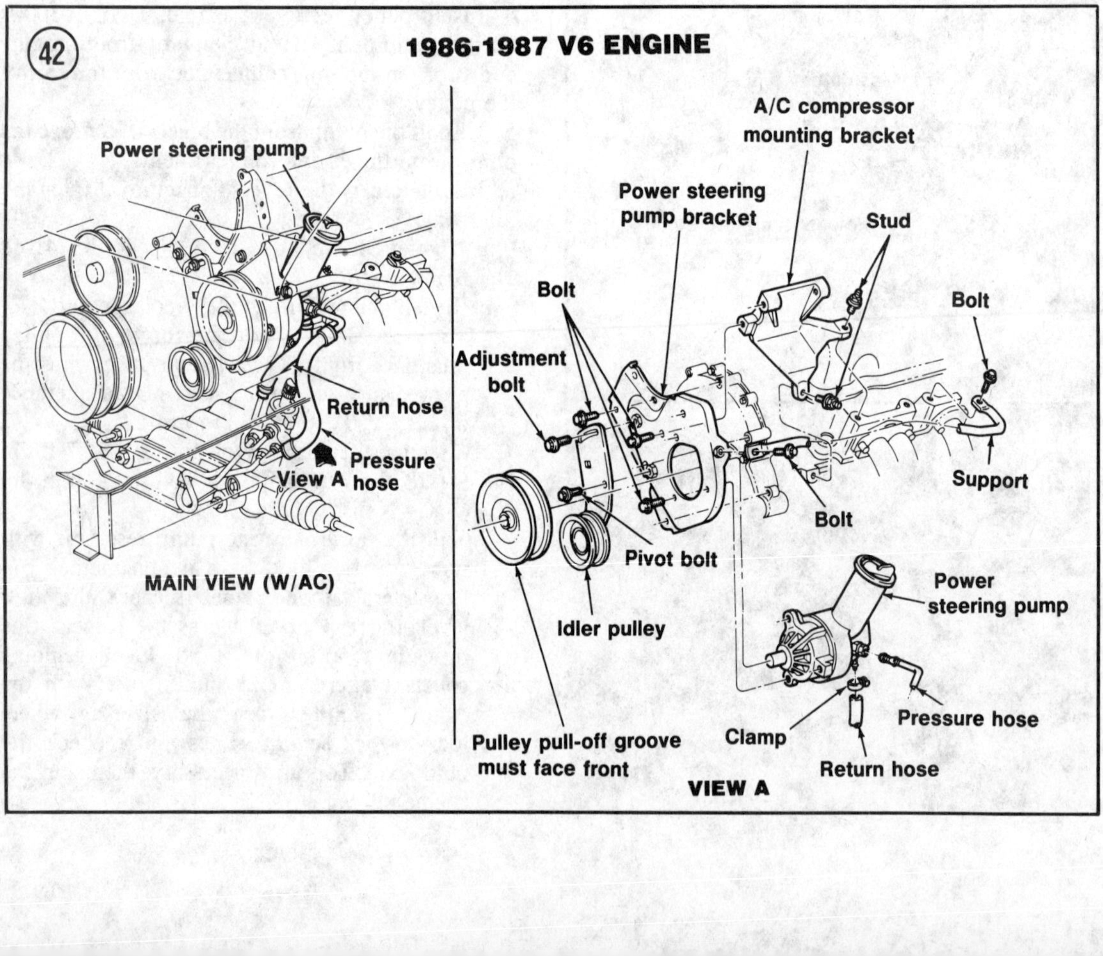

42
1986-1987 V6 ENGINE
Power steering pump
Return hose
Pressure hose
View A
MAIN VIEW (W/AC)
A/C compressor mounting bracket
Power steering pump bracket
Stud
Bolt
Bolt
Adjustment bolt
Support
Bolt
Pivot bolt
Idler pulley
Power steering pump
Pressure hose
Clamp
Pulley pull-off groove must face front
Return hose
VIEW A

V6 Power Steering Pump Removal/Installation

Refer to **Figure 42** (1986-1987) or **Figure 43** (1988) for this procedure.

1. Disconnect the fluid return hose at the power steering pump reservoir and drain the fluid in the hose into a suitable container.
2. Disconnect the pressure hose at the pump.
3. Loosen the idler pulley pivot and adjusting bolts. Remove the drive belt from the power steering pump pulley.
4. Install pulley remover part No. T69L-10300-B on the pump pulley. Hold the pump from moving and turn the tool nut counterclockwise to remove the pulley.
5. Unbolt the support. Unbolt the pump from the bracket. Remove the pump from the engine compartment.
6. Installation is the reverse of removal, plus the following:

   a. Tighten pump bolts to 35-47 ft.-lb. (47-64 N•m). Tighten support to 35-47 ft.-lb. (47-64 N•m).
   b. Install pulley with pulley replacer part No. T65P-3A733-C. Pull-off groove on pulley must face front of vehicle and pulley must be pressed in place on the shaft with a tolerance of flush to 0.010 in. (0.254 mm).
   c. Fit belt over pulley, insert a 1/2 in. drive breaker bar in idler pulley slot and rotate

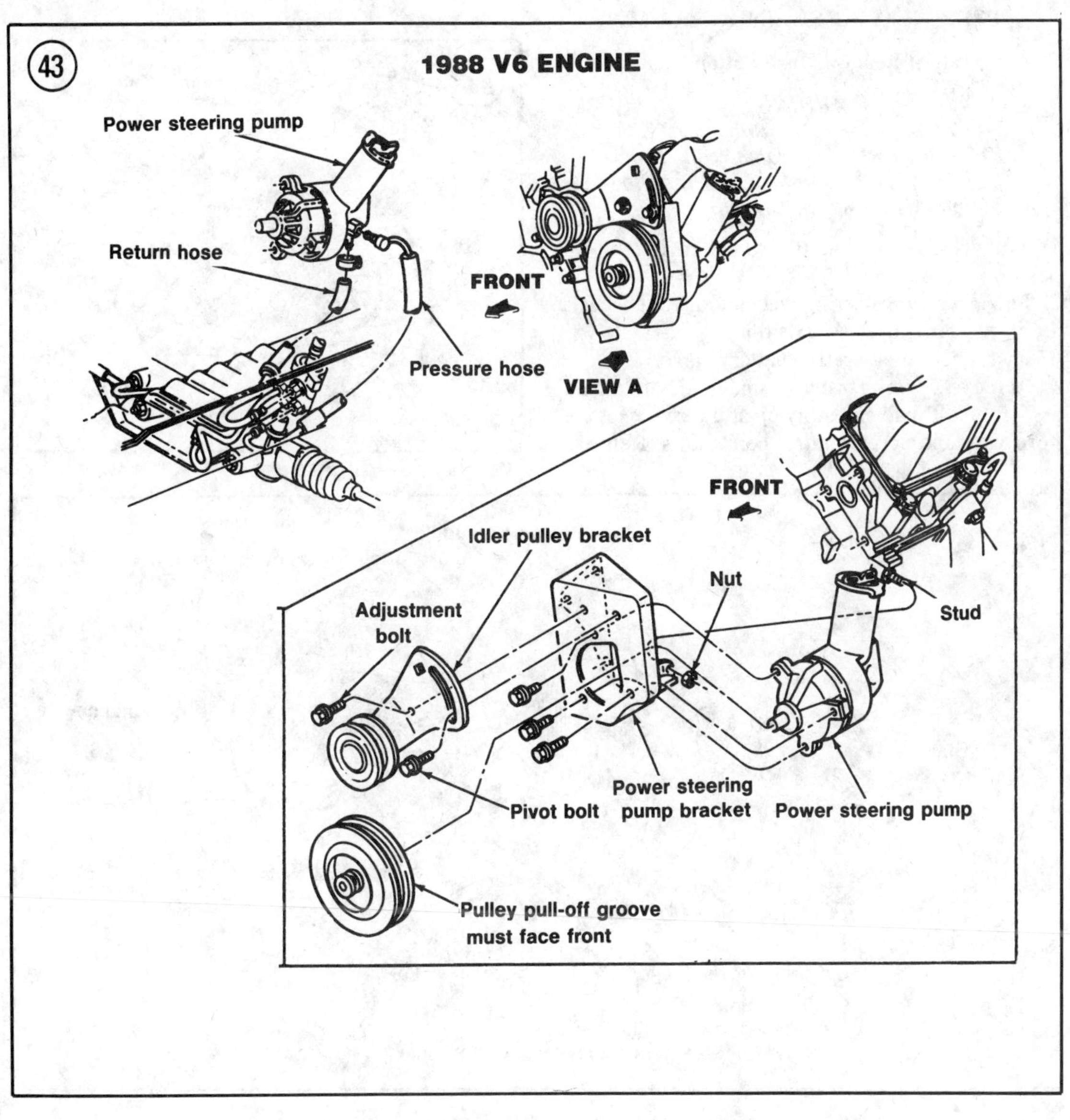

pulley assembly until 80-100 lb. tension is shown with a tension gauge, then tighten adjusting and pivot bolts to 35-47 ft.-lb. (47-64 N•m).

d. Fill the power steering pump reservoir with power steering fluid. Start the engine and run for several seconds, then recheck the fluid level and top up if necessary. Repeat this procedure until the fluid level remains constant after running the engine. With the engine running, turn the steering wheel lock-to-lock several times and recheck the fluid level. Top up if necessary, then shut the engine off.

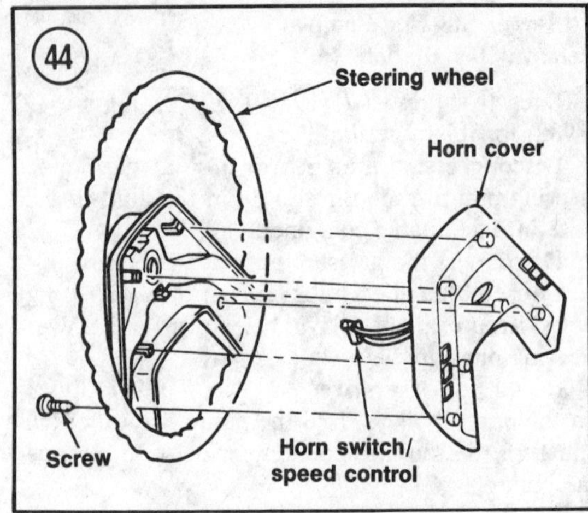

STEERING WHEEL AND COLUMN

Steering Wheel Removal/Installation

WARNING
Use of a puller other than part No. T67L-3600-A or equivalent can shear or loosen the plastic fasteners used to maintain steering wheel rigidity.

1. Tilt wheel—Position the wheel in its full-up position.
2. Make sure the steering wheel and front wheels are in the straight-ahead position.
3. Disconnect the negative battery cable.
4. Remove 2 screws from the underside of the pad assembly. Lift pad assembly up and disconnect the horn wire and speed control connectors. Remove

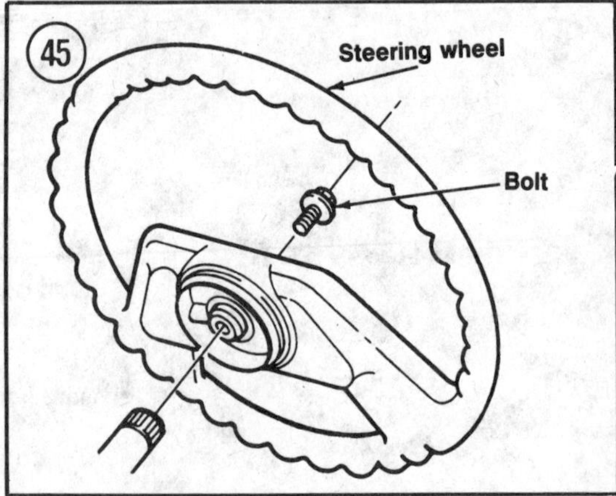

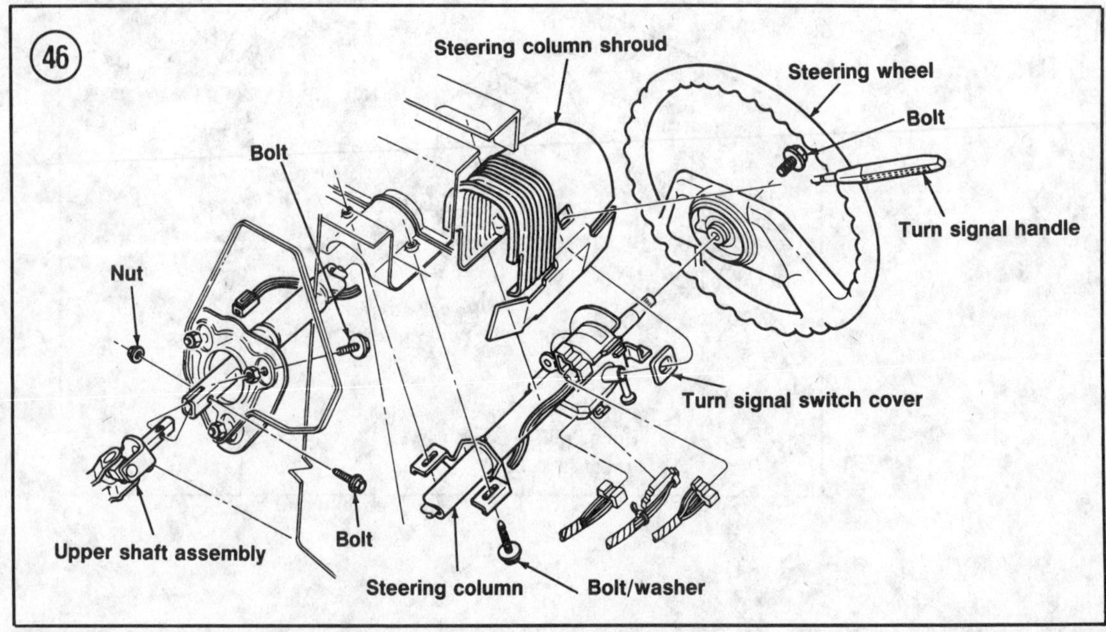

the horn cover assembly from the steering wheel. See **Figure 44**.

5. Remove the steering wheel attaching bolt (**Figure 45**).

6. Install wheel puller part No. T67L-3600-A or equivalent and tighten until the steering wheel comes free of the steering column upper shaft.

7. Remove the puller. Remove the steering wheel from the steering column.

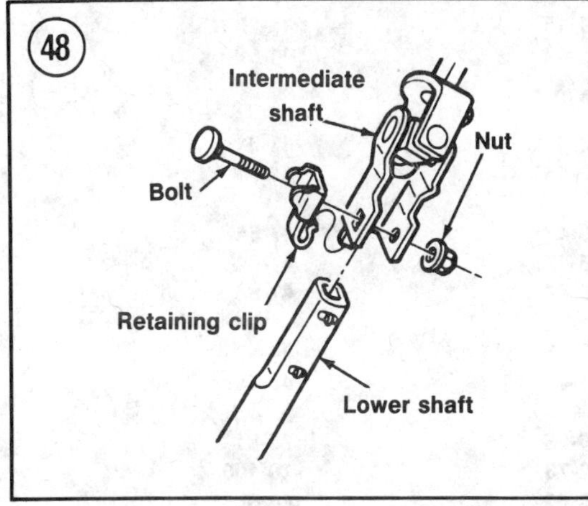

8. Installation is the reverse of removal. Align the notch on the steering wheel with the mark on the steering column. Install and tighten the steering wheel bolt to 23-33 ft.-lb. (31-45 N•m).

Steering Column Removal

WARNING

The steering column is very susceptible to damage during and after removal from the vehicle. Hammering, dropping or leaning on the column can damage internal plastic injections used to maintain rigidity.

This procedure applies to both standard and tilt-wheel columns. Refer to **Figure 46**.

1. Disconnect the negative battery cable.
2. Unbolt the steering column shaft from the intermediate shaft assembly. See **Figure 47**. Disconnect the shafts.
3. Remove the steering wheel as described in this chapter.
4. Remove the steering column trim shrouds.
5. Tilt wheel—Squeeze the upper extension shroud at the top and bottom and pop it free of the retaining plate.
6. Unbolt and remove the instrument panel cover directly below the column.
7. Unplug all electrical connectors to the column and column switches.
8. Loosen but do not remove the 2 bolts holding the column to the lower instrument panel bracket.
9. Remove the 3 screws holding the column toeplate/lower seal to the dash panel.
10. Remove the 2 bolts loosened in Step 8.
11. Lower the steering column and remove it from the vehicle.
12. Installation is the reverse of removal. Refer to **Figure 48** for correct installation of steering shaft attaching bolt and clip. Tighten all fasteners to specifications (**Table 1**).

Table 1 is on the following page.

Table 1 TIGHTENING TORQUES

Fastener	ft.-lb.	N·m
SUSPENSION		
Crossmember-to-frame rail	145-195	196-264
Cowl drain bracket-to-frame	10-14	14-18
Jounce bumper-to-frame	24-33	32-45
Lower control arm-to-crossmember	100-140*	136-190*
Rebound bumper-to-frame	15-21	20-28
Shock absorber		
Upper end	25-35	34-48
Lower end	16-24	22-33
Spindle		
To upper ball-joint	27-37	37-50
To lower ball-joint	80-120	108-163
Stabilizer bar		
To lower control arm	9-12	12-16
Mounting bracket-to-frame	16-24	22-33
Stabilizer link-to-stabilizer bar	9-12	12-16
Tie rod end-to-spindle arm	52-74	70-100
Upper control arm-to-adjusting arm	70-100	95-135
Wheel lug nuts	85-115	115-155
STEERING GEARBOX AND PUMP		
Attaching fasteners	80-105	108-142
Fluid line fittings @ gearbox	10-15	15-20
Intermediate shaft pinch bolt	30-42	41-56
Power steering pump		
2.3L		
Pump-to-support bracket	30-45	41-61
Support brcket-to-engine block	30-45	41-61
1986 V6		
Pump-to-support bracket	35-47	47-64
Idler adjustment/pivot bolts	35-47	47-64
Support brace bolts	35-47	47-64
1987-on V6		
Pump-to-bracket	25-35	34-47
Idler adjustment/pivot bolts	35-47	47-64
Tie rod		
Ball socket to rack	55-65	75-81
End to spindle nut	52-73	70-100
Jam nut	35-50	48-68
STEERING COLUMN AND WHEEL		
Column-to-brake/clutch pedal support	11-17	15-23
Column toeplate-to-dash	11-17	15-23
Intermediate shaft-to-column shaft	30-42	41-57
Flex coupling-to-steering gear bolt	30-42	41-57
Lock cylinder housing-to-bracket	12-21	17-28
Steering wheel bolt	23-33	32-45

* Tighten with axle in normal ride position.

CHAPTER ELEVEN

REAR SUSPENSION, DIFFERENTIAL AND DRIVE SHAFT

This chapter provides service procedures for the rear suspension, rear axle and axle shafts, drive shaft and differential. Tightening torques are provided in **Table 1** at the end of the chapter.

REAR SUSPENSION

A tri-beam rear suspension is used on all vehicles. This type of rear suspension consists of a single upper control arm, 2 lower control arms and 2 coil springs (**Figure 1**).

The coil springs are matched to the load capacity rate of the vehicle. If one coil spring is replaced, the replacement spring must have the same capacity rating as the remaining spring.

The upper and lower control arms position the rear axle in the vehicle. The upper arm locates the axle from side-to-side (laterally) while the lower arms locate it front-to-rear. All of the arms are sensitive to any braking or acceleration forces applied to the rear axle.

The upper control arm is attached at 3 points. The rear leg bolts to the rear axle housing through a bushing; the front leg bolts to the right-hand frame bracket through a bushing and the lateral leg has an integral stud which allows it to connect to the left-hand frame rail. The bushing used to attach the rear leg contains a cam adjuster which can be rotated to change the rear axle pinion angle.

The front of each lower control arm is fastened to a frame bracket with a special bolt (**Figure 3**); the rear of the control arm bolts to a bracket on the rear axle housing (**Figure 4**). Each lower control arm contains the lower seat for the coil spring.

Rear axle travel during jounce is controlled by rubber bumpers attached to each side of the rear axle tube (**Figure 5**). These bumpers contact the vehicle frame rail during vehicle travel over rough terrain. Vehicles rated for a standard payload have 2 bumpers; those with the optional payload rating have 4 bumpers.

11

Telescopic shock absorbers containing low pressure nitrogen gas dampen road shock to provide road comfort. Shock absorbers are installed between the frame rail and axle housing bracket. They are tuned according to vehicle operation, which should be taken into account when replacing a defective unit.

Shock Absorber Inspection

Shock absorbers in doubtful condition can be inspected as described under *Front Suspension,* Chapter Eleven.

Shock Absorber Removal/Installation

Always use new rubber insulators/bushings when installing new shock absorbers. Refer to **Figure 2** (typical) for this procedure.

1. Securely block the front wheels. Raise the rear of the vehicle with a jack and place it on jackstands.
2. Place a hydraulic jack underneath the axle housing. Raise the axle to remove its weight from the coil springs and shock absorbers.
3. Remove the nut and bolt holding the shock absorber to its lower mounting bracket (**Figure 6**). Pivot the lower end of the shock absorber from the axle housing bracket.
4. Remove the bolt and washer holding the shock absorber to its upper mounting bracket (**Figure 7**). Remove the shock absorber from the vehicle.
5. Position the upper end of the shock absorber on the mounting bracket with the insulator/bushing and washer. Install the attaching bolt with washer. Finger-tighten the bolt.
6. Repeat Step 5 to attach the lower end of the shock absorber. The bolt should be installed with its head on the outer side of the vehicle. Tighten the nut to 41-65 ft.-lb. (55-88 N•m).
7. Tighten the upper attaching bolt to 25-35 ft.-lb. (38-48 N•m).
8. Remove the jackstands and lower the vehicle to the ground. Remove the wheel chocks.

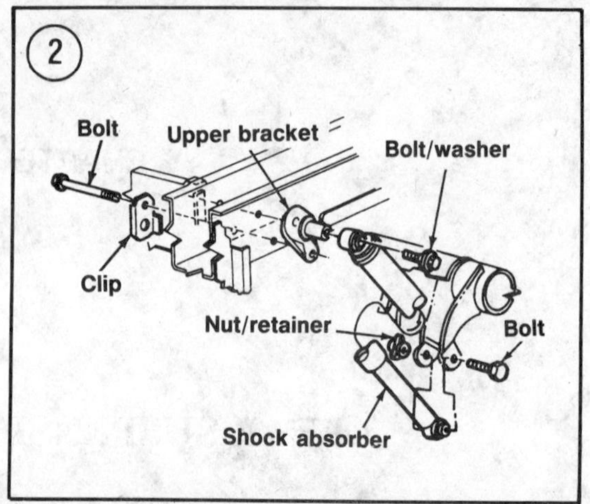

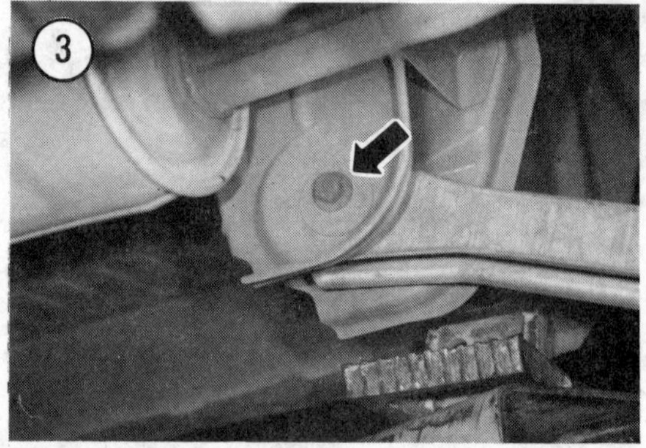

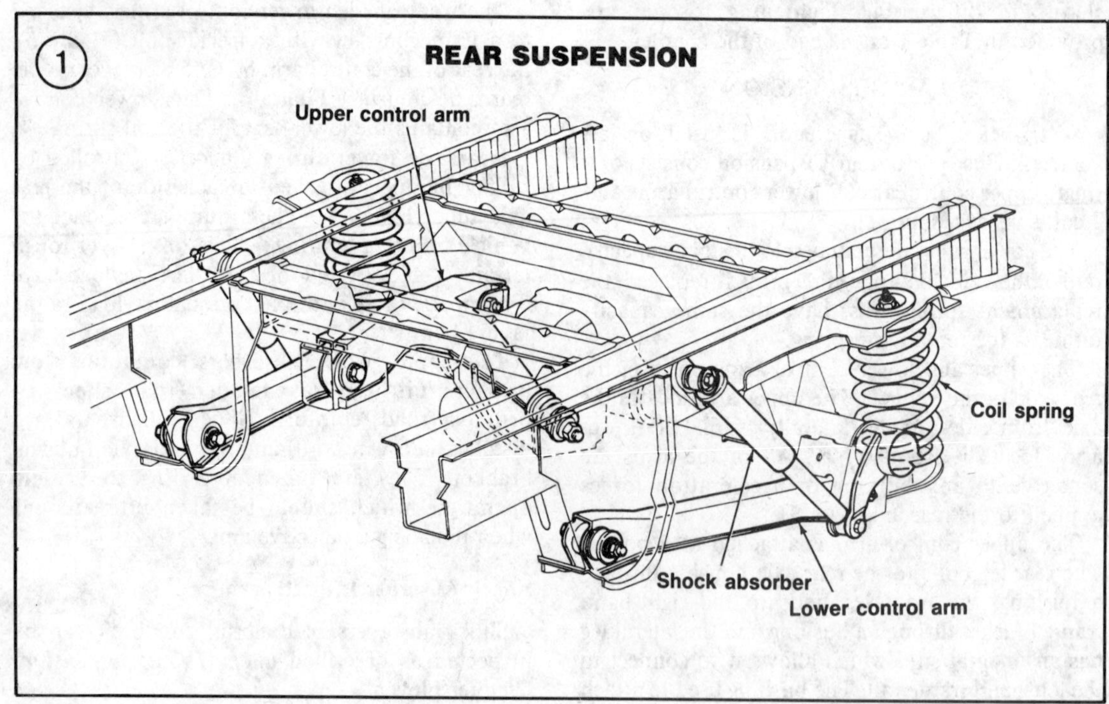

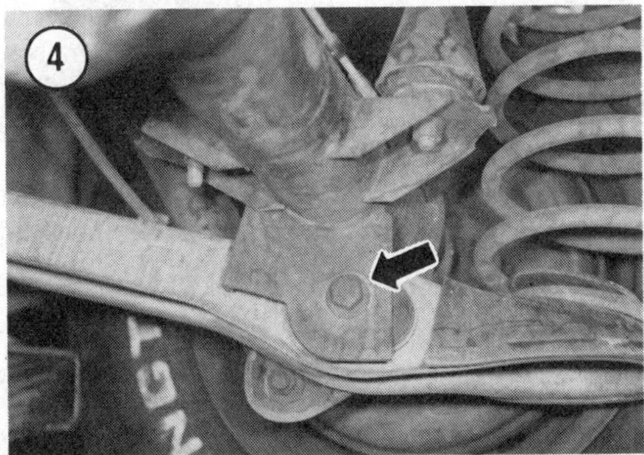

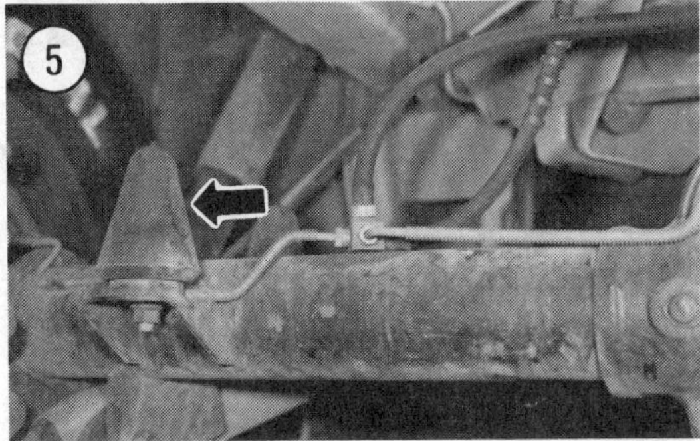

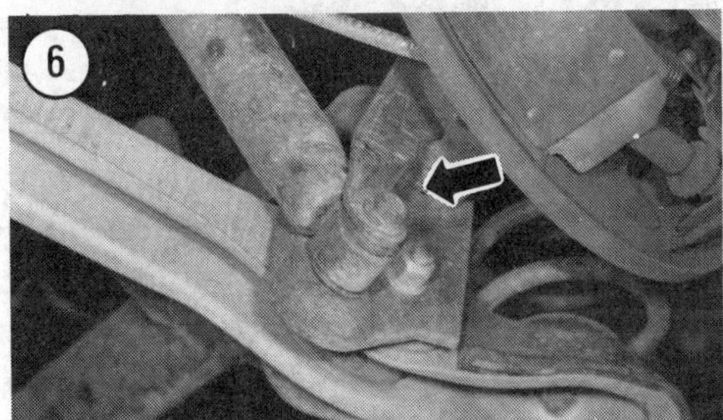

Coil Spring Removal/Installation

Remove and install springs one at a time. Refer to **Figure 8** for this procedure.

1. Loosen the rear wheel lug nuts.
2. Securely block the front wheels so the vehicle will not roll in either direction.
3. Raise the rear of the vehicle with a jack and place it on jackstands. Position the jackstands at the frame rear lift points (Chapter Three) or underneath the rear bumper support brackets.
4. Remove the wheel/tire assembly.
5. Remove the nut and bolt holding the shock absorber to its lower mounting bracket (**Figure 6**). Pivot the lower end of the shock absorber from the axle housing bracket.
6. Lower the jack under the rear axle enough to relieve coil spring tension (**Figure 9**).
7. Remove the nut holding the lower retainer and spring to the lower control arm.
8. Remove the bolt holding the upper retainer and spring to the frame.
9. Remove the spring, retainers and both insulators from the vehicle.

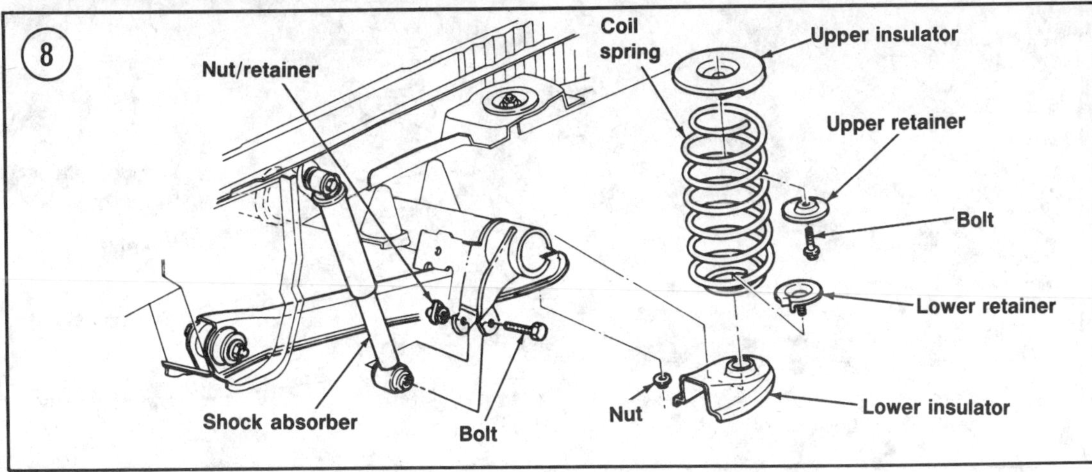

10. To reinstall the spring, position the lower insulator on the control arm and the upper insulator on the top of the spring.
11. Fit the spring with insulators in place between the frame and control arm.
12. Make sure the pigtail on the small diameter tapered coil rests against the rubber stop on the upper insulator, then rotate the spring and upper insulator until the pigtail on the lower end of the spring is pointing in the 3:00 position.
13. Install the upper retainer. Install and tighten the bolt to 30-40 ft.-lb. (40-55 N•m).
14. Install the lower retainer. Install and tighten the nut to 41-65 ft.-lb. (55-88 N•m).
15. Raise the jack under the rear axle to return the axle to its normal ride position.
16. Reconnect the lower end of the shock absorber to its mounting bracket. The bolt should be installed with its head on the outer side of the vehicle. Tighten the nut to 41-65 ft.-lb. (55-88 N•m).
17. Reinstall the wheel and tighten the lug nuts finger-tight.
18. Remove the jackstands and lower the vehicle to the ground. Tighten the wheel lug nuts to specifications (**Table 1**). Remove the jack under the axle and the wheel chocks from the wheels.

Lower Control Arm Removal

Refer to **Figure 10** for this procedure.

1. Loosen the rear wheel lug nuts.
2. Securely block the front wheels so the vehicle will not roll in either direction.
3. Raise the rear of the vehicle with a jack and place it on jackstands. Position the jackstands at the frame rear lift points (Chapter Three) or underneath the rear bumper support brackets.
4. Remove the wheel/tire assembly.
5. Remove the nut and bolt holding the shock absorber to its lower mounting bracket (**Figure 6**).

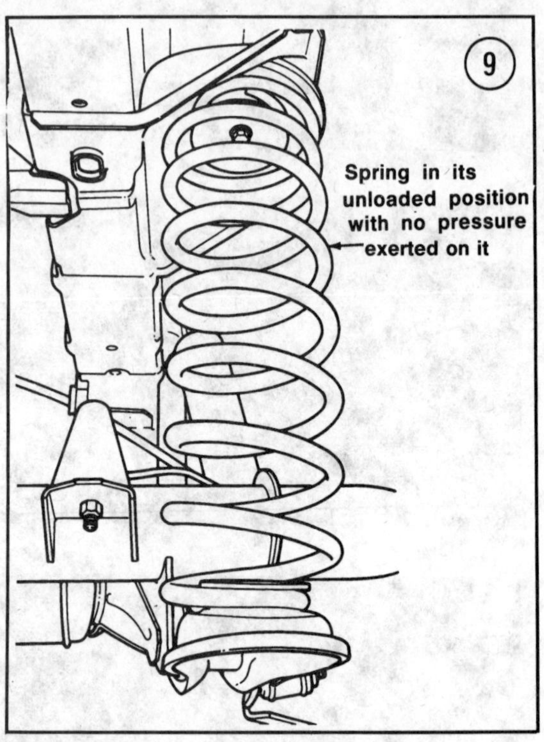

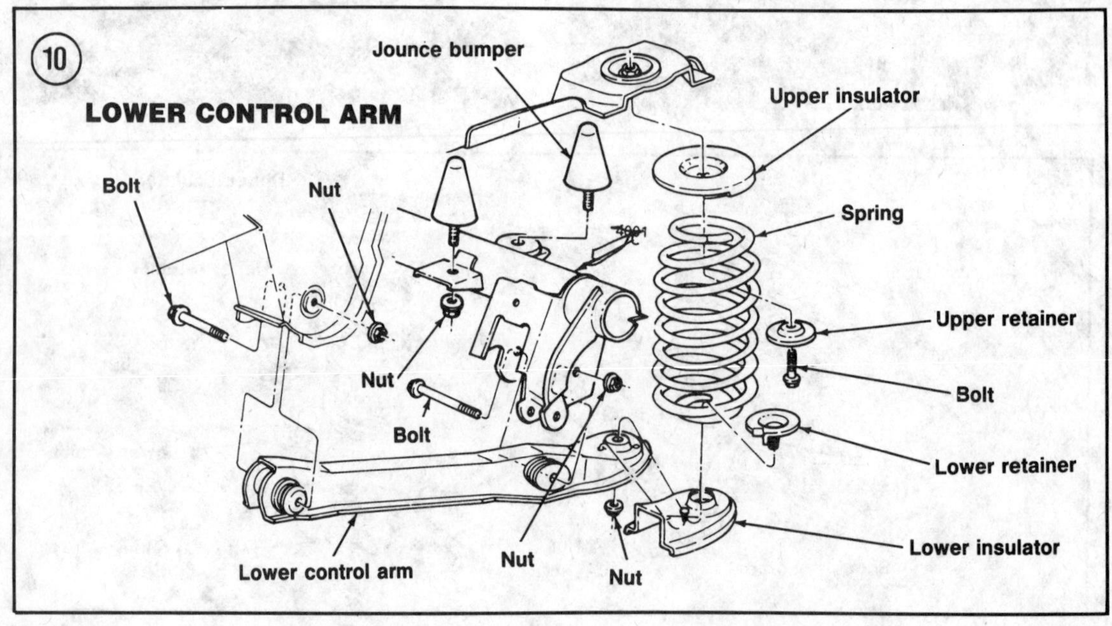

Pivot the lower end of the shock absorber from the axle housing bracket.
6. Lower the jack under the rear axle enough to relieve coil spring tension (**Figure 9**).
7. Remove the nut holding the lower retainer and spring to the lower control arm. Remove the insulator from the lower control arm.
8. Unbolt the lower control arm from the axle housing.
9. Unbolt the lower control arm from the frame bracket. Remove the lower control arm from the vehicle.

Lower Control Arm Installation

Refer to **Figure 10** and **Figure 11** for this procedure.

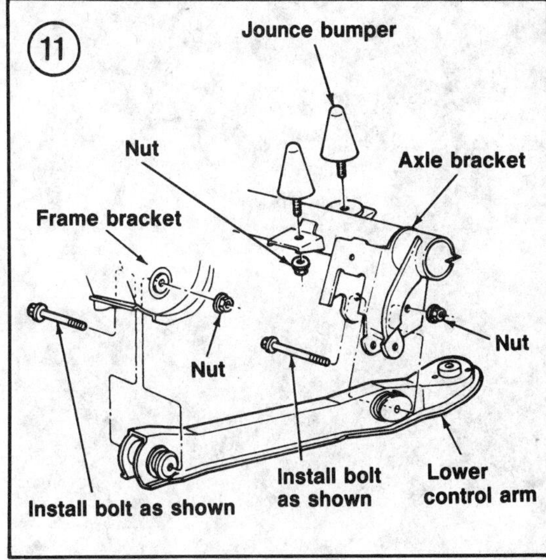

1. Fit the lower control arm into the frame bracket. Install the bolt with its head facing the inside of the vehicle (**Figure 11**) and finger-tighten the nut.
2. Fit the lower control arm into the axle housing bracket. Install the bolt with its head facing the inside of the vehicle (**Figure 11**) and finger-tighten the nut.
3. Install the lower control arm insulator.
4. Fit the coil spring and lower retainer on the lower control arm, then install and tighten the retainer nut to specifications (**Table 1**).
5. Raise the jack under the rear axle to return the axle to its normal ride position.
6. Tighten the lower control arm axle housing bracket fastener to specifications (**Table 1**).
7. Tighten the lower control arm frame bracket fastener to specifications (**Table 1**).
8. Reconnect the lower end of the shock absorber to its mounting bracket. The bolt should be installed with its head on the outer side of the vehicle. Tighten the nut to specifications (**Table 1**).
9. Reinstall the wheel and tighten the lug nuts finger-tight.
10. Remove the jackstands and lower the vehicle to the ground. Tighten the wheel lug nuts to specifications (**Table 1**). Remove the jack under the axle and the wheel chocks from the wheels.

Upper Control Arm Removal

Refer to **Figure 12** for this procedure.
1. Loosen the rear wheel lug nuts.
2. Securely block the front wheels so the vehicle will not roll in either direction.
3. Raise the rear of the vehicle with a jack and place it on jackstands. Position the jackstands at

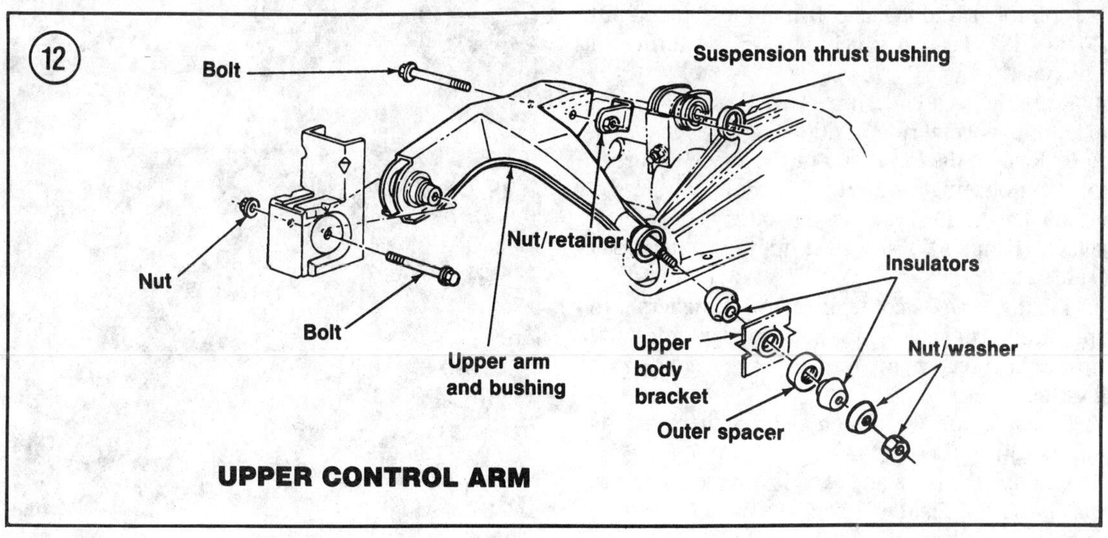

11

the frame rear lift points (Chapter Three) or underneath the rear bumper support brackets.

4. Remove the wheel/tire assembly.

5. Remove the nut and bolt holding the shock absorber to its lower mounting bracket (**Figure 6**). Pivot the lower end of the shock absorber from the axle housing bracket.

6. Lower the jack under the rear axle enough to relieve coil spring tension (**Figure 9**).

7. Unbolt and disconnect the upper control arm from the rear axle. See **Figure 13**.

8. Carefully scribe a mark indicating the position of the cam adjuster in the axle bushing.

9. Unbolt the upper control arm from the right frame bracket (**Figure 14**), then rotate the arm to disconnect it from the bracket.

10. Remove the nut, washer, outer insulator and spacer holding the arm to the left frame bracket (**Figure 15**). Remove the arm from the bracket, then slide the inner insulator off the arm stud. Remove the upper control arm from under the vehicle.

Upper Control Arm Installation

Refer to **Figure 12** for this procedure.

1. Slide the inner insulator onto the control arm stud. Install the control arm with its stud extending through the left frame bracket. Install the spacer, outer insulator, washer and nut on the stud. See **Figure 15**. Tighten nut snugly but do not torque at this time.

2. Fit the upper control arm into the right frame bracket. Install the bolt and nut (**Figure 14**). Tighten snugly but do not torque at this time.

3. Make sure that the marks inscribed on the cam adjuster and axle bushing are aligned, then attach the control arm to the axle. Install the bolt and nut (**Figure 13**). Tighten snugly but do not torque at this time.

4. Raise the jack under the rear axle to return the axle to its normal ride position.

5. Reconnect the lower end of the shock absorber to its mounting bracket. The bolt should be installed with its head on the outer side of the vehicle (**Figure 6**). Tighten the nut to specifications (**Table 1**).

6. Tighten the control arm fasteners to specifications (**Table 1**) in the following order: left frame bracket, right frame bracket and axle bracket.

7. Reinstall the wheel and tighten the lug nuts finger-tight.

8. Remove the jackstands and lower the vehicle to the ground. Tighten the wheel lug nuts to specifications (**Table 1**). Remove the jack under the axle and the wheel chocks from the wheels.

DRIVE SHAFT

An aluminum or graphite drive shaft assembly is used to transmit torque from the transmission to the rear axle. See **Figure 16** (typical). The drive shaft connects to the transmission and rear axle with a single cardan universal joint.

All vehicles covered in this manual use a 1-piece drive shaft. A universal joint and splined slip yoke are located on the transmission end of the shaft

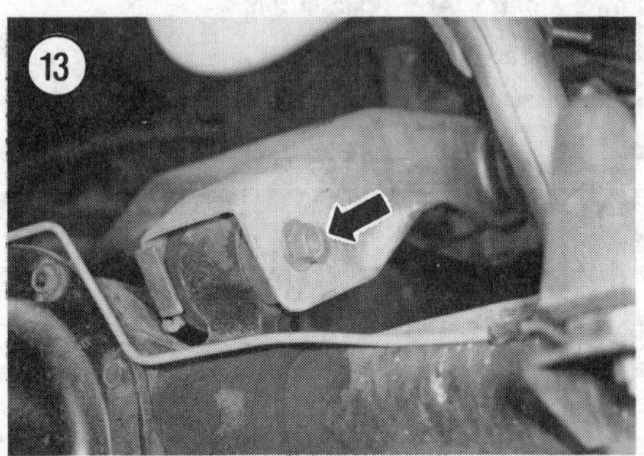

13

14

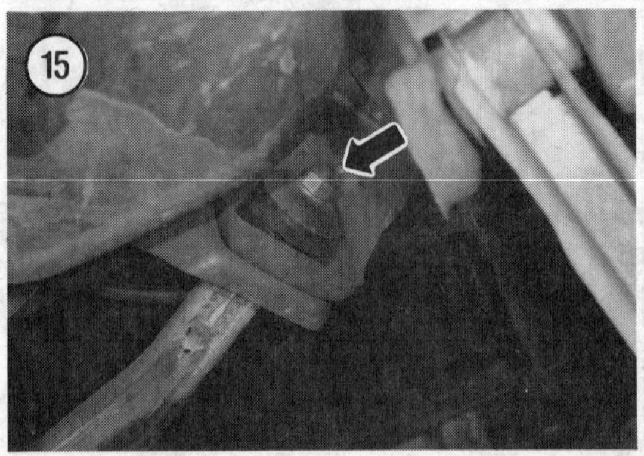

15

(**Figure 16**). A universal joint on the other end of the shaft connects to the rear axle end yoke with U-bolts and nuts. See **Figure 17**.

The universal joints are factory-lubricated and cannot be lubricated while on the vehicle. Universal joint bearings are factory-installed with snap rings. A repair kit containing a new spider with bearing assemblies and snap rings is available to overhaul worn universal joints.

The relationship of the front/rear universal joint angle is very important. The angle between the drive and driven yokes of the universal joint must be approximately the same in order for the alternating acceleration/deceleration of one joint to offset the alternating acceleration/deceleration of the other joint. If these angles are not almost identical, rough operation and vibration will result. Whenever the drive shaft is removed or replaced, a driveline angularity check should be performed. Since this requires the use of a special pinion angle level gauge (part No. T68P-4602-A), it should be performed by a dealer.

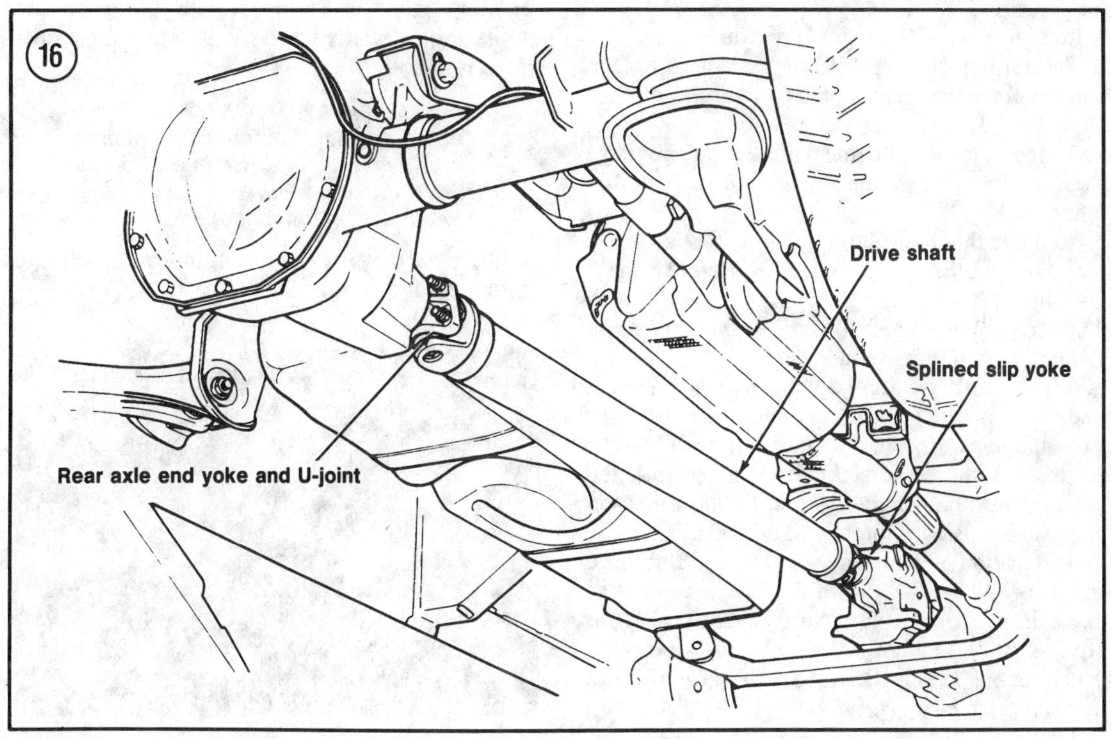

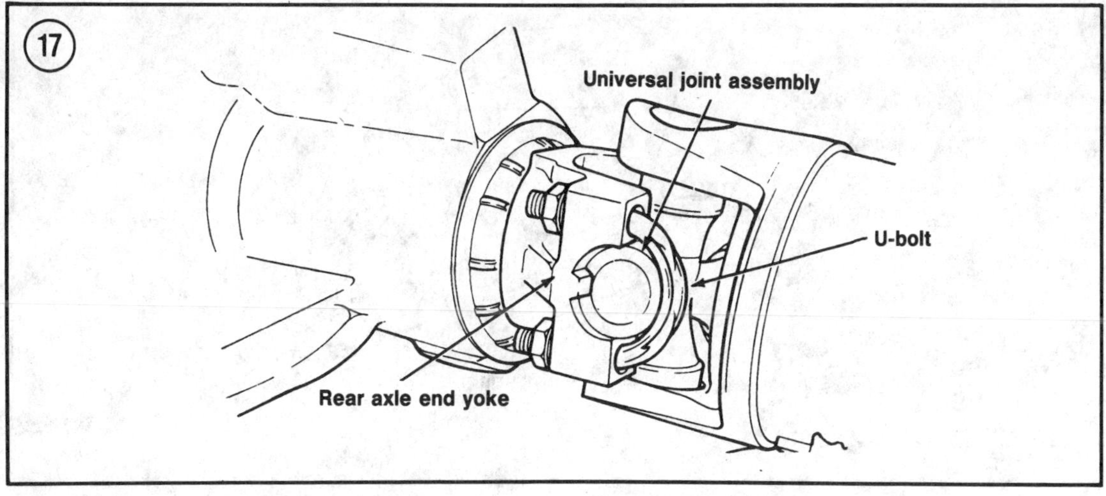

11

Drive shafts and coupling shafts are balanced assemblies and must not be painted or undercoated. Correct alignment is required when a drive shaft is removed and reinstalled to prevent drive line vibrations. Correct phasing is also required. This means that the U-joints must be installed on the shafts in the same plane.

Removal/Installation

If the drive shaft must be disconnected but need not be removed from the vehicle, perform Steps 1-4 and wire the end of the shaft to the underbody for support.

Refer to **Figure 16** for this procedure.

1. Securely block the wheels that remain on the ground. Raise the vehicle with a jack and place it on jackstands.
2. Scribe or chalk alignment marks on the drive shaft and rear axle end yoke for reassembly reference.
3. Remove the 4 nuts holding the 2 U-bolts at the rear axle end yoke. See **Figure 18**. Remove the 2 U-bolts.
4. Slide the drive shaft forward to disconnect the U-joint from the axle end yoke.
5. Move the drive shaft to the rear and pass it under the axle housing to disengage the slip yoke from the transmission.
6. Remove the drive shaft from underneath the vehicle. Install a suitable plug in the transmission extension housing to prevent fluid leakage.
7. Installation is the reverse of removal. Lubricate the slip joint splines with Ford Multi-purpose Long-life Lubricant (part No. C1AZ-19590-B) or equivalent. Tighten the U-bolt nuts to specifications (**Table 1**). Have a dealer perform a driveline angularity check.

Single Cardan Universal Joint Service

The single cardan joint consists of a single spider and 4 sets of needle bearings, bearing seals, caps and cap retainers. If the specified tools are not available, the bearings can be pressed out with suitable size sockets and a C-clamp.

Disassembly

Refer to **Figure 19** (typical) for this procedure.

1. Remove the drive shaft from the vehicle as described in this chapter.
2. Make the position of all parts to be disassembled relative to the drive shaft for proper reassembly.

CAUTION
Clamping the aluminum or graphite drive shaft tube in a vise in Step 3 can distort the tube and result in drive line vibration after installation.

3. Place the drive shaft on a clean workbench—do not clamp it in a vise.

18

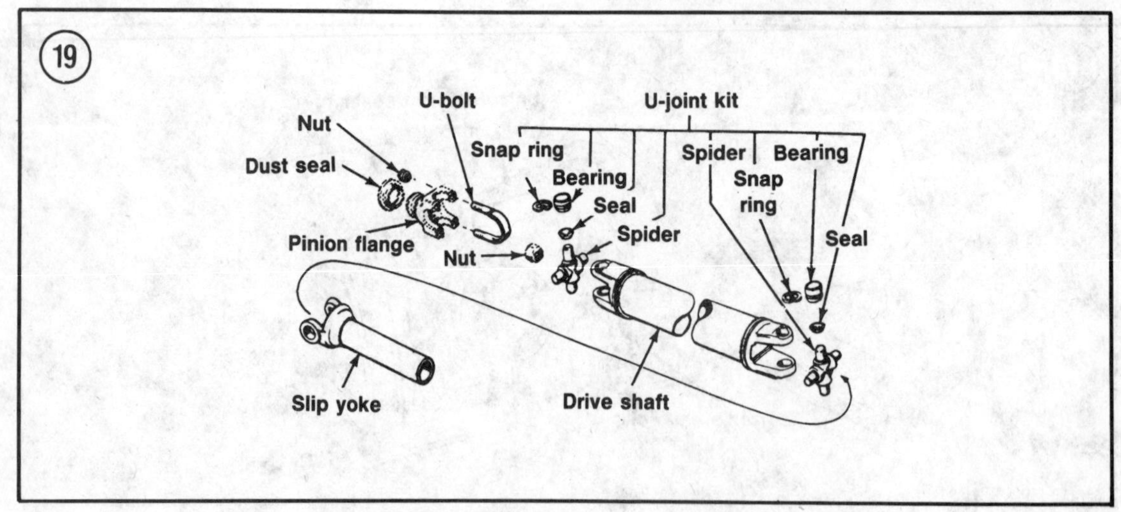

4. Remove the bearing cup snap rings with a screwdriver blade.
5. Install receiver part No. T74P-4635-C or equivalent on the slip yoke as shown in **Figure 20**. Press the bearings out.
6. If the bearing cup cannot be pressed out of the slip yoke, remove it with locking pliers.

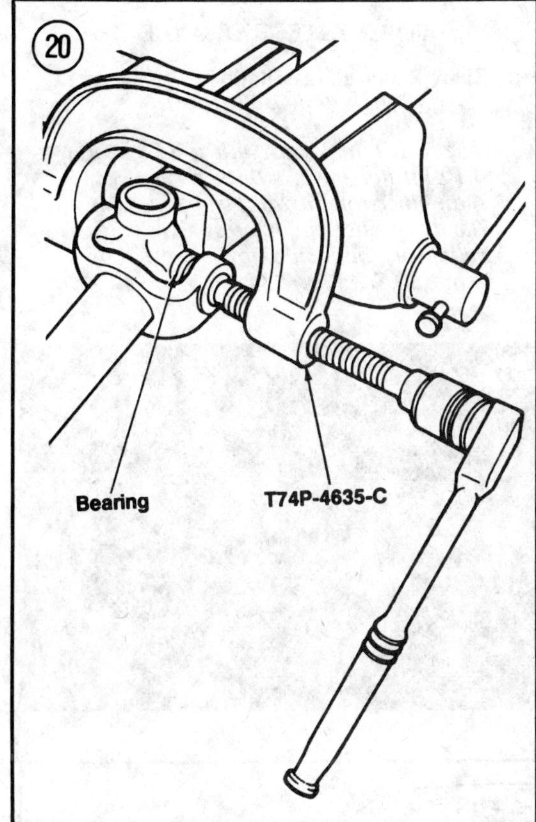

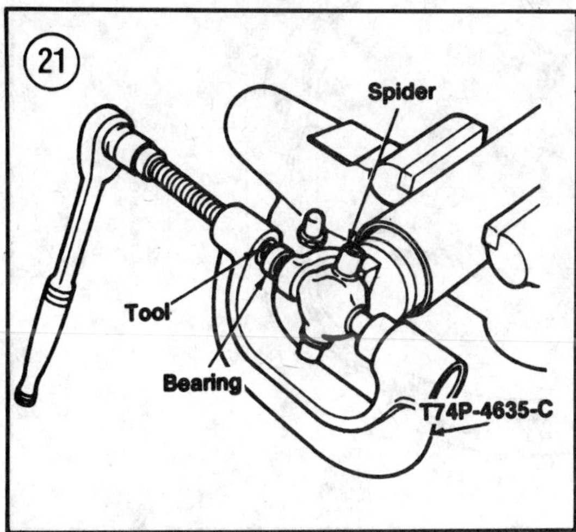

7. Reposition the tool 180°. Press on the spider and remove the remaining bearing cup from the opposite yoke.
8. Remove the slip yoke from the spider.
9. If universal joint service is also required at the other end of the drive shaft, remove the pinion flange in the same manner.

Cleaning and Inspection

1. Clean the yoke bearing cap bores with solvent and a wire brush.
2. Wash the bearing caps, bearings and spider in solvent. Wipe dry with a clean shop cloth.
3. Check the caps, bearings and spider for brinneling, flat spots, scoring, cracks or excessive wear. Replace the entire assembly if any part(s) show such conditions.

Assembly

Refer to **Figure 19** (typical) for this procedure.

1. Install a new bearing cup in the yoke.
2. Position the spider in the yoke and use tool part No. T74P-4635-C and a suitable spacer to press the new cap 1/4 in. below the yoke surface. See **Figure 21**.
3. Remove the tool and install a new snap ring.
4. Fit a new bearing cup into the opposite side of the yoke.
5. Install tool part No. T74P-4635-C as shown in **Figure 20** and press on the bearing cup until the opposite cup touches the snap ring.
6. Remove the tool and install a new snap ring.
7. Reposition the drive shaft 180° and repeat Steps 1-7 to install the remaining bearing cups and spider.
8. Check the assembled joint for free movement. If misalignment during installation has caused a bind, tap the drive shaft ears sharply with a brass hammer while supporting the shaft to seat the bearings. If this does not relieve the binding condition, disassemble the joint as described in this chapter and locate the cause of the problem.
9. Lubricate the new universal joint assembly with Ford Multi-purpose Long-life Lubricant (part No. C1AZ-19590-B) or equivalent.

REAR AXLE AND AXLE SHAFTS

This section includes removal, installation and inspection procedures for the standard Ford integral carrier and Dana Model 30 rear axles and axle shafts. Rear axle repair requires special skills and many expensive special tools. The inspection procedures will tell you if repairs are necessary. Refer service on locking rear axles to your dealer.

Carrier Gasket Replacement

1. Securely block both front wheels so the vehicle will not roll in either direction.
2. Raise the vehicle with a jack and place it on jackstands.
3. Clean all dirt from the axle housing and carrier cover sealing surfaces with a wire brush and cloth.
4. Place a clean container underneath the carrier housing.
5. Remove the cover bolts. See **Figure 22** (typical). One bolt is used to attach the rear axle identification tag. This bolt and tag should always be reinstalled in the same hole from which it was removed.
6. Carefully pry the cover loose with a screwdriver and let the lubricant drain into the container.
7. Remove the cover.
   a. Dana axle—Remove and discard the gasket. Clean the gasket sealing surfaces on the cover and carrier of all gasket residue.
   b. Ford axle—Clean all RTV sealant residue from the cover and carrier mating surfaces.

8A. Dana axle—Install the cover with a new gasket. Tighten the cover bolts to specifications (**Table 1**) in a crosswise pattern to assure a uniform draw on the gasket.

8B. Ford axle—Run a 1/8-3/16 in. continuous bead of RTV sealant on the carrier casting face. See **Figure 23**. The cover must be installed within 15 minutes after the sealant is applied to the casting face or the sealant must be removed and a fresh coat applied. Install the cover and tighten all cover bolts to specifications (**Table 1**).

9. Remove the fill plug from the front of the carrier (Ford axle) or rear cover (Dana axle) and fill the carrier with the recommended type and quantity of lubricant (Chapter Three) to within 3/8 in. of the fill plug hole. Reinstall the fill plug and tighten securely (Dana axle) or to specifications in **Table 1** (Ford axle).
10. Remove the jackstands and lower the vehicle to the ground. Remove the wheel chocks.

FORD INTEGRAL AXLE

Axle Shaft Removal/Installation

NOTE
*The 7 1/2 in. axles with a 3.73:1 or 4.10:1 ratio have a thicker ring gear than other ratio axles. For this reason, the differential pinion cross shaft has a relief on one side for axle C-clip removal. See **Figure 24**.*

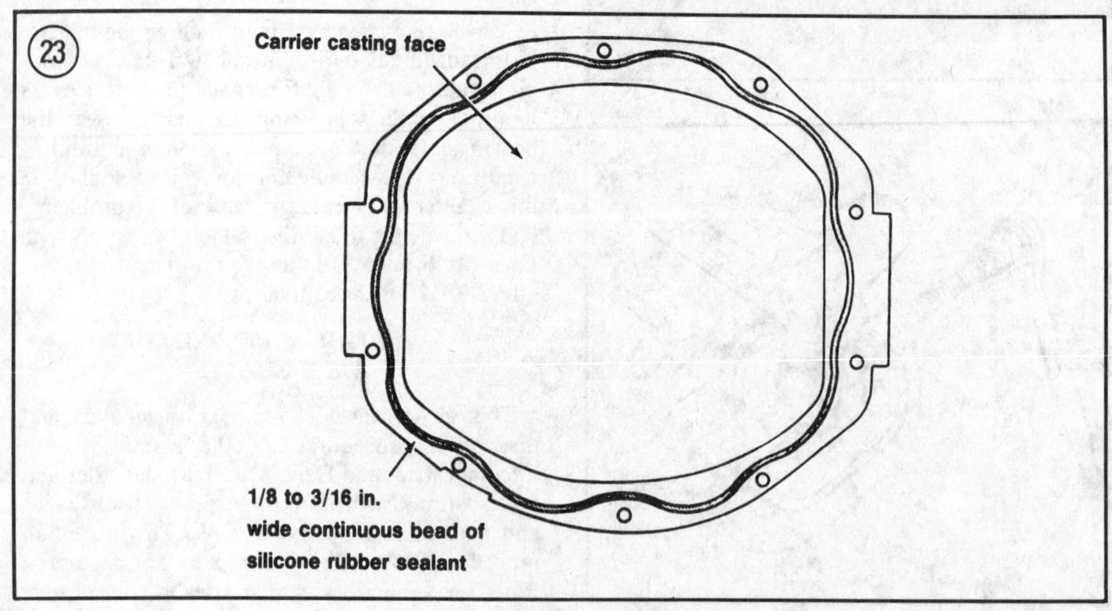

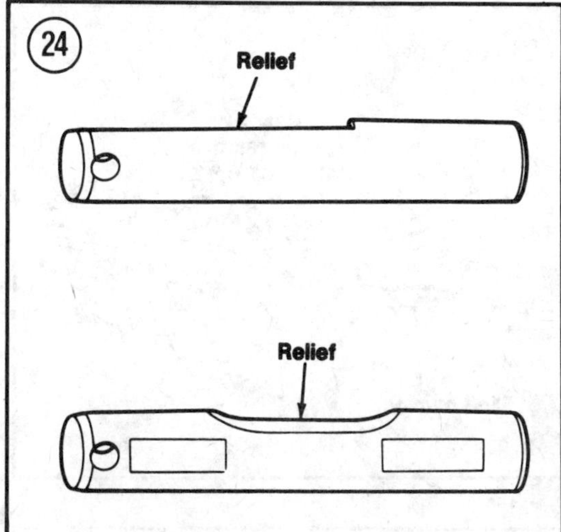

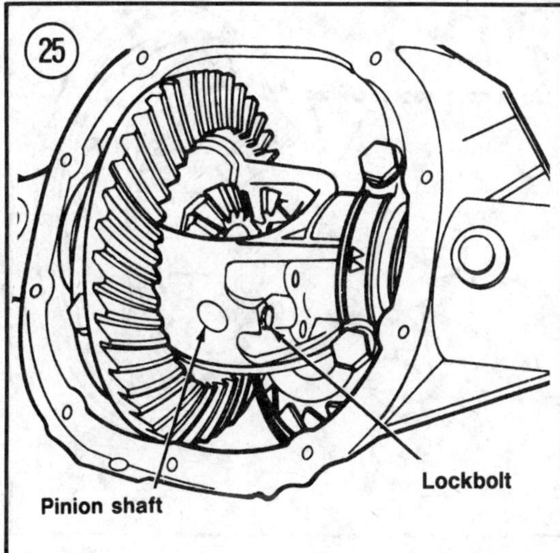

1. Securely block both front wheels so the vehicle will not roll in either direction.
2. Remove the wheel cover (if so equipped) and loosen the rear wheel lug nuts.
3. Raise the rear of the vehicle with a jack and place it on jackstands positioned under the rear frame crossmember.
4. Remove the wheel and tire assembly from the brake drum. Remove the brake drum.
5. Remove the carrier cover as described in this chapter.
6. All except 3.73:1 and 4.10:1 ratio axles:
   a. Remove the differential pinion shaft lockbolt and shaft (**Figure 25**).
   b. Apply pressure to the outer end of the axle shaft, pushing it inward toward the center of the vehicle, and remove the C-lock from the button end of the shaft (**Figure 26**).
7. 3.73:1 or 4.10:1 ratio axles:
   a. Remove the pinion shaft lockbolt.
   b. Reach behind the differential case and push the pinion shaft out until the relief step touches the ring gear (**Figure 27**).
   c. Remove the C-lock from the button end of the shaft (**Figure 26**).
   d. If both axle shafts are to be removed, rotate the pinion shaft 180° to position the relief in the shaft for C-lock removal.
8. Carefully withdraw the axle shaft from the carrier housing to prevent damage to the oil seal.
9. Installation is the reverse of removal. Tighten the pinion shaft lockbolt to 15-22 ft.-lb. (21-29 N•m). Fill the axle with the recommended type and quantity of lubricant specified in Chapter Three until the lubricant level reaches within 3/8 in. of the bottom of the fill plug hole. Install the fill plug and tighten to specifications (**Table 1**).

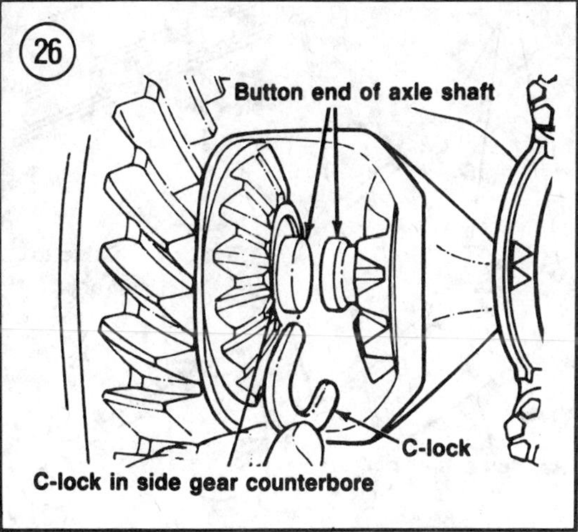

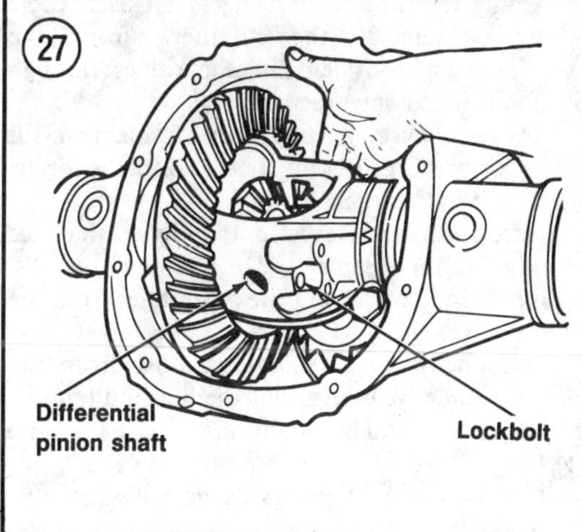

Axle Shaft Oil Seal and Bearing Replacement

The bearing and seal are replaced as a unit. Installation of a new bearing or seal without the specified tools can distort the assembly, cause leakage and result in premature bearing failure.

1. Remove the axle shaft as described in this chapter.
2. Attach bearing/seal remover part No. T85L-1225-AH to a slide hammer and insert it into the axle shaft bore until its tangs engage the bearing outer race. See **Figure 28** (typical). Remove the bearing and seal.
3. Lubricate a new bearing with rear axle lubricant. Install the bearing in the housing bore with tool part No. T78P-1225-A or equivalent.
4. Lubricate the new seal lips with Ford Multi-purpose Long-life Lubricant (part No. C1AZ-19590-B) or equivalent. Fit the seal in the housing bore and install with bearing replacer part No. T78P-1177-A or equivalent. See **Figure 29**.
5. Reinstall the axle shaft as described in this chapter.

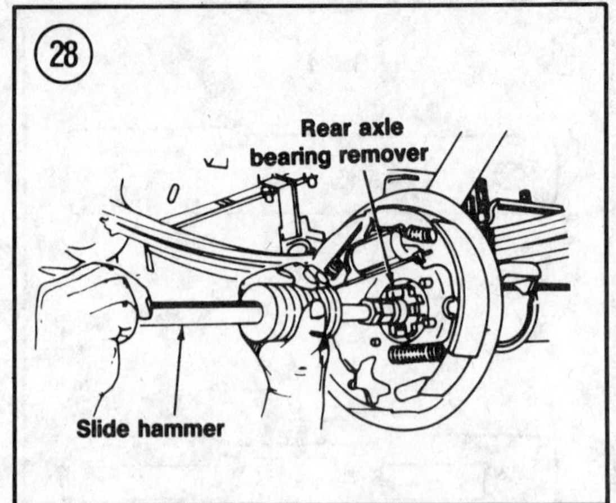

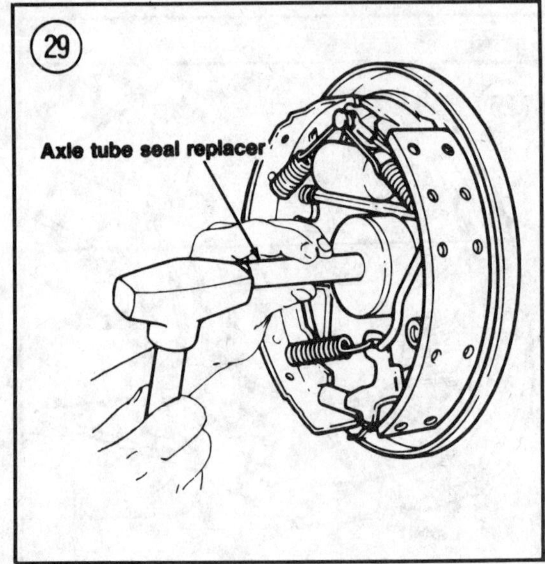

Axle Housing Removal/Installation

Ford Motor Company recommends the use of a twin-post type hoist for rear axle housing removal.

1. Loosen the rear wheel lug nuts, then raise the vehicle on a twin-post type hoist.
2. Refer to **Figure 30** and release the parking brake cable tension as follows:
   a. Grasp the front parking brake cable and pull it towards the rear of the vehicle about 2 in.
   b. Clamp the front cable to the crossmember, working carefully to avoid damage to the plastic coating on the cable.
   c. Disconnect the rear cables from the equalizer. Compress the retainer fingers on each cable and disengage the retainers from the crossmembers, then pull the cables through the rear crossmember.
3. Position jackstands under the frame rear lift points or underneath the rear bumper support brackets. See **Figure 31**.
4. Disconnect and remove the drive shaft as described in this chapter.
5. Remove the wheel and tire assemblies from the brake drums.
6. Disconnect the brake jounce hose from the master cylinder rear line. Plug the line and remove the jounce hose and bracket from the frame (**Figure 31**).
7. Remove the coil springs as described in this chapter.

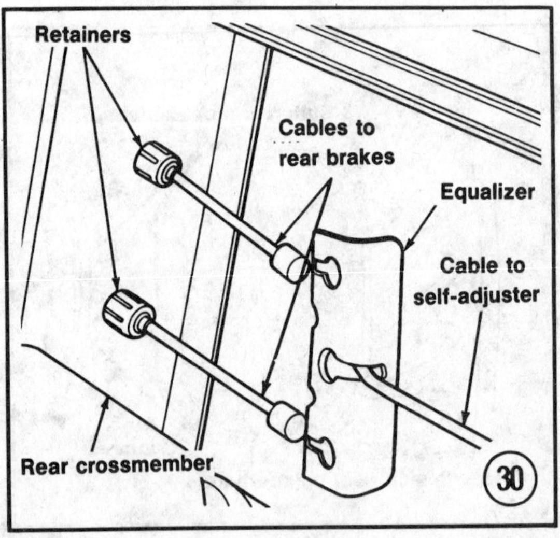

8. Unbolt and disconnect the upper control arm from the rear axle.
9. Carefully scribe a mark indicating the position of the cam adjuster in the axle bushing.
10. Carefully lower the rear of the hoist holding the axle housing. Remove the rear axle assembly from underneath the vehicle.
11. Installation is the reverse of removal. Bleed the brakes (Chapter Twelve).

DANA MODEL 30 AXLE

Axle Shaft Removal/Installation

Axle shafts are the same length and can be interchanged between the right and left side of a vehicle, but they are not interchangeable between vehicle models.

1. Loosen the rear wheel lug nuts.
2. Securely block both front wheels so the vehicle will not roll in either direction.
3. Raise the rear of the vehicle with a jack and place it on jackstands.
4. Remove the wheel and tire assembly from the brake drum. Remove the brake drum.
5. Working through the hole provided in the axle shaft flange, remove the nuts holding the bearing retainer plate in place. See **Figure 32**.
6. Attach puller part No. T66L-4234-A or equivalent to the axle shaft flange. Connect a slide hammer to the puller and carefully remove the axle shaft from the housing. Remove and discard the flange gasket.
7. Remove the backing plate and wire it to the frame out of the way.
8. Installation is the reverse of removal. Use a new gasket and carefully slide the axle shaft in place to prevent damage to the oil seal. Tighten all fasteners to specifications (**Table 1**).

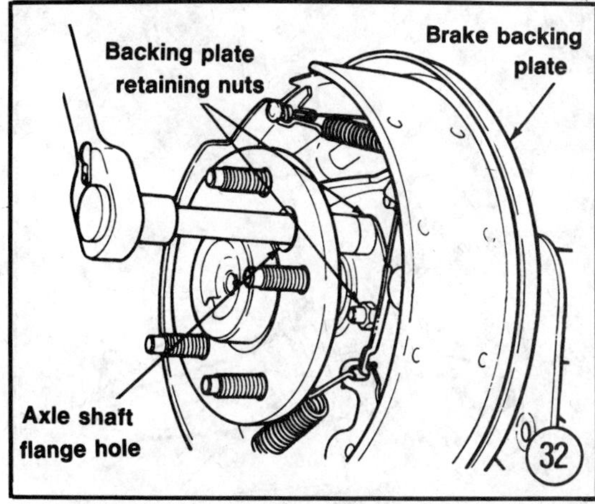

Wheel Bearing and Seal Replacement

The rear wheel tapered roller bearings are pressed onto the outer end of the axle shafts and ride in the outer ends of the axle housing.

1. Remove the axle shaft as described in this chapter.

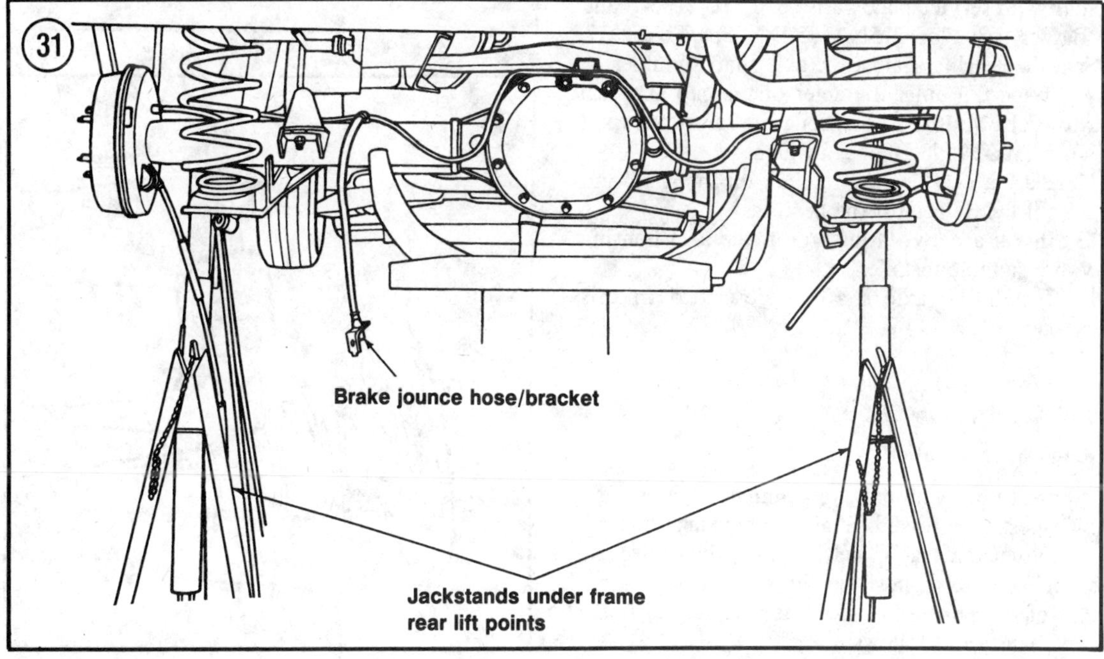

11

2. Remove the bearing cup from the axle housing with a suitable puller and slide hammer (**Figure 33**).

CAUTION
Do not drill the hole completely through the retainer ring in Step 3 or the axle shaft may be damaged.

3. Drill a 1/4 in. hole in the outer diameter of the inner retainer about 3/8 of the way through the retainer (**Figure 34**).
4. Break the retainer ring by placing a chisel across the drilled hole and striking it sharply with a hammer. See **Figure 35**. Remove and discard the retainer ring.

CAUTION
Do not use heat to remove the bearing in Step 5. This will distort the axle shaft.

5. Remove the bearing with a universal puller and an arbor press. Discard the bearing.
6. Check the axle shaft and housing bore for irregularities. Remove any slight nicks or burrs with emery cloth.
7. Lightly lubricate the wheel bearing bore with axle lubricant.
8. Slide the retainer plate over the axle shaft. Make sure it is not on backwards.
9. Install a new seal and bearing on the axle shaft. Make sure the cup rib ring faces the axle flange. See **Figure 36**.
10. Press the bearing/seal assembly on the axle shaft with service plate part No. T75L-1165-B and adapter part No. T75L-1165-DA. See **Figure 37**. Seat the bearing against the axle shaft shoulder.
11. Wipe the outer diameter of the cup and seal with Ford Multi-purpose Long-life Lubricant (part No. C1AZ-19590-B) or equivalent.
12. Place a new bearing retainer on the shaft and press it tightly against the bearing.
13. Install a new bearing cup in the axle housing with a suitable installer.
14. Install the axle shaft as described in this chapter.

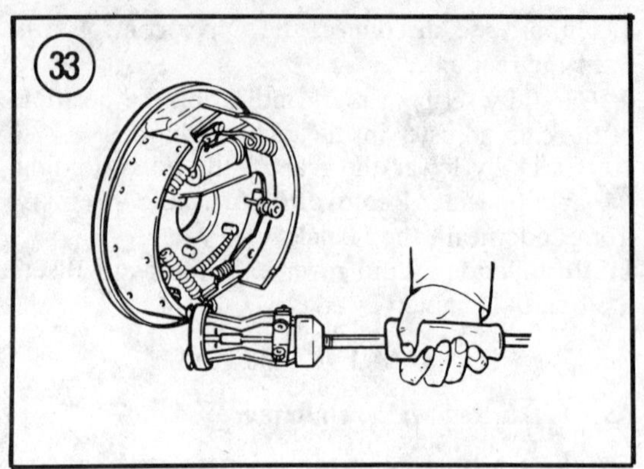

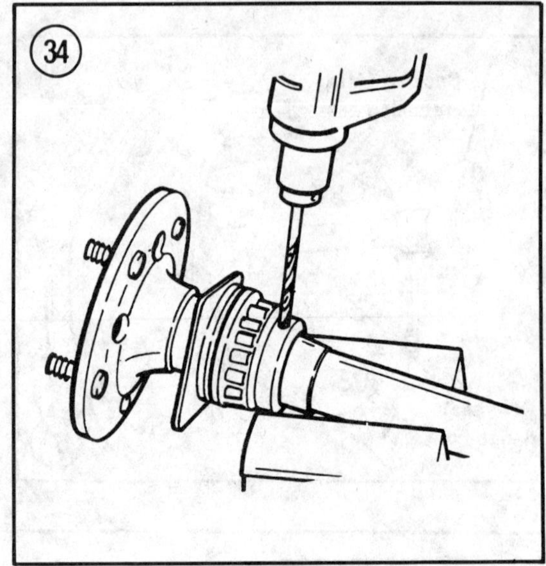

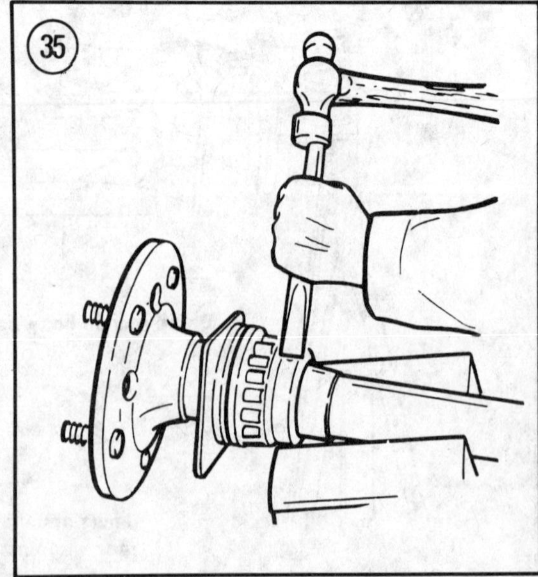

Axle Housing Removal/Installation

Ford Motor Company recommends the use of a twin-post type hoist for rear axle housing removal.

1. Loosen the rear wheel lug nuts, then raise the vehicle on a twin-post type hoist.
2. Refer to **Figure 30** and release the parking brake cable tension as follows:

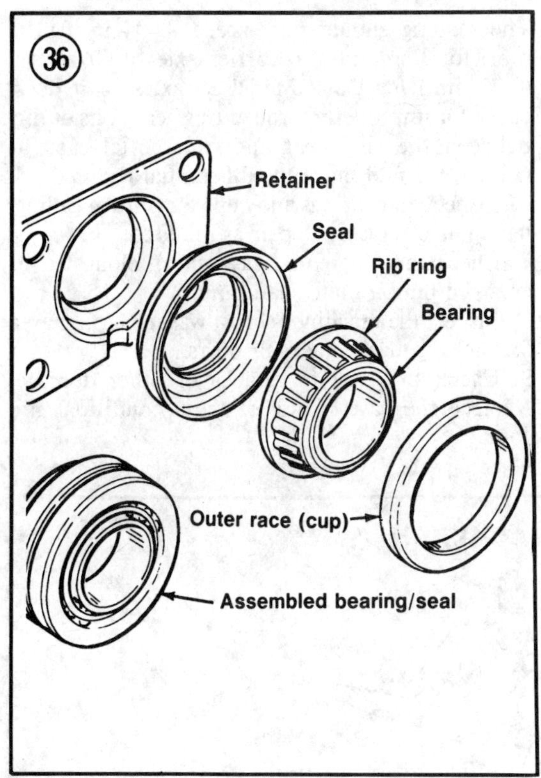

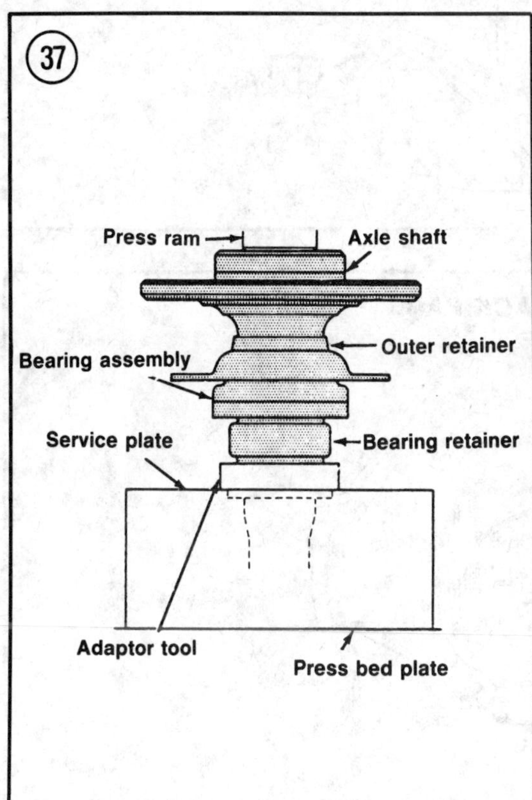

a. Grasp the front parking brake cable and pull it towards the rear of the vehicle about 2 in.

b. Clamp the front cable to the crossmember, working carefully to avoid damage to the plastic coating on the cable.

c. Disconnect the rear cables from the equalizer. Compress the retainer fingers on each cable and disengage the retainers from the crossmembers, then pull the cables through the rear crossmember.

3. Position jackstands under the frame rear lift points or underneath the rear bumper support brackets. See **Figure 31**.

4. Disconnect and remove the drive shaft as described in this chapter.

5. Remove the wheel and tire assemblies from the brake drums.

6. Disconnect the brake jounce hose from the master cylinder rear line. Plug the line and remove the jounce hose and bracket from the frame (**Figure 31**).

7. Remove the coil springs as described in this chapter.

8. Unbolt and disconnect the upper control arm from the rear axle.

9. Carefully scribe a mark indicating the position of the cam adjuster in the axle bushing.

10. Carefully lower the rear of the hoist holding the axle housing. Remove the rear axle assembly from underneath the vehicle.

11. Installation is the reverse of removal. Bleed the brakes (Chapter Twelve).

DIFFERENTIAL

The differential case assembly and drive pinion should be inspected while installed in the case. This inspection can assist in determining the cause of the problem and the corrective action required. If the inspection procedure indicates defects, take the axle housing to a Ford dealer or competent garage. Do not disassemble the axle carrier further without the necessary tools and experience.

Differential Inspection

1. Wipe as much lubricant as possible from the ring and pinion gears and other internal components. Use paper towels or clean lint-free cloths.

2. Visually check the components for signs of wear or damage.

3. Rotate the ring gear manually. Check ring gear teeth for abnormal wear, scoring, cracking or chipping. Any roughness during rotation indicates defective gears or bearings.

4. Mount a dial indicator as shown in **Figure 38** to measure ring gear backlash. The indicator plunger should touch the drive side of a ring gear tooth at right angles to the tooth. Hold the pinion from turning with one hand and rotate the ring gear against the dial indicator with the other. Backlash should be 0.008-0.015 in. with 0.012-0.015 in. preferred for Ford integral carrier axles. Backlash with Dana Model 30 axles should be 0.005-0.009 in. (0.13-0.23 mm). If the backlash reading is not as specified, have the differential disassembled and adjusted.
5. Remount the dial indicator as shown in **Figure 39** to measure ring gear runout. Set the indicator gauge to zero and rotate the ring gear one full turn. The reading should not exceed 0.004 in. (0.102 mm) for Ford integral carrier axles or 0.002 in. (0.05 mm) for Dana Model 30 axles. If it does, check for improperly torqued ring gear bolts or dirt between the ring gear and differential case. If neither is found, have the differential repaired.
6. Inspect all bearings and cups for pitting, galling, flat spots or cracks. Repair as required.
7. Check the differential case for an elongated or enlarged pinion mate shaft bore.
8. Inspect the machined thrust washer surface area for nicks, gouges, cracks or burrs.
9. Check the case for cracks or other damage. Replace the case if any of these conditions are found.

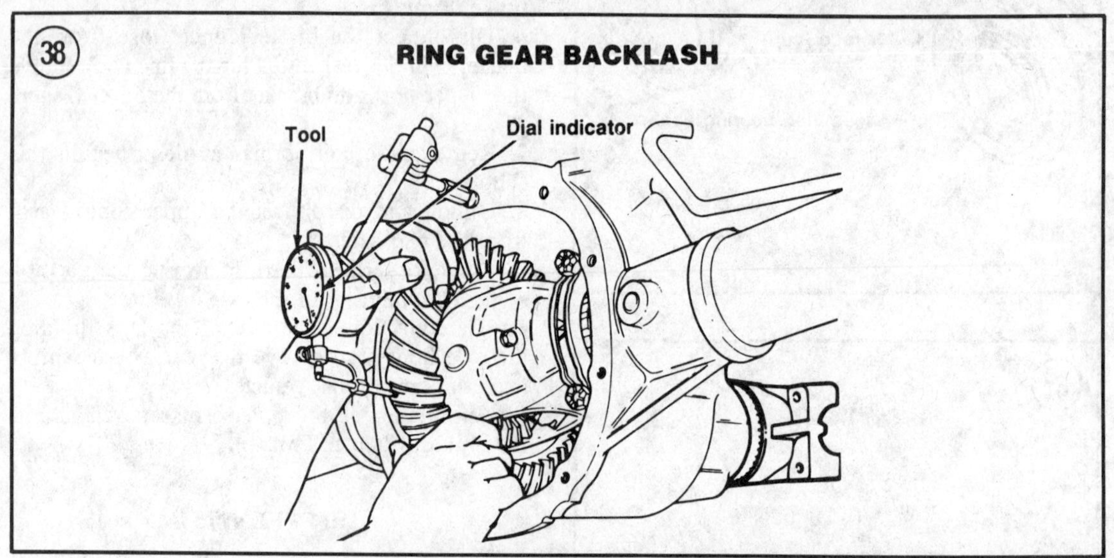

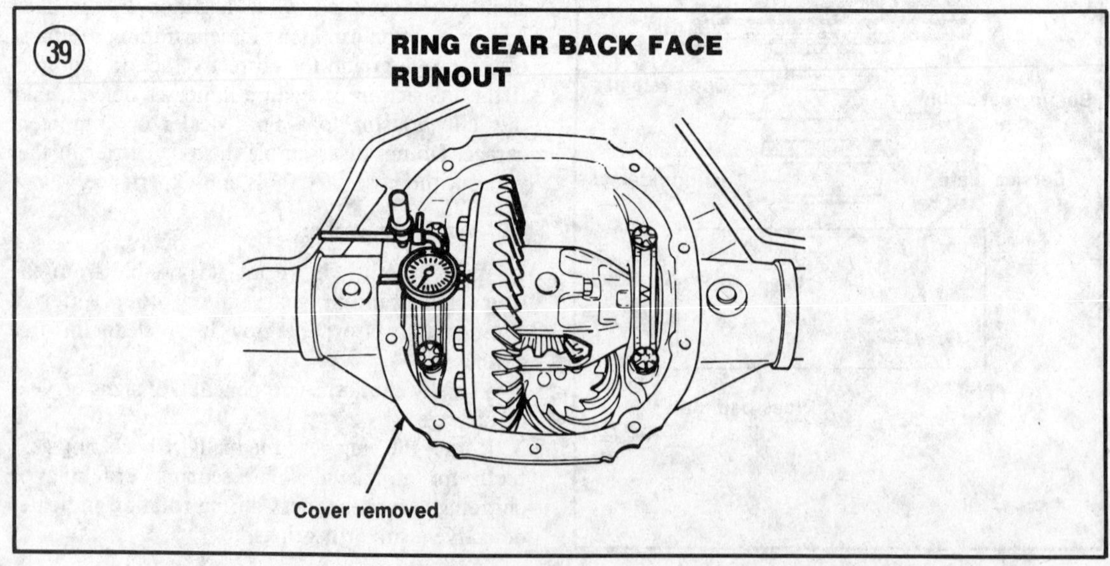

Tooth Contact Pattern Test

1. Wipe all oil from the axle housing. Clean each ring gear tooth carefully.
2. Apply a light coat of gear marking compound to the drive side of the ring gear teeth (**Figure 40**).

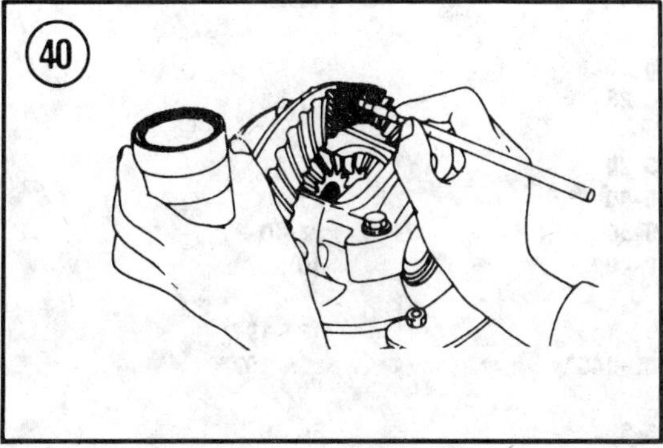

3. Rotate the ring gear slowly in both directions to press the contact pattern of the teeth into the gear marking compound. The contact pattern should have the following characteristics:
   a. Both drive and coast patterns should be fairly well centered on the teeth.
   b. Some clearance between the top of the teeth and the top of the pattern is desirable.
   c. There should be no distinct lines (indicating areas where pressure is high).
   d. Marks on adjoining gear teeth should be directly opposite each other.
4. Compare the contact pattern pressed into the marking compound with those shown in **Figure 41.** The pattern need not be exactly as shown or described to be acceptable. An erratic pattern indicates that repairs are needed. If the pattern is not correct, have the differential disassembled and adjusted.

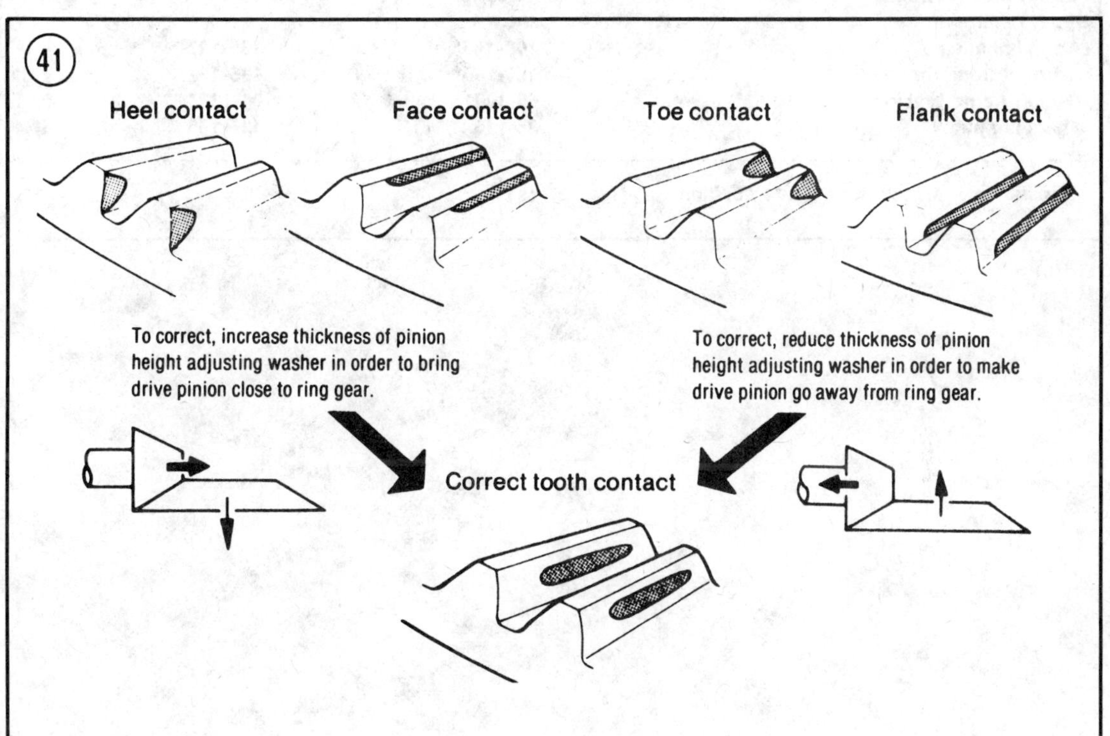

Table 1 is on the following page.

Table 1 TIGHTENING TORQUES

Fastener	ft.-lb.	N•m
Coil spring		
Lower retainer nut	41-65	55-88
Upper retainer nut	29-41	39-56
Drive shaft U-joint nut	8-15	11-20
Dana Model 30 axle		
Axle shaft retaining nuts	25-35	34-48
Cover	15-25	21-33
Ford integral axle		
Carrier cover	15-20	21-27
Pinion shaft lockbolt	15-30	21-40
Fill plug	15-30	21-40
Jounce bumper retaining nut	30-40	40-55
Lower control arm		
To axle housing	100-145*	135-197*
To frame bracket	100-145*	135-197*
Shock absorber		
Upper bracket bolt	25-35	34-48
Lower bracket bolt	41-65	55-88
Upper control arm		
To axle housing	100-145*	135-197*
To right frame bracket	100-145*	135-197*
To left frame bracket	60-100*	81-135*
Wheel lug nuts	85-115	115-155

* Tighten with axle in normal ride position.

CHAPTER TWELVE

BRAKES

Front disc brakes and self-adjusting rear drum brakes are standard on all models. All vehicles use a dual hydraulic brake system with 2 independent circuits. See **Figure 1** (typical). A failure in one circuit leaves the other circuit intact and functional. One circuit operates the front brakes and the other circuit operates the rear brakes. Failure of one of the brake circuits will normally be indicated by the instrument panel brake warning light turning on. However, if the light is burned out or the wiring faulty, the first indication of a brake failure may occur when the brakes are applied, requiring much more pedal pressure than normal.

Front disc brakes are a pin rail-type, single piston caliper design mounted on an integral cast iron rotor and hub assembly (**Figure 2**). When hydraulic pressure is applied, the caliper piston moves the inner pad against the rotor. This causes the caliper to move on the pin rails and pull the outer pad inward, clamping the rotor between the 2 pads.

Rear drum brakes are a single anchor, duo-servo design (**Figure 3**). When hydraulic pressure is applied, the wheel cylinder pistons apply pressure against the upper end of the primary and secondary brake shoes, expanding the shoes against the drum surface.

An aluminum master cylinder with a single see-through reservoir (**Figure 4**) is used. The reservoir contains a low fluid level indicator switch (arrow, **Figure 4**). The master cylinder services the front disc brakes through its 2 primary outlet ports (nearest the dash panel) and the rear drum brakes through its secondary outlet port (at the front). The primary and secondary ports are connected to a 3-way or combination valve on 1987 and later models. See **Figure 1**.

The combination valve (**Figure 5**) is bracket-mounted to the fender well and contains 3 sections: front system metering, rear system proportioning and an interconnected pressure differential shuttle. The metering valve delays disc pad application until the brake shoes contact the brake drums. The proportioning section of the valve balances braking pressure between the front and rear brakes to minimize rear wheel skidding or lockup during hard braking. The pressure differential shuttle performs a bypass function to permit full pressure at the rear brakes should front system pressure should be reduced significantly.

All vehicles are equipped with power brakes. A single diaphragm vacuum booster unit utilizes engine intake manifold vacuum and atmospheric pressure for its power. See **Figure 6**.

A ratchet-type hand-operated parking brake lever is mounted on the floor between the 2 front seats and is connected to the rear wheel brakes through a front and 2 rear cables connected to an equalizer unit underneath the floor pan. See **Figure 7**.

Tightening torques are provided in **Table 1** at the end of the chapter.

FRONT DISC BRAKES

The front disc brake assembly uses a single piston pin slider caliper. The caliper is located on abutment surfaces machined on the trailing edges of the front wheel spindle. No return spring is used in the caliper piston bore. Lining wear is compensated for by increased piston extension and the lateral sliding motion of the caliper. The caliper operates on an integral rotor/hub assembly retained on the spindle by the wheel bearing nut lock retainer.

Before replacing disc brake pads, remove the master cylinder cover and use a large syringe to remove and discard about 50 percent of the fluid from the reservoir. This will prevent the master

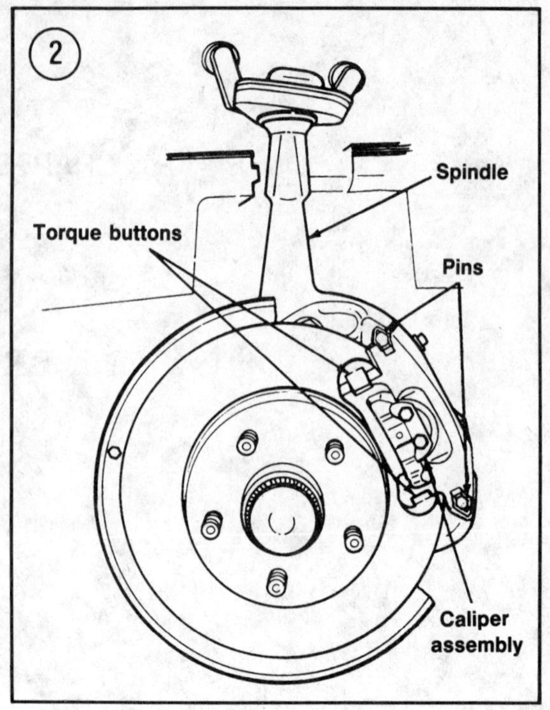

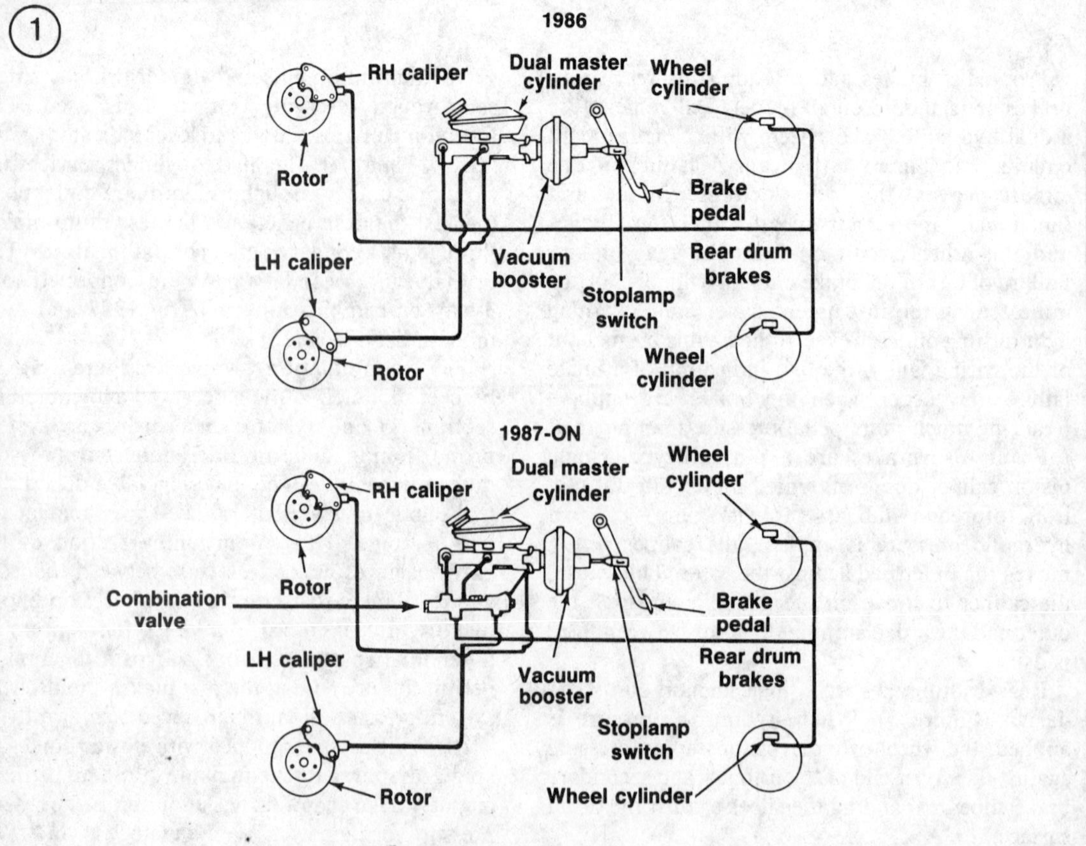

3

Anchor
Wheel cylinder
Retracting spring
Primary shoe
FRONT
Backing plate
Adjuster spring
Adjuster
Secondary shoe
Adjuster lever

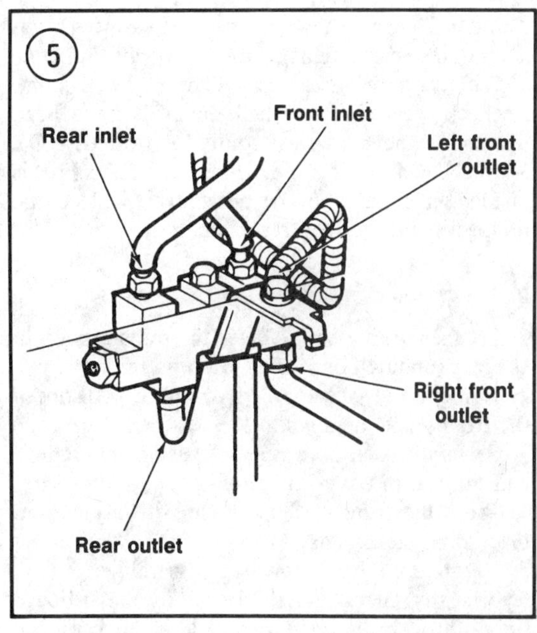

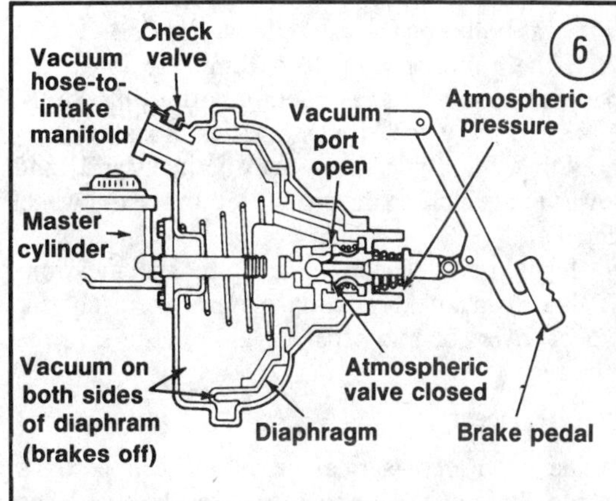

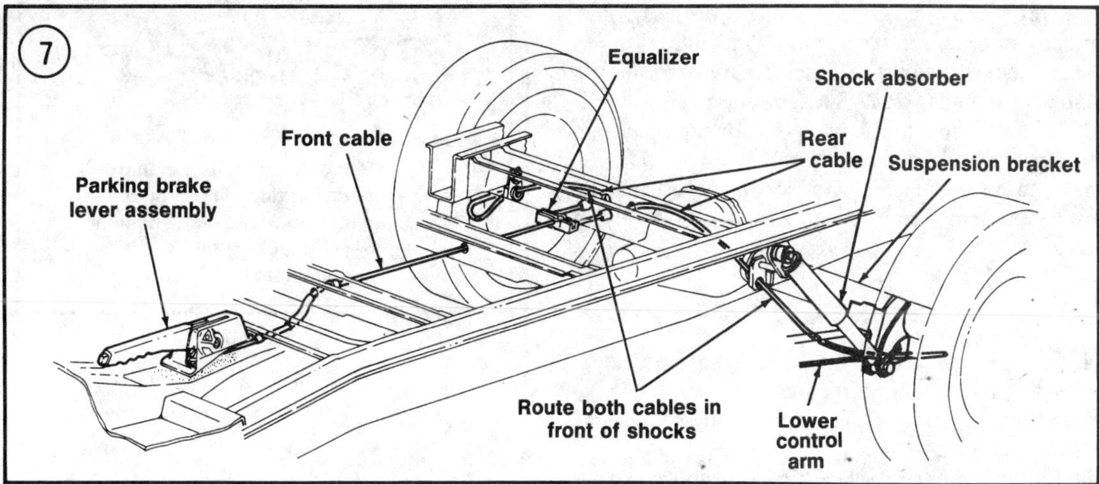

cylinder from overflowing when the caliper piston is compressed for reinstallation. *Do not drain the entire reservoir* or air will enter the system. Recheck the reservoir when the pads have been reinstalled and top up as required with fresh DOT 3 or DOT 4 brake fluid. If no hydraulic line is opened, it should not be necessary to bleed the brake system after pad replacement.

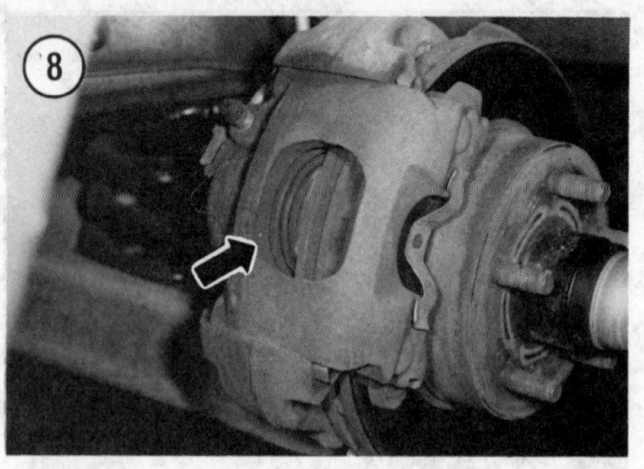

Pad Inspection

1. Set the parking brake. Place the transmission in 1st gear (manual) or PARK (automatic).
2. Remove the wheel covers or hub caps. Loosen the front wheel lug nuts.
3. Securely block both rear wheels so the vehicle will not roll in either direction.
4. Raise the front of the vehicle with a jack and place it on jackstands.
5. Remove the front wheel/tire assemblies.
6. Visually check the thickness of the inboard lining through the inspection hole in the center of the caliper. See **Figure 8**. Check the thickness of the lining at both ends of the outboard pads.
7. If the lining is worn to within 1/16 in. of the pad, replace the pads as a set on both front wheels.
8. Install the wheel/tire assemblies. Install the lug nuts finger-tight, then remove the jackstands and lower the vehicle to the ground. Remove the wheel chocks.
9. Tighten the wheel lug nuts to specifications (**Table 1**) in an alternating pattern. Reinstall the wheel covers or hub caps.

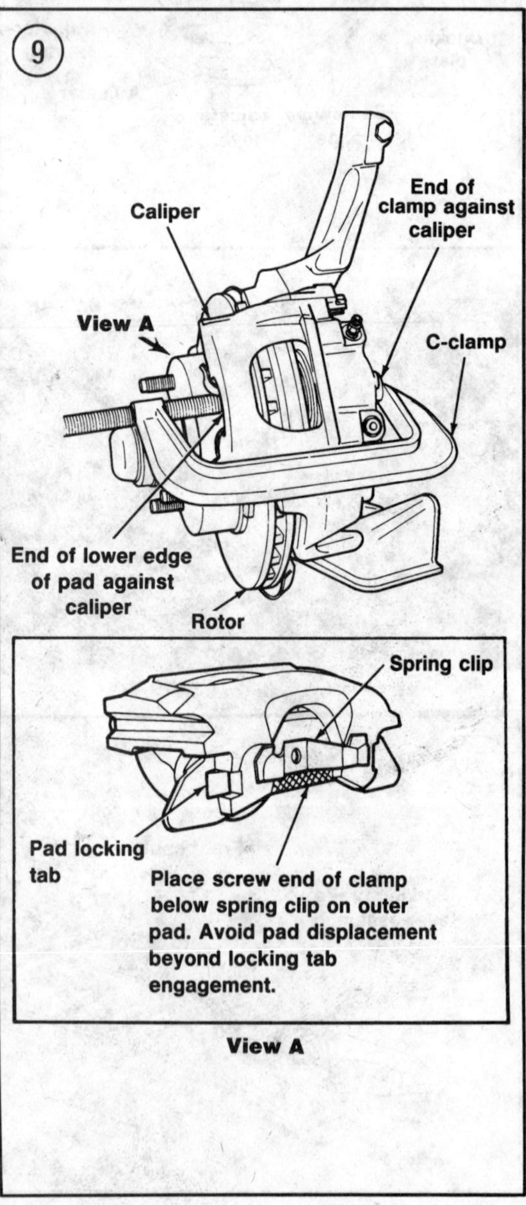

Pad Replacement

The outer pad is retained in the caliper by a spring clip and 2 rectangular torque buttons. The torque buttons must seat in the caliper notches and the spring clip must grasp the caliper properly. The inner pad has a replaceable anti-rattle clip.

1. Set the parking brake. Place the transmission in 1st gear (manual) or PARK (automatic).
2. Remove the wheel covers or hub caps. Loosen the front wheel lug nuts.
3. Remove the master cylinder cap and use a large syringe to remove about half the brake fluid in the reservoir.

WARNING
Discard this brake fluid. Do not reuse.

4. Securely block both rear wheels so the vehicle will not roll in either direction.
5. Raise the front of the vehicle with a jack and place it on jackstands.
6. Remove the front wheel/tire assemblies.

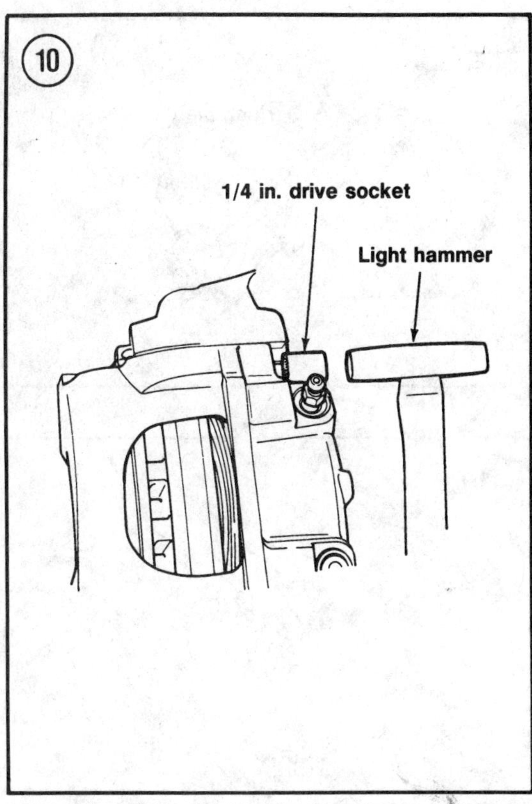

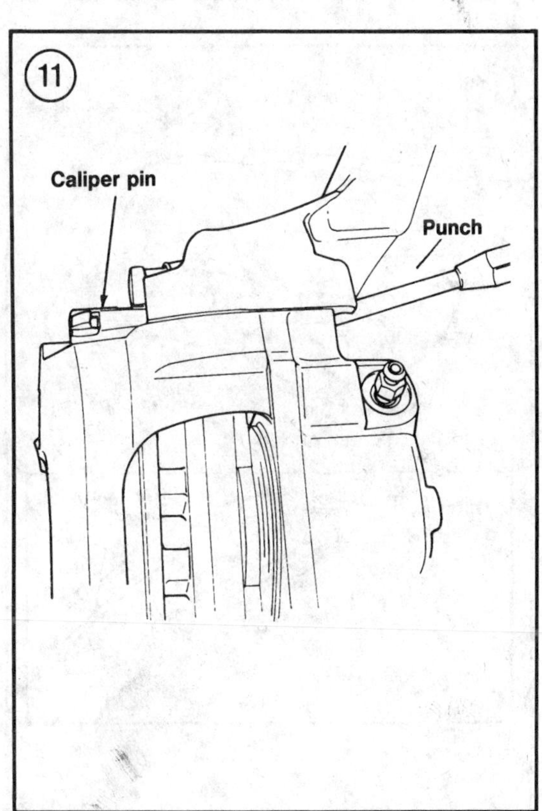

7. Install a C-clamp as shown in **Figure 9** and tighten until the piston bottoms in the bore (approximately 1/8 in.). Do not allow C-clamp to contact spring clip on outer brake pad. Remove the C-clamp.
8. Clean the area around the pin tabs to remove any contamination.
9. Drive the upper caliper pin towards the outside of the caliper with a suitable 1/4 in. drive socket and a light hammer until the tabs on the pin pass the face of the spindle. See **Figure 10**.
10. Using a suitable pair of pliers, compress and hold the pin tabs, then continue to drive the pin until the tab slips into the groove on the spindle.
11. Use a 7/16 in. or smaller punch to drive the pin out of the caliper slide groove (**Figure 11**).
12. Repeat Steps 9-11 to remove the lower caliper pin.
13. Remove the caliper from the rotor with an upward rotating motion. Suspend it from the suspension with a wire hook to prevent stressing the brake hose.
14. Compress the anti-rattle pin on the inner pad and remove the pad from the caliper.
15. Remove the outer pad from the caliper by pressing on each ear of the pad until the 2 torque buttons on the pad are released from their retention notches in the caliper. See **Figure 12**.

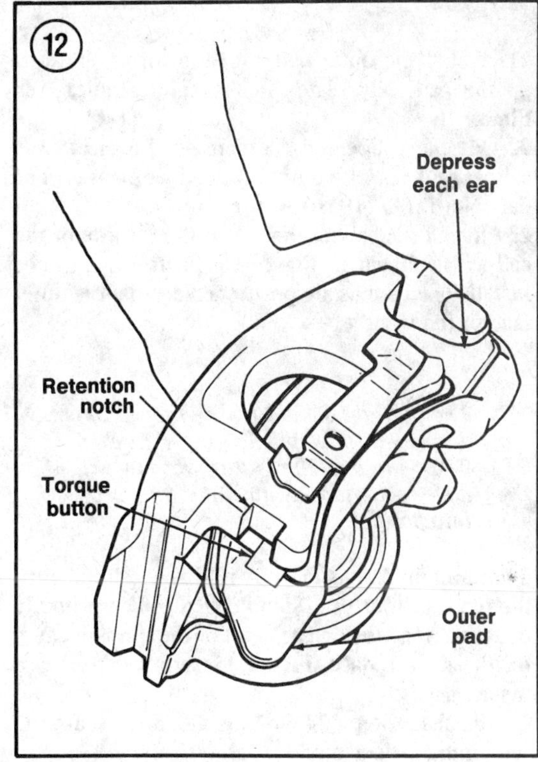

16. Inspect the pads. Light surface dirt, oil or grease stains may be sanded off. If oil or grease has penetrated the surface, replace the pads. Since brake fluid will ruin the friction material, pads must be replaced if any brake fluid has touched them.

17. Check the caliper piston seal and boot area for brake fluid leaks. If brake fluid has leaked from the caliper housing, replace the caliper. If the leak appears to come from the seal area, rebuild the caliper as described in this chapter.

18. Inspect the brake rotor as described in this chapter.

19. Install a new anti-rattle clip on the lower end of the inner pad (**Figure 13**). Make sure the clip tabs are properly positioned and the clip is fully seated.

20. Fit the inner pad and anti-rattle clip in the caliper pad abutment. The clip tab must rest against the shoe abutment and the loop-type spring must face away from the rotor. See **Figure 14**. Compress the clip and slide the upper end of the pad in place.

WARNING

The torque buttons on the outer pad must seat solidly in their respective notches in the caliper to prevent a possible temporary loss of braking power.

21. Install the outer pad with the torque buttons on the pad fully seated in the caliper holes. See **Figure 15**.

22. Fit the caliper on the spindle. Lubricate the caliper grooves with disc brake caliper grease (Ford part No. D7AZ-19590-A or equivalent).

23. Install the caliper pins from the outside of the caliper as shown in **Figure 16**. Each pin must be installed so its tabs are positioned against the outer face of the spindle.

NOTE

The pin tabs should not be tapped too deeply into the spindle groove in Step 24 or the opposite end of the pin will have to be tapped until the tabs snap into position.

24. Carefully drive the pin into the caliper until the pin tabs touch the spindle face. When properly installed, the tabs on each end of the pin will catch on the spindle face. **Figure 17** shows correct pin installation.

25. Repeat Step 24 to install and seat the remaining caliper pin.

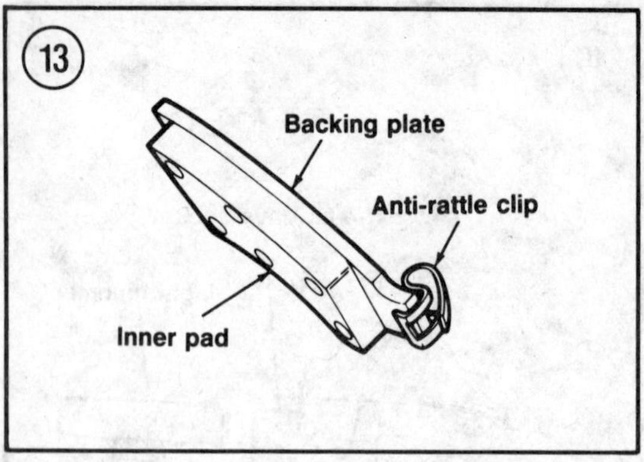

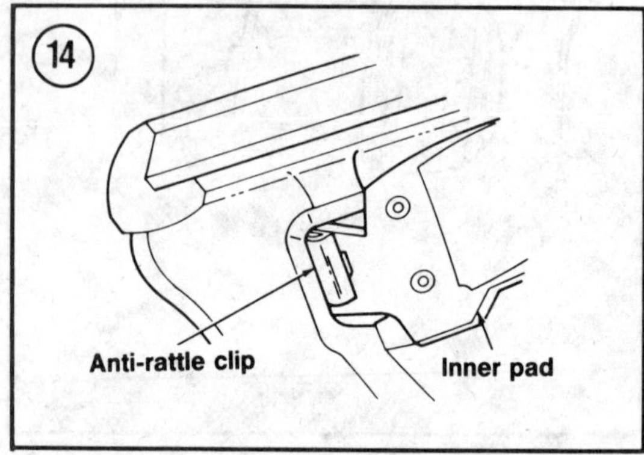

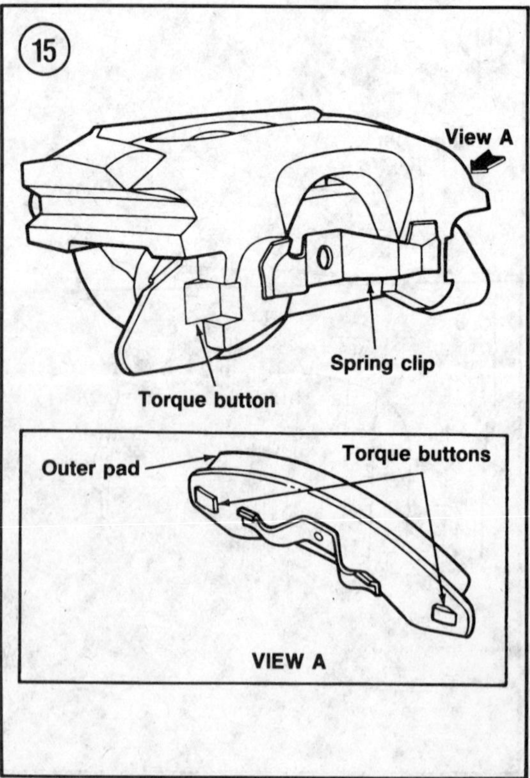

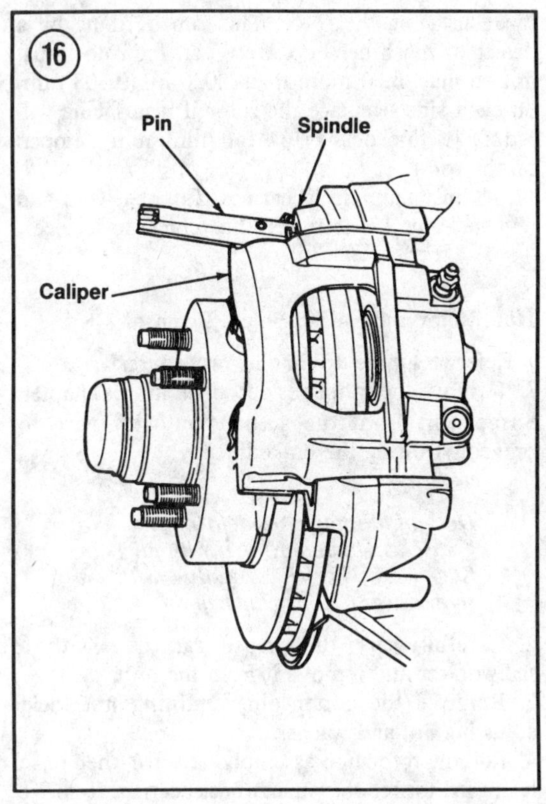
16
Pin
Spindle
Caliper

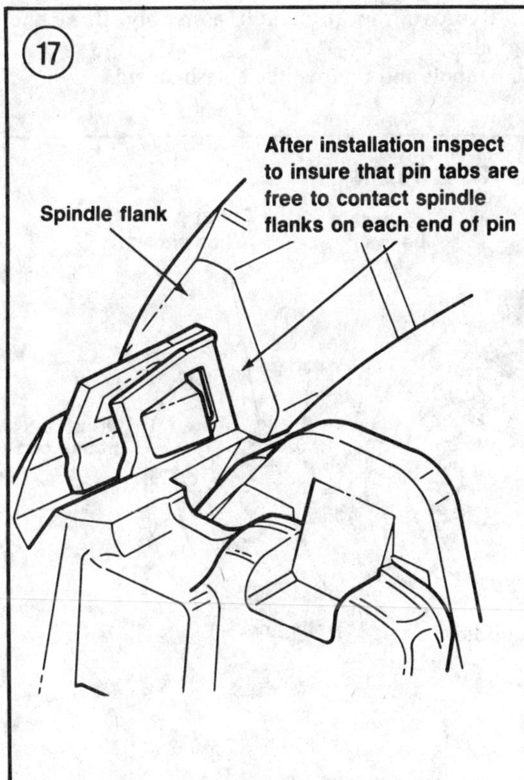
17
After installation inspect
to insure that pin tabs are
free to contact spindle
flanks on each end of pin
Spindle flank

26. If the caliper brake hose was disconnected for any reason, reinstall and bleed the brakes as described in this chapter.
27. Install the wheel/tire assemblies. Install the lug nuts finger-tight, then remove the jackstands and lower the vehicle to the ground. Remove the wheel chocks.
28. Tighten the wheel lug nuts to specifications (**Table 1**) in an alternating pattern. Reinstall the wheel covers or hub caps.

WARNING
Do not use brake fluid from a previously opened container in Step 29. Brake fluid absorbs moisture from the air and moisture in the hydraulic lines can result in erratic or slow braking.

29. Fill the master cylinder reservoir to the maximum level line with fresh DOT 3 or DOT 4 brake fluid from an unopened container.
30. Install the reservoir cap and check for leaks around the caliper and hoses.
31. Depress the brake pedal several times to position the caliper and pads and road test the vehicle to make sure the brakes operate properly.

Caliper Removal/Installation

1. Perform Steps 1-13 of *Pad Replacement* in this chapter.
2. Disconnect the brake hose from the caliper at the inlet fitting and discard the copper washers (if used). Plug the caliper inlet port and hose outlet to prevent fluid leakage or the entry of contamination.
3. Mark the left and right calipers for identification if both are removed.
4. Install the brake hose to the inlet fitting with new copper washers (if used).
5. Perform Steps 19-31 of *Pad Replacement* in this chapter to complete installation.

Rotor Inspection

1. Loosen the front wheel lug nuts.
2. Securely block both rear wheels so the vehicle will not roll in either direction.
3. Raise the front of the vehicle with a jack and place it on jackstands.
4. Remove the wheel/tire assemblies.
5. Tighten the wheel bearings just enough to remove all bearing free play.
6. Attach a dial indicator to the spindle knuckle assembly so that the indicator stylus touches the rotor surface approximately one inch from the outer edge of the rotor.

7. Set the dial indicator to zero, then slowly turn the brake rotor one complete revolution to check runout. If the total lateral runout exceeds 0.010 in. (0.254 mm), have the rotor resurfaced by a dealer (or replace it if the wear is excessive).

NOTE

If the rotor is resurfaced, no more than 0.020 in. (0.508 mm) should be removed equally from each side. The finished thickness of the rotor should not be less than 0.81 in. (20.6 mm) or the number cast on the inside of the rotor (if different).

8. Check the rotor for parallelism (thickness variation) with a micrometer at 12 equal points on the rotor. Take each reading with the micrometer positioned one inch from the edge of the rotor. If measurements vary more than 0.0005 in. (0.0127 mm), resurface or replace the rotor as required.
9. Use the micrometer to measure the thickness of the rotor at several points around the circumference and at varying distances from the center. If the rotor measures less at any point than the minimum stamped on the rotor, replace it.
10. Inspect the rotor for cracks, rust or scratches. Replace the rotor if cracked. Light rust can be removed with crocus cloth or medium emery paper. Light scoring of the rotor which does not exceed 0.015 in. (0.38 mm) results from normal operation and does not affect brake operation. Heavy rust or deep scratches should be removed by resurfacing the rotor. This can be done by a dealer or machine shop. However, the rotor must not be machined more than 0.020 in. (0.508 mm) on each side. Replace the rotor if resurfacing will reduce its thickness below the minimum stamped on the rotor.
11. Adjust the wheel bearings (Chapter Ten) and reverse Steps 1-4 to return the vehicle to service.

Hub, Rotor and Splash Shield Removal

Refer to **Figure 18** for this procedure.

1. Remove the caliper as described in this chapter. Suspend it from the suspension with wire to prevent stressing the brake line.

CAUTION

Do not damage or deform the hub grease cap by removing it with pliers in Step 2. Work carefully with a screwdriver and pry the cap off.

2. Carefully pry the grease cap free with a screwdriver and remove it from the hub.
3. Remove the cotter pin, retaining nut lock, adjusting nut and washer.
4. Pull the rotor/hub assembly outward, then push it inward to free the outer wheel bearing. Remove the bearing.
5. Remove the rotor/hub assembly from the spindle.
6. Unbolt and remove the splash shield.

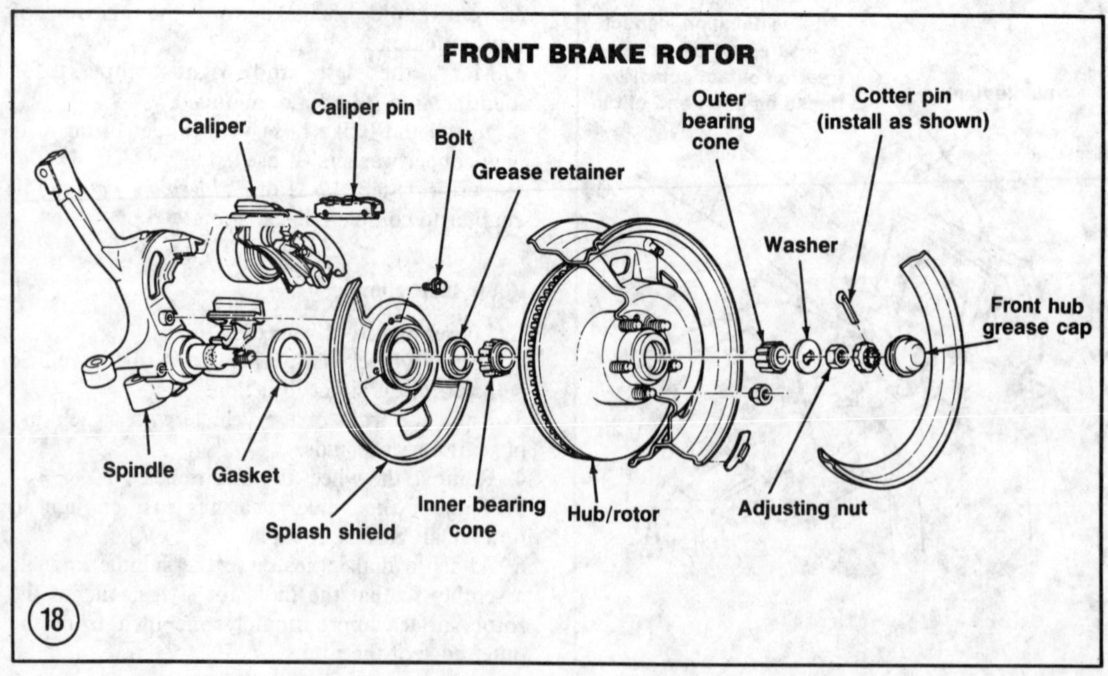

Hub, Rotor and Splash Shield Installation

Refer to **Figure 18** for this procedure.

1. Install the splash shield and tighten the attaching bolts to 13-19 ft.-lb. (18-25 N•m).

2A. If a new rotor is being installed, remove the protective coating on the rotor surfaces with aerosol brake cleaner. New wheel bearings must be installed, using the procedure described in Chapter Ten.

2B. If the original rotor is being installed, repack the wheel bearings with grease as described in Chapter Ten.

3. Slide the rotor/hub assembly and inner wheel bearing assembly onto the spindle.

CAUTION
Keep the rotor centered on the spindle to prevent damage to the grease seal and spindle threads.

4. Install the outer wheel bearing and washer. Install the adjusting nut and tighten it finger-tight. Make sure the rotor rotates freely.
5. Install the caliper as described in this chapter.
6. Adjust the wheel bearings as described in Chapter Ten.
7. Lower the vehicle and tighten all wheel lug nuts to specifications (**Table 1**).
8. Bleed the brakes as described in this chapter.

REAR DRUM BRAKES

The rear drum brakes are a self-adjusting duo-servo design. The drums fit over the rear wheel hub studs and are retained by the wheel/tire lug nuts. Vehicles may be equipped with a 9 in. (**Figure 19**) or a 10 in. (**Figure 20**) rear brake.

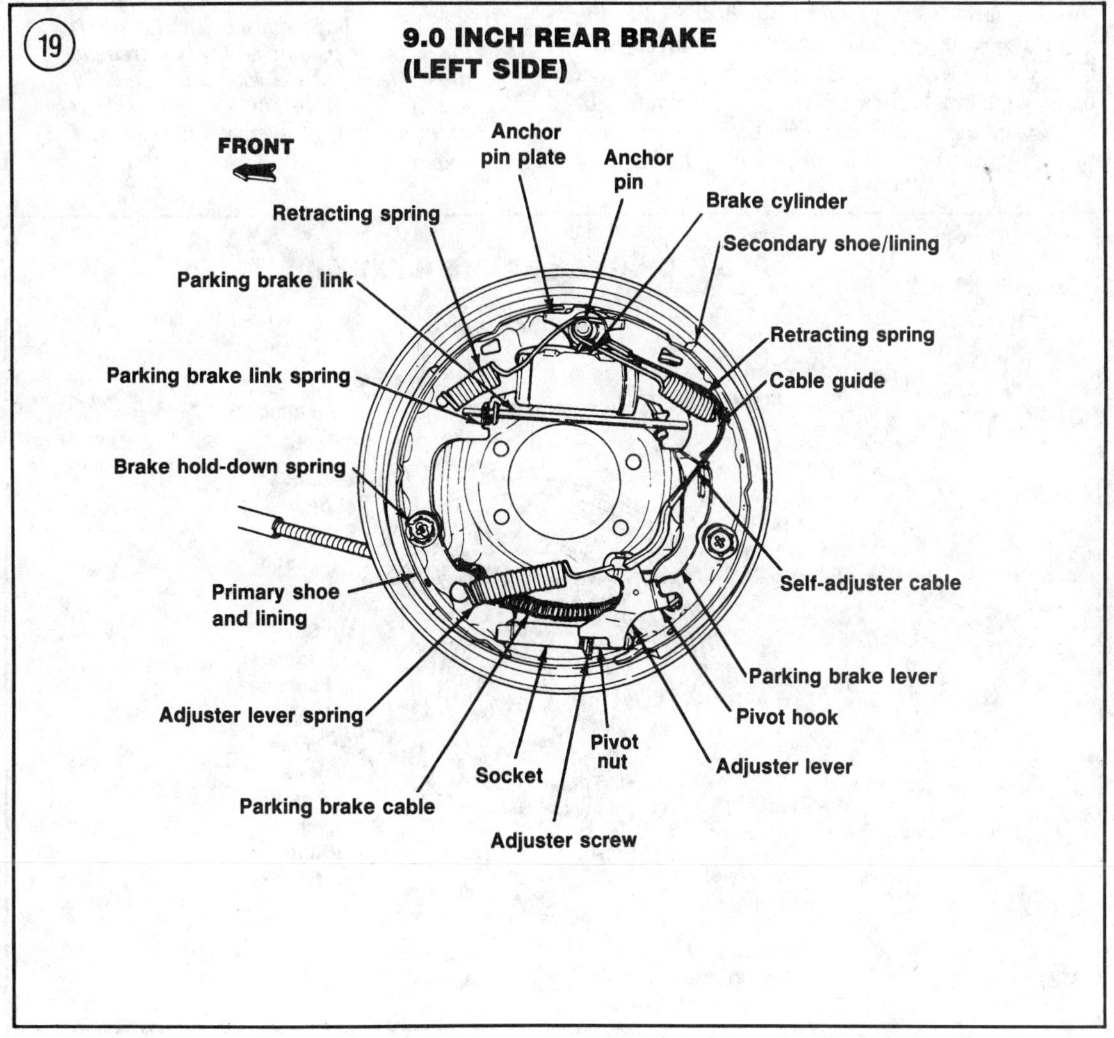

12

Brake Drum Removal/Installation

If the drum and lining on one side require cleaning and dressing, this service should be carried out on the opposite side also.

WARNING
Do not inhale brake dust. It may contain asbestos, which can cause lung cancer.

1. Set the parking brake and block the front wheels.
2. Remove the wheel covers or hub caps. Loosen the rear wheel lug nuts.
3. Raise the rear of the vehicle with a jack and place it on jackstands.
4. Remove the wheel/tire assembly. Remove the drum retainers and pull the drum free.
5. If the brake drum will not come off easily, remove the access hole plug from the support plate. Insert a narrow screwdriver through the adjusting hole, disengage and hold the adjusting lever away from the adjusting screw. Back off the screw with a brake adjusting tool. See **Figure 21**. Be careful not to damage the adjusting screw notches; otherwise, the self-adjusting mechanism will not function properly. If adjustment is backed off, make sure adjuster lever seats properly in the shoe web.
6. If a new drum is being installed, remove the protective coating with carburetor degreaser.
7. Install the brake drum with drum retainers. Install the wheel/tire assembly. Install the wheel lug nuts finger-tight.
8. Lower the vehicle to the ground and tighten the lug nuts to specifications (**Table 1**) in an alternating pattern. Reinstall the wheel cover or hub cap and remove the wheel chocks.
9. If brake adjustment was backed off to remove the drum, adjust the brakes as described in this chapter.

Drum and Shoe Inspection

WARNING
Do not clean brake drum or shoe assembly with compressed air in Step 1. Brake linings contain asbestos and the dust can be hazardous to your health. If the drum or shoe assembly is extremely dirty, clean with a vacuum cleaner or use an old paint brush and wear a painter's mask over your nose and mouth.

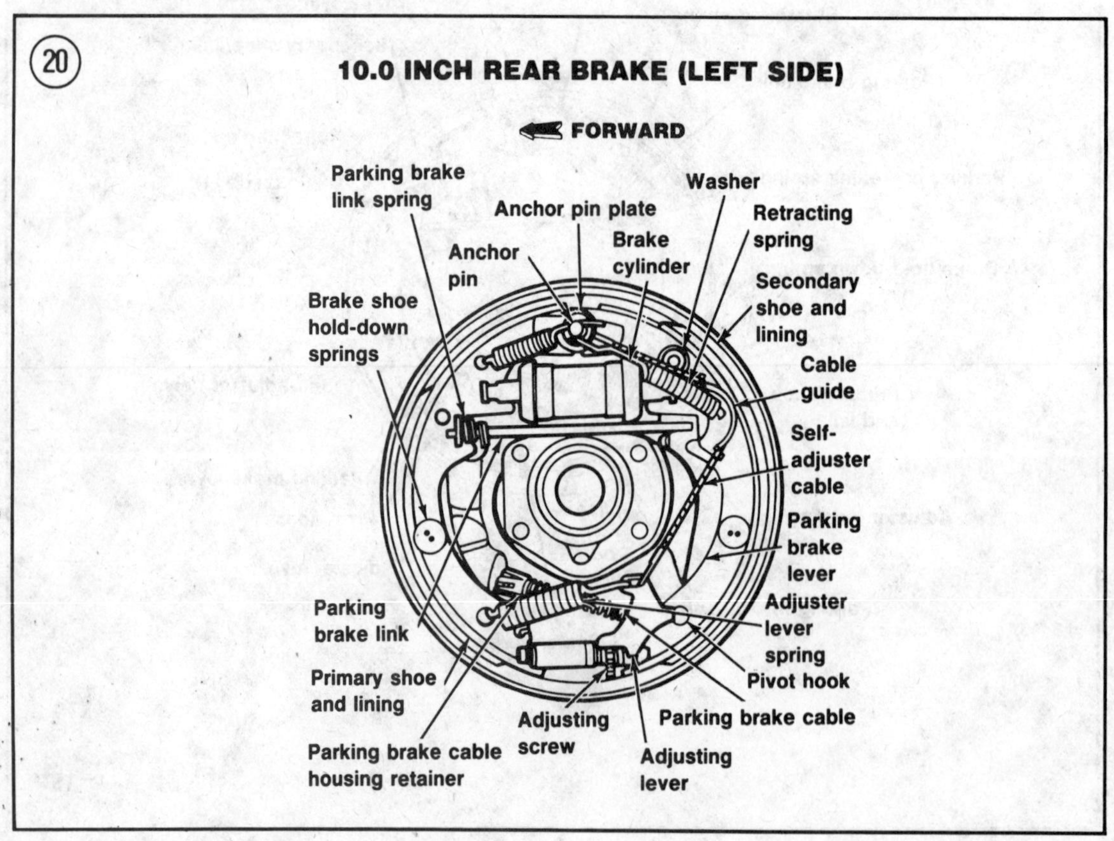

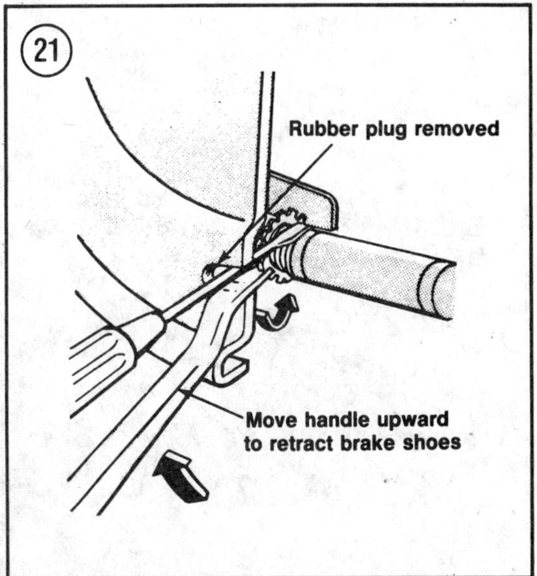

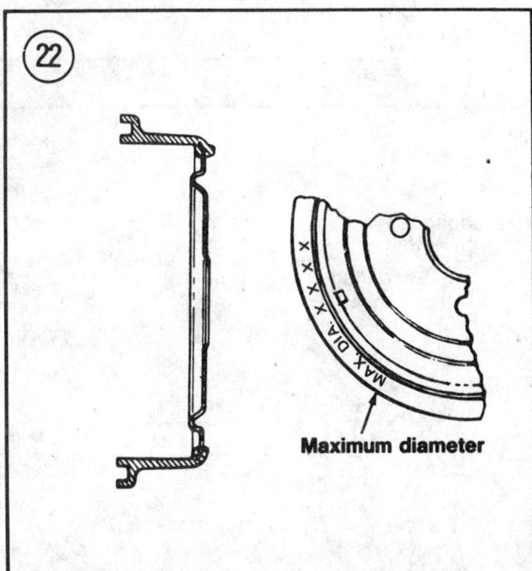

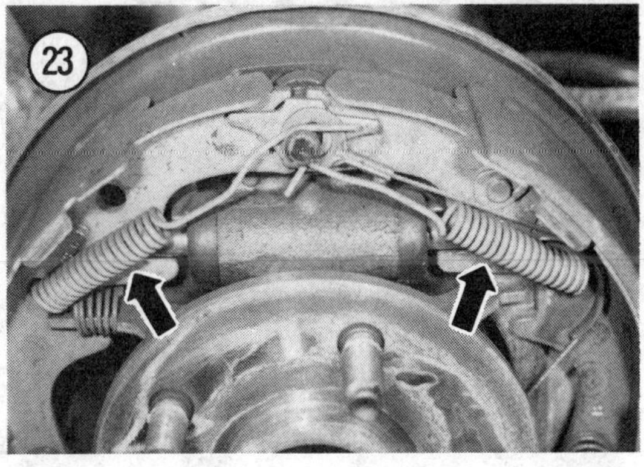

1. Wipe the inside of the drum with a clean dry cloth to remove any sand, dirt or other foreign matter. Clean all other parts (except the linings) with aerosol brake cleaner or new brake fluid. Do not use gasoline, kerosene or solvent as a cleaning agent.

CAUTION
If cleaning with brake fluid, keep it off the lining surfaces. Brake fluid will ruin the linings and they will have to be replaced.

2. Check drum for visible scoring, excessive or uneven wear, corrosion or glazed heat spots. Any scoring sufficiently deep to snag a fingernail is reason enough for having the drums turned and the linings replaced. Minor scratches or scoring can be removed with fine emery cloth. If this is done, clean thoroughly with compressed air to remove any abrasive. If heat spots (blue-tinted areas) are noted, replace the drum.
3. If you have precision measuring equipment, measure the drum for wear and out-of-roundness. If you do not have the equipment, this can be done by a dealer or machine shop. If the drum has surface damage or out-of-round exceeds 0.006 in. (0.152 mm), have it resurfaced on a lathe by a dealer or machine shop. However, the inside diameter after resurfacing must not exceed the maximum wear specification cast in the drum. See **Figure 22** (typical). If the drum would have to be cut larger than this to correct it, it must be replaced.
4. Inspect the lining material on the brake shoes. Make sure it is not cracked, unevenly worn or separated from the shoes. Dirt and foreign particles that are embedded in the lining can often be removed with a wire brush, but lining replacement is recommended instead. Light surface oil or grease stains may be sanded off. If oil or grease has soaked beneath the surface, replace the shoes. Since brake fluid will ruin the linings, the shoes must be replaced if brake fluid has touched them. Shoes must also be replaced if the lining material has worn to within 1/32 in. of a rivet (riveted lining) or the shoe (bonded lining).
5. Check all springs for signs of overheating, weakness or deformation (paint discoloration or distorted end coils indicate overheating). See **Figure 23** (typical). Replace as required.

Shoe Removal

Brakes should be reconditioned at least in pairs—both front or both rear—or all 4 wheels at the same time. In addition, new linings should be arced to the contour of the drums. This is a job for a dealer or automotive brake specialist.

Refer to **Figure 19** (9 in.), **Figure 20** (10 in.) or **Figure 24** (typical) for this procedure.

1. Remove the brake drum as described in this chapter.
2. Install a wheel cylinder clamp (**Figure 25**) or a heavy rubber band over the ends of the wheel cylinder.
3. Grasp the adjusting lever cable and pull it to the rear to disengage the lever from the adjusting screw, then move the outer side of the adjusting screw up and back off the pivot nut as far as possible. See **Figure 26**.

NOTE

Do not attempt to pry the pivot hook from the secondary shoe web hole in Step 4.

4. Disengage the pivot hook from the large hole in the secondary shoe web by pulling the adjusting lever, cable and spring down and toward the rear. Remove the adjusting spring and lever.

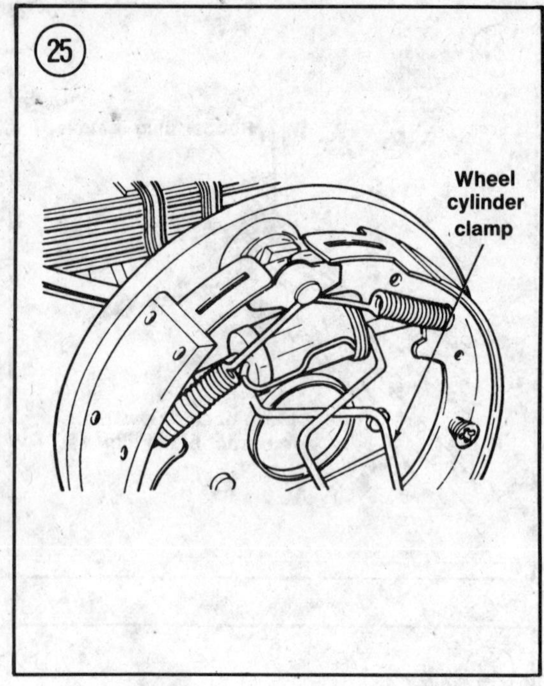

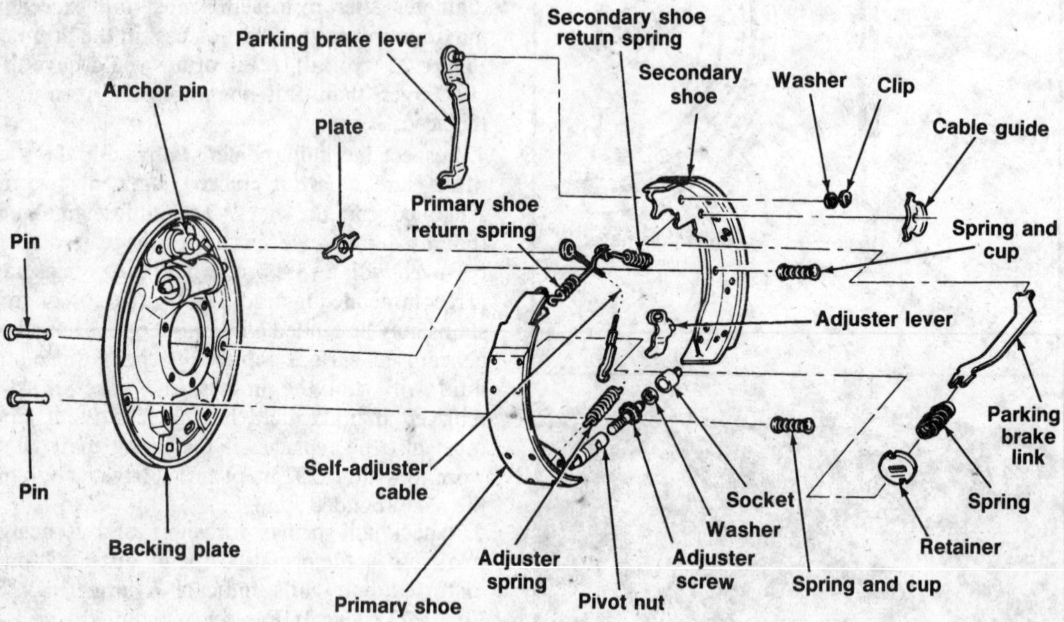

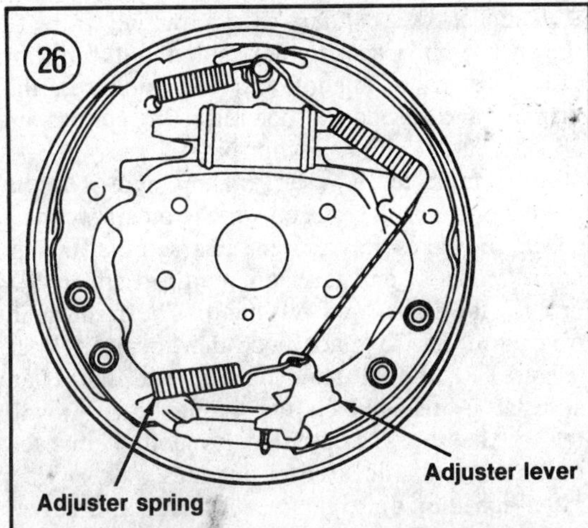

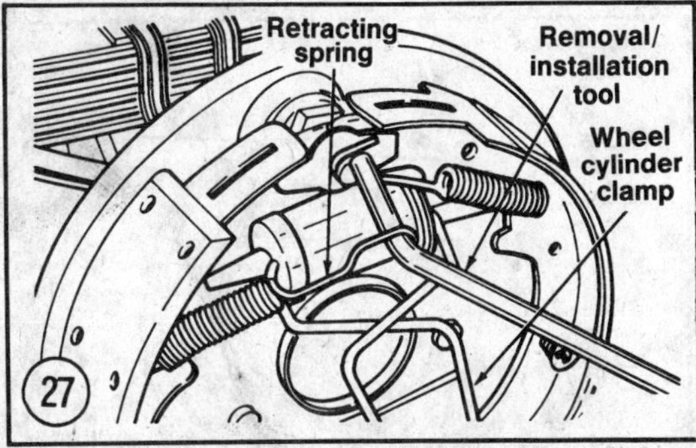

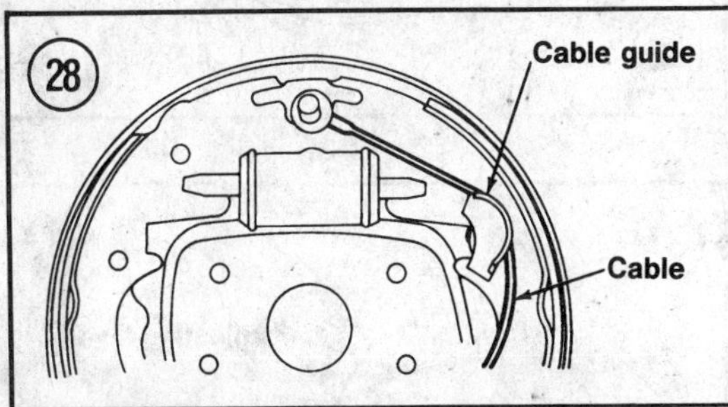

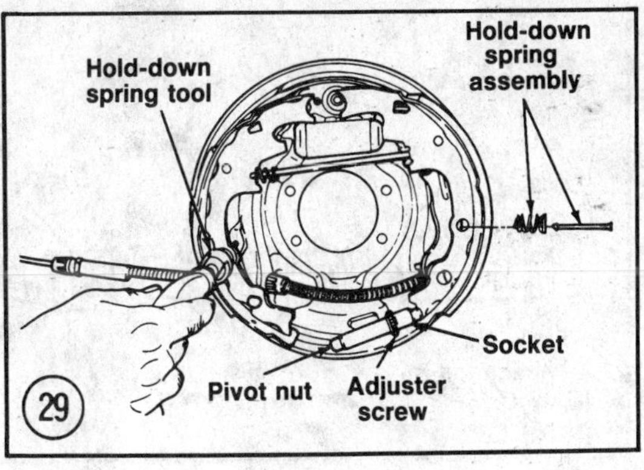

5. Unhook the secondary, then the primary shoe return springs with a brake tool (**Figure 27**). Large pliers can also be used, but a brake tool will make the job much easier. Unhook the cable anchor and remove the anchor pin plate, if so equipped.

6. Remove the cable guide (**Figure 28**) from the secondary shoe.

7. Depress the shoe hold-down spring cups and rotate 90°, then remove the hold-down springs and lever pivot from the hold-down pins. See **Figure 29**.

8. Remove the parking brake link and spring, then disconnect the parking brake cable from the lever. See **Figure 30**.

9. Remove the brake shoes.
   a. 9 in. brakes—Remove the parking brake lever from the secondary shoe.
   b. 10 in. brakes—Remove the retainer clip and spring washer holding the parking brake lever to the secondary shoe (**Figure 31**). Remove the lever from the shoe.

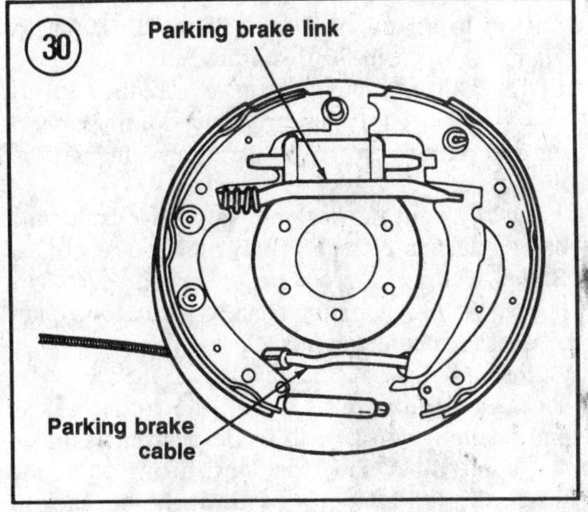

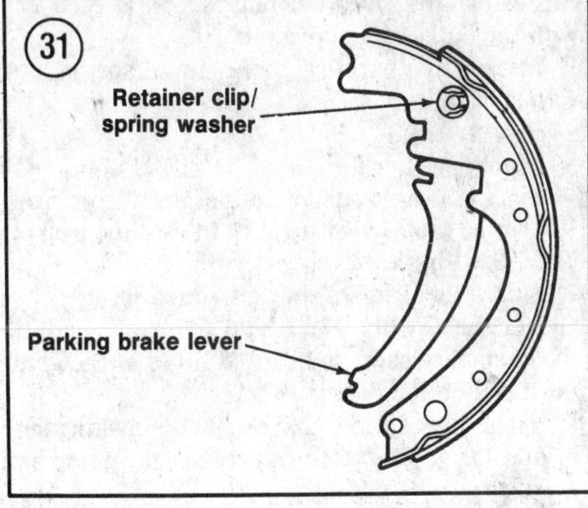

12

Brake Inspection

1. Carefully pry back the lower edge of each wheel cylinder boot and check for leakage. A slight film of brake fluid on the piston rods is normal, but if there is an excessive amount of fluid in the boots or wet stains outside the cylinder, it should be replaced as described in this chapter.
2. Inspect the backing plate for signs of oil that may have leaked past the axle seal. If oil is present, replace the seals. See Chapter Eleven.
3. Check and tighten the backing plate fasteners. Thoroughly clean the backing plate and all brake components. Use only aerosol brake cleaner—do not use mineral-based solvents. Clean the shoe contact surfaces to the bare metal with emery cloth. Make certain all loose dirt, rust, corrosion and abrasives are removed.
4. Check the adjuster screw operation. If it does not turn smoothly, disassemble, clean and lubricate it.

Shoe Installation

Refer to **Figure 19** (9 in.), **Figure 20** (10 in.) or **Figure 24** (typical) for this procedure.
1. Check the new linings to make sure they are not nicked or burred. If they are bonded linings, check for and remove any excess bonding cement along the edges.
2. Lightly sand the backing plate ledge pads until bare metal can be seen. Apply a light coat of Disc Brake Caliper Slide Grease (Ford part No. D7AZ-19590-A) or equivalent to the backing plate at the shoe contact points.
3. Install the parking brake lever on the secondary shoe. On 10 in. brakes, install the spring washer and retaining clip to hold the lever to the shoe.
4. Fit the brake shoes on the backing plate and insert the hold-down pins through the backing plate and shoes. Install the hold-down spring and cup assemblies over the pins. Depress each cup with the brake tool and rotate 90°.
5. Install the parking brake link, spring and washer. Connect the parking brake cable to the lever.
6. Install the anchor pin plate (if so equipped). Connect the cable anchor to the pin; the crimped side of the cable collar must be toward the backing plate. See **Figure 32**.
7. Attach the primary shoe retracting spring to the anchor pin (**Figure 27**). Install the cable guide in the secondary shoe; the flanged holes in the guide must fit into the hole in the web.
8. Route the cable around the guide, making sure it is in the groove and not between the guide and shoe.
9. Connect the secondary shoe retracting spring to the anchor pin. Check to make sure that the anchor pin plate, cable anchor and the hooks on the primary and secondary shoe retracting springs are all stacked flat on the anchor pin.
10. Assemble the adjuster, making sure it is the correct one for the brake on which you are working (if both brakes have been disassembled). The adjusting screw and lever are stamped either "R" or "L" for right- and left-hand. The right-hand pivot nut has 2 machined identification lines (**Figure 33**); the left-hand nut has one line. If an adjuster is installed on the wrong brake, it will retract the shoes rather than expand them each time the automatic adjuster operates.
11. Wipe the adjusting screw threads and socket with Ford Multi-purpose Lubricant (part No.

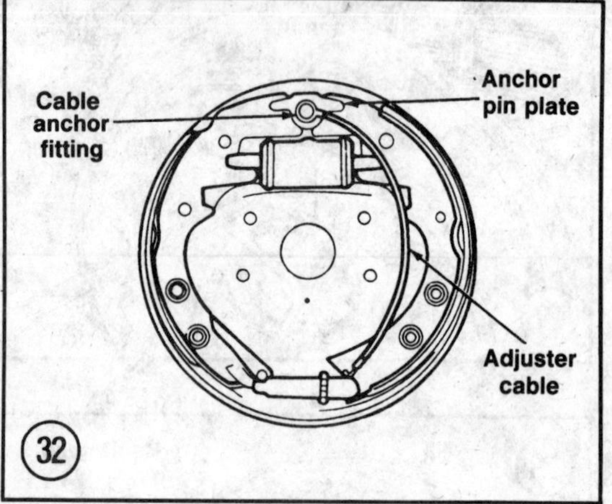

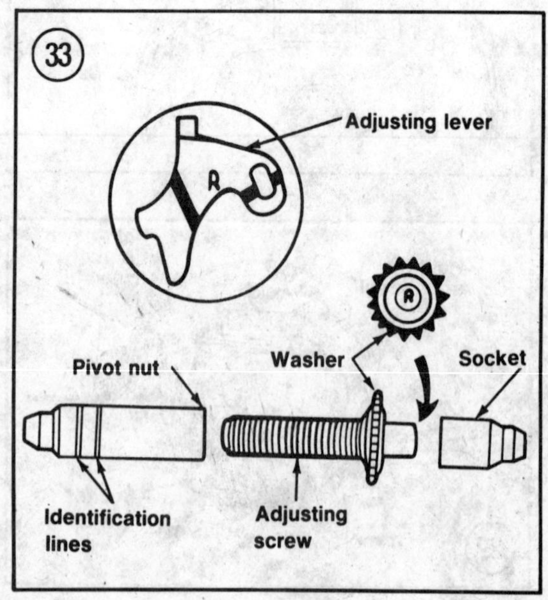

C1AZ-19590-B) or equivalent. Thread the adjusting screw all the way into the nut, then back it off 1/2 turn. Install the socket on the end of the screw. Install the adjuster between the shoes with the screw toward the secondary shoe. See **Figure 34.**

12. Connect the cable to the adjusting lever. Engage the hook on the lever in the secondary shoe hole, then connect the adjuster spring. Check the action of the adjuster by pulling the cable (between the guide and adjuster lever) toward the secondary shoe far enough to lift the adjuster out of engagement with the adjuster screw notches (**Figure 35**). Release the cable; the adjuster lever should engage the next notch in the screw. The adjuster spring should pull the lever down to its original position, turning the screw one notch.

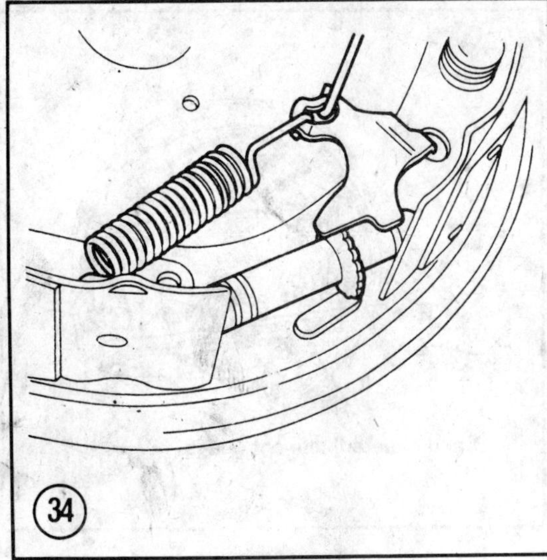

34

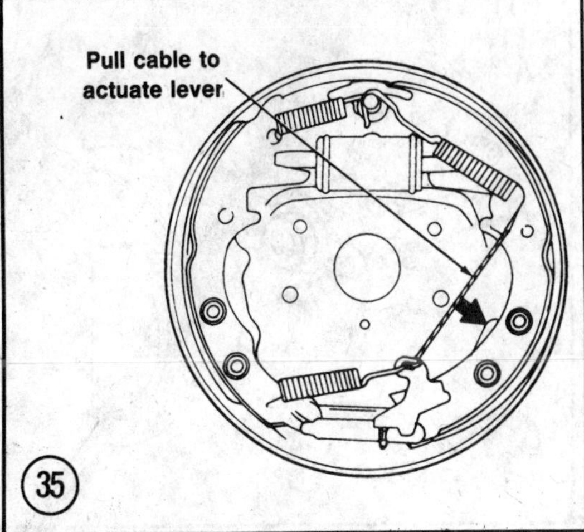
Pull cable to
actuate lever

35

13. If the adjuster does not operate correctly, check the following:
   a. Make sure the cable ends are not pulled out of the crimped collars. If they are, replace the cable.
   b. Make sure the groove in the cable guide is smooth. The groove must be parallel to the shoe and lie flat against the shoe web. Replace it if damaged.
   c. Make sure the hook on the lever is square and parallel with the lever. If not, it may be possible to bend it until it is correct. If not, replace the lever.

14. When both brakes on an axle have been assembled, make a preliminary adjustment. Pull the adjuster lever away from the adjusting screw just far enough to disengage it. Do not bend the lever. Turn the adjuster screw to expand the brakes just far enough so the drum can be installed with a slight drag, then loosen the adjuster screw 1 1/4 turns to retract the shoes. Install the drums and wheels.

15. Make a final brake adjustment by repeatedly driving the vehicle forward and backward and stopping in each direction with firm pedal pressure until the pedal height and resistance are satisfactory.

Wheel Cylinder Replacement

1. Remove the brake drum and shoes as described in this chapter.

CAUTION

Do not bend the brake line away from the wheel cylinder after unscrewing the nut in Step 2. Bending the brake line will make it difficult to reconnect and may cause it to crack. The wheel cylinder will separate from the brake line when it is removed from the backing plate.

2. Clean all dirt and contamination from the brake line fitting at the rear of the backing plate. Disconnect the brake line and cover the end of the line with a clean, lint-free cloth to prevent contamination from entering the hydraulic system.
3. Remove the bolts and lockwashers holding the wheel cylinder to the backing plate. Remove the wheel cylinder from the backing plate.
4. Install the new or rebuilt wheel cylinder to the support plate. Tighten the bolts securely.
5. Connect the brake inlet tube to the wheel cylinder and tighten the tube nut to specifications (**Table 1**).
6. Reinstall the brake shoes and drum as described in this chapter.

BRAKE ADJUSTMENT

Disc Brakes

Disc brakes are automatically adjusted. No adjustment procedure is necessary or provided.

Drum Brakes

Drum brakes are self-adjusting. Adjustment occurs when the vehicle is driven in reverse and the brakes are applied. If the brake pedal can be pushed within a few inches of the floor, the brakes should be adjusted by backing the vehicle up several times and sharply applying the brakes. Test the adjustment by driving the vehicle at about 20 mph and braking to a smooth stop. If the pedal travel is still excessive, repeat the procedure as required.

NOTE
Brake drums should be cold when adjusting the shoes. If the shoes are adjusted when the drums are hot and expanded, they may drag when the drums cool and contract.

Manual adjustment is unnecessary unless the brakes have been serviced. If so, proceed as follows:

Recommended procedure

1. With the brake drum off, disengage the actuator lever from the starwheel.
2. Measure the inner diameter of the brake drum with brake shoe adjustment gauge part No. D81L-1103-A or equivalent. See **Figure 36.**
3. Using the opposite side of the tool, position it against the linings (**Figure 37**) and rotate the starwheel with a small screwdriver blade as required until the tool just fits over the linings.
4. Install the brake drum as described in this chapter.

Alternate procedure

If the brake clearance gauge is not available, the brake drum can be used as an adjustment tool.

1. Rotate the starwheel with a small screwdriver blade as required until the drum slides over the linings with a slight drag.
2. Rotate the starwheel another 1 1/4 turns to retract the shoes. This will give enough clearance for final adjustment by driving the vehicle as described in this chapter.
3. Install the brake drum as described in this chapter.
4. Repeat the procedure on the opposite wheel.
5. Install the wheel/tire assemblies.

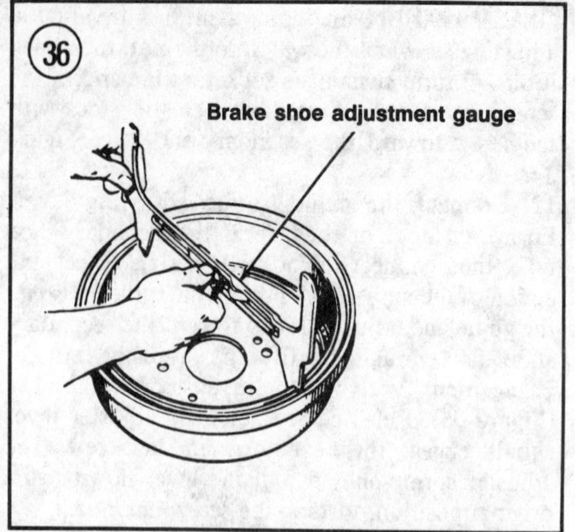

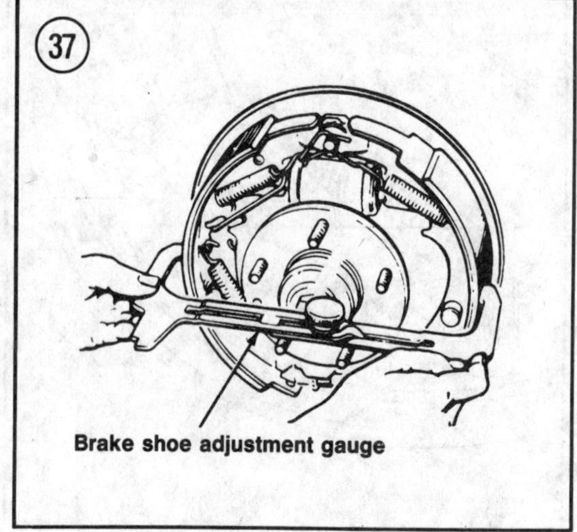

6. Remove the jackstands and lower the vehicle to the ground.
7. Make a final brake adjustment by repeatedly driving the vehicle backward and forward and stopping with firm pedal pressure until the pedal height and resistance are satisfactory.

Parking Brake

All vehicles use a hand-operated ratchet-type parking brake pedal mounted on the floor between the front seats. The parking brake is self-adjusting.

MASTER CYLINDER

The aluminum master cylinder uses a single plastic reservoir with a low fluid level indicator switch. The master cylinder is attached to the vacuum booster. **Figure 38** shows the operation of the master cylinder.

If the master cylinder is defective, it is safer and more economical to replace it with a new or professionally rebuilt unit than to attempt to overhaul the unit.

Removal/Installation

Refer to **Figure 39** (typical) for this procedure.

1. With the engine stopped, depress the brake pedal to expel any vacuum remaining in the brake booster system.
2. Disconnect the negative battery cable.

CAUTION
Brake fluid will damage paint. Wipe up any spilled fluid immediately, then wash the area with soap and water.

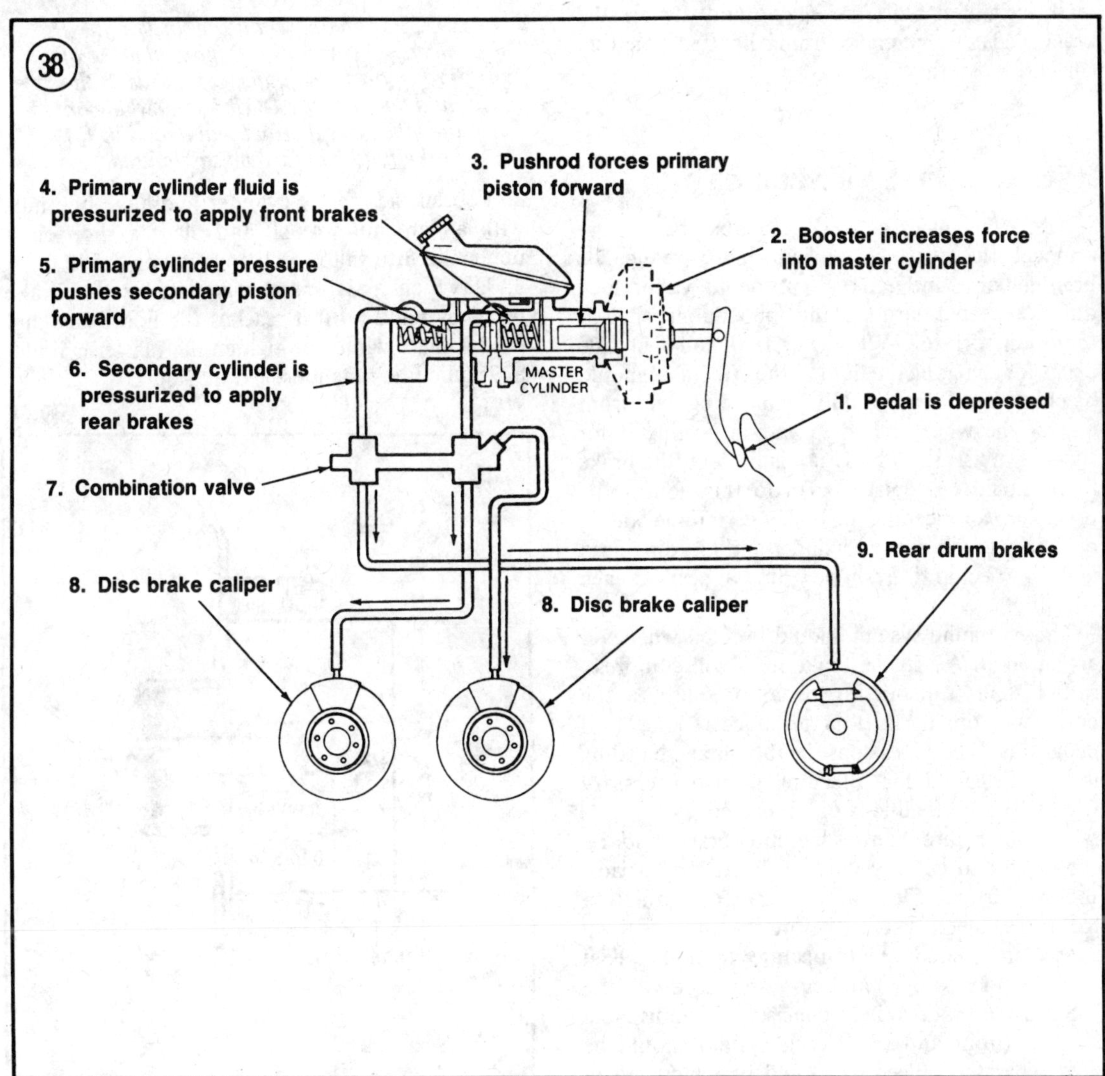

12

3. Disconnect the electrical leads and hydraulic lines at the master cylinder. Use a flare nut wrench to avoid rounding the fitting nuts. Cap the lines and plug the master cylinder ports to prevent leakage and entry of contamination.
4. Remove the 2 attaching nuts from the vacuum booster unit studs. Carefully remove the master cylinder from the engine compartment.
5. Before reinstalling the master cylinder, check the distance from the outer end of the pushrod to the front face of the booster assembly. Turn the pushrod in or out as required to obtain the specified length shown in **Figure 40**.
6. Installation is the reverse of removal. Tighten all fasteners to specifications (**Table 1**). Fill the master cylinder reservoir to the maximum level line embossed on its side wall with clean DOT 3 or DOT 4 brake fluid. Bleed the brakes as described in this chapter. Start the engine and depress the brake pedal to set the warning light in position. Check for external leaks.

BRAKE BLEEDING

After long usage, brake fluid absorbs enough atmospheric moisture to significantly reduce its boiling point and make it prone to vapor lock during repeated hard braking applications, such as mountain driving. While no hard and fast rule exists for changing the fluid in the system, it should be checked at least annually by bleeding fluid from one of the wheel cylinders and inspecting it for signs of moisture. If moisture is present, the brake fluid should be replaced. To do this, follow the procedure for bleeding the brakes. Continue adding new fluid to the master cylinder and bleeding fluid at each wheel until fresh, new fluid appears at each wheel.

The hydraulic system should be bled whenever air enters it. Air in the brake lines will compress, rather than transmitting pedal pressure to the brake operating parts. If the pedal feels spongy or if pedal travel increases considerably, brake bleeding is usually called for. Bleeding is also necessary whenever a brake line is disconnected.

This procedure requires handling brake fluid. Be careful not to get any fluid on brake discs, pads, shoes or drums. Clean all dirt and contamination from the bleed valves before beginning. Two people are needed: one to operate the brake pedal and the other to open and close the bleed valves.

Since the brake system consists of 2 individual systems (front and rear), each system should be bled separately. Bleeding should be conducted in the following order: master cylinder, right rear, left rear, right front, left front.

NOTE
Do not allow the master cylinder reservoir to run dry during bleeding.

Exhaust the vacuum reserve by applying the brakes several times.

Omit Steps 2-4 if the master cylinder was bench-bled before installation.

1. Clean away all dirt around the master cylinder. Remove the reservoir cap and diaphragm assembly. Top up the reservoir with brake fluid rated DOT 3 or DOT 4. Leave the cap off the reservoir and place a clean shop cloth over the top of the master cylinder to prevent any contamination from entering the fluid.

NOTE
DOT 3 means that the brake fluid meets current Department of Transportation quality standards. If the fluid does not say DOT 3 somewhere on the label, buy a brand that does. DOT 4 brake fluid can also be safely used.

2. Loosen the master cylinder hydraulic line nuts with a flare nut wrench and place a shop cloth under the fittings to catch any leaking fluid.
3. Have an assistant slowly depress the brake pedal by hand until it reaches the floorboard and hold it there while you tighten the master cylinder hydraulic line nuts loosened in Step 2.

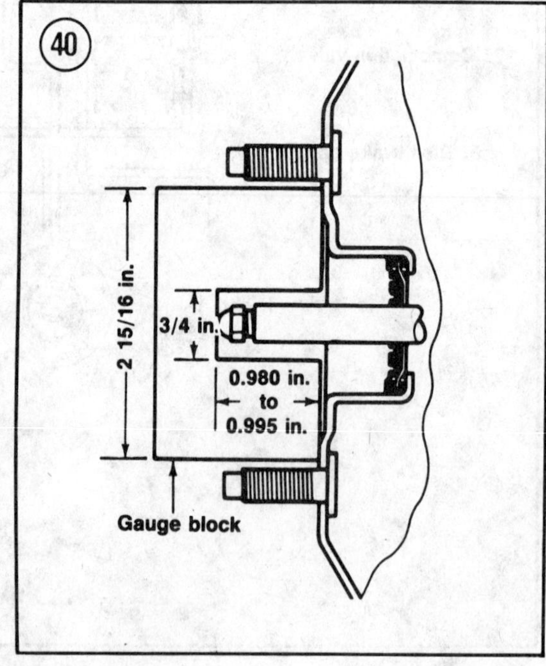

4. Repeat Step 2 and Step 3 as required until the brake pedal is firm and no air escapes from the fittings.
5. Fit an appropriate size box-end wrench over the bleed screw on the right rear wheel and attach a length of plastic or rubber tubing to the bleed screw. Be sure the tubing fits snugly on the screw. Submerge the other end of the tubing in a container partially filled with clean DOT 3 or DOT 4 brake fluid. See **Figure 41** (typical).

NOTE
Do not allow the end of the tubing to come out of the brake fluid during bleeding or the fluid level in the reservoirs to run dry. Either could allow air to enter the system and require that the bleeding procedure be repeated.

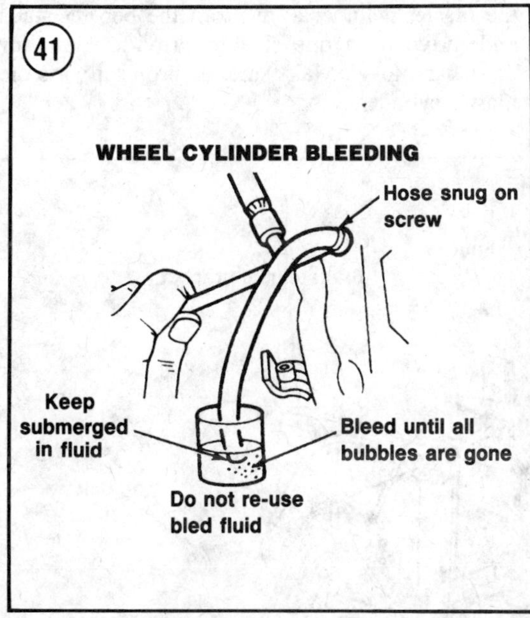

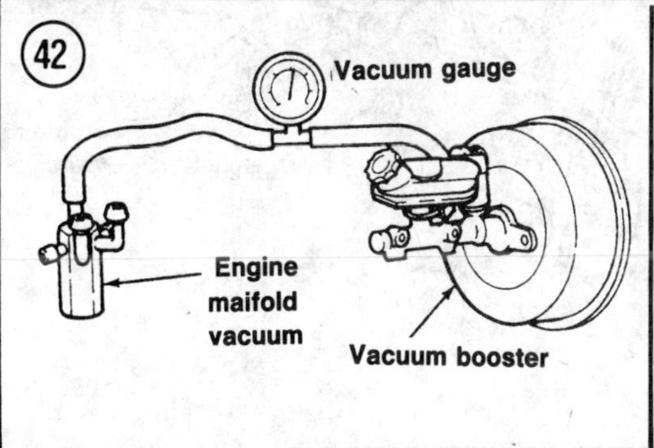

6. Open the bleed screw about 3/4 turn and have the assistant slowly depress the brake pedal to the floorboard. When the pedal reach the floorboard, close the bleed screw. After the screw is closed, have the assistant slowly release the pedal.
7. Wait 15 seconds and repeat Step 6 until the fluid entering the jar from the tubing is free of air bubbles.
8. Repeat this procedure at each of the remaining bleed screws. Top up the master cylinder after bleeding each wheel to prevent the reservoir from running dry.
9. Road test the vehicle to make sure the brakes operate correctly.

POWER BRAKE VACUUM BOOSTER

The vehicles covered in this manual use a single diaphragm vacuum booster unit mounted to the engine compartment cowl. The booster unit uses intake manifold vacuum and atmospheric pressure to reduce braking effort. The power booster is serviced as an assembly if defective. The only service possible to this unit is check valve replacement and pushrod adjustment.

Testing

1. Check the brake system for signs of a hydraulic leak. Make sure the master cylinder reservoir is filled to the maximum level line embossed on the side wall.
2. Start the engine and let it idle for about 2 minutes, then shut it off. Place the transmission in NEUTRAL and set the parking brake.
3. Depress the brake pedal several times to exhaust any vacuum remaining in the system. Once vacuum is exhausted, depress pedal and note amount of pressure required to hold it down. If pedal continues to move downward under pressure, there is a leak in the hydraulic system.
4. With the vacuum exhausted, depress and hold the pedal. Start the engine. If the pedal does not start to fall away under foot pressure (requiring less pressure to hold it in place), the vacuum booster unit is not working properly.
5. Disconnect the vacuum line at the booster check valve and connect a vacuum gauge with a tee fitting. See **Figure 42** (typical). Start the engine and check the gauge reading at idle with the transmission in neutral. If the gauge does not read at least 15-19 in. Hg (at sea level), tune the engine. See Chapter Three. If tuning the engine does not solve the problem, there is a vacuum leak in the system.

6. Shut the engine off and watch the vacuum gauge. If the reading drops by more than one inch in one minute, replace the check valve.
7. With the engine off, the vacuum gauge connected and the system holding vacuum as specified in Step 5, depress and hold the brake pedal for several seconds, then release it. If the vacuum reading drops to zero, replace the booster.
8. Run the engine for at least 10 minutes at fast idle. Shut the engine off and let it stand for 10 minutes. Depress the brake pedal with about 20 lb. of force. If the pedal feel is not the same as it was with the engine running, replace the vacuum unit.

Vacuum Hose and Check Valve Inspection

1. Check the vacuum hose between the booster unit and the intake manifold for leaks or a loose connection. Replace or tighten as required.
2. Disconnect the hose and remove the check valve from the booster unit. It should be possible to blow air into the brake booster end of the valve, but not into the intake manifold end. If air flows both ways or neither way, replace the check valve.

Booster Removal/Installation

Refer to **Figure 43** for this procedure.

1. With the engine stopped, depress the brake pedal to expel any vacuum remaining in the brake booster system.
2. Install a prop under the master cylinder for support.
3. Loosen the clamp holding the intake manifold vacuum line to the booster check valve. Disconnect the line at the check valve. Remove the valve from the booster unit.

CAUTION
Move the master cylinder carefully in Step 4 to prevent bending or stressing the hydraulic lines.

4. Remove the nuts and lockwashers holding the master cylinder to the booster unit. Carefully pull the master cylinder away from the booster studs and move it to one side to provide room for booster removal. Make sure the prop supports the master cylinder.

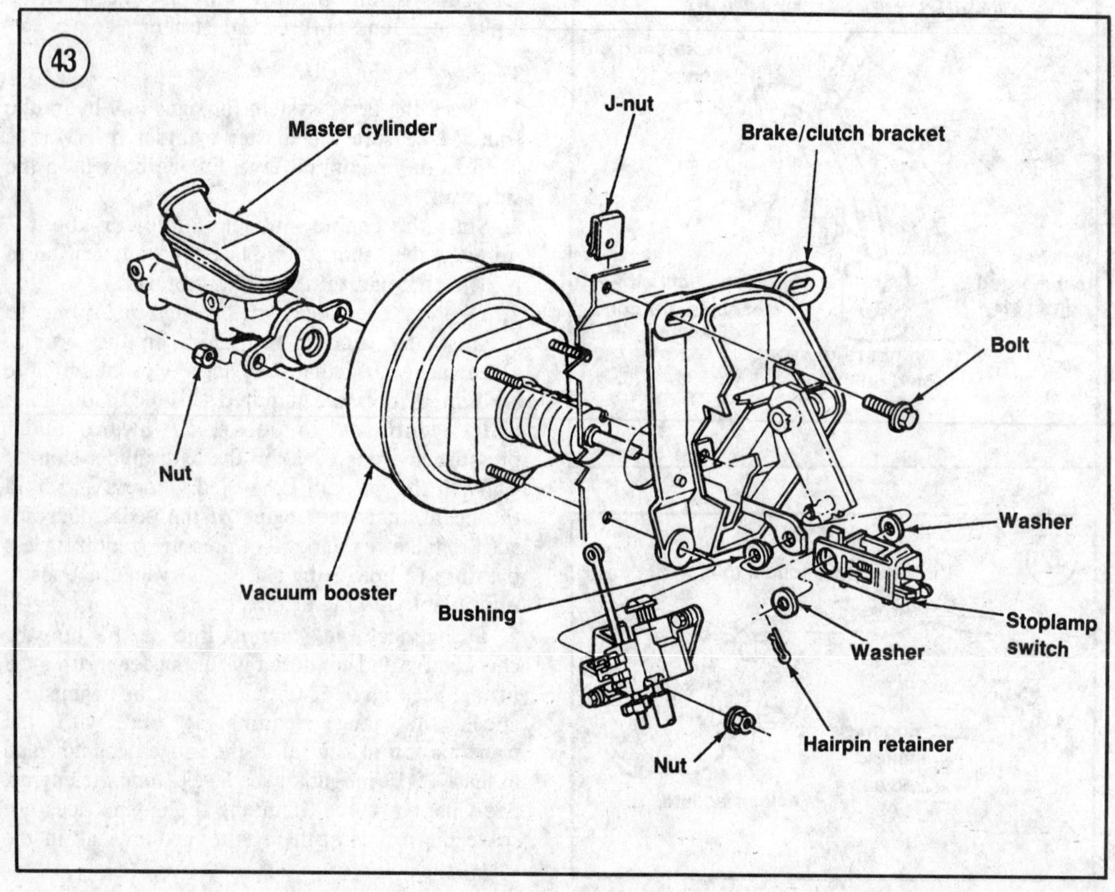

5. Working inside the cab, remove the pin holding the stoplight switch and pushrod to the brake pedal arm. Note the positioning of any spacers used, then slide the stoplight switch, pushrod, spacers and bushing off the pedal arm.
6. From inside the cab, remove the nuts holding the booster unit to the cowl. Remove the booster unit from the engine compartment.
7. Make sure the black reaction disc is positioned as shown in **Figure 44**. If the master cylinder pushrod was disturbed during removal, it will dislodge the disc. This will result in excessive pedal travel or improper operation when reinstalled.
8. Check the distance between the outer end of the booster unit pushrod and the front face of the booster unit with a gauge fabricated as shown in **Figure 40**. Turn the pushrod adjusting screw in or out until dimension A in **Figure 40** is 0.980-0.995 in.
9. Installation is the reverse of removal. Since the master cylinder lines are not disconnected during this procedure, it is not necessary to bleed the brake system. Start the engine and check brake operation. Road test the vehicle to make sure the brakes operate properly.

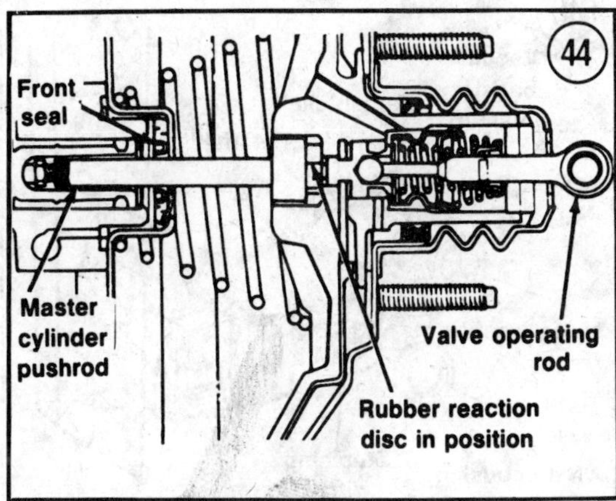

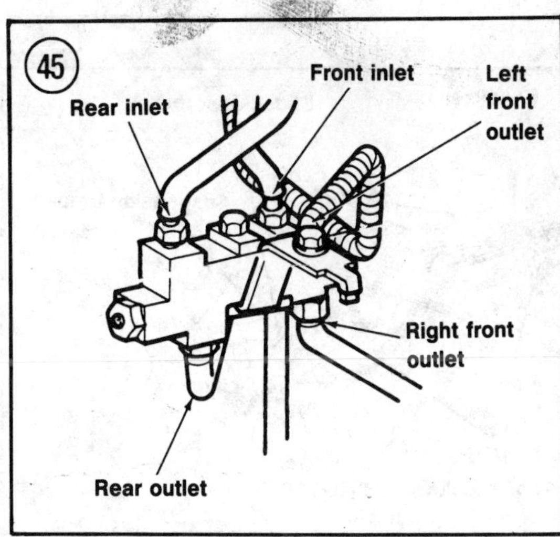

COMBINATION VALVE

The combination valve combines a front system metering system, rear brake proportioning system and pressure differential shuttle in a single unit bracket-mounted to the frame or fender well. The combination valve is not serviceable and must be replaced if any of its 3 functions do not work properly.

Replacement

Refer to **Figure 45** for this procedure.

1. Securely block both rear wheels so the vehicle will not roll in either direction.
2. Raise the front of the vehicle with a jack and place it on jackstands.
3. Disconnect and plug the hydraulic lines at the combination valve. Use a flare nut wrench to avoid rounding off the corner of the fitting nuts.
4. Remove the fasteners holding the valve to the fender well or frame bracket. Remove the valve.
5. Installation is the reverse of removal. Tighten the mounting fasteners securely. Bleed the brakes as described in this chapter.

DUAL BRAKE WARNING LAMP SYSTEM

A warning lamp on the instrument panel is connected to a low fluid level switch in the master cylinder reservoir and to the parking brake switch. The lamp should come on momentarily (as a self-test) whenever the ignition switch is turned to the START position. The lamp will also come on if the master cylinder fluid level is low or when the parking brake is applied.

Electrical Circuit Testing

1. If the warning lamp does not come on when the ignition switch is turned to the START position, check for a burned-out bulb or an open in the wiring between the lamp and ignition switch.
2. If the warning lamp does not come on when the master cylinder reservoir fluid level is low, check for a burned-out bulb, an open in the wiring between the lamp and low fluid level switch or a defective low fluid level switch.
3. If the warning lamp does not come on when the parking brake lever is activated, check for a burned-out bulb, an open in the wiring between the lamp and parking brake switch or a defective parking brake switch.

STOPLIGHT SWITCH

The stoplight switch is mounted on the brake pedal arm with a hairpin clip retainer (**Figure 46**).

Replacement

1. Working inside the cab, locate the wiring harness connector at the switch. Lift up the connector tab and disconnect the connector from the switch.
2. Remove the hairpin clip holding the stoplight switch on the brake pedal arm.
3. Slide the stoplight switch, vacuum booster pushrod, nylon washer and bushing away from the brake pedal pin. Disengage the switch from the pushrod and remove it from the vehicle.
4. Installation is the reverse of removal. Switch should be positioned with its U-shaped side facing the pedal and directly over or under the pedal pin. Make sure bushing and washers are properly positioned, then slide the switch over the booster pushrod and engage on the pedal pin. Make sure the wire harness is properly routed and will travel the full pedal stroke without binding before reconnecting it to the switch. If hairpin retainer is lost or must be replaced for other reasons, use only a factory-supplied retainer pin—do not use a cotter pin or other substitute.

PARKING BRAKE

All models use a manually operated, self-adjusting parking brake assembly. A cable connected to the parking brake lever is routed to the equalizer. Separate cables connected to the equalizer are routed to each rear wheel. See **Figure 47**. Cable routing and retaining clip usage may differ according to model year but cables can be replaced using the following generalized procedures.

Cable Tension Release

Cable tension must be released prior to servicing any component in the parking brake system. This is done by inserting a pin in the parking brake lever to release the self-adjusting pawl, then rotating the ratcheting wheel in the lever to allow insertion of a second pin to lock the wheel in the released position. Once service has been completed and the cables reconnected to the equalizer, cable tension must be reset.

1. Starting with the front screw, remove the screws holding the parking brake lever boot to the floorboard. Remove the parking brake lever boot.
2. Make sure the lever is in its fully released position.
3. Insert a suitable steel pin in the pawl lock-out pin hole (**Figure 48**) from the inner side of the control. The pin should be inserted at a slightly forward and upward angle, then moved downward

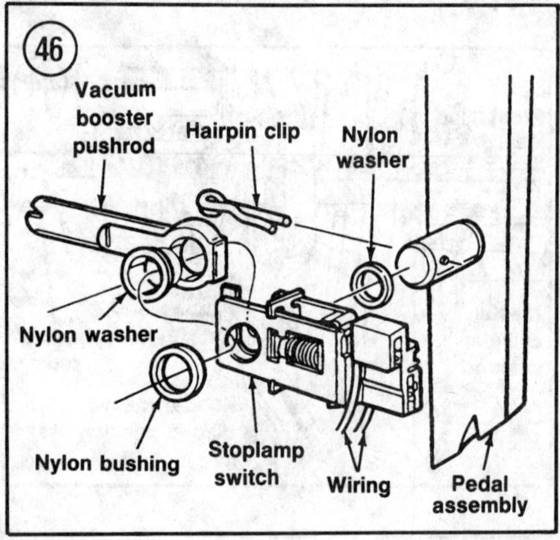

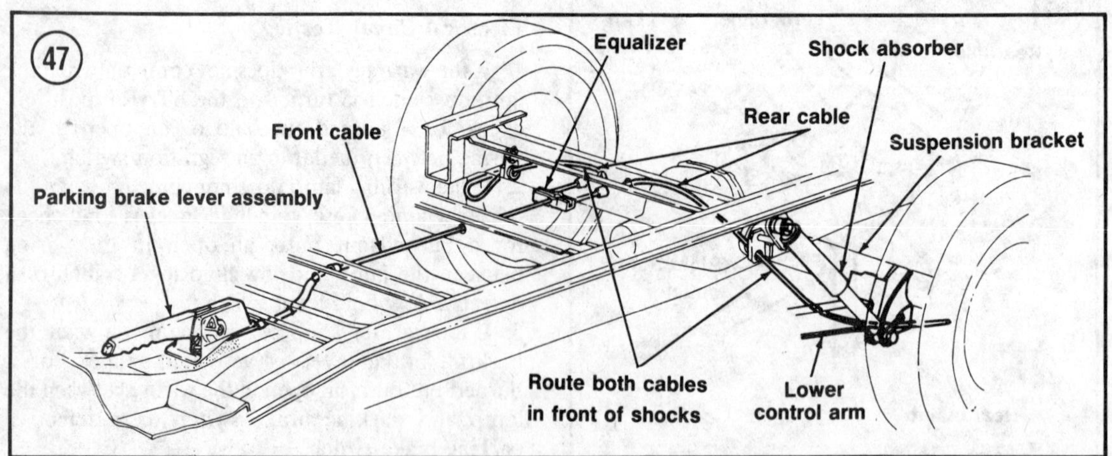

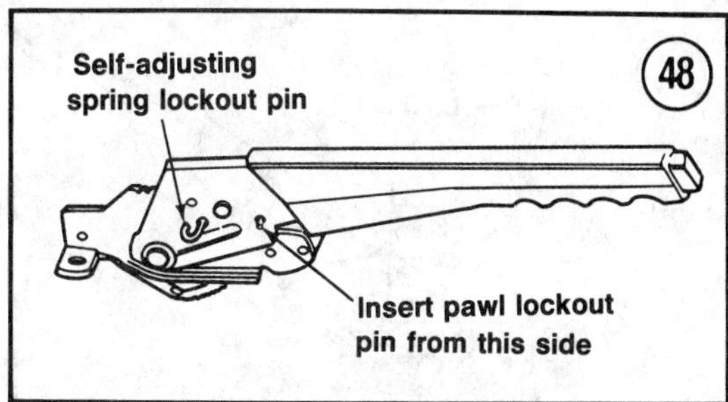

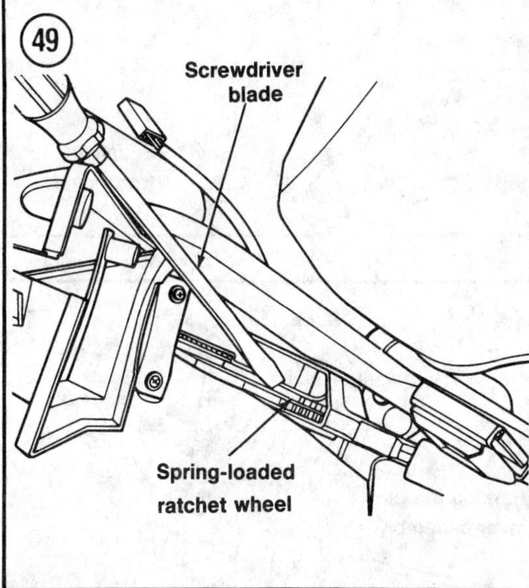

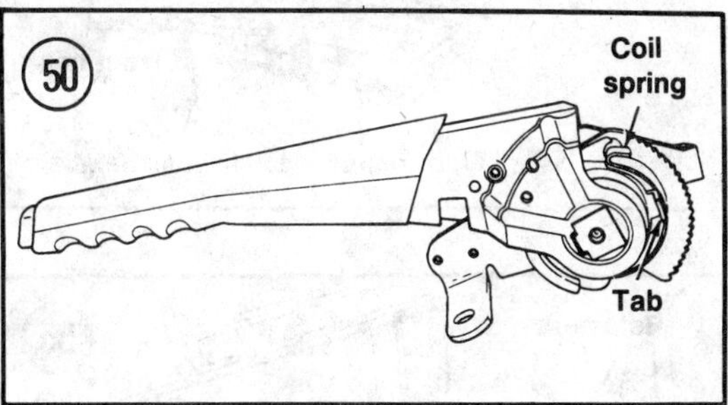

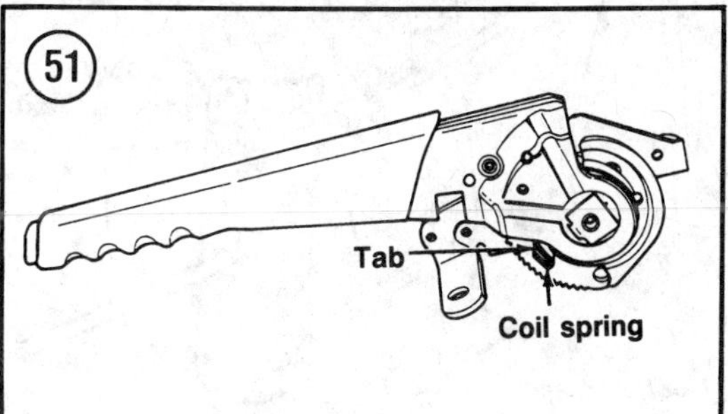

and to the rear. This displaces the self-adjusting pawl, allowing a pin to be inserted through the other hole and lock out the self-adjusting pawl.

4. Use a suitable screwdriver blade or punch to rotate the spring-loaded ratchet wheel in the self-adjuster mechanism back as far as it will go to release the cable tension. See **Figure 49**.

5. To reset the tension, make sure that the parking brake cables are properly connected to the equalizer.

6. Remove the steel pins from the lever pin holes in the same order as installed in Step 3.

7. Apply and release the parking brake lever several times to reset cable tension properly.

Resetting Parking Brake Lever Spring Tension

Spring tension in the parking brake lever may be lost if:

a. One of the cables breaks.

b. The lock pins are removed from the lever before the cables are properly reconnected.

c. The system is serviced without installing the lock pins in the lever. If the coil spring unwinds and disengages from the wheel tab (**Figure 50**), causing a loss of spring tension:

1. Remove the parking brake lever assembly as described in this chapter.

2. Re-engage the coil spring on the wheel tab (**Figure 51**).

3. Insert a suitable steel pin in the pawl lockout pin hole (**Figure 48**) from the inner side of the control. The pin should be inserted at a slightly forward and upward angle, then moved downward and to the rear. This displaces the self-adjusting pawl, allowing a pin to be inserted through the other hole and lock out the self-adjusting pawl.

4. Fit a spare cable over the pulley, inserting the cable anchor pin into the ratchet plate pivot hole (**Figure 52**).

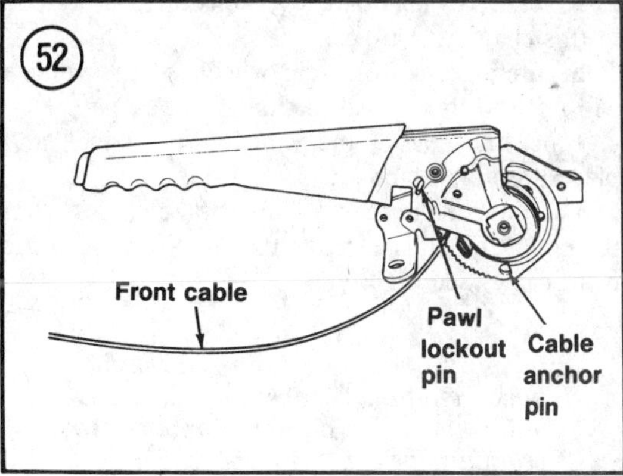

5. Step on one end of the cable on the floor (**Figure 53**) or clamp the cable end in a vise. Pull on the lever while holding the mounting bracket tightly against the lever. Cable tension should rotate the cable track unit enough to allow the insertion of a lock pin to hold the assembly in the "cable released" position.
6. Remove the spare cable and reinstall the parking brake lever assembly as described in this chapter.

Parking Brake Lever Removal/Installation

Refer to **Figure 54** for this procedure.

1. Starting with the front screw, remove the screws holding the parking brake lever boot to the floorboard.
2. Release the cable tension as described in this chapter.
3. Disengage the cable anchor pin from the ratchet plate pivot hole.
4. Disconnect the equalizer cable from the parking brake lever assembly.
5. Unbolt and remove the parking brake lever from the floorboard.
6. To reinstall, route the cable around the parking brake lever pulley, then engage the cable anchor pin in the ratchet plate pivot hole.
7. Install the parking brake lever to the floorboard. Tighten the retaining bolts securely.
8. Reset cable tension as described in this chapter.
9. Fit the boot over the parking brake lever. Install and tighten the screws securely.
10. Apply and release the parking brake lever several times to reset cable tension properly. Make sure the instrument panel warning lamp comes on when the parking brake is applied.

Front Cable Replacement

Refer to **Figure 47** for this procedure.

1. Make sure the parking brake is fully released.
2. Release parking brake lever tension as described in this chapter.
3. Securely block both rear wheels so the vehicle will not roll in either direction.
4. Raise the rear of the vehicle with a jack and place it on jackstands.
5. Disconnect the rear parking brake cables from the equalizer, then remove the equalizer from the front cable. See **Figure 55**.

NOTE
It may be necessary to loosen the fuel tank retaining straps and partially lower the tank on some models to provide sufficient access for Step 6.

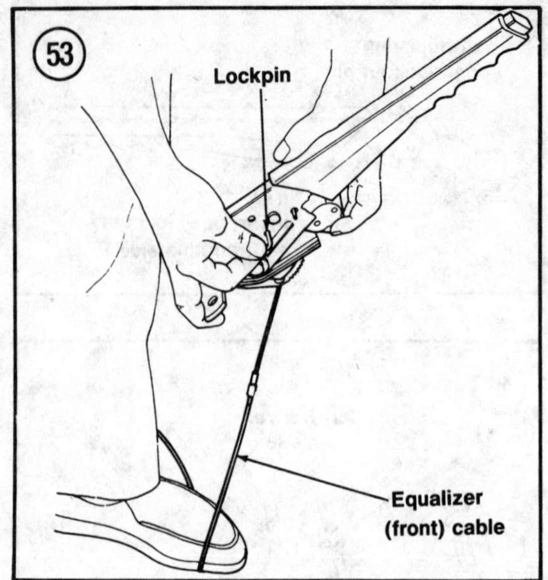

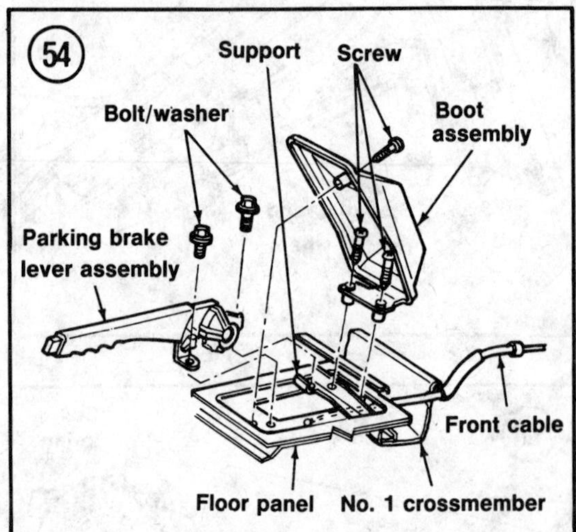

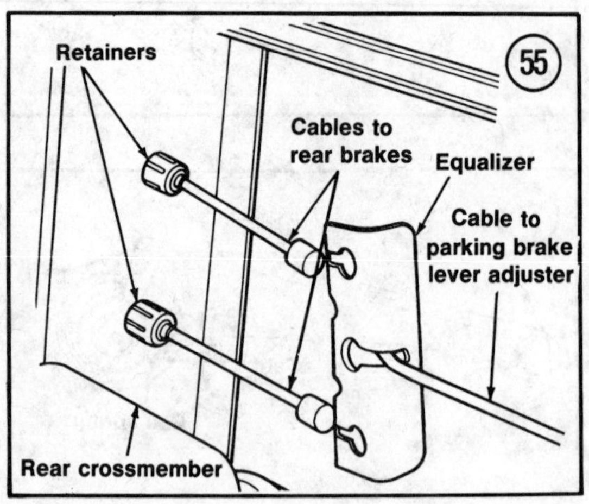

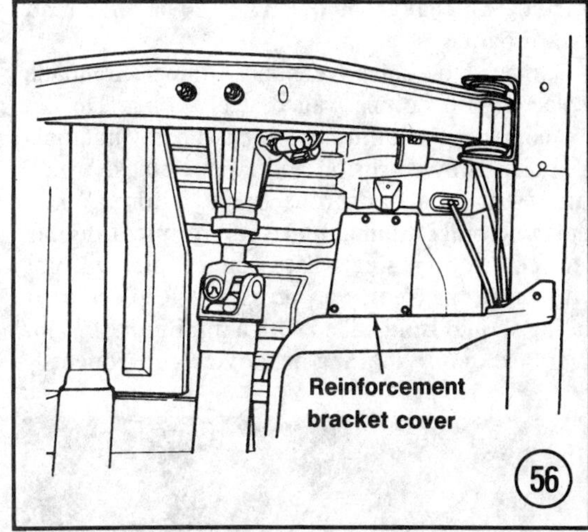

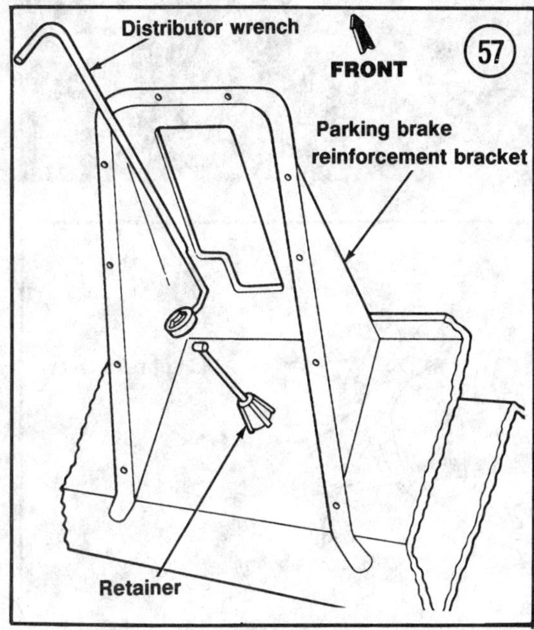

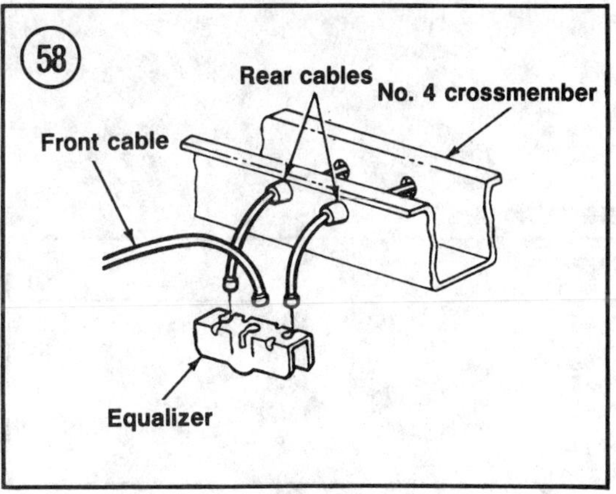

6. Unbolt and remove the reinforcement bracket cover (**Figure 56**).
7. Working in the cab, disengage the cable anchor pin from the ratchet plate pivot hole (**Figure 52**).
8. Remove the front cable from the lever control assembly.
9. Use a 1/2 in. 12-point box-end distributor lockbolt wrench to compress the cable retainer fingers in the front section of the U-shaped crossmember (**Figure 57**). Remove the retainer from the rear section of the crossmember, then pull the cable ends through the crossmember and remove it from under the vehicle.
10. To install the new cable, feed it through the holes in both crossmember sections, pushing the retainers through the holes to allow the fingers to expand over each hole.
11. Route the cable around the parking brake lever pulley, then engage the cable anchor pin in the ratchet plate pivot hole.
12. Position the equalizer as shown in **Figure 58**. Bend and insert the cables into the equalizer, then straighten the equalizer up to assume its normal position (**Figure 55**).
13. Reset cable tension by removing the lock pins from the parking brake lever assembly.
14. Make sure the front cable is connected to the parking brake lever, then reinstall the reinforcement bracket cover (**Figure 56**) and tighten the fasteners securely.
15. Fit the boot over the parking brake lever. Install and tighten the screws securely.
16. Apply and release the parking brake lever several times to reset cable tension properly. Make sure the instrument panel warning lamp comes on when the parking brake is applied.

Rear Cable Replacement

The following steps can be used to replace either the right- or left-hand cable. Refer to **Figure 47** for this procedure.

1. Make sure the parking brake is fully released.
2. Release parking brake lever tension as described in this chapter.
3. Remove the rear wheel hub cap. Loosen the wheel lug nuts.
4. Securely block both front wheels so the vehicle will not roll in either direction.
5. Raise the front of the vehicle with a jack and place it on jackstands.
6. Remove the rear wheel and brake drum as described in this chapter.
7. Disconnect the rear parking brake cables from the equalizer. See **Figure 55**.
8. Compress the retainer fingers and remove the cable retainer from the rear crossmember.

9. Remove the cable from the crossmember and the frame bracket.
10. Disengage the cable from its slot in the parking brake lever (**Figure 59**), then remove the cable through the hole in the backing plate.
11. Installation is the reverse of removal. Apply and release the parking brake lever several times to reset cable tension properly. Make sure the instrument panel warning lamp comes on when the parking brake is applied. If necessary, adjust the rear brakes as described in this chapter.

BRAKE PEDAL

The system is designed to provide a full stroke of the master cylinder when the brake pedal is fully depressed. The pedal height and travel are fixed and do not require adjustment.

BRAKE HOSES AND TUBING

The condition of all flexible brake hoses (A, **Figure 60**) and rigid tubing (B, **Figure 60**) should be checked at least twice a year to make sure they are properly connected and are not leaking or deteriorated. Check hoses for leaks, blisters, cracking or chafing of the outer cover and road hazard damage.

Damaged or defective brake tubing should be replaced with double walled steel tubing. Do *not* use copper or aluminum tubing. These materials are affected by corrosion and fatigue cracks which can result in a dangerous brake failure. When replacing brake tubing, make sure to use a double flare connection; single flare connections will not withstand the required pressure. Replacement tubing should be installed with a minimum 0.75 in. clearance to all vibrating or moving components.

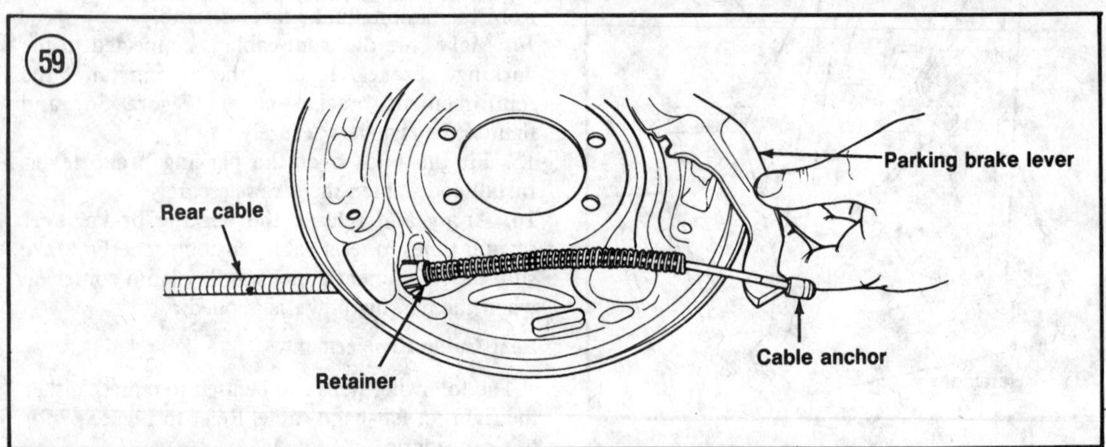

Table 1 TIGHTENING TORQUES

Fastener	ft.-lb.	N·m
Backing plate-to-axle housing	25-35	34-47
Master cylinder attaching nuts	13-25	18-33
Power booster-to-cowl	13-25	18-33
Splash shield	13-19	18-25
Wheel lug nuts	85-115	115-155

INDEX

A

Air cleaner system 153-156
Air conditioning 211-213
Auxiliary shaft 75-76
Axle
  Dana model 311-313
  Ford integral 308-311
Axle and axle shafts, rear 307-308

B

Battery
  Cables 221
  Care and inspection 216-217
  Charging 219-220
  Jump starting 220
  Open circuit voltage test
    (maintenance-free) 218
  Replacement batteries 220-221
  Safety precautions 219
  Testing maintenance-free 217-218
  Unsealed battery testing 218-219
Brakes
  Adjustment 332-333
  Bleeding 334-335
  Combination valve 337
  Dual brake warning lamp
    system 337
  Front disc 318-325
  Hoses and tubing 342
  Master cylinder 333-334
  Parking brake 338-342
  Pedal 342
  Power brake vacuum
    booster 335-337
  Rear drum 325-332
  Stoplight switch 338

C

Carburetor 159-162
  Cleaning and inspection 160
  Model identification 159
  Preparation for overhaul 159-160
  Removal/installation 159
Catalytic converter 180
Charging system 9-13
Clutch
  Components 253
  Disc inspection 261-262
  Installation 263
  Interlock switch 264-265
  Parts identification 253
  Pedal removal/
    installation 263-264
  Pilot bearing 265
  Pressure plate inspection 262
  Release bearing
    inspection 262-263
  Removal 261
  Troubleshooting 27-28

Clutch hydraulic system (1986-1987)
Bleeding ... 258-259
Master cylinder removal/installation ... 257
Master cylinder reservoir removal/installation ... 257
Release bearing replacement ... 258
Slave cylinder removal/installation ... 257-258
Clutch hydraulic system (1988-on)
Bleeding ... 261
Master cylinder removal/installation ... 259-260
Master cylinder reservoir removal/installation ... 259
Release bearing replacement ... 260-261
Slave cylinder removal/installlation ... 260
Combination valve ... 337
Coolant level check ... 187
Coolant temperature switch ... 239-241
Cooling system ... 183-192
Cooling fan ... 200-202
Checks ... 184-186
Drive belts ... 204-206
Flushing ... 187-192
Leakage test ... 186-187
Radiator ... 194-200
Refrigerant ... 212
Routine maintenance ... 212-213
Thermostat ... 192-194
Troubleshooting ... 26
Water pump ... 202-204

D

Differential ... 313-315
Drive belts ... 204-206
Drive shaft ... 304-307

E

Electrical accessories
Troubleshooting ... 25-26
Electrical circuit protection ... 248-250
Electrical system
Battery ... 215-221
Coolant temperature switch ... 239-241
Electrical circuit protection ... 248-250
Hazard flasher ... 251
Headlight switch ... 236-239
Horn ... 244
IAR charging system ... 221-228
Ignition system ... 236-237
Instruments ... 242-243
Lighting system ... 234-236
Oil pressure switch/sending unit ... 241
Starter ... 228-231
TFI-IV ignition system ... 232-234
Turn signals ... 251
Windshield wipers and washers ... 244-248
Wiper/washer switch ... 239
Emission control systems
Catalytic converter ... 180
Evaporative emission control (EEC) system ... 177-178
Exhaust gas recirculation (EGR) system ... 180
Oxygen sensor ... 180-181
Positive crankcase ventilation (PCV) system ... 178-179
Thermactor system ... 179-180
Troubleshooting ... 20-24
Engine, 4-cylinder OHC
Auxiliary shaft ... 75-76
Camshaft ... 81-83
Camshaft belt ... 73-74
Camshaft belt outer cover ... 72
Core plug replacement ... 92
Crankshaft ... 88-90
Cylinder block ... 91-92
Cylinder head ... 80-81
Disassembly checklists ... 68-69
Exhaust manifold ... 71
Flywheel or drive plate ... 90
Identification ... 61
Manifold inspection ... 71-72
Oil pan ... 76-79
Oil pump ... 79
Pilot bearing ... 91
Piston/connecting rod assembly ... 83-87
Rear main oil seal ... 87-88
Removal/installation ... 62-68
Service ... 61-62
Sprockets and engine front seals ... 74-75
Troubleshooting ... 14-18, 24-25
Upper and lower intake manifold ... 71
Valve cover ... 69-71
Valves and valve seats ... 83
Engine, 2.8L V6
Camshaft ... 122-125

Core plug replacement 142
Crankshaft 138-140
Crankshaft pulley and damper 117
Cylinder block 141-142
Cylinder head 127-130
Disassembly checklists 109
Flywheel or drive plate 140-141
Front cover and timing gears 118-120
Identification 98
Manifold inspection 116
Oil pan 125-126
Oil pump 126-127
Pilot bearing 141
Piston/connecting rod assembly 132-137
Rear main oil seal replacement 137
Removal/installation 99-104
Rocker arm assemblies 116-117
Rocker arm covers removal/installation 109-110
Service 98-99
Troubleshooting 14-18, 24-25
Valves and valve seats 130-131

Engine, 3.0L V6
Camshaft 122-125
Core plug replacement 142
Crankshaft 138-140
Crankshaft pulley and damper 117
Cylinder block 141-142
Cylinder head 127-129
Disassembly checklists 109
Flywheel or drive plate 140-141
Identification 98
Intake and exhaust manifolds 113-115
Manifold inspection 116
Oil pan 125-126
Oil pump 126-127
Pilot bearing 141
Piston/connecting rod assembly 132-137
Rear main oil seal replacement 137-138
Removal/installation 104-108
Rocker arm assemblies 117
Rocker arm covers removal/installation 110-112
Service 98-99
Timing cover, seal, sprockets, timing chain 120-122
Troubleshooting 14-18, 24-25
Valves and valve seats 130-132
Engine tune-up 52-55

Evaporative emission control (EEC) system 177-178
Exhaust gas recirculation (EGR) system 180
Exhaust system 175-176

F

Fuel system
Adjustments 57
Fuel injection, multi-point (2.3L EFI) 163-166
Fuel injection, multi-point (3.0L EFI) 166-170
Fuel quality 157-158
Pump 170-173
Quick-disconnect fittings 163
Tank and lines 173-175
Troubleshooting 18-20

H

Hazard flasher 251
Headlight switch 237-239
Heater system 206-210
Hoisting, jacking and lift points 33-35
Horn 244

I

IAR charging system 221-228
Ignition service 55-57
Ignition switch 236-237
Ignition troubleshooting 13-14
Instruments 242-243

L

Lighting system 234-236

M

Maintenance
Engine tune-up 52-55
Fuel system adjustments 57
Hoisting, jacking and lift points 33-35
Ignition service 55-57
Non-scheduled maintenance 48-52
Owner safety checks 41-44
Scheduled maintenance 44-48
Towing 35
Weekly checks 35-41

Master cylinder
Brake 333-334
Clutch 257, 259-260

O

Oil pressure switch/sending unit 241
Owner safety checks 41-44
Oxygen sensor 180-181

P

Parking brake 338-342
Positive crankcase ventilation (PCV) system 178-179
Power brake vacuum booster 335-337

R

Radiator 194-200
Refrigerant 212

S

Starter 228-231
Starting system 9
Steering system 29, 290-296
Steering wheel and column 296-297
Stoplight switch 338
Suspension, front
Coil spring replacement 278-280
Jounce bumper removal/installation 285
Lower control arm removal/installation 282-283
Rebound bumper removal/installation 285
Shock absorber operational check 276-277
Shock absorber replacement 278
Spindle removal/installation 281-282
Stabilizer bar removal/installation 280-281
Troubleshooting 29
Upper ball-joint/control arm
assembly/installation 285
removal/installation 283-284
Suspension, rear
Coil spring removal/installation 301-302
Lower control arm installation 303
Lower control arm removal 302-303
Shock absorber inspection 299
Shock absorber removal/installation 300
Troubleshooting 29
Upper control arm installation 304
Upper control arm removal 303-304

T

TFI-IV ignition system 232-234
Thermactor system 179-180
Thermostat 192-194
Tire wear analysis 29-32
Tools 4-8
Towing 35
Transmission, automatic
Installation 274
Kickdown cable 270-271
Manual linkage adjustment 269-270
Neutral start switch 269
Removal 272-273
Selector lever removal/installation 272
Troubleshooting 28
Tune-up 52-55
Transmission, manual 265-268
Troubleshooting 28
Tune-up equipment 5-8
Turn signals 251

W

Water pump 202-204
Weekly checks 35-41
Wheel alignment 285-288
Wheel balancing 32
Wheel bearings 288-290
Windshield wipers and washers 244-248
Wiper/washer switch 239